Morning Exercises

Calvary Press
PUBLISHING
AMITYVILLE, NEW YORK 11701
1 800 789-8175

Morning Exercises

William Jay

Calvary Press Publishing
P.O. Box 805
Amityville, NY 11701
U.S.A.
1 (800) 789-8175
ISBN 1-879737-33-7

Calvary Press can be found on the World Wide Web at:
www.calvarypress.com

Jacket Design by Anthony Rotolo

Jay, William, 1769-1853
Morning Exercises
Recommended Dewey Decimal Classification: 234
Suggested Subject Headings:
1. Bible—Meditations
2. Devotional calendars
I. Title

Manufactured in the United States of America
1 2 3 4 5 6 7 8 9 10 98 99 00 01

This book is dedicated to
David Straub:

lover of Jay,
lover of the lost,
lover of the brethren,
lover of Christ.

Introductory Word

William Jay (1769-1853) had a long and fruitful career as a preacher of the gospel by voice and pen. He pastored Argyle Chapel in Bath, a spa town in southwest England, from 1791 to the year of his death—more than six decades. A devoted evangelical of great ability and good sense, he was close to most of the evangelical leadership of his era—William Wilberforce, John Newton, Hannah More, Rowland Hill, Richard Cecil, Thomas Haweis, for instance, among the Anglicans, and John Foster, John Ryland, Sr., Robert Hall and Thomas Chalmers in Britain's other denominations. It is natural to see him as a link between the days of the original evangelical revival and England's nearest approach to a second great awakening, the decade 1855-65 that saw the first years of Spurgeon's amazing London-based ministry.

Mentored for the pastorate by Cornelius Winter, George Whitefield's travelling companion during the latter years of his life, Jay was distinctly Whitefieldian in his theology, fluency, insistence on the primacy of the pulpit, and total freedom from sectarianism and party spirit. On the other hand, the pattern of his ministry (a settled pastorate, with frequent travels, avid reading, rapid preparation for everything, a fruitful literary outflow, and sustained spirit of ardent, relaxed, joyful, shrewd Calvinistic piety) was in truth Spurgeonic on a smaller scale. Like Spurgeon and Whitefield, he was thirsty for souls, and had much fruit as an evangelistic preacher; like them he was genial and outgoing, and maintained friendships with individuals who did not share his faith. Sheridan, the playwright, described Jay as the most natural orator he had ever heard, and John Foster called him the prince of preachers. His greater predecessors and successors have overshadowed him, but he was a great man in Israel in his day.

His unspeculative, undisputatious practical Calvinism is a delight to discover. A quotation is in order here.

> "In my considerable acquaintance with the religious world [he was writing at the end of his life] some of the most exemplary individuals I have met with have been Calvinists. Of this persuasion were the two most extraordinary Christian characters I ever knew—John Newton and Cornelius Winter. They held its leading sentiments with firmness; but their Calvinism, like that of John Bunyan, was rendered, by their temper, milder than that of some of their brethren; and they were candid toward those who differed from them; and esteemed and loved them as fellow-heirs together of the grace of life.
>
> With this scheme of divinity my principles accord generally more than with any other ...
>
> Two grand truths have always seemed to me to pervade the whole Bible, and not to be confined to a few particular phrases, viz,., that if we are saved, it is entirely of God's grace; and if we are lost, it will be entirely from ourselves. I know full well, a man may easily force me into a corner with things seemingly or really related to the truth of either of these affirmations; but he will not shake my confidence in either, while I can read, 'O Israel, *thou* hast destoyed thyself: but in *Me* is thy help.' The connection is like a chain across the river; I can see the two ends, but not the middle; not because there is not a real union, but because it is under water ... Paley observes, that we should never suffer what we know, to be distured by what we know not."

Written in front of Jay's personal study Bible was the following:

> "In reading this Book, let me guard against four things—
> 1. The contractedness of the Systematic:
> 2. The mysticism of the Allegorizer:
> 3. The dogmatism of the Bigot:
> 4. The presumption of the Rationalist.

Let me tremble at God's word, and let me, in reading it, keep three purposes in view:

1. To collect facts rather than form opinions:
2. To regulate practice rather than encourage speculation:
3. To aid devotion rather than dispute."

Of the morning exercises here reprinted, it need only be said that they are vintage specimens of the kind of study that Jay outlines above. Read on, and you will see. And you will be fed, too.

J. I. Packer

CONTENTS OF VOLUME I.

JANUARY.

FEBRUARY.

MARCH.

APRIL.

MAY.

CONTENTS.

JUNE.

PREFACE.

A PUBLICATION is not rendered improper or needless, because works of a similar nature have preceded it. Little would ever issue from the press, if such a principle were admitted. For what new thing is there under the sun? Neither is an author in this case supposed to undervalue the labors of those who have gone before him. He only adds to their number, with his own probabilities of excitement. And *he* may awaken fresh attention in the minds even of those who have made use of his predecessors: while he may fall into the hands of some who have to begin this kind of reading. Every author, too, has not only his own connexions, but his own manner; and thus, as the taste of readers vary, all can be gratified.

The following pages, it is believed, will be found to differ a little from works of the same species; especially in making the exercises always express more fully the import of the textual motto at the head of them; in the arrangement of a greater diversity of subjects; in the selection of more passages from the less observed and improved parts of Scripture; and in the seizure of hints of instruction from the more indirect and incidental strokes of the sacred penmen.

The work has, in some measure, been its own reward: But it required the author to sacrifice almost needful repose and relaxation, in seizing every spare moment from the engrossing duties of a large and important station. And the work was, he confesses, much more arduous in the execution than he had apprehended in the prospect. The *chief* difficulty arose from the necessity of so much compression and brevity. It was found no easy thing, in two or three pages, not only to secure the spirit of the passage, but to give it some illustration and effect, by glimpses of scenery, and glances of historical facts and traits of character—where diffusion and particularity were forbidden. While he makes no scruple to avow that this was his wish and design, he laments sincerely that he has not more perfectly succeeded in accomplishing them. Leisure, and an *exclusive* dedication of himself to the plan, for some months, or even weeks, might have yielded something more satisfactory But complaint is useless; and apology vain. He has done, in his circumstances, what he could. And it yields him pleasure to think, that besides some other works of a general nature for the religious public, and especially several for the use of families, he has now done something more particularly for the Closet.

The writer has always been attached to publications of this kind; and, from his own experience, and observation, he is convinced of their adaptation to usefulness. He cannot but wish that Christians would read *the Scripture itself* more; and endeavor to *reflect themselves* on the passages, which, either in continued course, or in selections at the time, come before them. The power of doing this would improve by the use; and the pleasure and advantage resulting from the facility would amply reward any difficulty in the acquisition. But it is to be lamented, many do *not* reflect: and so the customary and cursory perusal for *want of thought* produces little impression, and the paragraph or chapter—or it may be even chapters—are immediately forgotten. But a verse or sentence, separately placed before the eye, is more distinctly remarked; and being illustrated in a brief and lively comment, is more easily remembered. To supply such assistance cannot be reckoned an attempt to lead people from the word of God, but to it: and it may teach those who use it, in time, to do for themselves what it may be necessary at first in another to do for them.

As to the subjects of these Exercises, the author has aimed to blend doctrine, experience, and practice together. There is danger of Antinomianism when the attention is too exclusively called to doctrinal points; of enthusiasm, when it is too exclusively attached to experimental; and of legality, when it is too exclusively drawn to practical. It is the proportionate admixture of sentiment, feeling, and duty, that qualifies each; and renders them all, not only safe, but profitable. The writer, also, has not confined himself to the usual mode of making the subjects of such meditations always of the *consolatory* kind. Christians, in the divine life, want something besides, comfort. They are to have their pure minds stirred up, by way of remembrance: to suffer the word of exhortation: to hear the reproofs of wisdom; to walk humbly with God; and wisely with men. Indeed, the best way to gain comfort is not always to seek it *directly;* but immediately; and the medium may require self-denial and patience. It is the same with comfort, as with reputation; it is more certainly secured as a consequence, than by making it a mere design.

The writer has not often put the exercise into the form of a soliloquy, or generally expressed himself in the language of the first person. He found the common mode of address better suited, especially to the explanatory and hortative parts of his design. Why should not the reader consider himself the *addressed*, rather than the *speaker?* and, by immediate application, make, as much as possible, the reflections his own?

As to the style itself, what was principally designed for pious use in retirement could not be too clear, and easy, and forcible, and pointed; too much abounding with terse briskness, niavete of expression; too free from the tameness and smoothness by which common, but important truths, are aided to slide down from the memory into oblivion.

In three hundred and sixty-five exercises, there may be some coincidences; and the same thought, image, or example, may occur more than once—It was hardly possible to prevent it, as the whole series could not be kept in memory, or be continually compared. As the work advanced, the subjects too frequently *increased* in length, beyond the bounds he had prescribed himself—The case was; the printer pressed upon him—and he had not time to be short. He *could* have introduced more of the exercises, in verse. If there be any blame arising from the few he *has* admitted, some friends ought to bear it, instead of himself.

But enough of this. The author commends the work to that part of the pious public who love and practice retreat; who wish not only to read the Scriptures alone, but to observe their beauties, and advantages; who, while they neglect not their own meditations, are thankful to derive help from others—and often exclaim, "A word fitly spoken, how good is it!" who wish to be in the fear of the Lord all the day long, who would not have their religion a visiter, but an inmate; who would speak of divine things, not by kind of artificial effort, but out of the abundance of the heart; and who know how much it conduces to our sanctification to keep the mind filled with good things, not only as these will exclude base intrusions, but will be sure to leave somewhat of their own tinge and likeness behind.

As to the readers of *this* character, the author trusts the materials here furnished will not be unacceptable, of whatever religious denomination they may be found. He considers the community in which, by the providence of God, he himself labors—not as a party—but only as a part; and he is not an enemy to the whole army, because he is attached to his own regiment. He does not oppose, but co-operate. He has not attempted in these volumes to conceal the leading sentiments which he holds; but he has not offensively obtruded them: nor has he availed himself of opportunities to bring forward those peculiar views, in subordinate matters, in which he may differ from others. He readily allows that every man has a right to state and defend the opinions which he has derived from conviction: but his love should abound in knowledge and in all judgment: and he should regulate the degree of his zeal by the importance of the subject. He is also persuaded that the statement and defence should be effected in a work avowedly for the purpose; and not be introduced into a publication adapted to general edification.

How much less circulation and usefulness would Doddridge's Rise and Progress of Religion, and Alleine's Alarm, and other good books, have obtained, had their authors inserted their own minor partialities, and attacked those of others! In reading a valuable volume where such things are found, we should resemble the ox in the meadow, who, when he comes to a tuft of grass he dislikes, does not grow angry and attempt to tear it up with his hoofs and horns, but placidly leaves it, and feeds on in the large and rich pasturage. But all have not this "meekness of wisdom." The prejudices of many are powerful, and quickly excited, and meeting with a passage in the beginning of a work—by no means essential to its design—they throw it instantly aside, and lose all the pleasure and benefit it would otherwise have afforded them.

The work will meet the wishes of those who have not the command of much time for private engagements. And this is the case with many in our day, not only from the avocations of civil life, but even from the calls of religious beneficence. More leisure, indeed, in many instances, may be secured, by earlier rising, and by more skill, and order, and diligence, in the management of all our affairs: yet the period in which we live is peculiar; and the calls of God to labor in doing good, in so many civil and sacred charities, leave it not our duty, to retire and read by the hour as our forefathers did.

He hopes a book of this nature will be a suitable companion to those whose advanced years and infirmities will not allow of deep, and laborious, and lengthened perusals. What is preferable for them, is something easy, and short, and *very Scriptural.* It is observable how much more aged believers delight in God's word, than in reading any other works. It is their "necessary food," and their "dainty meat," when their appetite for other things fails. It is their solace, when the evil days are come in which they have no pleasure. It is their support, and their reliance in weakness and weariness; and they use it, not for amusement, but for relief only. Thus we have seen a man walking forth gayly in the morning, carrying his staff under his arm, or twirling it in his hand—but, worn with the toils and fatigues of the day, we have seen him returning home in the evening, leaning and pressing it, at every weary step.

The work also, will suit the afflicted. Retirement and devotion seem congenial with trouble; and the sufferer naturally turns to them for succor and comfort. But many of the distresses of life prevent or abridge the resources they render so desirable and needful. What changes have many experienced, by losses and reductions! They are called from freedom and ease to the care of thought, the shiftings of contrivance, and the exertion of labor. Where now is the leisure they once enjoyed, for their secluded employments of piety? Their hours of composure are fled, and have only left them hurried and broken moments. They can only sip of the brook in the way.

May the author presume that he may be of some little service to some of his brethren in the ministry: not only by aiding their retirement, as Christians—and they to save themselves, as well as those that hear them—but by throwing out hints that may lead them to think for the pulpit, and furnishing, occasionally, outlines of discourses, which they can have the merit of filling up?

He cannot also but wish to be useful to another interesting class—the sources of our future families, and the hopes of our churches. Here he is tempted to insert an extract from one of the letters he received, stimulating him to this undertaking. The name of the writer would add weight to his remarks; but it is suppressed, because he is not apprised of the liberty now taken—and his hints were not intended to meet the public eye. This excellent, and learned, and judicious friend thus expresses himself—"I have ventured to put upon paper the idea I have conceived of a series of daily contemplations or reflections, which, among others, shall be adopted to be put into the hands of intelligent and educated *youth.* I have a sincere veneration for the intentions of Bogatzdy, and other similar authors: but there is such a paucity of thought, such a poverty of expression, such a narrowed range of ideas, such a ringing of changes incessantly, on a few topics, without gracefulness or variety, as to render the books exceedingly unattractive to the present rising generation. In these cases, I conceive we are bound to provide, as far as we can, that the food presented to their minds may not disgust, by the manner in which it is served up; and that, when we put important truth in their way, it should be encumbered with as few external obstacles as the case will admit. Good sense you have lately told us, is good taste; and that, I consider, is both good sense and good taste, in devotion, which would present to every mind, without the sacrifice of a particle of divine truth, such an exterior as may invite, rather than repulse. He who has once been effectually gained over to the love of the Gospel, will retain his affection for it under a very homely form; but he who has yet to be won, will require of us some attention, as to our first addresses, to his understanding and his heart. My view, then, my dear sir, is, that the selection of texts should involve the whole range of revealed truth; and should present it in that combined form in which the Scripture exhibits it; where doctrine, and duty, and privilege, blend like the colors that form the pure brightness of light: where religion is never exposed to view, as a bare skeleton, but as endued with all the properties of life, and in actual existence. Pithy sayings, wise experiences, urgent examples, faithful warnings, should revolve daily beneath the eye, and show the reader all that religion has done for others, all it aims to do for him, and all the evils that result from the absence of her beneficence. Testimonies, also, such as that of Chesterfield to the Vanity of the World, which he had so fully tried; dying experiences such as that of Rochester; confessions of the value of religion, such as are found in the Letters of Burns; and passages from eminent and striking lives, might be introduced in your own way, briefly prefaced or commented upon. Thus the whole might allure, by its variety; interest, by the reach of thought to which it leads; and profitably keep before the mind of youth, amidst daily temptations, what religion *can* do for them, and what the world and other things never can do."

Perhaps, however, if I am not accused of vanity, in making this extract from my correspondent, I shall be chargeable with imprudence, in publishing a recommendation, which, though I admire, I have so much failed in following.

Percy Place, Dec. 26th, 1828.

MORNING EXERCISES

FOR THE CLOSET.

JANUARY 1.—" On the first day of the first month shalt thou set up the tabernacle."—Exodus, xl. 2

AND why was this period chosen for the erection? God has always reasons for his conduct; but He does not always " give account of any of his matters." We may, however, make two remarks here. First. Things that are the same to God, are not the same to us. Our goodness extendeth not to Him: religion regards the exigencies of man; and when these are subserved, its provisions will be needless. John saw no temple in the New Jerusalem. All places are alike to God; yet we never feel, in a common dwelling, the solemnity that seizes us in the sanctuary. The first day of the year was no more to God than any other; but it would render the service more memorable and impressive to the people; therefore, says He, " On the first day of the first month shalt thou set up the tabernacle." Secondly. It is well to begin a new year with some good work; and to commence serving God after a new manner. And have *we* no tabernacle to set up on this first day of this first month?

Let us begin the year with solemn reflection—and say, with Job, " When a few years are come, I shall go the way whence I shall not return." Let me not only believe this; but think of it, and feel the importance of the sentiment. Yes, in a little time I shall be no more seen. How—where—shall I be disposed of? The seasons will return as before, but the places that now know me, will know me no more for ever. Will this be a curse? or a blessing? If I die in my sins, I shall return no more to my possessions and enjoyments; to the calls of mercy; to the throne of grace; to the house of prayer! If I die in the Lord, I shall (O blessed impossibility!) return no more to these thorns and briers; to this vain and wicked world; to this aching head; to this throbbing heart; to these temptations, and troubles, and sorrows, and sins.

Let us begin the year with self-inspection—and say, with the chief butler, " I do remember my faults this day." We are prone to think of the failings of our fellow-creatures, and often imagine, because we are free from *their* faults, that we are faultless; but we may have others; we may have worse; and while a mote is in our brother's eye, a beam may be in our own. Let us be open to conviction. Let us deal faithfully with our own hearts. Let us not compare ourselves with others, and especially the more vile; but with our advantages; with our knowledge; with our professions; with the law of God.

Let us begin the year with a determination to abandon whatever appears sinful—and say, with Elihu, "If I have done iniquity, I will do no more." If the evil course, or the evil passion solicits, let it plead in vain, while the Savior Judge says—"If thy right eye offend thee, pluck it out, and cast it from thee; for it is profitable for thee that one of thy members should perish, and not that thy whole body should be cast into hell. And if thy right hand offend thee, cut it off, and cast it from thee: for it is profitable for thee that one of thy members should perish, and not that thy whole body should be cast into hell."

Begin the year with pious and personal dedication—and say, with David, "Lord, I am thine, save me." Through Him, who is the way, yield yourselves unto God. It is your reasonable service. He has infinite claims to you; and you will never be truly your own till you are his.

Begin the year with relative religion; and if the worship of God has never been established in your own family, now commence it—and say, with Joshua, "As for me, and my house, we will serve the Lord." A family without prayer is like a house without a roof. It is uncovered and exposed; and we know who has threatened to pour out his fury upon the families that call not upon his name.

Begin the year with fresh concern to be useful—and ask, with Saul of Tarsus, "Lord, what wilt thou have me to do?" Let me look at my condition, my resources, my opportunities. How can I glorify God, and promote the welfare of my fellow creatures? Is there not a bible to spread? Are there not missionaries to support? Are there none perishing for lack of knowledge that I can instruct? Have I no irreligious neighbors to reclaim? Are there no poor to relieve? No widows and fatherless to visit?

Begin the year with more conduct in the arrangement of your affairs—and resemble Ezra and his brethren, who "did according to the custom, as the duty of every day required." God has said, let every thing be done decently, and in order. Much of your comfort will arise from regularity in your meals, in your devotions, in your callings, and your piety will be aided by it. Have a place to receive every thing; an end to simplify it; a rule to arrange it. Leave nothing for the morrow that ought to be discharged to-day; sufficient for each period will be its own claims; and your mind ought to be always at liberty to attend to fresh engagements.

Finally. Time, this short, this uncertain, this all-important time, upon every instant of which eternity depends, will not allow of our trifling away any of its moments. Resolve, therefore, to redeem it. Gather up its fragments, that nothing be lost. Especially rescue it from needless sleep; and if you have hitherto accustomed yourself to the shameful indulgence of lying late in bed, begin the new year with the habit of early rising; by which you will promote your health, and improvement of every kind, and live much longer than others in the same number of days—and say, with David, "My voice shalt thou hear in the morning, O Lord; in the morning will I direct my prayer unto thee, and will look up."

And if this be your determination, the season will be the date of your happiness; and God himself says, "From this day will I bless you."

JANUARY 2.—"I will surely do thee good."—Gen. xxxii. 12.

THIS is a blessed assurance with which to enter a new year, not knowing what a day may bring forth. But what have *we* to do with this promise? It was indeed given immediately to Jacob; but it equally belongs to every Israelite indeed; for he never said to the seed of Jacob, Seek ye me in vain. Promises made on particular occasions are intended for general use and advantage. Paul, referring to the words with which God had encouraged Joshua, applies them to the believing Hebrews: "Let your conversation be without covetousness, and be content with such things as ye have; for he hath said, I will never leave thee, nor forsake thee." So that *we* may boldly say, "The Lord is my helper, and I will not fear what man shall do unto me." And Hosea, alluding to God's intercourse with Jacob, even at Bethel, says, "And there he talked with *us*."

The very brevity of the promise is a recommendation. We complain of our memories; but surely we can retain these six golden words, "I WILL SURELY DO THEE GOOD." It is also the better for being indefinite. Some promises ensure an individual blessing: but we are a mass of wants; and this assurance is a comforter that meets every fear, every anxiety, every wish. It sets the mind completely at rest with regard to any possible contingencies. It tells us to be "careful for nothing;" "casting all our care upon Him, for *He* careth for us." But though specifying nothing in particular, it leaves our hope to range at large—yet it is within the compass of our welfare. "They that seek the Lord shall not want any *good* thing." "I will surely do thee *good*."

Now the meaning of this promise must be understood, or else we shall find it impossible to harmonize it with experience. The people of the world have often reproached those who profess to be the blessed of the Lord, with their poverty and distress; and have asked, "Where is *now* your God?" And they themselves have sometimes been perplexed and dismayed. Gideon said, "If God be with us, why then is all this evil befallen us?" And Jacob said, "All these things are against me." In an agreeable mansion, and enjoying all the comforts of life, no difficulty may be felt from the language of God: but what is Joseph in prison; what is Job among the ashes; what is he who says, "All the day long have I been plagued, and chastened every morning?" what is *he* to make of the promise, "I will surely do thee good?" We must confide in the judgment of God, and distrust our own. We are short-sighted; and easily imposed upon by appearances; and know not what is good for us in this vain life, which we spend as a shadow. But *He* cannot be mistaken. A wise father will choose far better for his infant, than the infant can choose for himself. We must always distinguish between what is pleasing and what is profitable. Correction is not agreeable to the child; yet it is so good for him, that he who spareth the rod, hateth his son. Medicine is unpalatable; but it is good for the patient, and renewed health will more than reconcile him even to pay for it. The vine-dresser does the tree good, not by suffering the wanton shoots to grow on, draining the sap, but by pruning it, that it may bring forth more fruit. What said David? "It is good for me"—

that I have prospered? that I have risen from obscurity? that I conquered Goliah? that I got such a victory in the Valley of Salt? No; but, It is good for me that Doeg impeached me, that Saul hunted me like a partridge on the mountains, that Absalom drove me from my palace, that Shimei cursed me on the hill, that sickness brought down my life to the ground: "it is good for me that I have been afflicted." We must also look to the conclusion of events. Things good in themselves, with regard to us, may result in evil; and things evil in themselves, may issue in good. Abraham spake according to our present estimations, when he said to the rich man, "Son, remember that thou in thy lifetime receivedst thy good things, and Lazarus evil things." But had we known them both before death, and been assured that soon would the one have been comforted, and the other tormented, we should have judged the poverty and distresses of Lazarus to have been the "good things," and the wealth and luxury of the rich man the "evil things." All is ill that ends ill; and all is well that ends well.

But let us believe the truth of this declaration. There are four steps by which we may reach the conclusion. The first regards his sufficiency. He is *able* to do us good. Nothing is too hard for the Lord. In the Lord Jehovah is everlasting strength: there is no enemy but he can conquer; no exigency but he can relieve. He is able to do exceeding abundantly above all we can *ask* or *think*. The second regards his inclination. He is *disposed* to do us good. His love is not only real, but passing knowledge. He feels toward us as his jewels, his friends, his children, his bride: he rests in his love, and joys over us with singing. The third regards his engagement. He is *bound* to do us good. We have not only his word, but his oath; an oath sworn by himself, because he could swear by no greater; and confirmed by the blood of an infinite sacrifice. The fourth regards his conduct. He *has* done us good. We have had complaints enough to make of others; but of Him we are compelled to say, "Thou hast dealt well with thy servant, O Lord." His goodness and mercy have followed us all the days of our lives. How often has he turned the shadow of death into the morning! But when I look at the cross, I see that he *has* done already far more than remains to *be* done. "He that spared not his own Son, but delivered him up for us all; how shall he not with him also freely give us all things?"

January 3.—"And the manna ceased on the morrow after they had eaten of the old corn of the land; neither had the children of Israel manna any more; but they did eat of the fruit of the land of Canaan that year."
Josh. v. 12.

This cessation of the manna is one of the several remarkable occurrences at the crossing of the river Jordan. God is every thing to his people. In the wilderness they had no pathway; but he led them in a pillar of cloud by day, and a pillar of fire by night. They were in danger; but he was their defence. They had no abode; but he was their dwelling-place. They had no water; but he gave them streams in the desert. They had no provision; but he rained down manna around their tents. So that what nature refused, Providence furnished; and what could not be derived from the ground, came from the clouds.

When the supplies they brought with them from Egypt were spent, they feared they were going to perish. They forgot the hand that had dried up the sea; and said, Can God furnish a table in the wilderness? But he gave them bread from heaven, and for forty years they did eat angels' food. What an abundance was necessary for such a multitude! And what a display of divine power was here witnessed! Nor less was it a proof of divine mercy. Had he dealt with them after their desert, fire would have come down from heaven, instead of food: but as the mother silences the fretful, angry child, by giving it, not the rod, but the breast, so did his gentleness indulge them. Hence, when they despised the manna as light food, it might have been suspended, and they might have been left to learn the worth of it by the want: but day after day, year after year, it continued to attend them, and ceased not till the day after they had taken possession of their inheritance, and they had eaten of the old corn of the land.

At length it *did* cease; and wisely too. What was necessary before, became needless now: and what want had endeared, abundance would have despised. This teaches us not to look for extraordinary supplies, when relief is to be had in an ordinary way. He who sustained Israel is as almighty as ever; but we must plough, and sow, and gather into barns. He who fed Elijah with ravens, commands us to labor, working with our own hand the thing that is good. If a man neglects the means of subsistence, he is not trusting Providence, but tempting it; and is likely to be reminded by something more than Scripture, that if any man will not work, neither shall he eat. Even in miraculous achievements, what human agency *could* do, was not done supernaturally. When Peter was in prison, the angel of the Lord opened the door, and broke off his fetters—for this Peter could not have done; but he did not take him up in his arms, and carry him out; but said unto him, "Follow me." Miracles were never needlessly employed; and had they been common, they would have ceased to be marvellous: the exceptions would have become a general rule; and the whole system of Nature and Providence have been deranged.

The manna was typical. "*I* am," said Jesus, "that bread of life." As the manna came down from heaven, and preserved the Israelites from famine, "God so loved the world, that he gave his only begotten Son, that whosoever believeth in him should not perish, but have everlasting life." And the Savior surpasses the emblem. The manna was for the body; he saves the soul. The manna could not preserve from death always; but they who partake of him, live for ever. The manna was confined to *one* people; he gave his flesh for the life of the world. He, therefore, is the *true* bread.

And shall this cease? Far from it. You shall live by him, as well as with him, for ever.

Yet there will be a great difference between your present and your future experience in reference to him. Many things now necessary, will then be done away. Conjecture, opinion, reasoning, will give place to knowledge. Now we walk by faith, then we shall walk by sight. Now we are saved by hope; then hope will cease in fruition. Love will continue for ever; but charity and mercy can have no object, no exercise there. We shall be still praising him; but prayer, and preaching, and baptism, and the Lord's supper, will have no place. We can dispense with the channels, when we are at the fountain head; and with the types, when we have the reality. We are now glad when they say unto us, "Let us go into the house of the Lord;" but says John, "I saw no temple there; but the glory of God and of the Lamb were the light thereof." When that which is perfect is come, that which is in part will be done away; and the fare of the wilderness will be superseded by the produce of Canaan.

January 4.—"As thy days, so shall thy strength be."—Deut. xxxiii, 25.

Dr. Doddridge was one day walking, much depressed, his very heart desolate within him. "But," says he, "passing a cottage door open, I happened at that moment to hear a child reading, 'As thy days, so shall thy strength be.' The effect on my mind was indescribable. It was like life from the dead." Much is often done by a word; and many can say, with Watts,

"And when my spirit takes her fill
"At some good word of thine,
"Not warriors, who divide the spoil,
"Have joys compared with mine."

And what does *this* word say to *us?* "As thy days, so shall thy strength be." There is strength bodily. The continuance of this is a mercy. How soon, how easily may it be crushed or reduced, so that we may be made to possess months of vanity; and endure wearisome nights; and feel every exertion a difficulty, and every duty a burden. But there is strength spiritual. This is very distinguishable from the former, and often found separate from it. The Lord does not always give his people a giant's arm, or an iron sinew; but *His* strength is made perfect in weakness. This is the strength here spoken of, and for two purposes his people will find it necessary: *service* and *suffering*.

Every Christian has a course of duty common to him as a man; which is to provide for his outward wants, and the support of his family. And this is done by labor, in which he is required not to be slothful. But there is a series of duties pertaining more immediately to him in his religious character; to believe, to pray, to deny ungodliness and worldly lusts, and to live soberly, righteously, and godly, in the present evil world. The discharge of this high calling is sometimes expressed by a race, which he is to run with patience. Sometimes, also, by the life of a soldier. A soldier must not be effeminate, but endure hardness and fatigue. Even his preparations and exercises are often trying—how much more his actual services! And the Christian's enemies possess every thing that can render them formidable; and so fights he, not as one that beateth the air.

Suffering is commonly connected with service in the divine life.

It was so invariably in the beginning of the gospel. Then it was deemed impossible for any one to live godly in Christ Jesus, and not suffer persecution. Therefore, no sooner was Paul converted, than he was told how great things he had to suffer. As real religion is always the same, some degree of the same opposition may be always looked for; and the hatred of the world *will* be shown, as far as they have liberty to express it, and are not restrained by law, or the usages of civilized life. But when the Christian has rest from such trials as these, God can subserve their purpose, by personal and relative afflictions, which are often severer, all things considered, than the endurings of a martyr. They are called chastenings and rebukes, which he is neither to despise, or faint under. They have been the experience of all his children from age to age. They are not wantonly inflicted; but there is a needs be for them, of which their heavenly Father is the unerring judge; and who, as far as their education and welfare will allow, will spare them as a man spareth his own son that serveth him.

Now, the prospect of all this, when he looks forward into life, is enough to awaken the Christian's anxiety; and nothing can effectually encourage him, but the discovery of strength equal to his exigencies. And this he finds not in *himself*. The natural man has no sensibility of his weakness, because he is not earnestly engaged in those applications which require divine strength. But the Christian is. He knows that he is as destitute of strength, as he is of righteousness. He feels himself entirely insufficient for all the duties and trials of the divine life. And the consciousness, instead of diminishing, grows with the experience of every day. And he need not be afraid of this—rather let him cherish it; for when he is weak, then he is strong. What he wants is provided and ensured by the promise of a God who cannot lie. "As thy days, so shall thy strength be." And as we have heard, so have we seen in the city of our God. His veracity has been attested by all his people, not one failing. And what says our own experience? Year after year I have been travelling in an enemy's country, and carrying with me an evil heart, prone to depart from the living God. I have often said, I shall one day perish. But where am I this morning! Following hard after God, his right hand upholding me. My prayers have not been always lively and delightful; but I have looked again toward his holy temple; and, through many a benighted hour I have waited for the Lord, more than they that watch for the morning. I have had no might of my own, and have been often faint; but he giveth power to the faint, and to them that have no might he increaseth strength. This is my testimony to the praise of the glory of his grace—and, at the beginning of another year I thank God, and take courage.

> "Here raise mine Ebenezer,
> "Hither, by thy help, I'm come,
> "And I hope, by thy good pleasure
> "Safely to arrive at home."

JANUARY 5.—"And they cast their crowns before the throne."—Rev. iv, 10.

RELIGION distinguishes and elevates. The possessors of it begin to rise on earth; but their dignity is perfected and displayed in heaven.

There they are *crowned*. Racers were crowned. Conquerors were crowned. Benefactors, who had saved the life of a fellow citizen, were crowned. Bridegrooms were crowned. Solomon's mother crowned him in the day of his espousals. Princes, on their ascension, were crowned. The saints on high are every one of these, in themselves; and the crown each wears is called "a crown of righteousness;" "a crown of life;" "a crown of glory that fadeth not away;" a crown divinely superior to the prize of mortal ambition. "Now they do it to obtain a corruptible crown, but we an incorruptible."

But if they are thus honored, "they cast their crowns before the throne," they approach; testifying, by this action, from whom they have received them, and confessing that they deem themselves unworthy to wear the honor "before the presence of his glory;" all, all in conformity with the peculiar design of the gospel constitution, "that no flesh should glory in *his presence*," but "according as it is written, He that glorieth, let him glory in the Lord."

It is no easy thing to bring a man to this temper of mind; for it is not natural to him. Naturally, he is as proud as he is poor. Therefore, he would be wise, though born as a wild ass's colt. Therefore, though poverty itself, he says, I am rich, and increased with goods, and have need of nothing. Therefore, though without strength, he trusts in his own heart; and, though guilty before God, he goes about to establish his own righteousness. Therefore, he is impatient under his affliction, as if he had a right to complain, and unthankful under his mercies, as if he deserved them.

The day of conviction is a day of self-abasement; and in that day the lofty looks of man are brought low. Then he submits himself to God, and begins to walk humbly with him; he admires the patience that was borne with him, and adores the abundant mercy that has saved and called him. The more he advances in the divine life, the more he sinks in his own estimation. "I, who am but dust and ashes." "Behold, I am vile." "Who am I, and what is my father's house?" "I am not worthy of the least of all thy mercies." "I am not worthy that thou shouldst come under my roof." The "latchet of whose shoes I am not worthy to stoop down and unloose." "I am not worthy to be called an apostle." "I am less than the least of all saints." These have been the self-annihilations of men who were all great in the sight of the Lord; and these must be the best proofs, as they will be the certain effects, of *our* growing in grace, and in the knowledge of our Lord and Savior.

Ignorance is the pedestal of pride: throw down the basis, and the figure falls. But here our knowledge is not complete; hereafter we shall see things in God's own light. Then we shall have other views than we now have, of the exceeding sinfulness of sin; of the number and aggravations of our offences; of the greatness of our guilt and desert; of the vastness of our obligations; of the wonders of that love that passeth knowledge in every part of our salvation. Thence will result that fine ingenuous feeling that shrinks back, and is ready to decline a distinguished privilege, not from dislike, or unwillingness to be under obligation, but from a sense of unworthiness, increased by immediate contrast with the object. Did Peter wish to be abandoned of Christ? Yea, he placed all his happiness in his presence: but it was under this feeling, on the sight of the miracle, he exclaimed, "Depart from me, for I am a sinful man, O Lord."

Some would not think of such abdications, were they to enter heaven with their present principles and dispositions; they would rather view their crowns as of their own deserving, and their own procuring: and feel the spirit of a late emperor, who, too proud to receive *his* diadem from any other hand than his own, placed himself the crown upon his head. But that world is a world of humility and gratitude. All the dignitaries there cast their crowns before the throne of the Savoir, in whose righteousness they are exalted—still praising *him*, and saying, "Not unto us, O Lord, not unto *us*, but unto thy Name give glory, for thy mercy and thy truth's sake."

But whatever heaven is, we must be disposed and prepared for it before we can enter it. Has then God wrought us for the self-same thing? Has he brought down the pride of our nature, and made us willing to "submit ourselves unto the righteousness of God?" Are we saying, "Blessed be the God and Father of our Lord Jesus Christ, who hath blessed us with all spiritual blessings in heavenly places in Christ?" Is the leading sentiment of the BLESSED, now living in our hearts, and reigning in our lives? "BY THE GRACE OF GOD I AM WHAT I AM. NOT I BUT THE GRACE OF GOD WHICH WAS WITH ME."

JANUARY 6.—"Unite my heart to fear thy name."—Ps. lxxxvi, 11.

THE fear of God does not here mean a particular grace of the Spirit, but religion at large. It is common to all writers to express the whole of a thing by a part; but then it ought to be an essential and a distinguishing part; and "the fear of the Lord is the beginning of wisdom;" and "we perfect holiness, in the fear of God."

Religion is nothing without the heart; yet naturally the heart is alienated from the life of God, and hangs off loosely and carelessly from all the spiritualities of his service. But it must be drawn and attached to divine things; and God alone can accomplish this union. Without his agency, indeed, there may be an outward and professional union; but the ligatures of faith and love which are in Christ Jesus, will be wanting. To him, therefore, must we give the glory of the work, if it has been effected, and to him we must repair, if we desire to experience it; encouraged by the assurance that he will not fail to give the Holy Spirit to them that ask him.

But how may I know that he has united my heart to his fear? When we are attached to a thing, we love to hear of it; we think much of it; speak much of it; we delight to remember it. If we are cordially united to an individual, he shares our sympathy; we feel his interests to be our own: we weep when he weeps, and rejoice when he rejoices. It is the same with a man that is cordially attached to religion; he feels himself to be one with it: when it is assailed, he will endeavor to defend it: when it is wounded in the house of his friends, he will feel the pain: the reproach of it will be his burden; he will pray for its success, and exult in its prosperity. Are we cordially united to any one? In the same degree we dislike absence, and dread separation. Thus the attached Ruth said to Naomi, "Entreat me not to leave thee, nor return from following after thee; for whither thou goest, I will go; and where thou lodgest, I will lodge: thy people shall be my people, and thy God, my God. Where thou diest, I will die, and there will I be buried." And what is the language of a soul under this divine influence? "Why shouldst thou be a stranger in the land, and as a wayfaring man that turneth aside to tarry for a night?" "Hide not thy face from me; put not thy servant away in anger; thou hast been my help; leave me not, neither forsake me, O God of my salvation." "Cast me not away from thy presence, and take not thy Holy Spirit from me."

But was not David's heart united to the fear of God BEFORE? It was. But he who has the dawn, wishes for the day. He in whom the good work is begun, will always pray, "Perfect that which concerneth me." And who can say here, I have attained, I am already perfect? David, as a backslider, prayed, "Create in me a clean heart, O God, and renew a right spirit within me:" but there was no period in his life, or advancement in his religion, at which he would not have used the very same prayer.

> **Whoever says, "I want *no more*,"**
> **Confesses he has *none*.**

The Christian, as long as he feels any reluctance to duty; any dullness in his work; any distraction in his worship; any law in the members warring against the law of his mind; any reason to sigh, "When I would do good, evil is present with me, and how to perform that which is good, I find not," will not cease to pray, "Unite my heart to fear thy name."

> **"Weak is the effort of my heart,**
> **"And cold my warmest thought;**
> **"But when I see Thee as thou art,**
> **"I'll praise Thee as I ought."**

JANUARY 7.—"Salute my well-beloved Epenetus, who is the first-fruits of Achaia unto Christ."—Rom. xvi, 5.

PAUL here remembers many, and speaks of them all with affection; but he salutes Epenetus as his WELL-*beloved*. We are not bound to love all in the same manner, or in the same degree.

The Apostle calls this convert, "fruits unto *Christ*," not unto *himself*. Yet he had been the means of bringing him to the knowledge of the truth. But Paul knew that *he* had not redeemed him; justified him; called him by his grace. And as to his conversion, he had only been the *instrument*, the Lord working with him, and confirming his word with signs following. In another place he says, "Who then is Paul, and who is Apollos, but ministers by whom ye believed, even as the Lord gave to every man?" If converted sinners are the seal, and reward, and glory, and joy of the preacher, they are infinitely more so of the Savior himself. *He* sees in them his agency; his image; the travail of his soul; the recompense of his sufferings. He will enjoy their blessedness, and receive their praises for ever.

Epenetus is here said to be the "*first*-fruits unto Christ in *Achaia*." Yet he says to the Corinthians, "Ye know the house of Stephanas, that *it* is the first-fruits of Achaia." The apparent difficulty is easily solved by the fact, that the house of Stephanas was the first family that was converted, but that Epenetus was the first convert in the family. Christians at first were few in number, and driven together by persecution. They were, therefore, well known to each other, and to their ministers. They were marked characters. The conversion of a man to Christianity in a heathen place, must have been peculiarly *observable*. It was the production of a "new creature," which would of course be greatly wondered at. It was displaying the "heavenly" where all was "earthly, and sensual, and devilish" before. And we see it was *worthy* of attention. Earthly minds are most interested by the events of this life: by the policy of statesmen, the exploits of heroes, the discoveries of philosophers—but what Paul noticed in Achaia, was the first man that was called there out of darkness into the kingdom of God's dear Son. He knew that the conversion of one soul far transcended in importance the deliverance of a whole kingdom from civil bondage. Kingdoms will soon be no more; but such a soul will shine a monument of grace and glory for ever and ever. "There is joy in the presence of the angels of God over one sinner that repenteth."

How long Epenetus, in the place and in the family, stood *alone* as a professed Christian, we know not; but it is no uncommon thing for an individual to be similarly situated. We have often seen single converts seeking and serving Christ, as the first-fruits of the neighborhood, or the household, wherein they lived. The way in which, and the means by which these persons are brought forward before others, would, if stated, be found to be various, and often remarkable. Hearing the Gospel while from home; visiting in a family where the worship of God is maintained; meeting with a good book; a letter from a friend; a conversation with a stranger; an affliction that made the heart bleed, and laid bare the prospects of life—where shall we end? "Lo! all these worketh God oftentimes with man, to bring back his soul from the pit, to be enlightened with the light of the living." For though the incidents upon which this mighty event hinged seemed perfectly casual, they were all arranged by his own purpose and grace.

And the circumstances in which these *first* converts are placed, are a post of *trial;* and sometimes the trial is very severe. They have to take up their cross daily, and hourly too; and a cross too heavy to be borne without divine aid. Little do many who have been religiously brought up, and whose relations and friends, if not decidedly pious, are not hostile; little do they know what some have to endure, especially at the commencement of their religious course; when, instead of assistance and countenance, (so much needed,) they meet with neglect, and opposition, and sneers, and reproach, from all around them—and from all that are dear to them.

—They are also in a post of *duty;* and are required to be not only harmless and blameless, but most exemplary in their language, temper, and conduct. The reason is, that they will attract peculiar notice. Every thing they do will be canvassed by a shrewdness sharpened by enmity, and ready to magnify every failing. *They* will be judged by their profession; and their religion will be judged by *them.* And they are to put gainsayers to silence, and constrain them, by their good works which they behold, to glorify God in the day of visitation. They are to adorn the doctrine of God our Savior in all things; and by walking in wisdom, to win those who are without. They are not to repulse by rudeness, or chill by disdain. They are never to betray a feeling that says, Stand by thyself; come not near to me—I am holier than thou. They are not, by stiffness, and affectation in little and lawful things, to lead people to suppose that their religion is made up of oddities and perverseness. Yet, in things of unquestionable obligations and real importance, they must be firm and immoveable, always abounding in the work of the Lord: for not only will conscience require this, in the testimony they are always to bear for God, but such *consistency* alone will enthrone them in the convictions and esteem of others.

—For they are also in a post of *honor*. They have a peculiar opportunity of showing their principles. Later converts may be equally conscientious, but *these* coming after, when they have the sanction and co-operation of others, cannot so obviously appear to be on the Lord's side, nor so fully evince the purity and power of their motives, as those who come forward *alone*, and say to all others, however numerous, however influential, however endeared—choose you this day whom you will serve; but as for me, I will serve the Lord. They have, therefore, the privilege of taking the lead, and of being examples, instead of followers. And they may be, and are likely to be, the means of prevailing upon others. We have seldom seen an instance of failure. The effect has not always immediately appeared; but where they have been enabled to walk worthy of God unto all pleasing, after a while they have no longer gone *alone* to the cross of Christ, to the throne of grace, to the house of God, but in company—in company with those who once stood aloof, or before even opposed. And " he that converteth a sinner from the error of his ways, shall save a soul from death, and shall hide a multitude of sins."

January 8.—" Beloved, I wish above all things that thou mayest prosper and be in health, even as thy soul prospereth."—3d Epis. John, 2.

It has been supposed from hence, that Gaius had an infirm and sickly constitution. This is probable, but it does not necessarily follow; for John might have wished him the continuance and increase of health, as well as the restoration of it.

However this may be, we learn from his language, that it is allowable for us to pray for temporal blessings, and that, of all these blessings, health is the most valuable and necessary.

But is outward prosperity—is even health itself the chief good—that " above all things" he wishes his friend to enjoy it? Some, therefore, have rendered it, " I wish above all persons;" others, " I wish in all respects;" that thou mayest prosper and be in health. But there is no need of criticism here. Gaius had grace already, and a high degree of it; and this one thing needful being secured, it was *then* supremely desirable that he should have health to enjoy and improve it—" even as his soul prospered."

John makes, also, his soul-prosperity the standard and rule of his prayer for other things. This would be a dreadful rule with regard to many. Such praying, if answered, would ruin them. Yes, if they were to prosper in temporal things *as* they prosper in spiritual, they would become the poorest, meanest wretches on earth; for they are strangers to every thing like the true riches. And if their bodies were to be as healthful *as* their souls, their dwellings would become an hospital—their bed of ease a bed of languishing; they would be blind, for they have no spiritual understanding—deaf, for they never hear the voice of God—dead, for the Spirit of God is not in them.

Yet this seems to be the only safe rule. For unless religion keeps pace with our outward good, our safety and welfare would be endangered by it. We are not afraid when we see Christians succeeding in life, if, at the same time, they grow in grace. But the peril is, when there is so much sail, and so little ballast. What can be more awful than to see those who too much mind earthly things, gaining abundantly; to see those who have a relish for the pride of life, enabled to be splendid; to see those much indulged, who cannot put a knife to their throat. If our plenty and dainties awaken in us no moral apprehensions, and if we can feast ourselves without fear, surely our table is likely to become a snare, and that which should have been for our welfare to become a trap. The prosperity of fools destroys them, and the prosperity of those who have not *much* wisdom injures them.

Let us, therefore, examine our wishes. Let us regulate them piously. Let us seek first the kingdom of God, and his righteousness. Let us ask for no more of other things than we can bear—ever praying for our friends and ourselves, that we may prosper and be in health even as our *souls prosper.*

JANUARY 9.—" He will be our guide even unto death.—Psalm xlviii, 14.

THIS assurance comes home to our case and feelings. We are strangers and pilgrims upon earth. We resemble the Jews in the wilderness; we are not in Egypt, and we are not in Canaan, but journeying from one to the other. We are delivered from our natural state, but before we can enter glory,

" We have this desert world to pass; " A dangerous and a tiresome place."

And as the Jews were not left to themselves, but had a conductor, so have we—" This God is our God for ever and ever; he will be our guide even unto death." How perfectly, how infinitely qualified is he for this office! In a journey it is unnecessary for the traveller to know the road, but the guide ought to know it; and when *he* is well acquainted with it, and we have full confidence in him, we shall feel satisfaction, notwithstanding our own ignorance. Abraham went out, not knowing whither he went, but he knew *with whom;* and Job, after expressing his perplexities, and the successlessness of his efforts to explore the dispensation he was under, relieves himself with this thought: " But he knoweth the way that I take."

" Oh, who so fit to choose our lot, " And regulate our ways,"

as he who sees the end from the beginning; who knows all our walking through this great wilderness; who cannot mistake as to what is good or evil for us, and who has said, " I will bring the blind by a way that they know not, I will lead them in paths that they have not known; I will make darkness light before them, and crooked things straight; these things will I do unto them, and not forsake them." If we had a wise and sure, but a sullen and silent leader, it would deduct much from the pleasure of the journey. But our guide indulges us with constant intercourse. He allows us to address *him* whenever we please, and in every thing by prayer and supplication to make known our requests; while he condescendingly addresses *us*, talking with us by the way, and opening to us the scriptures. He is also equal to all our exigencies. Do we want food, refreshment, rest? He can supply all our need, according to his riches in glory by Christ Jesus. Have we storms? "He is our refuge and strength, a very present help in trouble." Are we exposed to enemies? What David said to Abiathar who had fled to him in his jeopardy, HE says to us, "Abide with me, for he that seeketh thy life seeketh my life, but with me thou shalt be in safeguard." I should not be afraid of the sights and howlings of the wood, if I had a lion at my right hand every step, and could depend upon his fidelity; a lion is the strongest among beasts, and turneth not away for any. More than this is our privilege.

> "A thousand savage beasts of prey
> "Around the forest roam;
> "But Judah's Lion guards the way,
> "And guides the traveller home."

What human patience could bear with our manners and provocations? What creature conductor is there but would throw up his charge long before the journey's end? But he does not cast away his people. He *never leaves* nor forsakes them. This is their comfort; this is their hope; this is their security: the long-suffering of our God is salvation. "I, the Lord, change not; therefore ye sons of Jacob are not consumed."

Yes, he will be our guide "even unto death;" that is, till the journey is over, and all its cares cease. But is nothing more necessary? TO death is much, but THROUGH death seems better. When we come to the entrance of the gloomy passage, it is pleasing to think that he is at the other side, and will receive us to himself; that where he is, there we may be also. But how am I to get THROUGH? "My flesh and my heart faileth."

> "Oh, if my Lord would *come* and MEET—
> "My soul would stretch her wings in haste,
> "Fly fearless through Death's iron gate,
> "Nor feel the terrors as she pass'd."

Well, this case is provided for—all is insured. He will be with us THROUGH. "Yea, though I walk *through* the valley of the shadow of death, I will fear no evil, for thou *art with me:* thy rod and thy staff they comfort me."—*Amen.*

JANUARY 10.—"A devout man, and one that feared God with all his house, which gave much alms to the people, and prayed to God alway."—Acts, x, 2.

WE should beware of general and indiscriminate reflections upon communities and professions. They are injurious, and tend to make and keep the parties what they find they are generally supposed to be. They are unjust; for there are always exceptions. And they are ungenerous; for the more temptations men have to resist, the more evils they have to subdue, the more difficulties they have to struggle with—the more deserving and commendable is the individual that succeeds; or rather, the more is the grace of God glorified in him. Can there be no excellency connected with arms? In the New Testament we meet with no less than four centurions, and all are spoken of with approbation—the centurion who came to our Lord on the behalf of his servant—the centurion that watched and confessed at the cross—the centurion that behaved so courteously to Paul in his voyage, and Cornelius, here spoken of..

He is supposed to have been a proselyte, but he was not. Yet he worshipped God, the knowledge of whom he probably obtained by residing with his men in Judea. He was a " devout man," and three fine unions are mentioned in his character and conduct.

A union of *personal* and *relative duty:* " *He* feared God *with* all his house." This was like Joshua, who said, " As for me and my house, we will serve the Lord:" not my house without myself, nor myself without my house; but I, *and* my house. If we are godly ourselves, we shall surely give evidence of it by instructing, and admonishing, and impressing those who are placed under our care. And in vain shall we use the means, if we counteract them by our own example. We must do, as well as teach.

A union of *piety* and *morality; gave alms* and *prayed.* Piety is more than prayer, and morality is more than alms; yet alms and prayer are not only parts, but essential parts of them, and they can never be separated. Some talk of their love to the gospel, and their communion with God, who are hard-hearted, and close-handed. " But whoso hath this world's good, and seeth his brother have need, and shutteth up his bowels of compassion from him, how dwelleth the love of God in him?" Others stand fair with their fellow creatures, and are distinguished by liberality and kindness, yet they have no fellowship with the Father and his Son Jesus Christ; they live without God; they indulge their sensual passions, and imagine that charity covers a multitude of sins; " But pure religion, and undefiled before God and the Father is this, to visit the fatherless and widows in their affliction, and to keep themselves unspotted from the world."

A union of the *real* and *eminent* in religion: " He gave *much* alms to the people, and prayed to God *alway.*" There cannot be the eminence of grace without the reality; but there may be the reality without the eminence. We should be thankful for a day of small things, but we should seek after a day of great ones. We should add to the essentials of religion, its excellencies too. We should not only have life, but have it more abundantly.

As to our temporal condition, we should be content with such things as we have; but contentment does not become us in divine things. There we should be ambitious. There we should be covetous. We need more. And more is attainable. Let us, therefore, enlarge our desires and our hopes, and seek to be filled with all the fullness of God.

JANUARY 11.—" Where dwellest thou?"—John i, 38.

THIS question was addressed to our Lord by two of John's disciples. One of them was Andrew, Simon Peter's brother—of the other we are ignorant; but they were both following Jesus. Then Jesus turned, and saw them following, and saith unto them, " What seek ye?" They said unto him, " Rabbi, where dwellest thou?"

Let us consider the principle of the inquiry. It was not curiosity, but regard. It was as much as to say, We wish to be better acquainted. John had spoken of him highly, and they had just seen him; but this, instead of satisfying them, drew forth their desire after more intimacy. Now this is common to all the subjects of divine grace, and arises from *their love to him.* For love longs to be near the object of attachment; separation is painful; distance is intolerable; while intercourse yields a pleasure words can no more describe than paint can express light or heat. Hence the believer longs to be with the Savior. "Tell me, O thou whom my soul loveth, where thou feedest, where thou makest thy flock to rest at noon; for why should I be as one that turneth aside from the paths of thy companions?" The desire ariseth also from *the want of him.* What can I do, says the Christian, without him? he is my deliverer, my helper, my guide, my comforter. The earth can do better without the sun than I can do without him, the sun of righteousness. The body does not depend so much upon the soul as I do upon him, the quickening Spirit. Who can screen me from the condemnation of the law? Who can relieve my burdened conscience? Whose grace is sufficient for me, to sanctify me in prosperity, to sustain me in adversity, to crown me in death? "Oh, cast me not away from thy presence, and take not thy Holy Spirit from me." I must live in the same place, the same house, the same room, where thou dwellest—"Where dwellest thou?"

But let us find, if we can, an answer to this question. "He saith unto them, Come and see;" and they went, and "saw where he dwelt." In a general way, he had not where to lay his head. It is not probable he had now a house to himself, but only an apartment hired or borrowed. But how was that lodging sanctified and honored! They showed Alexander, when in Holland, a house where Peter the Great resided, and which is preserved in memory of him. Many have seen at Olney the alcove where Cowper wrote his "Task." Oh, to have seen a dwelling where Jesus resided! But where dwells he now? He *is* every where, but he is not said to *dwell* every where. Dwelling, with regard to him, implies preference, and abiding with him, delight. First, then, he dwells in heaven; and this marks the place, yea—this makes it. "Where I am, there shall my servants be" "Absent from the body, and present with the Lord." Secondly, he dwells in his Church. "This," says he, "is my rest for ever; here will I dwell, for I have desired it." Thirdly, he dwells in the sanctuary. "In all *places* where I record my name, I will come unto thee, and I will bless thee." "*Where* two or three are gathered together in my name, *there* am I in the midst of them." And there his people have found him, and exclaimed, "Surely, God is in this place." Fourthly, He dwells in the heart. He will reject every other residence you may offer him. "My son," says he, "give me thine heart;" and from every believer he obtains what he demands. Christ dwells in his "heart by faith."

This may be called *enthusiasm* by some; but it is the language of Inspiration. "Hereby we know that he abideth in us, by the Spirit which he hath given us." Let me forbear to injure and insult a Christian. Let me revere and honor him: he is a palace of the Prince of Peace; a temple of the Lord of all. Let me admire the condescension and kindness of Immanuel, God with us; and if I am the subject of this residence, let me not only rejoice in the dignity and privilege, but be concerned to discharge every duty I owe to such a distinguished guest, to such a divine inhabitant! "Let the words of my mouth, and the meditation of my heart, be acceptable in thy sight, O Lord, my strength and my Redeemer."

JANUARY 12.—"And it came to pass, when Pharaoh had let the people go, that God led them not through the way of the land of the Philistines, although that was near; for God said, Lest peradventure the people repent when they see war, and they return to Egypt: but God led the people about, through the way of the wilderness of the Red Sea."—Exod. xiii, 17, 18.

THERE were two ways which they might have taken to their destination. One was from the north of Egypt to the south of Canaan This was short and direct, and would have taken but a few days, as we see in the case of Jacob's sons, when they fetched corn, and in the rapid incursion of Bonaparte. The other was very much farther, and very indirect, and yet God took this; and instead of leading them to the Isthmus of Suez, he conducted them to the border of the Red Sea. He therefore declined the common road which the people would have chosen, and which every one else might have recommended, and selected the most unlikely.

For his thoughts are not our thoughts; neither are his ways our ways. And the promise is, "I will bring the blind by a way that they know not; I will lead them in paths that they have not known: I will make darkness light before them, and crooked things straight." It is well that we are under his guidance, for the way of man is not in himself; it is not in man that walketh to direct his steps. We know not what is good for us; and, like children left to themselves, we should soon run into mischief. We are too ignorant, too selfish, too carnally minded, to choose for ourselves safely. How was it with the Jews in the time of Moses? They must have flesh; and he gave them their hearts' desire, but sent leanness into their souls. And was it not the same in the days of Samuel? They would have a king, and he gave them a king in his anger, and took him away in his wrath. And how has it been with ourselves? Have we not often been imposed upon both by our hopes and fears? Have we not anxiously desired what we now see would have proved injurious? And have we not been eager to escape what we now know has proved a blessing? If our bones have not been broken, have we not been bruised by the falls of our own rashness and folly? If we have not been thrown out of the vehicle, have we not endangered it enough to induce us to give back the reins into the proper hands? Surely we are not *yet* leaning to our own understanding, but committing our way unto the Lord. Surely we are *now* saying, the Lord shall choose our inheritance for us.

"Since all the downward tracks of time,
"His watchful eye surveys;
"O who so fit to choose our lot,
"And regulate our ways."

It is acknowledged that the course declined "was near." But, God being the judge, the nearest way is not always the best. Jacob, in obtaining the blessing, went the nearest way to work in imposing upon his blind father; but God's way would have been better, though it would have taken more time. Joseph's dreams might have been fulfilled by constraining his brethren to pay him immediate obeisance. But more than twenty years must previously elapse, and he must be sold into Egypt as a slave, and be imprisoned as a criminal, and be released as an interpreter, and possess all the store of the land as a deliverer. The thing was true; but the time appointed was long.

Yet the Lord's time is the best; and the fruit we covet will be much more rich and wholesome when ripe, than if seized and devoured while green. He that believeth, therefore, maketh not haste. "This world is a Mesech, and my soul is vexed with the conversation of the wicked. Why is not my taste gratified? and why am I not allowed to enter the region of purity and peace?" Because your principles are to be tried and exemplified. Because you are to serve your generation by the will of God. "How long have I waited for an answer to prayer, for a deliverance from affliction, for a sense of divine favor?" And are ye not told that "it is good for a man not only to hope, but quietly to wait for the salvation of God?" and that "Blessed are all they that wait for him?" The order of nature is not to reap as soon as the seed is sown—weeks and months of varied weather, and some of it dreary and chilling, are introductory and preparatory to the harvest. It is the same with the order of grace. "Be ye also patient."

God doth all things well; and if he led them the longest way, it was the right way. He did not choose it arbitrarily, but for reasons founded in his wisdom and kindness. Some of these reasons are not mentioned, but they were afterward developed; and the motive here assigned is well worthy of our attention. It was to keep them from "seeing war"—especially "with the Philistines," into contact with whom they would have immediately come the other way. At present they were not fitted for serious conflict. Their spirits had been broken by oppression, and they partook of the timidity, as well as meanness of slaves. They were raw recruits, shepherds, brickmakers. It was better for them not to fight for awhile, or to have only a distant brush with Amalek, rather than be plunged at once into a sanguinary contest with veteran foes, inured to battle, and rendered courageous by victory. How instructive is this! What is the counterpart of it? He knows our frame; he remembers that we are dust. A bruised reed will he not break, and the smoking flax will he not quench. He gathers the lambs with his arm, and carries them in his bosom. He affords to young converts some peculiar encouragements to allure them on, till they have advanced too far to think of going back, whatever they meet with. From a regard to their weakness, and want of experience, for a time he hides or restrains many of their enemies, and thus secures them from encounters with which more aged Christians are familiar. When will ministers and Christians learn to be followers of God? Under their guidance, persons who have but just left Egypt are often involved in controversies even with Philistines. They have scarcely entered the grammar school of repentance, before they are sent to the university of predestination. Babes, instead of being fed with milk, have strong meat given them, and even bones. Their hope is shaken, and their comfort destroyed, because they have not the confidence and assurance required of them.

But if we turn to the conduct of our Lord, we shall see that every thing is not to be advanced at once—every thing is not to be exacted of all, and in all circumstances. Hear *him.* "I have yet many things to say unto you, but ye cannot bear them now." "And they said unto him, Why do the disciples of John fast often, and make prayers, and likewise the disciples of the Pharisees, but thine eat and drink? And he said unto them, Can ye make the children of the bridechamber fast, while the bridegroom is with them? But the days will come when the bridegroom shall be taken away from them, and then shall they fast in those days. And he spake also a parable unto them: No man putteth a piece of a new garment upon an old: if otherwise, then both the new maketh a rent, and the piece that was taken out of the new agreeth not with the old. And no man putteth new wine into old bottles; else the new wine will burst the bottles, and be spilled, and the bottles shall perish. But new wine must be put into new bottles, and both are preserved."

JANUARY 13.—"The goodness of God leadeth thee to repentance.—Rom. ii, 4.

REPENTANCE is indispensable to fallen creatures. And though it be from God, as well as all the blessings annexed to it, yet there is an order in his operations, and he must do some things for us before he can do others. He must give grace, before he can give glory; and before he makes us happy with himself, he must make us holy like himself. Hence we read of "repentance unto life."

But let us observe the manner of his producing this repentance. We are *led to it by his goodness*—not driven by the terrors of the Almighty. Cain, Pharaoh, Judas, were all terrified into repentance: and there was nothing in their experience ingenuous or saving. Peter was led to repentance. He had sadly sinned, and denied his Lord with cursings. But the Lord turned and looked upon Peter; and the look broke his heart, and "he went out and wept bitterly." And, says God, "thou shalt remember and be confounded, and never open thy mouth any more, because of thy shame, when I am pacified toward thee for all that thou hast done."

In the Gospel he draws with the bands of a man and with the cords of love. And the repentance here spoken of is the tender mother pulling her infant to her knee, while chiding him, and constraining the little offender to hide his blushing face, and to sob out his heart into her bosom—not the stern father, driving the transgressor from his face into distance, and concealment, and dislike, and falsehood, Or, if it be the father, it is the father of the prodigal. Impatient of paternal restraint, he asked for his portion of goods, and went away into a very far country. Soon all he had was spent: and there arose a famine in the land, and he began to be in want; and he went and hired himself to keep swine—and oft he looked at his grovelling charge, and said, "O that I was one of you, and could eat and die, and be no more." He even fed upon their vile fare, for no man gave unto him. At length he came to himself, and the thought of home struck him. "There is bread enough in my father's house, and I here perish with hunger. I will arise and go unto my father." While he was yet a great way off, hovering about, and afraid to draw nigh, his father saw him, and had compassion on him, and ran and fell on his neck and kissed him. He had prepared a confession, acknowledging the vilest guilt, and a petition, imploring the meanest favor; but forgiving, overflowing love prevented the expression of either. "Bring forth the best robe, and put it on him; and put a ring on his hand, and shoes on his feet; and bring forth the fatted calf, and kill it, and let us eat and be merry; for this my son was dead, and is alive again; he was lost, and is found."

He felt his unworthiness before, but he was a thousand times more penitent now. "What a father have I sinned against! What excellence have I contemned! What love have I abused!" How would he blush and weep, as he was not only clothed, but adorned; and not only fed, but feasted. How, as the ring touched his finger, and he was conducted into the room of mirth, prepared for *him!* how, almost sinking under the weight of obligation, would he be ready to say, "How can I bear all this?" And would not the father be more endeared to him by forgiveness than by birth? And after all this, would he be able to stab his father to the heart? To offend him? To grieve him? Must he not delight to obey him? and every moment ask, What wilt thou have me to do?

Despair hardens; but we are saved by hope. Threatenings may make us afraid to go on; but goodness makes us unwilling. Terrors may wrest the weapons of rebellion out of our hand; but goodness induces us to hate them, and throw them down—and weep over them—and return and vow, "O Lord, other lords beside thee have had dominion over us; henceforth by thee only will we make mention of thy name."

How mistaken then are many with regard to Christian repentance. It is not legal, but evangelical. It is not slavish, but filial. It is not degrading, but connected with the noblest feelings of the heart. It is not desponding and miserable, but lives in the comforts of the Holy Ghost. And "blessed are they that mourn, for they shall be comforted."

JANUARY 14.—"And it came to pass the third day, which was Pharaoh's birth-day, that he made a feast unto all his servants; and he lifted up the head of the chief butler, and of the chief baker, among his servants.—Gen. xl, 20.

If the chief butler had been falsely, and the chief baker had been justly accused, the providence of God was now seen in the clearing of the one, and the punishment of the other. If both were either equally innocent or guilty, here was an instance of the arbitrariness of a prince, who probably prided himself in his absolute authority, and in having it said, "Whom he would he slew, and whom he would he kept alive." Or, perhaps, he designed to show his subjects that he would be known both in the exercise of mercy and judgment. And hence, the *season* was his birth-day.

The birth-day of princes has been anciently and generally solemnized as a token of the respect due to their sovereignty: but it has often been abused, and given rise to wickedness and mischief. We see this in the case of Jeroboam. At the commemoration of his birth, intemperance rioted; and the intoxication of the king himself injured his health, and made him forget his dignity in his joining familiarly with low buffoons and jesters: "In the day of our king the princes have made him sick with bottles of wine: he stretched out his hand with scorners." And how was it on a similar occasion with Herod? "Herod on his birth-day made a supper to his lords, high captains, and chief estates in Galilee"—the daughter of Herodias danced—the king was excited—and John was beheaded!

But, in almost every rank of life, the usage prevails, of persons observing with some degree of festivity the day of their birth. The thing is lawful in itself, if it be used lawfully. It might be used profitably. But our pious forefathers made it a day of relative intercourse and congratulations, yet a day also of pious feeling and regard. And surely it should be made

—A day of thanksgiving to the Author and Giver of life—For our being—for the rank we occupy in the scale of creation—for the country and family in which we were brought forth—for our civil and religious advantages—and for our preservation through so many perils—and when so many have been cut off.

—A day of humiliation—That we were shapen in iniquity, and in sin did our mother conceive us—that we went astray from the womb—that our transgressions are innumerable, and our trespass is gone up into the very heavens—and that we have not improved, as we ought to have done, any of our privileges—"I do remember my faults this day."

—A day of reflection—That as there is a time to be born, so there is a time to die—that so much of life is already passed away as a shadow—that when a few years come, we shall go the way whence we shall not return—that our continuance here is as uncertain as it is short—that we may never see this day again—and if we do not—where shall we be when it returns?

—A day of prayer—That we may so number our days as to apply our hearts unto wisdom—that we may obtain pardoning mercy and renewing grace—that we may be prepared for all the duties and trials that lie before us—that whether we live we may live unto the Lord, or whether we die we may die unto the Lord; so that living and dying we may be the Lord's.

Happy they who, without complaining of their lot, or being impatient to be gone, yet know that the day of their death is better than the day of their birth. Though for them to live is Christ, to die is gain; and every returning birth-day tells them, "So much nearer your heavenly home."

But how dreadful the state of those who know, and if they consider, they must know—that every year advances them so much away from all they love; and brings them so much nearer a world in which, as they have no hope, so after which they can have no desire. If conscience be not stupified, and all thought banished by company and gayety—a birth-day to them is far from enviable. Verses may be written; addresses may be received; smiles may be put on: but even in laughter the heart is sorrowful, and the end of that mirth is heaviness.

What a difference in the two following references to the birth of the individuals.

"Who," says Voltaire, "can, without horror, consider the whole world as the empire of destruction? It abounds with wonders; it also abounds with victims. It is a vast field of carnage and contagion. Every species is without pity pursued and torn to pieces, through the earth, and air, and water. In man there is more wretchedness than in all the other animals put together. He loves life, and yet he knows that he must die. If he enjoys a transient good, he suffers various evils, and is at last devoured by worms. This knowledge is his fatal prerogative: other animals have it not. He spends the transient moments of his existence in diffusing the miseries which he suffers; in cutting the throats of his fellow creatures for pay; in cheating and being cheated; in robbing and being robbed; in serving, that he might command; and in repenting of all he does. The bulk of mankind are nothing more than a crowd of wretches, equally criminal and unfortunate; and the globe contains rather carcasses than men. I tremble at the review of this dreadful picture to find that it contains a complaint against Providence itself; and I WISH I HAD NEVER BEEN BORN."

Now let us hear the language of the excellent Hallyburton, who died as he lived, full of confidence in God. "I shall shortly get a very different sight of God from what I have ever had, and shall be made meet to praise him for ever and ever. O the thoughts of an incarnate Deity are sweet and ravishing. O how I wonder at myself that I do not love him more, and that I do not admire him more. What a wonder that I enjoy such composure under all my bodily pains, and in the view of death itself. What a mercy that, having the use of my reason, I can declare his goodness to my soul. I long for his salvation; I bless his name I have found him, and die rejoicing in him. O blessed be God that I WAS BORN! O that I was where he is. I have a father and mother, and ten brothers and sisters, in heaven, and I shall be the eleventh. O there is a telling in this Providence, and I shall be telling it for ever. If there be such a *glory* in his conduct toward me now, what will it be to see the Lamb in the midst of the throne? Blessed be God that—ever I WAS BORN."

JANUARY 15.—"Unto thee, O Lord, do I lift up my soul."—Ps. xxv, 1.

IT is not easy to do this. We are naturally sluggish and groveling. Who has not reason to acknowledge, with shame and sorrow, "My soul cleaveth unto the dust?" It is easy enough, in duty, to lift up our hands, and our eyes, and our voices; but it is another thing to come even to his seat, to enter into the secret of his tabernacle, and to hold intercourse with the God of heaven. And yet, without this, what is devotion? And how unanswerable will our services be to the requisition of Him who is a Spirit, and seeketh such to worship him as worship him in spirit and in truth?

And without this a real Christian is no more satisfied than God. He will not, indeed, from a principle of duty, undervalue the means of grace, and neglect private and public devotion; but he is disappointed unless he can lift up his soul unto God. And this marks the spiritual worshipper. He is not distinguished by always enjoying liberty and fervor in his holy exercises, but he mourns the want of them; while the formalist looks no further than the performance itself, and returns from the House and Throne of God, without ever inquiring whether he has had communion with Him.

It is the spirituality of religion that befriends enjoyment. Nothing yields us pleasure but in proportion as the heart is engaged in the pursuit. How dull, how tiresome are those tasks, in which,

"In vain to heaven we lift our cries, "And leave our souls behind."

But it is good to draw *near* to God. Then there is a sacred charm that keeps our thoughts from wandering, and we attend on the Lord without distraction. Then we feel no weariness of spirit. We call the Sabbath a delight. We find his words, and eat them. And our meditation of Him is sweet.

And when such a worshipper comes forth, he will be ready to say to all he meets, " That which we have seen and heard declare we unto you; that ye may have fellowship with us; and truly our fellowship is with the Father, and with his Son Jesus Christ. And *His* recommendations are likely to have some effect. For his profit will appear unto all men. His face shines. His heart speaks. His life speaks. His character speaks. He *must* be impressive and influential. He *will* be felt—in the family—in the church—and in the world. He cannot but do good, even without pretension—without effort.

" When such a man familiar with the skies,
" Has filled his urn where those pure waters rise;
" And once more mingles with us, meaner things,
" 'Tis e'en as if an angel shook his wings—
" Immortal fragrance fills the circuit wide,
" Which tells us whence his treasures are supplied."

JANUARY 16.—" I know the thoughts that I think toward you, saith the Lord; thoughts of peace, and not of evil, to give you an expected end." Jer. xxix, 11.

WHAT can the people of God desire more? They are here assured by Himself that he *thinks* of them; that he *knows* his thoughts toward them; that they are *kind* in their nature, thoughts of *peace*, and not of *evil;* and that they regard an *end*, allowing and requiring *expectation*, to bring them to an *expected end.*

He designed and procured the Jews good in Babylon; but the ransomed of the Lord were to return, and come to Zion. " After seventy years be accomplished at Babylon, I will visit you, and perform my good word toward you, in causing you to return to this place." Here we see what was *their* expected end. And what did it prefigure . .ut " the end of our faith, even the salvation of our souls"—" the end, everlasting life." The Christian is now on the sea, encountering many a wind, and feeling many a fear; but the voyage will end, and he will be brought into the desired haven. He is now on a journey, and he is often discouraged because of the way; but it will end in a better country, and at his Father's house, where are many mansions. He is now in a warfare; and though it be a good one, it is trying and painful. But the strife will soon end, and the head exchange the helmet for " the crown of glory that fadeth not away."

But what characterizes the posture of the believer's mind with regard to this? Expectation. He is looking for that blessed hope. He is waiting for the Savior from heaven. For he is now saved by hope. Every thing now leads him forward Creatures, ordinances, his connexions, his experience, every thing in his painful and in his pleasant feelings; all, all says, " Arise, and depart hence, for this is not your rest." Human expectation is seldom justified by the event. If the votary do not miss his aim, he is disappointed in his object, his heart sighs in the midst of his success. But let the Christian's expectation be as great as even the Scripture can make it, the blessedness itself will be much greater, and the fruition will induce the acknowledgment, "The half was not told me." Yet the expectation is very distinguishable from the confidence of the presumptuous. Natural men find it a very easy thing to hope, because they hope without any proper sense of their unworthiness and guilt; they hope without examination, without evidence, uninformed and unauthorized. It is one of the first works of the Spirit of God to break up this state of mind; and then the man can say with Paul, "I was alive without the law once; but when the commandment came, sin revived, and I died." Yet, while he for ever shuts this door of hope, he opens another; he turns him from the law to the gospel; from self to the Savior; from going about to establish his own righteousness, to submit himself to the righteousness which is of God. Hence arises what the apostle calls "*a good hope through grace*;" and the goodness consists not so much in the strength of the confidence, as in the solidity of the foundation, and the clearness and fullness of the warrant. Our Lord speaks of two builders, the one he calls a fool, and the other a wise man. But the difference between them was not so much in the edifices themselves, as in the ground-work. Both structures looked fair enough to the passenger, but the house of the former was built upon the sand, and the storm carried it away, while that of the latter stood every assault, for it was founded on a rock. What a sandy base has the hope of many. How certainly and easily will it be overthrown—the expectation of the sinner, the worldling, the hypocrite, and the Pharisee. But the Christian's hope maketh not ashamed; it rests on the foundation laid in Zion, and the possessor cannot be confounded, unless God can become a liar, and be chargeable with perjury; for he has not only promised, but sworn; and "because he could swear by no greater, he swore by himself."

Keep much alive this expectation. Let nothing shake its confidence. Let nothing obscure the object, or the ground of it. It can do wonders, and will produce a thousand advantages in proportion as it is realized.

I repair to the believer who is fully exemplifying it; and I find him dead to the world, and "all that earth calls good and great." And what is the cause? "An expected end." He has looked within the vail, and seen the glory that excelleth. The sun has rendered invisible the glow-worms, and the stars too.

I find him satisfied with an inferior condition in life, and though denied many indulgences with which the children of this generation abound. And what is the reason? "An expected end." There are at home, says he, but I am not.

> **"Their hope and portion lie below, "'Tis all the happiness they know."**

But I am a stranger and pilgrim, I am at an inn; it yields me but few entertainments, or even accommodations—so much the better. It might otherwise tempt and detain me: but now it urges me on.

And what makes him so cheerful in his trials? "An expected end."

> **"A hope so much divine, "May trials well endure."**

And this hope, says he, I have as anchor of the soul, both sure and steadfast: and "I reckon that the sufferings of the present time are not worthy to be compared with the glory which shall be revealed." This expected end, also, says he, animates me in all the difficulties attending a course of obedience. If hope actuates to such exertions, hardships, and sacrifices, the sons of learning, fame, and wealth, should *I* ever be cold, or discouraged, with the certainty before me of an eternity, an infinity of all good? This too, says he, composes me in the prospect, and reconciles me to the approach of death. In itself, it is far from pleasant, but it is the right way to a city of habitation; a departure to be with Christ, which is far better. He also can make the exit as gentle as the issue is glorious. However this may be,

" 'Tis there for ever I shall dwell,
" With Jesus in the realms of day;
" Then I shall bid these fears farewell,
" And he will wipe my tears away.

" Jesus, on thee our hope depends,
" To lead us on to thine abode;
" Assured our hope will make amends
" For all our toil upon the road."

JANUARY 17.—' The law was our schoolmaster, to bring us unto Christ.
Gal. iii, 14.

WHAT law? Three kinds of law were given to the Jews. It is not necessary to exclude either, though the last is principally intended.

The *judicial*. This regarded their policy as a nation; regulated their conduct toward each other; and determined their civil crimes and penalties. Even this led to Christ; especially the right of redemption, which lay with the nearest of kin; and the provision of the cities of refuge. Happy they who have fled for relief to him that was prefigured by them.

The *ceremonial*. This prescribed their worship, and enjoined a multitude of services and sacrifices which were all shadows of good things to come, but the body was Christ. It would be endless to particularize. The tabernacle, the mercy-seat, the altar, the table of shew-bread, the paschal lamb—all these led to him, and derived their importance from the relation. And hence those who deny their typical use have always spoken depreciatingly of them. The Jews were in the infancy of the Church; and these ceremonies were like pictures placed over the child's lessons: or the whole economy may be considered as a star to the travellers in search of the Consolation of Israel, going before them till it stood over where the young child was—and then disappearing.

The *moral*. This was of universal and perpetual obligation; being founded not on any positive appointment or authority, but in the nature of man, and the relations between him and God; and between him and his fellow creatures. The substance of it is, to love God supremely, and our neighbor as ourselves. Is this unreasonable? Can God himself dispense with it? Can he require less?

Now this leads us to Christ, first, by convincing us of sin; for by the law is the knowledge of sin. It is owing to men's ignorance of this law they think so well of themselves. Did they know that it ranks all omissions of duty in the number of sins; that it extends to the state of the heart, as well as of the life; and to our motives and principles, as well as our actions, self-abased they would cry out, " Enter not into judgment with thy servant, for in thy sight shall no man living be justified."

Secondly, by showing us our danger. This results from transgression: for the curse enters with all sin. "Cursed is every one that continueth not in all things written in the book of the law to do them." If you were in a room, where there was a dead lion, you need not be afraid. But if while you were walking by, he should come to life, and rise upon his feet, and glare his eye-balls, and begin to roar, as he revived, you would die with fear. So it was with Paul—"I was alive," says he, "without the law, but when the commandment came, sin revived, and I died."

Thirdly, by gendering despair of life by it. Here again the Apostle tells us, that his death *to* the law was also *by* it. "I *through* the law am dead unto the law, that I might live unto God." Thus the extremity of the danger makes us call out for a deliverer. Famine lectured back the Prodigal to his father's house; and disease drives the patient to apply to a physician, which he would otherwise neglect, and submit to a remedy which he would otherwise reject. "The law is our schoolmaster to bring us unto Christ."

The law, therefore, is good if it be used lawfully, and ministers ought to preach it. Some pass under a greater law work than others; but let none question the genuineness of the relief they have obtained, because they have not experienced much terror and distress. This terror and distress are but in the order of means; and the design of them is answered if we are brought to Christ, and acquiesce in *his* salvation.

—Every one, therefore, that hath heard and learned of the Father cometh unto him, and can find encouragement no where else. And him that cometh unto me, says the Savior, I will in no wise cast out.

JANUARY 18.—**"I had not thought to see thy face; and lo, God hath shewed me also thy seed."—Gen. xlviii, 11.**

THIS was the language of the dying Jacob, when Joseph presented to him his two sons, Manasseh and Ephraim.

We behold in it his *piety*. He owns God in his indulgences—*He* has shown me. Our comforts are sanctified and rendered doubly sweet when we receive them all from *his* hand. Let others live without God with them in the world; I would acknowledge him in all my ways. Let them ascribe their successes and enjoyments to chance, or to the power of their friends, or to their own diligence and skill; I would give him the glory that is due only to *his* name; and remember that whatever be the medium of my comfort, he is the source; that whatever be the instrument, he is the author. "The blessing of the Lord, it maketh rich, and he addeth no sorrow with it."

Observe, also, his *language;* his expectation was more than exceeded. We remember the sad relation of Joseph's loss, and the garment dipped in blood, by which his grief was deluded, though not relieved. "And he knew it, and said, It is my son's coat; an evil beast hath devoured him: Joseph is without doubt rent in pieces. And Jacob rent his clothes, and put sackcloth upon his loins, and mourned for his son many days. And all his sons and all his daughters rose up to comfort him; but he refused to be comforted; and he said, For I will go down into the grave unto my son mourning. Thus his father wept for him." For many years he never dreamed of his survival:

but added, "Joseph is not, and Simeon is not, and will ye take Benjamin away? All these things are against me." In process of time, however, all this gloomy conclusion was contradicted: "And they told him, saying, Joseph is yet alive, and he is governor over all the land of Egypt. And Jacob's heart fainted, for he believed them not. And they told him all the words of Joseph, which he had said unto them: and when he saw the waggons which Joseph had sent to carry him, the spirit of Jacob their father revived: and Israel said, It is enough; Joseph my son is yet alive: I will go and see him before I die." By and by this was fulfilled; "And Joseph made ready his chariot, and went up to meet Israel his father, to Goshen, and presented himself unto him; and he fell on his neck, and wept on his neck a good while. And Israel said unto Joseph, Now let me die, since I have seen thy face, because thou art yet alive."

Something, however, was still wanting. Joseph had sons; and these would be peculiarly endeared to Jacob. At length he embraces *them*, as well as the father—"I had not thought to see thy face; and lo, God hath shewed me also thy *seed*."

Is this the only instance in which God has not only frustrated the fears, but surpassed the hopes of his people? When Moses was in the ark of bulrushes, all his parents could have hoped for would have been his preservation, or falling into the hands of some kind individual, who, affected with his infancy and suffering, would have taken care of him—though they should never have seen him more. But Pharaoh's daughter finds him, and adopts him; and his mother becomes his nurse, and he is educated in all the learning of Egypt; and he appears the deliverer and leader of Israel! David said, I shall one day perish by the hand of Saul: but after a number of hairbreadth escapes, he was saved from *all* his enemies, and sat down upon the throne, "a wonder unto many."

How many are there in whose experience this remark has been exemplified, as to temporal things. They once had no inheritance, not so much as to set their foot on: and all they hoped to gain by their humble effors, was only bread to eat and raiment to put on; and lo! he has given them not only subsistence, but competency and affluence. And as to spiritual things—the penitent remembers how, when awakened out of his sleep, and he gazed on the horrors of his state, there seemed nothing left but a certain fearful looking for of judgment and fiery indignation. How hard did he find it to hope even for deliverance! But the Lord appeared to his joy; and not only spared and pardoned him, but enriched and ennobled him: and took him not only into his service, but into his house and into his bosom.

But in nothing has this observation been more frequently verified than in the dying experience of believers. They had all their lifetime been subject to bondage through fear of death; a thousand comforts had been imbittered by the apprehension—but this did not affect their safety then; and when their departure was at hand, they were filled with peace and joy; and had an abundant entrance ministered unto them into the Savior's everlasting kingdom. Some who had trembled at the shaking of a leaf before, have then displayed a courage amounting to more than heroism; and those who had shrunk back from speaking, especially concerning themselves, had shouted aloud upon their beds, and sung of His righteousness. "Ah!" says Dr. Goodwin, "Is this dying? How have I dreaded as an enemy this smiling friend!" To die is gain.

When the Queen of Sheba, though accustomed to royal magnificence, witnessed the glory of Solomon, she exclaimed, The half was not told me. So the believer, after all the reports of the Scripture, all the earnests and foretastes of Heaven, finds it to be a glory yet to be revealed; and when he arrives at the possession, he will acknowledge that eye had not seen, nor ear heard, nor had entered into the heart of man the things which God has prepared for them that love him.

Let all this scatter our doubts, and lead us to say, "Why art thou cast down, O my soul? and why art thou disquieted within me? Hope thou in God: for I shall yet praise him." Especially let us view, through the force of this truth, all our future duties and difficulties. We are not to limit the Holy One of Israel. What is impossible to us, is easy to him. His thoughts and ways are as far above ours as the heavens are higher than the earth; and he is able to do for us exceeding abundantly above all we can ask or think. We have read of an Emperor, who said, he delighted to undertake enterprises deemed by his counsellors and captains impracticable; and he seldom failed in them. God cannot fail; but he loves to surprise. He, therefore, turneth the shadow of death into the morning. At eventide, says He, it shall be light.

JANUARY 19.—"**And Noah walked with God.**"—**Gen. vi, 9.**

THE Apostle gives us a fine representation of religion, when speaking of God, he says, "with whom we have to do." We have to do with our fellow creatures in various relations: but morality must be supported by piety, and flow from it. It is with God we have principally to do. Our connexions with him, our expectations from him, our obligations to him, are infinitely supreme.

Three expressions are observable as to our walking with regard to God. First, we read of "walking *after* the Lord." This supposes him to be our leader and example; and requires us to be followers of him as dear children. "They shall walk after the Lord," says Hosea. Secondly, we read of walking *before* God. This supposes him to be our observer and witness—we are thus always in his sight. "Walk before me," said God to Abraham. "I will walk before the Lord," says David, "in the land of the living." We also read of "walking *with* God." So did Noah; so did Enoch; so does every partaker of divine grace. But this seems to hold him forth as our companion and friend. This is surprising; but so it is. There is an intercourse between us—we have fellowship one with another. In order to this, reconciliation is necessary: for "how can two walk together except they be agreed?" And this reconciliation must be mutual. It is not enough that God is reconciled to us through the blood of the cross—we must be also reconciled to God, and love his presence, and choose his way.

For walking *with* God implies a oneness of course; and supposes that we advance together toward the same end. God's aim is his own glory; and we are enjoined, "whether we eat or drink, or whatever we do, to do all to the glory of God." As far as we observe this rule, we walk with God; as far as we neglect it, we leave God, and go in another direction.

If we are familiar and conversant with any one, we unavoidably catch something of his spirit and manners. Hence it is said, "He that walketh with wise men shall be wise; but a companion of fools shall be destroyed." If I walk with God I shall resemble him, and all will take knowledge of me that I have been with Jesus.

How envied would the man be that was allowed to walk with the king. But I walk with the King of kings, and the Lord of lords. "Such honor have all the saints." What security have I in nearness to Him? "He is at my right hand; I shall not be moved." What can I want if I have Him? "My presence shall go with thee; and I will give thee rest."

"Were I in heaven without my God,
"'Twould be no joy to me;
"And while this earth is my abode,
"I long for none but Thee."

JANUARY 20.—"And praying, the heaven was opened, and the Holy Ghost descended in a bodily shape like a dove upon him."—Luke, iii, 22.

WE may consider this descent three ways: as an answer to prayer, as a miraculous testimony, and as a significant emblem.

He had just been baptized, and was now going to enter on his public office, and we are told he prayed. Whether he prayed vocally, or only mentally, we know not; but he prayed really. And if prayer was necessary for him, can it be needless for us? And he prayed exemplarily; and has taught us to pray after we have been engaged in any ordinance, and before we enter on any undertaking. He also prayed successfully. Indeed, the Father heard him always, because he always prayed according to the will of God. But how prompt was the answer! It reached him in the very act of devotion. "And *praying*, the heaven was opened, and the Holy Ghost descended in a bodily shape like a dove upon him." It was the same in the transfiguration. "*As* he prayed, the fashion of his countenance was altered, and his raiment was white and glistening." The prayer of faith is always immediately heard, and if it be not always immediately answered, it is not from a want of disposition in God to bless us, but because he is a God of judgment, and waits to be gracious. But if we consult the Scripture, and appeal to our own experience, and especially observe, not only the benefit we have derived *from* prayer, but *in* it, we shall know that he is a God at hand, and not afar off; and verify the truth of his own word: "It shall come to pass, that before they call, I will answer; and while they are yet speaking, I will hear."

It is to be viewed also as a miracle; and so it was an authentication of his divine mission. Hence the voice that accompanied it—"Thou art my beloved Son; in thee I am well pleased." Hence John was previously informed of this confirmation. For though his relation, yet (to preclude all collusion and management) John had not seen Jesus before this event; but was taught, when they met, to recognise him by it. "And John bare record saying, I saw the Spirit descending from heaven like a dove, and it abode upon him. And I knew him not; but he that sent me to baptize with water, the same said unto me, Upon whom thou shalt see the Spirit descending, and remaining on him, the same is he which baptizeth with the Holy Ghost." John, therefore, could not but be instantly and perfectly convinced: "And I saw," says he, "and bare record, that this is the Son of God." Nothing, therefore, could have been more unsuspicious and decisive. The sign was foretold—its brilliancy, form, and descent, were obvious to sense—it remained on him for a considerable time—and all was in the presence of a multitude of spectators! How different are the miracles of the gospel from the prodigies of heathenism, and the lying wonders of the church of Rome!

But in whatever visible form the Holy Ghost had alighted upon the Savior's head, the miracle would have been the same. But the symbol would not have been the same. His descending in "a bodily shape *like a dove*," was intended to be an emblem. First, an emblem of the dispensation he had to announce. The law is called a fiery law, and it worketh wrath to every transgressor. The nature of it was intimated even in the very manner of its promulgation. The mount shook, and burned with fire. There was blackness, and darkness, and tempest, and the sound of a trumpet, and the voice of words. The people could not endure that which was commanded. And so terrible was the sight, that Moses said, I exceedingly fear and quake. But grace and truth came by Jesus Christ. And how? The moment he is inaugurated, and is stepping forth to preach the kingdom of heaven, the heaven opens—not for the thunder to roll, and the lightnings to flash, but for the Holy Ghost to descend in a bodily shape like a dove upon him!

Did the dove return into the ark with an olive branch, thereby announcing that the flood had subsided? And has he, with a leaf in his mouth, ever since been viewed as the image of a messenger of peace? Who came and attested deliverance from the wrath to come? Who came and preached peace to them that were far off, and to them that were nigh? What says the Church? "Rise up, my love, my fair one, and come away: for lo, the winter is past, the rain is over and gone; the flowers appear on the earth, the time of the singing of birds is come, and the voice of the turtle is heard in our land?" But who was the harbinger of another spring—of a nobler renovation? Who cries, "Come, for all things are now ready?"

Secondly, an emblem of his personal character. All the love, tenderness, gentleness, mildness, for which the dove seems always to have been considered as a kind of representative, were to be found in him. So the prophecies going before had described him. And if we observe his miracles, if we enter into his life, his whole life on earth, we shall see him going about doing good. How kind to friends! How merciful to the distressed! How gracious to the guilty! How ready to forgive! How patient under provocation! He was compassion, alive and embodied.

Thirdly, an emblem of the temper of his disciples. For there must be a conformity between him and them. In all things he has the pre-eminence; but if any man has not the Spirit of Christ, he is none of his. He that is joined to the Lord is of one spirit—and how did the Holy Ghost descend upon him? As a *dove*.

Estimate, therefore, your religion by your resemblance to this image. Do not judge of your having the Spirit by opinions, but principles; by impressions, but dispositions; by gifts, but grace. Some fear they are strangers to the Spirit, because they have not received it in a particular way; that is, after great terror and anguish of soul. This is, indeed, sometimes the case; but it is not always so. In this manner the jailer's religion commenced; but it was not thus with Cornelius, nor Lydia.

Whatever distress or horror of conviction we have felt, they are nothing, if they have not brought us to Christ; and if we *have* been brought, let us be thankful and rejoice, "if by any means." The best thing is to judge, not by the manner of the operation, but the influence itself, and its effects, or by the fruit of the Spirit; and "the fruit of the Spirit is love, joy, peace, long-suffering, gentleness, goodness, faith, meekness, temperance. Against such there is no law." And as many as walk according to this rule, peace be on them, and mercy, and upon the Israel of God."

JANUARY 21.—" And the Lord said unto Moses, Get thee up into this mount Abarim, and see the land which I have given unto the children of Israel. And when thou hast seen it, thou also shalt be gathered unto thy people, as Aaron thy brother was gathered."—Numb. xxvii, 12, 13.

REFLECTIONS on death can never be unseasonable while we are in a dying world, and a dying church, and are conscious that we ourselves are dying creatures. It is said, God sees no iniquity in his people. But he has threatened to visit their transgressions with a rod. Some tell us, that sin never hurts a believer. But it hurt David and Eli. Moses was also severely chastised. He was very dear to God, and could plead great provocation; but because he rebelled against his commandment in the desert of Zin, in the strife of the congregation, he was excluded the land of Canaan; and though he was very importunate, he could not obtain a repeal of the trying sentence. But in judgment God remembers mercy. He here orders him to die; but the order is attended with three softenings to reconcile him to it.

First. He must die—but he shall previously go up, and "see the land which the Lord has given to the children of Israel." Some might suppose that this would tantalize him, and add to his affliction at the loss; but it was designed as an alleviation, and it was accepted by Moses as a favor. For this purpose his natural sight continued uninjured, and his extent of vision was perhaps also enlarged. Thus not only was his curiosity gratified, but he saw, with gladness and praise, the goodness and truth of God's promise to his people; while, in type, he hailed the prospect of a better country, even a heavenly, and which he was going to enter. O, say many, apprehensive now of the solemn event,

"O! could we make our doubts remove,
"These gloomy doubts that rise,
"And view the Canaan that we love,
"With unbeclouded eyes!

"Could *we* but climb where *Moses* stood,
"And view the landscape o'er;
"Nor Jordan's stream, nor death's cold flood,
"Should fright us from the shore."

And they are generally indulged. And often those have been peculiarly favored, who all their life-time have been subject to bondage through fear of death.

Secondly. He must die—but this will be "a gathering unto his people." To Abraham, and Isaac, and Jacob, and Joseph, and the Israel of God. These he so prized on earth, that he chose rather to suffer affliction with the people of God, than to enjoy the pleasures of sin for a season. Some had departed that he had known, and numbers that he had not known: but he was to join them—not in the same grave, for he was buried alone, and no one knows of his sepulchre unto this day; but in heaven—not as to his body, but as to his soul, which was to be united with the spirits of just men made perfect. The believer expects a family meeting. There, says he,

"There my best friends, my kindred dwell,
"There God my Savior reigns."

Thirdly. He must die—but "only as Aaron his brother was gathered." And are we better than those who have gone before us? And is there any reason why we should be exempted from their lot? The previous removal of the pious, especially those of our own relations, tends to render death more familiar. It comes near enough for us to view it. It enters our very apartments. It also tends to diminish our forebodings and despondency. We have seen that God was better to them than their fears. He was with them in the valley. Their end was peace. They were supported; they were comforted—and we thank God, and take courage. Why should it not be so with us? It also weakens our attachment to life. We have fewer attractions below, and so many more above. Who has not felt the sentiment, "Let us also go away, that we may die with him."

Surely the bitterness of death is past.

"I could renounce my all below,
"If my Creator bid;
"And run, if I were called to go,
"And die as Moses did."

JANUARY 22.—"And they said one to another, Did not our heart burn within us, while he talked with us by the way, and while he opened to us the Scriptures?"—Luke, xxiv. 32.

THAT is, we have *now* discovered him. How is it that we did not discover him earlier? and find him out upon the road! Why did we not distinguish him by his very speaking—the manner of it—the effect of it—in touching and animating the heart?

Ah! my soul, it is thus his teaching is to be known—it is always FELT. And while other teachers reach only the ear, he penetrates the heart, and causes it to burn with ingenuous shame, with abhorrence of sin, with holy revenge, with love to his name, with zeal for his glory, and earnestness to save sinners.

He *now* converses with us by the way, and he opens to us the Scriptures, and he does it in three ways.

First, by his dispensations. As the word explains Providence, so Providence illustrates the word. How many passages are there in the Bible, the beauty of which we should never have seen, the sweetness of which we should never have tasted, the force of which we should never have felt, had it not been for certain events, and those chiefly of an afflictive kind. These drive us to the book, never so valued as in the day of trouble, and enable us to read with other eyes, and with other light, than before.

Secondly, by the labors of his servants. He replenishes his ministers that they may dispense to others; he gives them the tongue of the learned, that they should know how to speak a word in season to him that is weary. It was in the temple David wished to inquire; it was when he went into the sanctuary of God, that he seized a clue which enabled him to unravel a mystery which had so confounded and distressed him before. And while hearing the word preached, have not our doubts been often solved, our fears dispelled, our faith and hope strengthened? That which was general before, has been particularized; that which was distant, has been brought home to our apprehensions; that which was read without impression or notice, has become significant and interesting. How often has the Angel of the Church, like Hagar's angel, opened our eyes, and shown us the well.

Thirdly, by the agency of his Holy Spirit. "He shall lead you into all truth." Means do not render his influence needless—revelation itself does not. David had the word of God, but he kneeled and prayed, "Open thou mine eyes, that I may behold wondrous things out of thy law." The dial tells us the time, but the sun must shine upon it; the compass enables the mariner to steer, but not if it be placed in the dark. "In thy light we shall see light." Here is the promise at once to direct and encourage. "If any man lack wisdom, let him ask of God, who giveth to all men liberally and upbraideth not, and it shall be given him." What is the reason why many, in the greatness of their folly, for ever go astray? They do not trust in the Lord with all their heart, but lean to their own understandings; while the way-faring man, though a fool, errs not therein; because, made sensible of his ignorance and insufficiency, he in all his ways acknowledges God, and God himself directs his paths.

JANUARY 23.—"Knock, and it shall be opened unto you."—Luke, xi, 9.

It is needless to prove, that by this action our Savior intends prayer. But see the simplicity and familiarity of *his* comparisons, and wonder not that the common people heard him gladly. Volumes have been written upon the subject of prayer; but he who spake as never man spake, comprises every thing in one word—*knock.* The allusion is to a person who wishes to excite attention, in order to obtain relief—he knocks.

Where are we to knock? "I am," says the Savior, "the door." "I am the way, the truth, and the life: no man cometh to the Father but by me."

When are we to knock? "Morning, and evening, and noon," says David, "will I pray and cry aloud." "Pray without ceasing," says Paul. And, says our Lord, "Men ought always to pray, and not to faint."

For *what* are we to knock? We may in every thing, by prayer and supplication, make known our requests unto God. But we are supremely to implore all spiritual blessings, because these are blessings for the soul and eternity. Seek ye first the kingdom of God and his righteousness.

How are we to knock? *Importunately*—we cannot knock too loud. Prayer is nothing, unless it be sincere and earnest. God will not regard the address we ourselves do not feel. Jacob said, "I will not let thee go, except thou bless me:" and he prevailed. How? *Perseveringly.* The Lord does not alway immediately appear to our joy. "I waited patiently for the Lord," says David, "and at last he inclined his ear unto me, and heard my cry." And, "blessed," it is said, "are all they that wait for him." But though it be a good thing for a man not only to hope, but quietly to wait for the salvation of God, it is often no easy thing. The delay is trying in itself; but circumstances may render it more so. While standing at the door, the weather may be foul; or those passing by may laugh and insult, for they are full, and have need of nothing: or, he may be weak, and ready to faint. And what, while thus exercised, can *keep* the man knocking and waiting? Nothing but a sense of his wants. They are so pressing that he *must* succeed or perish. Nothing, but hope, This hope may be sometimes very weak. But a degree of it, if it only amounts to a mere possibility, is necessary to preserve him from abandoning his suit, and saying, "What, should I wait for the Lord any longer?" More, however, is desirable and attainable: and here is enough to say to him, "Wait on the Lord, be of good courage, and he shall strengthen thy heart: wait, I say, on the Lord." Here is the *command*—"Knock." Here is the *promise*—"It shall be opened."

But how shall I plead? I knock and long for audience—and yet I draw back, and seem afraid to be seen. For, what can I say? What does the beggar say? He is not at a loss. He knows a fine dress is not necessary—it would be contemned. Yet he can express his meaning, and his wants and feelings make him eloquent. Begin, then, and say—

"Encourag'd by thy word
"Of promise to the poor,
"Behold, a beggar, Lord,
"Waits at thy mercy's door!
"No hand, no heart, O Lord, but thine,
"Can help or pity wants like mine."

Yet add—

"The beggar's usual plea,
"Relief from men to gain,
"If offered unto thee,
"I know thou would'st disdain;
"And pleas which move thy gracious ear,
"Are such as men would scorn to hear."

There are five of these pleas urged by others, which you must completely reverse.

How often does the beggar plead his former condition—"He has seen better days: and once had a sufficiency for himself and others." But this must be your language—

"I have no right to say,
"That though I now am poor,
"Yet once there was a day
"When I possessed more:
"Thou know'st that from my very birth
"I've been the poorest wretch on earth."

How often does the beggar plead his innocency or goodness—"I have been reduced, not by my fault, but by misfortune; and deserve pity rather than censure." But your language must be—

"Nor can I dare profess,
"As beggars often do,
"Though great is my distress,
"My faults have been but few:
"If thou shouldst leave my soul to starve,
"It would be what I well deserve."

How often does the beggar plead the unusualness of his application—"This is not my practice: it is the first, and shall be the last time of my importuning you." But your language must be—

"'Twere folly to pretend
"I never begg'd before;
"Or if thou now befriend,
"I'll trouble thee no more;
"Thou often hast reliev'd my pain,
"And often I must come again."

How often does the beggar plead the smallness of the boon—"A very little will suffice me: I ask only a trifle." But your language must be—

"Though crumbs are much too good
"For such a dog as I,
"No less than children's food
"My soul can satisfy.
"O do not frown and bid me go,
"I must have all thou canst bestow.'

Men, so limited are their resources, are afraid of more applications than they can relieve: and, therefore enjoin the suppliant secrecy; and he promises concealment. But your language must be—

"Nor can I willing be
"Thy bounty to conceal
"From others who, like me,
"Their wants and hunger feel;
"I'll tell them of thy mercy's store,
"And try to send a thousand more."

And he will be delighted with this. He commands you to spread his goodness, and to invite all the ends of the earth!!

"Thy thoughts, thou only wise!
"Our thoughts and ways transcend,
"Far as the arched skies
"Above the earth extend;
"Such pleas as mine men would not bear,
"But God receives a beggar's prayer."

JANUARY 24.—"Thy blessing is upon thy people."—Psalm iii, 8.

—HE has a people, and we need not ascend into heaven and examine the decrees of God to know who they are. The Bible is our book of life; there the heirs of glory are written, if not by name, yet by character; and "we are the circumcision," says the apostle—"who worship God in the spirit, and rejoice in Christ Jesus, and have no confidence in the flesh." By the Scripture let us judge ourselves, and be anxious to ascertain whether we are in the number of his people, for they are the most important and enviable people upon earth. They are not commonly distinguished by any worldly greatness, and they have many enemies who consult their injury; but the blessing of God is upon them.

—Upon their *mercies*. This takes the curse out of them, and gives them a relish never tasted in the comforts of others. "I will bless thy bread and thy water."

—Upon their *trials*. And they as much need a blessing upon their daily rod, as upon their daily bread. Without this our afflictions will do us no good, yea, they will prove injurious, and leave us more careless and impenitent; but by means of this they will turn to our salvation, and yield the peaceable fruits of righteousness to them that are exercised therewith.

—Upon their *labors*. "Thou shalt eat the labor of thy hands; happy shalt thou be, and it shall be well with thee." Without this, in vain we rise up early, and sit up late, and eat the bread of sorrows; it is he that giveth his beloved sleep. It matters not what we sow, if he does not give the increase; or what we bring home, if he blows upon it; or what we gain, if we "put it into a bag with holes." "The blessing of the Lord, it maketh rich; and he addeth no sorrow with it."

—Upon their *families*. The house of Obed Edom was blessed for the sake of the ark, and the thing was publicly known. "I have been young," says David, "and now am old, yet I have never seen the righteous forsaken, nor his seed begging bread." The generation of the upright shall be blessed.

—Upon their *souls*. Thus they are blessed with light, and liberty, and strength, and peace, and joy; yea, they are blessed with all spiritual blessings in heavenly places in Christ."

O, Christian, is this thy experience and portion? Rejoice and be grateful. What can equal the blessing of God!

But remember how it comes upon you. The source is his free and boundless grace. The medium is the Lord Jesus; he is the way from God to us, as well as from us to God.

Remember how it is insured—by the truth of His promise and His oath. Of this, reminding him, you may plead as Jacob did, "And thou saidst, I will surely do thee good."

Remember, also, how it is to be enjoyed—in the use of means, and in obedience to his will. "Blessed are they that do judgment, and keep his commandments at all times."

O my soul, put in for a share, and pray, "Bless me, even me also, O my Father." He will not, cannot refuse. "Their hearts shall live that seek God."

JANUARY 25.—"And it came to pass after these things, that one told Joseph, Behold, thy father is sick: and he took with him his two sons, Manasseh and Ephraim. And one told Jacob, and said, Behold, thy son Joseph cometh unto thee: and Israel strengthened himself, and sat upon the bed."—Gen. xlviii, 1, 2.

AFTER a very cloudy day, Jacob has a clear and calm evening, and it is but an evening. He is now called to go the way of all the earth: but his end is peace. Some die suddenly. But the more common road to the house appointed for all living, is down the narrow, miry, dark, dismal lane of sickness. The former is a privilege to the individual himself, saving him from "the pains, the groans, the dying strife:" but the latter befriends more his usefulness by affording him opportunities to exercise the graces of the Holy Spirit, and showing how religion can sustain when every other supply fails, and refresh when every other spring of comfort is dried up. But we are not to choose for ourselves; and if we can hope that the Savior will receive us to himself, we may well leave the when, the where, and the how, to his wise and kind care.

When sickness seizes persons in early life, and removes them in the midst of their days and usefulness, we seem surprised. Yet wherefore? Are not all our days vanity? And if, by reason of strength, they be fourscore years, is not their strength labor and sorrow? What, then, can we expect at one hundred and forty-seven?

Jacob had some time before kept his bed, and Joseph had visited him; but seeing no immediate danger of death, he had returned. Now the case assumes a more threatening character, and he is recalled. Doubtless they had sent to another being, saying, "Lord behold he whom thou lovest is sick;" but they do well to inform Joseph; and Joseph immediately leaves his public affairs, and hastens to visit him. To visit the sick is a duty. If it affords the sufferer no effectual relief, it is soothing to show our regard, our sympathy, and our readiness to help. It is alway profitable to ourselves, and far better than if going to the house of mirth. For here the heart is made better, more serious, and more soft. Hence the dying bed is shunned by infidel and worldly companions, who love not to be reminded how soon the condition of others may be their own.

How affecting is it to visit a fellow creature, the progress of whose disorder is saying to corruption, thou art my father, and to the worm, thou art my mother and my sister. But O! to see a dear friend, a beloved relation, a revered parent, sinking under the decays of nature, and the violence of disease! It is a sick, dying *father*, who had trained him up under an affection too partial, that Joseph visits. Though death does not follow the order of nature, but the appoint ment of God; yet, while parents are living, there seems to be something between us and death; but when they are removed, his course seems opens to us; and we naturally deem ourselves the next objects of assault.

Joseph goes not alone, but takes his two sons, Manasseh and Ephraim, with him. It was wise and well in Joseph to take these youths away from the splendor of a court, to see the end of all men; to view a dying bed dignified with more than a palace could bestow; to show them, at their entering the world, a servant of God departing out of it; to enable them to receive his admonition and blessing; and to be reminded, that though born in Egypt, Egypt was not to be their home, but while incorporated with strangers, they were to seek the heritage of Jacob, God's chosen.

How much wiser and better was this, than the conduct of many parents, who, instead of bringing them up in the nurture and admonition of the Lord, conduct their children into scenes of gayety and dissipation, exciting and feeding the pride of life, and making provision for the flesh to fulfil the lusts thereof. We mourn over children that are bereaved of their parents: yet one is sometimes tempted to wish the removal of some wretched fathers and mothers—hoping, that if these examples and teachers of evil were withdrawn, their children would find it good to bear the yoke in their youth, and that the Lord may take them up. The worst orphans are those who have wicked parents alive! What a dreadful meeting will there be hereafter between their offspring, and those fathers and mothers who not only neglected their souls, but taught and encouraged them to go astray! Not that we would have children confined to religious prisons, or even cells. Hinder them not from seeing and enjoying whatever is pleasing and instructive in the world of nature, and the wonders of art. Keep them not in a frozen region, that shall chill and check every harmless budding of mind and affection. Let your piety itself be inviting, not rebuking and repulsive. But, O ye parents, keep them from infidel books; from vicious associates; from every path of the destroyer. Allure them to the Bible, to the Throne of Grace, to the grave of friendship, to the chamber where a dying Jacob is waiting for God's salvation—to every place where they are likely to meet Him, who says, "I love them that love me, and they that seek me early shall find me."

JANUARY 26.—"**He that hath wrought us for the self-same thing is God, who hath also given unto us the earnest of the Spirit.**"—**2 Cor. v, 5.**

THIS self-same thing is nothing less than the final blessedness of the righteous, which, though it doth not yet fully appear, is expressed in the Scripture by various names and images. It is called in the preceding verses, "A building of God, a house not made with hands, eternal in the heavens;" and also "life." "Mortality shall be swallowed up of *life*."

With regard to this, the apostle reminds us of God's work, in our preparation for the whole; and of God's gift, in our possession of a part.

The preparation is not natural to us. We are not born Christians, but made such; and the operation is no less than divine. Creatures have not done it, nor have we done it ourselves. It is above the power of education, example, and moral suasion. *He that hath wrought us for the self-same thing is God.* But the work is as necessary as it is divine. In vain should we have a title to glory, without a meetness for it. Every office, every state, requires a qualification for it; and the higher the state and the office, the more important and difficult the qualification becomes. Happiness is not derivable from any thing, without a suitableness to it. It does not depend upon the excellency of the object, but the conformity of the disposition. The acquisition must be *wanted*, *desired*, *hoped for*, before it can gratify and content. Have I, then, any thing in me that could find happiness in the heaven of the Scriptures?

If He has wrought us for the whole, he has bestowed upon us a part. *He has given us, also, the earnest of the Spirit.* The earnest is not only to insure—it is a portion of the payment; and so is distinguishable from a pledge, which is returned at the completion of the agreement; for the earnest remains, and goes on as a part of the bargain. This is very instructive. It tells us that what the believer has here, in the possession and influence of the Spirit, is not only indicative of heaven, but like it, and a degree of it.

Is heaven perfect knowledge? The eyes of his understanding are now opened; already he spiritually discerns, and in God's light sees light.

Is it perfect holiness? He is already delivered from the power and love of every sin; he is renewed in the spirit of his mind; he delights in the law of God after the inward man.

Is it perfect happiness? exceeding joy? fulness of joy? pleasures for ever more? But even now, blessed are the people that know the joyful sound. There remaineth a rest for the people of God—but "we which have believed do enter into rest." They shall enter into peace—but now they have a "peace which passeth all understanding." They shall enter the joy of their Lord—but now, "believing, they rejoice with joy unspeakable, and full of glory." They will then join the spirits of just men made perfect—but the saints are now their companions and their delight. They will then dwell in his house, and be still praising Him—but they are already attempt ing and commencing this work. "I will bless the Lord at all times; his praise shall continually be in my mouth."

Such experience is it that weans them from the world, and makes them willing to depart. Heaven is not a distant, unknown good. They are come to the city of the living God. They are partakers of the glory that shall be revealed. They have everlasting life.

January 27.—"And the inhabitant shall not say, I am sick."—Isaiah xxxiii, 24.

Who can say so here? How many of our fellow creatures, the subjects of infirmity, languor, and nervous apprehension, are saying, "I am made to possess months of vanity, and wearisome nights are appointed to me. When I lie down, I say, When shall I arise, and the night be gone? I am full of tossings to and fro until the dawning of the day." Another is "chastened, also, with pain upon his bed, and the multitude of his bones with strong pain; his flesh is consumed away that it cannot be seen, and his bones that were not seen, stick out; yea, his soul draweth nigh unto the grave, and his life to the destroyer." There are few, perhaps none, who never feel indisposition or sickness.

Sickness is the effect of sin, which brought death into the world, and all our wo. It now (under the providence of God, which is not only punitive, but salutary) subserves various purposes. It is taken into covenant, so to speak, with the godly, and is one of the paths of the Lord, which *to them* are *all* mercy and truth. It checks them in going astray. It frees them from many a temptation arising from more intercourse with the world. It gives them the most sensible proofs of the care, and kindness, and fidelity of their Lord and Savior. He knows their frame, and has promised to be with them in trouble, and to comfort them on the bed of languishing—yea, to comfort them as one whom his mother comforteth; and she, while none of her children are neglected by her, will be sure to pay the most tender attentions to the poor little aching invalid.

Yet sickness is an evil in itself, and it is trying to flesh and blood. It not only deducts from the relish of all, and prevents entirely the enjoyment of some of our outward comforts; but it injures, it hinders the performance of a thousand duties, relative, civil, and religious. It also often brings a gloom over the mind, and genders unworthy apprehensions of God, and misgivings of our spiritual condition. It not only shuts us out from the loveliness of nature, but from the public means of grace, and fills us with a mournful pleasure at the thought of seasons when we went in company to the house of God, with the voice of joy and gladness to keep holy day. Hence Hezekiah, anxious to ascertain his recovery, asked, "What is the sign that I shall go up to the house of the Lord?" How feelingly has Watts described the Lord's prisoner when the Sabbath comes.

"Lo! the sweet day of sacred rest returns,
"———— But not to me returns
'Rest with the day. Ten thousand hurrying thoughts
"Bear me away tumultuous, far from heaven
"And heavenly work; alas! flesh drags me down
"From things celestial, and confines my sense

"To present maladies. Unhappy state!
"Where the poor spirit is subdued t' endure
"Unholy idleness; and painful absence
"From God and heav'n, and angels' blessed work;
"And bound to hear the agonies and woes,
"That sickly flesh, and shatter'd nerves impose."

Well, soon the warfare with the body will be accomplished, and we shall put off the flesh, and be in joy and felicity. And as there will be no more sin, neither will there be any more pain; for the former things are all passed away.

A union with the body, were it to rise as it now is, would be dreaded, rather than desirable. But the body will not only be raised, but improved; improved beyond all our present comprehension, but not beyond our present BELIEF. For we can trust Him who has assured us, that though it be sown in weakness, it shall be raised in power; though it be sown a natural body, it shall be raised a spiritual body; and that this corruptible shall put on incorruption, and this mortal shall put on immortality. We shall bear, not the image of the earthly, but of the heavenly. Our bodies will not be made like the body of Adam in Paradise, but like the Savior's own glorious body, according to the working whereby he is able even to subdue all things unto himself. No burdens, no depressions then! No clogs, no confinements! No animal wants! No debasing appetites! No unruly passions! No fluttering heart! No aching head! "The inhabitant shall no more say, I am sick."

"These lively hopes we owe
"To Jesus' dying love:
"We would adore his grace below.
"And sing his power above."

JANUARY 28.—"In the wilderness thou hast seen how the Lord thy God bare thee, as a man doth bear his son, in all the way that ye went." Deut. i, 31.

THE image is parental. In another part of this book the reference is to a parent *bird;* "As an eagle stirreth up her nest, fluttereth over her young, spreadeth abroad her wings, taketh them, beareth them on her wings, so the Lord alone did lead him." Here the allusion is to a *human* parent, and it is worthy of remark how often the allusion is made in the Scriptures. Thus to mention a few of them: "Like as a father pitieth his children, so the Lord pitieth them that fear him." "I will spare them, as a man spareth his own son that serveth him." "If ye, being evil, know how to give good gifts unto your children, how much more shall your Father, who is in heaven, give good gifts to them that ask him?" The softer sex is also adduced, and *maternal* tenderness supplies feeling, as well as thought. "As one whom his mother comforteth, so will I comfort you." "Can a woman forget her sucking child, that she should not have compassion on the son of her womb? Yea, she may forget, yet will not I forget thee."

Observe the image which Moses here employs. It regards a child, a young child; for it is too weak to go alone—it is borne. The father is here mentioned, not the mother; for the action of bearing requires strength, rather than tenderness. The mother may have been dead. When one parent is called to supply the place of both, an increase of care and kindness becomes necessary, and is soon felt.

Imagine, therefore, an Israelite—deprived in his journey through the wilderness of the companion of his life—perhaps as soon as she had brought him forth a son—perhaps in consequence of it. The child, thus bereaved, is endeared by the decease of the mother, and *he* takes it and bears it. How? Sometimes in his arms, and often in his bosom. How? Tenderly, softly—now pressing it to his lips, now soothing its cries, now lulling it to repose—feeding it, defending it, supplying all its wants!

All this God does in reality, and infinitely more. What is the goodness, the gentleness, the care of the tenderest being on earth, compared with the disposition and kindness of God toward his people! When an image is applied to God, we must separate from it all its imperfections. A father may be unable to defend a child; he is sometimes absent from it; he cannot always be awake, and inspecting it; he may be ignorant of the cause of its complaint; he may not know what is good for it; he may decline in affection, and become heedless and negligent; he may become cruel, and abandon his charge. But nothing of all this can apply to Him, who bears us in all the way that we go.

Yea, we must not only strip the image of imperfection, when we apply it to God, but we must attach to it divinity. Every human relation, however complete, is yet *finite* in its exercise and excellence; but his attributes are *infinite.* His love passeth knowledge. " He is able to do for us exceeding abundantly above all that we can ask or think."

Well, hast thou *seen* in the wilderness how the Lord thy God bare thee, as a man doth bear his son, in all the way that ye went? Let the sight affect your admiration, and induce you to exclaim, " Lord, what is man, that thou art mindful of him, or the son of man, that thou visitest him?" We talk of condescension; but what is the difference between one creature and another—one worm and another? But what is God! what are we! how mean, unworthy, guilty! Let it draw forth

Your gratitude, and call upon your soul, and all that is within you, to bless his holy name. " To him that led his people in the wilderness; for his mercy endureth for ever."

—Let it encourage you.

You are not yet come to the rest and the inheritance which the Lord your God giveth you; but he is with you in the way, and with you as your father; engaged to do all that such a relation requires. He has said, " I will never leave thee nor forsake thee." Reason from the past to the future, and " because he has been your help, therefore under the shadow of his wings rejoice." Let him be

Your example. Job was a *father* to the poor, not a tyrant, or an overseer. Be *kind,* as well as bountiful. Be ye followers of God. In him the fatherless findeth mercy; let him find it in you also. " Be ye merciful, even as your father in heaven is merciful." Recommend him to others, and say to them, " Come with us, and we will do you good, for the Lord hath spoken good concerning Israel." Oh that the young who are entering this wilderness world would place themselves under his care, and beseech him to be the guide of their youth. Oh that the bereaved would think of Him who can more than repair the losses which make them bleed. "When my father and my mother forsake me, the Lord will take me up."

January 29.—"And shall leave me alone; and yet I am not alone, because the Father is with me."—John, xiv, 32.

There is a relation between Christ and Christians, and a conformity founded upon it; so that what *He* says, *they* may subordinately adopt as their own language.

There are cases in which they *may* be alone—and there are cases in which they *ought* to be alone—and there is one case in which they *must* be alone; and yet they are not alone, because the Father is with them.

They *may* be alone by the dispensations of Providence. By death, lover and friend may be put far from them, and their acquaintance into darkness; and bereavements may force from solitude the sigh, "I watch, and am as a sparrow upon the house-top." They have often been driven out of society by the wickedness of power. Their connexions have abandoned them through falseness, or deserted them through infirmity. And this is no inconsiderable trial. Our Savior felt the desertion of his disciples, and said, "I looked for some to take pity, and there was none, and for comforter, and found none;" but looking upward, he said, "I am not alone, for the Father is with me." Joseph was separated from his family, and sold into Egypt; but the Lord was with Joseph. John was banished into the isle of Patmos; but there he had the visions of the Almighty, and was in the Spirit on the Lord's day. "At my first answer," says Paul, "no man stood by me, but all *men* forsook me; notwithstanding the *Lord* stood by me, and strengthened me." Yes, whoever dies, the Lord liveth. Whoever fails us, He is firm. "He is faithful that hath promised. He hath said, *I* will never leave thee nor forsake thee."

They *ought* to be alone by voluntary solitude. Not that they are to become recluses by abandoning their stations, and shunning intercourse with their fellow creatures. The Christian life is a candle; but a candle is not to be placed under a bushel, but on a candlestick, that it may give light to all that are in the house; and our light is to shine before men; and they are to see our good works, and glorify our Father who is in heaven. But *occasional* and *frequent* retirement for religious purposes is a duty, and it will be found our privilege. We shall never be less alone than when alone. "Go forth," saith God to Ezekiel, "into the field, and there will I talk with thee." Isaac, at eventide, was meditating in the field when the Lord brought him Rebekah. Jacob was left alone when he "obtained power with God," and with man, and prevailed. Nathanael was seen and encouraged under the fig tree. Peter was by himself praying upon the house-top when he received the Divine manifestation. If the twelve patriarchs, or the twelve apostles, lived near us, and their presence drew us off from our closets, their neighborhood would be a serious injury to us. No creature can be a substitute for God. And it is *alone* we hold the freest and fullest communion with him. It is there the secret of the Lord is with us, and he shows us his covenant.

There we become acquainted with ourselves. There we shake off the influences of the world. It is good to be there.

"Be earth with all her scenes withdrawn;
"Let noise and vanity be gone;
"In secret silence of the mind,
"My heaven, and there my God, I find."

—Men may live in a crowd, but they *must* die alone. Friends and ministers can only accompany us to the entrance of the pass. None of them can speak from experience, and tell us what it is to die. And it is a way we have not gone ourselves heretofore. But the Christian *here*, though alone, is not alone. "Yea," says David, "though I walk through the valley of the shadow of death, I will fear no evil, for thou art with me: thy rod and thy staff, they comfort me."

"Death is a melancholy day "To those that have no God."

But how must it be softened and cheered to those that have? O to have a God, the God of all grace, at hand, a very present help in that time of trouble; laying underneath his everlasting arms; shedding around the light of his countenance; communicating the joy of his salvation; and insuring the glory to be revealed—in ways beyond all our present experience and thought!

"O my God, what time I am afraid, I will trust in thee. Thou hast holden me by my right hand. Thou shalt guide me with thy counsel, and afterward receive me to glory. Whom have I in heaven but thee, and there is none upon the earth I desire beside thee. My flesh and my heart faileth, but God is the strength of my heart, and my portion for ever."

JANUARY 30.—**"And when the angel which spake unto Cornelius was departed, he called two of his household servants, and a devout soldier of them that waited on him continually; and when he had declared all these things to them, he sent them to Joppa."—Acts, x, 7, 8.**

SUCH was his obedience to the heavenly vision. It was immediate, and well executed.

He did not himself go for Peter. This he would have readily done, but was ordered by the angel *to send;* and *his* presence was proper and necessary at home. He was a man in office: and in command. He had a weighty trust reposed in him; and we are to abide with God in our callings.

The messengers he employed were two of his household servants, which shows him to have been a man of some estate, beside his profession, and a devout soldier of them that waited on him continually. Observe here—the officer himself was a devout man, and he has not only devoted, but devout soldiers. The master was godly, and the servants are the same: for it is said, Cornelius feared God with all his house; like Joshua, who said, "As for me, *and* my house, we will serve the Lord." This correspondence between the head and the members of the family, may be accounted for in two ways. First, such a man will choose, as far as he can, those that are religious to attend him—saying, with David, "Mine eyes shall be upon the faithful of the land, that they may dwell with me: he that walketh in a perfect way, he shall serve me. He that worketh deceit shall not dwell within my house: he that telleth lies shall not tarry in my sight."

And secondly, he will be likely to render them such, if they are not such when he engages them. For he will be sure to use all the means in his power: and his own temper and example will harmonize with his efforts: and the grace of God, which he will never fail to implore, will honor him. Thus, they who are blessed, are also blessings, and for them the desert rejoices as a rose. Some are favored by their opportunities and talents, to cultivate a large expanse of barrenness: but let us see, let us all see, whether we cannot convert a small spot at least, from waste, to smiling verdure: cultivate, if not the neighboring moor, yet a cottage garden, and let the traveller say, "The blessing of the Lord be upon thee." Many a domestic has been thankful that he ever entered a pious family: there he has been made wise unto salvation, and has become a child of God, by faith in Christ Jesus. What a disgrace is it for a Christian master and mistress to let a servant leave their family unable to read the Bible!

"So, having declared these things to them, he sent them to Joppa." Here we have, not a harsh injunction to a trembling slave; not a bare order, couched in a few unexplained terms; not the sealed instructions, the orders of a tyrant, who is to be implicitly obeyed, and is afraid to trust. Here is intercourse, openness; here is confidence in the master, reposing on principle in the servants. How happy, where the distinctions of life are preserved—and they are to be preserved; and yet there is union and harmony, and condescension, and kindness; and unreserve on the one side, and respect and obedience, without encroachment, on the other. How happy where authority is softened by gentleness, and submission by love: where indulgence breeds nothing like irreverence, and goodness is rewarded by diligence and fidelity. And in what connexions, in what families, is all this most likely to be found? "Men do not gather grapes from thorns, nor figs from thistles." Piety is the spring, the guard, the refinement, the glory of morality.

JANUARY 31.—"And he cried unto the Lord; and the Lord showed him a tree, which, when he had cast into the waters, the waters were made sweet."
Exodus, xv, 25.

It is useless to inquire what kind of tree this was, and whether the effect was produced by a quality inherent in the wood, or by a miraculous application—the latter is far the most likely. But it has been disputed whether this transaction was designed to be an evangelical type. Perhaps it is impossible to determine this, and it is unnecessary. We shall only derive from it an illustration of a very interesting subject, in which we are fully justified by the words of the apostle to the suffering Hebrews: "Consider him that endured such contradiction of sinners against himself, lest ye be wearied and faint in your minds."

We, like these Jews, are travelling through a wilderness. In our journey we meet with bitter waters. These are the troubles of life, personal and relative. These are very distasteful and offensive to flesh and blood. But they may be rendered drinkable. In other words, we may be able to endure the afflictions of life—yea, we may even acquiesce in them; and not only so, but glory in tribulation also. But how can this be done? Here is the secret—

"The cross on which the Savior died,
"And conquered for his saints;
"This is the tree by faith applied,
"That sweetens all complaints.

"Thousands have proved the bless'd effect,
"No longer mourn their lot;
"While on his sorrows they reflect,
"Their own are all forgot.

"While they by faith behold the Cross,
"Though many griefs they meet,
"They draw a gain from every loss,
"And find the bitter sweet."

Let us see how the Savior's sufferings will alleviate ours. It is some relief, in distress, that others are exercised in the same way. Individuality of wo looks ominous; it is appalling to be singled out like a victim deer from the whole herd, and suffer alone. Thus the apostle tells the Corinthians that no temptation had taken them but such as is common to man; and Peter also tells the sufferers he addressed, that the same afflictions were accomplished in their brethren that were in the world. So it is—whom the Lord loveth, he chasteneth. This has been the case with even his most eminent servants. And even his "dear Son," in whom his soul delighted—he, even he, did not escape. And shall we dread the fellowship of his sufferings?

But if there is something to affect the mind, even in the reality of his passion, there is much more in the greatness of it. In general, our groaning is heavier than our complaint; and we are prone, from our selfishness and ignorance, to imagine our trials pre-eminent. *He* could say, Behold, and see if ever there was sorrow like unto my sorrow. In our sorrows we have alleviations. Ours are not perpetual, but his continued through life. Ours are not universal; but he suffered in every part that was capable of suffering—he was a man of sorrows. Ours are not foreknown; but his were all laid out in prospect, and he suffered in apprehension, as well as reality. No tongue can express, no understanding conceive, what *he* bore when his soul was exceeding sorrowful, even unto death; and his sweat was, as it were, great drops of blood falling to the ground!

"Now let our pains be all forgot,
"Our hearts no more repine;
"Our sufferings are not worth a thought,
"When, Lord, compared with thine."

We must also think of the dignity of this sufferer. We commonly and properly feel more for those who are reduced in life, than for those who have never enjoyed a better estate, because the penury is imbittered by previous affluence. Job considers his former greatness as an enhancement of his fall, and contrasts, with the honors shown him in his prosperity, the insults now offered him by those whose fathers he would not have set with the dogs of his flock, "They were children of fools, yea, children of base men; they were viler than the earth. And now I am their song; yea, I am their by-word. They abhor me; they flee far from me, and spare not to spit in my face." Jesus was the Lord of all; and all the angels of God worshipped him. Yet was *He* despised and rejected of men; he was buffeted, scourged, spit upon; and not only the scribes and elders, but the soldiers, the common rabble, and the very thieves, set him at nought, and vilified him. But who and what are we? Our foundation is in the dust. Man is a worm, and the son of man is a worm; and it is condescension in God to have any thing to do with him, or to deign even to chastise him. "What is man that thou shouldest magnify him? and that thou shouldest set thine heart upon him? And that thou shouldest visit him every morning, and try him every moment?"

But the great may render themselves *worthy* of their humiliations, and often have been *righteously* punished. We suffer justly, because we suffer the due reward of our deeds. Good men themselves cannot complain, or even wonder, at their afflictions, when they consider their years of irreligion, and their sins, since they have known God, or rather have been known of him—for who can understand his errors? In the sudden and awful death of his two sons, Aaron held his peace; he had just before been aiding to make the golden calf. David had been recently guilty of adultery and murder; when, therefore, Absalom, his own son, as well as subject, rose against him, what could he but say of his offended God, Here I am; let him do to me what seemeth good unto him. This consciousness also induced him to say, Let him alone, for the Lord hath bidden him, when Shimei cursed him, and Joab offered to go and slay him. I will bear the indignation of the Lord, because, says the Church, I have sinned against him. But this man did nothing amiss; he was harmless, holy, separate from sinners. He could make the appeal to all his adversaries, Which of you convinceth me of sin? Yet he suffered—suffered, though *innocent;* and was led as a lamb to the slaughter.

His sufferings, therefore, were *for* us, only and entirely *for* us—and what can be more relieving in our sorrows, than to consider the *benefits* we derive from his? Such is the benefit of an atoning Sacrifice, by which we are delivered from all condemnation, and have peace with God, and access to him. What are trials? when there is no wrath in them; when they are only the effects of a father's care—the bitterness of death is past. Such is the benefit of a sympathizing Friend, who, from his own experience, can be touched with the feelings of our infirmities—for in that he himself hath suffered, being tempted, he is able also to succor them that are tempted. Such is the benefit of an Example, which shows us how to act and how to feel in the hour of trial—for he also suffered for us, leaving us an example, that we should follow his steps. Such is the benefit of Divine Influence; for by dying, he obtained for us the dispensation of the Spirit, which is therefore called his Spirit, and without the supply of which, we must fail and sink—but his grace is sufficient for us.

How encouraging, too, is it to think of the issue of his sufferings. For the joy that was set before him, he endured the Cross, despising the shame, and is set down at the right hand of the Throne of God Your sorrows also will have an end—and the same end. It is a faithful saying: for if we be dead with him, we shall also live with him; If we suffer with him, we shall also be glorified together.

FEBRUARY 1.—"Do ye now believe?"—John, xvi, 31.

THIS was in reply to the profession of his disciples. They had said unto him, "Now speakest thou plainly; now we are sure that thou knowest all things—by this we believe that thou camest forth from God."

It is not easy to lay the emphasis with perfect certainty; and yet according as it *is* laid, the language will strike us with some shades of difference.

We may consider the words as an *inquiry*. "Do ye now *believe?* I have a right to ask, and I do ask." He is not inattentive to our condition, and experience; our deficiencies, and improvements. And though he needeth not that any should testify of man, because he knoweth what is in man, yet he will know these things from ourselves; that we may be urged to consider—and be affected with our own communications.

We may consider them as a *censure*. "Do ye *now* believe? You ought to have believed long—yet, hitherto it would seem, according to your own avowal, you have not: that is, as you ought to have done, and as you might have done. How strange and blamable, that, with all your advantages, you have been, even down to this hour, filled with hesitation and doubts." For he can reprove, as well as encourage. Do ye not yet remember? Do ye not yet understand? After his resurrection, he upbraided them with their unbelief, and hardness of heart.

We may consider them as a *check to presumption*. "*Do* ye now believe? You think so; but have you not expressed yourselves with too much confidence? You now consider yourselves confirmed believers: and you suppose that you shall never err again; fail again. I know you better than you know yourselves. Imagination is not reality: and events will prove, that you have much less faith than you now suppose—Behold the hour cometh and is now come, that ye shall be scattered, every man to his own, and shall leave me alone."

There is a difference between hypocrisy and instability. We may feel what we utter at the time: but emotions are not principles, impulses are not dispositions. There may be goodness; but it is like the morning cloud and early dew, that soon passeth away. How often do we become a wonder, as well as a grief, to ourselves. How little do we know of our own hearts, till we are tried. The little ants disappear in the cloudy and rainy day; and the observer might suppose that they were all dead. But let the sun shine forth; and they are again all alive, and in motion. There is the same mud at the bottom of the water when calm; but the waves thereof cast up the mire and dirt.

Let us not therefore make too much of frames and feelings; nor imagine, because we are now walking in the light of God's countenance, that we shall never again mourn his absence. Behold, the hour cometh when we may consider all our present joy as only a delusion. Do we now believe? A change in the weather, a depression of animal spirits, may renew all our doubts and fears; and make us shiver again.

Therefore let us rejoice with trembling. Let us remember our own weakness; and instead of depending on the grace that is in us, be strong in the grace that is in Christ Jesus.

"Beware of Peter's word,
"Nor confidently say,
"I never *will* deny thee, Lord;
"But, grant I never may.

"Man's wisdom is to seek
"In God his strength alone;
"And e'en an angel would be weak
"That trusted in his own."

FEBRUARY 2.—" O that I had wings like a dove? for then would I be away, and be at rest."—Psalm lv, 6.

WHOSE exclamation is this? It is obviously the language of a man *not* at rest. And if we read the preceding and following verses we shall find that the complainant was, indeed, really in trouble. And so are many. It seems inseparable from humanity. Man that is born of a woman is of a few days and full of trouble.

But who was *this* man? One of those deemed the darlings of Providence: a man who had experienced one of the most marvellous revolutions recorded in history. For he was originally nothing more than a shepherd; but rose from obscurity, and became a hero, a renowned conqueror, a powerful monarch. He had given him, the necks of his enemies and the hearts of his subjects; and we might have supposed him sated with victory, and glory, and dominion, and riches. But from the midst of all this he sighs " O that I had wings like a dove, for then would I fly away, and be at rest!" For, with all his aggrandizements, how much did he suffer from implacable malevolence! How much also from some of his own officers, and especially his nephew, Joab, the commander-in-chief. After rearing his fine palace of cedar, he could not for a length of time take possession of it, for he was sick, nigh unto death, and week after week saw the grave ready for him. And suppose they had brought out his crown and imposed it upon him, would this have eased an aching head, or have relieved the anguish of a disordered body? What is an ornamented room in the rage of a fever? Then his own house was not so with God. What a distracted and wretched family! His daughter is humbled. The incestuous brother is murdered. The murderer becomes a traitor, and drives his father, as well as king, into exile. In his flight he is told that Ahithophel, his bosom friend and counseller, is among the conspirators with Absalom. Who can tell what other sorrows corroded him! The heart knoweth his own bitterness. There are griefs that we cannot pour even into the bosom of intimacy. There are thorns in the nest that pierce through the down that lines it, but are known and felt only by the occupier. Did David never regret the loss of the privacy of Bethlehem?

The spirit that is in us lusteth to envy. We are prone to think that, though *generally* men are born to trouble, there are some exempted individuals; and that though, commonly considered, this earth is a vale of tears, there are some privileged spots. And it is worthy our observation, that these exceptions always belong to *others*, and always to those who are *above* us. Is the servant happy? He will when he is master. Is the master happy? He will when he is rich. Is the rich man happy? He will when he is ennobled, and has distinction as well as gold. Is the nobleman happy? He will when he is king. Is the king—the king happy? Oh, says he, that I had wings like a dove, for then would I fly away and be at rest.

Let us remember this, and not be afraid when one is made rich, and the glory of his house is increased. Let us check the risings of ambition, and not seek great things to ourselves. Let us learn, in whatsoever state we are, to be content; and follow the moderation of the patriarch, who asked only for bread to eat, and raiment to put on, and a safe return to his father's house in peace.

Felicity depends not upon external condition, but the state of the mind. Paul was happy in prison, while Nero was miserable in a palace. Haman, after telling his wife and his friends all his promotion and glory, adds, Yet all this availeth me nothing, so long as I see Mordecai the Jew sitting at the king's gate. On that night could not the king sleep.

> "Tired Nature's sweet restorer, balmy sleep—
> "He, like the world, his ready visit pays
> "Where fortune smiles."

But is this true? No. Sleep, sound, wholesome, refreshing sleep, has least to do where fortune smiles. His ready visits are paid to the early rising, the temperate, the diligent: the sleep of a laboring man is sweet. "The wretched," indeed, "he forsakes." But where does he find them? Here is one of them—the ruler of one hundred and twenty-seven provinces—on that night could not the king sleep. Ahab, the monarch of Israel, is melancholy, and sick, and cannot eat, because he cannot obtain Naboth's little parcel of ground for a garden of herbs; and neither his happiness nor health could go on till his worthy helpmate taught him to gratify his wish by the destruction of the noble-minded peasant. How wise was the answer of the Shunamite, when Elisha offered to speak for her to the king, "I dwell among my own people." If we are not content with such things as we have, we shall never be satisfied with such things as we desire. If there is a difference in outward conditions, it lies against those who fill the higher ones. Their want of occupation—the listlessness, far worse than any labor, they feel—the little relish they have of natural refreshments—their sufferings from weak nerves and timid spirits—their squeamish anxieties about their health—the softening of their disposition by indulgence and ease, so that they are unable to endure—their sensibility under trifling vexations, which others despise—their leisure to brood over and hatch a progeny of dangers—the envies to which they are liable—their cares, fears, responsibilities, and dependence—the unreasonable things expected from them, and their inability to give satisfaction to expectants. Where shall I end? These, and a thousand other things, are enough to show the poor and the busy that those who are placed above them are proportionably taxed.

Neither, however, is the opposite state the most desirable. As far as happiness depends on any outward condition, there lies between the extremes of prosperity and adversity, penury and affluence, the most eligible choice. If life be a pilgrimage, man, the traveller, is best prepared for advancing, not when the shoe pinches, or when it is large and loose, but when it fits; not when he is destitute of a staff, or when he has a large bundle of staves to carry, but when he has one which affords him assistance without incumbrance. Pray we, therefore, "Remove far from me vanity and lies; give me neither poverty nor riches; feed me with food convenient for me: lest I be full, and deny thee, and say, Who is the Lord? or lest I be poor, and steal, and take the name of my God in vain."

February 3.—"Thou shalt remember that thou wast a bondman in Egypt, and the Lord thy God redeemed thee thence."—Deut. xxiv, 18.

The bondage of Egypt, under Pharaoh's tyranny and task-masters, was nothing to the bondage of corruption in which sinners are naturally held, and the power of darkness, from which we are translated into the kingdom of God's dear Son. And the freedom the Jews obtained, when they were delivered by a strong hand and a stretched-out arm, was not to be compared with the glorious liberty of the sons of God—for if the Son makes us free, we are free indeed.

And this redemption is what we are called to remember. The admonition may seem needless. For can such a deliverance be ever forgotten? We should once have deemed it impossible; but we are prone to forget his works, and the wonders which he has shown us. The event, indeed, can never be completely forgotten. But we need to have our minds stirred up by way of remembrance. And for four purposes, "Thou shalt remember that thou wast a bondman in the land of Egypt, but the Lord thy God redeemed thee thence."

First, for the purpose of humility. We are prone to think more highly of ourselves than we ought to think; but with the lowly is wisdom. God resisteth the proud, but giveth grace unto the humble; and surely we have enough to hide pride from us, if we reflect properly. If we are now wise, we were once foolish: if we are now justified, we were once condemned; if we are now the sons of God, we were once the servants of sin. Let us look to the rock whence we were hewn, and to the hole of the pit whence we were digged.

Secondly, we should remember it for the purpose of gratitude. If we are affected with the kindness shown us by our fellow creatures, shall we overlook our infinite Benefactor? Were they under no obligation to relieve us? Had we forfeited our lives to them? Did they deliver us from the lowest hell? Did they become poor to enrich us, and die that we may live? We have no claims upon *Him* for the least of all his mercies; and, therefore, should be thankful for all his benefits. But *herein* is love. Thanks be unto God for his unspeakable gift. Blessed be the Lord God of Israel, for he hath visited and redeemed his people.

Thirdly, we should remember it for the purpose of confidence. David argued from the past to the future, and said, Because thou hast been my help, therefore, under the shadow of thy wings will I rejoice. But here we have a peculiar reason for encouragement. For what were we when he first took knowledge of us? Was he not found of them that sought him not? Was the want of worthiness a bar to his goodness then? And will it be so now? Is there with him any variableness or shadow of turning? Is there not the same power in his arm, and the same love in his heart? Did he pardon me when a rebel, and will he cast me off now he has made me a friend? "If, when we were enemies, we were reconciled to God by the death of his Son, much more, being reconciled, we shall be saved by his life." "He that spared not his own Son, but delivered him up for us all, how shall he not with him also freely give us all things?"

Fourthly, we should remember it for the purpose of piety and zeal. How many are there all around you in the gall of bitterness, and the bond of iniquity, ready to perish! You know the state they are in, and you know the blessedness of a deliverance from it. You are witnesses for God of what he is able and willing to do. Invite the prisoners of hope to turn to him—you can speak from experience. Say to others, That which we have seen and heard, declare we unto you, that ye also may have fellowship with us. O taste and see that the Lord is good: blessed is the man that trusteth in him.

FEBRUARY 4.—**"And Jacob said, O God of my father Abraham, and God of my father Isaac, the Lord, which saidst unto me, Return unto thy country, and to thy kindred, and I will deal well with thee; I am not worthy of the least of all thy mercies, and of all the truth which thou hast showed unto thy servant; for with my staff I passed over this Jordan, and now I am become two bands. Deliver me, I pray thee, from the hand of my brother, from the hand of Esau; for I fear him, lest he will come and smite me, and the mother with the children. And thou saidst, I will surely do thee good, and make thy seed as the sand of the sea, which cannot be numbered for multitude."—Gen. xxxii, 9—12.**

WE cannot too much admire the conduct of Jacob on this trying occasion, when he had to meet his enraged brother Esau. The religion that, aiming at something uncommon and preternatural, disregards the plain dictates of reason and revelation, is always to be suspected; and, on the other hand, caution and exertion, unaccompanied with a devout dependence upon God, is the wisdom of the world, which is foolishness with him; and he will take the wise in their own craftiness. Therefore prudence and piety should always be connected together. Accordingly, Jacob sends forward a deputation with a soft answer, that turneth away wrath, and arranges his company and cattle in the wisest order. But what does he then? When we have done all that we can do, to what does it amount? "Except the Lord build the house, they labor in vain that build it; except the Lord keep the city, the watchman waketh but in vain;" and unless he gives his beloved sleep, "in vain we rise early, and sit up late, and eat the bread of sorrows." When we have planned, and are setting all our measures in motion, then is the time to take hold of God, and to say, "O Lord, I beseech thee, send *now* prosperity." Jacob, therefore, now prays; and as this prayer was heard, and he who teaches us how to pray is our best friend, let us glance at the particulars which God has here noticed.

Observe the relation under which he addresses the Supreme Being: "O God of my father Abraham, and God of my father Isaac." As much as to say, my family God, and my God in covenant. This was laying hold of his faithfulness, as well as goodness, and asking *in faith*. We have another title under which to bespeak attention—the God and father of our Lord Jesus Christ. This inspires more abundant hope, and involves more exceeding great and precious promises, and reminds us of a covenant made with *him*, and *so* with us, everlasting, ordered in all things and sure.

He appeals to the will of God in his present difficulty: "Thou saidst unto me, Return unto thy country, and to thy kindred, and I will deal well with thee;" I am now in a strait, but I have been brought into it by following thee. This was wise. They that suffer according to the will of God, may commit the keeping of their souls to him in well doing; and it affords great relief to the mind, and much aids our confidence, when we are conscious that the embarrassments we feel have not been brought upon ourselves, but have befallen us in the path of duty. And how does it add to the pressure of the burden, and the bitterness of the cup, when God asks, "What dost thou here, Elijah?" and conscience cries, "Hast thou not procured this unto thyself?" Let no man, therefore, suffer as a murderer, as a thief, or as a busy-body in other men's matters. We complain of the world; and there are many unavoidable evils in life; but there is a large multitude entirely of our own producing, and God is no otherwise accessary to them, than as he has, in the nature of things, and the course of providence, established a connexion between folly and misery.

He shows his humility. "I am not worthy of the least of all thy mercies, and of all the truth which thou hast showed unto thy servant." This temper is not natural to us; but grace brings us down, and keeps us from thinking more highly of ourselves than we ought to think. And we cannot have too much of this self-abasing disposition; it will keep us from exercising ourselves in great matters, and in things too high for us; it will keep us from murmuring under our trials; it will teach us, in whatever state we are, therewith to be content; and it will dispose us in every thing to give thanks—for only in proportion as we are humble can we be thankful.

Jacob, therefore, acknowledges the kindness of God toward him. More than twenty years before, he had crossed the same river where he now was. At that time he had no inheritance; no, not so much as to set his foot on. He was going forth, a poor pilgrim, in search of subsistence; and all that he ever stipulated for was bread to eat, and raiment to put on, and a return to his father's house in peace. From this condition he had been raised to affluence, and his family and his flock had equally multiplied. Therefore says he, "For with my staff I passed over this Jordan, and now I am become two bands;" alluding to the division which he had just made of his household and his substance. We should do well often to review life, and to mark the changes which have taken place in our stations and circumstances. Have not many attained conditions, which would once have appeared the most improbable? Yet the Lord has made windows in heaven—and such things have been. Yet he has brought the blind by a way that they knew not, and made darkness light before them. Those born in the lap of ease, and whose course has been always even, cannot enter into the feelings of those who have found themselves advanced, without any designs formed by their friends, or expectations indulged by themselves. But how sad will it be, if they want the disposition of Jacob, and, forgetting that the blessing of the Lord maketh rich, sacrifice to their own net.

Observe his petition. "Deliver me, I pray thee, from the hand of my brother, from the hand of Esau; for I fear him, lest he will come and smite me, and the mother with the children." Here nature speaks; and we are allowed to feel, and even to desire the cup may pass from us, with submission to the will of God. How much was there here to awaken anxiety and dread! Not only his own death, but the destruction of each of his wives—and each a mother too—

and of his children also—and of the mother *with* the children; or, as it is in the margin, the mother upon the children. So it would have been. On the approach of the executioner she would have thrown herself upon them, to cover and defend them, and in vain would he have endeavored to pull her away; she would have been slaughtered upon their bodies.

Finally, his argument. "And thou saidst, I will surely do thee good, and make thy seed as the sand of the sea, which cannot be numbered for multitude." He had mentioned this before—Thou saidst, I will deal well with thee; and now he repeats it. It was a sweet morsel, and he rolls it under his tongue. It was a breast of consolation, and he sucks till he is satisfied. It shows us that promises do not supersede prayer. If God has engaged to do a thing, it will indeed be accomplished, but in his own way; and he has ordained the means as well as the end. The promises furnish us both with matter and encouragement when we pray; and we cannot do better than to pray them over, and to plead them with God. This, says an old writer, is sueing God upon his own bond. "Remember thy word unto thy servant, on which thou hast caused me to hope."

FEBRUARY 5.—**"That, whether we wake or sleep, we should live together with him."—1 Thess. v, 10.**

How well does the Apostle call the Redeemer "our life." There are three modes of expression by which our relation to him under this character is held forth; and they all furnish matter for the most important meditation. We are said to live *by* Him—"He that loveth me, even he, shall live *by* me." We are said to live *to* Him—"They that live, should not live unto themselves, but *unto* Him that died for them, and rose again." And we are said to live *with* Him—"That whether we wake or sleep, we should live together *with* him."

To judge of this state, we must consider where he lives; and how he lives; and what he is; and how far he is able by his presence, to bless us, and make us happy. For though our happiness, with such a nature as ours, must be social, it is not a privilege to live with every one. With some, it would be a misery to dwell even here; and to have our "portion with the hypocrites and unbelievers;" and to be with "the devil and his angels;" this will be hell hereafter. But O, to unite with those who will be all loveliness; to embrace, without any fear of separation, those who were endeared to us on earth; to sit down with Abraham, Isaac and Jacob, in the kingdom of God; to join the innumerable company of angels! But, above all, to live with Jesus! To be with him, where he is, to behold his glory! To walk with him in white! To reign with him!—for ever and ever!—this is far better.

The season for enjoying it is, "whether we wake," *i. e.* live, or "whether we sleep," *i. e.* die. It takes in, therefore, time and eternity; our living with him in earth and in heaven; in the communions of grace, and the fellowships of glory. These are inseparably connected, and are essentially one and the same condition with regard to him; but they differ in degree as the bud and the flower, the dawn and the day, the child and the man, differ. His people live with him now, but not as they will live with him hereafter. Now he is invisible—then they will see him as he is. Now their intercourse with him is mediate, and often interrupted—then it will be immediate, and free from any annoyance. Now they are with him in the wilderness—then they will be with him in the land flowing with milk and honey. Now they groan, being burdened with infirmities, and cares, and troubles—then they will be presented faultless before the presence of his glory, with exceeding joy. Yet, whether they *wake* or *sleep*, they live together with him.

And does not this more than indicate his divinity? How else can they live with him *now?* He is no more here, as to his bodily presence, for the heavens have received him. Yet, where two or three are gathered together in his name, he is in the midst of them. Yet he said, Lo! I am with you always, even unto the end of the world. Yet, says the apostle, We live with him even while we *wake!* Yet, at the same time, others live with him when they *sleep*—The dead are with him above, while the living are with him below! How? unless he pervades all periods, and occupies all places? How? unless he can say, "Do not I fill heaven and earth?" It is obvious the apostle viewed him as omnipresent, and could say, "Whom have I in *heaven* but Thee? and there is none upon *earth* I desire beside Thee."

Here is your happiness Christians; it is your union with Christ. This prepares you for all seasons, and all conditions. Do you think of life? This is sometimes discouraging; especially when you contemplate the prospect in a moment of gloom. But why should you be dismayed? If you *wake* you will live together with him. If your continuance here be prolonged, you will not be alone; He will always be within call, and within reach. He will render every duty practicable, and every trial supportable, and every event profitable. And, therefore, whatever be your circumstances, you may boldly say, "Nevertheless I am continually with thee; thou hast holden me by my right hand. Thou shalt guide me with thy counsel, and afterward receive me to glory." Do you think of death? This is often distressing, and there is much in it to dismay—if viewed separate from Him. But if you *sleep*, you will live together with him. Death, that severs every other bond, cannot touch the ligatures that unite you to him. As you leave others, you approach nearer to him; you get more perfectly into his presence—you are for ever with the Lord.

Voltaire more than once says, in his Letters to Madame Duffand, "I hate life, and yet I am afraid to die." A Christian fears neither of these. He is willing to abide, and he is ready to go. Life is his. Death is his. Whether we wake or sleep, we shall live together with him.

FEBRUARY 6.—"And, behold, two of them went that same day to a village called Emmaus, which was from Jerusalem about three score furlongs. And they talked together of all these things which had happened. And it came to pass, that while they communed together and reasoned, Jesus himself drew near, and went with them."—Luke, xxiv, 13—15.

THE name of the one was Cleopas; of the other we are ignorant. We are also unacquainted with the design of this journey; but it betrayed the imperfection of these disciples. For is it not astonishing that they could leave Jerusalem *before* they had *ascertained* an event so interesting as his resurrection; especially as he had more than once assured them that he should rise again the third day; and certain women, early at the sepulchre, had reported that the body was missing, and that they were informed by a vision of angels that he was alive; and, also, some from among themselves had gone to the grave, and found it even as they had said; yet they walk off into the country in the midst of all this perplexity! Such is our impatience! Such is our fear! Such is our despondency! But he that believeth maketh not haste.

Yet a drop *is* water, and a spark *is* fire, and a little grace *is* grace, and perfectly distinguishable from mere nature. And we have here, not only infirmity, but excellency. Their minds cleave unto him still, and they can talk about nothing else—and he joins them. Let me not pass over this without remark.

It shows the Savior's kindness and tenderness. He does not despise the day of small things, nor cast off those who have a little strength. I know not what kind of person he had. But if he had not bodily beauty, in his mind he was fairer than the children of men. I am sure of his temper; I can look into his heart, and see that it is made of love: "A bruised reed will he not break; and the smoking flax will he not quench; but will bring forth judgment unto victory."

It shows me the truth of the promise. "*Where*"—let it be where it will, in the temple, the private dwelling, the field, the road: "where *two* or three" (if there are no more; for, as he is not confined to place, so neither to number) "are gathered together in my name, *there* am I in the midst of them."

I also learn, that the way to have him for our companion, is to make him our theme. No theme ought to be so dear—no theme can be so excellent, so profitable.

Let worldly minds pursue the things of the world. But let Christians abundantly utter the memory of *his* great goodness, and mention the loving kindnesses of the Lord. And then he will be present. He *is* there.

"We'll talk of all he did and said,
"And suffer'd for us here below;
"The path he mark'd for us to tread,
"And what he's doing for us now.

"Thus, as the moments pass away
"We'll love, and wonder, and adore;
"And hasten on the glorious day,
"When we shall meet to part no more."

FEBRUARY 7.—"Take up thy bed and walk."—John, v, 8.

WE are too prone to overlook the circumstantial and incidental instruction of the sacred writers—forgetful that every word of God is pure, and that whatsoever things were written aforetime, were written for our learning. Let us not lose any of this hid treasure for want of observing and applying what we read.

Our Savior met with this man at the pool of Bethesda; but no sooner had he pronounced the word of healing, than he orders him to take up *his bed* and walk. He has always reasons for his conduct, though they are not always perceptible. But I think we can see four reasons for this command.

First, it was to evince the perfection of the cure. His walking, indeed, would prove this; but his taking up his bed, and being able to carry that in which he had been carried, would display it still more, as it showed his strength, as well as health. We often refer to miracles, and they are the witness of the Spirit. But the question is, were they true? Never could any thing have been more remote from imposition than the miracles recorded in the Gospel. Examine them. They were many—they were public—they were performed before witnesses interested in their detection, had they been false. The circumstances, too, were always corroborative. Does he raise the dead? The young man was carrying to his burial, attended with much people. Lazarus was in his grave, and had been dead four days. Does he recover the infirm and the diseased? The man whose eyes he opened was born blind. And this paralytic had been afflicted thirty-eight years; and in a moment he was made whole, and was seen by all going home with his bed upon his shoulders.

Secondly, it was to teach him to be careful, and to waste nothing. The bed probably was not very valuable, but he was not to throw it away. In correspondence with this, after the miracle of the loaves and fishes, even then, when he had shown with what ease he could multiply resources, and support his creatures, he said, "Gather up the fragments that remain, that nothing be lost." Christians should avoid closeness and meanness, lest their good be evil spoken of; but there is another extreme they should be anxious to avoid: it is profusion—yea, negligence and carelessness. They ought not to love money; but they should know the use and worth of it, and remember that they are responsible for all they have. How needy are many, and how ready would they be to call down the blessing of heaven upon you for a few pence, for the remnants of your wardrobe, for the refuse of your garden, for the crumbs that fall from your table. Be examples of economy yourselves. Teach your children to be prodigal of nothing. You would dismiss a servant that purloined; keep no one that wastes. How unfrugal, often, are the poor. How few of them seem to know how to make the most of any of their pittances. Let them be instructed personally, and by tracts.

Thirdly, as a memento of his deliverance and duty. When at home, and looking on this bed, he would say, "Ah! there I lay, a poor enfeebled creature; and said, My strength and my hope is perished from the Lord, remembering mine affliction and my misery, the wormwood and the gall: my soul hath them still in remembrance, and is humbled within me. This I call to mind; therefore have I hope." It is a sad charge against Israel, that they *soon* forgat His works, and the wonders that he had shown them. We are prone to the same evil, and need every assistance to aid recollection. Joseph and Moses made the very names of their children remembrances. Samuel set up a stone, and called it Ebenezer. Some have set apart particular days. Some have kept diaries.

"Why should the wonders He has wrought,
"Be lost in silence, and forgot?"

Fourthly, to try his obedience. Carrying his bed was a servile work; and it was now the Sabbath, on which day no burden was to be borne. He seemed, therefore, to oppose the law of Moses, and accordingly the Pharisees were offended, and murmured. But works of necessity and mercy were *always* proper, and the Sabbath was made for man, and the Son of Man was Lord even of the Sabbath day. And it is pleasing to find that the man's mind was informed, as well as his body cured, and to hear him reasoning with the objectors as he does. "He answered them, He that made me whole, the same said unto me, Take up thy bed and walk." How fine, how instructive is this. We are not to judge the Lord's commands, but to follow them. His orders may be trying, and in obeying them we may give offence; but we need not mind the revilings of men, while we can plead his authority. It is our Deliverer, our Benefactor, who enjoins, and what has *He* said unto us? He that died for us, and saved us from the wrath to come, what will *He* have me to do? He that made me whole, the same says unto me, "If ye love me, keep my commandments."

FEBRUARY 8.—**"And he was there in the prison."—Genesis, xxxix, 20.**

—BUT he was not there *criminally*, but under an imputation as false as it was infamous. How little can we judge of character from outward condition. At one time the best people in the country were to be found at the stake or in prison. But it is the cause, and not the cross, that makes the martyr. Let us see, that, like Daniel, we are accused only in the law of our God, and resemble Paul, who suffered *as* an evil doer, even unto bonds, but was *not* one. Let us beware of drawing upon ourselves deserved reproach or persecution, by imprudent or immoral conduct.

"For what glory is it, if, when ye are buffeted for your faults, ye take it patiently?"

"And he was there in prison;" but he was not *alone* there. But the Lord was with Joseph—no doubt of it; for he hath said, "I will *never* leave thee, nor forsake thee." No situation can exclude God from access to his people, or keep them from intercourse with God. Jeremiah found him in the deep dungeon; John in the isle of Patmos, and Paul on the sea. His people sometimes wonder at this; the experience is beyond their expectation; and they say with Jacob, "Surely God is in this place, and I knew it not." But they might know it; especially if it be a scene of distress; for has He not said, "I will be with thee in trouble!"

"And he was there in the prison;" but he was not miserable there. All was peace within. His rejoicing was thus the testimony of his conscience. How much happier was he in this respect than his vile mistress, who had knowingly belied him; and his brethren who had cruelly sold him; how galled often would they be by reflection and self-reproach. How much happier was he, the suffering slave, than Potiphar, his prosperous master—yea, than Pharaoh upon the throne! Strange as it may seem, this prisoner, in this wretched confinement, was by far the happiest man in Egypt. But he had the presence of God. This presence makes the fullness of joy above, and this presence here, turns a prison into a palace—into a temple. The world marvels to see how Christians are sustained and consoled in their afflictions; but the reason is, they cannot see all; they can see their burdens, but not the everlasting arms underneath them; they can see their sorrows, but not the comforts of the Holy Ghost shed abroad in their hearts; but they themselves know, that as the sufferings of Christ abound in them, the consolation also aboundeth by Christ.

"And he was there in the prison;" but he was not there in *vain*. He was a witness for the God of Israel; and the very manner of his suffering, his temper, his carriage, if he had said nothing, would have impressed all that beheld him. But he would also speak a word in season, and his addresses, enforced by his example, would carry weight with them. He taught the master of the prison, and his fellow sufferers, and explained the dreams of the chief baker and butler, and thus raised wonder and gained confidence, which he failed not to turn to advantage. There, also, he was himself at school, and gained much useful knowledge, while "the word of the Lord tried him." His tribulation wrought patience, and patience experience, and experience hope. In the prison he was prepared for the palace, and by his adversity he was made meet for prosperity. He could well say, "It is good for me that I have been afflicted."

"And he was there in the prison;" but he was not there *always*. Nothing could detain him when the word of the Lord came and commanded his deliverance. Till then he relied on God's promise; but his confidence was sorely exercised; the event was not only delayed, but seemed to grow less probable, and the gloom thickened. But he found that it is good for a man not only to hope, but quietly wait for the salvation of the Lord. At length, and not a moment beyond his own appointed time, and not a moment beyond the best time, the Lord appeared, and from the prison he steps into the second chariot in Egypt.

Christians, the God you serve is continually able to deliver you. If you have his word, lay hold of it, and let it keep your mind in perfect peace, being stayed on Him. You have nothing to do with difficulties; indeed there are none where the truth of God is concerned. You believe in God the Father Almighty, Maker of heaven and earth; He turneth the shadow of death into the morning. At evening tide it shall be light.

FEBRUARY 9.—"My soul shall make her boast in the Lord; the humble shall hear thereof, and be glad."—Psalm xxxiv, 2.

WE are prone to boast, and there is scarcely any thing that does not often call forth the tendency. Some boast of their beauty—some of the multitude of their riches—some of their pedigree and rank—some of their genius, and learning, and knowledge. Some boast of their wickedness, which is glorying in their shame. Some boast of their goodness, when, too, they *have* none; for there is a generation who are pure in their own eyes, and are not washed from their filthiness. But they who have "the root of the matter" in them—have *they* any right to boast? Is their religion derived from themselves? Is it self-sustained? Is it perfect? Where is boasting then? It is excluded. By what law? The law of faith, for "it is of faith, that it might be of grace." And this is its language: "God hath chosen the foolish things of the world to confound the wise, and God hath chosen the weak things of the world to confound the things which are mighty; and base things of the world, and things which are despised hath God chosen, yea, and things which are not, to bring to nought things that are, that no flesh should glory in his presence. But of Him are ye in Christ Jesus, who of God is made unto us wisdom, and righteousness, and sanctification, and redemption; that according as it is written, He that glorieth, let him glory in the Lord."

But here we see that we may glory in Him, though we are forbidden to glory in creatures, or in ourselves. Accordingly, David says, "My soul shall make her boast in the Lord." And so ought we to resolve. And there are moments and frames when, surveying Him in his works, and perfections, and promises, the believer can exult with joy unspeakable and full of glory.

"All my capacious powers can boast,
"In thee most richly meet;
"Nor to my eyes is light so dear,
"Nor friendship half so sweet."

"What a Friend have I—a tried, kind, almighty, everlasting Friend—a Friend who loveth at all times, and has sworn that he will never leave me nor forsake me. 'This is my Beloved, and this is my Friend, O ye daughters of Jerusalem.' What a Shepherd have I! The Lord is my Shepherd, I shall not want. He maketh me to lie down in green pastures; he leadeth me beside the still waters. He restoreth my soul; he leadeth me in the paths of righteousness, for his name's sake. Yea, though I walk through the valley of the shadow of death, I will fear no evil; for thou art with me; thy rod and thy staff, they comfort me. What a God is mine! The God of truth; the God of all grace; a God in covenant; a God in Christ—this God is my God, for ever and ever: he will be my guide even unto death. What a portion is mine! The Lord is the portion of mine inheritance, and of my cup; thou maintainest my lot. The lines are fallen unto me in pleasant places; yea, I have a goodly heritage."

But not only is included here the elevation of joyous feeling, arising from the view and possession of magnificent good, but also the breaking forth of gratitude and praise. The selfish and the proud dislike the thought of dependence, and wish every acquisition to be considered as of their own procuring: "therefore they sacrifice unto their net, and burn incense unto their drag." But pious minds ever delight to own that they have nothing but what they have received. It is very painful to be under obligations to an enemy, but how pleasant it is to be indebted to one we admire and love! They who, therefore, supremely love their God and Savior, make their boast in the Lord. They will hereafter cast their crowns before the throne, and their language now is, "By the grace of God I am what I am." "In the Lord have I righteousness and strength." "I will greatly rejoice in the Lord; my soul shall be joyful in my God; for he hath clothed me with the garments of salvation; he hath covered me with the robe of righteousness, as a bridegroom decketh himself with ornaments, and as a bride adorneth herself with her jewels."

David supposes that his doing this would be known. "The humble shall hear thereof." They would possibly hear it from others, for the godly have their observers, and "are men wondered at."

They were likely to hear it from himself. Therefore, says he, "O magnify the Lord with me, and let us exalt his name together. I sought the Lord, and he heard me, and delivered me from all my fears;" "Come and hear, all ye that fear God, and I will declare what he hath done for my soul. I cried unto him with my mouth, and he was extolled with my tongue." Spiritual sadness seeks seclusion and concealment. Then, as the stricken deer leaves the herd, the man sitteth alone and keeps silence, because he has borne it upon him. Peter went out and wept bitterly. But spiritual freedom and joy soon discover themselves. Like the return of health, and of day, it says to the prisoners, Go forth; to them that are in darkness, Show yourselves. When Hannah was in bitterness of soul, and prayed unto the Lord, and wept sore, it is said she prayed in her heart, only her lips moved, but her voice was not heard. But when she had succeeded, she broke forth into a song, and said, "My heart rejoiceth in the Lord, mine horn is exalted in the Lord; my mouth is enlarged over mine enemies, because I rejoice in thy salvation."

David also inferred the effect this knowledge would produce in them—"The humble shall hear thereof, and be *glad*." He could reckon upon this from his own disposition, and from the connexion there is between all the subjects of Divine grace. They are all one in Christ Jesus. They belong to the same family; they are parts of the same body; and if one member suffers, all the members suffer with it: and if one member be honored, all the members rejoice. They who have prayed for me, will not refuse to praise. "Bring my soul out of prison, that I may praise thy name; the righteous shall compass me about, for thou shalt deal bountifully with me." What sight can be so gratifying to a good man, as to see a convert leaving the world and entering the Church; a backslider returning into the path of peace; a believer walking worthy the vocation wherewith he is called; a dying saint joyful in glory, and shouting aloud upon his bed? They that fear thee will be glad when they see me, because I have hoped in thy truth.

—The Lord's followers are supposed to be mopish and melancholy, but they have a thousand sources of joy which others know not of. How great is the pleasure they derive even from others. Indeed they can often rejoice on the behalf of their brethren, when they fear things are not going on well with themselves. But what a proof is this feeling that their heart *is* right with God!

—Envy is the rottenness of the bones, and the temper of the devil. To rejoice in another's good is Christian—angelical—divine. God is love; and he that dwelleth in love, dwelleth in God, and God in him.

FEBRUARY 10.—"Be sober."—1 Thess. v, 8.

THIS stands opposed to bodily excess, and especially to drunkenness. It is painful to think that it should be ever necessary even to mention such a subject among those who ever profess to be Christians. The Spartans presented to their children intoxicated slaves, that, seeing their beastly demeanor, they might detest the vice.

Some pagan legislators inflicted a double punishment upon crimes committed in a state of drunkenness. Christian lawgivers and judges are not equally wise and just; for how scandalous is it to hear men, in a court of justice, allege their intoxication to extenuate, if not to justify their conduct. Drunkenness takes away the man, and leaves the brute. It dethrones reason from its seat. It covers the wretch with rags, and reduces his wife and children to want and beggary. It impairs appetite, produces trembling of limbs, and such sinking of spirits as almost compels to the repetition of the offence—so that, physically, as well as morally, it is next to impossible to cure it.

Let me therefore guard against it, and not only in the *grossness*, but the *guilt*. Some professors of religion seem to think they are *not* chargeable with the sin, if they can keep their eyes open, and walk from the dining-room to the tea-table, not considering that every indulgence beyond natural relief and refreshment is vicious; and that the Scripture peculiarly condemns those who, by gradual training, have made themselves *strong* to drink wine, and to mingle strong drink. Let me therefore beware of the encroaching *degree*, and put a knife to my throat, if *given* to appetite. And instead of being filled with wine, wherein is excess, let me be filled with the Spirit.

But the pure and holy religion of Jesus, when it says, "Be sober," forbids much more than this vile and offensive practice. It enjoins temperance in *all* our appetites, desires and affections. It extends even to businesses. As a man may be entangled, so he may be intoxicated with the affairs of this life; and how often do the cares of this life, and the deceitfulness of riches, choke the word, and it becometh unfruitful. A Christian may be too mindful of earthly things, too alive to fame, too anxious to join house to house, and add field to field, and to load himself with thick clay. As a man inebriated is unfit for the duties of his station, and is obliged to be confined, so it is with those who set their affection on things below. They are unqualified for their high calling, and cannot walk as becometh the Gospel.

"Seekest thou great things to thyself?" says Jeremiah to Barach, "seek them not." Let me reflect, in the light of Scripture and observation, on the vanity of worldly things; their unsatisfactoriness in possession; their perishing in the using; and the many and hurtful lusts to which they expose; and let my conversation be without covetousness, and let me be content with such things as I have, for He hath said, I will never leave thee, nor forsake thee.

Sleep is a natural and necessary refreshment. But we may be excessive in this, as well as in any other indulgence. And, alas! how often are we, even to the injury of our health, as well as the waste of our time.

Recreation is allowable and salutary; but we may exceed the bounds which the redemption of time, and the repairing and refitting us for duty can only allow.

Paul exhorts Timothy to be "sober-minded." How intemperate are some in their opinions; and opinions, especially in religion, that regard inferior truths, and subjects concerning which the understanding meets with the greatest difficulties. Some are eager, and rash, and positive in all their judgments, and nothing is too absurd or ridiculous for their adoption.

Again, let me hear the apostle; "I say to every man that is amongst you, not to think of himself more highly than he ought to think, but to think soberly;" *i. e.* not overrating his station, his connections, his abilities, his usefulness, his performances. "For if a man think himself to be something when he is nothing, he deceiveth himself."

Finally, let me not forget how *obviously*, as well as extensively, I am to discharge this obligation; nor lose sight for a moment, of the *argument*, by which it is enforced—"LET YOUR MODERATION BE KNOWN UNTO ALL MEN—THE LORD IS AT HAND."

FEBRUARY 11.—"The children of the day."—1 Thess. v, 5.

THREE distinctions may be here made. The first, regards heathens. The second, the Jews. The third, Christians.

Heathens are the children of *night*. With regard to them, darkness covered the earth, and gross darkness the people. What did they know of God; of themselves; of their origin; their fall; their recovery; their duty? What did they know of a future state? A few of their philosophers spoke of the immortality of the soul; but none of them thought of the resurrection of the body, unless to turn it into ridicule. And what they expressed, they did but conjecture: they could prove and establish nothing. And they held it in unrighteousness; it had no influence over them as a motive; for wanting the certainty of a principle, it wanted the efficacy. And they kept it from the people at large, and employed no means to inform the multitude, who, as quite sufficient for them, were abandoned to every kind of superstition.

The *Jews* were all children of the *dawn;* an intermediate state between night and day; better than the former, and very inferior to the latter. Hence the Savior alluding, not to the state of pagans, but to the disadvantages of Judaism, said to his disciples, "Many prophets and righteous men have desired to see the things that ye see, and have not seen them." They had the law, which was given by Moses; but we have grace and truth that came by Jesus Christ. They had the shadows, we have the substance. They had the types, and the promises; we, the realizations, and the accomplishment. To them, the Sun of Righteousness was below the horizon; on us, he has risen with healing under his wings—God having provided some better thing for us, that they, without us, should not be made perfect. For

Christians are the children of the *day*. It is their privilege to have the system of Revelation complete; and to be blessed with the full dispensation of the glorious Gospel. They have the servants of the Most High God, which show unto men the way of salvation.

Every thing with us is made clear, in proportion as it is important. And with regard to the acceptance of our persons with God, the renovation of our nature, our title to eternal life, our meetness for glory, our supplies of grace, and all spiritual blessings in heavenly places in Christ; the darkness is entirely past, and the true light now shineth, and we are the children of the day.

Therefore let us hail it with gratitude. And what thanks can ever equal the benefit? A mud cottage with the Scriptures in it, is more ennobled in the view of an angel, than the palace of the richest emperor upon earth. David would have descended from his throne, and have passed his days in a poor-house, to have enjoyed our advantages. Abraham, at the distance of near two thousand years, rejoiced to see our day, saw it, and was glad.

Therefore let us receive it with joy. Nature shows off her beauties: the lambs play; the birds carol their notes; every thing seems to welcome the approach of day. Truly light is sweet, and a pleasant thing it is for the eyes to behold the sun. And shall the Gospel, this day of good tidings, inspire us with dread and gloom? Is it not intended, is it not adapted to make even our spirits rejoice in God our Savior? And was it not thus always originally regarded?

Therefore we should improve it with diligence. The sun ariseth, and man goeth forth to his work and to his labor until evening—the night is for inaction. They that sleep, sleep in the night; and they that are drunken, are drunken in the night. But let us, who are of the day, be sober. And knowing the time, let us cast off the works of darkness, and let us put on the armor of light. Advantages infer obligations, and produce responsibility. Where much is given, much will be required. What do ye more than others? asks the Savior. And he has a right to ask. He also says, Yet a little while is the light with you. Walk while ye have the light, lest darkness come upon you. Blessed Jesus! possess me with thy own Spirit; and, henceforth repelling every interruption, and crushing every indecision and delay, may I make thy purpose and zeal my own: "I must work the works of Him that sent me while it is day—the night cometh wherein no man can work."

FEBRUARY 12.—" And he said, Leave us not, I pray thee; forasmuch as thou knowest how we are to encamp in the wilderness, and thou mayest be to us instead of eyes."—Numbers, x, 31.

SUCH was the language of the Jewish leader to Hobab, the son of Raguel the Midianite, Moses' father-in-law. How numerous are our wants, in whatever condition we are found. We need not food to nourish us, apparel to cover us, sleep to refresh us, friendship to succor us. We need the heart of one of our fellow creatures, and the hand of another. One must be feet to us, another eyes. Who is self-sufficient? Who, but under the delusion of pride and vanity, would ever affect independence? The eye cannot say unto the hand, I have no need of thee. Nor, again, the head to the feet, I have no need of you. Nay, much more those members of the body which are feeble, are necessary. Above others in circumstances, we may be inferior to them in grace or experience, or some particular attainment. David was superior to Jonathan in divine things; yet "Jonathan went to David in the wood, and strengthened his hands in God." I long to see you, says Paul to the Romans, that I may impart unto you some spiritual gift, that ye may be established; but they aided and confirmed him first; for they came down to meet him as far as Appii Forum and the Three Taverns; and when he saw them *he* thanked God, and took courage.

Here we see the advantages of society. A God of knowledge and truth has said, It is not good for man to be alone; and if it was so with regard to Paradise, how much more with regard to a wilderness. Half the pleasure of solitude, it has been remarked, arises from our having a friend at hand to whom we can say, How delightful this retirement is! Ointment and perfume rejoice the heart, so doth a man his friend by hearty counsel. Why, but to encourage social devotion, did our Savior say to his disciples, "If two of you shall agree on earth as touching any one thing that they shall ask, it shall be done for them of my Father which is in heaven. For where two or three are gathered together in my name, there am I in the midst of them." Why did he send forth the seventy, two by two, in their mission through Judea, but to comfort each other in distress; to confer with each other in cases of perplexity; to stimulate each other in cases of languor; to check each other in cases of temptation." "Two are better far than one, because they have good reward for their labor. For if they fall, the one will lift up his fellow; but wo to him that is alone when he falleth; for he hath not another to help him up."

Let none despond. As all are required to be useful, so all may be serviceable, if they will; and often, far, beyond the probability of their condition, or their own hopefulness; for humility makes a good man modest in his expectations, as well as in his pretensions.

We also see here, that confidence in God is not to lead us to disregard any advantages we can derive from ordinary resources. Moses had the engagement of God, and was even under a miraculous guidance; yet he does not overlook the assistance he could derive from his father-in-law, as to his advice in difficulties, and those instructions which, from his knowledge of the Wilderness, he could give him, with regard to particular situations, and their conveniencies or inconveniencies. The religion of the Bible is always a reasonable service. It does not keep a man's eyes upon the stars, while he falls over every stumbling block in his way, but says to him, "Let thine eyes look right on, and thy eyelids straight before thee; ponder the path of thy feet, that thy goings may be established." It places our dependence upon God, but that reliance is favorable to activity—it is the spring of it. In Him we live, move, and have our being; but this does not supersede eating and drinking. He teaches us; but we are to read and hear his word. He promises, but he will be inquired of for the performance. And none of the aids he affords us render needless the exercise of prudence, the exertion of our faculties, the offices of friendship, or the means of grace. "Draw nigh to God, and he will draw nigh to you."

February 13.—**"Turn thee unto me, and have mercy upon me: for I am desolate and afflicted. The troubles of my heart are enlarged: O bring thou me out of my distresses."—Psalm xxv, 16, 17.**

Surely this book is addressed to the heart? and requires sensibility rather than talent to understand and explain it. How tender here is the language of David, and how instructive too. He was a sufferer, though a king, and a man eminently godly. And his sorrows were not superficial, but deep and depressing, "the sorrows of the heart."

And while hoping for their diminution they were "enlarged." But he is a petitioner, as well as a sufferer, and those sorrows will never injure us that bring us to God. Three things he prays for.

First. Deliverance. This we are allowed to desire consistently with resignation to the divine will. But we must seek it, not from creatures, but from God, who has said, "Call upon me in the day of trouble, and I will deliver thee." Nothing is too hard for Him; He can turn the shadow of death into the morning—Therefore, says David, "O bring thou me out of my distresses."

Secondly. Notice. A kind look from God is desirable at any time, in any circumstances; but in affliction and pain, it is like life from the dead. Nothing cuts like the neglect of a friend in distress; nothing soothes like his calls, and inquiries, and sympathy, and tears, then. But to say, Thou, God, seest me; thou knowest all my walking through this great wilderness—to be assured that he is attentive to my condition, and is smiling through the cloud; fills the heart, even in tribulation, with a peace that passeth all understanding—Therefore, says David, "Look upon mine affliction and pain."

Thirdly. Pardon. He does not think himself sinless: and trials are apt to revive a sense of guilt, and to make the sufferer fearful, and to induce the prayer, "Do not condemn me." We will also venture to say, that however a Christian may feel his sorrows, he will feel his sins much more: these, these are the burden and the grief—Therefore, David says, "Forgive all my sins."

This was his meaning, and I hope I can make it my own. If it be thy pleasure, release me from my complaint. If not, and the distress is continued to try me, be near to afford me a sensible manifestation of thy favor; let me see thy countenance; let me hear thy voice, saying, "I remember thee still." Or, if this be denied, and I have no claim upon thee for such an indulgence, let me, for the Redeemer's sake, be absolved and justified. Remove my guilt, whatever becomes of my grief—grief *then* cannot be penal—cannot be injurious—

> "If sin be pardon'd, I'm secure;
> "*Death* hath no sting beside:
> "The law gives sin its damning pow'r;
> "But Christ, my ransom, died"

February 14.—"Ye are my friends, if ye do whatsoever I command you."
John, xv, 14.

He does not say, ye are the subjects of my love; but, "Ye are my friends," if ye do whatsoever I command you. You may love an animal, a slave, an enemy; but neither of these can be your friend; for friendship implies and requires what their condition does not admit. It is a remarkable expression that Moses employs when he says, "If thy brother, the son of thy mother, or thy son, or thy daughter, or the wife of thy bosom, or thy FRIEND who is as thine OWN SOUL." It seems to place a friend above all the relations of kindred, and Solomon does not scruple to say, "There is a friend that sticketh closer than a brother." Friendship has always been deemed essential to the happiness of human beings, and, indeed, to their very honor; for it would be thought as disgraceful as it is disconsolate to have no friend. No peculiarity of condition, nor elevation of rank, sets a man above the attraction and utility of friendship. Kings have laid aside their royalties to indulge in it, and Alexander would have found a conquered world a kind of desert, without an Ephestion.

But it is needless to enlarge on the excellency and value of this blessing. Who is not ready to acknowledge that friendship is the delight of youth, the pillar of age, the bloom of prosperity, the charm of solitude, the solace of adversity, the best benefactor and comforter in this vale of tears. But the question is, where a friend is to be found? It will be allowed that many who wear the name are unworthy of the title, and that even those who are sincere in professions may be chargeable with infirmities. Yet even human friendship is not a utopian good. He who says all men are liars, says it in his haste, or from a heart that judges of others by itself. They who complain most are commonly the most to be complained of; for there is *real* friendship to be found on earth. But there is better in heaven; and in our text we have the advantage in the highest of all examples. In others we may have the reality, and even the eminency of friendship, but in Him we have the perfection, the divinity of it.

But what is necessary to our claiming it? Ye are my friends, says He, "If ye do whatsoever I command you." But this he shows us, that though he is the friend, he is also the lawgiver. Under whatever character he reveals himself, we are never to lose sight of the Sovereign. His goodness is to display his greatness, not to weaken it. He is the Prince as well as the Savior; He "commands" his friends. And nothing less than obedience to his will is required of us. It is not enough to read it, and hear it, and know it, and talk of it, and profess it; we must "*do*" it. And our obedience must be impartial; we must do "whatsoever" he commands us. Obedience may be sincere without being perfect in the degree; but it cannot be sincere without being universal in its principle and disposition. For if I do some things which he enjoins me, and not others, it follows, that what I do, I do from some other motive than his authority; for this would lead me to observe all he enjoins. True obedience will not suffer me to select, any more than to dictate; its only inquiry is, "Lord, *what* wilt thou have me to do?" He who commands me to enter his gates with thanksgiving, tells me also to enter my closet. He who forbids me to steal, tells me to speak evil of no man. Can I say with David, "I esteem *all* thy commandments concerning all things to be right, and I hate *every* false way?"

With regard to the connexion, however, between this friendship and this obedience, let it not be supposed that it is a meritorious one, as if the practice deserved the privilege. This is impossible, and would subvert the gospel of Christ. Yet it is a certain connexion, and as certain, both in its exclusion and inclusion, as the nature of things, and the word of truth, can make it. And it is an encouraging connexion. Had the requisition turned on worldly honor, or wealth, or genius, or science, many must have despaired. But the essential is not derived from condition, but conduct. It is, therefore, within the reach of the poor, as well as of the rich, and of the illiterate, as well as the learned. All may be great in the sight of the Lord, and he is the greatest, whatever be his circumstances in life, who best obeys his Lord and Savior. Mary was blessed in being his mother; but this was a privilege necessarily confined to one individual. He, therefore, when he heard the exclamation of the woman, Blessed be the womb that bare thee, and the paps which thou hast sucked! instantly mentions a way to a higher privilege, and which lies open to every one: "Yea, rather, blessed are they that hear the word of God, and keep it."

Pray, therefore, "O that my feet were directed to keep thy precepts!" "Many will entreat the favor of the prince, and every one is a friend to him that giveth gifts." But when you seek the regards of the great, what base compliances are often necessary to please them—and then you are never sure of succeeding—and when you succeed, what have you gained? But his work is honorable and glorious. If you seek, you are sure to find. And whoso findeth Him, findeth life, and shall obtain favor of the Lord. However unobserved or neglected among men you may be, no one can pass your door and say, "There dwells a friendless person."

Lord Brook was so charmed with that rare and accomplished personage, Sir Philip Sidney, that he would have no other inscription on his tomb than this, "Here lies the friend of Sir Philip Sidney."

Ah! says the Christian, I envy not those whose sepulchre will be adorned with the trophies of war, the pride of heraldry, or the renown of science, if my humble grave can tell, and tell truly, "Here lies the friend of Christ."

FEBRUARY 15.—"And all the people saw him walking and praising God; and they knew that it was he which sat for alms at the Beautiful Gate of the temple; and they were filled with wonder and amazement at that which had happened unto him."—Acts, iii, 9, 10.

HIS walking was a proof of the reality and perfection of the cure. His praising God was the proper improvement of it.

But what an attestation was here to the divine mission of the apostles, and so to the truth of Christianity itself! We *speak*, said they, in His name who was crucified—and if you ask for a proof of it, we will *act* in His name. Bring forth your dumb, and we will give them speech; your blind, and we will open their eyes; your sick, and we will heal them; your lame, and we will make them leap as a hart. This was evidence adapted to persons of every rank and capacity; it required no labored process of reasoning and eloquence—it was the broad seal of heaven, which all could see and understand.

And there was nothing like artifice or collusion in these miracles. Take the case before us. The patient resided, not in a remote place, but in Jerusalem, that is, in the midst of their enemies. He had been lame from his mother's womb, and was now upward of forty years old. He was well known; he was a beggar. Multitudes had seen him; many had relieved him; and many had handled him—for he was carried daily to the place of begging. And this was not an obscure corner, but the entrance into the temple. And the thing was not done in the night, but at nine o'clock in the morning, when there was a concourse of people.

Put all this together, and then ask whether any thing could have been fairer. Could any thing have been more open to detection, had there been any imposture? Compare such an achievement with the prodigies of heathenism, and the miracles of the Romish church.

And see, also, what can equal the *credulity* of unbelievers! What is the faith of a Christian to their belief? Christians believe difficulties, because they are abundantly confirmed; but *they* swallow improbabilities, and impossibilities. Their rejection of the Gospel cannot arise from an intellectual, but a moral cause. They do not want evidence, but disposition—they receive not the love of the truth, that they might be saved. Therefore, How can they escape, if they neglect so great salvation; which at the first began to be spoken by the Lord, and was confirmed unto them by those that heard him: God also bearing them witness, both with signs and wonders, and with divers miracles, and gifts of the Holy Ghost, according to his own will?

Need I tremble for the cause of Christianity? Need my reason be ashamed of my faith?

"Hence, and for ever from my heart,
"I bid my doubts and fears depart;
"And to those hands my soul resign,
"That bear credentials so divine"

FEBRUARY 16.—"They serve not thy gods, nor worship the golden image which thou hast set up."—Daniel, iii, 12.

THE refusal of these three young men was as trying as it was noble. The resolution has immortalized them. But let us observe how much they had to overcome in adhering to it.

They could plead *authority*. Here was the command of their sovereign; and good men are to be good subjects, to honor principalities and powers, to obey magistrates, and to be ready to every work But there is a difference between civil and spiritual claims. We are, indeed, to render unto Cæsar the things that are Cæsar's· but we must also render unto God the things that are God's. If any being requires us to do what is opposed to the revealed will of God, we are prevented by an authority from which there can lie no appeal, and we ought to obey God rather than man. Thus the midwives did not as the king of Egypt commanded them, but saved the men-children alive. "And it came to pass, because the midwives feared God, that He made them houses."

This conscientiousness, however, has often given the conduct of God's servants an appearance of insubordination and revolt; and their enemies have not failed to seize it, and turn it to their discredit. Jesus was not Cæsar's friend; and stirred up the people. The Apostles turned the world upside down. And, doubtless, Shadrach, Meshach, and Abednego, were censured and vilified for their disloyalty.

They could plead *obligation*. Nebuchadnezzar was not only their sovereign, but their friend and benefactor. He had educated them in a princely manner, and advanced them to the most honorable charges. And nothing tries like tenderness. Benefits attract and attach the heart, and good men are the most susceptible of grateful impressions. One of the most painful things in the world, to an ingenuous mind, is to refuse the wishes of one who has done much for him; for there is nothing in which he would more delight, were he not restrained by principle. Suppose a dutiful child. He loves and honors his parents; and he ought to honor them. These parents, in other respects, are kind and good, but they are worldly, and require him to go into the dissipations of life; they are irreligious, and forbid him to attend what, according to his conviction, is the truth of God; and, instead of threatening, they weep over him, and beseech him by every tender motive, not to break their hearts, nor bring down their gray hairs with sorrow to the grave. Now to loosen from such embraces and entreaties, and act a part that *looks* like disrespect; at the hearing of a voice that cries, "He that loveth father or mother more than me, is not worthy of me:" here is a trial hardly supportable. And much of this, these young men would feel, at the thought of the favors which had been heaped upon them.

They could plead *universality of compliance.* All besides obey, and why should they stand alone, and affect to be better than any one else? How often is this objection thrown out? Singularity, for its own sake, argues a little and vain mind: vain, because it seeks notice; and little, because it can attain it in no better way. In things harmless and indifferent, we may lawfully conform to the usages of the day and place wherein we live; but where truth, and duty, and conscience are concerned, we must be steadfast and immovable, though deserted, opposed, ridiculed by all, and by unsought, but indispensable singularity, evince the purity of our motives, and the dignity of our principles. So did Abdiel.

> "——— Faithful found
> "Among the faithless, faithful only he
> "Among innumerable false, unmov'd,
> "Unshaken, unseduced, unterrified:
> "His loyalty he kept, his love, his zeal.
> "Nor number, nor example with him wrought
> "To swerve from truth, or change his constant mind,
> "Though single."

So did Joshua, and Caleb, and Lot, and Noah. And all Christians are required not to be conformed to the world. And Jesus died to redeem and purify unto himself a peculiar people—and peculiar they must be while the multitude do evil. Well, said these sufferers, if all yield, we must not—will not—whatever be the consequence.

And they could plead the *dreadfulness of the penalty.* We are often ready to justify or excuse our conduct by the pressure of circumstances; and to allege, that the trial is too great for our virtue. And what is the trial? What are our difficulties and perils in the path of duty? If we follow such a course—Well, shall we be bound to the stake? or thrown into a lion's den? or a fiery furnace? No. Shall we then be deprived of our liberty? and confined in prison? or be stripped of our property, and reduced to beggary? No such thing. Blessed be the laws of this happy land. Behold our jeopardies and sacrifices! We may lose a trifle of our profit by not selling or working on the Sabbath. We may have less to hoard by giving alms to the needy. If we follow our convictions, we may lose the smile of a friend, or incur the sneer of a fool. By the redeeming our time, we may even be constrained to leave the bed of sloth a little earlier in the morning.

These are our tribulations because of the Word! These are the martyrs of our day! Ye professors of religion, who can exercise no self-denial, who can take up no cross; "If thou hast run with the footmen, and they have wearied thee, then how canst thou contend with horses? And if, in the land of peace, wherein thou trustest they wearied thee, then how wilt thou do in the swellings of Jordan!" Look at these youths. What had they to lose! What to suffer! A fiery furnance before their eyes, into which they were to be instantly thrown!

FEBRUARY 17.—" Rejoice the soul of thy servant."—Psalm, lxxxiv, 6.

THE Queen of Sheba not only admired Solomon, but hailed his attendants. "Happy are thy men, and happy are these thy servants that stand continually before thee." What then is it to be a servant of the King of kings and Lord of lords!

A servant of God, however, is not one that only subserves his designs. This, by an over-ruling Providence, all do, even the wicked themselves. But one, who, from conviction and disposition, resigns himself to his will, and holds himself at his disposal, always asking, "Lord, what wilt thou have me to do?" always praying, "Let the words of my mouth, and the meditation of my heart, be acceptable in thy sight, O Lord, my strength, and my redeemer."

And can such a man as this want spiritual joy? Yes. Even David himself, that eminent servant of God, does; and therefore prays, "Rejoice the soul of thy servant." We ask, if I am his, why I am thus? We think our course of experience singular; but while we complain, we are passing by the very landmarks which those who have gone before us have set up to tell us that we are right. Our state is one thing, our joy is another: the former remains always the same, the latter often varies. Our safety does not depend upon our knowledge, but our comfort is much affected by it; and sometimes a servant of God has but very imperfect views of those glorious truths which make us "free indeed." Sometimes he may be depressed by his bodily frame and infirmities. Sometimes, too, he is under Divine rebuke for sin—for this it is that separates between God and the soul. We should therefore search and try our ways. Is there not a cause? If the consolations of God are small with us, is there no secret thing with us? Is there no worm at the root of our withering gourd? No Achan in the camp, the troubler of Israel? Joab besieges Abel, and threatens to destroy it. A woman cries out to him to know the cause. He answers, there is one Sheba, the son of Bichri, a traitor to the king. Cast him over the wall, and I will withdraw. And so it was. And thus, if we would have peace with God, we must sacrifice every usurper, saying,

"The dearest idol I have known,
"Whate'er that idol be,
"Help me to tear it from thy throne,
"And worship only thee."

But a servant of God will value what he may want. He prizes it not only because God has commanded and promised it, but because he knows, from experience, that the joy of the Lord is his strength. He has seen how it emboldened his profession, and enlivened his zeal, and weaned his heart from the world, and revived him in the midst of trouble. He has tasted its sweetness; this he can never lose the relish of, and this excites him to pray, "Restore unto me the joy of thy salvation."

For he is sure that God is alone the source and giver of it, and therefore to *Him* he goes. "Rejoice the soul of thy servant." It is very desirable to see the morning after a dark night, and the spring after a cold barren winter. But what makes the morning and the spring? Not all the lamps or fires in the world, but the sun. And the Lord God is the Sun, as well as the Shield of his people. All our light, and heat, and bloom, are from Him, and in Him is our fruit found. He is the God, not only of all grace, but of all comfort.

It is He that comforts us in any of our common mercies; otherwise our sleep would not refresh us, nor our food nourish us, nor friends cheer us. And what would the means of grace be, if He was not in them? God, says the apostle, comforted us by the coming of Titus—not Titus, but God *by* Titus. Who, then, is Paul, and who is Apollos, but ministers *by* whom he believed, even as *God* gave to every man? Luther says, it is as easy to make a world, as to ease a troubled conscience. But,

The troubled conscience knows thy voice;
Thy cheering words awake our joys;
Thy words allay the stormy wind,
And calm the surges of the mind.

FEBRUARY 18.—"Making request, if by any means now at length I might have a prosperous journey by the will of God to come unto you. For I long to see you, that I may impart unto you some spiritual gift, to the end ye may be established."—Romans, i, 10, 11.

AT this time Paul had not seen Rome. But how natural was it in a man of his taste and intelligence to wish to see it. Nothing had made such a figure in history as this imperial city. From a kind of village it extended, in a course of years, till it had become the mistress of the nations, and the metropolis of the world. How powerfully must curiosity have been awakened by its extent, its majesty, its edifices, its institutions, laws, and customs. Paul was also a citizen, and while some, with a great ransom, purchased this privilege, he was free-born. Yet his longing to see it was not to indulge the man and the Roman, but the Christian and the apostle. He longed to impart to the beloved and called of God there, "some spiritual benefit."

But see the order of divine grace. Before he was useful to them, *they* imparted some spiritual benefit to him, and established his wavering confidence. For when he had landed at Puteoli, and advanced towards Rome, the brethren came to meet as far as the Appii Forum and the Three Taverns, "whom, when Paul saw, he thanked God, and took courage." Here we see that the most eminent servants of God may be depressed and desponding, and that it is possible for them to derive assistance and comfort from those who are much inferior to them in office, condition, abilities, and grace. There is no such thing as independence. Let none be proud. Let none despair. The Christian church is a body, and the body is not one member, but many. "If the foot shall say, Because I am not of the hand, I am not of the body, is it therefore not of the body?" The eye cannot say to the hand, I have no need of thee; nor the head to the feet, I have no need of you.

But how was this prosperous journey, according to the will of God, for which he made so many requests, accomplished? How little did he imagine the way in which he was to visit this famous city. He enters it, indeed, but in the character of a prisoner, driven thither by persecution, and after being shipwrecked upon a certain island. So high above ours are God's thoughts and ways! So little do we know what we pray for! So often by strange, and sometimes by terrible things in righteousness, does He answer us as the God of our salvation. So fulfils He the promise, "I will bring the blind by a way that they knew not; I will lead them in paths that they have not known; I will make darkness light before them, and crooked things straight. These things will I do unto them, and not forsake them."

February 19.—" And when he thought thereon he wept."—Mark, xiv, 72.

Doddridge supposes that this is intended to express, not only the immediate sensibility of Peter, but his feeling through life, and that he always wept at the thought of his vile and ungrateful conduct. His sin was certainly very aggravated; and, with all his failings, he was a man of very tender affections and great ingenuousness.

But sorrow arising from such a source is not peculiar to our apostle; all the people of God should feel a penitent disposition at the review of their sin.

And who, when they look back, can be at a loss for materials of accusation and contrition? There are the sins of our unregenerate condition. There are the sins we have been capable of since we have been called to the knowledge of the truth. All these we are to judge of, not by their grossness, but by their guilt. In the number of our sins we are to rank our omissions of duty; our non-improvement of our time and talents; the defectiveness of our aims and motives; and the departures of our heart, in love and confidence, from the blessed God.

Some would prevent the effect of such self-inspections, by the notion that there is no evil in the sins of God's people. But their sins are worse than those of others, by reason of the nearer relations in which, and the greater obligations under which, they are committed. They have, also, in sinning, greater difficulties to overcome. They have not only to sin against greater love, but greater light; and they have been convinced of the evil and bitterness of sin; and have had a wounded spirit, which they could not bear. Their sins, also, are more injurious with regard to others: distressing the strong; stumbling the weak; confirming the prejudiced; hardening the wicked; causing the enemies of the Lord to blaspheme, and the way of truth to be evil spoken of. And is all this nothing? Micah did not think so. Who, says he, is a God like unto him, who passes by the transgression of the remnant of his heritage?

But suppose the Christian is led to see that his standing is secure, and that God is pacified toward him. Will he weep then? Yes; he will weep the more. The goodness of God will lead him to repentance; and he will sorrow after a Godly sort—like a dying saint, who, being asked why he so wept? answered, I weep not that my sins may be pardoned, but because I hope they are pardoned.

Let us then never be ashamed or afraid of such tears as Peter shed. Nothing is so becoming and reasonable. Other grief may be excused; but this can be justified. Other sorrow may render us amiable in the eyes of our fellow creatures; but this is extolled of God. "The sacrifices of God are a broken spirit; a broken and a contrite heart, O God, *thou* wilt not despise." This brings us within the reach of the promises. "They that sow in tears, shall reap in joy." "Blessed are they that mourn, for they shall be comforted." It is not easy, or perhaps possible, to make others comprehend this—but there is a pleasure even in the frame itself; and they who are the subjects of it well know that their happiest moments are their most tender; and, with Augustine, they can bless God for "the grace of tears." Here is a proof of our being under the renewing of the Holy Ghost. If the heart of stone was not taken away, how could I feel and grieve? And if there was nothing in me but nature, how could I feel and grieve for sin? There is nothing more useful in the divine life than this disposition. It endears the Savior, and his atonement, and his righteousness, and his intercession, and his grace. It makes me cautious and circumspect; in this temper of mind I cannot expose myself to temptation, or trifle with sin, but be always watchful and prayerful. Blessed is the man that feareth always.

"'Tis joy enough my all in all,
"At thy dear feet to lie;
Thou wilt not let me lower fall,
"And none can higher fly."

FEBRUARY 20.—"Ye shall go forth, and grow up as calves of the stall.'
Malachi, iv, 2

THEY were before in *darkness* and *disease*, both of which *confine*. But the Sun of Righteousness arises, and with healing under his wings; and thus, the true light now shining, and health being restored, they become free and active. They go forth and grow up as calves of the stall.

For even now they have not attained, they are not already perfect. Nor are they to remain what they are, but to increase with all the increase of God. Some tell us, there is no growth in grace—as if Christians could not be more wise, more humble, more patient, more zealous, than they are—as if Paul's commendation of the Thessalonians was a falsehood, when he told them, that their faith grew exceedingly, and the charity of every one of them toward each other abounded—as if Peter enjoined an absurdity, when he admonished Christians to grow in grace, and in the knowledge of their Lord and Savior—as if God himself mocked or trifled, when he said, "The righteous shall hold on his way, and he that hath clean hands shall wax stronger and stronger!"

We are not to deny what God has done for our souls; yea, we ought to be thankful, if we have only light enough to see our darkness, and feeling enough to be sensible of our hardness.

"Cold as I feel this heart of mine,
"Yet since I *feel* it so,
"It yields some hope of life divine
"Within, however low."

But though we must not despise the day of small things, we are not to be satisfied with it. A day of greater things is attainable; and if we do not aspire after it, we have reason to suspect even the reality of our religion. Spiritual principles may be weak, but if they are divine, they will evince it by a tendency to growth.

The sacred writers express this progression by every kind of growth. By human—we read of babes, little children, young men, and those of full age, who have their senses exercised, by reason of use, to discern both good and evil. By vegetable growth—Thus we read, first the blade, then the ear, and after that the full corn in the ear; they shall spring as among the grass, as willows by the water-courses; they shall grow as the lily, they shall grow as the vine. Here we have animal growth. They shall grow up as calves of the stall. No creatures perhaps increase so rapidly and observably as these, especially when, as here, they are well attended and fed, and for the very purpose of growth.

We have sometimes been reminded of the truth of this image by the spiritual reality. We have seen those, who, in a little time, have surprised all around them by their progress in the divine life. So clear and full have been their views of the things of God. So established have their hearts been with grace. So simply and entirely have they depended upon the Savior. So decided have they been in their separation from the spirit of the world; and yet so concerned to be useful in it. So spiritual have they been in their conversation; and yet so free from all religious grimace and affectation. So ready have they been to do good and communicate, in the cause of the poor, and the cause of Christ. Such a living sacrifice have they presented in their bodies and spirits. So have they adorned the doctrine of God our Savior, in all things.

But alas! as to many of us, we have reason to exclaim, "My leanness, my leanness!" How little progress have we made in religious knowledge, experience, practice, and usefulness, though we have possessed every advantage, and long enjoyed the means of grace. After all the discipline of his family, the instructions of his word, the ordinances of his house, how dull are our ears of hearing; how slow of heart are we to believe; how much do our souls cleave unto the dust; how affected are we with the things of time and sense; and how little actuated by the powers of a world to come. At present, the comparison reproves us.

—But let it also excite and encourage. It not only reminds us of our duty, but of our privilege This growth is not only commanded, but promised. It is, therefore, attainable—and we know the way to our resources. *He* came, not only that we might have life, but have it more abundantly. "He giveth power to the faint; and to them that have no might he increaseth strength. Even the youths shall faint and be weary, and the young men shall utterly fall; but they that wait upon the Lord shall renew their strength; they shall mount up with wings as eagles; they shall run and not be weary, and they shall walk and not faint."

FEBRUARY 21.—**"And the soul of the people was much discouraged because of the way."—Numbers, xxi, 4.**

THE people of God are held forth under various characters in the Scriptures; and no one of them all is more common, more just, more pleasing, more instructive, than the image of strangers and pilgrims upon earth. And who knows not what a beautiful use Bunyan has made of it.

> **" Ingenious dreamer, in whose well-told tale,**
> **" Sweet fiction and sweet truth alike prevail.**
> **" ——— where PILGRIM marks the road,**
> **" And guides the PROGRESS of the soul to God."**

But what is there in the way to discourage the souls of the travellers heaven-ward? Much. Sometimes they are affected by the length of the way. For hope deferred maketh the heart sick. This was the case with Israel at this time; for instead of passing through the land of Edom, they had to fetch a compass all around the borders; and all this in a wilderness too, and under a burning sky. If a traveller, after supposing he was near his journey's end, was to learn that it was yet many miles off, all worn and weary, his heart would be ready to faint, and utter the sigh of despondence, "Oh, I shall never reach it!" What Isaiah says, "They shall behold the land that is very far off," may be applied to the experience of Christians with regard to heaven. It is often remote in fact; that is, it is frequently long before they arrive there. For they are not removed hence as soon as they are converted; but detained here to be made meet for their destination, and to honor their Redeemer, and to serve their generation. Hence many of them are longer on earth after they are called by grace, than the Jews wandered in the wilderness after leaving Egypt. But we refer to the slowness of their progress, the smallness of their attainments, and the nature of their apprehensions. "Once," says the soul, "I was ready to receive the blessing; but now it seems to recede as I advance; yea, the distance between me and the attainment seems to increase daily." "How long wilt thou forget me, O Lord? for ever? How long wilt thou hide thy face from me? How long shall I take counsel in my soul, having sorrow in my heart daily?" "My soul waiteth for the Lord more than they that watch for the morning." "O, when will it dawn? When wilt thou come unto me?"

Sometimes they are discouraged because of the way, owing to the enemies that infest it. In the re-building of the second temple, we are told, that every man with one hand wrought in the work, and with the other held a weapon—this was sore labor. But the Christian's life is a warfare as well as a pilgrimage; he moves on, bearing his sword, as well as his staff—now to walk and fight too—and to contend every step of the way—and with adversaries possessing every thing to render them formidable—and as soon as one is vanquished to see another rising up—this is arduous and trying. And what wonder, when, if, without are fightings, within are fears?

Then the way shows many that are turning back in it; and this is often discouraging. We had heard of their setting off. Some of them had passed us near enough to be observed. They soon left us, seeming to surpass us, not only in gifts, but grace—and we not only hailed, out envied them. How wonderful and grievous to see them returning vicious, or infidel, or lovers of this present world. We instantly remember, and apply to *them* the awful declaration, "If any man draw back, my soul shall have no pleasure in him." But who can help thinking of *himself?* And what am I? And may not I also prove a cast-way?

Besides, these revolters never come back silent. They solicit us to return too. They assure us the way is impassible. They have tried it; and hope their experience will make us wise. Once they thought certain notions to be erroneous; and certain indulgences to be sinful; but they are more enlightened and liberal now. Such persons, too, never subside into neutrals. From friends, they necessarily become enemies. They persecute, if it lie in their power. They always reproach and villify—even in their own defence, defaming the party and the cause, to justify their secession from them.

It is often discouraging, also, to find the way so narrow "Narrow is the way that leadeth unto life." The difficulty, therefore, of getting on is great. A way is made narrow by the near approximation of the sides, whether walls, ditches, or hedges; so that we have to press through, and can hardly do it without some injury on the right hand or on the left. In the exercise of every grace, and the performance of every duty, a Christian has to keep between two extremes. As to the use of the means of grace, he must neither neglect them nor idolize them. As to connexions and relations in life, we may sin by not loving them enough, or by loving them too much. Courage lies between rashness and fear, and frugality between profusion and niggardliness, and confidence between presumption and despondency, and patience, between despising the chastening of the Lord, and fainting when we are rebuked of him. And is it easy always to go, not only in the way of righteousness, but in the *midst* of the paths of judgment?

So far generally of the road. But there are particular parts that are peculiarly trying; such as the Slough of Despond, the Valley of Humiliation, the Hill Difficulty with the lions, and the deep cold River to be waded through before the Shining City can be entered. A Christian knows what all this means, and sometimes finds it hard to believe that the way to glory lies through it all.

Am I then setting out for the heavenly world? Let me not prepare myself for surprise and disappointment, by expecting that every thing will be smooth, and flowery, and delightful. I cannot, indeed, look for too much from the promises of God, they are so exceeding great and precious; but I must look for it in God's own order. I must deny myself and take up my cross, and not be slothful; but be a follower of them who through faith and patience have reached the prize of their high calling.

Have I professed, and hoped that I am a Christian? Let me not conclude that I have no part nor lot in the matter, because my soul is sometimes cast down and disquieted within me. Have not those who have gone before me wept and groaned also? Are not the subjects of divine grace represented by their fear, as well as their confidence? by their sorrow, as well as their joy?

Yet let me endeavor to go on my way rejoicing. Let me remember that there is much to encourage me, because of the way. An unerring guide—an almighty guard—companions—strength to hold on—refreshments along the road—and the end of it perfect rest, and peace, and glory, and joy.

"Our journey is a thorny maze,
"But we march upward still!
"Forget these troubles of the way,
"And reach at Zion's hill.

"See the kind angels at the gates
"Inviting us to come:
"There Jesus, the forerunner, waits
'To welcome travellers home.

" There, on a green and flowery mount,
" Our weary souls shall sit,
" And with transporting joys recount
" The labors of our feet."

FEBRUARY 22.—" Ye shall serve the Lord your God, and he shall bless thy bread, and thy water."—Exodus, xxiii, 25.

OUR chief concern should be to secure those blessings which will supply the soul, and endure for ever. He only is truly blessed who is blessed with all spiritual blessings in heavenly places in Christ. Our Savior therefore says, " Seek ye first the kingdom of God and his righteousness;" yet he does not scruple to say, " And all *these* things shall be added unto you." Temporal benefits are not beneath the attention of our kind Father. He knoweth that we have need of these things before we ask him. He knoweth our frame, and he knoweth our fears. And not only under the law, but under the gospel, godliness is profitable unto all things, and has promise of the life that now is, as well as that which is to come.

The promise before us extends to all the temporal support of his people; but there is wisdom in the language. In another place it is also said, " Thy bread shall be given thee, and thy water shall be sure." Is not the specification designed to check not only anxiety, but ambition? Does it not say, " Seekest thou great things for thyself? Seek them not." " Let your conversation be without covetousness, and be content with such things as ye have."

Nothing can do us good without the blessing of God; but his blessing commands what it announces; and what He blesses *is* blessed. Hence a *little* that a righteous man hath, is better than the riches of many wicked. It is more *efficient*. It goes further; as Philip Henry was wont to say to his family, " My dear children, the grace of God will make a little go a great way." It is surprising to see with what a slender income many Christians keep up a decent appearance, and owe no man any thing, and even give to him that needeth. The thing is, " The secret of the Lord is upon their tabernacle." But while he blesses the habitation of the just, his curse is in the house of the wicked. And then nothing prospers, and they seem a wonder to themselves and others; they get much, and gain nothing. So it was with the selfish and illiberal Jews when they came back from Babylon, and built their own ceiled houses, while the house of God lay waste. Had they minded his affairs, He would have minded theirs, and have proved that we cannot serve God for nought But now, says God, " Ye have sown much, and bring in little; ye eat, but ye have not enough; ye drink, but ye are not filled with drink; ye clothe you, but there is none warm; and he that earneth wages, earneth wages to put into a bag with holes."

It is also more *satisfying*. For the state of the mind conduces to the relish of every outward comfort; and in the Christian this state of mind is grateful, and peaceful, and cheerful, arising from a hope of reconciliation with God. His frown would darken a thousand suns. But every thing smiles when He smiles.

" How sweet our daily comforts prove, | " When they are seasoned with his love."

And when we see the dear medium through which they come as covenant blessings.

"*He* sunk beneath our heavy woes,
"To raise us to his throne;
"There's not a gift his hand bestows,
"But cost his heart a groan."

—The wicked feast without fear; but there is reason enough why they *should* fear. Neglecting his service, they are strangers to his blessing, and, left to themselves, every advantage and indulgence, operating upon their depravity, contributes to their guilt and misery. Their table becomes a snare before them, and that which should have proved for their welfare becomes a trap. The prosperity of fools destroys them. Now consider this ye that forget God, and, without delay, seek to be numbered with the seed which the Lord hath blessed.

FEBRUARY 23.—**"Let him know, that he which converteth a sinner from the error of his way shall save a soul from death, and shall hide a multitude of sins."—James, v, 20.**

AND can *we* convert the sinner from the error of his way? Yes, or the language would be futile. But *how* can we do this? Not meritoriously; this would invade the office and glory of the Lord Jesus; for He only delivers us from the wrath to come; He only saves his people from their sins. Not efficiently; this would invade the work and honor of the Holy Spirit; for we are saved by the washing of regeneration, and the renewing of the Holy Ghost. There is, therefore, only one way in which *we* can convert a sinner, and that is instrumentally. But this does not detract from divine agency; there is no inconsistency between agency and instrumentality. A pen is nothing without a hand to use it. An instrument always supposes and requires an agent. But is the converse of this proposition true? Does an agent always require an instrument? It is so with us, but not with a Being whose will is efficiency, and who said, Let there be light, and there was light. Yet what God is not compelled to do from weakness, he chooses to do from wisdom. He, therefore, works by means. We know of nothing that he does immediately. He fans us by the breeze, and warms us by the sun, and refreshes us by sleep, and sustains us by food. And as it is in nature, so it is in grace. Among the Corinthians. God gave the increase, but Paul planted, and Apollos watered. Their faith came not *from* them; but Paul and Apollos were ministers *by* whom they believed. We mean not, however, by this reference, to confine this work to ministers. James alludes not only or chiefly to them, but to Christians at large. All may be useful here, and in a thousand ways exert themselves to accomplish this blessed and glorious design.

For he who effects it is the greatest of all benefactors, for "He saves a soul from death, and hides a multitude of sins!" And what is every other achievement compared with this? Nothing, less than nothing, and vanity. So will all those judge who walk by faith, and believe the testimony of God concerning the value of a soul; the dreadfulness of eternal death, and the absolute necessity of forgiveness, in order to the man's escape from the damnation of hell.

The work, therefore, is its own reward. Spurious beneficence always wishes to excite notice; and the man, in some way or other, aims (or he will do nothing) to make it conducive to his own interest. But true charity seeketh not its own, but the welfare of the object;

and if *that* end be answered, the benefactor is satisfied. James knew this, and mentions nothing else, by way of motive, but the thing itself. He does not tell his brethren, that if they convert a sinner they shall be applauded here, or recompensed at the resurrection of the just. It is true that they *will* derive honor and advantage from their usefulness. They that water shall be watered also. The sinners they save will pray for them; and if they die first, when they fail, will receive them into everlasting habitations; and in the day of the Lord Jesus they will be their joy and crown. But this is the effect, and nct the principle of their zeal. It is enough if they succeed—enough if they can save a soul from death, and hide a multitude of sins.

And the prospect of success in such a case, however limited, should be sufficient to animate. Some may be privileged to bless numbers. But James speaks of "the sinner," and "a soul." This agrees with the language of our Lord, who tells us, "There is joy in the presence of the angels of God over *one* sinner that repenteth." This brings the encouragement home to all. All cannot be Luthers, to reform countries; or Whitfields, to preach to thousands; or Careys, to translate the Scriptures into other tongues. But can we do nothing? Surely some one soul is thrown in our way to whom we may be useful; a child, a servant, a relative, a neighbor.

James would have us *think* of this, and think *much* of it. "Let him *know* that he which converteth the sinner from the error of his way shall save a soul from death, and shall hide a multitude of sins." And who does not know this? Yea, were we to judge from their practice, we should be ready to ask, Who does know it? What is the knowledge that answers no end? It is not enough to believe—we must remember, and reflect; we must follow out our convictions. This fine sentiment must be present to the mind at all times, and in all conditions—when we are alone, and when we are in company—when we pray, and when we speak—when we sit in our house, and when we walk by the way—and when we lie down, and when we rise up—we must bind it as a sign upon our hand, and wear it as a frontlet between our eyes, and write it upon the posts of our door, and upon our gates. "Let him KNOW that he which converteth a sinner from the error of his ways shall save a soul from death, and shall hide a multitude of sins."

FEBRUARY 24.—**"They shall be as the stones of a crown, lifted up as an ensign upon his land."—Zech. ix, 16.**

HERE we see the dignity of the Lord's people. They are "stones," precious stones, set in the "crown" of the King of kings. For such is the infinite goodness of God, that he not only spares, but pardons and justifies. In his righteousness they are exalted. They are not only saved, but ennobled. With kings are they upon the throne. They are naturally in a low estate, and are viler than the earth; but he raiseth the poor out of the dust, and lifteth up the beggar from the dunghill. And though the world knoweth them not, and they are little and low in their own eyes, and it doth not yet appear what they shall be; yet now are they the sons of God; and since they have been precious in his sight, they have been honorable, and he has loved them, and calls them his jewels, and a peculiar treasure unto him. And all those who in his light see light, view them in the same way. They remember the time when they began to honor them that fear the Lord; when they took hold of the skirt of him that is a Jew, and prayed to see the good of his chosen. Then they seemed to regard them as more than human beings; and while above all things they desired communion with them, they felt unworthy of their presence and notice. And though, since then, they have found that they are not already perfect, yet they know they are the excellent of the earth, and that they are more excellent than their neighbors. There is often more real virtue in their failings than in the very devotions of others, and "the gleaning of the grapes of Ephraim is better than the vintage of Abiezer."

Here is also their exhibition; these stones of a crown are "lifted up." They are not to be concealed. Our Savior compares them to a city set, not in the valley, but on a hill, which cannot be hid, and to a candle placed, not under a bushel, but on a candlestick, that it may give light to all that are in the house. And when he calls them by his grace, he says to the "prisoners, Go forth; and to them that are in darkness, Show yourselves; they shall feed in the *ways*, and their pastures shall be on all *high* places." Christians need not be concealed; every thing in their religion will bear examination, and challenges the eyes of all, whether infidels, or philosophers, or politicians, or moralists. They ought not to be concealed; every thing in their religion is adapted to do good; but for this purpose it must be known. They cannot be concealed; their principles must operate, and the sun cannot shine without showing itself.

Here is also their utility; these stones of a crown are to be lifted up "as an ensign upon his land." An oriflamme suspended over the royal tent, and designed to attract and aggregate followers to the cause in which he is engaged. Thus the Savior himself is spoken of: "And in that day there shall be a root of Jesse, which shall stand for an ensign of the people; to it shall the Gentiles seek, and his rest shall be glorious." But what Christ is, Christians are—subordinately, indeed, yet really. Hence their calling to hold forth the word of life. They are placed and displayed to reprove, and convince, and excite, and encourage others, to seek and serve God. They are witnesses for him. They are trophies of the power, and greatness, and riches of his grace. They proclaim what he is able and willing to do; and saved by him, they are all employed for him. "Instead of the thorn shall come up the fir-tree, and instead of the brier shall come up the myrtle-tree; and it shall be to the Lord for a name, for an everlasting sign, that shall not be cut off."

FEBRUARY 25.—"Salute Philologus, and Julia, Nereus, and his sister, and Olympus, and all the saints which are with them."—Romans, xvi, 15.

ADMITTING that the Bible be the word of God, we might have inferred, from his wisdom and goodness, that no part of it can be useless; but we are expressly assured, that "All Scripture *is* profitable for doctrine, for reproof, for correction, for instruction in righteousness."

Therefore this long postscript, this catalogue of particular salutations, has its uses. It certainly shows us the principle that actuated the first Christians—all men were to know that they were the disciples of Christ by their loving one another. It shows, also, how mistaken they are, who think the New Testament does not sanction private friendship. It also proves how impossible it was to forge this epistle. abounding, as it does, with so many specific allusions; for these not only render detection possible, but easy. Hence Paley much avails himself of this chapter, in his Horæ Paulinæ, a work of uncommon excellence, and which deals only in the argument derivable from *incidental* evidence.

—Neither is it improper to observe from it the error of Popery. Papists say that Peter was the Bishop of Rome, but had he been there, is it credible, for a moment, that *he* would have been overlooked by an apostle? The probability indeed is, that he never was there. There is no evidence of it in the Scripture, and we know for what purposes of delusion it has been pretended, viz. to prove the Roman succession of bishops from him.

—But who can help observing how many females are mentioned here? Phebe, Priscilla, Mary, Junia, Tryphena, Tryphosa, Persis, the mother of Rufus, Julia, the sister of Nereus. All these, with the exception of two, are not only mentioned, but commended; and these two would not have been saluted by name, unless they had been persons of religious excellence; for Paul valued no other qualities compared with this. But all the rest of these worthies have ascribed to them some attainment or service, "in the Lord."

Let not, therefore, females suppose that they are cut off from usefulness, and usefulness even in the cause of Christ. The most eminent servants of God have acknowledged their obligations to them, and ascribed no little of their success to their care and kindness. The public ministry, is not, indeed, open to them—neither is the army or navy, or the senate; and good sense will acquiesce in the distinctions and determinations of heaven, especially when it is seen that they are not founded on any principle of degradation, but in the obvious proprieties of life. If they have not authority, they have influence, which is far better, and more deeply effective. Servants have blessed God for pious mistresses. Children have been prepared for the preaching of the word, and the devotion of the sanctuary, by the earlier but important efforts of a mother. How much does even the religious public owe to a Mrs. Newton, a Mrs. Cecil, and a thousand more, from whom the churches have derived such able ministers. To Hannah we owe a Samuel; and to Lois and Eunice, his mother and grandmother, we owe a Timothy.

They are at home in almsdeeds, like Dorcas, who made garments for the poor; and are peculiarly adapted to visit the sick and the afflicted. The wife may win the irreligious husband without the word; and fan his devotion, and give speed to his zeal, when he is in the way everlasting. Who would keep them from those public meetings where feelings are to be excited, which they will be sure to carry away, and improve at home? In a word, women have the finest heads, and hearts, and tongues, and hands, for usefulness, in the world. Who does not wish to see them always under a religious principle? Who would not have them *appropriately* more encouraged and employed as workers together with the servants of Christ? "Help," therefore, says the apostle, "those women that labored with me in the Gospel, whose names are in the book of life."

FEBRUARY 26.—**"When he was come near, he beheld the city, and wept over it."—Luke, xix, 41.**

AN ordinary mind would have been engrossed and elated by the actions and acclamations of the multitude, who cut down branches from the trees, and strewed them in the way; and spread their garments on the ground for him to ride upon, and filled the air with hosannas, crying, Blessed is he that cometh in the name of the Lord! But he wept—wept at the sight of Jerusalem, whose visitation was now closing, and whose judgment was hastening on, saying, "O that thou hadst known, even thou, at least in this thy day, the things that belong to thy peace; but now are they hid from thine eyes."

Surely these tears teach us, that there is nothing degrading in sensibility. Indeed, all true greatness is tender and sympathetic. Jonathan and David, the heroes of the age, one of whom had slain a whole garrison, and the other killed Goliath, both wept, till each exceeded. Homer, that exquisite painter of nature, considers Ulysses as excelling all men in wisdom, yet represents him as weeping three times in six lines. Achilles, too, so extraordinary in courage, he describes as weeping often and plentifully. Let not, therefore, the unfeeling pride themselves as superior in fortitude and philosophy. Feeling is the noblest distinction and ornament of humanity, and in proportion as we lose it, we cease to be men. There is a moral ossification of the heart as well as a physical; and the one is as pitiable as the other. He who was fairer than the children of men was often known to weep.

As these tears were honorable, so they are exemplary. For whom did he shed them? The inhabitants of Jerusalem, who, after every kind of insult, were going to put him to death. At the grave of Lazarus he wept for friends; here, for adversaries. And does he not, by this, tell us to be tender-hearted? to weep with them that weep? That we should bewail the miseries of others, and not confine our compassion to our own connexions, but love our enemies, bless them that curse us, and do good to them that persecute us? Does he not enforce this, not only by precept, but example? And can we be his disciples, unless we follow him? "He that saith he abideth in Him, ought himself so to walk even as He walked." "If any man have not the spirit of Christ, he is none of his."

These tears are encouraging. Tears are generally considered proofs of concern. Human tears, indeed, it will be allowed, are not infallible tokens; but the tears of Christ may be safely trusted. They show his compassion, the sincerity, the greatness of his compassion. They tell us that his love passeth knowledge, and therefore they call upon us to repair to Him, telling us that He is not willing that any should perish; that, as He lives, He has no pleasure in the death of him that dieth.

"'Give me thine heart, my son,' he cries,
"And kindly waits to take thee in:
"With love and pity in his eyes,
"He weeps to save thee from thy sin."

Finally, they are awful and foreboding; admonishing us of the dreadfulness of their doom on whose behalf they are shed. It is affecting to see a man weep, and especially a great man. You would naturally suppose that something vast and momentous was necessary to move to tears such mighty minds as those of a Bacon or a Newton. And could a trifle move the Son of God to weep? And if the temporal calamities coming on the Jews affected him, how much more would their eternal perdition! What were the Roman eagles, compared with the wrath to come! O, these tears say plain enough, "There is something divinely, infinitely pitiable in the loss of a soul! It is a fearful thing to fall into the hands of the living God! Who knoweth the power of his anger!"

May we not fairly infer from hence, what his feeling is in the recovery of a sinner? If he weeps over those who are ready to perish, surely he will rejoice over those that are saved. "He will rejoice over them with joy; he will rest in his love; he will rejoice over them with singing."

FEBRUARY 27.—"Increasing in the knowledge of God."—Col. i, 10.

DOES this mean the knowledge of which God is the author, or the knowledge of which he is the subject? In reality, this is the same thing. The Gospel contains the knowledge which God has communicated to the children of men; and this principally discovers *himself;* so that it is at once a revelation *from* God, and a revelation *of* him. All his works, the largest and the least, praise him. If we take up the telescope, or the microscope, we alike exclaim, "This is the finger of God;" but we take up the Gospel, and say, "No man hath seen God at any time, the only begotten Son, which is in the bosom of the Father, he hath declared him." Here we look into his very heart, and see that it is the dwelling-place of pity—Here we know the thoughts he thinks toward us, and find that they are thoughts of peace, and not of evil.

With regard to this knowledge, we may make out four classes.

—Some are *destitute of this knowledge* of God. Some! There are at present more than five hundred millions lying in darkness, and the shadow of death! These have never heard of the name of Jesus, and know not that there is such a being in the universe. Yet Christians have it in their power to inform them; and a few are exerting themselves. Prosper, O God, their endeavors—that thy way may be known on earth, thy saving health among all nations.

—Some *reject it.* This is one of the things we should deem incredible; but we have undeniable, as well as mortifying evidence How many refuse to hear! How many never read the word of God! Others even sneer at its inspiration, and ridicule its contents! Whatever difficulties may attend the doom of the former class, justice admits of none with regard to this; "How can we escape if we neglect so great salvation?"

—Some *hold it in unrighteousness.* They profess to know God; but in works deny him. Some of these have clear views of the way of salvation; and even contend for the faith once delivered to the saints. The Gospel has taught them every thing—except to deny themselves, and take up their cross, and follow the Savior in the regeneration. They would be offended to be placed near the former class. "We are not unbelievers." No—you have denied, and are "worse than an Infidel."

—Some *receive it in the love and the influence of it.* Their faith is more than notion; their worship is not formality; their hope is not delusion—they live in the Spirit, and walk in the Spirit. Though these are still comparatively few, yet, blessed be God, their number is daily and greatly enlarging; and the Lord add to his people, how many soever they be, a hundred fold!

Art thou, my reader, one of them? Remember four things.

First. That thou hast *any* of this knowledge—should make thee thankful.

Secondly. That thou hast *so little*—should make thee humble.

Thirdly. That more is *attainable*—should make thee hopeful.

Fourthly. That it is attainable only in the *use of means*—should make thee diligent.

Consider what I say; and the Lord give thee understanding in all things.

FEBRUARY 28.—"Having loved his own which were in the world, he loved them unto the end."—John, xiii, 1.

THESE words refer immediately to the twelve disciples of our Lord. But what said he in his intercessory prayer? "Neither pray I for these alone, but for them also which shall believe on me, through their word." And what part of the statement here will not extend beyond his first followers?

Is it the *relation?* These are called "His own;" and they were indeed his own, by extraordinary office; but they were far more importantly his own, by saving grace. And thus he has a propriety in all Christians. If ye are Christ's, then are ye Abraham's seed. They that are Christ's have crucified the flesh. He has a peculiar right to them, from covenant donation, and the execution of his trust. They were given him as so many sheep to feed; as so many scholars to teach; as so many patients to heal; as so many captives to redeem. They are therefore, not their own, but bought with a price; and the ransom was no less than his own blood. The connexion between Him and them is so intimate and entire, that they are called his heritage, his children, his bride; the members of his body, of his flesh, and of his bones; yea, they are joined to the Lord, and of one spirit with him.

Is it the *condition?* They "were in the world." He was leaving it, and they were to be left in it; and from what it had been to him, they could judge what it would be to them; according to his own intimation, "The servant is not greater than his Lord. If they have persecuted me, they will also persecute you." They found themselves, therefore, as lilies among thorns; as sheep among wolves. And he prayed not to have them taken out of the world, but only kept from the evil. And thus it is with his people now. They are in the world; and this is their field of action, and this is their sphere of duty and trial for a season. There they are to serve their generation; there they are to glorify God, by doing and suffering his will.

"But the world is much improved." It has advanced much in science and civilization; but it retains the same disposition toward real godliness as formerly, and is more perilous in its smiles than in its frowns, in its treacherous embraces than in its avowed hostilities. But if you are "His own" while you are "in the world," you will not be of it; and He, whose you are, will not only keep you from falling, but render you useful in it, and bring you honorably out of it. Be of good cheer, says He, I have overcome the world.

Is it the *reality of his regard?* "He *had loved* his own which were in the world." What other principle could have actuated him in selecting them, calling them, informing them, employing them, adopting them, honoring them, blessing them with his constant intimacy? They had not chosen Him but he had chosen them, and ordained them, that they should go and bring forth fruit. He treated them not as servants, but as friends; and all things that he had heard of the Father, he made known unto them. He could say, As the Father hath loved me, so have I loved you. And is not this true of all his people? Who said, Deliver them from going down into the pit? Who bore their sins in his own body on the tree? Who shut the mouth of hell? Who opened the kingdom of heaven to all believers? O Christian, who sought—and who saved thee? Whatever you are, whatever you have, is the effect of the love of Christ, that passeth knowledge.

Is it the *permanency of this affection? Having* loved his own which were in the world, he *loved them unto the end.* They tried him, and proved themselves very unworthy of his continued attachment. But he bore with their dullness and imperfections. He chided and reproved them; but this was not only compatible with his constancy, but resulted from it; for as many as he loves he rebukes and chastens, and faithful are the wounds of this Friend. And now we see him at the last all alive to their welfare, teaching and comforting them, washing their feet, and praying for them. In the garden, when he found them sleeping, he extenuated the infirmity. The spirit, indeed, is willing, but the flesh is weak. When he surrendered himself to his enemies, he stipulated for their exemption. Let these go their way. He died with them in his heart. He arose and appeared to them; and though they had all forsaken him, and fled in the hour of trial, he said, Be not afraid; peace be to you. He laid his hands upon them, and while he blessed them he was taken up into heaven. And did he forget them then? He sent them another Comforter, that should abide with them for ever. And was this peculiar to them? He is the same yesterday, to-day, and for ever. He rests in his love. He hath said, I will never leave thee, nor forsake thee. A true friend loveth at all times. But there are few such friends to be found. But He abideth faithful. Job's brethren proved like a summer's brook. One told David in his distress, Ahithophel is among the conspirators with Absalom. At my first answer, no one, says Paul, stood by me, but all men forsook me; but he adds, Nevertheless, the Lord stood by me, and strengthened me. So will it be with all those who trust in Him. "They shall not be ashamed or confounded, world without end."

"This God is the God we adore,
"Our faithful unchangeable Friend;
'Whose love is as great as his power,
"And neither knows measure nor end.

"'Tis Jesus, the First and the Last,
"Whose Spirit shall guide us safe home
"We'll praise him for all that is past,
"And trust him for all that's to come."

MARCH 1.—" And it shall be, if thou go with us, yea, it shall be that what goodness the Lord shall do unto us, the same will we do unto thee."—Numbers, x, 32.

WHILE this invitation is founded in benevolence, it also displays humility. Christians are convinced that *they* can only give according as they have received. But, from God's communications to them, they know that they *can* be useful, and that they *ought* to be useful to others. They never receive grace for themselves only. If the glory of the Lord has risen upon them, they are to arise and shine. If they are converted, they are to strengthen their brethren. If they are comforted, they are to comfort with the same comforts those who are in any trouble. If they are rich in this world, they are to do good, and be rich in good works, ready to distribute, willing to communicate. "As every man hath received the gift, even so minister the same one to another, as good stewards of the manifold grace of God." Hence says Moses to Hobab, "If thou go with us, what goodness the Lord shall do unto us, the same will we do unto thee."
—And he repeats the assurance: "It shall be—yea, it shall be." And was it not so? Did he repent of his adhering to Israel? See what is said in Judges, and in Samuel, of his descendants. And was Obed-Edom a loser by the ark? Did not the sacred guest more than pay for its entertainment? "It was told David, saying, The Lord hath blessed the house of Obed-Edom, and all that pertaineth unto him, because of the ark of God." Who is likely to be injured by casting in his lot with the followers of the Lamb? Will his family suffer? Many a wretch has reduced his wife and children to penury and ruin by his vices, but every principle of a good man will lead him to provide for his own, and the generation of the upright shall be blessed. Will his substance? The play-house, the ale-house, the gaming-house, the house of her who lives in the way to hell, going down to the chambers of death, will injure a man much more than the house of God. Will his health? Is *this* likely to be injured, or benefited, by temperance, and calm temper, and cheerful confidence, and benevolent feelings? Religion must befriend reputation, as it produces and guards all the elements from which it is derived, while the name of the wicked shall rot.

Therefore come with us, and we will do you good; for the Lord hath spoken good concerning Israel. We cannot promise you great things in the world, but the Lord will bless your bread and your water; and a little that a righteous man hath, is better than the riches of many wicked. We cannot promise you exemptions from affliction, but nothing shall befall you but what is common to man; and God is faithful, who will not suffer you to be tempted above that ye are able, and will, with the temptation, also make a way for your escape. We cannot secure you from privations and sacrifices, but we can promise, that you shall be more than indemnified for every thing you do or suffer, or lose, for the cause of God. He will not be unrighteous to forget your work of faith, and labor of love. A cup of cold water, given to a disciple in the name of a disciple, shall not lose its reward. "There is no man," saith the Savior, "that hath left house, or parents, or brethren, or wife, or children, for the kingdom of God's sake, who shall not receive manifold more in this present time, and in the world to come life everlasting." We can assure you, that if you travel with us, you shall feed on the manna, and drink of the rock, and be guided by the cloud, and behold the glory of the Lord, in the wilderness; and then you shall share with us, beyond Jordan, the land flowing with milk and honey. How blessed are they whose transgressions are forgiven, who have peace with God, who are delivered from the sting of a guilty conscience, and the torment of fear, who walk in the comforts of the Holy Ghost, who rejoice in hope, who know that death is their friend, and heaven their home, who have their fruit unto holiness, and the end everlasting life! "Lo, this, we have searched it, so it is, hear it, and know thou it for thy good."

Lord! I have often heard this invitation; I now accept it. I am a companion of them that fear thee, and of them that keep thy precepts. "Remember me, O Lord, with the favor that thou bearest unto thy people; O visit me with thy salvation, that I may see the good of thy chosen, that I may rejoice in the gladness of thy nation, that I may glory with thine inheritance."

MARCH 2.—"But Peter followed him afar off."—Matt. xxvi, 58.

THIS, too, was better than forsaking him and fleeing, as the rest did. Here was the working of some degree of principle. Here was some love to the Savior, or he would not have followed him at all—the lingering of that affection which may be seemingly smothered in the Christian, but can never be extinguished, and will soon be blown again into a flame.

But he was overcome by fear. His Lord was apprehended, and going to be tried and crucified. What if I, said Peter, should be found in the same doom as one of them! The fear of man bringeth a snare. Skin for skin, yea, all that a man hath, will he give for his life.

Yet this was very unbelieving in him. He had seen his Lord's miracles, and knew what he could do. He knew that he had actually stipulated for their release in the garden, as the condition of his own surrender. He knew that he had assured them, that after he was risen from the dead he would appear to them, and employ them as his witnesses, which involved their preservation. What a difference between Peter and Paul—Paul, who said, "None of these things move me; neither count I my life dear unto myself, so that I may finish my course with joy." And between Peter and Luther—Luther, who, when informed of his dangers, said, If there were as many devils in Worms as there are tiles upon the houses, I would go. But Peter followed him afar off!

This was also very ungrateful. The Savior had done much for him. He had healed, by a miracle, his wife's mother; he had called him to the apostleship, the highest honor on earth; He had singularly distinguished him with James and John on several occasions; He had saved him by his grace, and enlightened him from above, and was now going to suffer and die for him. And a friend is born for adversity. Then, instead of keeping at a distance from us, we look for his attendance and sympathy. Peter could have unequivocally testified in favor of suffering innocence; but he hangs off! And Patience itself complains, "I looked for some to take pity, and there was none! and for comforters, but I found none!"

All this, too, was in violation of his own profession and vows—that he was willing to follow him to prison and to death—that he would die with him rather than deny him; and all this had scarcely left his lips, and was uttered just after our Savior had so solemnly forewarned him. Yet Peter followed him afar off.

This led to something worse, and I wonder not at the sequel. His after conduct in denying him, and thrice; and swearing with oaths and curses, was only the continuance and the increase of his present reluctance. So it is, the way of error and sin is always downhill; and, once in motion, who can tell when and where he will stop? You follow him afar off this hour, the next you are ashamed of him. You trifle with the sabbath to-day, to-morrow you profane it. You now endure evil company; you will soon choose it; so true is it, "They proceed from evil to evil."

And yet who of us can cast a stone at him? Are not we verily guilty, as well as Peter? Let us see whether, though as yet we have not begun to curse and to swear, saying, I know not the man, we have not been following him afar off. Here let us not depend upon the opinion of our fellow creatures—we may stand fair with them. But what do they know of us? of our inward state? of our principles and motives? What says the *heart?* "If our heart condemn us not, then have we confidence toward God." Yet even on this testimony we must not absolutely rely. "*God* is greater than the heart, and knoweth all things." The Laodiceans were satisfied with themselves at the very time when He charged them with every one of the evils from which they supposed themselves free. Has *He* not somewhat against us? May we not continue to read and hear his word, and keep our places in the sanctuary, and even at his table; and yet feel very little of that sacred fervor and delight that once accompanied our devotions? Attendance upon the Savior in the means of grace, is very distinguishable from spiritual worship. We may draw nigh to him with our mouth, and honor him with our lips, while the heart is far from him. Does the *heart* lag behind? Then are we following him afar off.

His people are himself. He that receiveth them, receiveth him; and what we do not, to the least of one of all his brethren, we do not to him. In the distance of our regard to them, and especially our backwardness to notice, and relieve, and visit the poor and afflicted, are we not following him afar off?

Above all, does not the evil appear in the remoteness of our resemblance? We are commanded to follow him, and our conformity to him is essential to all religion, and we may always judge of the degree, as well as the reality of our religion by it. How far short of the model do we come? How distantly do we resemble that condescension, which washed the disciples' feet; that self-denial, which pleased not himself; that fervor, which led him to say, The zeal of thine House hath eaten me up; that delight in obedience, which led him to say, My meat is to do the will of Him that sent me, and to finish his work—

And thus, by our negligence and indifference, we grieve his Holy Spirit, and rob our own souls; for he is all in all; he is the fountain of life, and it is good for us to draw *near* to Him. But when we follow him afar off, we cannot see him, and hear him, and converse with him. And wo unto us if trouble befalls us, or the enemy meets with us, and he is most likely to do so then, when we are absent from him.

Let me *sigh*—

"Prone to wander, Lord, I feel it;
"Prone to leave the God I love."

And let me *sing*—

"Thou Shepherd of Israel divine,
"The joy of the upright in heart,
"For closer communion I pine,
"Still, still to reside where Thou art.

"'Tis there I would always abide,
"Nor ever a moment depart;
"Preserved evermore by thy side
"Eternally hid in thy heart."

MARCH 3.—"Yea, let God be true, but every man a liar."—Rom. iii, 4.

BUT cannot God be true, and man be true also? Does the veracity of the one infer the falsehood of the other? Not absolutely, but in particular instances. There may be, and there often is, an opposition between their testimony; and when this is the case we are not to hesitate a moment by whose claims we shall be decided. If the whole world was on one side and He on the other, Let God be true, but every man a liar. And, comparatively, the credibility of the one, must always be nothing to that of the other. If we receive the witness of men, the witness of God is greater. And this will appear undeniable from four admissions.

The first regards the ignorance of man and the wisdom of God. Man is fallible. He not only may err, but he is likely to err. He may be deceived by outward appearances; by the reports of others; by his own reasonings. His powers are limited; his researches in every direction are soon checked; there are depths which he cannot fathom, heights which he cannot scale, complications which he cannot unravel. Let not the wise man glory in his wisdom. How much of it is mere opinion and conjecture! With what follies have the greatest minds been charged! Where is the wise? Where is the scribe? Where is the disputer of this world? Hath not God made foolishness the wisdom of the world? But His understanding is infinite. He knows all things. He cannot be mistaken.

The second regards the mutability of man, and the unchangeableness of God. Creatures, from their very being are mutable. Many of the angels kept not their first estate. Adam fell from his original condition. Who needs to be told that man never continues in one stay? New views gender new feelings, and these new pursuits. What pleases to-day may offend to-morrow. Many are unstable as water; and no one is immutable. But God changes not; what he thinks now of any subject he always thought, and always will think, for with Him there is no variableness, neither shadow of turning.

The third regards the weakness of man, and the all-sufficiency of God. Man may threaten in fury, but be unable to execute. He may promise sincerely, and his promises be vain words; he *cannot* fulfill them. In this respect he is not always to be judged of by his conduct. There are cases in which we censure, when, if we knew all, we should only pity. The man struggles with difficulties which have unexpectedly come upon him; and yields to dire necessity, and provides things honest in the sight of the Lord, who has seen all his heart and his hardships, though not in the sight of men. But God is almighty. He who made and upholds all things by the word of his power, speaks every thing in the Scriptures.

The fourth regards the depravity of man, and the rectitude of God. Man goes astray from the womb, speaking lies. He often intentionally deceives; it is his aim and study; and he rejoices in his success. Even men who are influenced by religious principles may be overcome by evil, and occasion our saying, Lord, what is man! How far from truth was the sentiment of Jonah, "I do well to be angry, even unto death." How lamentable was the falsehood of Abraham, when he said of his wife, She is my sister. How dreadful was the perjury of Peter, when he swore, "I know not the man." But God is holiness itself. He is incapable of a wrong bias, he cannot be tempted to deceive.

When, therefore, we look at man, ignorant and fallible, varying according to his excitements, often unable to make good his engagements; yea, accessible to the influence of evil motives; and then contemplate God, in all the glories of his wisdom, immutability, almightiness, and rectitude; each being an everlasting and infinite preservative of truth—who can view these competitors for our belief, and not join with the apostle, "Yea, let God be true, but every man a liar."

And the use to which this fact should be applied, is to reduce our confidence in man, and increase our confidence in God—

"Then let us trust the Lord alone,
"And creature-confidence disown:
"Sure as on creatures we depend,
"Our hopes in disappointment end."

And yet the reverse of this is our practice. We yield where we should be cautious, and we hesitate where it is impossible for us to err. We turn from the Rock of Ages, and lean on the broken reed. And what is the consequence? "Thus saith the Lord, Cursed be the man that trusteth in man, and maketh flesh his arm, and whose heart departeth from the Lord; for he shall be like the heath in the desert and shall not see when good cometh; but shall inhabit the parched places in the wilderness, in a salt land, and not inhabited. Blessed is the man that trusteth in the Lord, and whose hope the Lord is; for he shall be as a tree planted by the waters, and that spreadeth out her roots by the river, and shall not see when heat cometh, but her leaf shall be green, and shall not be careful in the year of drought, neither shall cease from yielding fruit."

Let us cease then from man. Not that we are to become universally suspicious, and suppose there is no sincerity in the world. It was David's error to say in his haste, All men are liars. And when the Scripture says, "There is no faithfulness in them; men of low degree are vanity, and men of high degree are a lie; it must be taken with qualification. Yet instances of inflexible integrity are not abundant. And we should not implicitly rely upon any one, especially in divine things. Let us respect great and good men, but not be enslaved by them. Let us not pin our faith to the sleeve of any authority merely human. Let us suffer no man to have dominion over our conscience; always searching the Scriptures to see whether these things are so *there*.

For God is entitled to our absolute confidence. "God is not a man, that he should lie; neither the son of man, that he should repent; hath he said, and shall he not do it? or hath he spoken, and shall he not make it good?" Let us trust him as he deserves. Let us always place a ready and unshaken reliance on his word. Let God be true, in its doctrines, and let us receive them, however mysterious. Let God be true, in its predictions; and whatever difficulties stand in the way, believe that the whole earth shall be filled with his glory. Let God be true, in its threatenings; and let us flee from the wrath to come. Let God be true, in its promises; and let us be strong in faith, giving glory to God.

"O for a strong and lasting faith
"To credit what th' Almighty saith!
"T' embrace the message of his Son,
"And call the joys of heaven our own."

MARCH 4.—"All his saints are in thy hand."—Deut. xxxiii, 3.

THESE *holy ones* are distinguished by many things from each other. Some of them are in public life, and some in private. Some are rich and some poor. Some are young and some old. But all are equally dear to God; and partakers of the common salvation; in which there is neither Jew nor Greek, neither bond nor free, neither male nor female, for we are all one in Christ Jesus. They pass under various denominations among men; and these too often keep them at a distance from each other, and lead them to mistake and censure each other; and often they would seem to wish to draw *Him* along with them, and confine his influences within their respective exclusivenesses. But no. He owns them all: and they are all children of the same family, and going to the same temple to worship; and however they may differ in dress, or age, or stature, they all stand in the same relation to each other, and to himself. Some of them are strong, and others are weak in faith: he has in his fold lambs as well as sheep, and in his family babes as well as young men—but a bruised reed will he not break, and the smoking flax will he not quench, but will bring forth judgment unto victory. This honor have *all* his saints. "*All* his saints are in thy hand."

—In his fashioning hand. They are the clay, and he is the potter, and he makes them vessels of honor, prepared unto every good work. He fearfully and wonderfully made them as creatures. But they are his workmanship by another and a nobler creation. "This people have I formed for myself—they shall show forth my praise."

—In his preserving hand. For now they are precious, they are the more exposed. They are called a crown and a diadem; and the powers of darkness would gladly seize it; but observe where it is placed for security—"Thou shalt be a crown of glory in the hand of the Lord, and a royal diadem in the hand of thy God;" and there they are safe, perfectly safe; safe, not owing to their strength, but to their situation. By another image the Savior establishes the same confidence. "My sheep hear my voice, and I know them, and they follow me; and I give unto them eternal life; and they shall never perish, neither shall any man pluck them out of my hand. My Father which gave them me, is greater than all; and no man is able to pluck them out of my Father's hand."

—In his guiding hand. To lead a blind man, you take him in your hand. Thus the Lord leads his people. He knoweth the way that they take, but they do not. I will bring the blind by a way that they know not; I will lead them in paths that they have not known. You take a little child in your hand to lead him. Though God, says Bishop Hall, has a large family, none of his children are able to go alone; they are too weak, as well as too ignorant. But fear not, says God; I will strengthen thee, yea, I will help thee, yea, I will uphold thee with the right hand of my righteousness.

—In his chastening hand. They are sometimes alarmed at their afflictions, and cry, Do not condemn me—as if they were in the hand of an enemy. But he is their Father; and not like fathers of our flesh; for they verily, for a few days, chastened us after their own pleasure, but he for our profit, that we may be partakers of his holiness. Luther therefore said, Strike on, Lord, strike on; for now I know I am thy child. We deserve to lose the rod, and by our improper behavior we forfeit all claim to his correction; and we may well wonder, and exclaim, Lord, what is man, that thou shouldest magnify him, that thou shouldest set thine heart upon him, that thou shouldest visit him every morning, and try him every moment? But so it is; for he does not deal with us according to our desert. And therefore, rather than leave us to make flesh our arm, or the world our portion, he will remove every prop of support, and dry up every spring of comfort. But he does not afflict willingly. If needs be only, we are in heaviness; and when we mourn our faults, the rod drops upon the ground, and he hastens to wipe away our tears.

"Is Ephraim my dear son? Is he a pleasant child? For since I spake against him, I do earnestly remember him still; therefore my bowels are troubled for him; I will surely have mercy upon him, saith the Lord."

—Whatever, therefore, Christians have to distress and perplex, here is enough to comfort and to satisfy them. "For all this I considered in my heart, even to declare all this, that the righteous and the wise, and their works, are in the hand of God."

MARCH 5.—" So then, with the mind I myself serve the law of God; but with the flesh, the law of sin."—Romans, vii, 25.

So ends this chapter, concerning which there has been much dispute. For some have contended, that the apostle does not here speak of himself, but personates another. They suppose that he refers to a Jew—under the law, but not under grace—awakened, but not renewed—convinced, but not converted. But can any unregenerate person, with truth say, not only, "I consent to the law, that it is good," but "with my mind I serve the law of God," and "I delight in the law of God after the inward man?" an expression of godliness that characterized the temper of the Messiah himself. *He* could say nothing more than, "I delight to do thy will, O my God; yea, thy law is within my heart."

At first view the language of complaint may seem much too strong to apply to the experience of a real Christian. But what real Christian would find it too much to utter when placed in the same state, and occupied in the same way, with the apostle? That is, viewing himself before that God in whose light the very heavens are not clean, and who charges his angels with folly, and who sees more pollution in our duties than we ever see in our sins—that is, comparing himself with the rule of all rectitude, the divine law, whose spirituality is such as to extend to the thoughts and the desires of the mind, as well as the actions of the life, and which considers anger as murder, and the lusts of the eye as adultery. What must the highest attainments of mortals be, compared with this absolutely perfect standard of holiness; yea, or even with the elevated and vast desires of a renewed soul!

We need not wonder that many are astonished and perplexed here. "The spiritual judgeth all things, but he himself is judged of no man." They who are strangers to the warfare in which he is engaged, can never clearly comprehend his language, or enter into those feelings which produce such a depth of confession and abasement. Those who have never been in the field may be surprised at many things related by a veteran in describing the campaigns he has passed through, but his old scar-worn comrade can attest the truth of them. In religious matters, more than in any other, the heart knoweth his own bitterness, and a stranger intermeddleth not with his joy. But the secret of the Lord is with them that fear him.

We allow that this chapter has been much perverted. There is no part of the Bible that Antinomians so much delight in, or which ungodly men, who turn the grace of God into lasciviousness, so often quote. Such persons wrest, also, the *other* Scriptures to their own destruction. And are we to argue against the use of a thing, from the abuse of it? What good thing is not abused? Yet we do not refuse raiment to the naked, because there are some who glory in what ought to remind us of our shame; or food to the hungry, because some make a god of their belly. And shall we refuse to sincere and humble souls, mourning over the evils of their own heart, the instruction and consolation here provided for them, for fear the interpretation should be applied to an improper purpose? No one really taught of God *will* abuse it; nor *can* he be more reconciled to his corruptions, or more satisfied with his deficiencies, in consequence of being able to adopt the language as his own. For shall they continue in sin that grace may abound? God forbid. How can they, who are dead to sin, live any longer therein? We are not to make sad the hearts of God's people, but to comfort them; for the joy of the Lord is their strength. And only the last day will show how much this section of Scripture has strengthened the weak hands, and confirmed the feeble knees of those who were deeming their experience peculiar, and concluding that they had no part with the Israel of God, till they had heard Paul bewailing and encouraging himself thus: For to will is present with me, but how to perform that which is good I find not. I find then a law, that when I would do good evil is present with me. O wretched man that I am! who shall deliver me from the body of this death? I thank God, through Jesus Christ our Lord. So, then, with the mind I MYSELF serve the law of God, but with the flesh the law of sin.

MARCH 6.—" Behold, the Lord thy God hath set the land before thee: go up and possess it, as the Lord God of thy fathers hath said unto thee: fear not, neither be discouraged."—Deut. i, 21.

WE may, we ought to transfer what is here said to the Jews concerning Canaan, to ourselves with regard to a better country, that is, a heavenly; for the one was designed to be typical of the other.

Observe the exhibition: " Behold, the Lord thy God hath set the land before thee." Where? In the Scriptures: not in its full developement, for so it is a glory to be revealed, for it doth not yet appear what we shall be; but in its general nature, and in a way adapted to our present apprehensions, and likely to take hold of our mind. Hence so many figures are employed, all of which aid our conceptions, while they fall short of the subject.

But does he place it before our eyes to tantalize us, by awakening our notice, and drawing forth our admiration, and exciting our desire, when the boon is not within our reach?

Observe the command: " Go up and possess it, as the Lord God of thy fathers hath said unto thee." This supposes it to be attainable: yea, it makes the attainment our duty. Our missing it is not only our misery, but our crime. We shall be punished for neglecting so great salvation. It is our guilt—the guilt of the vilest disobedience to the most gracious authority: for he not only allows, but he enjoins us to seek first his kingdom and righteousness, and commands us to believe on the name of his Son Jesus Christ. Are we doing *this?* For *He* is the way; and we come *unto God by him.*

Observe the encouragement: " Fear not, neither be discouraged." To this we are liable on two accounts. First. By a sense of our unworthiness. The greatness of the blessedness, when combined with a sense of our desert, astonishes the mind into a kind of credulity, and makes hope seem no better than presumption. But every thing here is free, and designed to show the exceeding riches of his grace in his kindness toward us. We are as welcome as we are unworthy. Why then should we refuse to be comforted? Secondly. By a sense of our weakness. Who is sufficient for the distance, the difficulties, and the dangers? The Jews were dismayed by the report of the spies. The towns, said they, are walled up to Heaven. There are the Anakims, in whose sight *we* were but as grasshoppers. The people were disheartened. But said Caleb, " Let us go up at once, and possess it, for we are able." How did he mean? Without God? No. But with him, as their leader and keeper—and this he had promised. And is he not with you? Has he not said, " Fear not, for I am with thee; be not dismayed, for I am thy God: I will strengthen thee, yea, I will keep thee; yea, I will uphold thee with the right hand of my righteousness!" We cannot be too sensible of our weakness; but let us remember that his grace is sufficient for us. Has it not been sufficient for all those who have gone before us?

> "Once they were mourning here below,
> "And wet their couch with tears;
> "They wrestled hard, as we do now,
> "With sins, and doubts, and fears."

But their fears were vain. They overcame, and now are more than conquerors through him who loved them. But Jordan rolls between. So it was with the Jews, and it was even overflowing its banks at the time. But the ark divided the waters; they went through dry-shod, and their enemies were as still as a stone—till they were clean passed over.

MARCH 7.—"**I have called you friends.**"—**John, xv, 15.**

WHAT condescension, and kindness, and grace are here! For these must be the principle of this friendship, whether we consider His greatness, or our meanness and unworthiness. Lord, what is *man*, that *thou* art mindful of him? and the *son* of man, that *thou* visitest him? Yet he *is* mindful of us; he *does* visit us—yea, he calls us his FRIENDS. And names and things, professions and realities, are the same with Him. If he calls us friends, he will treat us accordingly, and we may expect from him whatever the most perfect friendship can ensure.

For instance. He will honor us with his confidence; the very thing he here mentions, "Henceforth I call you not servants; for the servant knoweth not what his Lord doeth; but I have called you friends; for all things that I have heard of my Father I have made known unto you." A servant is intrusted, not with secrets, but orders, and he is seldom informed of the reasons, even of these. Turning him into a confidant, is one of the ways to exemplify Solomon's observation: "He that delicately bringeth up a servant, shall have him for his son at length;" and he will take greater liberties than a child. There is, indeed, respect due to a servant; but it is respect of another kind. We do not like a master or mistress, who is above speaking to a domestic, unless in the language of menace or authority. Good sense will find out a happy medium between distance and fondness; between haughtiness, and a familiarity that inspires no deference. But unreserved confidence is for friends. Nothing is concealed between them. Abraham is called the friend of God: and, says God, "Shall I hide from Abraham the thing that I shall do?" How did our Lord unbosom himself to his disciples? To you, said he, is given to know the mysteries of the kingdom of heaven. When he was alone he expounded all things unto them; he manifested himself to them, and not unto the world. And so now; the secret of the Lord is with them that fear him, and he will show them his covenant.

If he calls us friends, he will give us freedom of access to him. The distance and ceremonies which may be necessary to regulate the approach of others, are laid aside with a friend; the heart, the arms, the house, are all open to him. And does the Lord keep us at a distance? His language is invitation. "Come unto me." He allows us to come even to his seat, and to enter the secret of his pavilion. He permits us, at all times, to spread our most minute affairs before him; yea, he indulges us to live in his house, to sit at his table, to walk with him, to lean upon his bosom. Such honor have all his saints.

—If he calls us friends he will reprove us. Whenever friendship is founded on proper principle, reproof will be found one of its chief duties, and privileges too. Faithful are the wounds of a friend; and so David valued them. "Let the righteous smite me, it shall be a kindness; and let him reprove me, it shall be an excellent oil which shall not break my head; for yet my prayer also shall be in their calamities." Moses makes the omission the proof of hatred, "Thou shalt not hate thy brother in thine heart; thou shalt in any wise rebuke thy neighbor, and not suffer sin upon him." But the Savior will never incur this reproach: As many as I love, I rebuke and chasten.

—If he calls us friends he will counsel us. There are passages in the life of every man sufficient to confound a single understanding. But how pleasing is it, in doubts and perplexities, to fetch in aid from the judgment or experience of another, and who we know is concerned for our welfare? But He is "*The* Counsellor." "Counsel," says he, "is *mine*, and sound wisdom." He is a light to them that sit in darkness; a dissolver of doubts. The meek will he guide in judgment, and the meek will he teach his way, and they that follow it will find it to be pleasantness and peace.

—If he calls us friends he will sympathise with us. There is no true friendship, unless we make the pleasures and the pains of our connections our own, rejoicing when they rejoice, and weeping when they weep. To him that is afflicted, pity should be showed from his friend. The natural language of the sufferer is, "Pity me, pity me, O ye my friends, for the hand of God hath touched me!" Hence the complaint of the Savior, "I looked for some to take pity, and there was none; and for comforters, but I found none," for even all the disciples forsook him and fled. But he will never inflict what he endured. In all our affliction he is afflicted. To exemplify this he assumed our nature. He became a man to be a friend. For in that he himself hath suffered, being tempted, he is able also to succor those that are tempted; and, therefore, though he is passed into the heavens, we have not a High Priest who cannot be touched with the feeling of our infirmity. Yea, "He that toucheth them, toucheth the apple of his eye."

—If he calls us friends he will afford us assistance and succor. And this is the grand test of friendship. A friend loveth at all times; but is born for adversity; and he has forfeited all claim to the character, who says, in the hour of application, Go in peace; be ye warmed, and be ye filled, while he gives not the things that are needful! Yet, how often is this the case; and the words of Solomon verified, "Confidence in an unfaithful man in the time of trouble, is like a broken tooth, or a foot out of joint." Many are very friendly when you want not their aid, especially while you are imparting instead of receiving. You are their garden; they walk in you in summer, but abandon you in winter—then you have no flowers or fruits. You are their scaffold; they build with you, but the work done, they take you down, and lay you aside. But though the Savior will never leave us nor forsake us, he has emphatically said, I will be with you in trouble. And his people have always found him a present help, when every other resource has failed. Some may really feel for us, but be unable to help us. But nothing is too hard for the Lord. Even in death he will be the strength of our heart, and our portion for ever.

Thus he treats his friends. How do they treat him? Have we never given him cause to say, "Is this thy kindness to thy friend?" Have we never betrayed a want of confidence in him? Have we never been ashamed of him? Never denied him before men? Have we not often preferred our own ease and honor to his cause and glory? We can never make him adequate returns for his goodness, but have we made him suitable returns? Rather will not an honest review of our temper and conduct constrain us to blush and say,

> "O were not I so vile and base,
> "I could not thus my friend requite;
> "And were not he the God of grace,
> "He'd frown and spurn me from his sight."

March 8.—"Behold, the eye of the Lord is upon them that fear him, upon them that hope in his mercy."—Psalm xxxiii, 18.

This is a very encouraging character. They who cannot claim the higher distinctions of religion, may surely know that they "fear God, and hope in his mercy."

Some may wonder at the combination, and suppose that the qualities are incompatible with each other. But the first Christians "walked in the fear of the Lord, and in the comforts of the Holy Ghost." They may think that the fear will injure the hope, or the hope the fear. But they are even mutually helpful, and they are not only never so beautiful, but never so influential as when they are blended. The fear promotes hope by the evidence it affords; and by keeping us from loose and careless walking, which must affect our peace and pleasure. And hope no less befriends this fear. For never is God seen so glorious, so worthy of all our devotedness to him, as when we hope in his mercy; and even the more assured we are of his regard, the more we shall inquire, Lord, what wilt thou have me to do? The more we shall tremble at the thought of offending and grieving him, the more we shall continue upon our knees, praying, Let the word of my mouth, and the meditation of my heart, be acceptable in thy sight, O Lord, *my* strength, and *my* redeemer. It is called "a lively hope;" and Christians know, by experience, that upon all their principles and duties, it has the same influence as the spring has upon the fields and the gardens.

Despondence of mind has the same effect upon our feelings and obedience as frost upon the stream; it chills, hardens, and stagnates. But divine love dissolves the ice, and the waters flow.

God is a Spirit, and has none of our senses and members; but in speaking to us, he makes use of language that we can understand. His *eyes* are upon them that fear him, and hope in his mercy. The eyes of his *knowledge* are upon them. Every thing in their affairs comes under his notice. He knows all their walking through this great wilderness, and nothing befalls them without their heavenly Father. Parents cannot always have their eye upon a child. They may be engaged, or be afar off, or asleep. But He is always at hand; He is never diverted or perplexed; He never slumbers or sleeps.

The eyes of his *affection* are upon them. The eye not only affecteth the heart, but follows it. It turns with the object of attachment; it sparkles with delight while dwelling upon it; and when deprived of the sight, continues looking in the direction of departure, as the disciples stood gazing up toward heaven after their blessed Savior. Oh! to be the object of God's love! To be precious in his sight, and honorable! But he "takes pleasure in them that fear him, in those that hope in his mercy." "He will rest in his love; He will joy over them with singing." The eyes of his *providence* are upon them. Therefore it is added, "To deliver their soul from death, and to keep them alive in famine." That is, for a part is put for the whole, to secure them from all danger, and to supply all their wants. In cases the most perilous and extreme, He is able to do for them exceeding abundantly above all they can ask or think. We are not to look for miracles; but it is only because the power and truth of God can do without them.

"For sooner all Nature shall change,
"Than one of God's promises fail.
"How safe and how happy are they,
"Who on their good Shepherd rely!
"He gives them out strength for their day,
"Their wants he will surely supply.
"He ravens and lions can tame;
"All creatures obey his command;
"Then let me rejoice in his name,
"And leave all my cares in his hand."

March 9.—"Be strong in the Lord, and in the power of his might." Ephesians, vi, 10.

To this we must be brought. Nature can never do the work of grace. Reason cannot be a substitute for faith. Education cannot render needless the teaching of the Spirit. Vain must all our exertions be, without his agency. Without his influence, we may have the form of godliness, but not the power; we may be reformed, but not renewed; we may become other creatures, but not new ones.

What is the use we are to make of this admission? Are we to derive from it ease in sin? self-justification? excuses for indolence? reasons for despair? Self-despair, indeed, grows out of it; but no other. There is a hope in Israel concerning this thing. We *have* a resource, and it is *accessible;* and we are commanded to "be strong in the Lord, and in the power of his might."

When we plead for this doctrine, we are often charged with enthusiasm. But the Scripture asserts, that we are his workmanship, created in Christ Jesus; that it is God who worketh in us to will and to do of his good pleasure; that hereby we know that he abideth in us by the Spirit which he hath given us. And we retort the charge upon those that would exclude this influence. For what is enthusiasm, but visionary hope, groundless expectation? And what can be more delusive, than looking for an end, without suitable and adequate means? a mighty effect, without a more powerful cause? a practice, the most alien from our depraved nature, without a divine principle? a gathering of grapes from thorns, and figs from thistles? And this is the case with those who deny the operations of that grace which is alone sufficient for us. We allow that we draw the character of the Christian high, and expect from him great things; that he should be renewed in the spirit of his mind; that he should walk by faith, and not by sight; that he should overcome the world, and have his conversation in heaven. But then we have means answerable to all this; we have a principle adequate to the practice; and we have a cause far superior to all these grand results. We allow that the work of a Christian, as it is described in the Bible, looks fitter for an angel than for a fallen, weak man; but this fallen, weak man has more than the sufficiency of an angel for the discharge of it—his sufficiency is of God!

Such a discovery, such an assurance is necessary. We are depraved creatures, and must be conscious of it; we have inward repugnancies to spiritual duties; we are surrounded with outward difficulties; on the side of sin there is number, example, constant solicitation; our slothful heart cries, "There is a lion in the way: I shall be slain in the streets." With all this known and felt, who could enter a religious course with pleasure or vigor, without the certainty of effectual aid? Possibility, probability, is not enough; mere hope is not enough; our hands hang down, our knees tremble, our very souls are chilled, unless we have a full and express persuasion that God will be with us and bear us through. And here, therefore, he meets us, and says, "Fear not, for I am with thee; be not dismayed, for I am thy God; I will strengthen thee, yea, I will help thee, yea, I will uphold thee with the right hand of my righteousness. Rely on me. Nothing is too hard for the Lord. I can enlighten the darkest understanding. I can turn the heart of stone to flesh. Take hold of my strength, and be more than a conqueror. I will never leave thee, nor forsake thee."

At the sound of this animation, every thing revives in me, like vegetation at the call of spring. I am filled with confidence and courage—weak in myself, I am strong in another, and almighty in the God of my salvation.

And is it not better for me that I should be a constant suppliant at the mercy-seat, than have no reasons for calling upon God, being able to do without him? Is it not better for me to depend upon the God of all grace for the continual supplies of the Spirit of Jesus Christ, than to have a fund of my own? The sufficiency lodged in me must have been limited and finite: but in the Lord Jehovah I have everlasting strength. I can rely upon his word—I could not trust in my own heart. I can never be so willing to supply myself, as he is ready to succor me.

"Though in ourselves we have no stock,
"The Lord is nigh to save;
"The door flies open when we knock,
"And 'tis but ask, and have."

MARCH 10.—"Will a man rob God?"—Malachi, iii, 8.

—Is it probable? Is it possible?

Can he be so disingenuous? What! rob a father, a friend a benefactor! The best of all fathers! The kindest of all friends! The most generous of all benefactors!

Can he be so daring? To rob a Being so high and sacred, and whose glory so enhances the offence? To injure a fellow-subject is felony; but to injure the king is treason. To steal from a man is injustice; but to steal from God is sacrilege: and the wretch adds profaneness to violence, when he breaks, not into a house, but a temple, and takes off things dedicated to the service of the Deity.

Can he be so irrational? To rob a Being—not absent, for he never is absent, but in his presence—not in the night, but in the day; for darkness and light are both alike to him—not when he sees not, observes not, but while he is looking on, and *must* look on—for his eyes are upon the ways of man, and he pondereth all his goings!

Can he be so desperate? To rob One who can, who will punish; and whose punishment is not only unavoidable, but intolerable? It is a fearful thing to fall into the hands of the living God.

Yet, says God, and he cannot be mistaken, or accuse unrighteously, "Ye have robbed *me*." But on whom falls the charge? A Pharaoh only, who would not let the people go? A Nebuchadnezzar, who carried away the vessels of the sanctuary? A Belshazzar who profaned them? An Ananias and a Sapphira, who kept back part of the property they had sold? A Herod, who beheaded John? Or a Nero, who slew Paul? Alas! the criminals were less obvious characters, and are found much nearer home; they are to be found in our own houses—they are to be found in the house of God.

Who has not robbed God of *property?* Our wealth is not our own. We are only stewards. It looks suspicious when a gentleman's steward becomes very rich, and dies affluent. It is even so with professors of religion. It would be better for them to die *comparatively* poor; it would be better for their reputation, and for their relations; a little would be more efficient than a large accumulation embezzled from God. Substance is intrusted to its occupiers for certain purposes plainly laid down in the Scripture; and the providence of God is perpetually calling upon you for it. Do you discharge these claims? or do you alienate from them by hoarding or extravagance? How much do some *unjustly* expend in table luxuries, in costly dress, in magnificent furniture? And they are fond of displaying these. They have little reason. They glory in their shame—for these are all robberies. They are purloined from God's cause, or God's poor.

Who has not robbed God of *time?* The *Sabbath* he expressly claims for himself, and it is called the Lord's day. Have we not often robbed him of much of this—perhaps of all—by worldly accounts, by evil company, by idle visits, by doing our own ways, and finding our own pleasures? *Youth* is the morning, the spring of life; it is our best season, and, therefore, God has a right to it, and calls upon us to remember his demands. But have we not partially or wholly robbed him of these days, squandering them away in vanity, folly, and vice? *All* our moments and opportunities are his, and he commands us to redeem the time; but who lays to heart the brevity and uncertainty of life? Who values it as "the day of salvation?" Who seizes it as the only season of usefulness? Who rises early?

> "Where is that thrift, that avarice of time,
> "(O glorious avarice!) thought of death inspires?"

Where is *He* in all our ways, who said, "I must work the work of Him that sent me while it is day; the night cometh wherein no man can work."

Who has not robbed him of the *heart?* This was made for him, and he demands it: "My son, give me thine heart." But the fear of the heart, the confidence of the heart, the gratitude of the heart, the attachment of the heart, we have transferred to the creature from the Creator, God over all, blessed for evermore.

And may not the same be said of our *talents*—whether learning, or the powers of conversation, or the retentiveness of memory, or our influence over others? Let us not affect to deny the charge, and ask, wherein have we robbed thee? But let us repair to the footstool of Mercy, and cry, "If thou, Lord, shouldest mark iniquity, O Lord, who shall stand?"

But there is forgiveness with Him that he may be feared, and with him there is plenteous redemption. There is. And we may, and we ought to approach him with the encouragement of hope. But this hope must be founded on his own invitations and promises. It must bring us "unto God *by Him*," who said, "No man cometh unto the Father but by me." To pray to God to save such creatures in any other way, is to disobey his dearest command, and to affront and insult him, by beseeching him to be untrue and unrighteous; to frustrate his grace, and to make Jesus Christ to be dead in vain. But in him he can be just, and yet the justifier. He can redeem Jacob, and glorify himself in Israel.

We shall also be turned away from all iniquity; for he that confesseth and forsaketh his sin, shall find mercy. We shall also sorrow after a godly sort; and instead of complaining of any of them, we shall acquiesce in all the methods of his grace and providence—and remember, and be confounded, and never open our mouth more, because of our shame, when He is pacified toward us for all that we have done.

MARCH 11.—"I will mention the loving kindnesses of the Lord."—Isaiah, lxiii. 7.

THERE are three ways in which we should resolve to do this. To others. To ourselves. And to God.

To others we should mention the loving kindnesses of the Lord in the way of conversation. "Let no corrupt communication," says the apostle, "proceed out of your mouth;" but where there is nothing immoral or indecent, there may yet be much that is trifling and vain; he therefore adds, "But that which is good, to the use of edifying, that it may minister grace unto the hearers." And here is a subject for discourse, not only innocent, but profitable. A *saying*, not only faithful, but worthy of all acceptation, and such as Moses and Elias would delight to join in were they in company with us. We should also mention them to others, in a way of recommendation. Some are convinced of sin, and ready to despair, and nothing but the exceeding riches of this grace can keep them from it. And some are seeking happiness where we know they can never find it. Let us, therefore, say to them, "Wherefore do ye spend money for that which is not bread, and your labor for that which satisfieth not? Hearken diligently unto me, and eat ye that which is good, and let your soul delight itself in fatness." "O taste and see that the Lord is good; blessed is the man that trusteth in him." This coming from our own experience, and enforced by our own example, may save a soul from death. Especially, too, if we can bear a *final* testimony to the truth, and say, with the departing Henry, "You have heard the dying words of many—These are mine: I have found a life of communion with Christ the happiest life in the world."

—We should also mention the loving kindnesses of God to ourselves. There is such a thing as self-converse; and we wish it were more common. It is said, fools talk much to themselves—but wise men will talk more. David enjoins this: "Commune with your own heart upon your bed, and be still:" and he also was an example of it; "I commune with my own heart, and my spirit made diligent search." Yet the Lord will command his loving kindness in the day-time, and in the night his song shall be with me. Hence he chides his own soul: "Why art thou cast down, O my soul? and why art thou disquieted within me? Hope thou in God, for I shall yet praise him who is the health of my countenance, and my God." Are you discouraged by your unworthiness, and the greatness of your guilt? Bring before your minds the freeness and fullness of his mercy and his loving kindnesses to others, who had no more claim upon him than yourselves. Are you in trouble? Recal his goodness in former difficulties; and say, O my desponding soul!

"Did ever trouble yet befall,
"And he refuse to hear thy call?
"And has he not his promise pass'd,
"That thou shalt overcome at last?"

Mention them also to yourselves, to excite you to imitation. Has he been so ready to forgive, and daily loaded me with his benefits? and shall I, O my soul, be implacable and uncharitable? Let me be a follower of God. Let me be merciful, even as my Father who is in heaven is merciful.

—We should mention his loving kindnesses to God himself, in the various exercises of devotion. In expostulating with him: "Look down from heaven, and behold from the habitation of thy holiness and of thy glory: where is thy zeal and thy strength, the sounding of thy bowels, and of thy mercies toward me? are they restrained?" In pleading with him: If we fill our mouth with arguments, they must be fetched from his own goodness; "For thy name's sake, O Lord, pardon mine iniquity, for it is great." In praying for ourselves: "I stretch forth my hands unto thee: my soul thirsteth after thee, as a thirsty land. Hear me speedily, O Lord; my spirit faileth; hide not thy face from me, lest I be like unto them that go down into the pit. Cause me to hear thy loving kindness in the morning; for in thee do I trust: cause me to know the way wherein I should walk; for I lift up my soul unto thee. Deliver me, O Lord, from mine enemies; I flee unto thee to hide me. Teach me to do thy will; for thou art my God: thy Spirit is good; lead me into the land of uprightness. Quicken me, O Lord, for thy name's sake: for thy righteousness' sake bring my soul out of trouble." In interceding for others—the conversion of our kindred, the salvation of sinners, the prosperity of the Church: "Do good in thy good pleasure unto Zion; build thou the walls of Jerusalem." In thanksgiving: "O Lord, I will praise thee: though thou wast angry with me, thine anger is turned away, and thou comfortest me."

Alas! how seldom does God hear this from us! There was a time when this heavenly exercise commenced—and O that it had been earlier! But it will never end. They that dwell in his house will be still praising Him.

Because my finite capacity will not admit of blessedness infinite in the degree, it shall be infinite in the duration; and, by happy reviews of the past, and unbounded prospects of the future, I shall feel perpetually growing beatitudes, and shall be always singing a new song. My mourning days, and my warring days, and my watching days, and my praying days, will soon be past. But,

> "My days of praise shall ne'er be past,
> "While life, or breath, or being last,
> "Or immortality endures."

MARCH 12.—"By love serve one another."—Galatians, v, 13.

THIS admonition implies our connexion with, our dependence upon, and our obligation to, each other. The service it enjoins is levied upon all, without exception, and is to be displayed in every way in which we can afford each other assistance.

But let me observe what it requires as the *principle* of the practice. Love. "By love serve one another."

The principle may be wanting, where the service is not. And this may be easily proved and exemplified. A man has a sum of money to dispose of. He hears of a person by whom it is desired, and to whom it will be useful, and he advances it on proper security. But is the borrower's need, or his own gain the motive? A hospital is built for the reception of poor patients. A rich man in the neighborhood becomes a subscriber and a patron. "He is so charitable!" Nay; he wishes to maintain the character of a man of liberality; and he fears appearing to disadvantage when compared with the 'Squire, or Sir Thomas. Hence some who give, give in a way that will be sure to make it known; they therefore impart it through the medium of some other—in spite of the admonition, not to let the left hand know what the right hand doeth. Some would never give, if the name was not printed Some connect themselves with public institutions, and labor to establish and enlarge them, who would individually do nothing—but here they are put upon the committee, and gain distinction. But love seeketh not her own. It regards only the good of the recipient. There are four reasons why we should serve from this principle.

First. Without it, the service has no value or excellency in the sight of God. It may be useful to the beneficiary; but it will be nothing to the benefactor. Though I speak with the tongue of men and of angels, and give all my goods to feed the poor, and even give my body to be burnt, and have not love, it profiteth me nothing. The Lord looketh to the heart; if this be right, the least service is regarded by him; and where it is not, the most costly sacrifices are disdained. "For if ye love them which love you, what thank have ye? for sinners also love those that love them. And if ye do good to them which do good to you, what thank have ye? for sinners also do even the same. And if ye lend to them of whom ye hope to receive, what thank have ye? for sinners also lend to sinners, to receive as much again. But love ye your enemies, and do good, and lend, hoping for nothing again; and your reward shall be great, and ye shall be the children of the Highest, for he is kind unto the unthankful and to the evil. Be ye therefore merciful, as your Father also is merciful."

Secondly. This will render the service pleasing to the performer. It is the nature of love to make even difficult things easy, and bitter ones sweet. This made the seven years of hard labor, which Jacob served for Rachel, seem to him as so many days. Every thing follows the heart, not only really, but cheerfully.

Thirdly. What is done from love will excel in the manner. Being done willingly and pleasantly, it will be done more gracefully and welcomely. What a man does grudgingly he does disagreeably, harshly, repulsively. He puts on a northeast face, turns himself half round, murmurs and complains; perhaps reproaches too; and if he yields at last, you feel no more obliged than if he refused. The ungracious, unfeeling mode, spoils the thing. Men may act the hypocrite, but it is almost impossible, without love, to act *courteously* and *kindly*. But where love actuates, the sufferer is not insulted while he is relieved. Alms are not flung at him instead of being given. The wound of distress is not torn open, but gently touched with an angel-hand. Oh, I have seen, I have heard some, refuse entirely, or in a degree, in a way that has soothed, and even satisfied the unsuccessful petitioner—"I wish it *was* in my power—I lament my inability—I wish this trifle was ten times more—such as it is, the blessing of God go with it, and with thee." I wonder not that love is called a *grace*, I am sure it deserves the name, not only for its origin, but for its carriage and behavior.

Lastly. This will make the service more efficient. It will constantly excite us, and we shall think we have done nothing while any thing remains to be done. For love is generous; it does not stand conditioning. It will not be stinted by rules and set measures, it does not want urgings and excitements, like reluctance and taskings. The person influenced by love cannot, without shame, sit and enjoy the luxuries of his table while penury and distress are his next door neighbors. He cannot go out of his road to preserve his sensibility from being shocked at the sight of a bleeding traveller. He will let his eye affect his heart. He will not say to the hungry and naked, Be ye warmed, and be ye fed, while he gives them not such things as are needful. He will give to his power, yea, and beyond his power, if some were to judge. He will not incapacitate himself for beneficence, by indulging extravagance of any kind. He will labor with his own hands, and guide his affairs with discretion, to increase his means. He will not grow weary in well-doing, and when he meets with instances of ingratitude, though he will lament the depravity, he will not suffer them to justify illiberality.

"All this is trying and difficult." It is. And therefore love is necessary. "By love serve one another."

This sweet little verse, if universally acted upon, would immediately turn this earth into a paradise. "Owe no man," therefore, "any thing, but to love one another; for he that loveth another, hath fulfilled the law." And the Gospel too; for "the end of the commandment is charity, out of a pure heart and a good conscience, and faith unfeigned."

—You know the grace of our Lord Jesus Christ. How did he, in the face of our unworthiness, and foreseeing our sad returns, how did he look at Bethlehem and Calvary; how did he, by love, serve us? Be ye, therefore, followers of God, as dear children: and walk in love, as Christ also loved us, and gave himself for us, an offering and a sacrifice to God of a sweet-smelling savor.

MARCH 13.—"When thou goest out to battle against thine enemies, and seest horses, and chariots, and a people more than thou, be not afraid of them; for the Lord thy God is with thee, which brought thee up out of the land of Egypt."—Deut. xx, 1.

ISRAEL was now a camp, rather than a nation. Though Canaan was given them, they were to take and defend it by force of arms. Hitherto they had seen little of war, having had only a few brushes in their journey with inferior adversaries. But things would soon become more serious; and they would see horses and chariots, and a people more than themselves. Hence they would be liable to alarm; and it was necessary for them to know what they had to embolden them. Moses therefore admonishes and encourages them, and both the admonition and encouragement will apply to ourselves.

Religion is a state of conflict. All Christians are soldiers. They wage, indeed, a good warfare. It will bear examination. Every thing commends it, and every thing *requires* it; it is not only a just, but a *necessary* war; all that is valuable is at stake; and we must conquer or die. But it is a trying warfare. It continues through every season, and in every condition. It is here admitted, that the forces of their enemies may be very superior to their own, in number, wisdom, vigilance, and might.

Hence the danger of apprehension and alarm. And fortitude is the virtue of a warrior, and none needs it more than the man who wrestles with all the powers of darkness. And none has more grounds for courageousness than he. If he considers his foes and himself only, his confidence must fail him; but he has something else to consider.

First, The Divine presence: "For the Lord thy God is with thee." And, "How many," said Antigonas to his troops, dismayed at the numbers of the foe, "How many do you reckon me for?" But God is all-wise, and almighty. Nothing is too hard for the Lord; and if He be with us, "they that be with us are more than they that be with them." "Greater is He that is in us than he that is in the world."

Secondly, His agency: "Who brought thee up out of the land of Egypt." This, to the Jew, was not only a proof, but a pledge; it not only showed what he *could* do, but was a voucher of what he *would* do. For He is always the same, and will not suffer what he has done to be undone. It would have been strange, after opening them a passage through the sea, to have drowned them in Jordan. What would he have done for his great Name, after placing himself at their head to lead them to the Land of Promise, if he had suffered them to be overcome by the way? He who begins the good work, is not only able to finish, but begins it for the very purpose. "He that spared not his own Son, but delivered him up for us all, how shall he not with him also freely give us all things?" "For if, when we were enemies, we were reconciled to God by the death of his Son; much more, being reconciled, we shall be saved by his life."

"Grace will complete what grace begins,
"To save from sorrows or from sins;
"The work that Wisdom undertakes,
"Eternal Mercy ne'er forsakes."

MARCH 14.—"That I may win Christ."—Philippians, iii, 8.

Is this the language of Paul? Is *he* the candidate for Christ? How well might he say, that in the subjects of Divine Grace old things are passed away, and all things are become new. What a change must have taken place in his own experience! Compare the man with himself. Now a blasphemer of the name of Jesus, and now asking, at his feet, "Lord, what wilt thou have me to do?" Now persecuting his followers, and now preaching the faith that once he destroyed. Now living a Pharisee, and boasting of his Jewish privileges and attainments; now saying, What things were gain to me, these I count loss for Christ. Yea, doubtless, and I count all things but loss, for the excellency of the knowledge of Christ Jesus my Lord; for whom I have suffered the loss of all things, and do count them but dung, that I may *win Christ.*

But had he *not* won him *already?* Yes, for many years he had known, and served, and enjoyed him. But intense affection makes us think that we are never sure enough of the object. Intense delight in any good, makes us long after more fruition. There is this difference between a convinced sinner and an experienced believer in Christ; the former desires only from a sense of want; the latter desires also from the relish of the enjoyment; for *he* has tasted that the Lord is gracious, and hence he the more earnestly cries, Lord, evermore give me this bread, for taste provokes appetite. Advancement, by increasing knowledge, and improving skill, produces humility and dissatisfaction. Hence the nearer any one approaches completeness in any thing, the more easily he discerns, and the more mortifyingly he feels his remaining deficiencies. And no wonder, therefore, the apostle should here say, "I have not attained, I am not already perfect;" for here, so immense is the blessing, that what is possessed will never bear a comparison with what remains; and as the object is infinite, and the faculty finite, there will always be a possibility of addition, and the happiness derivable from the Savior will not only be eternal, but eternally increasing.

But is this prize attainable by us? How is He placed before us in the Scripture? Is He exhibited only to our view, or proposed to our hope? Are not *all* allowed, invited, commanded to seek him? And all *without exception?* And could *any* be condemned for rejecting him, if he was not placed within their reach?

But what is necessary to make him our own? Not *desert.* Witness the characters of those who are encouraged to hope in him; he came to seek and to save that which was lost; He died for the ungodly. Indeed, if any meritorious qualifications were to be possessed, or conditions to be performed, in order to our obtaining him, our case would be desperate.

But *desire* is necessary. Ask, and ye shall have; seek, and ye shall find. Warrant is one thing, disposition is another: unless we are convinced of our need of him, we cannot long after him; and unless we value him, the blessing could not gratify and content us if acquired.

Sacrifice is, therefore, needful; and when the desire is supremely urgent and active, and nothing can be a substitute for the object, we shall be ready to part with whatever stands in competition with him. Hence we read in the Scripture of selling all to buy the pearl of great price. Buying, here, does not signify giving an equivalent for him—who could think of this? But, as in buying, something is parted with for the purpose, so it is here. And whether it be the pride of reason, or self-righteousness, or our worldly connexions and interests, or our sins, that keep us back from him, we must forsake them all, and follow him. And shall we not be more, infinitely more than indemnified, if we *win Christ?*

MARCH 15.—" That I may win Christ."—Philippians, iii, 8.

—AND what a prize is He! The tongue of men and of angels would infinitely fail to do *Him* justice. The sacred writers, though inspired, labor for language and imagery to aid us to conceive a little of his worth. He is the hope, the Savior, the consolation, the glory of his people Israel. He is Lord of all. In Him all fullness dwells. In winning Him we gain all pure, spiritual, durable, satisfying good; a way to God; a justifying righteousness; a sanctifying Spirit; a sufficiency of grace to help in time of need; a peace that passeth all understanding; a joy that is unspeakable and full of glory; we are blessed with all spiritual blessings in heavenly places in Christ.

If an ancient philosopher had been asked, what one thing would entirely have met all his wants, and satisfied all his hopes and desires? he would have been at a loss for an answer. But ask a Christian this question, and, without a moment's hesitation, he replies, " All I need, all I wish, is to win Christ." Let me attain Him, and I shall—I can look no further.

How blessed, then, is the winner! He is happy now. Happy alone. Happy in trouble Happy in death. How much more happy will he be hereafter! By this acquisition he is raised above the condition of Adam in Paradise—above the estate of angels in heaven. *His* portion is to be judged of by what *Christ* is, and has—for he has gained *Him*—he has won *Christ!!*

But how foolish the despiser! How poor! How wretched! How miserable in time! How much more miserable in eternity! How *can* we escape, if we neglect so *great* salvation? O my soul, hear him and live—" He that findeth me, findeth life; and shall obtain favor of the Lord; but he that sinneth against me, wrongeth his own soul; all they that hate me, love death."

MARCH 16.—" When it pleased God, who separated me from my mother's womb, and called me by his grace."—Galatians, i, 15.

PAUL is here referring to two events—his natural birth, and his spiritual birth; the one connecting him with the world, the other with the church. The former of these is common to all men; the latter is confined to a few. The former affords us no security from the wrath to come, "Because they are a people of no understanding, therefore he that made them will not have mercy on them, and he that formed them will show them no favor." The latter makes us heirs according to the hope of eternal life.

Both these, therefore, are important; but the one is far more momentous than the other. The multitude do not think so. They keep the day of their birth, and are thankful for the continuance of life; but never inquire, Has He, who separated me from my mother's womb, called me by his grace? Has He made me not only a creature, but a new creature? Am I not only a partaker of that life whose days are few and evil, but the life which the just live by faith, and which shall endure for ever?

Yes, *this* is the main thing. And you will deem it so when conscience shall be awakened; when heart and flesh shall fail, and the cold hand of death lays hold of you, to bring you into the presence of the Judge of all. To this, therefore, attend, and regard it without delay. We would not have you indifferent to the beauties of Nature, and the bounties of Providence; but let it be your chief concern to be blessed with all spiritual blessings in heavenly places in Christ. Say, with David, "I will praise thee; for I am fearfully and wonderfully made; marvellous are thy works; and that my soul knoweth right well." But O, rest not satisfied till you can say, with Paul, "He called me by his grace."

Regeneration is necessary. The nature of religion demands it. The nature of God demands it. The nature of heaven demands it. Ye *must* be born *again*. Observe *again*. Paul, you see, had been born twice; and if you are not born twice before you die once, it had been good for you if you had never been born. Those born once only, die twice—they die a temporal, and they die an eternal death. But those who are born twice, die only once—for on them the second death hath no power.

Paul was as fully persuaded of his being called by grace, as he was of his having been separated from his mother's womb. What a satisfaction must this be to the assured individual! All are not equally privileged. Some have fears concerning their conversion. But even this anxiety is a token for good. And let them remember, that there is a certainty attainable not only in Christian doctrine, but in Christian experience; and give all diligence to the full assurance of hope unto the end. Let them wait on the Lord and keep his way, and read the things that are written unto them that believe on the name of the Son of God, that they may know that they have eternal life.

—Little, when Paul was born, did any know what he was destined to be. The father embraced him, the mother forgot her anguish, for joy that a man was born into the world. His birth was no way distinguished from any other. His religious friends could not look into the future, nor conjecture the powers he was to develope, the space he was to occupy in history, the labors he was to perform, the advantages he was to render the human race to the end of time; nothing of all this could they foresee in this helpless babe. But here was the acorn of the oak. God sees the end from the beginning. Gamaliel's pupil, the zealous Pharisee, the bloody persecutor, the praying penitent, the Christian disciple, the inspired apostle—all, all were present to His view when He separated him from his mother's womb. And even then He had done virtually what He did actually in the journey to Damascus—call him by his grace. Time is nothing with Him. Design is accomplishment. Every thing has its season. All the circumstances of life, and godliness; of our birth, and our conversion, are arranged by Infinite Wisdom and Goodness. Just and true are all thy ways, O thou King of saints. He hath done all things well.

Heaven, earth, and sea, and fire, and wind,
" Show me thy wonderous skill;
" But I review myself, and find
" Diviner wonders still.

" Thy awful glories round me shine;
" My flesh proclaims thy praise:
" Lord, to thy works of Nature join
" Thy miracles of grace."

MARCH 17.—" The same Lord over all is rich unto all that call upon him."—Romans, x, 12.

POWER and benevolence are rarely united in our fellow creatures. Here is one who has abundance, but he has no disposition to do good; he turns away his ear from hearing the poor, and seems to live as if he was born for himself only. Yea, the disposition often decreases as the capacity increases; so that there are some who not only give less comparatively, but less really, than they did when they were poorer. Then it hardly seemed worth their while to be covetous and to hoard, but now they have the means, and the temptation conquers them; and in their commerce of charity, silver is used instead of gold, and copper instead of silver. On the other hand, there is many a one who has bowels of mercies, but he can only pity and shed unavailing tears over victims of distress. He is compelled to say only, Be ye warmed and be ye filled, for he has it not in his hand to give such things as are needful for our body—his hand is shortened that it cannot save, though his ear is not heavy that it cannot hear. But some few there are, in whom the means, and the mind to use them, are found united. The Lord increase their number! These are little images of Himself, in whom we equally find greatness and goodness, the resources and the readiness of compassion. " He is over all, and he is rich unto all that call upon him."

Let me look at his greatness. He is over all. All beings of every rank are under his absolute control. He rules over all *material* agents; over all *animal* agents; over all *human* agents; over the best of men; the greatest of men; the worst of men: over all *invisible* agents; over devils; over angels; over departed spirits. He is Lord both of the dead and the living. How astonishing then are his possessions and his dominions! A nation seems a great thing to us. But what is the greatest nation to our earth? And what is our earth to the luminaries of heaven? Many of these are discernible by the naked eye. When this fails, art assists nature; and Herschel seems innumerably more. When the telescope fails, the imagination plunges into the immensity beyond, and we exclaim, Lo! these are parts of his ways. But how small a portion is known of Him.

" And will this mighty Lord
" Of glory condescend;

" And will he write my name,
" My Father and my Friend?"

Yes, for his mercy equals his majesty—and the *same* Lord who is over all, "is rich unto all that call upon him." His goodness has three characters.

First. It is plenteous. "He is *rich* unto all that call upon him." Some, if they are bountiful, are poor in bounty. And this appears not only in the smallness of their gifts, but in the mode of giving. It seems done by constraint, not willingly and of a ready mind. It does not drop from them as honey from the comb, or flow like water from a spring—it seems an unnatural effort. You feel no more respect when they give much, than when they give little; every thing like nobleness is destroyed by the manner; the meanness of the disposition is betrayed, and the poor spirited mortal can no more give kindly and generously than a clown can dance gracefully. But the Lord God is a sun; He gives grace and glory; and no good thing will he withhold. He is abundant in goodness and in truth. He abundantly pardons. And while he gives liberally he upbraideth not.

Secondly. It is impartial. He is rich *unto all* that call upon him. For there is no difference between Jew and Greek. And the same will apply to sex, and age, and calling, and condition, and character. The proclamations of divine grace exclude none, whatever be their circumstances—and it is well they do not. If *any* were excluded, awakened souls would be sure to find themselves among the exceptions. But what exceptions can any find when they read, "Preach the Gospel to every creature;" "Whosoever will, let him take of the water of life freely." Evangelical mercy is like Noah's ark; that took in the clean and the unclean, only with this difference in favor of the truth of the above type: there all the beasts came out as they went in; whereas, if a man be in Christ, he is a new creature. He changes all he receives, and sanctifies all he saves.

Thirdly. It is wise. He is rich unto all that *call* upon him. This is required, and cannot be dispensed with. Not because God wills it; but because it seemeth good in his sight. He knows that we should never praise him for blessings which we do not value; and that we never could be made happy by them; for that which gratifies is something that relieves our want, fulfils our desire, accomplishes our hope, and crowns our endeavors. God's way, therefore, is to make us sensible of our state, and to cause us to hunger and thirst after righteousness; and then we shall be filled: for whoso asketh receiveth; and he that seeketh, findeth; and to him that knocketh, it shall be opened.

God reveals himself, not only for our encouragement, but imitation; and vain is our confidence in him without conformity to him. Therefore, says the apostle, Be ye followers of God, as dear children. How? In what? and walk in love, as Christ also hath loved us, and given himself for us, an offering and a sacrifice to God for a sweet-smelling savor. Men would be like God, as the greatest of beings; but we are to be like him, as the best of beings. They would resemble him in his natural perfections; but we are to resemble him in his moral. They would, as He is, be over all, and gladly have every thing at their own disposal; but we are to be holy, and true, and patient, and forgiving, and tender, as He is; and, according to our resources, to be rich unto all that call upon us.

March 18.—"Now Peter and John went up together into the temple at the hour of prayer, being the ninth hour."—Acts, iii, 1.

The associates here were Peter and John. We should not have noticed this particularly, did we not find them so frequently and constantly together in the Scripture. The instances will readily occur to all attentive readers of the New Testament. But the reasons of this peculiar intimacy are not mentioned. Each of the two had a brother among the Apostles. But there is an amity superior to relationship; there is a friend that sticketh closer than a brother. It is commonly supposed, that those who attract each other and unite, very much resemble each other: whereas, Peter and John seem to have been more dissimilar than any other two of the Apostles that could have been selected. But may not the unlikeness be considered as one of the causes of this friendship? Peter knew the excellencies of John were the opposites to his imperfections, and would tend to rectify them. Peter was eager and severe. John was more patient and affectionate. Peter was the hand, John the eye—but they were the more mutually necessary to each other.

Peter had denied his Lord, and rendered his attachment to him questionable. Perhaps John had been more compassionate toward him after his fall, and more ready to restore him in the spirit of meekness. David, after his backsliding, prayed, "Let them that fear Thee turn unto me"—and some do this much more freely than others.

But connexions and intimacies are not always accountable: they often depend on things impossible for us to describe; they come from God, who has peculiar purposes to answer, and link us together by invisible chains. See an instance of this. "It came to pass, when he had made an end of speaking unto Saul, that the soul of Jonathan was knit with the soul of David, and Jonathan loved him as his own soul. Then Jonathan and David made a covenant, because he loved him as his own soul. And Jonathan stripped himself of the robe that was upon him, and gave it to David, and his garments, even to his sword, and to his bow, and to his girdle." Though an heir apparent, Jonathan was at once attached to a man who was to exclude him from the succession: but the thing was of the Lord. How often do we read of God's giving a man favor in the eyes of another.

We have here a word in recommendation of friendship. It is sanctioned by Scripture and example. It is not good for man to be alone; but we are not required to put even every one we love into our bosom. Peter had many colleagues, but one companion, one friend.

Their friendship was religious; and instead of leading them to walk in the counsel of the ungodly, or stand in the way of sinners, or sit in the seat of the scornful; it took them to the House of God in company. Those connexions are the most valuable in which the Bible is a witness between us; in which another world is not forgotten; in which we are bound by faith and love which are in Christ Jesus; in which we walk together as heirs of the grace of life, that our prayers are not hindered.

We see that public devotion has claims upon us. God has commanded us not to "forsake the assembling of ourselves together, as the manner of some is;" and he has said, "In all places where I record my name, I will come unto thee, and I will bless thee." The worship of the Sanctuary enlivens our feelings; endears us to each other; and keeps the distinctions of life from becoming excessive. There the rich and the poor meet together; and seek and serve a Being with whom there is no respect of persons. Happy they who love the place where his honor dwelleth! Let me always avail myself of the duty; the privilege: and be glad when they say unto me Let us go up into the House of the Lord.

MARCH 19.—**"Ask thy father, and he will show thee; thy elders, and they will tell thee."—Deut. xxxii, 7.**

THERE is much truth in the proverb, he that will learn of none but himself, is sure to have a fool for *his* master. The way to advance in knowledge is to be sensible of our own deficiencies, and willing to avail ourselves of assistance. The cause of all errors is pride; for though we are ignorant, and unable to guide ourselves, there is an infallible Instructor, under whose teachings we may place ourselves. "If any of you lack wisdom, let him ask of God, that giveth to all men liberally, and upbraideth not; and it shall be given him."

And there are others that may be subordinately consulted: they possess, and can impart a little of His judgment: for in his light they see light. The priests' lips should keep knowledge; and they should seek the law at his mouth: for he is the messenger of the Lord of Hosts. And not only ministers, but—common Christians may be useful—yea, and unlearned Christians, and poor and afflicted Christians, who walk much with God, and draw in their irradiations immediately from the Scriptures. Indeed, there is hardly a being, however inferior to ourselves in some respects, but being versed in others, can teach us something. A wise man can learn more from a fool than a fool will learn from a thousand wise men. The Scripture sends us even to the brute creation: "Ask now the beasts, and they shall teach thee; and the fowls of the air, and they shall tell thee." "Go to the ant, thou sluggard; consider her ways, and be wise."

But I said, days should speak, and multitude of years should teach wisdom. It is true, great men are not always wise, neither do the aged understand judgment: yet they must have had many more opportunities for observation and decision than others; and God obviously intended to place some under the tuition of others. We were designed to live in a state of connexion with, and dependence upon each other: and while the old need the strength and activeness of the young, the young need the prudence and counsel of the old. Therefore says Peter, "Ye younger, submit yourselves unto the elder." Nothing can be more offensive in them than self-sufficiency. Surely they must acknowledge, that those who are much older than themselves, have at least the advantage of *experience*, which is commonly the slow growth of time, and is the most valuable of all knowledge. And when young people so often err in the connexions they form, and the steps they take, and the hazards they run, is it not from that self-confidence which deems advice needless? They are sober-minded: but think more highly of themselves than they ought to think.

But what advantage do we derive from writing and printing? The birds and beasts are no wiser now than when they went to Noah for shelter, and to Adam for names. It is nearly the same with savage life; knowledge is not preserved, transmitted, and increased, for want of books. But in consequence of them the improvements of one age flow into another, and the stream is continually enlarging by the influx of additional discoveries. By means of them we can consult the dead, as well as the living; for though dead, they yet speak. And we can hold converse with Bacon and Boyle, with Luther and Leighton, and can be *alone* with them, and in their best moments, and when they are most ready to communicate. Yea, by the Scriptures we can associate with Paul and Isaiah, with Moses and the patriarchs; and can sit down with Abraham, and Isaac, and Jacob, in the kingdom of God.

MARCH 20.—**"Be merciful unto me, O Lord; for I cry unto thee daily."**
Psalm lxxxvi, 3.

So David, though a man after God's own heart, and perhaps the greatest proficient in experimental and devotional piety before the coming of Christ, felt *his* need of mercy, and sought it daily, or every day, as it in the margin. Let us follow his example, and cry daily.

—For pardoning mercy. He is ready to forgive, and it is well for us he is. Who can understand his errors? In many things we offend all. What omissions of duty are we chargeable with! If our actions are materially good, how defective are their principle and motive! The sins of our holy things would condemn us. Usher, one of the best, as well one of the greatest of men, therefore said, He hoped to die with the words of the publican in his mouth, God be merciful to me a sinner; and he died pronouncing them. And Paul, after eulogizing Onesiphorus so highly for his good works, adds, "The Lord grant that *he* may find mercy of the Lord in that day"—he, even he, would need mercy—to the last, and, above all, at the last. And where is the man who, in prospect of *that* day, must not fall upon his knees and pray, "Enter not into judgment with thy servant, O Lord, for in thy sight shall no flesh living be justified!"

—Let us cry daily for sanctifying mercy. We cannot be in a proper state of mind if we only see the guilt of sin, and not the pollution also; if our fear only be excited, and not our aversion; if we are concerned to be delivered from the wrath to come, but not to be "saved by the washing of regeneration, and the renewing of the Holy Ghost." "I want," says the Christian, "true holiness. I want to bear more of the image of the heavenly. I want to be purified even as he is pure"

—Let us cry daily for assisting mercy. What can we do *alone* in these trials and these duties; in our calling as men, and our vocation as Christians? We cannot see to-morrow with the light of to-day; nor will our present food yield us future support; we must have fresh supplies of light and of food. And we must have fresh supplies of the Spirit of Jesus Christ, to help our infirmities, to renew our strength, and to enable us to adorn the doctrine of God our Savior in all things. We must live in the Spirit, that we may walk in the Spirit.

—Let us cry daily for preserving mercy. Our reputation, our substance, our business, our health—every thing is exposed; and He is the preserver of men. But the great thing is the soul. To what dangers is not this liable? And he who knows not only his perils, but himself, will not only watch, but pray, lest he enter into temptation. He knows that God alone can keep him from falling, and that without Him he can no more stand than a staff when the hand is withdrawn. And, therefore, his language will be, "Hold thou me up, and I shall be safe."

—Let us cry daily for providing mercy. He has taught us this. When ye pray, say, Give us day by day our daily bread. Bread signifies sustenance at large; but the word employed is wisely chosen to teach us moderation, and not to pray for dainties, but to be fed with food convenient for us. Our necessity, as well as safety, if properly consulted, will keep us from seeking great things to ourselves. Nature wants but little, and grace less.

—Let us cry daily for guiding mercy. How much depends, not only upon a wrong course, but even a wrong step! It may give a new cast to my condition, and quarter upon me repentance for life. And the way of man is not in himself; it is not in man that walketh to direct his steps. What a privilege that He who cannot err is as willing as He is able to lead me. To Him alone let me repair, and on him alone depend, saying, as the language both of choice and of confidence, *Thou* shalt guide me with thy counsel, and afterward receive me to glory. Then prayer will be turned into praise, and I shall sing of the mercy of the Lord for ever.

March 21.—"The Lord thy God in the midst of thee is mighty; He will save, He will rejoice over thee with joy."—Zeph. iii, 17.

It is obvious He *can* save, for He is in the *midst* of them, and *mighty*. Here is nearness and power; He is, therefore, able to save to the uttermost—whatever be the heinousness of guilt, or the depravity of nature, or the extremity of danger, or the depth of distress.

—But He *will* save—He is inclined, He is engaged, He is bound by promise, oath, and blood—

—Neither does He repent of the obligation under which He has been pleased to bring Himself—neither does He perform the work with reluctance. He will save, He will *rejoice over them with joy.*

—Are they his vineyard? I the Lord do keep it; I will water it every moment; lest any hurt it, I will keep it night and day. Are they his sheep? "The Lord shall save them in that day as the flock of his people; neither shall the beast of the field devour them; but they shall dwell safely in the wilderness, and sleep in the woods."

But what is this salvation? It does not exclude temporal preservation and deliverance. He knows how to deliver the godly out of temptation; so that if he does not find a way, he can easily make one. Thus he saved Joseph from prison, and David from the paw of the lion and the bear, and the uncircumcised Philistine, and Elijah from famine, and Jonah from the belly of hell.

"Blest proofs of power and love divine,
"That meet us in his word;
"May every deep felt care of mine
"Be trusted with the Lord."

We are not to look for miracles, but we may look for Him who performed them; who has said, I will be with thee in trouble; and who has all events at his control. He is always the same. His hand is not shortened that it cannot save; neither is his ear heavy that it cannot hear. Here, however, a distinction is to be observed. Temporal deliverances are promised *conditionally*. He could not have promised *them* otherwise—it would be rather a threatening than a promise, were He to engage to relieve and indulge you, whether it be good for you or evil. And it *might* be evil; and though you may not be aware of it, He can foresee it, and will prevent it; and, therefore, He has said, They that seek the Lord shall not want any *good* thing. As to your property, He can make a hedge about all that you have. As to your reputation, He can hide you in the secret of his pavilion from the strife of tongues. As to your body, He can keep all your bones, so that not one of them shall be broken; and if it be good for you, He will, He must do it; but if it would be otherwise, He will disappoint your wishes and hopes, and make the privation—the privilege.

But as to the *soul!* Ah! what did you mean when you first asked, "What shall I do to be saved?" When you first prayed, "Save me and I shall be saved?" You thought of nothing earthly then, but of redemption from the curse of the law; of deliverance from the powers of darkness; of freedom from the sting of death; of release from the dominion and being of sin; and it was said unto you, "Believe on the Lord Jesus Christ, and thou shalt be saved." And *this* salvation is insured; *this* salvation is begun. You are already justified by his blood, and saved from wrath through Him. You are already renewed in the spirit of your mind. You have already the earnest of your inheritance, and taste some of the grapes of Eshcol. And as to the completion, now is your salvation nearer than when you believed; the night is far spent; the day is at hand. And what is all beside! well with the soul! well for eternity! a smiling God! an opening heaven.

"A hope so much divine, | "May trials well endure"

MARCH 22.—"Think it not strange concerning the fiery trial which is to try you, as though some strange thing happened unto you."—1 Peter, iv. 12.

ARE we, then, before we really suffer, to suffer in imagination; tormenting ourselves with gloomy fears, and embittering present comfort with future apprehension? No. But neither are we to indulge presumption. We are to consider difficulties, as well as advantages; and though light is sweet, and a pleasant thing it is for the eyes to behold the sun, yet we are to remember also the days of darkness, for they shall be many. If we do not admit the possibility of disappointment and distress, we shall, when they occur, be dismayed and confounded, and say, If I am his, why am I thus? What is unexpected is overpowering; it does not leave us, for the time, the use either of reason or religion; and we resemble a soldier, who, while seeking his weapons, gives the enemy an advantage against him. But to be forewarned is to be forearmed; and what we reckon upon in the course of an enterprise, confirms, by the event, the reasonableness of our scheme. The apostle would not have us to be surprised, or deem it a strange thing, even if our trial should be fiery. A strange thing is a thing unlooked for, and which we had no reason to expect. But is this the case with our afflictions?

—Think of the ordinary state of humanity. Man is born to trouble as the sparks fly upward; and is it strange that he should inherit? How numerous and how delicate are the organs of the body, yet they are constantly in use, and in danger. To how many accidents are we exposed! How many seeds of disorder are lodged within us! Every possession makes us capable of loss; every connexion, of bereavement; every enjoyment, of grief; every hope, of fear; the wonder is, that we are ever free.

—Hear the declaration of Scripture: "Many are the afflictions of the righteous." "In the world ye shall have tribulation." "Through much tribulation you must enter the kingdom." Are these the true sayings of God?

—Trace the history of His people. However dear to God, or eminent in grace, which of them escaped?

"The path of sorrow, and that path alone,
"Leads to the land where sorrow is unknown;
"No traveller e'er reach'd that bless'd abode,
"Who found not thorns and briers on the road."

Is this only the language of poetry? "What son is he," asks the apostle, "whom the father chasteneth not?" "As many as I love," says God, "I rebuke and chasten."

Consider the disposition of the world; "Marvel not if the world hate you." If they hate the light, they are not likely to love those who diffuse it. The principles and walk of the Christian reproach and condemn not only the profane, but many who would pass for religious, but who deny the power of godliness, while they have the form. The mere moral and pharisaical are often the bitterest enemies of evangelical piety. The rule was once deemed without exception: "Yea, and all that will live godly in Christ Jesus shall suffer persecution." The absence of it now is owing, not to the want of disposition, but power. Many things restrain it; yet it is restrained only in the degree. The hand is tied, but the tongue is free; and how does it deal with the decided followers of the Lamb? And what is the carnal mind, but enmity against God?

—Survey the Christian's spiritual imperfections and necessities. Without suffering how can they resemble the Savior? and be weaned from the world? and be witnesses for God? and be prepared for usefulness? Can the welfare of the year dispense with winter? Is it a strange thing for the husbandman to plough up the fallow ground to receive the seed? or for the vine dresser to prune the vine? or for the refiner to put his gold into the furnace? Such a needs be is there for all our afflictions, and he only who is ignorant of it can wonder at the fiery trial.

But, Christians, while you look for it, so as not to be astonished at the experience, remember, you have enough to encourage you. He who died for you, and rose again, and rules over all, has made provision for every condition in which you shall be found. As the sufferings abound, the consolation shall abound also. If the way be rough, thy shoes shall be iron and brass; and as thy day, so shall thy strength be. Till the last tear is wiped away, and all shall be peace, and quietness, and assurance for ever.

March 23.—"I know whom I have believed."—2 Timothy, i, 12.

Or trusted, as it is in the margin. And this is better, for the apostle is referring to an act of confidence rather than belief; and which was expressed by his intrusting the Savior with a deposit, or committing his soul into his hands.

The knowledge of which he speaks is not only, or principally, the knowledge he had of the Lord Jesus *before* he believed on him. He had indeed such a knowledge, and he *must* have had, for how can we believe on him of whom we have not heard? Who would commit a jewel to a stranger? Who would walk over a deep abyss without inquiring whether the plank was sound or rotten? Ignorance, in such a case, would render confidence the act of a fool; whereas faith in Christ is wisdom; and when a man commits his eternal all to Him, he has the highest reason in the world for so doing. This previous knowledge, however, is derived entirely from testimony.

But there is also a subsequent knowledge derived from experience, and he that believeth hath the witness in himself. He knows the bitterness of gall, and the sweetness of honey, not from report, but from taste. My conscience, says he, was burthened, and I found no relief till I applied to the Blood of Sprinkling. Without Him I can do nothing; but I know that His grace is sufficient for me; for I have made trial of it, both in duty and in distress. I have read and heard much of His excellency; and I have put it to the proof; He is now a tried friend and benefactor. I have tried, much, and often, his power, faithfulness, and care, and have found them trust-worthy. I therefore feel satisfaction in reviewing what I have done. I have often been imposed upon, and have played the fool; but not here. Of many things I have repented, but the longer I live, the less I am disposed to repent of this. I have examined it in the retirement of the closet; in the light of Scripture; in the view of death and eternity; and the more I consider it, the more I approve and glory in the deed. And I will recommend the same to others; and I can speak with the boldness and earnestness of conviction, for I know whom I have believed.

And here we see the value of this knowledge. It increases reliance and confidence. Hence, says David, " They that know thy name will put their trust in thee: *i. e.* they will trust with more ease and more firmness. Whence arise many of the doubts and fears of Christians, but from their living more upon their frames and feelings than upon the clear and full views of the truth as it is in Jesus? As soon as ever you have committed a valuable treasure to any one you become alive to his character, and unless you are well acquainted with it, every surmising, every loose report, every dark and unexplained circumstance, may trouble and terrify the heart, even though the deposit may be secure. For though the safety of the deposit depends on the goodness of his character, your satisfaction depends upon your knowledge of it.

Let me therefore be concerned to grow in grace; and also, and for this very purpose, in the knowledge of my Lord and Savior Jesus Christ. Let me search the Scriptures, for they are they that testify of him. Let me attend his house, and the preaching of his word. Let me converse much with those who have been much with him. Let me earnestly implore the influence of the Holy Spirit, who, says the

Savior, shall glorify me, for he shall take of mine, and shall show it unto you. Paul, after such a length of acquaintance, and such a depth of intimacy, not only said, I count all things but loss for the excellency of the knowledge of Christ my Lord, but that I may know him and the power of his resurrection, and the fellowship of his sufferings, being made conformable unto his death.

MARCH 24.—"I will walk in thy truth."—Psalm lxxxvi, 11.

EVERY resolution expressed by a good man, in a proper frame of mind, will be founded, not in self-confidence, but in dependence on divine grace. *Then* it will be useful; it will tend to stimulate, and to humble; to bring to remembrance, and to bind; it will be like a hedge that defends the field; or like the hemming that keeps the robe from ravelling out. "I will walk in thy truth," is a noble resolution, and worthy of our imitation.

Walking, in the Scripture, takes in the whole of our conversation or conduct; and to walk *in* any thing, intends a fullness of it. For a man to *walk in* pride, is something more than to be proud; it says, that pride is his way, his element—that he is wholly under the influence of it. So we say, a man is in love, or in liquor. Four ways we should thus walk in God's truth.

—We should walk in the belief of his truth. It deserves our credence. It is a faithful saying, as well as worthy of all acceptation. If we receive the witness of man, the witness of God is greater. Men are very tenacious of the honor of their word. If their veracity be denied, they instantly demand satisfaction for the insult. How often is God made a liar! How slow of heart are we to believe all that the prophets have spoken! Lord increase our faith.

—We should walk in the practice of his truth. This is as necessary as the former, and the evidence of it—for we are to show our faith by our works. Faith without works is as the body without the soul there is nothing vital, or operative in it. The Gospel is a doctrine according to godliness. Every part of it has a practical tendency, and we are required to obey it from the heart. It is well to hear; but hearing is to be viewed in the order of means, and not as an end. Blessed are they that hear the word of God, and *keep it.* If ye know these things, happy are ye if ye *do* them.

—We should walk in the enjoyment of his truth. For it is not only of a sanctifying, but a consolatory nature; it brings us glad tidings of great joy; it is all written for our learning, that we, through patience and comfort of the Scriptures, might have hope. If, therefore, our conversation *becometh* the Gospel, it will be happy, as well as holy. Thus it was with the first Christians: they walked, not only in the fear of the Lord, but in the comforts of the Holy Ghost. They were not free from trouble; but, as the sufferings of Christ abounded in them, the consolation also abounded by Christ. They were not free from complaint and self-abhorrence; but in his name they rejoiced all the day, and in his righteousness were exalted. Of themselves they felt they could do nothing, but they were strong in the grace that is in Christ Jesus, and through Him they could do all things. They knew not what a day would bring forth; but they were careful for nothing, casting all their care on Him who cared for them. The Gospel did not shut them up in a dungeon of doubts and fears; they knew the truth, and the truth made them free indeed; and they walked in the glorious liberty of the sons of God.

—We should walk in the profession of his truth. If we know the joyful sound, so as to be blessed by it, we shall feel this yoke easy, and this burden light. We shall not act to be seen of men: but we shall have no objection that men should see us. Praise will not draw us out of a corner; and fear will not drive us into one. We shall be willing for all to know that we are not our own, but his who bought us with a price; and that we are not only bound, but determined to glorify Him in our bodies and spirits. For his love will constrain us, not only to confess Him with the mouth, but with the life, (for actions speak louder than words,) despising in our eyes a vile person, but honoring them that fear the Lord; attending only where his truth is preached, and his glory is maintained; and going forth to Him without the camp, bearing his reproach.

If we are thus governed, we shall be a credit and a comfort to our ministers, who have no greater joy than to hear of their children walking in the truth. We shall hold forth the word of life, and cause them to rejoice in the day of Christ, that *they* have not run in vain, nor labored in vain. We shall adorn the doctrine of God our Savior in all things, and be fellow-helpers to the truth—while He will *graciously* say, "They shall walk with me in white, for they are worthy."

MARCH 25.—"The Lord knoweth the days of the upright; and their inheritance shall be for ever."—Psalm xxxvii, 18.

EVERY thing here requires attention—

—The *persons*—"The upright." The upright mean those who are sincere: sincere in their dealings with their fellow creatures, with their own souls, and with their God. The character is equally rare and excellent. It admits of imperfection, but not of partiality; and is never separate from the renewing of the Holy Ghost.

—The *period*—"Their days." These are "known of God." This knowledge being spoken of as a privilege, something more than mere intelligence must be intended; for in this sense, He knows the days of the wicked, as well as of the upright. The meaning is, that he knows them kindly, and graciously; that He feels, and will acknowledge his concern in them, and make them all work together for their good. He knows their number. This is with him. He has appointed it; friends cannot enlarge, enemies cannot reduce it. Whenever they die, they have filled their days, and are immortal till their work is done. He knows the nature of them—and he determines it.—

"If light attends the course they run,
"'Tis He provides those rays;
"And 'tis his hand that veils their sun
"If darkness clouds their days."

Have they days of affliction? He knows them—knows their source their pressure, how long they have continued, the support they require, and the proper time to remove them. Have they days of danger? He knows them, and will be a refuge and defence in them. Have they days of duty? He knows them; and will furnish the strength and the help they require. Have they days of inaction, when they are laid aside from their work, by accident, or disease? He knows them; and says to his servants, under every prevention, It is well that it was in thy heart. Have they days of privation? when they are denied the ordinances of religion, after seeing his power and glory in the temple, and going with the voice of gladness, to keep holy day? He knows them; and will follow his people when they cannot follow him, and be a little sanctuary to them in their losses. Have they days of declension and of age? in which their strength is fled, and their senses fail, and so many of their connexions have gone down to the dust—evil days, wherein they have no pleasure? He knows them; and says, I remember thee, the kindness of thy youth. Even to old age I am He, and to hoar hairs will I bear and carry you.

—The *portion*—"Their inheritance shall be for ever." So was not the inheritance of many of the angels in Heaven; for they kept not their first estate. So was not the inheritance of Adam in Paradise; for the Lord drove out the man. So was not the inheritance of the Jew in Canaan; for the glory of all lands was made a desolation. So is not he inheritance of the man of the world. His portion is in this life. And what is this but a vapor, a shadow! Yet, at the end of it, he is stripped of all, and departs as naked as he came. Yea, and before the close his hopes and comforts may be all laid bare. For—

> "Short liv'd as are *we*, yet our pleasures, we see,
> "Have a much shorter date. and die sooner than we."

And the Christian has not only being, and health, and riches, and honor, and peace, and joy, and friendship, but all these for ever!

Indeed, the more important and valuable the acquisition, the more miserable he would feel if there was any uncertainty in the continuance. The thought of loss, and even of danger, would imbitter all. But it is for ever—for ever! Yea, it will be always increasing. After millions of years we shall be singing a new song.

In the world we have losses, but they cannot affect our estate. I, one day, says Mr. Newton, visited a family that had suffered by a fire, which had destroyed all their house and goods. I found the pious mistress in tears. I said, I give you joy, madam! Surprised, and ready to be offended, she exclaimed, What! joy that all my property is consumed! No; but I give you joy that you have so much property that no fire can touch. This turn checked the grief, and she wiped her tears, and smiled like the sun shining after an April shower. Thus the Hebrews took joyfully the spoiling of their goods, knowing in themselves that in heaven they had a better and an enduring substance.

MARCH 26.—"And now I have told you before it come to pass, that, when it is come to pass, ye might believe."—John, xiv, 29.

HE refers to what he had said concerning his death and resurrection, his sufferings and glory. As nothing befel him by chance, so nothing took him by surprise. All was laid out in his view, and he saw the end from the beginning, and foretold it all before any of it had come to pass. For what purpose? "That, when it is come to pass," says he, "ye might believe."

Hence we see the importance of faith. This is what he always required in those he healed. Only believe, said he, to the ruler of the synagogue. He said to his disciples, with regard to the death of Lazarus, "I am glad for your sakes that I was not there, to the intent ye may believe." If a man wishes a tree to grow, he waters not the branches, but the root. Holy tempers, and good works, are the fruits of religion—faith is the root, and as this is enlivened, every thing in the divine life prospers. Unbelief makes God a liar, renders the Scripture a nonentity, and leaves the soul open to every sin. But he that believeth shall be saved. Yea, he hath everlasting life. By faith we stand, walk, live. We are justified, we are sanctified, by faith. Faith purifies the heart, and overcometh the world. Unless we believe, we shall not be established. We are filled with all joy and peace in believing. We read of the joy of faith, the prayer of faith, the work of faith, the obedience of faith, the fight of faith—every thing is ascribed to it in the word of God. And yet some are afraid of having it much preached!

—Here we learn, also, that there may be an improvement in faith, where the principle is already found. Did not these disciples believe at this very time? They had been with him from the beginning; they had heard his sayings, and witnessed his miracles, and seen his glory—yes, and they believed on him too, and had left all to follow him. But they did not sufficiently believe. Their faith was too obscure in its views, too feeble in its hold, too powerless in its operation. Are there not, then, degrees in godliness? May there not be a growth in grace? Does not Paul tell the Thessalonians, that their faith grew exceedingly? And how desirable is this progress! The strong in faith have a thousand advantages above the weak. The latter have a heaven hereafter, the former have a heaven here too. And if the apostles were defective, and said, Lord, increase our faith, what need have we to cry out, with tears, like the father of the child, "Lord, I believe; help thou mine unbelief!"

—We remark, also, that one of the best means of increasing and establishing our faith, is to compare the word and the works of the Lord together. This was the help and advantage he would here insure to his disciples: "And now I have told you before it come to pass, that when it is come to pass ye might believe." So did the church in the time of David; "As we have heard, so have we seen in the city of our God." We have heard the promises, and we have seen the fulfilment. We have heard the threatenings, and we have seen the execution. We have heard the doctrine, and we have seen the practice. As soon as Jesus had said, "Go thy way, thy son liveth," the nobleman "believed, and went his way." "But as he was now going down, his servants met him, and told him, saying, Thy son liveth! Then inquired he of them the hour when he began to amend. And they said unto him, Yesterday at the seventh hour the fever left him. So the father knew that it was at the same hour in which Jesus said unto him, Thy son liveth; and himself believed, and his whole house." That is, he now believed more firmly and impressively; and this was the consequence of comparison. And thus facts are yielding us constant and growing evidence of the truth of God's word. Upon this principle, apostates and scoffers do not scandalize us—the Scripture tells us they will come. We read in the Scripture, the way of transgressors is hard; that he who walketh uprightly walketh surely; that the merciful shall obtain mercy; that the way of the slothful is a hedge of thorns; and how little must he have observed the experience of others, or consulted his own, who is not every day more convinced of this!

—Finally: Does not this clearly intimate, that the benefit to be derived from prophecy is subsequent to its accomplishment? "And now I have told you before it come to pass, that, when it is come to pass, you might believe. He mentions the same thing in several other places, and we are informed, in more than one instance, of the result. Thus we read—"When, therefore, he was risen from the dead, his disciples remembered that he had said this unto them; and they believed the Scripture, and the word which Jesus had said." So also, when they had witnessed his "zeal" in purifying the temple, his disciples remembered that it was written, "The zeal of thine house hath eaten me up." Thus we see our remark justified. Indeed, how can it be otherwise? Where is the evidence of the truth of prophecy before it come to pass? You say, a God who cannot lie has spoken it. But God himself does not demand our faith on the announcement, but on the event. And how little can it be understood beforehand, unless as to its general bearings? A definite and particular acquaintance with the contents of divine predictions would derange the order of Providence, and in many cases hinder the effect. Had this fact been duly considered, much time and attention would have been more profitably employed than in attempts to open the seals, and blow the trumpets and pour out the vials of the Apocalypse. There is no prophet among us, nor any that telleth how long; yet there are, as Fuller calls them, "fortune-tellers of the Church." Pastors have been drawn away from their proper work. And "the hungry sheep look up, and are not fed." And sinners are not converted from the error of their ways. For even allowing the views advanced with so much presumption to be just and true, they are not repentance toward God, and faith toward our Lord Jesus Christ. "Him crucified," the apostles preached, and determined to know nothing else. It is not for us to know the times, or the seasons, which the Father hath put in his own power. He has intrusted us with his commands, but not with his decrees. "The secret things belong unto the Lord our God; but those things which are revealed belong unto us and our children for ever, that we may do all the words of this law."

MARCH 27.—"He hath done all things well."—Mark, vii, 37.

A GREAT commendation; but deserved. Human excellences are rare and individual. One man does one thing well, another does another thing well; but He does *all* things well. The little men do well, is only *comparatively* well; all He does is *absolutely* so. And this will appear, whether we consider him as the Creator, and survey the works of nature; or as the Savior, and contemplate the wonders of grace; or as the Governor, and examine the dispensations of his providence.

We have some fine specimens of his agency recorded in the Scripture. Take, for instance, the history of Joseph. Read it over again and again, and then ask, Could any link in this chain, any stone in this structure, have been omitted? In this achievement could any thing have been added to the plan, or the execution? From a part, we may estimate the whole; and what applies to his dealings with others will apply to his dealings with us; for all the ways of the Lord are mercy and truth. But whence, then, is it, that we cannot really and readily, with regard to his concern in our affairs, and especially those of a trying nature, adopt the acknowledgment and say, He hath done all things well.

—The reason is, we judge *atheistically*. Every unregenerate sinner lives without God in the world. But does a Christian? Is he not made to differ from others, and from himself? He is. Yet his sanctification is not complete. Something is left in him of all the old kinds of leaven, and therefore something of this atheism. He is in a good frame, when with Eli he can say, of whatever befalls him, "It is the Lord, let him do what seemeth him good." But he does not always see Him. He sometimes stops at the instrumentality employed—"Oh, it was that unlucky accident, it was that heedless servant, it was that perfidious neighbor, it was that cruel enemy." No wonder *he* does not *all* things well, when he is not acknowledged as doing *any thing*.

—We judge *selfishly*. We are not to view ourselves as detached individuals. We are parts of a whole, and variously connected with others; and what is not good for us personally, may be good for us relatively. Suppose a trying dispensation makes us more tender and compassionate toward our fellow creatures and our fellow Christians; suppose a distressing experience gives us the tongue of the learned, and enables us to speak a word in season to him that is weary: suppose, as witnesses and examples of the power and excellency of the Gospel, we arouse the careless, and confirm the wavering; is there not enough here to call for resignation and praise? Ezekiel was deprived of the desire of his eyes with a stroke; to himself this was painful; but it was profitable to his ministry, and useful to his charge; and this was the design of it. No man liveth to himself, and no man dieth to himself.

We judge *carnally*. What is not pleasing may yet be beneficial; and natural evil may be moral good. When things are agreeable to our wishes, we never think of any difficulty in the divine proceedings. While we have ease, and health, and friends, and success in business, we never complain of the darkness of providence. But as soon as there is any reverse, O then we groan out, "His way is in the sea, his path in the deep waters, and his footsteps are not known," as if every thing was to be estimated by our accommodation and convenience, as if God acted wisely or unwisely, righteously or unrighteously, just as his doings affect us; and affect, too, not our best interests, but our present and temporal! Is it wonderful that we, who deserve stripes, should feel the rod? that we, who need correction, should meet with chastisement? Is it mysterious that the vine should be pruned? the ground ploughed? the gold tried in the fire? If the child now thinks certain restraints, and privations, and rebukes, to which the father subjects him, needless and harsh, he will more than approve of them when he comes to years.

—We judge *prematurely*. He that believeth maketh not haste. It is good for a man not only to hope, but quietly wait, for the salvation of God; and one reason is, because it will prevent a wrong conclusion. Therefore, says the apostle, judge nothing before the time until the Lord come. You would not judge of the abilities of the limner from the unfinished sketch, but you would wait till the canvas had received the last touches of his masterly pencil. You would not judge of the perfection of a building from the digging of the foundation, and coarse materials lying in a kind of disorder all around, especially if you had ever seen the model; but you would stay till the parts were all put together in their places, and the top-stone brought forth with shouting; let us stay till God has done. What I do, says he, thou knowest not now, but thou shalt know hereafter. Then every thing will speak for itself. Then we shall walk, not by faith, but by sight. Then we shall see what we now believe, and for ever acknowledge, "He is the rock; his work is perfect; for all his ways are judgment: a God of truth, and without iniquity, just and right, is he."

MARCH 28.—"Hereafter I will not talk much with you; for the prince of this world cometh, and hath nothing in me."—John, xiv, 30.

THERE are many talkers—profane talkers—indecent talkers—foolish talkers—vain talkers. And there are some who are wise and good talkers; their lips are as a well-spring of life. But *He* was perfectly wise and good; oh! to have heard him "talk!" The term is applied to his more public teaching, "While he yet talked to the people." And had some of his ministers spoken more in a familiar and conversational mode, then they would have resembled him more, and the poor would have had the gospel preached unto them, and the common people would have heard them gladly, and the children would have cried hosanna.

It is here intimated that he *had* talked "much" with them. He was never reserved. If he kept any thing back from them, it was because they could not, at the time, bear it. He treated them not as servants, but friends; for all things that he had heard of the Father he made known unto them. He always instructed, and reproved, and encouraged them, as the occasion required. He seized every opportunity for religious discourse, and levied a tax of spiritual profit upon every natural object or providential occurrence. He could not see a sower going forth to sow, or a fisherman dragging his net, or a woman drawing water, but he derived from it a parable or an illustration; teaching his followers to be social and communicative in divine things; and, for this purpose, to cultivate their understanding, and to be filled with the Spirit. For out of the abundance of the heart the mouth speaketh. How can much religious discourse be expected from those who have so little of the life of God in them? If, for the sake of consistency, they sometimes make the attempt, it must be a task; and they will soon drop into what is more natural to them, a conversation empty as the wind, and barren as the sand.

—But "hereafter" he *would* not talk much with them; not from disinclination, but for want of intercourse. Their opportunities would soon be over, for he was going to leave them. With regard also to us, it is probable as to some, and certain as to others, that we have heard and read much more than we shall ever read or hear in future. Yet a little while is the light with us.

The way in which he refers to his removal from them by his suffering and death is remarkable, "For the prince of this world cometh, and hath nothing in me."

He marks, first, the character of his adversary—the prince of this world. He is not so by right, but usurpation; and by God's allowing him power over those who provoke Him. When the traitor had received the sop, then Satan entered into him. He was in him before; but his agency was under restraints. These restraints were then all taken away, and the devil had his victim entirely to himself. Israel would have none of him, so he gave them up to their own hearts' lust. All who walk according to the course of this world, walk according to the prince of the power of the air, the spirit that now worketh in the children of disobedience. They may imagine themselves to be free, and many of them make a figure in the eye of sense; but faith sees them taken captive by the devil at his will, and held in the vilest subjection; he is their prince; yea, according to the apostle he is the God of this world; and in reality they not only obey, but worship him.

—Secondly, he sees his approach: "He cometh." Not personally; so he had come to him in the wilderness and been foiled; but in his instruments. In Judas that betrayed him; in Peter that denied him; in his disciples that forsook him and fled; in Herod that threatened him; in Pilate that condemned him; in the Jews that clamored for his blood; and in the Romans that shed it. "One of you," says our Lord, "is a devil;" he gives him the name, because he bore his image and did his work. "The devil," we read, "shall cast some of you into prison." Is the devil a justice of the peace? No; but if he acts unrighteously and cruelly, the justice of the peace is the devil. The devil is not Voltaire; but by poisoning and destroying the souls of men, Voltaire is the devil, who was a murderer from the beginning, and abode not in the truth.

—Thirdly, he is confident of the result of the conflict: "And hath nothing in me." He has enough in us. First, enough of guilt. Hence he can alarm and dismay us. In the conscience of some he produces such terror and anguish that the man chooses strangling and death rather than life. He is also the accuser of the brethren, and in their sins, and the sins even of their holy things, he finds enough against them to perplex and distress them in their afflictions, and in their approaches to God. But he could find no guilt in Jesus, and, therefore, he could stir up no feeling of self-remorse or despair. Secondly, enough of corruption. Hence he can easily draw us aside by laying hold of our envy, pride, avarice, impatience. Owing to the remains of unmortified passions, or, as the apostle calls it, the sin that dwelleth in us, we are always in danger from outward things. We may be ensnared by our dress, our table, our business, and our friends; what is innocent and good itself, may become to us injurious and evil. Here the sparks fall upon tinder. But there was nothing inflammable in him, and, therefore, no unhallowed fire could be kindled. He was the Holy One of God. "He *did* no sin," and "in him *was* no sin!"

a proof that if he was stricken, smitten of God, and afflicted, he was wounded for our transgressions, and bruised for our iniquities; the chastisement of our peace was upon him, and with his stripes we are healed. We also see that there must be a great difference between him and ourselves, as to moral danger. He was safe every where, and in all circumstances. We must watch and pray, lest we enter into temptation; the spirit, indeed, is willing, but the flesh is weak.

March 29.—"God hath not appointed us to wrath, but to obtain salvation by our Lord Jesus Christ."—1 Thessalonians, v, 9.

—No: "he has not appointed us to wrath." He might have done it. We deserved it, and were by nature children of wrath, even as others. But He has delivered us *from* the wrath to come. We have trials, but there is no curse in them. They come from a Father who corrects, not from a judge who punishes. We may sometimes fear his wrath, but this is our infirmity. Flesh cries, do not condemn me; but faith says, There is no condemnation to them that are in Christ Jesus.

—But "to obtain salvation." We are often said to be saved already; and we are so as to our state, but not as to possession and enjoyment. This is a future blessedness. It is, indeed, begun here; but that which is held up to the hope of the believer, is the accomplishment of all that God has promised—the reception of the soul at death; the resurrection of the body at the last day; the glorification of the whole man for ever. Oh! what an object of expectation! How poor and pitiful is every thing seen and temporal, compared with this! Some are destined to shine in courts; some to stride over the heads of others; some to amass heaps of shining ore; but, if a Christian, thou art destined to an inheritance beyond the skies, and a crown of glory that fadeth not away. What is life, however, indulged and endowed, that is, at its best estate, altogether vanity! What are the pleasures of sin for a season! What are riches and—death! a title and—damnation at the end of it! And what are losses and afflictions to a man who is going to obtain SALVATION!

But by what medium will he acquire it? "Through our Lord Jesus Christ." To seek it in any other way is a vain pursuit. There is salvation in none other. I am the way, said He, the truth, and the life: no man cometh unto the Father but by me. Yea, it is not only useless, but sinful. It opposes God's revealed will and express command; it robs the Lord Jesus of his highest glory; it frustrates his grace, and makes Him to be dead in vain. Much comes to some through others. We have had friends and benefactors, but, after all, what have they done for us? What self-denial have they exercised? What sufferings have they endured? But *He* knew what would be required of Him in opening for us a passage to glory. Yet He readily consented, and said, Lo! I come. Behold, and see if ever there was sorrow or love like his; He became poor that we might be made rich, and died that we might live.

The apostle does not forget to tell us, that we are *appointed* to obtain this salvation through our Lord Jesus Christ. As men we are not the creatures of chance. There is an appointed time to man upon earth; and He has appointed the bounds of our habitation. And as Christians, are we the offspring of contingency? Is conversion a happy accident? It is the work of God, and He does nothing without foreknowledge and design. Four things may be observed with regard to this appointment. The *earliness* of it—in hope of eternal life, which God, who cannot lie, promised before the world began. The *freeness* of it—it was not founded on the foresight of any worthiness or works of ours; He hath saved us, and called us, not according to our works, but according to his own purpose and grace given us in Christ Jesus before the world began. Its *efficiency*—it will not, cannot fail; the counsel of the Lord standeth for ever. "I will make an everlasting covenant with them, that I will not turn away from them to do them good; but I will put my fear in their hearts, that they shall not depart from me." Its *appropriation*—blessed are the poor in spirit, for theirs is the kingdom of heaven. Blessed are they that mourn. Blessed are they that hunger and thirst after righteousness. Go back from effects to causes. Prove your calling, and thus make your election sure.

And remember one thing; be simple, and receive the kingdom of God as a little child, not only as to doctrines, but as to its invitations and promises. The writer one day attended the dying bed of a young female. I have little, said she, to relate as to my experience. I have been much tried and tempted, but this is my sheet anchor; He has said, Him that cometh unto me I will in no wise cast out. I know I come to Him, and I expect that He will be as good as his word. Poor and unworthy as I am, He will not trifle with me, or deceive me. It would be beneath his greatness, as well as his goodness. I am at his feet, and you have often said:

"'Tis joy enough, my All in all,
"At thy dear feet to lie;
"Thou wilt not let me lower fall,
"And none can higher fly."

MARCH 30.—"When they saw Him, they besought Him hat He would depart."—Matthew, viii, 34.

HE had now entered the country of the Gadarenes, and cured two demoniacs. The people should have deemed themselves honored by his presence, and have thanked Him for relieving their wretched neighbors from the most dreadful malady. But He had, in correction of an unlawful traffic, destroyed their swine. They, therefore, preferring their sins to their souls, feared and hated Him, and desired Him to withdraw. He took them immediately at their word, and went, and returned no more. Oh! when He comes to us, and convinces us of sin, and reproves us from our evil passions and vile courses; when He comes and makes us uneasy by the admonitions of conscience, of friendship, of Scripture, of Providence, and instead of yielding to his merciful design, we regard Him as an irksome intruder, and entreat Him (and He hears our meaning without speech) to leave us, He will comply with our desire, and say, They are joined to idols, let them alone, and wo unto them when I depart from them! This is an awful truth.

But it is an equally pleasing one, that if we desire his presence, He will indulge our wish. And, therefore, when the two disciples, going to Emmaus, reached the illage whither they went, and He made as if He would have gone farther, they constrained Him, saying, Abide with us, for it is toward evening, and the day is far spent. And, it is said, He went in to tarry with them. So when the women of Samaria had persuaded many of their neighbors to come to the well to see Him, they besought Him that He would tarry with them: and He abode there two days.

Savior Jesus! cast me not away from thy presence, and take not thy Holy Spirit from me. Thou art all in all. Come and dwell in our country; come and dwell in our churches; come and dwell in our houses; come and dwell in our hearts, for ever!

"I cannot bear thine absence, Lord;
"My life expires if thou depart:
"Be thou, my heart, still near my God,
"And thou, my God, be near my heart."

MARCH 31.—"But that the world may know that I love the Father; and as the Father gave me commandment, even so I do. Arise, let us go hence." John, xiv, 31.

WHEN He says, "Arise, let us go hence," He shows his readiness to suffer. "I will not wait for the enemy; I will go and meet him. I will go to the place where Judas will look for me. I will go to the garden of Gethsemane, where I am to agonize; and from thence to Calvary, where I am to die. I have a baptism to be baptized with, and how am I straitened till it be accomplished!" We always see in Him this disposition, a proof that He was not compelled to engage; that he did not undertake the case from ignorance; and that He did not repent of his work, even in the sight of enduring all its expensiveness of wo; He loved us, and gave himself for us.

Yet this alacrity was not rashness, but obedience, "As the Father gave me commandment." Though in his higher character He had the disposal of Himself; in his human nature, and in his mediatorial office, He was obedient unto death, even the death of the cross. He felt no inconsistency in this, and why should we? No man taketh my life from me. I lay it down of myself; I have power to lay it down, and I have power to take it again. This commandment have I received of my Father. So mistaken should we be in supposing that the Father was less disposed to save us than the Son, or that his love was purchased by that death which was really the effect of it, and designed to be the medium through which it should operate. Herein God hath commended his love toward us, in that while we were yet sinners Christ died for us. And therefore did the Father love Him, because He laid down his life that he might take it again; and for the suffering of death, He crowned Him with glory and honor. Though there was something here peculiar in our Savior's obedience, there is something also exemplary in it. He did not expose Himself before his hour was come, but cheerfully submitted to the divine will when it was come. So we are not to turn aside in search of trials, but to take up our cross when it is fairly in our way. We are not to be impatient to suffer, but when we are called to it, the *call* should bear us up, and bear us through, for God is with us.

And this obedience resulted from love—"I love the Father." I delight, said He, to do thy will; yea, thy law is within my heart. My meat is to do the will of Him that sent me, and to finish his work. His people, in their measure and degree, can say the same. As obedience is the best evidence of love, so love is the best spring of obedience. It is love that makes it pleasant to ourselves, and acceptable to God. With Him nothing can be a substitute for it. Indeed, we ourselves, in the conduct of our fellow creatures toward us, judge not by the bulk of the action, but the disposition from which it proceeds. The estimate is taken, not from the service, but the principle; not from what is given, but from what is implied. The smallest donation is welcomed as a token of cordial regard; while, like God, we abhor "the sacrifice where not the heart is found."

Jesus would have all this known, not to his disciples only, but to others—and to all: "But that the *world* may *know* that I love the Father, and as the Father gave me commandment, even so I do. Arise, let us go hence." And the world ought to know it, and in due time will know it. They are deeply concerned in it. At present a very large majority of mankind have never heard of his name, or of his salvation. But his cause is spreading. The Scriptures are entering all languages. Missionaries are visiting all climes. The church is praying that his word may have free course and be glorified. And God has said, "It is a light thing that thou shouldest be my servant, to raise up the tribes of Jacob, and to restore the preserved of Israel; I will also give thee for a light to the Gentiles, that thou mayest be my salvation unto the ends of the earth." It must therefore by-and-by be said, without a figure, "Behold! the world is gone away after Him."

But blessed are our eyes, for they see, and our ears, for they hear. We already know these things. But *how* do we know them? Do we feel, as well as understand them? Are we, like a December's night, as cold as we are clear? Shall we be found in the number of those who behold, and wonder, and perish? Or, filled with admiration, and gratitude, and confidence, and zeal, are we, beholding as in a glass his glory, changing into the same image, from glory to glory, even as by the Spirit of the Lord?

• April 1.—"His sweat was as it were great drops of blood falling down to the ground."—Luke, xxii, 44.

It is a question whether this sweat was blood comparatively, *i. e.* whether it resembled blood, whose drops are denser, heavier, and larger than those of common perspiration, or really blood. The latter is possible, and there have been instances of it well authenticated, and the opinion early and generally prevailed, and nothing was more common among the fathers than to consider this as one of the times when He bled for us, each of his pores as a kind of wound, flowing with that blood without which there is no remission. It is, perhaps, impossible to determine this absolutely. But even allowing, what we by no means consider as proved, that it was only blood in resemblance, it must have been most extraordinary. For He was abroad in the open air, upon the cold ground, the night far advanced, and the weather chilling, for the high priest's servants made a fire to warm themselves; here was enough to have checked perspiration; yet his sweat was, as it were, great drops of blood falling down to the ground!

And what could have caused it? Surely not the mere circumstance of dying. Socrates, Seneca, did not sweat thus; they were cool and calm. Look at the martyrs, and even those of the more timid sex, they were tranquil in the prospect, and, in many instances, came forth from prison smiling, and blessed the instrument of death. Yes, but they had not to contend with the powers of darkness; but this was their hour, and the power of darkness. They had not to bear the sins of others, nor yet their own; whereas the Lord laid on Him the iniquities of us all.

We indulge here no curious speculations, and we require the definitions of no human creeds, but neither will we be reasoned out of the plain language and meaning of the Scriptures. We believe God, and not as some believe him, *i. e.* as a jury in a court believe the testimony of a suspected, a discredited witness, relying no further upon his deposition than it is collaterally supported, and thus yielding no honor to himself. We do not found our belief on knowledge, but derive our knowledge from belief. We believe in the unerring wisdom and veracity of God, and he has told us that Christ also suffered for sins, the just for the unjust; that He bore our griefs, and carried our sorrows; that the chastisement of our peace was upon Him, and that by his stripes we are healed.

Men think lightly of sin, but an awakened conscience feels it a burden too heavy to bear. It has made the whole creation groan. But see Jesus bearing it in his own body, and his sweat falls as great drops of blood down to the ground! What, then, if you should bear it in your own person, O sinner! Why it will sink thee to the lowest hell. But bear it you must, if you reject or neglect him, for there remaineth no more sacrifice for sin. He that believeth on the Son of God hath everlasting life; and he that believeth not the Son of God, hath not life, but the wrath of God abideth on him. But,

> " Each purple drop proclaims there's room,
> " And bids the poor and needy come."

Oh! let me look on Him who suffers thus. Oh! let me mourn over my sins, which caused his anguish.

> " 'Twere you that pull'd the vengeance down
> " Upon his guiltless head;
> " Break, break, my heart; and burst, my eyes,
> " And let my sorrows bleed?"

But let me also rejoice. That bloody sweat proclaims my discharge from condemnation, and tells me the law is magnified and made honorable.

And can I help loving Him? Love begets love. And what can evince love like suffering; and such suffering, and for such wretches, and not only without their desert, but their desire! Lord! what wilt thou have me to do?

APRIL 2.—" Then asked He them again, Whom seek ye? And they said, Jesus of Nazareth."—John, xviii, 7.

EVERY thing here is remarkable.

—In the very family of Jesus, how wonderful that any should be base enough to betray Him! But here we find Judas, who had been called to the apostleship, and invested with power to work miracles, and a few hours before had partaken of the holy supper, heading a band of men and officers, which he had obtained from the chief priest and Pharisees, and betraying his Master and Benefactor into their hands with a kiss

—How wonderful was the courage of Jesus, who, though he knew all things that should come upon him, not only remained in the place, but came forth from the retreat, and presented himself. This was the effect of a love stronger than death. Perfect love casteth out fear.

—How wonderful was the rebuke, and the repulse, which his enemies met with. No sooner did he pronounce the words, "I am he," than they went backward, and fell to the ground. Whether some rays of glory broke from his sacred body, or whether he immediately, by his power, impressed their minds, we know not; but surely here was enough to induce them to discontinue the unhallowed enterprise.

—Yet, how wonderful, that in a few moments they rise, and recover heart enough to approach him a second time. So that he asks them again, Whom seek ye? And they said, Jesus of Nazareth. This was partly the influence of numbers. A man alone may be often easily deterred from an evil action. But it is otherwise where hand joins in hand, and the sinner is seen and supported, and stimulated or reproached by his fellow creatures. It shows us, also, the hardening nature of sin. When the men of Sodom were smitten with blindness, they even then groped by the wall to find the house where the heavenly visitants were. Upon the removal of each plague, when Pharaoh saw there was respite, he hardened his heart. And Ahaz, in his affliction, sinned yet more and more against God. And of how many may it be said, "Thou hast stricken them, but they have not grieved; thou hast consumed them, but they have refused to receive correction; they have made their faces harder than a rock; they have refused to return."

Neither means, nor even miracles, will avail, when God leaves a man to himself. Persons often think, that a dreadful event will do what ordinances have failed to accomplish. But we have known many who have been stripped, and reduced, and yet their minds have not been humbled before God. They have resembled fractions of ice, or stone, broken, but not changed, each piece retaining the coldness and hardness of the mass. They think that a spectre would be much more efficacious than a preacher. Vain hope! if they hear not Moses and the prophets, neither would they be persuaded though one rose from the dead.

O thou God of all grace, fulfil in my experience the promise, "A new heart, also, will I give you, and a new spirit will I put within you, and I will take away the stony heart out of your flesh, and I will give you a heart of flesh. And I will put my spirit within you, and cause you to walk in my statutes, and ye shall keep my judgments, and do them."

April 3.—"Jesus answered, I have told you I am he: if therefore ye seek me, let these go their way."—John, xviii, 8.

Here we see the Savior's readiness to suffer. He makes not the least attempt to escape from the hands of his enemies; but tells them a second time that he was the victim they sought after, and yielded himself up to be bound and led away without murmuring or complaint. This willingness was magnified by the greatness of his sufferings, his knowledge of all he was to endure, his deserving it not, but bearing it for others, and his power of escape.

Here we see his tenderness toward his disciples. He would not have them die, or suffer, or at present even be apprehended and alarmed. They were unable to bear it, and could not follow Him now. He has the same heart still, and from this instance of his conduct we may conclude that He will suffer no affliction to befall his disciples, unless for some wise and useful purpose; that He will sympathize with them in their suffering; that He will afford them support and comfort, and in due time wipe away all their tears.

Here, also, we see his authority and dominion over their adversaries. We are mistaken if we suppose that He presented a request when He said, If ye seek me, let these go their way. A request would have been nothing in the present state of their minds, and provided, as they were, with officers, and an armed band of Roman soldiers. It was in the nature and force of a command. It was an absolute injunction. "I will not surrender unless these are allowed to depart. You shall not touch a hair of their head." Accordingly they make not the least objection, and suffer them to retire unmolested.

This was in character with his whole history. In his penury He always displayed his riches; in his deepest abasement He emitted rays of his glory. The manhood was seen; but it was, so to speak, deified humanity. What majesty was combined with the humiliations of his birth, and of his death. Does He here submit? It is a conqueror demanding his own terms, and obtaining them.

And did not this serve to enhance the sin of his disciples in denying and forsaking Him. They were overcome by the fear of man. But what had they to fear? Did they not here see that their enemies were under his control, and could do nothing without his permission? Did He not here obtain for them a passport, insuring their escape and safety? Yet they have not courage and confidence enough to declare themselves on his side, and to stand by Him. And do we not resemble them? How often do we shrink back from the avowal of our principles, or turn aside from the performance of some trying duty? And wherefore? We also yield to the fear of man that bringeth a snare. Yet what can man do unto us? or what can devils do? Satan could not sift Peter, nor touch an article of Job's estate, till leave was granted him. Our foes are all chained, and the extent of their reach is determined by the pleasure of Him who loved us well enough to die for us. If He careth for us it is enough. When shall we realize this, and go on our way rejoicing? If He says to events, "Let that man succeed in his calling," opposition and difficulties are nothing—he gets forward; the blessing of the Lord maketh rich. If He says to sickness, "Touch not that individual," the pestilence may walk in darkness, and the destruction rage at noon-day; a thousand may fall at his right side, and ten thousand at his right hand, it shall not come nigh him. If He has any thing more for us to do or suffer, though life be holden by a rotten thread, that thread is more than cable; we are immortal till our change come.

"Hast thou not given thy word,
"To save my soul from death?
"And I can trust my Lord
"To keep my mortal breath.
"I'll go and come,
"Nor fear to die,
"Till from on high
"Thou call me home."

APRIL 4.—"Christ died for us."—Romans, v, 8.

So have many. All those who have paid their lives to the injured laws of their country, have died for us; and if we derive not improvement from it the fault is our own. The world drowned in the deluge, perished for us. The Jews, whose carcasses fell in the wilderness, suffered, as the apostle tells us, as ensamples and admonitions to us, we have buried friends and relations; but—

"For us they languish, and for us they die."

That husband of *her* youth; that wife of *his* bosom; that child of *their* love, have been removed, to wean their hearts from earth, and to show how frail *they* are. But are we going to rank the death of Christ with such deaths as these? We would rather class it with that of an apostle: "If I be offered," says Paul to the Philippians, "upon the sacrifice and service of your faith, I joy and rejoice with you." This was noble. But was Paul crucified for us?

—No—"It is *Christ* that died." *His* death is peculiar and pre-eminent—infinitely peculiar and pre-eminent. This was indicated by the prodigies that attended it. But on these we shall not enlarge. Neither shall we dwell on the many touching circumstances of his death. Such a tragical representation may be derived from the history as would draw tears from every eye, while the heart may be unaffected with, and the mind even uninformed of, the grand design of his death. What was *this?*

Some tell us, that it was to confirm the truth of his doctrine by the testimony of his blood, and to suffer, leaving us an example, that we should follow his steps. Now this is true, and we believe it as fully as those who will go no further; but the question is, whether this be the whole, or the principal part of the design. We appeal to the Scriptures. There we learn that He died for us as an expiation of our guilt, and to make reconciliation for the sins of the people. There we see, that He died for us, as a sacrifice, a ransom, a substitute; that He redeemed us from the curse of the law, being made a curse for us; that He once suffered for sins, the just for the unjust, that He might bring us unto God. Exclude this, and the language of the Bible becomes perfectly embarrassing and unintellible. Exclude this, and what becomes of the legal sacrifices? They were shadows without a substance; they prefigured nothing; for there is no relation between them and his death, as he was a martyr, and an example; but there is a full conformity between them and his death, as he was an atonement. Exclude this, and how are his sufferings to be accounted for at all? for He did not die for the sins of others, and He had none of his own. Where, then, is the God of judgment? That be far from

Him, to do after this manner, to slay the righteous with the wicked. So far the Jews reasoned well; they rejected Him, for they considered Him stricken, smitten of God, and afflicted. And so He was; but "He was wounded for our transgressions; He was bruised for our iniquities; the chastisement of our peace was upon Him; and with his stripes we are healed. All we, like sheep, have gone astray; we have turned every one to his own way, and the Lord hath laid on Him the iniquity of us all." Exclude this, and with what can we meet the conscience, burdened with guilt? With what can we answer the inquiry, How shall I come before the Lord? With what shall we wipe the tear of godly grief? But we have boldness to enter into the holiest, by the blood of Jesus. Surely He hath borne our grief, and carried our sorrow. His death was an offering and a sacrifice to God, for a sweet-smelling savor. The all-sufficiency and the acceptableness were evinced by his discharge from the grave, and his being received up into glory. There, within the veil, our hope finds anchorage

"Jesus, my great High Priest,
"Offer'd his blood, and died;
"My guilty conscience seeks
"No sacrifice beside:
"His powerful blood did once atone,
"And now it pleads before the throne."

But even this is not all the design. Christ died for us, not only to reconcile, but to renovate; not only to justify, but to sanctify. The one is as necessary to our recovery as the other, and equally flows from the cross. For He gave himself for us, that He might redeem us from all iniquity, and purify unto Himself a peculiar people, zealous of good works.

"Oh! the sweet wonders of that cross,
"Where God, my Savior, groan'd and died!
"My noblest life her spirit draws
"From his dear wounds and bleeding side."

APRIL 5.—"He was buried."—1 Corinthians, xv, 4.

THE resurrection of our Savior necessarily presupposes his death, but not his burial. His burial was an additional thing; and, as his flesh could not see corruption, *seemed* an unnecessary one. But it is worthy of our notice.

Who begged his body for interment? It was Joseph and Nicodemus. And here, can we help remarking these petitioners themselves? Not many wise men after the flesh, not many mighty, not many noble, are called; but these men were of distinguished rank and condition in life. A few of these there have been in every age of the church; sufficient to show, not that the cause of God depends upon *them*, but to redeem religion from the prejudice, that it suits the vulgar only; and, also, to prove the power of divine grace in counteracting temptation. But, down to this period, Joseph and Nicodemus had not been persons of much promise; so far from it, that they were ashamed and afraid to have their regard to our Lord known, when his disciples were professing their resolution to follow him to prison, and to death. Behold the change! The latter, in the hour of trial, forsake Him, and flee; the former come, and openly acknowledge Him. Let us all seek after more grace; but let none trust in themselves, or despise others. "The strong may be as tow," and "the feeble may be as David." The man of whom we now think nothing may acquire confidence and zeal, and not only pass us in the road, but leave us very far behind in attainments and usefulness. "Who hath despised the day of small things?" "A bruised reed shall He not break, and the smoking flax shall He not quench, till He send forth judgment unto victory."

—Who attended as mourners? "The women, also, which came with Him from Galilee, followed after, and beheld the sepulchre, and how his body was laid." With us some days elapse before interment; but here only two hours were allowed between his execution and his burial. If indeed, his body had not been implored by Joseph and Nicodemus, It would have been interred at Golgotha—thrown into a hole, dug under the cross.

—Who carried the sacred corpse we know not; but they had not far to bear it—"for the sepulchre was nigh at hand." This was not a grave of earth, but of stone, and hewn out of a rock. Thus there was only one avenue leading to it; no one, therefore, could approach it from the sides, or behind; and the entrance was watched, guarded, and sealed. It was also a new tomb, in which never man was laid. And here, again, we see the hand of God; for had there been other bodies, some would have pretended collusion, and the evidence could not have been so simple and complete as it now was, when the body lay alone there. Finally, it was not his own. His followers are mad after the honors and riches of the world; but, living and dying, He had not where to lay his head. He was born in another man's house, and was buried in another man's grave.

—But why was He buried at all? First. His burial was an additional confirmation of his death, upon which every thing depended. An examination was made while he was upon the cross; and finding him dead already, they brake not his legs, but a soldier pierced his side, and forthwith came there out blood and water. But now his mouth, and nostrils, and ears, were all filled with the odors and spices—and who can question a man's death when he is buried? Secondly. It was the completion of his humiliation. "They have brought me into the dust of death." "Now, that He ascended, what is it but that He descended first into the lowest parts of the earth?" Thirdly. By this, He sanctified the grave, and prepared it for his people. They would have been afraid to go in, but He entered it before them. They can lie in this bed after Him. He has freed it from every horror. He has softened it, and made it easy for them.

—"And there was Mary Magdalen, and the other Mary, sitting over against the sepulchre." Let us sit by them, and contemplate. *There* lies in that rock He who made it. *There* are sealed up the lips which said, Come unto me, all ye that labor and are heavy laden, and I will give you rest. *There* are closed, the eyes which always beamed compassion, and wept for human wo. *There*, cold, are the hands which were laid on little children, to bless them, and that delivered the widow's son to his mother. *There* lies the Life of the world, and the Hope of Israel. He was fairer than the children of men—He was the image of the invisible God—He went about doing good—He was rich, and, for our sakes, became poor.

"Come, saints, and drop a tear or two,
"For Him who groan'd beneath your load,
"He shed a thousand drops for you,
"A thousand drops of richer blood"

On the tombs of mortals, however illustrious, the humbling sentence is inscribed, "Here he *lies*." But I hear the angel saying, "Come, see the place where the Lord *lay*." He *was* dead—but is alive again—and because He lives, we shall live also.—

"Break off your tears, ye saints, and tell
"How high your great Deliv'rer reigns;
"Sing how He spar'd the hosts of hell,
"And led the monster, Death, in chains.
"Say—'Live for ever, wondrous King!
"Born to redeem, and strong to save.'
"Then ask the monster, 'Where's thy sting!
"And where's thy victory, boasting grave?'"

APRIL 6.—"After that he was seen of above five hundred brethren at once; of whom the greater part remain unto this present; but some are fallen asleep."—1 Corinthians, xv, 6.

As the resurrection of our Lord and Savior is of such unspeakable importance, it cannot be too clearly and fully ascertained. Now the way to prove a fact, is to call in evidence: and if in the mouth of two or three witnesses every word shall be established, what shall we say when we meet such a cloud of witnesses as the apostle here brings forward—witnesses the most competent—eye-witnesses; ear-witnesses; witnesses who even handled the Word of Life—men, not of hasty credence, but slow of heart to believe; men, whose despondence was only to be done away by proof the most undeniable, and upon which they hazarded every thing dear to them, and braved reproach, and suffering, and death.

—This interview took place in Galilee, where our Lord had principally resided, and preached, and done his wonderful works. There He was best known, and chiefly followed. Before his death he had said, "After I am risen again, I will go before you into Galilee." On the morning of his resurrection, we find the angel knew of this design; and, therefore, meeting the women, he said, "Go quickly and tell his disciples that He is risen from the dead; and, behold, He goeth before you into Galilee; there shall ye see Him; lo! I have told you." Influenced by this authority, "the eleven disciples went away into Galilee, into a mountain where Jesus had appointed them." From whence it appears that the very spot had been named. And, from the words of the apostle, it is certain that the disciples did not repair to it alone; but having made known among their connexions the approaching interview with a risen Savior, they enjoyed the privilege in company with this large assembly. "He was seen of above five hundred brethren at once; of whom the greater part remain unto this present; but some are fallen asleep." Every thing here is striking.

The *name*—"Brethren." O, lovely distinction! When will it swallow up every other? When shall the religious world remember that all real Christians, notwithstanding their differences, are all justified by the same blood; sanctified by the same grace; travelling the same way; heirs of the same glory; children of the same Father, of whom the whole family in heaven and earth is named?

The *number*—" Above five hundred." We were not aware that he had so many adherents. In Jerusalem they could only bring together one hundred and twenty. But there were more in the country. Let us not judge of our Lord's followers by a particular place or party. Let us remember that He has his hidden ones, whom circumstances may never bring to our notice. How surprised should we be, if any event was to draw them together from their various retreats. " These, where have they been?" What a multitude, then, which no man can number, will there be, when they shall be all assembled, out of all nations, and kindreds, and people, and tongues?

The *ravages of time*—" Some have fallen asleep." And no wonder in the lapse of six-and-twenty years. Who has not, during such a period, been summoned to the grave to weep there? Whose heart within him has not been desolate at the loss of friends and relations? Even the church has not been a sanctuary from the robber and spoiler. The wise and the good, the holy and the useful, the followers and witnesses of the Redeemer, have finished their course and their testimony, and have slept the sleep of death.

Distinguished preservations—" The greater part remain unto this present." The majority of five hundred spared so many years! when, from the numberless perils of life, it was marvellous that any *one* of them should have lived even a *week*, or a *day!* Have we survived others? Let us not ascribe it to our own care, or the goodness of our constitution, but say, with Caleb, when so many carcasses fell in the wilderness, " The Lord hath kept me alive."

And let us be concerned that protracted life be devoted to Him, who is " the length of our days," and " the God of our salvation."

April 7.—" Thou wilt not leave my soul in hell, neither wilt thou suffer thine Holy One to see corruption. Thou wilt show me the path of life: in thy presence is fullness of joy; at thy right hand there are pleasures for evermore."—Psalm xvi, 10, 11.

Our Lord tells us of many things concerning Himself, not only in the law of Moses, and in the prophets, but in the Psalms. Some have contended that He is immediately regarded in every passage. This error, arising from a noble truth carried too far, has led the holders of it to take liberties with the translation, and with the original too. We may safely follow the applications of the Holy Ghost; and we are sure, from the language of Peter, in the Acts of the Apostles, that, in the words before us, David speaks of the Messiah, or rather introduces the Messiah himself as the speaker.

Jesus knew that he was to suffer and die; but He knew, also, that death could not feed upon Him. He knew He should be laid in the grave; but He knew, also, that He should not remain there. Thou wilt not leave my soul in hell. Hell, here, does not mean the place of the miserable, but the abode of the dead. This He entered, but continued not long enough there for dissolution to commence: " Neither wilt thou suffer thine Holy One to see corruption."

The path of life was his passage from the sepulchre to glory; from the tomb of Joseph to the palace of the great King. This path no one had yet trod. Enoch and Elias had entered heaven, but did not go in from the grave. Thousands had entered heaven, but left their bodies behind; but He did not leave his. He is, therefore, called the first born from the dead, because He was the first that entered heaven after lying in the grave. He was the first born, too, in the dignity and influence of the life He realized. Lazarus, and the widow of Nain's son, and others, though they were revived, died again. But He, being raised from the dead, dieth no more; death hath no more dominion over Him. He lives as no one else ever lived, or ever will live. He lives, having the keys of hell and of death. He lives in the possession of all power in heaven and in earth. He lives as our Head and Representative; as the source of all spiritual influence; as the Father of the everlasting age. And He shall see his seed, and shall prolong his days; and the pleasure of the Lord shall prosper in his hand.

And because He lives, we shall live also. His resurrection is the model, the cause, the proof, and the earnest of our own. For there is a union between Christ and Christians, by which they are federally and vitally one. When, therefore, He died, they were crucified with Him; and when He arose and ascended, they were quickened together with Him, and raised up, and made to sit with Him in the heavenly places. And though their bodies return to the dust, *they* will not see corruption *for ever;* for this corruptible shall put on incorruption, and this mortal shall put on immortality.

The believer, therefore, can also say, Thou wilt show *me* the path of life. This life means the blessedness reserved in heaven for the people of God after the resurrection. David here describes it, In thy presence is fullness of joy; at thy right hand there are pleasures for evermore. It has three characters. The first regards its *source.* It flows from "his presence." He is the fountain of life, and the supreme good of the mind.

The second regards its *plenitude.* It is *fullness* of joy. In this vale of tears every pleasure has its pain, and every comfort its cross. We pursue satisfaction, but we grasp vanity and vexation. We look to Jesus, and find Him the consolation of Israel. But consolation supposes trouble. His followers are described, not only by their rejoicing, but their mourning—without they have fightings, and within they have fears. They have blessed frames, and in some religious exercises they seem to be partakers of the glory that shall be revealed. And so they are; but it is by a glimpse, a taste, a drop—the fullness is above.

The third regards its *permanency.* The pleasures are *for evermore.* Uncertainty, as well as deficiency, attaches to every thing here. We embrace our connexions, and lo! they are gone. We set our hearts on that which is not.

If there was a possibility of the destruction or loss of the blessedness above, we should be miserable in proportion to its greatness. From the moment of knowing it the thought would poison all the fullness of the joy. But no; it is a crown of glory that fadeth not away. It is everlasting life!

April 8.—" If by any means I might attain unto the resurrection of the dead."—Philippians, iii, 11.

Here the subject of consideration is, *the resurrection of the dead!* But it is obvious the apostle does not refer to it as an event; for as an event it will be universal, and we shall be the subjects of it, whether we are willing or unwilling; for there will be " a resurrection of the dead, both of the just and of the unjust." But he refers to it as a privilege. That can hardly be called a deliverance that takes a man out of a bad condition, and consigns him to a worse. What is it for a criminal to be led out of prison to be tried, and condemned, and executed? What is it for the body to be revived and not renovated; inheriting the principles of all the evils entailed upon it by sin, and rendered immortal for the duration of misery. The grave is better than hell. But while some will come forth unto the resurrection of damnation, others will come forth unto the resurrection of life; a resurrection that shall change the vile body, and fashion it like the Savior's own glorious body, and complete all that the Savior has procured for us, and the gospel has promised to us.

With regard to the acquisition of a share in this blessedness, the apostle makes use of language that implies valuation, difficulty, variety, submission: " *If by any means* I might attain unto the resurrection of the dead."

—It implies valuation of the object. Things may be important in themselves, and not prized by those whom they concern. And we see this with regard to the blessings of the gospel; for, though they are as superior to all worldly good as the heavens are higher than the earth, yet men make light of them; and were we to judge of eternal salvation by the regard paid to it by the multitude, we should consider it a trifle unworthy a moment's serious thought. But what is it in the view of awakened souls? The " pilgrim," when leaving the City of Destruction, and implored by his friends and family to return, put his fingers in his ears, and ran, crying, Life! life! eternal life! Such wait for the Lord more than they that watch for the morning. They hunger and thirst after righteousness. They count all things but loss for the excellency of the knowledge of Christ Jesus their Lord. " Every thing," says Paul, " compared with this is nothing." *This* is the prize of my high calling. If I miss it I am undone for ever. If I reach it the possession will realize all my hopes and desires. The very prospect, as I can make it my own, enlivens and cheers me in all my labors and sufferings. " If by any means I might attain unto the resurrection of the dead."

— It implies the difficulty of the acquirement. All excellent things require application and diligence; and he who rationally expects success must be *determined*, and bring his mind to exertion and endurance. What pains and patience are necessary to attain human learning! " There is no royal way to geometry." And is divine wisdom the prey of the idle and careless? Must we labor for the meat that perisheth, and can we, without labor, obtain that meat which endureth unto everlasting life? No, says the Savior, even in the very passage in which He speaks of " giving it;" where it is obvious, therefore, that the giving is not opposed to diligence, but desert. How readest thou? " Strive to enter in at the strait gate." " Work out your salvation with fear and trembling." "Fight the good fight of faith, and lay hold on eternal life." But take those who, in their religion, know nothing of the privations and hardships of the soldier; nothing of the unbending alacrity of the racer; who never redeem their time; whose day is only distinguished from their night by the substitution of sloth for sleep; who exercise no self-denial; who never modify the deeds of the body; whose souls do not follow hard after God; would it not be perfectly absurd for one of these to say, "If by any means I might attain unto the resurrection of the dead?"

—It implies variety in the manner of reaching glory. This does not apply to the procuring of the blessing. This is done already. Jesus said, as He expired, "It is finished." He made peace by the blood of his cross, and brought in everlasting righteousness; and all that believe on Him are justified from all things. At the deluge, people could be drowned any where, but there was only one ark. The way of salvation has been always the same from the beginning; but the methods by which this salvation is applied are various. Various are the means employed in our conversion, and various are the courses of duty in which we actually obtain the promise. All the Lord's people obey; for he is the author of eternal salvation only to them that obey him; but they are called to obey in very different ways. One is required to act the Christian in single, another in relative life. One fills a public station, another a private. Some are to receive with gratitude, others are to give with cheerfulness. Some must discharge the duties of prosperity, others those of adversity. Our sufferings, too, vary, as well as our services. One glorifies God by bearing reproach and persecution, another by enduring bodily pain and infirmities. These have much outward trouble; and those, more inward conflict; each is to take up *his* cross, and to follow the Lamb whithersoever he goeth. For,

Finally, it implies submission; not prescribing, not objecting, but referring every thing to the divine pleasure. "If by any means I might attain unto the resurrection of the dead." Whatever they are, I bow to them. This implicit submission is necessary to evince the earnestness, and even sincerity of our conviction. Dr. Chyne often said to his patients, when they objected to the strictness of his regimen, "I see you are not bad enough for me yet." For if a patient really believes and feels his disease and danger, he will show it by readiness to yield to the remedies the physician enjoins, however trying they may be. Here, indeed, the great contention lies with many. It does not regard the end; they would have heaven but not by *any* means; it must be by those of their own devising or choosing. Are not the rivers of Damascus better than all the waters of Jordan? May I not wash in them and be clean? But when a man is at the point to die—for ever—he will acquiesce in any means of deliverance, however mysterious to his reason, however humiliating to his pride, however adverse to his sin and sloth. God will have the whole management of our case, or he will have nothing to do with it. And He ought to have it; for this submission is an homage due to his sovereignty. We have no claim upon Him; and it is wonderful mercy and grace that he will save and bless us at all. We owe it also to his wisdom and goodness; for though he is a Sovereign, in the exercise of his prerogative he does not act arbitrarily, but does all things well; his work is perfect. The issue, too, is such as to justify our submission to *any* means in securing it. In earthly things, the honey does not always pay for the sting, nor the rose for the thorns. But here the success will infinitely more than remunerate all our services and sacrifices. And the success, also, is sure. How many cases are there in which means, any means, may be used in vain! The race is not always to the swift, nor the battle to the strong. In every department of human enterprise the successful candidates are few. Yea, the event in *no* other pursuit is infallible. But if you are like-minded with Paul, you need not fear the result. The gate of mercy was never yet shut against a returning sinner. Their heart shall live that seek God.

APRIL 9.—"Now, if we be dead with Christ, we believe that we shall also live with him."—Romans, vi, 8.

THE death and the resurrection of Christ constitute the substance of the Gospel; and our concern with them includes more than our admitting them into our creed as doctrinal truths. They must become internal principles, and produce in us corresponding effects. He died, and we must be dead; dead to the law, not as a rule of life, but as a covenant of works. Dead to the world; not as the scene of God's wonderful works, nor as a sphere of duty, or a field of usefulness, but as the enemy of God and our portion. Dead to sin—this includes nothing less than our avoiding it, but it intends much more; we may be alive to it, even while we forsake it. But we must no longer love, or relish it; and *thus* no longer live in it. How shall we that are dead to sin, live any longer therein!

We must be dead *with Him*. We are dead with Him *virtually*. For He is the head and representative of his church, and therefore what He did for his people is considered as done by them. We are dead with Him *efficiently*. For there is an influence derived from his cross which mortifies us to sin, and this influence is not moral only, consisting in the force of argument and motive, though this is true; and nothing shows the evil of sin, or the love of the Savior like Calvary. But it is spiritual also. He died to purify as well as to redeem; and He not only made reconciliation for the sins of the people, but received gifts for men, and secured the agency of the Holy Spirit. There is no real holiness separate from the grace of the cross. There He draws all men unto Him. We are dead with Him as to resemblance. We are planted together in the likeness of his death, and therefore our death is called, as well as his, a crucifixion. "Knowing this, that our old man is crucified with Him, that the body of sin might be destroyed, that henceforth we should not serve sin." I am, says the apostle, not only dead, but crucified with Christ. That mode of dying was a painful one, and a visible one, and a gradual one, and a sure one; for the moment the body was fastened to the cross, it was as good as dead; the bones might be broken to accelerate the event, but it was never taken down alive. All this is easily applied to the crucifying of the flesh, with the affections and lusts.

But He rose, and now lives, and we shall live *with Him*. That is in consequence of his living. Because He lives, we shall live also. For we are quickened together with Christ, and are raised up, and made to sit together in heavenly places. That is, in his company. Where I am, there shall also my servant be. We have much in heaven to endear it. How delightful will it be to join our friends with all their infirmities done away. But to depart, to be with Christ, is far better. That is, in fellowship with Him. We may live with another, and not live like him. We may be with another, and behold his estate, but not share it. But when He who is our life shall appear we also shall appear with Him in glory. I appoint unto you, says He to his disciples, a kingdom, as my Father hath appointed unto me; that ye may eat and drink at my table in my kingdom, and sit on thrones judging the twelve tribes of Israel. Even our vile body shall be fashioned like his own glorious body. And the same duration attaches to his blessedness and ours. I am alive, says he, for ever more, and our end is everlasting life.

Finally, Paul *believed* all this. And let us do the same; but let us believe it *as* he did. That is, let us believe that we shall live with him *if* we be dead with him. Some believe it without this. But their faith is only presumption. Whatever they rely upon, whether their knowledge, or orthodoxy, or talking, or profession, they are only preparing for themselves the most bitter disappointment, if they are not dead unto sin, and delivered from the present evil world; for if any man have not the Spirit of Christ he is none of his.

—But let us also believe, that if we be dead with Him, we *shall* also live with Him. The inclusive is as sure as the exclusive, and takes in every diversity and degree of grace. Whatever be their apprehensions of themselves, none of them all shall come short of this glory. It is as certain as the promise, and oath, and covenant of God, and the death and intercession of the Savior, and the pledges and earnests of immortality, can render it. Therefore be not faithless, but believing. It was used by Christians to animate and encourage each other in the apostles' days, as a common and familiar aphorism; and they gave it full credit. "It is a faithful saying, for if we be dead with Him, we shall also live with Him."

APRIL 10.—"The sufferings of Christ, and the glory that should follow."
1 Peter, i, 11.

CONNECTED with the sufferings of Christ there was a three fold glory.

—There was a glory that *preceded* his sufferings. This is implied in his language—"I came forth from the Father:" "I came down from heaven." But it is expressly mentioned, when He says, "The glory that I had with thee before the world began." What condescension can there be where there is no previous dignity; and what possessions can a being claim before his existence? But He was rich, and for our sakes became poor. He was in the form of God, and thought it no robbery to be equal with God. He took upon Him the form of a servant, and made himself of no reputation.

There was a glory that *accompanied* his sufferings. There is often much parade at the death of a monarch, and, by a show of greatness, an attempt is made to conceal or alleviate the disgrace of real littleness. But what are the suspensions of business, the splendid equipage, the tolling of bells, the solemn music, the discharge of artillery—

"He dies; the heavens in mourning stood."

The sun was darkened; the earth shook; the rocks rent; the graves were opened; the dead arose. Spiritual trophies blended with the prodigies of nature. Peter's heart was broken at a look. The centurion, watching, exclaimed, Surely this man was the Son of God. All the people that came together to that sight smote their breasts and returned. The dying thief believed with the heart, and confessed with the tongue, unto salvation, and received an assurance of an immediate place in Paradise. And what a scene of moral glory was here also displayed—in his readiness to suffer; his apology for his slumbering disciples; the order to Peter to put up his sword; his healing the ear of his enemy's servant; his stipulating for the safety of his apostles; his confessing before Pontius Pilate; his bearing, without resentment, the mocking, the spitting, the scourging; his sympathy with the weeping daughters of Jerusalem, in his way to Calvary; his tender concern for his widowed mother, in his agony on the cross; his prayer for his murderers, "Father, forgive them, for they know not what they do!" Where shall we end? Here Celsus endeavors to turn his glory into shame. Having represented Him as despitefully used, arrayed in purple robes, crowned with thorns, and nailed to the tree, he cries out, in the name of wonder Why, on this occasion at least, does he not act the God, and hurl some signal vengeance on the authors of his insults and anguish? But, O Celsus, He does act the God. Any madman on earth, or fury in hell, is capable of anger, and wrath, and revenge. But to bear the most shocking provocations, and, though commanding the thunder and the flame, forbear to punish, and only pity! If it be the glory of a man to pass by a transgression, and the noblest triumph to overcome evil with good, He died gloriously beyond all example. Yes—says even a Rosseau—If the death of Socrates was the death of a sage, the death of Jesus was the death of a God.

There was also a glory that *followed* his sufferings. From the clouds that had concealed Him, He issues forth, in all the radiance of immortality, declared to be the Son of God with power, by the Spirit of holiness, in his resurrection from the dead. An angel descends, and rolls away the door of the sepulchre, and sits in glory upon it, and shakes the ground, and causes the Roman guards to flee for fear. His disciples are reanimated, and reassembled; to whom, also, He showed Himself alive, after his passion, by many infallible signs, being seen of them forty days, and speaking of things pertaining to the kingdom of God. See Him ascend into heaven, far above all principality and power, and every name that is named, not only in this world, but also in that which is to come. Were there glories on the day of Pentecost? *He* shed forth that which was seen and heard. He filled the apostles with the Holy Ghost, according to his promise, so that they spake with new tongues, and all the people heard, in their own language, the wonderful works of God. And three thousand were converted under one sermon. All the miracles his servants performed were done in his name, and were rays of his glory. The establishment of the Gospel then, and the spread of it since, and every soul called by grace, is a part of the joy set before him, wherein he sees of the travail of his soul, and is satisfied. And, Oh! the glories that are yet to follow—when the nations of them that are saved shall walk in the light of the Lamb—when he shall sprinkle many nations—when all nations shall fall down before him, and all kings shall serve him! And, Oh! the glories that are yet to follow, when his mediation shall be completely accomplished, and he shall come to be glorified in his saints, and admired in all them that believe, and attract every eye, and fill every heart, and employ every tongue, for ever!

Savior Jesus! may I be with thee, where thou art, to behold thy glory!

April 11.—" In that day, saith the Lord of Hosts, shall ye call every man his neighbor under the vine, and under the fig tree,"—Zechariah, iii, 10.

Thus inspiration characterizes the reign of the Messiah. It was to be distinguished by three things.

First. Its *enjoyment*. The very image is delightful. Vines and fig-trees were much prized in the East. They afforded at once delightful fruit for the taste, and refreshing shade from the heat. Persons therefore regaled themselves under their branches and leaves—and thus the expression in time came to signify happiness. And what said our Lord to his disciples? Blessed are your eyes, for they see; and your ears, for they hear. Because Christians do not run to the same excess of riot with others, and turn their back on the pleasures of sin, and the dissipations of the world, many think they are mopish and melancholy. But blessed are the people that know the joyful sound. It was so in the beginning of the Gospel. Wherever it came, it was received as good news, as glad tidings; and it was said of the receivers, that they walked, not only in the fear of the Lord, but in the comforts of the Holy Ghost. It not only relieved but delighted them. It not only tranquillized them, but inspired them with joy unspeakable and full of glory. Have we the same Gospel? Or do we embrace it properly, if, instead of being thus *blessed*, it leaves us in a dungeon of gloom, the victims of sadness, and care, and apprehension?

Second. Is *liberty*. Slaves and captives did not sit under their vines and fig-trees. Nor did proprietors in time of war. When invaded, they were liable to the surprises of the enemy. Then the inhabitants disappeared from these loved, but no longer safe retreats; and longed for the time when, released from perils and alarms, they should go forth with joy, and repose and refresh themselves again. Therefore Rabshakeh, to urge the Jews to a surrender said, "Make an agreement with me by a present, and come out to me; and eat ye every one of his vine and every one of his fig-tree, and drink ye every one the waters of his own cistern." Hence we read, "There was peace all the days of Solomon, and from Dan to Beersheba the people sat every man under his vine and under his fig-tree." But a greater than Soloman is here. In "his days Israel shall be saved, and Judah shall dwell safely." What have his subjects to fear? If God be for us, who can be against us? What shall separate us from the love of God? Who is he that condemneth? It is Christ that died; yea, rather, that is risen again; who is even at the right hand of God; who also maketh intercession for us. Christians may therefore give up themselves to holy confidence. Their souls may dwell at ease. They are free indeed. They are kept by the power of God. They shall never perish, neither shall any pluck them out of his hand. Let them realize this, and feel a peace that passeth all understanding, keeping their hearts and minds through Jesus Christ. Let them say, "I will trust, and not be afraid, for the Lord Jehovah is my strength and my song, he also is become my salvation."

The third is *benevolence*. Ye shall *call* every man *his neighbor* under the vine, and under the fig-tree. There is nothing like selfishness here; they are anxious that others should partake of their privileges. There is no envy here; there is no room for it. Here is enough, not only for ourselves, but for our neighbors; and for all of them. And if we are Christians indeed, our happiness, instead of being impaired by the experience of others, will be increased by it. Let us therefore remember the lepers. They had discovered plenty, and were regaling themselves, while their fellow citizens were perishing with famine in Samaria. But conscience smote them, and "they said one to another, We do not well; this day is a day of good tidings, and we hold our peace; if we tarry till the morning light some mischief will come upon us; now therefore come, that we may go and tell the king's household." Thus the first subjects of Christianity said to the spiritually destitute and dying, "That which we have seen and heard declare we unto you, that ye also may have fellowship with us; and truly our fellowship is with the Father and with his Son Jesus Christ." Cursed be the temper of the elder brother that turned wretched at the tears of joy that bedewed the beard of an aged father, and the ecstacies of a family thrown into transport at the return and reception of the prodigal. Let me resemble, in every feeling of my soul, those happy beings who rejoice in the presence of God over one sinner that repenteth. Let me invite all that come within my reach to that mercy which I have found. Let me say, O taste and see that the Lord is good; blessed is the man that trusteth in him, and do this not only by my lips, but by all my temper and all my conduct, holding forth the word of life.

APRIL 12.—**"Being justified freely by his grace, through the redemption that is in Christ Jesus."—Romans, iii, 24.**

HERE we have an answer to the most important and interesting of all inquiries, "How shall man be just with God?"

To be justified is to be acquitted from the charge brought against us, and absolved from the condemnation with which we were threatened. With regard to us the condemnation was deserved, and the charge was true. This renders the case so difficult and peculiar, and calls for the apostle's developement.

But in exposing the source of the privilege, he seems to use a tautology, "Being justified *freely by his grace*." If it be done freely, it must be of grace; and if it be gracious, it must be free. Yet this is not saying too much. Paul knew that men were proud and vain; and that, as Simon Magus thought of purchasing the Holy Ghost with money, so they, in dealing with God about their souls, wish to be merchants, rather than suppliants, and would buy, while they are compelled to beg. But, surely, if it be not saying too much, it is saying enough. Surely, after this, the freeness and graciousness of the thing cannot be questioned. It is not only free and gracious, as opposed to constraint, but as opposed to worthiness. Merit in a sinner is impossible; *his* desert lies on the other side. *There* he is worthy, and worthy of death. A man who asks a favor may have no claim upon you, but you may also have no demand upon him; and, therefore, though you may justly refuse him, yet you have no right to apprehend and punish him. But God has a right to punish and destroy *us;* and it is of his mercies that *we* are not consumed. It is also free and gracious, as opposed to *desire.* This is undeniable with regard to the constitution and accomplishment of the plan itself, for these long preceded even our being. But is it true with regard to the application of it? The publican prayed, God be merciful to me a sinner, and went down to his house justified. And you sought, and found. But what induced you to seek? A sense of your want of the blessing. But how came you to feel this, after being so long insensible of it? Hearing such a preacher. But who made this preacher, and sent him, and placed him in your way, and applied what he said to your heart? And the same may be asked with regard to any other instrumentality. Go as far back as you please; when you arrive, you will find him there before you, with all his preparations and excitements, and will hear him say as you approach, "Come, for all things are now ready."

"No sinner can be
"Beforehand with thee:
"Thy grace is preventing, almighty, and free."

But the apostle tells us of the medium of the privilege, "Through the redemption that is in Christ Jesus." And it is obvious *he* did not deem this inconsistent with the former. He knew that it was still freely by his grace. It was with God to determine whether the law should take its course, or the penalty be transferred to the surety; for the sentence was, "The soul that sinneth, *it* shall die." It was, therefore, an instance of his sovereign grace to admit a substitute. Besides, if he required reparation, he himself provided the Lamb for a burnt offering. Herein "God hath commended his *love* toward us, in that while we were yet sinners, Christ died for us;" and hence the exclamation, "Herein is love; not that we loved God, but that he loved us, and sent his Son to be the propitiation for our sins." We have an illustration of this in the case of Job's friends. They had displeased God, and yet he was willing that they should be reconciled. *He,* therefore, ordered a proceeding that should be available: "Therefore, take unto you now seven bullocks and seven rams, and go to my servant Job, and offer up for yourselves a burnt offering; and my servant Job shall pray for you; for him will I accept: lest I deal with you after your folly." The sacrifice and the intercession of Job did not *dispose* God to show them mercy, for he prescribed them; but they were the way in which he chose to exercise it. And thus "*He* laid on him the iniquities of us all." "*He* made him, who knew no sin, to be a sin-offering for us, that we might be made the righteousness of God in him." This redemption, therefore, is the effect of his goodness. He loved the Son *because* he laid down his life for us; and highly exalted him, *because* he was obedient unto death, even the death of the cross.

We cannot say too much of God's mercy; this is the origin of all our hopes. But, surely, he had the right to determine the way in which it should be extended toward those who had no claims upon it; and of the propriety of the way, both with regard to himself and us, he was the only competent judge. And, therefore, if he has appointed a way, and revealed it in his word, ignorance, pride, or rebellion only, can lead us to oppose or neglect it, and wretchedness and ruin must be the sure result. If we could not see the reasonableness of the dispensation, yet, if He has declared that it "became him," we should be bound to acquiesce and adore. But we can see that he has herein abounded toward us, in all wisdom and prudence; that here mercy and truth meet together, righteousness and peace kiss each other; that the law is magnified, and made honorable; that sin is condemned in the flesh; that God is just, while he justifieth the ungodly who believeth in Jesus; and that every end that could have been answered by the destruction of the sinner has been equally, better, infinitely better answered by the death of the Savior.

And now what wait we for? We are accepted in the Beloved. Let us come in his name. Let us draw near in full assurance of faith. Let us joy in God, through our Lord Jesus Christ, by whom we have now received the atonement. And let us not conceal, but zealously and gladly make known, the blessedness that has made us free indeed.

April 13.—"Upon one stone shall be seven eyes."—Zechariah, iii, 9.

The Lord Jesus is often called a stone, and seldom without some attribute of distinction. Thus Peter calls him "a living stone," and Isaiah "a tried stone, a precious corner stone, a sure foundation." And here the use of him is announced. He is the basis to sustain the complete salvation of the church of God, which is his house—his temple. Of such a structure how great would be the fall! The crash would be heard beyond the stars. But what can bear up for ever the weight of such an edifice? Our worthiness and works? Our righteousness and strength? Better would the sliding sand, the leaf of autumn, the down of the thistle, support St. Paul's cathedral, or one of the pyramids of Egypt, or the pillars of the earth. But He is infinitely equal to the importance of his station, and whoso believeth on him shall not be ashamed.

But let us observe the notice he was to excite and engage. Upon one stone shall be seven eyes. Seven is not to be taken here literally; it is what the Jews call a perfect number, and is designed to indicate a great multitude. Thus God says, If ye walk contrary to me, I also will walk contrary to you, and will punish you seven times for your iniquities; that is, often and severely. Shall I forgive my brother, says Peter, until seven times?

Let us look at a *little* of the accomplishment. The eye of God was upon him. No finite understanding can conceive the complacency He had in contemplating him, while achieving the redemption of his people, and finishing the work that was given him to do: "In whom," says He, "my soul delighteth."

We read of an innumerable company of angels. The eyes of these were upon him. He was seen of angels. They announced and carolled his birth. They ministered to him in the wilderness.

"Through all his travels here below
'They did his steps attend!
"Oft gaz'd, and wonder'd where at last
"The scene of love would end."

"Around the bloody tree
"They press'd with strong desire,
"That wond'rous sight to see—
"The Lord of life expire;
"And could their eyes have known a tear,
"Had dropp'd it there, in sad surprise."

—The eye of Satan was upon him. He watched him through life, hoping to make a prey of him, as he had done of the first Adam. But here was the Lord from heaven. And he found nothing in him.

—The eyes of men were upon him. Simeon saw him, and wished to see nothing else. Blind Bartimeus saw *him*, and followed him in the way. Judas saw him closely, for three years, and confessed that he had betrayed innocent blood. Pilate saw him judicially, and said, I am pure from the blood of that just man. The centurion watched him in death, and said, This man was the Son of God. And all the people that came together to that sight, beholding the things which were done, smote their breasts, and returned. Mary, his mother, was standing by the cross. *She* saw him; and what were her emotions when she viewed the head that had oft reposed upon her bosom, fall upon his shoulder, and yielding up the ghost! After his resurrection, then were the disciples glad when they saw the Lord. Have not I seen Christ? says Paul: yes, and even at mid-day he shone above the brightness of the sun.

—And, how many thousands and millions have seen him since!—not with the eye of the body, but of the mind; not with the eye of sense, but of faith. Indeed, this—this is the grand essential: "He that seeth the Son, and believeth on him, hath everlasting life." The one single design of the Gospel, and all the ordinances of religion, is to bring the eyes of men to fix upon him; for there is salvation in no other. He, therefore cries, "Behold me! behold me!" Every minister only endeavors to awaken attention to him; saying, with John, "Behold the Lamb of God, that taketh away the sin of the world!"

—Ah! Christians, it is your grief, not that you are so little known and regarded, but that so few eyes are upon him. But more are viewing him than you are aware of. And, soon, Jews shall look upon him whom they have pierced; and Gentiles shall come to his light, and kings to the brightness of his rising. Yea, all kings shall fall down before him, and all nations shall serve him.

—And, in another world, he is all in all. There he draws every eye, and employs every tongue. There his servants shall serve him, and they shall see his face, and his name shall be on their forehead. O glorious hope! It doth not yet appear what we shall be; but this we know, that when he shall appear, we shall be like him, for we shall SEE HIM AS HE IS.

APRIL 14.—"The breath of our nostrils, the anointed of the Lord, was taken in their pits, of whom we said, Under his shadow we shall live among the heathen."—Lamentations, iv, 20.

THE words are spoken of Zedekiah, the last king of Judah. And two things are to be noticed and improved. First, How his people regarded him—they called him "The breath of their nostrils." That is, he seemed as dear and necessary as the air they respired. How prone are we to make too much of creatures. To love them properly is a duty; to over-value them is folly and sin. Yet even Christians are in danger of this, according to the apostle John, "Little children, keep yourselves from idols." And who can cast stones at Zedekiah's subjects? Is there no being who is the breath of our nostrils? Have we never made flesh our arm? Never said of a child, "This same shall comfort us?" Never called gold our hope? What is all sin, but a departure from God; a transferring of that fear, and confidence, and dependance, and homage, to the creature, which are due to the Creator, God over all, blessed for evermore? Religion is nothing but a compliance with the demand—"My son, give *me* thine heart."

Secondly; observe how he disappointed them. They reposed their trust in him, and expected that under his empire they should enjoy security and happiness among the surrounding nations: "We said of him, under his shadow we shall live among the heathen—but he was taken in their pits." Alluding to his unsuccessful effort to escape, when Jerusalem was broken up; "all the men of war fled, and went forth out of the city by night, by the way of the gate between the two walls which was by the king's garden: but the army of the Chaldeans pursued after the king, and overtook Zedekiah in the plains of Jericho; and all his army was scattered from him. Then they took the king, and carried him up unto the king of Babylon to Riblah, in the land of Hamah; where he gave judgment upon him." Thus painfully were their hopes deceived: and their idol, instead of defending and blessing them, was himself bereaved, and blinded, and imprisoned, for life: "And the king of Babylon slew the sons of Zedekiah before his eyes; he slew, also, all the princes of Judah in Riblah. Then he put out the eyes of Zedekiah; and the king of Babylon bound him in chains, and carried him to Babylon, and put him in prison till the day of his death." Thus liable are we to disappointment, when we confide in creatures. "The inhabitant of Maroth looked carefully for good; but evil came down from the Lord unto the gate of Jerusalem." "Behold," says Hezekiah, "for peace I had great bitterness."

The young are peculiarly exposed here, owing to their ignorance and inexperience. Yet the old are not always wise. But we are the authors of our own disappointments. We disregard the notices of history and observation, and the word of truth; and look for that from creatures which they are neither designed nor able to afford. There is no assurance of any of our earthly possessions or enjoyments; they are liable to outward violence; they are corruptible in their qualities; they perish in the using. And there is not only a physical, but a moral uncertainty in their duration: for when we look to them rather than God, God will either take them away, that we may make Him the only strength of our heart, and our portion for ever; or if he leaves them, he will take away the comfort from them, and render them our rebukes. For whatever we make the means of our forsaking or forgetting God, God will make the instrument of chastising us. We may therefore often read our sin in our sufferings; and it will be well if the remnant of Israel no more shall stay upon him that smote them; but shall stay upon the Lord, the Holy One of Israel, in truth.

Many have had reason to say, It is good for me that I have been afflicted. The dispensation that removed a creature introduced them to the God of all grace; and the Valley of Achor became the door of hope. And so it has been, not only in the commencement, but in the progress of the divine life. The Lord's people have been enriched by their worldly losses; and in the failures of human dependence, they have taken a fresh hold of his arm, and said, "I will trust, and not be afraid, for the Lord Jehovah is my strength and my song; He also is become my salvation." When a good man was observed to be as cheerful in adversity as he had been in prosperity, he assigned as the reason, When I had every thing about me, I enjoyed God in all, and now I have nothing, I enjoy all in God. And happy he, who, when he abounds, can say, with the poet,

"To Thee we owe our wealth and friends,
"Our health, and safe abode:
"Thanks to thy name for meaner things;
"But they are not my God."

And who, when he is abased, can say, with the prophet: "Although the fig tree shall not blossom, neither shall fruit be in the vine; the labor of the olive shall fail, and the fields shall yield no meat; the flock shall be cut off from the fold, and there shall be no herd in the stalls; yet I will rejoice in the Lord, I will joy in my salvation."

April 15.—"Then all the disciples forsook him and fled."—Matthew, xxvi, 56.

Let us look at this lamentable fact, in connexion with the disciples, the Savior, and ourselves.

—With regard to the disciples, it shows us their weakness and depravity. They fled from fear; but their fear was needless, for he had stipulated for their safety when he surrendered himself in the garden: "If, therefore, ye seek me, let these go their way; that the saying might be fulfilled, Of them which thou hast given me, I have lost none." They were under great obligations to him. He had done much for them in calling them by his grace, and dignifying them with the apostleship. And he was now going to bleed and die for them. And they had professed a great attachment for him; for when Peter said, Though I should die with thee, I will not deny thee; so said all the disciples, yet they all forsook him, and fled! Lord, what is man! Yet this culpable cowardice was overruled for good. For their declension made their witness, after his resurrection, the more unexceptionably credible; and the weakness of their faith is the strengthening of ours. They were not persons of hasty belief. They had doubted, and, for the time, abandoned the cause, saying, "We trusted it had been he which should have redeemed Israel;" and were repairing to their former home and callings. What could have rallied them, and brought them back, and inspired them with courage to go forth, and bear reproach, and persecution, and death, in his name, but a conviction that nothing could resist!

—With regard to the Savior, this was a part, and a very trying part of his abasement and passion. A friend is born for adversity. Then his presence, his sympathy, his countenance, is peculiarly desirable and necessary. Common humanity says, To him that is afflicted, pity should be showed of his friend. But *he* looked for some to take pity, and there was none, and for comforters, and he found none. These men had been three years with him; they could have borne witness to his freedom from sedition; his innocency; his piety. They could have cheered him by their standing at his side, determined to suffer with him. But one betrayed him, another denied him, and all forsook him, and fled. Behold, and see if ever there was sorrow like unto his sorrow! And he foresaw and foretold this: "Behold, the hour cometh, and is now come, that ye shall be scattered every man to his own, and shall leave me alone." This enhanced his anguish, as he suffered in the apprehension, as well as in the reality; but it also enhanced his love. He was not drawn into any part of his suffering by ignorance or surprise—he knew all—all was before him; but he turned not his back.

—With regard to ourselves, it may teach us not to sink or wonder, if we should be deserted by those from whom we had reason to look for better things. Did not one tell David, "Behold, Ahithopel is among the conspirators with Absalom?" And did not he groan, "It was not an enemy that reproached me; then I could have borne it! neither was it he that hated me that did magnify himself against me; then I would have hid myself from him. But it was thou, a man mine equal, my guide, and mine acquaintance. We took sweet counsel together, and walked unto the house of God in company." Did not Job complain, "My brethren have dealt deceitfully as a brook and as the stream of brooks they pass away, which are blackish by reason of the ice, and wherein the snow is hid; what time they wax warm, they vanish; when it is hot, they are consumed out of their place." Did not Paul say, "At my first answer, no man stood by me, but all men forsook me; I pray God that it may not be laid to their charge?" Above all, consider the Lord Jesus, "lest ye be wearied, and faint in your minds." Is the servant above the master? "Then all the disciples forsook him and fled."

APRIL 16.—"I will not leave you comfortless; I will come to you."—John, xiv, 18.

THESE tender words are part of our Savior's farewell address to his disciples, immediately after the holy supper.

We see in them his kindness. These disciples had shown many defects, and had very little improved any of their advantages; but loving his own who were in the world, he loved them unto the end. They were now going to prove themselves very unworthy, and he foresaw and foretold what, according to their present views and feelings, seemed perfectly incredible to themselves; that they would all forsake him in the hour of trial, notwithstanding their obligations and professions. They were going to leave *him* comfortless, as far as it depended upon them; and to induce him to complain, "I looked for some to take pity, and there was none, and for comforters, and I found none." But, much as they deserved it, "I will not," says he, "leave you comfortless." "I will, not to punish, or upbraid, but to relieve and encourage, I will come to you."

Here, also, we perceive his greatness. When we are going away from our connexions to some distant place, we may speak of our return; but it must be conditionally; for we are not sure of the event; it does not depend upon us, and we ought always to say, "If the Lord will, we shall live, and do this or that." But when we die, we know our return is impossible, and our friends know it, and weep most of all that they will see our faces no more. The dying pastor cannot say to his anxious flock, I will not leave you comfortless; I will come to you, and again feed you with the bread of life. The dying father cannot say to his family, mourning around his bed, I will come again, and provide for you. One of the most touching circumstances in the beautiful lines of Cowper on his mother's picture, is the delusion employed to comfort him.

> "Thy maidens griev'd themselves at my concern,
> "Oft gave me promise of thy quick return:
> "What ardently I wish'd, I long believ'd,
> "And disappointed still, was still deceiv'd.
> "By disappointment ev'ry day beguil'd,
> "Dupe of *to-morrow*, even from a child—
> "Thus many a sad to-morrow, came and went
> "Till, all my stock of infant sorrow spent,
> "I learn'd at last, submission to my lot;
> 'But, though I less deplor'd thee, ne'er forgot."

And the same lesson we must all learn, with regard to every dear delight we here enjoy. The departing Joseph said unto his brethren, "I die: and God will surely visit you." He does not say, I will visit you—he knew he was going the way whence he could not return. But Divinity *here* speaks, as well as friendship. "I will not leave you comfortless; I will come to you." This is the language, not only of foreknowledge, but of sovereign dominion; the language of one who had the keys of hell, and of death; of one who said, No man taketh my life from me; I lay it down of myself—I have power to lay it down, and I have power to take it again. Even death would not interrupt his goodness, nor his entering another world affect his intercourse with his people in this. His presence with them was not confined to his bodily residence. While on earth, he said, "The Son of man, who is in heaven." And now, though in heaven, he is no less on earth. Lo! said he, I am with you alway, even unto the end of the world.

—And can we help perceiving, here, how indispensable he is to the happiness of his people? The disciples were comfortless in the view of his absence; and it is easy to account for this, from their attachment to him, and from the pleasure and profit they had derived from him. We feel, and tremble, and groan, at parting with a friend or relation. What must the feelings of the disciples have been at the thought of losing *him!* They would be left in the world like sheep without their shepherd; like travellers in a wilderness without their guide, like orphans bereaved of the father's care, and the mother's bosom. And what could comfort them, but the promise of himself again? Had he said, I will not leave you comfortless, I will send you riches and honors, princes shall be your friends, and angels your servants; what would all this have been without the assurance, "I will come to you?" But this is sufficient. Here is a resource equal to the exigency; a consolation adequate to all the distress.

The good found in creatures is always finite, and very limited. It is also much dispersed, so that we must apply to many to contribute their part to make up one comfort. The happiness we derive from creatures is like a beggar's garment, it is made up of pieces and patches, and is worth very little after all. But the blessedness we derive from the Savior is single and complete. In him all fullness dwells He is coeval with every period. He is answerable to every condition. He is a physician to heal; a counsellor to plead; a king to govern; a friend to sympathize; a father to provide. He is a foundation to sustain; a root to enliven; a fountain to refresh. He is the shadow from the heat; the bread of life; the morning star; the sun of righteousness; all, and in all. No creature can be a substitute for him; but he can supply the place of every creature. He is all my salvation, and all my desire; my hope, my peace, my life, my glory, and joy.

Whom have I in heaven but thee? and there is none upon earth that I desire beside thee. My flesh and my heart faileth, but thou art the strength of my heart, and my portion for ever. I cannot be exposed; I cannot be friendless; I cannot be poor; I cannot be fearful; I cannot be sorrowful, with thee.

"If thou, my Jesus, still art nigh,
"Cheerful I live, and cheerful die;
"Secure, when mortal comforts flee,
"To find ten thousand worlds in thee."

APRIL 17.—"Behold, I will engrave the graving thereof, saith the Lord of hosts."—Zechariah, iii, 9.

THAT is of the stone, upon which were to be seven eyes, and which intends the Messiah, the foundation laid in Zion.

To engrave, is to pierce and cut. When he became a man of sorrows, when he said, Reproach hath broken my heart; when he gave his back to the smiters, and his cheek to them that plucked off the hair; when the crown of thorns entered his temples, and the nails his hands and feet, and the spear his side—then, O my soul, was this Scripture fulfilled.

As there is no engraving without wounding, so to engrave is to embellish and beautify. And he was made perfect through suffering. Hence, "I do cures," said he, "to-day and to-morrow, and the third day I shall be perfected." Hence he calls the season of his passion the hour in which he was to be "glorified." Hence he adds, "Now is the judgment of this world; now shall the prince of this world be cast out; and I, if I be lifted up from the earth, will draw all men unto me." And the richest display of his graces, and the acquirement of the dispensation of the Spirit; and the dominion he exercises in our nature; and the prerogative of judging the world in righteousness; and the praises he will inhabit through eternal ages—all these resulted from his sufferings, according to the language of divine prophecy and history: "When thou shalt make his soul an offering for sin, he shall see his seed, he shall prolong his days, and the pleasure of the Lord shall prosper in his hand. He shall see of the travail of his soul, and shall be satisfied. By his knowledge shall my righteous servant justify many, for he shall bear their iniquity." "Because he was obedient unto death, even the death of the cross, therefore God hath highly exalted him, and given him a name above every name."

And as is the heavenly, such are they also that are heavenly. To a person unacquainted with the process, the pruning of the tree, the cleaving of the ground with the ploughshare, the operation of the chisel on the stone, would look like an effort to injure or destroy. But look at the thing afterward. Behold the vine, adorned with purple clusters. Survey the field, yielding the blade, the ear, the full corn in the ear. Examine the carved work when the sculptor has achieved his design, and fixed it in the proper place!

Christians are sometimes perplexed, and discouraged, because of their trials. They know not what God is doing with them. They fear he is angry, and going to crush and destroy. But they are his workmanship. He is preparing them for their destination in the temple of his grace. These trials are applied to qualify and advance them, and will all perfect that which concerneth them. Howard was taken by the enemy, and confined in prison. There he learned the heart of a captive; and this experience, originating in his suffering, excited and directed his thoughts, and led him into all his extraordinary course of usefulness and fame. It is good for me, says David, that I have been afflicted. I know, says Paul, that this shall turn to my salvation. For our light affliction, which is but for a moment, worketh for us a far more exceeding and eternal weight of glory.

April 18.—"Another parable spake he unto them: The kingdom of heaven is like unto leaven, which a woman took, and hid in three measures of meal, till the whole was leavened."—Matthew, xiii, 33.

We may consider the kingdom of heaven as intending the empire of the Gospel in the world; and also the empire of grace in the heart. Let us confine our attention to the latter.

The leaven in the meal is a foreign importation. It is not naturally in the meal, nor derived from it. It is the same with divine grace. Though it resides in us, it does not arise from us; for in our natural state dwelleth no good thing. It is altogether a new production, and so alien is it from the man himself, who is the subject of it, that the introduction of the principle occasions a ferment, or contest, that lasts for life; the flesh lusting against the Spirit, and the Spirit against the flesh.

The leaven in the meal is active and operating. There it works, and evinces it residence by its agency. And the grace of God, is this a dead, powerless thing? Is it a notion, or a principle? We read of the work of faith, the labor of love, the patience of hope. The same may be said of repentance: "What carefulness it *wrought* in you! yea, what zeal! yea, what revenge!" I will show thee, says James, my faith by my works: I will show thee the sun by its shining, and the spring by the streams. Faith justifies the soul, but works justify faith, and prove it to be of the operation of God.

The leaven is assimilating. It converts, it changes; not by destroying the substance of the meal, but the quality, communicating its own property, tincture, relish. It is the same here. We are transformed by the renewing of the mind. The man remains physically the same as he was before; the same in his relations, talents, condition, business. Yet he is another man; a new man. He is evangeized. He has something of the holy and heavenly nature of divine truth in him. If the grace of God be light, it enlightens him. If salt, it seasons him. If glory, it glorifies him. If leaven, it leavens him.

The operation of the leaven is gradual. The effect in the meal is not produced at once, but by degrees. And do we not read of being renewed day by day? of going from strength to strength? of being changed into the same image, from glory to glory, as by the Spirit of the Lord? The work would want the evidence of analogy, if it were instantaneous. In the family we see children becoming young men, and young men becoming fathers. In the field, we see first the blade, then the ear, and after that the full corn in the ear. Some are not sensible of their religious advancement; and the reason is, they judge by the growing rather than by the growth. The one escapes us, the other is perceptible. Were you to stand by the side of the most rapidly growing plant, you would not see it grow, but you would see when it was grown. Thus judge yourselves, and see whether there is not an increase in your convictions of sin, and the vanity of the world, and the preciousness of the Savior. Thus look at your dispositions, your dependence, your taste, your diligence, your self-denial, in the service and ways of God.

The influence of the leaven is diffusive. Commencing from the centre, it reaches, in due time, to the extremities, and penetrates every particle of the meal. The grace of God is lodged in the heart; but it is not confined there. It reaches all the powers of the man's mind and all the senses of his body. It enters all his situations and circumstances in life. It affects him in the field, in the shop, in the family, in all his connections, in all his civil and common actions, and whether he eats, or drinks, or whatever he does, he does all to the glory of God. And, as the leaven ultimately attains its object, and leavens the whole, so here the issue of the grace of God will be universal and complete holiness. It will sanctify us wholly, body, soul, and spirit. It will perfect that which concerneth us, and the result is sure, even now. How small soever the leaven is, compared with the mass, the less will prevail, and subdue the greater. The dawn will chase away the night, and blaze in full day. "He which hath begun a good work will perform it." Let us not despise, therefore, the day of small things, either in ourselves or others.

April 19.—"We ought to lay down our lives for the brethren."
1 John, iii, 16

In the beginning of the Gospel this test of love was frequently required: and Christians not only dared to be companions of them that suffered, but were ready to suffer for them. So Paul testifies of Priscilla and Aquila, his helpers in Christ: "Who," says he, "have for my life laid down their own necks; unto whom not only I give thanks, but also all the churches of the Gentiles." It is well the providence of God does not call us to such a severe trial. But surely the principle requires us to be ready to do *every thing in our power* on their behalf: and will not allow us to refuse any *service* or *sacrifice* for our brethren, however *arduous*.

We may do much for their minds; by dissipating their doubts, removing their fears, and bringing them comfort in their spiritual distresses. Thus Jonathan went to David in the wood, and strengthened his hand in God. Ointment and perfume rejoice the heart, so doth a man his friend by hearty counsel. A Christian is self-suspicious, and is afraid of every conclusion in his own favor drawn by himself; he sees not the consolation to which he is entitled, though so near him—But another, like the angel to Hagar, may open his eyes, and show him the well. Sometimes he is cast down, supposing many things are peculiar to himself; especially those painful feelings which arise from the assaults of Satan, and his conduct with in-dwelling sin, more and more of which he is continually discovering. But you can relieve him, by opening your own experience, and letting him know that it is so with you. There is another important case: "Brethren, if a man be overtaken in a fault, ye which are spiritual, restore such a one in the spirit of meekness; considering thyself, lest thou also be tempted."

What can be dearer to man than reputation? A good name is rather to be chosen than great riches: but it may be injured various ways. And surely we ought to be alive to a brother's character; and willingly throw ourselves between him and the strife of tongues. When any thing is said to his disparagement, we should show that charity which rejoiceth not in iniquity, but hopeth all things. We should frown away the slander of insinuation. We should not allow a relater to go on, without inquiring whether he will allow us to name it to the person aggrieved, or the person from whom he affirms to have derived it. What a world of calumny and mischief would this prevent! He that helps not in the circulation of the report, yet, if he pleasingly, or even patiently, sits to hear it, shares half the blame; and, as Dr. South says, the tale-bearer and the tale-hearer should be both hanged up, back to back, only the one by the tongue, and the other by the ear.

The body may need help. And our Savior bore our infirmities, and sicknesses, by compassion and sympathy. *His* commiseration could bear them away from the sufferers. We cannot perform miracles. But we may be useful by medical aid, and by personal attendance, and succor. And where the malady cannot be removed, the enduring may be alleviated. Is it nothing to the patient that you visit him in his affliction? that he sees you at the side of the bed of languishing? that, by your tears and prayers, you are answering to the address—Pity me, pity me, O ye my friends! for the hand of God hath touched me?

The state of our brethren may call for assistance; and is to be relieved according to our ability. It will be as base in us as unprofitable to them, to say, Depart in peace; be ye warmed and filled, while we give them not those things which are needful to the body. "Whoso hath this world's good, and seeth his brother have need, and shutteth up his bowels of compassion from him, how dwelleth the love of God in him?" Job could say, The blessing of him that was ready to perish came upon me, and I caused the widow's heart to sing for joy. It was the saying of our Lord, It is more blessed to give than to receive. It was the glory of Christianity, in its first powerful effect, that none who embraced it "lacked." As glory in heaven, and as grace on earth, so the blessings of providence were free, and open to all. The property of Christians went along with their affections; "and distribution was made to every one as he had need." And so tender were they of each other, that "the multitude of them that believed were of one heart and of one soul: neither said any of them that aught of the things which he possessed was his own; but they had all things common." "O, this is no rule for us." Well; take it, and interpret it in your own way. Yet will not what even you infer from it as a duty, include much more than is now found in the temper and practice of Christians? "But we are not able." This is commonly the language of those who *are* able, but not willing. Some *incapacitate* themselves. A decent distinction above the vulgar will not satisfy them: they must be splendid in dress, and luxurious in table, and magnificent in furniture. Others are disabled by hoarding. If accumulation be not condemned by Christianity, the extent of it is. A man may decently provide for his family, without wishing to leave them in the snares of affluence, and with a heap, which if they do not dissipate by vice and excess, they are likely only to be concerned to enlarge. And may not persons increase their powers of beneficence, by diligence, and economy, and *self-denial?* And is not self-denial the first lesson in the school of Christ? And you know the grace of Him, who, though he was rich, yet for your sakes he became poor, that you, through his poverty, might be rich. "WE OUGHT TO LAY DOWN OUR LIVES FOR THE BRETHREN."

APRIL 20.—" And being in an agony, he prayed more earnestly."—Luke, xxii, 44.

AND what must this agony have been, when it is added, that "his sweat was as it were great drops of blood falling down to the ground?" What, my soul, could have caused this?

"Oh! what wonders love has done!
"But how little understood;
"God well knew, and God alone,
"What produced that sweat of blood
"Who can thy deep wonders see,
"Wonderful Gethsemane?"

—But let us now observe his deportment. For we are not only to view him as our mediator in his passion, but as also suffering for us, to leave us an example that we should follow his steps: "In his agony he prayed more earnestly." Not that he was cold and formal before in his devotions; but as the hour and power of darkness advanced, and he began to be sore amazed, and very heavy, and his soul was exceeding sorrowful, even unto death; there was more excitement in his feelings, and vehemency in his manner of expression. Now were the days of his flesh, in which, with strong cryings and tears, he made supplications to Him who was able to save him from death. So it is to be with us. Prayer is never out of season. We see this in his life. On what occasion did not he pray? But there is a time when it is specially seasonable. Therefore, says God, "Call upon me in the day of trouble." "Is any afflicted? Let him pray." Prayer is the design, the refuge, the solace, the improvement of affliction; and the greater the distress and anguish we are in, the more necessary will it be, both for our satisfaction and support. Let us, therefore, be the more importunate. In the greatness of our distress,

—Let us not, like Adam and Eve, flee, and endeavor to hide ourselves from God, but pray.

—Let us not, like Cain, begin to build, and try, by worldly objects, to dissipate our grief, but pray.

—Let us not, like Jonah, fret under the loss of our gourds, and tell God himself, that we do well to be angry, even unto death, but pray.

—Let us not, like Ephraim and Judah, repair to creatures: "When Ephraim saw his sickness, and Judah saw his wounds, then went Ephraim to the Assyrian, and sent to King Jareb; yet could not he heal them, or cure them of their wound," but pray.

—Let us not, like Saul, who went to the witch of Endor, repair to the devil himself, by error, drunkenness, and sin, but pray.

—Let us not, like Ahithophel and Judas, have recourse to suicide, and plunge into hell for relief, but pray, saying, with the Church, "Come, and let us return unto the Lord; for he hath torn, and he will heal us: he hath smitten, and he will bind us up;" or, with Job, "Though he slay me, yet will I trust in *Him*."

"I seem forsaken and alone,
"I hear the lions roar;
"And every door is shut, but one,
"And that is Mercy's door.

"*There*, till the dear Deliv'rer comes,
"I'll wait with humble pray'r:
"And when he calls his exile home,
"The Lord shall find me *there*"

APRIL 21.—**"Fear not ye; for I know that ye seek Jesus which was crucified."—Matthew, xxviii, 5.**

THIS was the address of an angel to Mary Magdalene, and the other Mary, that had come to see the sepulchre before break of day They were last at the cross, and first at the tomb. Favors are given sovereignly by the Lord, but honor is conferred according to a rule; and the rule is this: "Them that honor me, I will honor." These women were informed of his resurrection before the apostles; the apostles received the intelligence from them, but they received it from an angel. At first these pious visitants were afraid. And what wonder when we consider that they were females; that all their sensibilities were alive; that they were in another's garden; that they were alone; that the earth was reeling under them; that the guards were fleeing, and perhaps shrieking; that it was early in the morning, and the remaining darkness rendered more visible and awful the divine messenger sitting at the door of the tomb—his countenance as lightning, and his raiment white as snow! But, says the angel, "*You* have nothing to apprehend from *me*. He is my master, as well as your Savior. I serve him whom ye seek; and having attended his resurrection, I now announce it to you. He is not here; he is risen, as he said; step forward; come, see the place where the Lord lay."

And it is true, in its most extended application, that they who seek Jesus Christ which was crucified, have really nothing to fear, whatever at first may dismay them. But who are entitled to this assurance? Do you feel your need of him as once you did not, for all the purposes of salvation? Have you desires after him so peculiar that nothing else can satisfy them; so powerful as to make you willing to part with whatever stands in competition with him? Are you determined to press through all difficulties, and be found in the use of all means which he has appointed? Are you submissively asking, Lord, what wilt thou have me to do? depending on the aid of his Holy Spirit? and looking for his mercy unto eternal life? If you can answer these questions in the affirmative, *I know that ye seek Jesus which was crucified.*

—And I also know, that ye have nothing to *fear*. "Fear not *ye*." Fear not that you have a graceless heart; the very seeking is a token for good. It cannot be the effect of nature; that which is of the flesh, is flesh; but that which is of the Spirit, is spirit. They that are after the flesh, do mind the things of the flesh; but they that are after the Spirit, the things of the Spirit. Fear not that your search will be successless. Had he a mind to kill you he would not have shown you such things as these. His aim in making you sensible of your condition, was not to render you miserable, but to endear himself, and to draw forth your souls after him. You shall not be disappointed. You may be tried, but he will appear to your joy. Did any ever seek him in vain? Can he deny himself? They that sow in tears shall reap in joy. Blessed are they that do hunger and thirst after righteousness, for they shall be filled. Fear not that you shall fall under the power of any evil. From what are you not secured? Is it temporal want? The young lions may lack, and suffer hunger; but they that seek the Lord shall not want any good thing. Is it the penalty of the law? He has redeemed you from the curse of the law, having been made a curse for you. Is it sin? Sin shall not have dominion over you; for ye are not under the law, but under grace. Is it the world? This is the victory that overcometh the world; even our faith. Is it Satan? The God of peace will bruise Satan under your feet shortly. Is it death? He has abolished death. O death, where is thy sting? O grave, where is thy victory? "Nay, in all these things we are more than conquerors, through him that loved us. For I am persuaded, that neither death, nor life, nor angels, nor principalities, nor powers, nor things present, nor things to come, nor height, nor depth, nor any other creature, shall be able to separate us from the love of God, which is in Christ Jesus our Lord."

APRIL 22.—" And it came to pass, when the ark set forward, that Moses said, Rise up, Lord, and let thine enemies be scattered; and let them that hate thee flee before thee. And when it rested, he said, Return, O Lord, unto the many thousands of Israel."—Numbers, x, 35, 36.

WE might have expected that Aaron would have done this, as he was the high priest. But Moses was the leader and commander of the people, and he was not offering sacrifice, or burning incense, in which he would have offended; but performing a duty of natural, as well as revealed religion. This is binding upon all, and especially upon public men. Thus Solomon, though a king, kneeled on a scaffold of wood at the dedication of the temple, and led himself the prayers of the nation. Princes, officers, magistrates, masters of families, should all be men of prayer. Relative, as well as personal claims, press on them.

It would seem that Moses always, on those occasions, employed the same terms. Our Lord, also, in the garden, prayed three times, saying the same words. It is obvious from hence, that whatever advantages extemporaneous prayer possesses, and it has many, yet forms of prayer cannot be in themselves improper, in public or in private.

As Moses thus addressed God at the commencement and the conclusion of every march, does it not behoove us to acknowledge Him in all our ways? and with prayer to begin and end every day? every meal? every ordinance? every enterprise? every journey? every going out, and every coming in?

Especially let us think of these short and sublime addresses in our travelling heavenward through this wilderness world.

Here is the marching prayer, "Rise up, Lord, and let thine enemies be scattered; and let them that hate thee flee before thee." That is, "Before we move we commend ourselves to thy guidance, and guardian care, and almighty agency. We are passing, not only through strange, but hostile regions. There are foes, open or concealed, which would hinder our progress, rob us, wound us, destroy us. But we are thy charge, and engaged in thy cause. They that hate us, hate thee; our enemies are *thy* enemies. And, formidable as they are, Thou canst as easily vanquish them, as the sun rising in his strength can disperse the shadows that seem to oppose his march." Let us realize this, and we shall feel enough to animate us to go forward, though men, though devils beset our path. "The Lord is my light and my salvation, whom shall I fear? The Lord is the strength of my life, of whom shall I be afraid? Though a host should encamp against me, my heart shall not fear; though war should rise against me, in this will I be confident."

Here is the resting prayer, "Return, O Lord, unto the many thousands of Israel." That is, "If *Thou* goest on, in vain we are left. What can we do without thee in our encampment, any more than in our march? Thy presence is our security, our treasure, our glory, our joy. What is any station without thee? How can its duties be discharged? its trials be endured? its comforts be sanctified? But every residence with thee is ennobled and blessed." Heaven is only the tabernacle of God with men. Thus the two disciples, when the Lord made as if he would have gone further, constrained him, saying, It is toward evening, and the day is far spent; and did he refuse? He went in to tarry with them. Do we thus prize him? Do we thus pray that he would go where we would go, and dwell where we dwell? If not, we have a poor prospect before us. If we *can* live without God with us in this world, we *must* live without him in another. But if our souls cleave to Him, and cry, "Cast me not away from thy presence, and take not thy Holy Spirit from me," we may rejoice in the promise, "I will never leave thee nor forsake thee."

—But let me not here overlook two things. First, the number of his people, "The many thousands of Israel." "For," unless we send out ignorance and bigotry to count them, "who can count the dust of Jacob, and the number of the fourth part of Israel?" And the Lord added to his people, how many soever they be, a thousand fold! Secondly; We shall be concerned for the whole Israel of God. We are parts of them, and they all belong to us. They are all fellow citizens of the same community; branches of the same household; members of the same body. They are more intimately related, and ought to be more endeared to us, than any earthly friends, or natural relations—Pray, therefore, for the peace of Jerusalem. For your brethren and companions' sakes, say, Peace be within thy walls, and prosperity within thy palaces. "Return, O Lord"—not unto our family, or tribe; not unto the thousands of episcopalians, or dissenters—but "unto the many thousands of Israel." "Grace be with all them that love our Lord Jesus Christ in sincerity." And, "As many as walk according to this rule, peace be on them and mercy, and upon the Israel of God."

APRIL 23.—"From the end of the earth will I cry unto thee, when my heart is overwhelmed: lead me to the Rock that is higher than I. For thou hast been a shelter for me, and a strong tower from the enemy."—Psalm lxi, 2, 3.

HE does us the most important service who instructs us to pray. We may here learn much from the example of David.

—*How* would he pray? "I will *cry* unto thee." Crying is a substitute for speech; and also the expression of earnestness. A child can cry, long before it can articulate; and its cries as much move the parent as any eloquence of words. A person in great danger, or want, or pain, not only utters himself, but cries out, and often aloud, according to the pressure of his feelings. Let me pray as I can. I may not be able to express my desires as some do; but, if I am deeply affected by them, and they spring from a broken heart and a contrite spirit, they shall not be despised.

—*Where* would he pray? "*From the end of the earth* will I cry unto thee." He means any condition, however desolate, or distant —distance of place being put for greatness of extremity. Sometimes we may be thrown into situations the most trying, and remote from human aid; but wherever we are, God is *there*, to hear and succor us. Thus Joseph found him, when sold into Egypt; and John, when he was exiled in Patmos; and Paul, when tossed far off upon the sea. We are as near the throne of grace in one place as another. Prayer can reach Him, wherever we are, in a moment, in the twinkling of an eye. "While they speak I will answer; and before they speak I will hear."

—*When* would he pray? "When my *heart is overwhelmed.*" Not that he would restrain prayer at other times; we are to pray without ceasing. It is the character of a hypocrite, that he will not always call upon God. There are birds that only make a noise at the approach of bad weather; and there are persons who only pour out a prayer when God's chastening hand is upon them. But what should we think of a neighbor, or friend, who never called upon us but when he wanted to borrow or beg? Yet what is always proper, may be sometimes peculiarly seasonable, natural, and necessary. And this is the case when we are in trouble and affliction. Therefore, says God, Call upon me in the day of trouble. The answer will, in due time, relieve and deliver. The exercise will immediately soothe and sanctify. Is any afflicted? Let him pray.

—*For what* would he pray? "*Lead me to the Rock that is higher than I.*" What means he by this Rock, but something which could afford him support, when he was ready to be swallowed up? the perfections of Jehovah; the everlasting covenant; the doctrine of providence; the Lord Jesus, who is our hope. This is the rest, and this is the refreshing. And yet, when the relief is provided and when we see it too, we cannot reach it of ourselves. We need a divine agency to conduct us to it. We live in the Spirit, and walk in the Spirit.

—*Whence* does he derive his encouragement to pray? "For thou *hast been* a shelter for me, and a strong tower from the enemy." Nothing can be more confirming and exciting, than the review of God's former interpositions on our behalf; and to reason from what he has been, to what he will be, and from what he has done, to what he will do. For he is the same yesterday, to-day, and for ever. And they that know his name will put their trust in him.

"His love, in time past,
"Forbids me to think
"He'll leave me, at last,
"In trouble to sink.

"Each sweet Ebenezer
"I have in review,
"Confirms his good pleasure
"To guide me quite through."

APRIL 24.—"But now they are hid from thine eyes."—Luke, xix, 42.

WHEN Pharaoh saw there was respite, he hardened his heart. Solomon tells us, Because sentence against an evil work is not executed speedily, therefore the hearts of the sons of men are fully set in them to do evil. But God's keeping silence is not approbation. His long-suffering is not even connivance. Cannot he be merciful unless he allows us to trifle and insult him for ever? His patience has its rules and its bounds. And Jerusalem knew this.

—Much has been said on what is termed a day of grace; and much which we neither admire nor believe. We are not authorized to say any one is beyond hope, while he is yet in life. Manasseh would have seemed very likely to be such a desperate character; but *he* obtained mercy.

"And while the lamp holds out to burn,
"The vilest sinner may return."

If we cannot view any of our fellow creatures as beyond the possibility of salvation, so we have no rule by which we can absolutely determine against ourselves. Yet there are several things of fearful import, to which we do well to attend.

First. The language of the word of God is fearful. "Ephraim is joined to idols; let him alone." "Israel would none of me; so I gave them up to their own hearts' lust." "In thy filthiness is lewdness: because I have purged thee, and thou wast not purged, thou shalt not be purged from thy filthiness any more, till I have caused my fury to rest upon thee." "If we sin wilfully after that we have received the knowledge of the truth, there remaineth no more sacrifice for sins: but a certain fearful looking-for of judgment and fiery indignation, which shall devour the adversaries." "Because I have called, and ye refused; I have stretched out my hand, and no man regarded; but ye have set at nought all my counsel, and would none of my reproof; I also will laugh at your calamity; I will mock when your fear cometh." "Behold, now is the accepted time; behold, now is the day of salvation." We offer no commentary on these passages—but, surely, their language is fearful.

Secondly. We know that final impenitency is irrecoverably hopeless; and *with life* all our opportunities end; and this is fearful. It would not be kindness, but cruelty, to flatter men with a contrary expectation. Search the Scripture, and you will always find a difference between the present and the future. One is a state of trial, the other of decision. The one is sowing, the other reaping; and whatsoever a man soweth that shall he also reap. Is not this sufficient to induce us to seek the Lord while he may be found, and to call upon him while he is near?

Thirdly. This life, upon which every thing depends, is very brief—this is fearful. Look at the images of Scripture; a flower of the field, a flood, a watch in the night, a dream, a vapor. Consider the deaths that come under your own observation. Observe the frailty of your frame. Remember the numberless diseases and accidents to which you are exposed. Think of your pulse, where the question is asked sixty times every minute, whether you shall live or die, and then you may well exclaim,

"Great God! on what a slender thread
"Hangs everlasting things!
"The eternal state of all the dead
"Upon life's feeble strings!"

Fourthly. Our continuance here is as uncertain as it is short—this is fearful. "I have not had," said a good man, "a to-morrow for years." It would be well if we had not. Indeed, we have not in *reality*, whatever we may have in imagination. "Boast not thyself of to-morrow, for thou knowest not what a day may bring forth."

Fifthly. Before this short and uncertain period terminates, many opportunities and advantages may elapse, to return no more—this is fearful. Many convictions may die away, no more to be renewed again unto repentance. We may be deprived of reason, and religion can only operate through the medium of that. Old age helps on insensibility, and before we are aware, though unpardoned and unrenewed, we may become incapable of a moral change. The Gospel may be removed from us. We may be placed where it is not in our power to attend it. We may become deaf, or blind. Sickness may confine us to a room of pain, or a bed of languishing. The influences necessary to render the means of grace effectual may be withholden. Though Paul plants, and Apollos waters, God alone gives the increase; and though we can do nothing to deserve his grace, we may provoke his anger, and he may judicially give us up. The heart is hardened through the deceitfulness of sin, and no less so by familiarity with divine things. And is not this the case with many? Once their consciences smote them. They dropped a tear upon their Bible. When walking alone, among the works of God, they prayed, "Lord, I am thine; save me." But Felix no more trembles, and neglects to send for Paul. And the Gadarenes have besought the healer of their neighbors, and the reprover of their sin, to depart out of their coasts.

April 25.—" And in the morning, rising up a great while before day, he went out, and departed into a solitary place, and there prayed."—Mark, i, 35.

And yet he had been greatly occupied the whole of the day preceding this. We think little of time, but he never passed an idle hour. The whole of his life said, I must work the works of Him that sent me, while it is yet day; the night cometh wherein no man can work. He was really a man; he took our infirmities; and wearied nature required repose: but he distinguished between the necessary and the needless; and even between refreshment and indulgence; and while he enjoined self-denial upon his disciples, as the very first lesson in his school, " He pleased not himself."

It is allowed, that as to the measure of sleep, no one rule can be laid down for all. Some require more than others. But it is questionable whether they require *much* more. Yea, it may be questioned whether they require *any* more as to *length*. What they want more of is better sleep; and the quality would be improved by lessening the quantity. Let those who are now so wakeful, and restless, and can only sleep sound when they ought to be rising, let them try the experiment, and see whether a few hours of sweet and solid sleep be not preferable to the protraction of being bed-ridden, rather than of enjoying repose.

We should also inquire too, whether we have not produced the habit itself that *now* demands so much to satisfy it. If so, we are accountable for the cause as well as the effect.

—We should also be always fearful and suspicious when our reasonings and pleadings are on the side of gratification and ease. It is here, where nothing sinful is thought of, and no danger appears; it is here, we peculiarly need the admonition, Watch and pray, lest ye enter into temptation. The spirit indeed is willing, but the flesh is weak.

—Some live only to do evil. We do not wish *them* to rise early—they are only harmless while they sleep.

—Some live a life of mere indolence and ease. They are indeed free from vice, but they have no useful employment. It is of little importance at what time *they* rise. There is very little difference between their sleeping and wakeful hours. The one is as barren as the other of any active endeavors to glorify God, or serve their generation, or work out their own salvation.

But surely there are some who feel that life is infinitely important; who know that they are placed here to gain good, and to do good; who remember that the only opportunities they have for both are short and uncertain. Surely these will say, Let us not sleep as do others. Surely these will feel the excitement and reproach. It is high time to awake out of sleep. They that sleep, sleep in the *night*.

—In a word, has not early rising every recommendation? Is it not *physically* advantageous? Is it not better for health? Consult your strength, your appetite, your nerves, your spirits, your complexion. Ask your physician. Is there a medical man upon earth that would risk his reputation by a contrary opinion? Sinclair, in his volumes on health and longevity, remarks, that though those who lived to a very great age differed in many things, they all resembled each other here. There was not one of them but rose early.

—Is it not as desirable to our *civil* concerns? What an advantage has a tradesman by early rising, in planning and arranging his concerns for the day; in forwarding his work, and placing it under his command, and in having leisure for any incidental engagement, without stopping or deranging the usual course of his calling? While another, who has said, A little more sleep, a little more slumber, and who begins at ten what he should have commenced at six, is thrown into haste and confusion, hurries on to overtake himself, finds, through the day, his duty a turmoil, and feels himself a drudge. If we turn from the shop and look into the family, what a difference between the early and late mistress! and the early and the late servant! Even those who do not practise early rising themselves plead for the importance of it in their domestics, and would never engage them without it. Indeed, the reputation of every individual, whatever be his condition in life, is concerned in it; and his character, in the feelings of others, is unavoidably lowered by late rising, unless there be a known and justifiable cause.

—Above all, is it not *morally* important? The heathens said, the morning was the friend to the muses. It is surely a friend to the graces. If it be the best time for study, it is also the best time for devotion. It is better to go from prayer to business, than from business to prayer. Intercourse with God prepares us for our intercourse with our fellow creatures, and for every occurrence, whether pleasing or painful. Who would go out in the morning, not knowing what a day may bring forth, and feeling his ignorance, and weakness, and depravity, and danger, without retiring first, and committing himself to God? Boerhaave, the celebrated physician, rose early in the morning, and through life his practice was to retire an hour for private prayer and meditation. This, he often told his friends, gave him firmness and vigor for the business of the day. He commended it, therefore, from experience, as one of the best rules of life. The great Judge Hale, too, rose early, and retired for prayer, and read a portion of God's word; without which, he said, nothing prospered with him all the day. But see the Lord of all!! What did *He?*

APRIL 26.—**" Sitting at the feet of Jesus."—Luke, viii, 35.**

—THIS was a place of nearness. Love longs to be near its attraction, and this man now loves his benefactor, and feels his obligation to his pity and power.

—It was a place of safety. He naturally dreaded the return of the malady, and the devils gaining possession of him again; he, therefore, keeps close to his Deliverer.

—It was the place of instruction. The two former purposes might have been answered by his sitting at the side of Jesus. But sitting at his feet was the position and posture of a learner. " They sat down at his feet," says Moses, when God was on the top of Horeb, and the people at the bottom, and received of his words. Isaiah, speaking of Abraham, says, " God called him to his feet." Martha had a sister, " who also sat at Jesus' feet." Saul of Tarsus " was brought up at the feet of Gamaliel." In all these instances there is a reference to the ancient and Eastern custom; when the master occupied a higher seat, and the scholars were sitting at his feet; as hereby he had them in view, and they were reminded, by their very place, of the reverence and submission which became them as learners.

This is the place we should all be found in. But how is it possible for us to sit at his feet now? He said, I am no more in the world; and the heavens have received him till the restitution of all things. It is true, he is no longer here corporeally, but he is here spiritually. He is not visible, but he is accessible; and,

"Where'er we seek Him he is found, | "And every place is holy ground."

We have his throne, and his house, and his word, and his ministers, and his ordinances. We have himself; for he has said, Lo! I am with you alway, even unto the end of the world. Where two or three are gathered together in my name, there am I in the midst of them. *We* can, therefore, sit at his feet. And in recommendation of this place, let us observe the excellencies of the Master, and the advantages of his disciples, for the one involves the other.

And here we must not overlook the dignity of his character. A tutor seems to shed lustre over his pupils; and scholars have always prided themselves in the name of an illustrious preceptor. A young Israelitish prophet would have boasted in having been in the school of Samuel, or Elijah. How far did the queen of Sheba come to hear the wisdom of Solomon! But, behold, a greater than Solomon is here! one fairer than the children of men; He is Lord of all. See that poor, despised Christian. He is debarred every seat of learning among men, but he is under a divine instructor; such honor have all his saints. For so highly are they related; so peculiar is their destination; so sublime are the stations they are to fill, and the functions they are to discharge, as kings and priests unto God for ever, that their education is not intrusted to a creature. All thy children shall be taught of the Lord.

There is, also, the perfection of his ability. In him are hid all the treasures of wisdom and knowledge. Other teachers may be mistaken, and they may deceive us. They cannot, therefore, deserve our implicit and absolute confidence. But he does. He knows every thing, and every thing perfectly. We cannot, therefore, rely too much on his decisions. Heaven and earth may pass away, but his word shall not pass away.

There is the kindness of his manner. Men often discourage and intimidate learners by their distance, hastiness, and austerity. They have not long-suffering, and gentleness, and tenderness enough to attract and attach the very soul of the pupil, to soften and shame him, if perverse; to fix him, if roving and volatile; to inspire him with confidence, if timid; and to produce in him at once that freedom and application of mind, so essential to improvement, and so incompatible with agitation and confusion of spirit. For something besides talent; and may we not say something beyond talent? is required in a teacher. In proportion to the greatness of his knowledge, and the quickness and facility of his apprehension, a master will be tried by the imperfections of his scholars, and the scholars will be the more liable to be abashed and depressed. Conscious of their ignorance, and inability, and slowness, they will be reluctant, and afraid to give up themselves to such a superior tutor, unless he has other qualities; and such a tutor would not be very likely to waste, as he would suppose, *his* time and talents upon such unpromising subjects. But *we* sit at the feet of One, whose condescension equals his greatness. He will stoop to teach me, even where I must *begin*. He will accommodate himself to my wants and weakness. He will repeat his lessons. He will give me line upon line, precept upon precept, here a little, and there a little; and upbraid not. Thus he taught his immediate disciples as they were able to bear it, and loved them to the end, notwithstanding their mistakes and infirmities. And thus he said to his hearers, Learn of *me*, for I am meek and lowly in heart. Does he not refer to himself in these attributes as a motive as well as an example? As much as to say, "You need not be afraid to place yourselves under my care, I will deal tenderly with you."

—There is also the efficiency of his tuition. None teaches like him. Other masters teach, but they cannot make their pupils learn. They can improve, but they cannot impart ability; and without some aptitude for art or science, little progress will be made under the best efforts. What could Handel or Haydn have done with a clown without any taste or ear for music? But Jesus gives the capacity, and the disposition he requires. He furnishes not only the medium but the faculty of vision. He makes the blind to see, and the deaf to hear. He gives us a new heart, and puts a new spirit within us, and causes us to walk in his statutes. And though, like the morning, we set off with a few rays only, our path is like that of the shining light, that shineth more and more unto the perfect day.

But Oh! what are the instructions he gives! What is all other knowledge compared with this? Ask Paul: he was a man of genius and learning; he did not despise science; yet he exclaims, "Yea doubtless, and I count all things but loss for the excellency of the knowledge of Christ Jesus my Lord." Of other knowledge we may be destitute, and yet safe. But this is life eternal. Other knowledge leaves us as it finds us; yea, it often injures the possessor, and talent caters for depravity. But a man at his feet feels his words to be spirit and life. He is taught to deny ungodliness and worldly lusts, and to live soberly, righteously, and godly in the present world. In other cases, "In much wisdom there is much grief; and he that increaseth knowledge increaseth sorrow;" but, "Blessed are the people that know the joyful sound." The burden of guilt is removed, and they enter into rest. They cast all their care on Him who careth for them. Their minds are kept in perfect peace. They can not only bear, but enjoy solitude. Even in the midst of trouble they are revived, and rejoice in hope of the glory of God. How sweet are his words unto their taste! yea, sweeter than honey to their mouth!

No wonder, therefore, the disciple prizes his privilege, and cannot be seduced from his Master's feet. He has been taught the truth as it is in Jesus. He knows the truth, and the truth has made him free. And, therefore, upon the question, when others are offended, "Will ye also go away?" he answers, with Peter. Where can we do so well? Lord, to whom shall we go? To sin? That has ruined us. To the world? That has deceived us. To the heathen philosophers? Their foolish hearts are darkened. To the chief priests and Pharisees? They are the blind leading the blind. To the law? That roars and flames despair. To Moses? He wrote of thee. To thee gave all the prophets witness. Lord, to whom should we go, but unto thee? *Thou* hast the words of eternal life.

APRIL 27.—"**Members one of another.**"—**1 Corinthians, xi, 20.**

ALL mankind are joined together by a connection which only death can dissolve. The remoteness of the situation in which we are placed does not hinder this connection, but rather strengthens it, as we see in the traffic of different nations, and their mutual exchange of commodities. The inhabitants of one region cultivate the productions of the ground, and produce articles of manufacture for the use of those of another; and those of another do the same in return for them; and we sometimes find the four quarters of the globe in the furniture of one house, or the provisions of one table. The sea, which seemed likely to separate the dwellers upon earth, in the progress of science and arts, has rendered them accessible to each other, and navigation has become the principal medium of trade.

There are various distinctions in life, and the Scripture does not discountenance them, neither are we to view them as selfish, or terminating only in the advantage of the superior ranks. The lowest are useful as well as the highest. The rich benefit the poor, and the poor labor for the rich. The king is the protector of his subjects; and every subject contributes to the support of the king. The king is served by the labor of the field. There is no such thing as independence; and were it not for ignorance and pride, we should never think of it. The under ranks are even the basis of the community; the lowest parts of the wall sustain the higher. The more we rise, and possess, the less claim have we to independence; as a larger building requires more support than a smaller. A nobleman employs a thousand hands; a peasant wants but two; and these are his own.

—If this reasoning be true as to men, it is more so as to Christians. And it is in this light Paul so frequently and largely speaks of it: "I say, through the grace given unto me, to every man that is among you, not to think of himself more highly than he ought to think; but to think soberly, according as God hath dealt to every man the measure of faith." To show how important it is to display a mutual dependence, he remarks, "The eye cannot say unto the hand, I have no need of thee; nor again, the head to the feet, I have no need of you. Nay, much more those members of the body which seem to be more feeble, are necessary." They have all their respective places and uses. Each is necessary; necessary to each, and necessary to the whole; necessary to the beauty, the strength, the happiness, the perfection of the whole; why, then, should we set at nought a brother?

Yet the harmony is often broken, and a schism found in the body. The Christian church would never have been reduced to its present disjointed state, if the members had not been beguiled from the simplicity that is in Christ. The first wrong step took them at a distance from the Spirit, and as though Christ had been divided, and had imparted himself and his gospel to some, exclusively of others; the names of creatures became noted as the sources from which particular doctrines were derived, and by whom particular modes of discipline were established. The words the Holy Ghost used were less regarded than the words which man's wisdom teacheth. The worthy name by which Christians were originally called, was no longer sufficient. They ranged themselves under different leaders, and called "Rabbi," forgetting who had forbidden this; and that one was their Master, even Christ, while all they were only brethren. Hence feuds and animosities followed, and the professors of meekness itself learned to bite and devour one another. The consequences of such measures are known and felt even at the present day; and though much of the violence of religious parties has subsided, distinctions unscriptural and unnecessary, (in the degree, if not in the existence,) are supported; and though all hold the same head, the members of one community often look for no more honor and assistance from those of another, than if they were not of the body. But "if the foot shall say, Because I am not the hand, I am not of the body, is it, therefore, not of the body? And if the ear shall say, Because I am not the eye, I am not of the body, is it, therefore, not of the body?" "But now are they many members, yet but one body;" "that there should be no schism in the body; but that the members should have the same care one for another. And whether one member suffer, all the members suffer with it; or one member be honored, all the members rejoice with it." "For by one Spirit are we all baptized into one body, whether we be Jews or Gentiles, whether we be bond or free; and have been all made to drink into one Spirit."

—Christians are not only so many members in a natural body, but are so many members in a civil or domestic state. However different and distant they were by nature from each other, an effectual method has been taken by divine grace to bring them together. They are reconciled in one body on the cross. They are no longer strangers and foreigners, but fellow citizens with the saints, and of the household of God. Therefore they are one in Christ, by obligation, as well as by connexion and dependence. Christ over his own house, has a right to enact a law for the well ordering and governing of those placed under him. This law is clearly contained in the Scripture, and vain is every other proof of our belonging to him, unless we obey it. And what says He? "Then are ye my disciples, if ye love one another." According to this, we must not live to ourselves. Each is to live for the good of each, and of all. Even a gratification, harmless in itself, is to be avoided, if the peace of a weak conscience will thereby be destroyed. Such was the example of Paul; yea, and of Christ also: "Let every one of us please his neighbor for his good to edification; for even Christ pleased not himself; but as it is written, The reproaches of them that reproached thee fell on me."

"Now, by the bowels of my God,
"His sharp distress, his sore complaints,
"By his last groans, his dying blood,
"I charge my soul to love the saints."

APRIL 28.—"When Jesus knew that his hour was come that he should depart out of this world unto the Father."—John, xiii, 1.

—"His hour" means the period of his death. In another place it is called the hour of his enemies: "This," said he, "is *your* hour, and the power of darkness." It is called *their* hour, because they seemed to have every thing their own way. They apprehended him, and mocked and scourged him, and nailed him to the cross. All their purposes and wishes succeeded, and they considered his cause as annihilated. But their triumph was short and foolish. What they had done was provided for, was admitted into his plan, and the very means of accomplishing his design.

—It was "*His* hour." He was delivered by the determinate counsel and foreknowledge of God. There was nothing casual in his death. The time was appointed, and till this arrived the attempts of his adversaries were vain: "They could not lay hands on him, because his hour was not yet come." It was not only *his* hour by appointment, but by importance. No such hour had been witnessed since time had commenced. No hour of his own life would bear a comparison with it. It was infinitely unique, wonderful, and interesting, in its design and effects. Now was the judgment of this world. Now was the prince of this world cast out. Now was the ceremonial law abolished. Now was the moral law magnified and made honorable. Now he was to finish transgression; now he was to bring in everlasting righteousness. Now he was to open the kingdom of heaven to all believers. Now he was to get himself a name above every name.

—He *knew* that his hour was come—and so perfect was his foresight of the event, that he knew not only the fact itself, but the incidents attending it; and knew the whole before there was any appearance of the thing, before his enemies had formed the design, before Judas had felt the thought of treason. And thus he evinced his devotedness to his work. He saw the hour was at hand, but he seeks no hiding-place, nor attempts to escape, though he had so many means in his power. It does not affect this to say, that in another sense he was unable to have released himself; because he was bound by covenant engagement; and if he saved others, himself he could not save. For his engagement was made in the full prospect of all he was to endure; and as the tremendous suffering approached, so far was he from repenting of what he had brought upon himself, that he said, "How am I straightened till it be accomplished!"

—But how is his passage through this dreadful scene expressed? "That he should depart out of this world unto the Father." Here let us think of his people, as well as of himself. In all things he must have the pre-eminence, but they resemble him. What is here said of his death, will, in a pleasing degree, apply to their own. Their death is not, indeed, like his, mediatorial; neither know they the hour when it will take place. But all their times are in God's hand; and the circumstances of their death, as well as of their life, fall under his arrangement. They know they have their hour, and are immortal till it arrives. They know that enemies cannot hasten it, that friends cannot retard it. They know also that it is approaching; that it cannot be far off; that it may be very near—and therefore that it requires a constant readiness. But was *his* death a "departing out of this world?" So is theirs. He was in it for three and thirty years. Many of them are in it a shorter, and many a much longer period. It was a sad world to him. It knew him not, but despised and rejected him. It hated him without a cause. It persecuted him from his birth, refused him a place where to lay his head, and could not be satisfied till it had shed his blood. And *they* find it a vain and deceitful world, a vexing and injurious world, a vile and wicked world. Every thing in it cries, Arise, and depart hence; for this is not your rest, because it is polluted. And are we unwilling? Yes—

"Thankless for favors from on high,
"Man thinks he fades too soon;
"Though 'tis his privilege to die,
"Would he improve the boon.

"But he, not wise enough to scan
"His best concerns aright,
"Would gladly stretch life's little span
"To ages, if he might—

"To ages, in a world of pain—
"To ages, where he goes,
"Gall'd by affliction's heavy chain,
"And hopeless of repose.

"Strange fondness of the human heart,
"Enamor'd of its harm!
"Strange world, that costs it so much smart,
"And yet has power to charm!"

We do not wonder, indeed, that this should be so much the case with "men of the world." They have "their portion in this life," and no hope of a better. Bad as it is, they know that it is the best world they will ever be in, and that whatever be its troubles, to them they are only the beginnings of sorrow. But it is otherwise with Christians. They are here like Israel in Egypt; and death is their departure for the land of promise. They are like strangers in an inhospitable country, and travellers at a cheerless inn; and death is their departing to their delightful home.

Was *his* death a "going to the Father?" So is theirs. That is, going to heaven; for the Father is there, and in his presence there is fullness of joy, and at his right hand there are pleasures for evermore. He went to the Father, to carry on their cause, and to possess his own reward; but he had been there before. Hence he said, "I came forth from the Father, and am come into the world; again I leave the world, and go unto the Father." Hence he speaks of heaven without wonder. He had been at court. He had resided there, and had only left it for a season. His return, with all the glories that should follow, was the joy set before him, for which he endured the cross. And, as love delights in the welfare of its object, he expected that his discipies would rejoice when he said, "I go unto the Father; for the Father is greater than I." But they were never there before; all will be new and surprising to them. But they, also, will have their work, and will be still praising him; they, also, will drink of the rivers of his pleasure; they will have immediate and uninterrupted access to his Father and our Father, to his God and our God. And with Him is the fountain of life.

April 29.—"And there appeared an angel unto him from heaven, strengthening him."—Luke xxii, 43.

Thus, though the cup was not taken from him, he was heard, in that he feared, according to the promise: "I have heard thee in a time accepted; and in the day of salvation have I succored thee." We may be heard, when we are not delivered; and succored in distress, when we are not saved from it. And if the burden be not diminished, yet, if our ability to endure it be increased, the effect is the same. Paul was a witness of this. When he besought the Lord thrice, that the thorn in the flesh might depart from him, the Savior said, My grace is sufficient for thee; for my strength is made perfect in weakness. And says David, In the day that I cried, thou answeredst me, and strengthenedst me with strength in my soul.

—Here we see the humiliation of the Savior. He who was rich, for our sakes became poor. He was in the form of God, but took upon him the form of a servant. He was Lord of all, but had not where to lay his head, and was relieved by the creatures of his power: "Certain women which had been healed of evil spirits and infirmities, Mary, called Magdalene, out of whom went seven devils, and Joanna, the wife of Chuza, Herod's steward, and Susanna, and many others, ministered unto him of their substance." He was the Lord of angels, but he was made a little lower than they; yea, he received assistance from them: "There appeared unto him an angel from heaven, strengthening him."

—What a contrast is here! His apostles, who had been so much honored by him, forsook him; and even Peter, James, and John, who had been admitted to the transfiguration, and now were selected to be with him in the garden, slumbered and slept. And though, when he came to them and found them in this condition, he pitied them, and said, The spirit, indeed, is willing, but the flesh is weak; yet he felt it, deeply felt it, and said, "What! could ye not watch with me one hour?" But if earth disowns him, heaven does not. If men abandon him, angels cry with a loud voice, Worthy is the Lamb! "He was seen of angels." One of them announced his approaching conception; another proclaimed his birth; a multitude of them carolled his advent. In his temptation in the wilderness, "Behold, angels came and ministered unto him." An angel rolled away the stone from the door of the sepulchre, and said to the women, "Fear not *ye*, for I know that ye seek Jesus, which was crucified: he is not here;" "Come, see the place where the Lord lay." And here "an angel appeared unto him from heaven, strengthening him."

He could have asked the Father, and he would have given him twelve legions of angels, and rescued him. What are we saying? *One* of these would have been sufficient; the least of them could have looked all his adversaries into nothing. But how then could the Scriptures be fulfilled, that thus it must be? And how could he have put away sin by the sacrifice of himself? Or how could he have sympathized with us, if he had never suffered? The angel, therefore, only *strengthened him*. Reminding him of the joy that was set before him; telling him of the result of his passion, the effect of it in the glory of God, and the salvation of the world; spreading before him the promises, perhaps reading to him the prophecy of Isaiah, "When thou shalt make his soul an offering for sin, he shall see his seed: he shall prolong his days, and the pleasure of the Lord shall prosper in his hand; he shall see of the travail of his soul, and shall be satisfied." Raising him up from the cold ground; supporting his fainting head; wiping away the bloody sweat from his dear face. So that he appeared fresh, and fair, and glorious in his visage, and made those who came to apprehend him go backward, and fall to the earth, when he only presented himself, and said, "I am he."

—In all things he has the pre-eminence, and how willing are his people to acknowledge it! But while he is the first born among many brethren, all of them are predestinated to be conformed to him. Angels, therefore, who attended him, attend them also. "Are they not all ministering spirits, sent forth to minister unto them that are the heirs of salvation?" Their attendance is no less real than formerly, though it is no longer visible, according to the principle of the economy under which we live, and which is to walk by faith, and not by sight. They delight to do the will of their Lord and ours. These blessed beings have no envy, no pride. They are enemies to his enemies, but they are friends to his friends. They rejoice when a sinner repenteth, and carry the dying saint into Abraham's bosom.

APRIL 30.—" But go your way; tell his disciples, and Peter, that he goeth before you into Galilee; there shall ye see him, as he said unto you."—Mark, xvi, 7.

THESE are the words of the angel who had descended from heaven to attend his rising Lord. They were addressed to Mary Magdalene, and Mary the mother of James, and Salome. These women had honored the Savior, and he honored them. They were the first to receive the announcement of his resurrection, and the first to report it.

But observe, they were to carry the news, not to the chief priests, and scribes, and Pharisees, not to Pilate, not to Herod. It was just to leave these men in the darkness they loved. They rebelled against the light, and no evidence would have convinced those who had already seen his miracles, and believed not. But his disciples, though timid, and weak, and imperfect, were sincere. They had forsaken all to follow him. Their very doubting arose from the greatness of their love, and sorrow had now filled their hearts. They would, therefore, welcome the intelligence, and be influenced by it, as his followers and witnesses.

—But why is Peter distinctively mentioned? Because he was the chief of the apostles? So far from it, the distinction reminds us of his humiliation. He had fallen by his iniquity; and after the most solemn warnings and professions, he had denied his Master, with oaths and curses. But the look in the judgment-hall had broken his heart, and made him go out, and weep bitterly. He was now on the verge of despair, and ready to say—perhaps was even now saying—Ah! he will disown me—and righteously—for ever! The angel's *naming* him, therefore, on this occasion, was as much as to say, The Savior has not cast thee off; he has not forgotten to be gracious; he does not break a bruised reed, nor quench the smoking flax, but will send forth judgment unto victory—while it conveyed an intimation to his brethren that they were to follow his example, and endeavor to restore such a one in the spirit of meekness, considering themselves, lest they also were tempted.

—The message, more than announcing his resurrection, added, that he would go before them into Galilee. In vain we ask how he passed thither. He had the power to appear and disappear, and to transport himself from place to place as he pleased, in a moment of time. But what led him down so many miles from Jerusalem? Was it to intimate his forsaking that guilty city? Wo unto you when I depart from you! Or was it to call them off from the strife and cruelty of their enemies? It was comparatively a place of security and concealment. Or was it, that their journeying down separately, or with each other, might bring them to recollection, and recover them from their late cowardice and unbelief? Was it to tell them to withdraw, in order to be in the way of intercourse with him? It was a despised place—would he teach them to rise above local and vulgar prejudices, and to call nothing common or unclean? It is certain that he had been much in Galilee himself, and had many followers there. And this accounts for the largeness of the assembly; for the apostles would naturally inform his friends there of this expected interview, and hence he was now seen of above five hundred brethren at once, many of whom were living when Paul wrote to the Corinthians, though some had fallen asleep.

—His promise, that they should see him there, would prove a test of their faith and affection. If they valued the sight of him, and believed his word, they would certainly repair thither. Accordingly they did repair thither; and there was he! Let us apply this to ourselves. There are means and ordinances which he has established. In these he has engaged to be found of those that seek him. If we rely on his truth, and desire communion with him, we shall gladly avail ourselves of them. And shall we—can we be disappointed—if we do? Has he ever said to the seed of Jacob, Seek ye me, in vain? He has often been better than his word; but who ever found him worse? Let us go, therefore, to his throne, and to his house, with full and lively expectation. In all places where I record my name, I will come unto thee, and I will bless thee; for where two or three are gathered together in my name, there am I in the midst of them. There shall we see him, as he has said unto us.

—He is also gone before us into heaven. Let us arise, and depart hence, and seek him *there*. *There* shall we see him in all his glory, according to his promise—Where I am, there shall also my servants be. Oh! to join him there! To be for ever with the Lord!

"O glorious hour! O bless'd abode!
"I shall be near, and like my God:
"And flesh and sin no more control
"The sacred pleasures of my soul."

MAY 1.—"And I will give her her vineyards from thence."—Hosea, ii, 15.

—OBSERVE the author of these favors. *I* will do it, says God. Every good gift and every perfect gift is from him; and his people will readily acknowledge that all they enjoy is not only from his agency, but his grace.

—Observe also the richness of the supplies—I will give her—not her corn—corn is for necessity, but grapes are for delight. Yea, it is not a vine, but a vineyard—yea, vineyards! He engages to give, as if he could not do too much for them; being concerned—not only for their safety, but for their welfare—not only for their relief, but enjoyment—and not only for their tasting consolation, but their being filled with all joy and peace in believing.

—Observe, also, the strangeness of the way in which these indulgences are to be communicated. For *whence* are these supplies to come? From a *wilderness*. "I will allure her, and bring her into the *wilderness*, and speak comfortably unto her; and I will give her her vineyards from *thence*." What could be looked for in a wilderness, but loneliness, and mazes, and danger, and beasts of prey, and reptiles, and sand, and briers, and thorns? Who would expect to find the vineyards of Engedi there? But "He only doeth wondrous things; he is God alone." He turneth the shadow of death into the morning. He makes rivers in high places, and streams in the desert. He makes the wilderness to rejoice, and blossom as the rose—and gives us vineyards from *thence*.

The region through which his people passed, in their way from Egypt to Canaan, was a wilderness. Here read the words of Jeremiah; "Who led us through the wilderness, through a land of deserts, and of pits, and of the shadow of death; through a land that no man passed through, and where no man dwelt." Moses also calls it that terrible wilderness, wherein were fiery serpents, and scorpions, and drought; where there was no water. But He gave them their vineyards from thence. Though the place yielded them nothing, they were well supplied from above. Though they had no rivers or springs, he smote the rock, and the waters gushed out, and followed them in all their journeyings. Though they had no food, the clouds poured down manna, and they did eat angels' food. Though they had no road, they had a guide to lead them the right way, in a cloud of fire which shaded them by day, and comforted them by night. The tabernacle of God was in the midst of them. From the mercy-seat he communed with them. He sent them Moses, and Aaron, and Miriam. He gave his good Spirit to instruct them. They had grapes from Eschol. They had a view of the glory of all lands, and at length the possession of it—where they sang, "To Him that led his people through the wilderness; for his mercy endureth for ever!"

—Earth is a wilderness; and he gives them their vineyards from thence. It was not designed to be a wilderness; but by one man sin entered into the world; and it was said to the transgressor, "Cursed is the ground for thy sake; in sorrow shalt thou eat of it all the days of thy life. Thorns also, and thistles, shall it bring forth to thee;" and there are enough of these.

"Lord, what a wretched land is this,
"That yields us no supply!
"No cheering fruit, no wholesome trees,
"Or streams of living joy.

"But pricking thorns, through all the ground,
"And mortal poisons, grow!
"And all the rivers that are found,
"With dangerous waters flow."

Such it is, as the fall left it. Such it now would be, but for divine grace. How discontented and miserable are the men of the world who have nothing else! especially in their afflictions—and man is born to trouble. But to the Christian the curse is turned into a blessing. He has not only before him a land of promise, but even now—even here, he has a thousand alleviations, and succors, and even delights.

"The men of grace have found
"Glory begun below;
"And heavenly fruits on earthly ground,
"From faith and hope may grow."

And if earth *be* a wilderness, when they attend divine ordinances, and hear the joyful sound, and embrace the promises, and rejoice in hope of the glory of God, and walk in the comforts of the Holy Ghost, they have their vineyards from thence.

Solitude is a wilderness, and He gives them their vineyards from thence. There is not only much to be done alone, but gained alone, and enjoyed alone. There we gain much of our best knowledge, and our richest experience. There we enjoy the freedom of prayer, and the most unreserved intercourse with God. There his secret is with them that fear him, and he shows them his covenant. They are never less alone than when alone. "Go forth into the plain, and I will there talk with thee." David said, "My soul shall be satisfied as with marrow and fatness, and my mouth shall praise thee with joyful lips, when I remember thee upon my bed, and meditate on thee in the night watches." Nathanael under the fig tree found something more refreshing than the shade of its leaf, more delicious than the taste of its fruit.

Outward trouble is a wilderness. Many have been afraid to be brought into it; yet He has given them their vineyards from thence, and the Valley of Achor for a door of hope. They have been saved by their undoing, and enriched by their losses. Manasseh, in his affliction, sought and found the God of his father. And David, though he was converted before, could say, It is good for me that I have been afflicted. What proofs have all his people had that he was with them in trouble! What discoveries! what supports! what tendernesses of comfort have they had there! As the sufferings of Christ have abounded in them, the consolation hath also abounded by Christ.

—The state of mind produced by conviction of sin is a wilderness. A wounded spirit who can bear? Who does not remember the surprise, the confusion of mind, the terror, the anguish, the self-despair he once felt, and who can forget the feelings induced by a discovery of the cross, and the joy of God's salvation! Many are afraid when they see their relations and friends trembling at God's word, and broken in heart at his feet, but Christians hail it as a token for good. They know that he gave *them their* vineyards from thence.

The same may be said of that soul-abasement and distress the believer himself may feel, from increasing views of his unworthiness, depravity, and guilt. And this may be the case, and often will be the case after he has been for seventy years in the way everlasting, and hoping better things of himself. This is truly lamentable and humbling, but will the humiliation hurt him? He giveth grace unto the humble. The rain falls upon the mountain tops, as well as in the valley, but the valleys are fertilized; they are also covered with corn; they shout for joy; they also sing.

"The more his glories strike mine eyes,
"The humbler I shall lie.
"But, while *I* sink, my *joys* shall rise
"Unmeasurably high."

—The valley of the shadow of death is the last wilderness. There is much to render it uninviting and awful; and yet, when it has been actually entered, the apprehension and the gloom have fled. And this has been the case generally, even with those who were most subject to bondage by the fear of it. The place has been made glad for them. They have had an abundant entrance into the joy of their Lord. And what vineyards does he give them from THENCE!!

May 2.—" A psalm and song at the dedication of the house of David." Psalm xxx.

This he built for himself as soon as he was established king over Judah and Israel. It was, doubtless, very different from the cottage he occupied when a shepherd. But there was no impropriety in this. A man may alter his mode of living with his rising condition in the world. The gradations of life are not discountenanced in the Scriptures, and we have never seen any advantage arising from the neglect of them. Good men ought to avoid extravagance; but by being mean or parsimonious they may cause their good to be evil spoken of.

David, as a king, was obliged to do many things from a regard to his station, rather than from personal choice. But godliness is to show itself in all circumstances. Therefore, when he took possession of his dwelling place he consecrated it to God. At entering a new house an entertainment is often given, and dissipation and excess follow. Many are invited, but God is not of the number; yea, they say unto God, Depart from us; for we desire not the knowledge of thy ways. But every thing is to be sanctified by the word of God, and prayer. Our religion is to be exemplified in little and common things. We are to sanctify the week, as well as to remember the Sabbath, and to walk with a perfect heart in our own dwellings, as well as to worship in the temple of God. All we have is the Lord's, and nothing is a blessing till he blesses it. And we know not what may befall us in our new abode. Here our children may be about us, or here we may weep because they are not. Here we may find a house of mourning for the desire of our eyes, or the guide of our youth. Here we may enjoy health, or be made to possess months of vanity, and have wearisome nights appointed unto us. Here we may live many years, or our sun may go down at noon. Let it, then, be our concern, that the place may be the house of God while we live, and the gate of heaven when we die.

David was a poet, and was accustomed to indulge his pious genius on any particular occurrence. Here are the lines he composed on the present occasion. "I will extol thee, O Lord, for thou hast lifted me up, and hast not made my foes to rejoice over me. O Lord, my God, I cried unto thee, and thou hast healed me. O Lord, thou hast brought up my soul from the grave. thou hast kept me alive that I should not go down to the pit. Sing unto the Lord, O ye saints of his, and give thanks at the remembrance of his holiness. For his anger endureth but a moment; in his favor is life; weeping may endure for a night, but joy cometh in the morning."

All we notice here is, that previously to his occupying this fine mansion, he had been suffering under a dangerous disease. For kings are as mortal as their subjects, and exposed to the same evils of life. And what would a house of cedar be to one who carried into it a body full of pain? But God had recovered him speedily, and while renewed health enabled him to enjoy the blessings of Providence, divine grace taught him to value life, as a privilege for religious purposes, prolonging his opportunities to glorify God, and serve his generation according to his will.

Nothing is more interesting than little casual insights into the his tory, and above all, the experience, of good and great men. And in this ode we see the workings of David's mind, before, and under, and after the affliction.

—Before the affliction: "And in my prosperity I said, I shall never be moved. Lord, by thy favor thou hast made my mountain to stand strong." He had not said this in words, but his views, and feelings, and actions, were all vocal with God. And do we not here see the danger of indulgence? How little can we bear without self-security, without presumption, without losing the heart of a stranger! Hence the necessity of a change, and the advantage of those trials that cry to our hearts, "Arise, and depart hence, for this is not your rest."

—Under the affliction: "Thou didst hide thy face, and I was troubled. I cried to thee, O Lord; and unto the Lord I made supplication. What profit is there in my blood, when I go down to the pit? Shall the dust praise thee? Shall it declare thy truth? Hear, O Lord, and have mercy upon me: Lord, be thou my helper." Cain, in his distress goes to building. Saul sends for music. Few turn to Him that smiteth them. But prayer is the design, the sanctification, the resource of affliction. Is any afflicted? let him pray.

—After the affliction: "Thou hast turned for me my mourning into dancing; thou hast put off my sackcloth, and girded me with gladness, to the end that my glory may sing praise to thee, and not be silent. O Lord my God, I will give thanks unto thee for ever." *He* has done it—

"His hand has loosed my bonds of pain,
"And bound me with his love."

Therefore I will serve him with my best powers, and for ever—

And his practice corresponded with his profession. No sooner had he taken possession of his new palace than "the king said unto Nathan the prophet, See now, I dwell in a house of cedar, but the ark of God dwelleth within curtains." And then it was that he availed himself of a pious and ardent frame of mind, to swear unto the Lord, and vow unto the mighty God of Jacob, "Surely I will not come into the tabernacle of my house, nor go up into my bed; I will not give sleep to mine eyes, or slumber to mine eyelids, until I find out a place for the Lord, a habitation for the mighty God of Jacob." How different the disposition of the selfish Jews on their return from Babylon! "Is it time for you, O ye, to dwell in your ceiled houses, and this house lie waste?" And what gained they? Them that honor me, says God, I will honor. "Ye looked for much, and, lo! it came to little; and when ye brought it home I did blow upon it. Why? saith the Lord of hosts. Because of mine house that is waste, and ye run every man unto his own house."

May 3.—"To reveal his son in me."—Galatians, i, 16.

To reveal is to lay open something which, though in existence before, was yet unknown. The knowledge of the Son of God is necessary to all the use we can make of him. And we may observe a fourfold revelation of him. The text only speaks of one of these, but they are all true, and they are all profitable.

There is a revelation of the Savior *to* us. This is found in the

Scripture, which therefore we often call emphatically "revelation." It discovers many things, but he is the principal subject; and we are persuaded nothing has found a place in it, but has some relation to him. This revelation early began. It dawned in paradise and the light continued to shine more and more unto the perfect day. All the Jewish ordinances and sacrifices prefigured him. Of him Moses in the law and the prophets did write: and the testimony of Jesus was the spirit of prophecy. He came personally as a preacher, and he was his own subject. He unbosomed himself to his disciples, as far as they were able to bear it; and promised them a fuller manifestation. This was done when the Holy Spirit taught them all things, and brought all things to their remembrance that he had said unto them, and inspired them to communicate the information to others, that all may read and understand their knowledge in the mystery of Christ.

There is a revelation of the Savior *in* us This is more than the former; for many who have access to the Scriptures will perish, and all their knowledge will only prove the savor of death unto death. There is, however, as to information, nothing in the internal relation that is not in the external. It is not, therefore, a new revelation in itself, for the truths themselves are as old as the creation; but it is new as to our perception and experience. If a man born blind were to receive his sight, he would not see a new sun, but it would be new to him. Even in a land of vision, we may be called out of darkness into his marvellous light; because the eyes of our understanding may be opened. We heard of these things before, but now in God's light, we see them; and this illumination shows us, not only their reality but their excellency; and, with their glory, fixes, and replenishes, and sways the soul. Be not satisfied with any thing short of this. Distinguish between a Christian in name, and a Christian indeed. Do not place your religion on any thing without you. Have you the witness in yourselves? Is Christ revealed in you? Have you such a sight of him, by faith, as to see that he is fairer than the children of men? as to feel him infinitely endeared? as to count all things but loss for the excellency of his knowledge? This is what he himself means, when he said, "He that seeth the Son, and believeth on him, hath everlasting life."

There is a revelation of him *by* us. It is our destiny, our duty, our privilege, to make him known. This is done by our being the subjects of his agency, as the work displays the attributes of the author, and the streams proclaim the quality of the fountain. We should discover him by our resemblance, as his followers, and by our testimony, as his witnesses. We can speak upon other subjects, why not upon this? Who has not opportunities to extol him among children, servants, friends, neighbors? What do seeking souls want, but to see Jesus? Or doubting ones, but to be assured of his love? Have we been freely healed by him? Let us tell the deceased and dying of the physician. Let us zealously aid every institution that aims to show forth his praise. Pray that his glory may be revealed, and that all flesh may see the salvation of our God.

There is also a revelation of him *with* us. The world knoweth us not; it knew him not. We are now hid, and he is hid, and both are to be displayed at the same time. The day of the manifestation of the sons of God is also the revelation of Jesus Christ. And when he, who is our life, shall appear, we also shall appear with him in glory. Them that sleep in Jesus will God bring with him. They suffered with him, and they shall be glorified together.

We wish to be distinguished. We want something exclusive; half the relish and value is gone, if others share with us. But *his* benevolence, *his* condescension are such, that he cannot be satisfied unless we partake with him: "I appoint unto you a kingdom, as my Father appointed unto me, that ye may eat and drink at my table in my kingdom, and sit on thrones, judging the twelve tribes of Israel." "To him that overcometh will I grant to sit with me in my throne, even as I also overcame, and am set down with my Father in his throne." But where will the ungodly and the sinner appear?

MAY 4.—"For even Christ pleased not himself."—Romans, xv, 3.

—NOT as if his undertaking our cause was against his will, or that he ever felt it to be a task and a grievance. He was voluntary in the engagement, and cheerful in the execution; and could say, I have a baptism to be baptized with, and how am I straitened till it be accomplished! But he never followed the indulgence of his natural inclination in the days of his flesh. He preferred the glory of God, and our benefit, to his own gratification. He did not consult his ease, but denied the demands of sleep when duty required exertion. He rejected, with anger, Peter's proposal to spare himself from suffering. He did not consult ambitious feeling, but refused the people when they would have made him a king. He stood not upon rank and consequence, but washed the disciples' feet, and was among them as one that serveth. He was far more delighted with Mary's reception of his word, than with Martha's preparation for his appetite. He was not only thirsty, but hungry, when the disciples left him at the well to go and buy meat; but when they returned, and said, Master, eat; he replied, "I have meat to eat which ye know not of. In your absence I have had something above corporeal satisfaction; I have been saving a soul from death, and hiding a multitude of sins. My meat is to do the will of Him that sent me, and to finish his work." When the collectors of the temple tax came to Peter, he said to him, "What thinkest thou, Simon? Of whom do the kings of the earth take custom or tribute? Of their own children, or of strangers? Peter saith unto him, Of strangers. Jesus saith unto him, Then are the children free. The temple is the house of my heavenly Father, and I am his only begotten Son." But, though not bound like others, he foregoes his right, in order to avoid offence; "Nevertheless, lest we should offend," *i. e.* excite pain, or dislike, or reflection, by their thinking we have not a proper regard to the sanctuary and ordinances of God, "Lest we should offend them, go thou to the sea, and cast a hook, and take up the fish that first cometh up, and when thou hast opened his mouth thou shalt find a piece of money; that take, and give unto them for me and thee." This he exemplified all through life; He was, therefore, well prepared, and authorized to say, "If any man will be my disciple, let him deny himself, and take up his cross and follow me."

—And observe the use the apostle makes of it. Because Christ pleased not himself, therefore, "let the strong bear the infirmities of the weak, and not please themselves;" "Let every one of us please his neighbor, for his good to edification." He, indeed, limits the duty. We are not to humor our brethren in a sinful course, but only in things innocent and lawful; and we are to do this with a view to secure and promote his welfare, and not any advantage of our own. But we are not to consult our own little conveniences, and appetites, and wishes. We are not even to follow our convictions in every disputed matter. "Let us not, therefore, judge one another any more; but judge this rather, that no man put a stumbling block, or an occasion to fall, in his brother's way. I know and am persuaded, by the Lord Jesus, that there is nothing unclean of itself; but to him that esteemeth any thing to be unclean, to him it is unclean. But if thy brother be grieved with thy meat, now walkest thou not charitably. Destroy not him with thy meat for whom Christ died." Here, again, the apostle calls in Jesus, as a motive, and an example. He denied himself so as to die for this weak brother, and will you, says he, refuse to deny yourselves in a trifling forbearance on his behalf? "It is good neither to eat flesh, nor to drink wine, nor any thing whereby thy brother stumbleth, or is offended, or is made weak."

Herein, too, Paul enjoins no more than he practised; for he drank deep into the Savior's spirit: "I please all men in all things, not seeking my own profit, but the profit of many, that they may be saved." If "meat make my brother to offend, I will eat no flesh while the world standeth, lest I make my brother to offend." And how noble does he here look! And how below his principles does a Christian act when he thinks of himself only, his own accommodation; yea, even his own conscience. He is to regard the satisfaction of another's mind, as well as his own; and is to walk, not only righteously, but charitably. Yet some say, "*I* do not *think* it sinful; therefore I am not obliged to abstain." And was Paul obliged to abstain? All things were pure to him; but he would not eat with offence. Some seem never to regard how their conduct will affect others; but the Book says, "Give none offence; neither to the Jews, nor to the Gentiles, nor to the church of God." Asaph was checked in his improper language by remembering, that if he so spake, he should "offend against the generation of the upright." Let us, therefore, beware of throwing stumbling blocks in the way of the blind. Let us make straight paths for our feet, lest that which is lame be turned out of the way; but let it rather be healed.

—Christianity is designed to refine and soften; to take away the heart of stone, and to give us hearts of flesh; to polish off the rudenesses and arrogancies of our manners and tempers, and to make us blameless and harmless, the sons of God, without rebuke. Lord Chesterfield, in one of his letters to his nephew, finely says, "Politeness is benevolence in little things." Religion should make us the most polite creatures in the world; and what persons of rank do from education, we should do from principle; yielding our own desires and claims to become all things to all men, if by any means we may gain some, and be not only sincere, but without offence, until the day of Christ.

—If so, some professors of religion have much to learn. They think of nothing but their own indulgence. They know nothing of bearing with infirmity; of waiting for improvement; of watching for opportunity. They are decisive, and dictatorial, and hasty, and severe, and pride themselves only on what they call faithfulness, and which is the easiest thing in religion to them, because it falls in with their own natural temper; not to say, that frequently what they mean by fidelity, is only rudeness and insolence. But while we can do nothing against the truth, but for the truth, we are required to be courteous, and to pursue whatsoever things are lovely, and of good report.

—And without this, professors will not only render religion unamiable and repulsive, but will lower themselves in general estimation, and lose the influence which is derivable from reputation and esteem. Who can regard the haughty and the selfish? But for a good man some would even dare to die. An inoffensive, self-denying, lovely disposition and carriage, wins the heart. It is not in our power to love, but it is in our power to be loved. Our loving another depends upon him; and here we have no control; but another's loving us, depends upon ourselves; and he that will have friends, must show himself friendly.

Doddridge buried a most interesting child at nine years of age. The dear little creature was a general favorite; and he tells us in his funeral sermon, that when he one day asked her how it was that every body loved her—I know not, she said, unless it be that I love every body. Tell your children this. Also read to them, " The child Samuel grew on, and was in favor both with the Lord, and also with men."

" For he that in these things serveth Christ, is acceptable to God, and approved of men. Let us, therefore, follow after things which make for peace, and things wherewith one may edify another."

May 5.—" If thou knewest the gift of God."—John, iv, 10.

As if he had said to the woman, Thou mistakest me for a mere Jew, wandering and weary, and sitting thus on the well, and asking for the refreshment of water, seemingly dependent on the kindness of a stranger. But if thou wert acquainted with me—that I am the mercy promised from the beginning; the only begotten of the Father, full of grace and truth; that I am come into the world to save sinners; and that in me all fullness dwells; what an opportunity wouldst thou find was now afforded thee, " If thou knewest the gift of God."

He calls himself the *gift of God*, because he came not according to the course of nature. A body was prepared him. A virgin conceives, and bares a Son; and the holy thing born of her is called the Son of God. We go also further. A preternatural interposition might have taken place in a way of wrath; and this is what seemed most probable in the case, and would have been the foreboding of our guilty minds. But God sent not his only begotten Son into the world to condemn the world, but that the world through him might be saved. He, therefore, came not according to any rule of desert. A few years ago we heard much of the rights of man, and though the expression was abused, and brought into contempt, there is a propriety in it. Man has rights, with regard to his fellow creatures. Children have rights, with regard to parents; and subjects, with regard to sovereigns. A man has a right to enjoy the fruit of his labor; he has a right to worship the Supreme Being according to his conscience. But what were his rights, with regard to God? What right to protection has a subject that has become rebellious? What right to wages has a servant that has run away from his master? As sinners, we had forfeited all expectation from God—except a fearful looking for of judgment and fiery indignation. We could have no right to the bread we eat, or the air we breathe. What claim, then, had we upon God for the Son of his love? He was a gift infinitely free; and not only free as opposed to desert, but also as opposed to desire. Was he withholden till we felt our need of him, and became suppliants at our offended Maker's feet? Ages before we were born, the plan was formed, and accomplished, and announced. And when we are desirous of obtaining the blessings of it, we find them provided, and hear a voice, saying, Come, for all things are now ready. All other good too, is insured by him. He that spared not his own Son, but delivered him up for us all, how shall he not with him also freely give us all things? Yea, he has given us all things in him; and whatever a perishing sinner needs, even to life eternal, is to be derived from him.

And if you *knew* the gift of God—surely you would say with the apostle, "Thanks be unto God for his unspeakable gift." You should overlook nothing in his bounty; but gratitude should bear some proportion to the favor it acknowledges. What is the sun in nature, to this Sun of Righteousness! What is our daily bread to this Bread of Life! Here are the exceeding riches of his grace—in his kindness toward us by Christ Jesus.

—If you knew the gift of God, surely you would avail yourselves of it. You would consider a participation of him as the one thing needful; and receive him as he is presented in the gospel; and as Zaccheus received him, who made haste, and came down, and received him joyfully.

—If you knew the gift of God, you would not yield to despondency. You would not say, by way of objection, I have no money, no worthiness. This is supposed. Who thinks of buying a gift; of deserving a gift—especially such a gift!

—If you knew the gift of God, you would make him known. You would commend him to your children, your relations, your friends, and your neighbors—You would pray, "Let the whole earth be filled with his glory"—

"His worth if all the nations knew,
"Sure the whole earth would love him too."

MAY 6.—"Therefore hath thy servant found in his heart to pray this prayer unto thee."—2 Samuel, vii, 27.

WHERE did he find his inclination, and power to pray? "In his heart." The heart is every thing in religion. Man judgeth according to the outward appearance; but the Lord looketh to the heart; and requires it—My son, give me thy heart. Where he does not find this, *He* finds nothing. Where this speaks, words are needless: he knows what is the mind of the Spirit. Hannah, she spake in her heart; only her lips moved, but her voice was not heard—yet what a prayer she prayed! and how successful! It is a blessed thing, therefore, to find it in our heart to pray—so that, while it is with many a bodily exercise only, a task which they would gladly decline, an effort forced upon them from something without—some danger, or trouble, we may do it naturally, and therefore constantly and pleasantly, from a principle in us, like a well of water springing up into everlasting life.

And what was the prayer he found there? It was *this*—"Let the house of thy servant David be established before thee." David had a peculiar concern for his family; and, from his character, we may be assured he wished it to be not only or principally glorious, but *good*. It is a man's duty to seek to promote the temporal welfare of his house; for he that provideth not for his own, especially those of his own house, hath denied the faith, and is worse than an Infidel. But the wish of many is not to build up their house in Israel, but in the world. They are only anxious for an increase of earthly wealth and honor. And how injurious have such risings in life proved to the comfort and religion of the family. And how inconsiderate and inconsistent are parents, especially if they are pious ones, in longing for such perils, when they know the depravity of human nature, and the snares of prosperity. How much better is it to see, and to leave their household great in the sight of the Lord; and under the blessing of that providence which will make all things work together for their good.

And what produced *this* prayer? "*Therefore*"—"For thou, O Lord of Hosts, God of Israel, hast revealed to thy servant, saying, I will build thee a house:" "*therefore* hath thy servant found in his heart to pray this prayer unto thee." He had refused him the pleasure and honor of building the temple which he had purposed. But he should be no loser. The will should be taken for the deed. Though he did not build God a house, God would build him a house—and except the Lord build the house, they labor in vain that build it. But all things are possible with him: and them that honor him, he will honor. What the king said to his prime minister—"You mind my affairs, and I will mind yours"—he says to each of his servants. Serve me yourselves, and be persuaded that my blessing is upon my people, and that the generation of the upright shall be blessed.

—But see—the certainty of a thing does not supersede the use of the means in attaining it. Why should David pray for it, when God had pledged himself to do it? So some would argue: but it would be the arguing of folly. The Scripture, the wisdom of God, knows nothing of this perversion. No doctrine there leads to enthusiasm. There the means and end are connected. There activity grows out of dependence; and zeal, out of confidence. There God says, after he has promised the thing, "I will yet be inquired of by the house of Israel to do it for them." Yea, we see prayer is not only consistent with the promise, but derived from it. It is this that furnishes the matter of our petitions, and gives us all our encouragements.

Therefore, let us be thankful for the promises. Let us search them out. Let us place them opposite all our wants. Let us plead them, and say, Remember the word unto thy servant, upon which thou hast caused him to hope. And, as *then* we can ask in faith, so we may pray with confidence: for whatsoever we ask according to his will, we know he heareth us.

MAY 7.—"The Sun of Righteousness shall arise."—Malachi, iv, 2.

HE is called the Sun of Righteousness, to intimate that he is the same in the righteous world as the orb of day is in the natural. The importance of the latter is acknowledged by all, but the value of the former is infinitely greater; for what are the interests of time and sense to those of the soul and eternity! We know there is only one sun in our system; and there is one Mediator between God and man. Neither is there salvation in any other. I am the way, the truth, and the life; no man cometh unto the Father but by me. The vastness of the sun is surprising; but Jesus is the Lord of all. His greatness is unsearchable. The beauty and glory of the sun are such that, in the absence of Revelation, and when creatures were idols, we can scarcely wonder that this illustrious display of Deity should have been adored. But He is fairer than the children of men. Yea, he is altogether lovely; and all the angels of God are commanded to worship him. But, oh! the inestimable usefulness of this luminary! How he enlightens! warms! fructifies! adorns! blesses! What changes does he produce! How he fills the air with songs, and the gardens with fruit and fragrance! How he clothes the woods with foliage, and the meadows with grass! How he fills the valleys with corn, and makes the little hills rejoice on every side, and crowns the year with his goodness! And this he has always done. The sun that ripened Isaac's corn ripens ours; and though he has shone for so many ages, he is undiminished, and is as all-sufficient as ever. What an image of Him, who is the same yesterday, to-day, and for ever! who has always been the source of light, life, relief, and comfort! the hope, the consolation of Israel! the desire of all nations! Truly light is sweet, and a pleasant thing it is for the eyes to behold the sun. But he that seeth the Sun of Righteousness, and believeth on Jesus, hath everlasting life.

—The *rising* of the sun is the finest spectacle in the creation. I fear some never saw it; at least at the most interesting season of the year. What to them are a thousand rising suns, to the sublimity of lying late in bed! But when and how does this Sun of Righteousness arise? His coming was announced immediately after the fall, when God said, the seed of the woman should bruise the serpent's head. This was the very first ray of the early dawn of that light which was to shine more and more unto the perfect day. His approach obscurely appeared in the types and services of the ceremonial law. In the clearer discoveries of the prophets, the morning was beginning to spread upon the mountains. But to the Jews he was below the horizon; they longed to see his day; and kings and righteous men pressed forward to the brightness of his rising. At length, he actually arose; and when the fullness of time was come God sent forth his Son. A messenger from heaven proclaimed him to the shepherds, and said, I bring you glad tidings of great joy. The Savior is born.

Oh! the splendor of that morning! It brought glory to God in the highest, and on earth peace, good will toward men—GOD WAS MANIFEST IN THE FLESH.

—He rises in the dispensation of the Gospel. Whenever this enters a nation, or a village, *He* is evidently set forth, and the savor of his knowledge diffused; and it is then said to the place, and to the people, Arise, shine, for thy light is come, and the glory of the Lord is risen upon thee. He rises in spiritual illumination. Then he is revealed in us. He is presented to the eye of the soul. He is seen in a new manner, so as to fix and fill the mind, and govern the life. He rises in renewed manifestations. For sometimes he hides his face, and we are troubled. Then we anxiously ask, O when wilt Thou come unto me? Then we wait for him more than they that watch for the morning—and when we behold him again, find a brighter day. He rises in ordinances. What fresh and enlivening views of him have we often in meditation and prayer; in his own supper; in reading and hearing his word!

" Sometimes a light surprises
" The Christian, while he sings:
" It is the Lord that rises
" With healing in his wings."

But how will he arise in the irradiations of heaven; in the morning of immortality; making a day to be sullied with no cloud, and followed with no evening shade! Then their sun shall no more go down.

" God shall rise, and, shining o'er you,
" Turn to day the gloomy night;
" He, your God, shall be your glory,
" And your everlasting light."

MAY 8.—" I will look for him."—Isaiah, viii, 17.

THIS is peculiar language. It is the language of none in *heaven*. There all have found him, and are for ever with the Lord. It is the language of none in *hell*. There they are only concerned to escape from his hand, and to elude his eye. It is not the language of any in the WORLD. There they are active and eager enough, but they rise early, and sit up late, and eat the bread of sorrow, to gain some temporal advantage, honor, or pleasure, but none saith, " Where is God my Maker, who giveth songs in the night?" It is not the language of all in the CHURCH. There are some happy souls who know the joyful sound, and walk in the light of God's countenance; in his name they rejoice all the day, and in his righteousness they are exalted. But there are others whose desire is to his name, and to the remembrance of him, whose wish is, " O that I was as in months past, when the candle of the Lord shined upon my soul, and the Almighty was yet with me." These, these are the persons saying, and they cannot do better than say, " I will look for him."

It is here supposed that God may hide himself from his people. Indeed, it is expressly asserted in the former part of the verse, " I will wait upon the Lord, who hideth himself from the house of Israel." Sometimes he does this as to providential dispensations, suffering them to fall into trouble, and for a while leaving them, as if he had no regard for them, and had forgotten to be gracious. But we now refer to spiritual manifestations. Sometimes they are so in the dark that they are unable to perceive their condition, or enjoy the comforts of the Holy Ghost. God loves them always, and they cannot serve him in vain; but they cannot always see this, as they once did. The sun is as really in his course in a dark day as in a bright one, but his face is hid by fogs and clouds; and, says David to his God, "Thou didst hide thy face, and I was troubled." For when we are in the dark with regard to him, other things come forth and dismay us; and it is true, morally as well as physically, "Thou makest darkness, and it is night, wherein all the beasts of the forest do creep forth."

But the subjects of divine grace cannot rest satisfied without God. We see this in Job: "Oh that I knew where I might find him. Behold, I go forward, but he is not there; and backward, but I cannot perceive him; on the left hand, where he doth work, but I cannot behold him; he hideth himself on the right hand, that I cannot see him." This anxiety and restlessness to find him results from three things. LOVE, that longs to be near the object of attachment, and cannot endure separation. CONVICTION, which tells him of God's infinite importance to his case, and of his own entire dependence upon him. I am sick, says he, and he is my only physician; I am a traveller, and he is my only guide. I have nothing; he possesses all things. EXPERIENCE, he has tasted that the Lord is gracious, and the relish of the enjoyment adds to the sense of want; for that which indulges the appetite, provokes it also. Hence, though the believer does not desire more *than* God, he desires more *of* him.

Well, this restlessness is a token for good. Henry says, "a Christian is always on the perch, or on the wing; he is always reposing in God, or in flight after him; and the latter is as good an evidence of religion as the former; for delight is not only a part of complacency and affection, but also fear, complaint, desire; fear of losing the object; complaint of our enjoying so little of it; desire to attain and feel more."

Therefore be of good comfort; and if you ask where you are to look for him, look for him in Christ, where he is reconciling the world to himself. In him he is well pleased. Look after him in the promises; there you will find him, pledged in every readiness of power and compassion. Look after him in his ordinances; where two or three are gathered together, there is He in the midst of them. And not only look for him in the temple, but in the closet; pray to thy Father who *is* in secret, and thy Father who seeth in secret shall reward thee openly. Look after him in thy former experiences. Call to remembrance thy song in the night.

' Did ever trouble yet befall, | " And he refuse to hear thy call?"

Can all your former views and feelings be a delusion?

" Could you joy his saints to meet? | " Choose the ways you once abhorred.'

Would he have shown you such things as these, and also have accepted many an offering at your hands, if he had been minded to kill you?

And when you have found him whom you are looking after, fall at his feet, and ingenuously confess your unworthiness in causing him to withdraw from you. Complain not of him; justify him; but condemn yourselves. And instead of thinking he has dealt hardly with you, wonder that he has not cast you off for ever, and be thankful that he has been found of you again. Again you have morning; again you have spring; but the rising and shining of the sun has made it. "Thou hast turned for me my mourning into dancing; thou hast put off my sackcloth, and girded me with gladness; to the end that my glory may sing praise to thee, and not be silent. O Lord my God, I will give thanks unto thee for ever." Cleave to him with purpose of heart. Resolve rather to die, than again to grieve his Holy Spirit. And say,

'Till thou hast brought me to thy home,
'Where doubts and fears can never come;
"Thy countenance let me often see,
"And often thou shalt hear from me."

MAY 9.—"So Daniel was taken up out of the den, and no manner of hurt was found upon him, because he believed in his God."—Daniel, vi, 24.

HIS case at first seemed very hard to flesh and blood; but we here see the end of the Lord. All was so overruled, that Daniel had no reason to repent of his conduct, or lament the result of it. It is true, the God he served continually did not preserve him from the den of lions, but he delivered him out of it. He could have made a way for his escape; but the prevention of the trial would not have been half so impressive and useful as the issue. What a night did he pass there! What hours were they of prayer and praise, of peace and joy! What reflections did he make upon the power and goodness of his God; while the hungry lions (and they had been prepared to devour) looked on, and snuffed his flesh, but felt an invisible Restrainer, who said, Touch not mine anointed, and do my prophet no harm. How would he resolve to confide in him, and confess him, and serve him in future! How would the multitude be impressed! Those who doubted would be convinced. The timid would be emboldened. Many proselytes would be made to the religion of Daniel, while the king said, "I make a decree, that in every dominion of my kingdom men tremble and fear before the God of Daniel; for he is the living God, and steadfast for ever, and his kingdom that which shall not be destroyed, and his dominion shall be even unto the end. He delivereth and rescueth, and he worketh signs and wonders in heaven and in earth, who hath delivered Daniel from the power of the lions."

How much, therefore, did his steadfastness conduce to the glory of God, and the advancement of his cause! Christians never honor God more than in the fires; when they suffer like themselves; when they are witnesses for God; when they show that his service is too dear to be forsaken; and that they are willing to follow him to prison, or to death; and the religion they more than *profess*, enables them to glory in tribulation also; men see that there is a reality in it—a vital—a blessed reality, and that the righteous is more excellent than his neighbor.

But the result equally terminated in Daniel's own honor and welfare. When taken up, how would every eye be drawn toward him! How breathless would be their gaze! How would every tongue extol him! With what shoutings would they follow him home! When they met him, how ready would every man be to say, There is the man who would rather enter a den of hungry lions than violate his conscience, or sin against his God! What influence would be attached to his character! what weight to his advice and counsel! His reputation is perfected, and a good name is rather to be chosen than great riches. And his attainder is revoked, and he is restored; he is promoted by his sovereign to a higher station.

—And who would not have done what Darius did? He who had been faithful to his God, was more likely to be faithful to his king. This is, indeed, one of the ways in which godliness *naturally* conduces to a man's present advantage. It gains him confidence, and this is the lever of elevation. Constantius, the father of Constantine the Great, while as yet this prince was a heathen, wished to know the *character* of those about him. He therefore called together before him all the chiefs in his suit, and ordered them to offer sacrifices to his gods, on pain of being deprived of all their honors and functions. This trial was severe. Many sunk under it. They could not give up every thing that was dear and valuable. But some were inflexible. They had bought the truth, and they would not sell it for any price. Whatever they suffered, they were resolved to have a conscience void of offence. What happened! Those who basely complied he drove from his presence; while those who nobly refused he intrusted with the care of his person, and placed them in the most important offices, saying, On these men I can depend—I prize them more than all my treasures. And we know who hath said, Them that honor me I will honor; but they that despise me shall be lightly esteemed.

May 10.—"And the children of Israel went up harnessed out of the land of Egypt. And Moses took the bones of Joseph with him; for he had straitly sworn the children of Israel, saying, God will surely visit you; and ye shall carry up my bones away hence with you."—Exodus, xiii, 18, 19.

Here are two circumstances not to be overlooked, because God has deemed them worthy of record.

The first is not easily understood from the present version. It is said, They went up out of Egypt *harnessed*. The word harness, when the Bible was translated, signified not the furniture of a horse, but of a soldier—or armor; and this is the first sense the term bears in Johnson's dictionary; and to check the presumption of a warrior it was once said, "Let not him that putteth on the *harness* boast himself like him that putteth it off." The translators therefore meant to say, that they went out *armed*. Yet this is not at all probable. Such a jealous tyrant as Pharaoh would, by his spies, have prevented the Israelites from manufacturing, or purchasing, or hoarding up, weapons. We find, in after-times, when the Philistines held the Jews in subjection, they would not allow a smith to live in the country, and only permitted them to sharpen their agricultural implements at particular places. "But they had arms in the wilderness, when they fought Amalek and others." Yes, they had carried away a few weapons concealed, and made others out of the materials they had with them; and above all, they furnished themselves from the spoils of Pharaoh's army thrown on shore. But they were now only going out from Egypt. The margin is, they marched "*five* in a rank." But this would have extended the train more than fifty miles in length. Others, therefore, have rendered it, "in five squadrons." But all the meaning seems to be, that they moved out, not armed, but in soldier-like order, as regularly organized and slowly, as disciplined troops, and not like a rude rabble, or a huddled, jostling multitude. It shows that they did not go out by "haste or by flight:" and this is very remarkable, considering their numbers and the quality of the people, and how natural it was for those behind to dread lest their task-masters should overtake them, and therefore to press forward, to get before. But there was nothing of this; they moved with such steadiness, and stillness, that "against none of them did a dog move his tongue." We are also informed that "there was not found one feeble among them." Indeed, they had enough to do to take care of themselves and their goods, without being incumbered with invalids. But did ever such an immense multitude leave a place before without one individual unable to follow? It was the Lord's doing, and it is marvellous in our eyes.

The other circumstance in this march regards "the bones of Joseph, which Moses took with them." This rendered it a kind of funeral procession, and such as no other history relates. Much people of Nain followed the bier of the widow's son; but Joseph's corpse was accompanied with every man, woman, and child, of a whole nation. There is generally some time between death and interment, though in warm climates this is very short: here was an intervention of near two hundred years. Other bodies may have been carried as far, but were never so long in their conveyance to the grave—for here forty years were taken up in bearing Joseph to his burial.

We read at the death of Joseph, that "they embalmed him, and he was put in a coffin in Egypt:" and when we consider that he was the prime minister, and the savior of the country, and the most popular man in the realm, we may be assured that this was done in a manner the most perfect and sumptuous. The descendants of his own family would be likely to have the care of this precious deposit; and they would feel a peculiar veneration for it. But it was dear to all, and useful to all. It was a memento of the vanity of all human greatness. Joseph had risen in life to an unexampled degree of eminence. But what, where now is the governor and idol of Egypt? Mummied within those few inches of board! It was also a moral, as well as a mortal memento. Joseph was a very pious character; he had been highly exemplary in every relation and condition of life; and much of God, of Providence, and of grace, was to be read in his history. What an advantage to be always reminded of such a man, in having his remains always in the midst of them! But the body would be, above all, valuable, as a pledge of their future destination. It was a present palpable sign of God's covenant with their fathers, on their behalf.

For observe how they came in possession of this treasure.

It was according to the dying wish and prophecy of Joseph: "For he had straightly charged the children of Israel, saying, God will surely visit you; and ye shall carry up my bones away hence with you." His charge did not arise from a superstitious principle, as if it were better or safer to moulder in one place than another—nor even from a principle of natural or relative affection. This feeling, indeed, is often strong, and the wish to lie with their kindred seems to grow with the decline of life. How affectionately does Jacob express this sentiment, when dying! "I am to be gathered unto my people: bury me with my fathers in the cave that is in the field of Ephron the Hittite, in the cave that is in the field of Machpelah, which is before Mamre, in the land of Canaan, which Abraham bought with the field of Ephron the Hittite, for a possession of a burying place. There they buried Abraham, and Sarah his wife; there they buried Isaac, and Rebekah his wife; and there I buried Leah." This, however, was more than the language of nature in the father—and so it was in the son. The apostle tells us, "By faith Joseph, when he died, made mention of the departing of the children of Israel; and gave commandment concerning his bones." If he did it by faith his faith must have had a divine warrant; and it had. It was the promise of a God that cannot lie, that he would give Canaan for a possession to the seed of Abraham.

"And he said unto Abram, Know of a surety that thy seed shall be a stranger in a land that is not theirs, and shall serve them; and they shall afflict them four hundred years; and also that nation, whom they shall serve, will I judge: and afterward shall they come out with great substance." And this was, at the very time, ratified by a solemn covenant. Joseph knew of this engagement, and believed it; and though the time was remote, and the difficulties in the accomplishment many, like a true son of Abraham, he staggered not at the promise of God, through unbelief, but was strong in faith, giving glory to God. This raised him above the treasures of Egypt; this kept him from naturalizing there amidst all his prosperity—*there* he was only a stranger and a sojourner—another nation was his people—another land was his home: and therefore, instead of being entombed in an Egyptian pyramid, he ordered his body to be immediately taken to Goshen, and kept by them till they should go as a body to possess their inheritance, and then bury him with his fathers.

And behold the fulfillment! Enslaved as they were, they are delivered. Their enemies perish. They live by miracle for forty years in the wilderness. The Jordan is crossed. Canaan is taken—and, says the Conqueror to the people he had led to victory, "Behold, this day I am going the way of all the earth: and ye know in all your hearts, and in all your souls, that not one thing hath failed of all the good things which the Lord your God spake concerning you; all are come to pass unto you, and not one thing hath failed thereof." "So Joshua made a covenant with the people that day, and set them a statute and an ordinance in Shechem." What more? "And the bones of Joseph, which the children of Israel brought up out of Egypt, buried they in Shechem, in a parcel of ground which Jacob bought of the sons of Hamor, the father of Shechem, for a hundred pieces of silver: and it become the inheritance of the children of Joseph." Here we leave his hallowed remains till the resurrection of the just; inscribing over his sepulchre—A MEMORIAL OF THE FAITHFULNESS OF GOD.

"O for a strong and lively faith,
"To credit what the Almighty saith:
"To embrace the message of his *Son*,
"And call the joys of heaven our own"

MAY 11.—"The lame man which was healed held Peter and John."
Acts, iii, 15.

How perfectly natural and picturesque are the narratives of the Bible; serving at once to vouch for their truth, and to leave their representations fixed in the memory.

The circumstance here mentioned is too simple, striking, and touching, to be overlooked. The poor man had been lame from his mother's womb, and was placed daily at the Beautiful Gate of the Temple, to ask alms of the worshippers. Silver and gold, Peter and John had none: but they gave him something far better. In the name of the Lord Jesus, said they, rise up, and walk. And immediately his feet and ankle bones received strength. And he, leaping up—stood—and entered with them into the temple—walking—and leaping—and praising God. The people, also, seeing what was done, hastened to Solomon's Porch, greatly wondering—But the man that was healed *held Peter and John.*

Was this the effect of apprehension? Did he imagine their influence was confined to their bodily presence; and that if he let them go, his lameness would return?

Or did this result from a wish to point them out to the multitude? "Are you looking after the wonderful men who have made me whole?" eager and proud to proclaim to them; "Here," says he, "here they are—these are they."

Was it not still more the expression of his attachment? "O my deliverers and benefactors, let me attend upon you; and enjoy the happiness to serve you. Entreat me not to leave you, nor to return from following after you. Let me live, let me die with you." So it is in our spiritual cures. It is natural to feel a regard for those who have been the means of our recovery; and to keep hold of them—But let us remember, we may hold them too closely. And we do so, if we suffer them to draw us away from the God of all grace. For whoever are the instruments of doing us good, He is the agent; and he will have us know, that the excellency of the power is of Him, and not of them. Hence the reproof; "For while one saith, I am of Paul; and another, I am of Apollos; are ye not carnal? Who, then, is Paul, and who is Apollos, but ministers by whom ye believed, even as God gave to every man? I have planted, Apollos watered; but God gave the increase. So, then, neither is he that planteth any thing, neither he that watereth, but God that giveth the increase." They are something in the order of means, and a proper respect is due to them in this character: but they are nothing as to efficiency and success—this is entirely from God; and his glory will he not give to another. To idolize a minister, is the way to have him removed from us, or rendered unprofitable to us; "Nor by might, nor by power, but by my Spirit, saith the Lord of hosts." We can never honor God so much as by dependence upon him. And them that honor him he will honor; and they that despise him shall be lightly esteemed.

MAY 12.—"And sent messengers before his face: and they went, and entered into a village of the Samaritans, to make ready for him. And they did not receive him, because his face was as though he would go to Jerusalem. And when his disciples James and John saw this, they said, Lord, wilt thou

that we command fire to come down from heaven, and consume them, even as Elias did? But he turned, and rebuked them, and said, Ye know not what manner of spirit ye are of. For the Son of man came not to destroy men's lives, but to save them."—Luke ix, 52—56.

WHY did our Savior send a message to "make ready for him?" It could not be from a principle of self-indulgence; he had blamed Martha for her too much serving, when she entertained him. Neither was it for the purpose of show and ostentation. But it was from a motive of civility, not wishing to put them to trouble and confusion by his sudden arrival, especially as he travelled not alone, but with his disciples, and probably others; and also, as he purposed paying for the accommodations he ordered, to *try* their dispositions. Accordingly they displayed themselves.

But why "would they not receive him?" There had always been an implacable aversion between them and the Jews; it appeared on all occasions, and even hindered, as we find in the woman's answer at the well, the common offices of civil life. But to this ordinary dislike something peculiar was here added. They knew that our Lord was a public teacher, and had heard of his miracles; but his services had been with their enemies. They also had *their* temple, and their festivals, which were held at the same time; and one of these was at hand. But they saw he was bound, not to mount Gerizim, but to mount Zion; therefore "they did not receive him, because his face was as though he would go to *Jerusalem*."

Not far from this very place Elijah had punished Azariah's captains and companies sent to take him. John and James, therefore, ask, "Lord, wilt thou that *we* command fire to come down from heaven to consume them, even as *Elias* did?" The very infirmities of good men are peculiar; they are the spots of God's children. Here was something excusable; yea, even commendable—such was their acquaintance with Scripture—their applying to our Lord for his permission and approbation; their faith and confidence in his power, that, if *He* willed the thing, it must take place; and their attachment to him; for they could not bear to see one so dear to them insulted, in being refused the common rights of strangers. But evil blended with the good. Their zeal was not according to knowledge. The punishment was also extreme; for though the people had shown their rudeness and prejudices, they had not offered him violence; yet they must be destroyed, and sent down quick into hell in their sins; and *all* of them, though some of them might have been far less blameable than others. The cases, too, were not parallel. Elias had a call—the very impulse in him was supernatural, and was justified by the event; for fire from heaven would not have obeyed private passion. *He* acted from a regard to the glory of God and the welfare of Israel. But these men had no call, and were urged on too much by their own feelings.

He therefore rebukes them: "Ye know not what manner of spirit ye are of." They little suspected how much their own tempers had to do in the proposal. When the Gadarenes besought him to depart out of their coasts, and when the Nazarenes took him to the brow of the hill to cast him down, these disciples did not call for such vengeance then; no—*they* were Jews, but these offenders are *Samari-*

tans. How insensibly does something of our selfish and carnal feelings creep in and assume a religious pretension! None of our passions justify themselves so much as anger; we think we do well to be angry. But the wrath of man worketh not the righteousness of God. We may offer strange fire on God's own altar; but it is not thereby sanctified. The Author of peace and Lover of concord requires us to "show out of a good conversation our works with meekness of wisdom. And the fruit of righteousness is sown in peace of them that make peace."

How much does it become us to study our own spirits, and watch over the springs of our actions! A Jehu may say, "Come, see my zeal for the Lord," when he was only removing God's enemies to clear his own way to the throne. What do some mean by dealing faithfully with others, but indulging their dislike and insolence? Some professors of religion never reprove their servants and children, but in fretfulness and ill humor; and then their temper is discharged in a kind of spiritual scolding. Who can understand his errors? "Search me, O God, and know my heart; try me, and know my thoughts, and see if there be any wicked way in me, and lead me in the way everlasting."

Our Lord knew James and John better than they knew themselves; and in further reproof, he refers to himself as their example: "For the Son of man is not come to destroy men's lives, but to save them." He came indeed to seek and to save the soul principally; but he did not overlook the body. He healed the diseased; he fed the hungry; and has taught us to be merciful to the temporal wants of our fellow creatures. And even in carrying on his own peculiar cause, and endeavoring to promote the religion of the Bible, he allows us not to employ force, or to impoverish, or imprison, or in any way persecute. The weapons of his warfare are not carnal, but spiritual. "My kingdom," said he, "is not of this world: else would my servants fight"—indeed they would. Yea, they have fought—men, women, children have fought. They have fought with more than the courage of heroes. They have *prayed*, and *lived*, and *taught*, and *wept*, and *bled*, and *died!*

MAY 13.—"I thank God, through Jesus Christ our Lord."—Romans, vii, 25.

THE experience of the Christian, while in this world, is of a mixed nature. It resembles the day spoken of by Zechariah, which was neither dark nor clear. Whatever advantages he attains at present, there is always enough to tell him that this is not his rest. But, under all his complaints, he has reason to take courage and be thankful. So it was with Paul: for these words are to be taken in connection with his language in the preceding verse, where he groans, being burdened with the remains of indwelling sin; "O wretched man that I am! who shall deliver me from the body of this death? I thank God, through Jesus Christ our Lord."

—Yes, even in the midst of such an experience as this, there is a fourfold ground of thankfulness, and the Christian may say—First, I thank God, through Jesus Christ our Lord, that my corruption is my complaint. It was not so once—neither is it so with many now.

They drink in iniquity as the ox drinketh in water. It is their element; but it is not mine. They roll it as a sweet morsel under their tongue; but I have been made to see and taste that it is an evil thing, and bitter. I loathe it, and abhor myself for it, repenting in dust and ashes. The heart of stone has been taken away, and I have a heart of flesh—a heart affected with the guilt, the pollution, and the vileness of sin. I have nothing to boast of; every view I take of myself is humbling; but my desire is before him, and my groaning is not hid from him.

"Marks of grace I cannot show;
"All polluted is my best;
"Yet I weary am, I know—
"And the weary long for rest."

And they are invited to obtain it.

Secondly, I thank God, through Jesus Christ our Lord, that though I am in the conflict, I am not conquered. Though yet alive, the enemy is dethroned. Though it rages, it does not reign. It threatens to resume its ascendancy, and has sometimes alarmed my fears. I have said, I shall one day perish; but having obtained help of God, I continue to this day, faint, yet pursuing, and feeling no disposition to turn back.

Thirdly, I thank God, through Jesus Christ our Lord, that deliverance is sure.

"What though my inbred lusts rebel;
"'Tis but a struggling gasp for life:
"The weapons of victorious grace
"Shall slay my sins, and end the strife."

The victory in this case may be inferred from the reality of the conflict. It is as certain as the word of God can render it. The result is left to no precariousness, but secured in the everlasting covenant. He who made his soul a sacrifice for sin, shall see his seed, and be glorified in them. Their help is laid on One that is mighty. His blood cleanseth from all sin. His righteousness justifies the ungodly. His grace is sufficient for the most weak and exposed. They shall never perish; neither shall any pluck them out of His hand. And they may anticipate this, and rejoicing in a hope that maketh not ashamed, say, I know whom I have believed; and am persuaded that He is able to keep that which I have committed to him against that day. Yea,

Finally, I thank God, through Jesus Christ our Lord, that the deiverance is near. Were it remote, I ought to wait for it with patience Others wait. The husbandman waiteth for the precious fruit of the earth, and hath long patience until he receive the early and the latter rain. But it will not tarry. If life be short, the conflict cannot be long. Soon the warfare must be accomplished; and the enemies I have seen to-day, I shall see no more for ever. My salvation is nearer than when I believed. The night is far spent. The day is at hand—

"Though painful at present,
"'Twill cease before long;
"And then, O how pleasant
"The Conqueror's song!"

May 14.—"I will cause you to pass under the rod."—Ezekiel, xx, 37.

Three things in the Scripture go by this name. A father's scourge, a king's sceptre, and a shepherd's crook. All these will apply in the present instance; and all of them are necessary to do some justice to the subject.

—There is a paternal rod. Thus we read, He that spareth the rod hateth his son. I will visit their transgressions with a rod, and their iniquities with stripes. There can be no mistake here. The idea is correction, and the rod means the instrument with which the father chastises. God is a father, and he has a rod. This rod is made up of any kind of affliction—outward troubles—bodily pains—family bereavements. Even men, wicked men, reproaching and injuring us, and undeservedly too, as to *them*, may be God's scourge, to make us suffer for something else. Thus he said of the Assyrian: "O Assyrian, the rod of mine anger, and the staff in their hand is mine indignation. I will send him against a hypocritical nation, and against the people of my wrath will I give him a charge, to take the spoil, and to take the prey, and tread them down like the mire of the streets." Our friends, our children, our dearest comforts in life, God can make the means of chastising us, if needs be. Who comes not under this rod? "As many as I love, I rebuke and chasten." They are not all exercised in the same way: but "what son is he whom the father chasteneth not?" And who, painful as the exercise may be, cannot acknowledge in the review, if not in the enduring—

"Yet I have found 'tis good for me
"To bear my Father's rod;
"Afflictions make me learn thy law,
"And live upon my God?"

And as they are useful in our progress in the divine life, so they have frequently been the means of first awakening the desire, "Where is God my Maker, who giveth songs in the night?" The failure of the human arm has made them feel after the divine. The desolations of earth have said to purpose, "Arise and depart hence; for this is not our rest." What sent the prodigal home? He began to be in want. What brought Manasseh to repentance? In his afflictions he sought the Lord God of his father.

"Father, I bless thy gentle hand:
How kind was thy chastising rod,
"That forced my conscience to a stand,
"And brought my wandering soul to God!"

—There is a regal rod. So we call a sceptre. Of the Messiah, the King on his holy hill of Zion, it is said, "He shall rule them with a rod of iron;" but this refers to his adversaries. He has another kind of rod for his subjects. The Lord shall send the rod of his strength out of Zion. And what *was* sent out of Zion but the Gospel? The Gospel, therefore, is his rod; and this rod is his sceptre, the emblem of his authority, displaying his majesty, and maintaining his rule. Hence it is added, "Rule thou in the midst of thine enemies;" meaning, over his subjects, though surrounded with foes; for they are brought under his sway, and feel and acknowledge their subjection, as it follows, "Thy people shall be willing in the day of thy power." Though once they said, Who is the Lord? and we will not have him to reign over us; they are all brought under the rod of his strength. The Gospel has come to them, not in word only, but in power. It has awakened their consciences; it has changed their dispositions; it has made them submit to the righteousness which is of God, and to yield themselves to his service, as those who are alive from the dead. They *were* the servants of sin; but they *now* obey, from the heart, the form of doctrine which was delivered them.

—There is a pastoral rod. Of this David speaks: when addressing the Lord as his shepherd, he says, "Yea, though I walk through the valley of the shadow of death, I will fear no evil; for thou art with me; thy rod and thy staff, they comfort me." This refers to the crook with which the shepherd both walks as he follows, and uses as he manages the sheep. It is the symbol and instrument of his charge and office. The people of God are naturally like lost sheep going astray, wandering upon the mountains of barrenness and danger. But He seeks them, and finds them out, and brings them all under his rod. And happy are they who are under his care. *He* is their shepherd, and they shall not want. He will make them to lie down in green pastures; he will feed them beside the still waters. He will restore their souls, and lead them in the path of righteousness, for his name's sake. He will gather the lambs with his arm, and carry them in his bosom, and gently lead those that are with young. And the privilege commenced in grace, will be continued and completed in glory. "Therefore are they before the throne of God, and serve him day and night in his temple; and He that sitteth on the throne shall dwell among them. They shall hunger no more, neither thirst any more; neither shall the sun light on them, nor any heat. For the Lamb, which is in the midst of the throne, shall feed them, and shall lead them unto living fountains of waters; and God shall wipe away all tears from their eyes."

May 15.—"I will bring you into the bond of the covenant."
Ezekiel, xx, 37.

What is this *covenant?* Some always consider it a kind of stipulation between God and us, in which he proposes to do so much, if we will do so much: thus representing the Supreme Being as a bargainer, getting as good terms as he can, while man, the other high contracting party, agrees to them. But God is said to make a covenant with the earth; yea, and with the beasts of the field. This cannot intend a reciprocal negotiation, but the engagement of God only; and which is called a covenant, allusively, to signify its stability and certainty, the effect in the one instance being put for the cause in the other. For the same reason, this name is given to that gracious constitution for the salvation of sinners through the Mediator, made known in the Scripture for the obedience of faith: and is the very same with what is also called "the mercy promised to the fathers," and "the hope of eternal life which God, that cannot lie, promised before the world began."

The *bond* of this covenant is the obligation which it lays upon God who makes it, and upon those who are saved by it. We could not, without profaneness, have talked of *binding* God; but he has been pleased, in his infinite condescension, to bind himself. His heart could have been trusted; but he knew our frame, and our weakness; and to remove all our fearful misgivings, arising from our meanness and guilt, he has brought himself under a covenant engagement. And if it be but a man's covenant, yet if it be confirmed, no man disannulleth it. And he has confirmed his engagement, by an oath—and because he could swear by no greater, he sware by himself; and also by a sacrifice—and the victim was no less than his only begotten Son, and whose blood, therefore, is called the blood of the everlasting covenant. Thus he is bound to be the God of his people; bound to save them, to pardon, to sanctify, to help them. Bound to make all things work together for their good. Bound to give them grace and glory, and to withhold no good thing from them.

It also binds them—not to atone for their sin—this is already expiated; nor to produce a righteousness to justify them before God—this is already brought in, and on this their hope only relies—but they are bound to obey, and serve, and glorify Him who has done such great things for them. Surely evidence, consistency, gratitude, justice, require it. They feel the obligation, and acknowledge it, and wish all to know that they are not their own, but bought with a price. They feel the obligation; and it is not irksome; for though they are bound, it is with the cords of a man, and the bonds of love. It is the obligation of a mother to press to her bosom her sucking child; it is the obligation of a hungry man to eat his pleasant meat—My meat is to do the will of Him that sent me. It is a yoke; but it is like the yoke of marriage to the happy pair who daily bless the bonds. It is a burden; but it is like the burden of wings to the bird, which, instead of confining him, gives him the freedom of the skies—Well, says the Savior, my yoke is easy, and my burden is light.

Blessed are the people that are in such a case! Their humble confidence can authorize them in every trouble to say, "Yet hath he made with me an everlasting covenant, ordered in all things and sure; for this is all my salvation and all my desire;" and their affectionate zeal, in every temptation, will constrain them to sing,

"All that I have, and all I am,
"Shall be for ever thine;
"Whate'er my duty bids me give,
"My cheerful hands resign.

"Yet if I might make some reserve,
"And duty did not call;
"I love my God with zeal so great,
"That I should give him all."

May 16.—"And it came to pass, when the time was come that he should be received up, he steadfastly set his face to go to Jerusalem."—Luke, ix, 51.

Whither he was to be received up, is not mentioned; but it is easily understood, especially if we compare the words with other passages. Accordingly the margin refers us to two places: in the first of which Luke says, "Until the day in which he was taken up;" and in the second, Mark says, "So then, after the Lord had spoken unto them, he was received up into heaven, and sat on the right hand of God." The event, therefore, was his ascending to his Father and our Father; to his God and our God. There was the home where he originally dwelt. He speaks of a glory which he had with the Father before the world was. Thus he was rich; but for our sakes he became poor, and made himself of no reputation. He resided on earth for three-and-thirty years in a kind of exile: a Prince higher than the kings of the earth, in disguise, and the world knew him not. But having accomplished the work that was given him to do, he entered into his glory.

—And if nothing is left to chance in our minutest affairs, surely there was nothing unarranged with regard to his leaving this world to go unto the Father. Accordingly, we here read of the *time* for his being received up. And if they have chronicles above, and days, as we have—what a memorable day would that have been, in which, after such an absence, and after such astonishing exploits, and completely vanquishing all the powers of darkness, the everlasting doors were opened, for the King of glory to enter in!

—On this, therefore, the Savior fixed his eye; and this emboldened him to *set his face steadfastly to go to Jerusalem.* For, what zeal, what courage did the determination require! He knew the perilous nature of the journey. He apprehended all that awaited him when he should arrive—That there he should be forsaken—and betrayed—and apprehended—and mocked—and scourged—and crucified. Yet his resolution does not fail him. Lo! I come, says he, to do thy will, O God! I have a baptism to be baptized with, and how am I straitened till it be accomplished! For he looked beyond, and regarded the blessed result. And this was the glorification of his human nature; the acquirement of his mediatorial reward; the dispensation of the Holy Spirit; the government of the world; the salvation of the church; the enjoyment of the praises of the redeemed for ever! This was the joy set before him in covenant engagement; and for this he endured the cross, and despised the shame. For though his soul was to be made a sacrifice of sin, yet he knew that he should rise from the dead, and see of the travail of his soul, and be satisfied. Therefore, as the season drew near, he looked to the issue, and triumphed in the prospect. Now, says he, is the hour that the Son of man shall be—not abased, but—glorified. *Now* is the judgment of this world; *now* is the Prince of this world cast out; and I, if I be lifted up from the earth, will draw all men unto me.

—So, Christian, should it be with you. There is a time appointed, when you also shall be removed from this vale of tears, and be for ever with the Lord. Think of it; and set your face boldly and firmly to go, whenever duty calls. The man who has an amputation to suffer, must not dwell on the operation, but must pass beyond, to the restoration of health, and the continuance of life. This, Christian, is the way to endure, and to be more than a conqueror. It is to reckon that the sufferings of the present time are not worthy to be compared with the glory that shall be revealed—You may sow in tears, but you shall reap in joy. The road may be rough, but it will soon bring you home.

"Yet a season, and you know
"Happy entrance will be given;
"All your sorrows left below,
"And earth exchang'd for heaven."

MAY 17.—"If it be so, our God whom we serve is able to deliver us from the burning fiery furnace: and he will deliver us out of thine hand, O king. But if not, be it known unto thee, O king, that we will not serve thy gods, nor worship the golden image which thou hast set up."—Daniel, iii, 17, 18.

CONDUCT so tried and triumphant in the trial, must have had some principle to produce it. He who acts without principle is the slave of impulse, humor, accident, custom; and you can no more rely upon him than upon a wave of the sea, driven with the wind and tossed. But when a man is governed by principle, he will be consistent in his practice: he may have infirmities, but a sameness pervades his character; he may err, but he is conscientious: and his excellencies will appear even in his mistakes and failings. Can we find a principle adequate to *this* heroism? The apostle tells us it was faith. But faith must have something to lay hold of; and the faith of these young men seizes three things.

The first is, the *power* of God. Our God whom we serve is *able* to deliver us from the burning fiery furnace. They knew nothing was too hard for the *Lord*. And we believe in the Father Almighty, Maker of heaven and earth. We, indeed, are not to look for miracles: but the power of God is the same as formerly: and there are cases in which the view of it can alone inspire relief. When difficulties multiply, and means fail, and creatures say, help is not in me—then we must lay hold of his strength, and remember that he is able to do for us exceedingly abundantly above all we can ask or think.

The second is, his *disposition*. And he *will* deliver us out of thine hand, O king. This they deemed probable—perhaps they had a persuasion of it, derived from a divine impression, or deduced from the character of God, and the records of his word. They had read in the Scriptures, along with the experience of his people, the assurance, "Call upon me in the day of trouble, and I will deliver thee:" "When thou passest through the waters I will be with thee; and through the rivers, they shall not overflow thee: when thou walkest through the fire, thou shalt not be burnt; neither shall the flame kindle upon thee." Here is another argument of faith. His people eye his goodness, as well as his power; and know that he *will* appear for them, and save them, in his own way, and in his own time.

The third, is a future state. "But if *not*, be it known unto thee, O king, that we will not serve thy gods, nor worship the golden image which thou hast set up." What! would they refuse, even if death was the consequence? Yes. But this shows undeniably, that they did not consider death as annihilation. They would not have acted thus, had they believed that there was nothing beyond the grave. Had they perished in the furnace, their martyrdom *could* not have been their duty—it would have been the sacrifice of fools—their end would have been madness.

This is the very case argued by the apostle, "If in this life only we have hope in Christ, we are of all men the most miserable:" "Else what shall they do which are baptized for the dead, if the dead rise not at all? why are they then baptized for the dead? And why stand we in jeopardy every hour?" God does not require us to sacrifice our being and happiness for ever, to his pleasure. It is *not* his pleasure; it *cannot* be his pleasure. By the law of our nature, and the authority of his word, we are even *commanded* to seek our welfare, and to seek *first* the kingdom of God and his righteousness; and therefore to be willing to give these up, would be disobedience and contempt. But the language was wise and noble, when they knew, that though they fell in the conflict, they should *yet* be more than conquerors; and that, if they lost a dying, they would obtain an immortal life.

It is absurd to suppose the Jews of old had no knowledge of a future state. Search the Scriptures, says the Savior, for in them ye think ye have eternal life. Abraham, and his fellow heirs of the same promise, said such things as declared plainly that they sought a country, even a heavenly. David said, Thou shalt guide me with thy counsel, and *afterward* receive me to glory. Shadrach, Meshach, and Abednego, *acted* upon this belief, and *must* have acted upon it. They endured, as seeing Him who is invisible. And what was Nebuchadnezzar, compared with *Him?* What was this furnace, compared with the lake that burneth with fire and brimstone, which is the *second* death? What could they gain by complying, compared with what they would for ever lose? And what could they lose by refusing, compared with what they would for ever gain? We reckon, said they, that the sufferings of the present time are not worthy to be compared with the glory that shall be revealed in us.

—And our faith must regard the future, or we shall be often perplexed and vanquished. This is the victory that overcometh the world, even our faith. Moses chose rather to suffer affliction with the people of God, than to enjoy the pleasures of sin for a season; for he had respect unto the recompense of the reward. This, believed and realized, explains all; harmonizes all; indemnifies all; glorifies all. "For our light affliction, which is but for a moment, worketh for us a far more exceeding and eternal weight of glory; while we look not at the things which are seen, but at the things which are not seen: for the things which are seen, are temporal; but the things which are not seen, are eternal." Lord, I believe; help thou mine unbelief.

MAY 18.—"Then answered Peter, and said unto Jesus, Lord, it is good for us to be here: if thou wilt, let us make here three tabernacles; one for thee, and one for Moses, and one for Elias."—Matthew, xvii, 4.

—"NOT knowing," we are assured by the Holy Ghost; "not knowing what he said." For had the motion been complied with, how could our Savior have suffered and died? And if Peter had continued there, how could he have attended to his wife and children? Besides, he was mistaken as to the nature and design of the dispensation, which was only for a confirmation of their faith, by making them witnesses of his glory, and to afford them a glimpse or taste of the heavenly blessedness. The full fruition is for another world. If ever we think of building tabernacles here, we shall soon hear a voice saying, "Arise and depart hence, for this is not your rest."

But though he did not know what he said, he knew *why* he said it. Two things caused his bliss. First, the communion of saints. And here were not only John and James, but Moses and Elias; and these were not shining statues, but they spake, and spake of the Savior's decease. What a subject! What speakers! How delightful must have been intercourse with them! But the second was the presence of Jesus. And surely it cannot be a question, why it is good to be where He is. With him we are safe, and no where else. He is the source of all light and knowledge. He is the fountain of honor and excellency. He is the consolation of Israel. He is all, and in all.

But where is he with his people? we do not mean as to his essential presence, this is universal; but as to his special and gracious. He is with them in the *closet.* There he manifests himself to them, as he does not in the world. There they enjoy an intimacy, a freedom, an unrestrained intercourse with him, such as other company will not allow. Could these beams and rafters, said a good man, pointing to an unceiled roof, speak, they would testify what hours of enjoyment I have had here, in communion with Him. Of the closet, therefore, they can say, It is good for us to be *here.*

—He is with them in his temple. Where would you look for a man, but in his own house? And the sanctuary is the place where the Lord's honor dwelleth. In all places where I record my name, I will come unto thee, and I will bless thee. And have they not found the promise true? Have they not seen his power and glory in the sanctuary? Of his house, therefore, they can say, It is good for us to be *here.*

—He is with them at his table. His cross is every thing to a Christian; and here, before our eyes, Jesus Christ is evidently set forth crucified among us. What a sublime duty; what an exalted privilege is the commemoration of his death! His flesh is meat indeed, and his blood is drink indeed! Who has not peculiarly found him in this exercise the Tree of Life? Who has not said, I sat down under his shadow with delight, and his fruit was sweet to my taste? It is good for us to be *here.*

—He is with them in the furnace. There the three Hebrew children found him. The flames only consumed their bands, and set them free; and they were seen walking in the midst of the fire, with the Son of God! I will be with thee, says He, in trouble. And if this be fulfilled, and it must be fulfilled, they will have reason to say, however deep the distress, Lord, it is good for us to be *here.*

—He is with them in the vale of death. How much will they need him then! Then all other friends and helpers leave them. Then heart and flesh will fail them. What shall we do, they have often said, what shall we do without him then? But they will not be without him. He knows their frame, and his grace is sufficient for them; and his strength shall be perfect in their weakness. Yea, though they walk through the valley of the shadow of death, he is with them; his rod and his staff they comfort them; and then they have cause to say, Lord, it is good for us to be *here.*

—How much more will they be justified in saying this in heaven! There he is with them immediately. There they will see him as he is; there, before the presence of his glory, they will possess fullness of joy, and pleasures for ever more.

But none will be translated thither in person, whose hearts are not sent off first. None will have their residence in heaven hereafter, who have not their conversation in heaven here. None will be with the Lord for ever, but those that find it their happiness for the Lord to be with them now.

MAY 19.—"He riseth from supper, and laid aside his garments; and took a towel, and girded himself. After that he poureth water into a basin, and began to wash the disciples' feet, and to wipe them with the towel wherewith he was girded."—John, xiii, 4, 5.

THAT he designed this to be exemplary is obvious, from his own declaration after the action had been performed. "Know ye what I have done to you? Ye call me Master and Lord: and ye say well; for so I am. If I then, your Lord and Master, have washed your feet, ye also ought to wash one another's feet. For I have given you an example, that ye should do as I have done to you. Verily, verily, I say unto you, The servant is not greater than his Lord; neither he that is sent greater than he that sent him. If ye know these things, happy are ye if ye do them." Now it is not necessary that we should resemble him in the very circumstances of the action, but only in the spirit of it. In popish countries, the ceremony of washing the feet of another, is often performed by persons not *very* lowly in heart—sometimes by a cardinal—yea, and by the pope himself. But the design is to enforce the *humility of brotherly love;* and to teach us that no service is to be deemed too mean for Christians to perform, when Providence brings it in their way, and the condition of a fellow creature requires it. We may profess to do this in the abstract, but refuse to afford the assistance called for in particular instances, because the office is too mortifying to the pride of our feelings or manners. But this is not to love without dissimulation. This is to love in word and in tongue, but not in deed and in truth. Many have lost all credit here, by their unfeeling, distant, and disdainful conduct towards their inferiors, when they had the finest opportunities to evince their condescension, if they had any.

It would be well, if all who name the name of Christ would attend to the admonition of his apostle; "In honor, preferring one another—Mind not high things, but condescend to men of low estate." Job was the greatest man in the East; yet he could say, "If I did despise the cause of my man-servant, or of my maid-servant, when they contended with me; what then shall I do when God riseth up? and when he visiteth, what shall I answer him? Did not he that made me in the womb, make him? and did not one fashion us in the womb?" And with regard to those sufferers, generally overlooked by greatness, yea, and by mediocrity too; and those instances of humbler kindness, which splendid beneficence never thinks of; he could make this affecting appeal: "If I have withheld the poor from their desire, or have caused the eyes of the widow to fail; or have eaten my morsel myself alone, and the fatherless hath not eaten thereof; (for from my youth he was brought up with me as with a father, and I have guided her from my mother's womb;) if I have seen any perish for want of clothing, or any poor without covering; if his loins have not blessed me, and if he were not warmed with the fleece of my sheep; if I have lifted up my hand against the fatherless, when I saw my help in the gate; then let mine arm fall from my shoulder-blade, and mine arm be broken from the bone."

A great man seldom wants more help than he can purchase or procure. Though he has wasted his substance, and reduced himself so as to deserve starvation; his utmost extremity is superfluous subsistence, compared with the suffering of a worthy character, who is neglected because originally indigent. But the industrious poor should be the objects of our attention, whose distress is brought upon them, not by vice, extravagance, and speculation, but by the providence of God; and whose condition sinks them below observation; so that, in the midst of their trouble, none careth for them.

Services, small in their nature, are greatly esteemed by those who are commonly neglected. And in those offices you perform for them, you serve the Lord Christ. They cannot recompense you; but he will graciously say, "Inasmuch as ye did it unto one of the least of these my brethren, ye did it unto me."

Let me, then, hear his blessed invitation—Take my yoke upon you, and learn of me; for I am meek and lowly in heart; and ye shall find rest unto your souls. Let the same mind be in me, which was also in Christ Jesus: who, being in the form of God, thought it not robbery to be equal with God; but made himself of no reputation, and took upon him the form of a servant, and was made in the likeness of men; and being found in fashion as a man, he humbled himself, and became obedient unto death, even the death of the cross.

MAY 20.—"Thanks be to God for his unspeakable gift."—2 Corinthians, ix, 15.

THIS gratitude, no doubt, must be due, infinitely due. But to excite and increase our thankfulness, it is desirable to know, not only that the Son of God has been given *for* us, but *to* us; and that he is now actually our *own*. There are some who are satisfied here. They can say, This *is my* beloved, and this *is my* friend: the strength of *my* heart, and my portion for ever. But this is not the case with all. Some are asking, with all the anxiousness the importance of the subject requires, Is this unspeakable gift, for which eternity will be too short to praise God, *mine?* In answer to which, allow me to ask,

Do you approve of the design for which he was given? He came into the world to save sinners, in a way equally *gracious* and *holy*. Do you acquiesce in a purpose which involves the destruction of *self* and of *sin?*

Have you received him? In the word and means of grace he is presented to us. We read of some who have received Christ Jesus the Lord; and as many as received him were privileged to become the sons of God. Has this act been yours? When Laban saw Abraham's servant laden with presents, he said, "Come in, thou blessed of the Lord." Did you ever give Christ such an invitation? "Zaccheus made haste, and came down, and received him joyfully." Did you ever give him such a welcome? And are you willing to receive him wholly? For is Christ divided? Can you receive him as your prophet, and not as your king? as your priest, and not as your example? Can you enjoy him in his sacrifice, and refuse him in his service? Can you entertain him in spiritual privileges, and cast him out in spiritual duties?

—Have you given yourselves to him? I do not say your substance only, or your time only. You may subscribe to religious institutions, and attend the means of grace—and keep back the main thing. But have you given him yourselves? The Corinthians gave their own selves unto the Lord. Can you remember such a surrender? An evening, perhaps, when, like Isaac in the field, you said, "Lord, I am thine, save me." The close of a Sabbath, perhaps, when in your closet, you read, and wept, and kneeled—and then rose, and wept, and kneeled again, and said, "O Lord, other lords beside thee have had dominion over me—henceforth by thee only will I make mention of thy name."

—Do you supremely prize him? To them that believe, he is precious. Paul longed to depart, to be with—James? Isaiah? Moses? No—but to be with Jesus. You have some who are dear to you on earth—you have more in heaven. Perhaps you have a child there—lovely here, but a cherub there; perhaps you have a mother there, whose knees were on the altar on which you laid your little hands to pray; perhaps you have there the dear minister who turned your feet into the path of peace. But, thinking of *Him*, can you say, "Whom have I in heaven but thee? and there is none on earth I desire beside thee?" Answer these inquiries, and claim this unspeakable gift as your own for ever.

But here is another question, What use should the possessor make of it? If you are Christians, though you were once darkness, you are now light in the Lord, and must walk as children of light. And much of your wisdom must appear in knowing what a prize you have in your hand. Make use of him, then, in all your duties. Meditation is a duty—let him enrich and enliven it, and sweeten it. Prayer is a duty—do it always in his name. Make use of him in all your wants. You want cleansing—use him as the fountain open for sin and uncleanness. You want safety—flee to him as your refuge. You want food—and his flesh is meat indeed, and his blood is drink indeed: feed on it. Make use of him in all your afflictions. Are you bereaved? are you poor? Hang upon him, in whom you possess all things. You know that your Redeemer liveth.

—We have one question more. What can we think of those who disregard this unspeakable gift? What can we think of their ingenuousness, in contemning such infinite goodness and mercy? Of their danger? How can they escape, if they neglect so great a salvation? Of their misery? What can a wretch do without him in death, and at the judgment-day? It is awful to think—but the Saviour may become the destroyer. The greatest blessing may prove the greatest curse.

May 21.—"That I may rejoice in the day of Christ, that I have not run in vain, neither labored in vain."—Philippians, ii, 16.

This is mentioned as an argument, to enforce the duties he had just recommended: "Do all things without murmurings and disputings; that ye may be blameless and harmless, the sons of God, without rebuke, in the midst of a crooked and perverse nation, among whom ye shine as lights in the world, holding forth the word of life." And surely we are to know them that labor among us, and to esteem them very highly in love for their works' sake, and to co-operate with them, and to be zealously concerned to promote their usefulness and comfort. There is a peculiar relation between a minister and the people of his charge; and, as a well conditioned flock is the credit of the shepherd, and a well ordered family the commendation of the master, and the moral and prosperous state of his subjects the praise of the ruler; so a wise, holy, consistent, amiable, lively, useful church, is the honor and happiness of the preacher. He lives, if they stand fast in the Lord, for they are his glory and joy.

But why, for this satisfaction, does the apostle refer to so *late* a period as the day of Christ? Had he no present rejoicing from their excellencies and exertions? He had. But he knew that he must *now* rejoice with trembling. He had known many who did run well, but were hindered; who began in the Spirit, but ended in the flesh. He had seen many moral blossoms perishing without fruit; and experience taught him to distinguish between the hope of the spring, and the richness of autumn. Persons, for a season, may rejoice in a minister's light, but in time of temptation fall away. They may hang on his lips, and then break his heart. He only that endureth to the end shall be saved; and then are we made partakers of Christ, if we hold the beginning of our confidence steadfast unto the end; and "the day will declare it."

—And till then the true character and condition of those among whom he has labored will not be completely ascertained and developed.

—Till then, also, his hearers will not be placed beyond the reach of moral harm, or be incapable of injuring the cause they profess.

—Till then, also, his aim will not be fully accomplished, which is, to "present every man perfect in Christ Jesus," and "filled with all the fullness of God."

—Then, also, many will acknowledge their obligations to his instrumentality for their conversion or edification, which he knew nothing of here; and it will be safer and better for him not to know the extent and degree of his usefulness, till he is secure from the possibility of vanity and pride. Then is the period for rejoicing, when there can be no mistake, no excess, no danger in the joy.

—Oh! may he that watches for my soul as one that must give an account, do it with joy, and not with grief!

What a proof is here that there will be a knowledge of each other in heaven! How else could the apostle say of converts, "What is our hope, or joy, or crown of rejoicing? Are not even ye in the presence of our Lord Jesus Christ at his coming? For ye are our glory, and our joy?"

MAY 22.—"Justified by the faith of Christ."—Galatians, ii, 16.

LET me remark here the blessing, and the way in which it is obtained.

What is justification? It is not the making us righteous in person, but in state. The Papists confound it with sanctification, and some Protestants do the same; but justification stands opposed to *condemnation.* It is the absolving a man from a charge, the acquitting him when accused, and pronouncing him righteous. Only as we are really guilty, we cannot be justified by disproving the offence, but by the non-imputation of it, and treating us as innocent. The manner is described by the apostle: We are justified freely by his grace, through the redemption that is in Christ Jesus, whom God hath set forth as a propitiation for sin. The blessing is full and complete; for we "are justified from all things." It is permanent and irreversible: "Their sins and iniquities will I remember no more." It is also a present benefit. The perception of it may be wanting, but the state is real; they have passed from death unto life—they are accepted in the beloved. And blessed, says David, is the man whose transgression is forgiven, whose sin is covered: blessed in his duties; blessed in his comforts. Blessed in his trials. For him affliction has no curse, death no sting, eternity no terror.

This inestimable blessing is obtained by the faith of Christ. We are often curious, and ask for reasons when we should be satisfied with facts. It is not necessary to be able to explain precisely how faith justifies the soul. It should be enough for us to know that it is a truth clearly revealed.

And since, O my soul, none are justified that do not believe, and all that believe are justified, let me apply my heart unto his wisdom; and, instead of losing myself in subtle inquiries, and angry disputes, let me do two things: let me observe, first, the importance of this faith. It is, in a sober sense, as important as Christ; and what is ascribed to him meritoriously, is ascribed to faith instrumentally. He is the well; but by faith we draw water out of it. He is the refuge; but a refuge cannot screen us, unless it be entered. He is the bread of life; but food cannot nourish us, unless it be eaten—and all this is done by faith only.

Let me, secondly, ask seriously and earnestly, have I this faith of Christ? Do I believe the record, that God hath given us eternal life, and that this life is in his Son? And am I repairing to him, and trusting in him alone for salvation? How does my faith sow? Does it "sow in tears?" How does it rejoice? Does it "rejoice in Christ Jesus?" and has it "no confidence in the flesh?" How does it work? Does it "work by love?" How does it travel? How plead? Can I say, "I will go in the strength of the Lord God; I will make mention of his righteousness only?"

MAY 23.—"Be not ye called Rabbi; for one is your Master, even Christ and all ye are brethren."—Matthew, xxiii, 8.

RABBI signifies Master; not a domestic or civil master, having servants or subjects under him, but a master of pupils; a leader, a teacher, having disciples who admire and follow him. It was not an ancient title; we scarcely read of it before the coming of the Messiah But the Scribes and Pharisees were exceedingly fond of the name "They love," says our Lord, "greetings in the markets, and to be called of men, Rabbi, rabbi." "But," adds he, "be not ye called Rabbi."

The apostles followed this admonition. "We have no dominion," said they, "over your faith, but are helpers of your joy." They did not lord it over God's heritage, but fed them with knowledge and understanding, and were ensamples to the flock. They considered themselves as messengers, deriving all their authority from their employer, and always referred their people from themselves to him. They delivered nothing but what they had received, and called upon those they addressed not to believe in them implicitly, but to search the Scriptures, and see whether the things were so; to prove all things, and hold fast that which was good. They were offended if persons thought too highly of them, or wished to be named after them. "Was Paul crucified for you? or were ye baptized in the name of Paul? Who then is Paul, and who is Apollos, but ministers by whom ye believed, even as God gave to every man?" "So, then, neither is he that planteth any thing, neither he that watereth; but God that giveth the increase."

—It is now hardly possible to avoid religious names, but we lament that they were ever introduced. Why should parties be called Calvinists, Arminians, Lutherans, Baxterians, or any other denomination? If the sentiments held by any of these men are not found in the Sacred Writings they are not binding upon the conscience, whoever sanctions them; and if they are, why should it be intimated that they have any other origin? Let us be satisfied with the words the Holy Ghost useth, without attaching salvation or damnation to men's definitions of them. The documents are divine and infallible; but who can pronounce the explications to be so?

If we call ourselves by the name of any human authority, let it be an inspired one. Let us call ourselves Paulites, after Paul; or Johnites, after John. But no. The worthy name by which we will be called is *Christians—after Christ.* All we are brethren—but he *is* our Master; and the voice from the most excellent glory cries, "Hear ye *him.*" His authority was proved by miracles, wonders, and signs. In him are hid all the treasures of wisdom and knowledge. All he delivers to us is truth—truth unmixed with error—truth of the mightiest importance—truth that can make us free—truth that can make us holy—truth that can make us blessed for evermore. And as to the mode of this tuition, none teaches like him; so tenderly, so effectually, so perseveringly.

—Will ye also go away? Lord, to whom should we go, but unto thee? Will ye also be his disciples? O, my soul! refuse not the privilege; and henceforth may I hear him, watching daily at his gates, and waiting at the posts of his doors. Lead me in thy truth, and guide me; for thou art the God of my salvation; on Thee do I wait all the day.

MAY 24. "I pray thee let me go over and see the good land that is beyond Jordan; that goodly mountain, and Lebanon.—Deuteronomy, iii, 25.

THIS desire seemed improper. For God had expressly said unto Moses and Aaron, "Because ye believed me not, to sanctify me in the eyes of the children of Israel, therefore ye shall not bring this congregation into the land which I have given them." We are poor creatures, and often insensibly transfer to God the effects of our own feeling and conduct. Did Moses, then, through infirmity, think that God was changeable? No; but he thought whether the threatening was absolute, especially as it was not ratified by an oath, as the exclusion of the people was. For many of God's denunciations, as we see, for instance, in the sentence with regard to Nineveh, have a condition implied, though not expressed; *i. e.* they will be executed *unless* repentance intervenes; upon this principle it was possible for Moses to hope for a retraction of the interdict.

But the desire was a very natural one. It was natural for him to desire to enter Canaan, even as an object of curiosity, of which he had heard so much; but still more as an object of hope, which had been so long promised with every enhancement. This it was that had animated the people to leave Egypt. This had encouraged them in all their travels in the desert. This was the end, the recompense of all their toils and sufferings for forty years, and they had now nearly reached it! How painful to miss the prize—when the hand was in the very act of seizing it; and to have the cup dashed—even from the lip!

—Yet the desire was refused. And the Lord said unto him, Let it suffice thee—speak no more to me of this matter. For he sometimes refuses the desires of his servants, and the most eminent and endeared of them too. And he does this in two ways. Sometimes he does it in *love.* He denies, because what is desired would prove dangerous and injurious. We should think badly of a father who, if a son asked bread, would give him a stone; or if he ask a fish, would give him a scorpion. But suppose, through ignorance, his son should ask for a scorpion instead of a fish; or suppose he should cry for a sharp instrument, or beg to climb up a steep ladder, *then* would he not hate his child, unless he rejected his wish? In how many cases must a wise and good parent distinguish between a child's wishes and his wants? He may wish for liberty, but he wants restraint: he may wish for holidays, but he wants schooling: he may wish for dainties, but he wants medicine. Here the love of the parent must appear in acting—not according to the wish, but the welfare of his child. And—

"God's choice is safer than our own:
"Of ages past inquire,
"What the most formidable fate?
"To have our own desire!"

How well would it have been for the Jews, had he more than once turned a deaf ear to their importunity! But they would have a king—and he "gave them a king in his anger, and took him away in his wrath." They would have flesh—and he gave them their hearts' desire, but sent leanness to their souls. On the other hand, who does not see, in looking back upon life, how well for him it was that such a scheme failed; that such a hope was crushed!—so much evil lurked under the specious appearance, or would have resulted from the indulgence. Who knows what is good for a man in this life? No one but God—the *good* God—

"Good when He gives, supremely good,
"Nor less when He denies;
"E'en crosses from his sov'reign hand
"Are blessings in disguise."

He also sometimes refuses in anger. Wrath is incompatible with love; but anger is not: anger may even flow from it. Though Christians cannot be condemned, they may be chastened: and the Law of the house is, that if his children walk not in his commandments, he will visit their transgression with a rod, and their iniquities with stripes. Hence those who shall be saved eternally may lie under the present rebukes of Providence; and be refused many things on which they have set their heart, as to station, business, connexions, and usefulness—for them that honor him he will honor. They may think hard of this at first; but as they discover their unworthiness and desert, they will bow to the dispensation, and say, with David, "I know, O Lord, that thy judgments are right, and that thou in faithfulness hast afflicted me." By such conduct, too, Providence reads lessons to others. See, it says, the evil of sin. See how severely God deals with it, even in his own people. And if these things are done in the green tree, what shall be done in the dry! If judgment begins at the house of God, what shall the end be of them that obey not the Gospel of our Lord Jesus Christ! And if the righteous scarcely are saved, where shall the ungodly and the sinner appear!

—Yet his desire was partially indulged: "Thou shalt not go over this Jordan; but get thee up into the top of Pisgah, and lift up thine eyes westward, and northward, and southward, and eastward, and behold it with thine eyes." This was obviously intended, not to tantalize him, but to be a *mitigation* of the severe sentence. The preservation of his good sight to so great an age, fitted him for the gaze; and probably it was also strengthened and enlarged for this very purpose. The prospect showed him how worthy the country was of all that God had said concerning it; and would give him high and honorable views of the truth and goodness of God, in his covenant with Abraham, and Isaac, and Jacob. Along with this, too, there was exerted the influence of divine grace, which soothed and satisfied him. For by this, God can make us easy and contented under the refusal or loss of any comfort, however essential to our happiness it appeared before: so that we behave and quiet ourselves as a child that is weaned of his mother; our soul is even as a weaned child. While, also, his mind was raised to things above, and, in type and emblem, to a better country, into which he was immediately to enter—and then there would be no want of Canaan.

—Thus, in the midst of judgment, He remembers mercy; and though he cause grief, yet will he have compassion. Like as a father pitieth his children, so the Lord pitieth them that fear him: for he knoweth our frame; he remembereth that we are dust.

MAY 25.—"**Grieve not the Holy Spirit of God.**"—**Ephesians, iv, 30.**

THE expression is not to be taken properly and literally, as if the Holy Spirit of God was capable of vexation or sorrow. The Divine Nature is not subject to human passions. God's condescension is not to rob him of his glory. When the Scripture ascribes to him actions or affections that imply imperfection, it is in accommodation to our weakness of apprehension; as we lisp with infants; and unable to view the shining sun with the naked eye, we survey it in a vessel of water, or through obscured glass.

We grieve a friend when we neglect him, or go contrary to his wishes and interests. And when he is grieved, he betrays it; his countenance is not toward us as aforetime; frowns succeed to smiles; complaint and reproof are administered; or there is a discontinuation of visits and correspondence. All this will apply to the grieving of the Holy Spirit of God. And there are three reasons why we should not grieve him. Nothing can be more unbecoming—ungrateful—unwise.

—Nothing can be more unbecoming if we consider his greatness. The Holy Spirit is deserving in himself of all the regard we can express. If a nobleman was calling upon you, common civility would teach you not to hurt his mind: and if the king honored you with his presence, how anxious would you feel not to offend him; how studious would you be to please him in all your actions, and words, and looks. Here all comparisons fail. No mortal is honored like the Christian, with whom the King of kings and Lord of lords deigns even to dwell.

And will he not be sensible of this? Will he not exclaim, "Lord, what is man, that thou art mindful of him, or the son of man, that thou visitest him?" Will he not fall upon his knees, and pray, "Let the words of my mouth and the meditation of my heart, be acceptable in thy sight, O Lord, my Strength, and my Redeemer?"

—Nothing can be more ungrateful, if we consider his goodness. What obligation was he under to you? You were not worthy of the least of all his mercies; you deserved that his wrath should have come upon you as children of disobedience. Had he therefore left you to perish, you would have had no reason to complain. But who remembered you in your low estate? Who quickened you when dead in trespasses and sins? Who unstopped your deaf ears, and opened your blind eyes? Who turned your feet into the paths of peace? Who enabled you to believe on the Lord Jesus Christ to life everlasting? Who gave you a disposition, a taste, congenial with the work and enjoyment of heaven, and sealed you unto the day of redemption? But for his gracious agency, where, and what, would you now have been? And are you forgetful of all this? Are you grieving such a benefactor? Is this thy kindness to thy friend?

—Nothing can be more unwise, if we consider his importance to you. As you are deeply indebted to him for the past, so are you entirely dependent upon him for the future. You live in the Spirit, you walk in the Spirit. Grieve the Holy Spirit of God! What! would you grieve your *leader*, and be left to travel alone? Can you find your way without him? Can you learn without this teacher? Must not he guide you into all truth? What! would you grieve your *helper*, and be left to act alone in your work? Can you worship without the preparation of the heart and the answer of the tongue, which are from him? Without him can you order speech by reason of darkness? Can you know what to pray for as you ought, unless the Spirit helpeth your infirmities? What power have you in any duty, unless you are strengthened with might by the Spirit in the inner man? You may spread your sails, but he must fill them. What! would you grieve your *preserver*, and be left to contend by yourself against your enemies? Are you a match for the power of darkness, and the devices of satan? Why, the first temptation that assaults you alone may occasion your sinning and falling, and by this you may cause the way of truth to be evil spoken of—ministers to be discouraged—your fellow Christians to be grieved—that which is lame to be turned out of the way, and your sin to be ever before you. What! would you grieve your *comforter*, and lose your hold of the promises, and be unable to discern your evidences of heaven, and feel your hope decline, and your heart sink in the day of adversity, and be in bondage through fear of death, and groan, "O that it were with me as in months past, when the candle of the Lord shined upon my head, and when by his light I walked through darkness, while as yet the Almighty was with me?"

The comforts of the Holy Spirit can afford such strong consolation as will revive us in the midst of trouble. According to the Savior's assurance, when leaving this world, *his* being with the disciples can more than make up for the loss of his own bodily presence. But, "When he hideth his face, who can behold him?" Vain then are friends, ministers, ordinances. "For these things," says the church, "I weep: mine eye runneth down with water, because the Comforter that should relieve my soul is far from me." What infatuation to grieve him!

Yet if there were no danger of this, the admonition would not have been given. Let me not therefore be high-minded, but fear. "Blessed is the man that feareth alway." I have always at hand an active adversary, the devil. I am passing through a world lying in wickedness. I carry within me an evil heart of unbelief, and every thing without is rendered dangerous by the sin that dwelleth in me. They who far surpass me in every thing, have been overcome. Let me therefore watch and pray, "Hold thou me up, and I shall be safe." Nor let me be satisfied with negative religion. Let it not, O my soul, be enough that I grieve him not. Let me cherish all his motions. Let me walk so as to please God. Let me abound therein more and more.

MAY 26.—"Ask of me, and I shall give thee the heathen for thine inheritance, and the uttermost parts of the earth for thy possession."—Psalm ii, 8.

"THE Heathen"—"the uttermost parts of the earth;" viewed in the representations of Scripture, and the reports of historians, travellers, and missionaries, seem a very unenviable acquisition. If it be true that the whole world lieth in wickedness, it seems fitter to be for the inheritance "and the possession" of Satan, than the Son of God. But two things are to be taken into account. Notwithstanding the present condition of the estate, it contains very *valuable* and *convertible* materials.

Every human being, however depraved and degraded, is a creature of God. He is the work of his hands, and is fearfully and wonderfully made: and he has a soul of more value than the material world. The child of a savage is a richer production than the sun. The sun sees not his own light, feels not his own heat, and with all his grandeur is doomed to perish; but that child is the subject of reason, the heir of immortality. That child is capable of knowing, and serving, and resembling God, and of filling a sphere of everlasting action and enjoyment. That child will hear the heavens passing away with a great noise, and see the elements melting with fervent heat, and stand with all the dead, small and great, before God.

—And we are also to consider what they may, and will become. Thus the Savior viewed them when they were surrendered to him. He pitied them, and he knew he was able to bless them, and he knew that they would not remain what they were; but that for him the wilderness and solitary place should be made glad, and the desert rejoice and blossom as the rose. He knew it had been said, be Faithfulness and Truth, "Ye shall go out with joy, and be led forth with peace; the mountains and the hills shall break forth before you into singing, and all the trees of the field shall clap their hands. Instead of the thorn shall come up the fir tree, and instead of the brier shall come up the myrtle tree; and it shall be to the Lord for a name, for an everlasting sign, that shall not be cut off." The more desperate the condition of the patient, the more pleasure does his recovery afford the physician, and the more does it display his skill and ability.

So here. All these captives the Redeemer ransoms; and each of them, as a justified, sanctified, glorified being, will for ever reflect his honor. He found them at hell's dark door; but he raises them above the heavens. He found them in the likeness of the devil, and he adorns them with the image of God. He found them the disgrace of the universe, and he makes them an eternal excellency, the joy of many generations. What is so interesting and delightful to a man of taste, as alteration and improvement! With what pleasure does he view a piece of rude and barren soil, under his cultivation, looking forth, dressed in living green, and abounding with trees and flowers! What pleasure does a benevolent mind feel when he views the child he has taken up, exchanging rags for decency, ignorance for knowledge, vicious and idle habits for virtue and industry, and contemplates his comfort, usefulness, and respectability, as the fruit of his kindness and labor! What satisfaction must the Savior feel, to behold, as the effect of his cross, and his grace, the renewal of human nature; the deliverance of province after province from the power of Satan, and the kingdoms of this world coming under the influence of the Gospel! What an inheritance—what a possession will the heathen, and the uttermost parts of the earth be to the Messiah, when paganism, and Mahommedanism, and the man of sin, shall perish! when the Jews shall come in with the fullness of the Gentiles! when, in every place, incense shall be offered unto him, and a pure offering! when the nations shall learn war no more! when the people shall all be holy, trees of righteousness, the planting of the Lord, that he may be glorified!

We read of two vast gifts of God in the Scripture: the gift of his Son to the world, and the gift of the world to his Son. The first of these is the greatest; and we ought never to think of it without exclaiming, Thanks be unto God for his unspeakable gift! But let us think of the other also, and rejoice that our earth is to come under the dominion of the Messiah, and is given to him for this purpose. It is thus to him, as Canaan was to the Jews. Canaan was to them the Land of Promise; and God having promised it, in vain was every attempt made to keep them from obtaining it. Egypt was plagued; Pharaoh and his army were destroyed; the sea opened a passage for the heirs of promise; Jordan was driven back, and they were brought in triumph to the rest and the inheritance which the Lord their God had given them. So will it be here. All opposition will be as vain as it is unreasonable. His enemies shall lick the dust. The word is gone out of God's mouth, and shall not return; that to him every knee shall bow, and every tongue confess. I will overturn, overturn, overturn, until he shall come whose right it is, and I will give it him.

Let us think of his prospects. We have sympathized with him in his agony and bloody sweat; in his cross and passion. Let us exult at the thought that he is crowned with glory and honor, and has the heathen for his inheritance, and the uttermost parts of the earth for his possession. And what an immensity of subjects will he derive from them! and what an infinity of services! and what an eternity of praises and delights! It was the joy set before him, and he shall see of the travail of his soul, and shall be satisfied.

We ought also to rejoice from a principle of benevolence. His dominion involves the happiness of the human race. Nebuchadnezzar, and other conquerors, had nations given into their hands; but they only enslaved, and impoverished, and cursed their subjects. But,

"Blessings abound where'er He reigns;
"The pris'ner leaps to loose his chains:
"The weary find eternal rest,
"And all the sons of want are blest."

MAY 27.—"The dumb spake."—Matthew, ix, 33.

THIS was a natural dumbness, the cure of which was to be one of the miracles attending the Messiah's advent: "Then the eyes of the blind shall be opened, and the ears of the deaf shall be unstopped: then shall the lame man leap as a hart, and the tongue of the dumb sing."

But there is a moral dumbness, and the Savior heals this when he makes us new creatures. Then old things pass away, and all things become new; not physically new, but spiritually; each faculty becoming new in quality, application, and use. Thus the man has a tongue before, but not a religious one. He speaks before, but now his speech is with grace. Now he speaks—of God—for God—and to God.

—He speaks *of* God; of his perfections; of his designs; of his works, and ways, and word; of his commands and promises—a theme for angels.

He speaks *for* God; "on his behalf," as Elihu says; in defending his truth; in justifying his people; in recommending his service; in pleading his cause. Wisdom is necessary here; and we are to distinguish between places, and seasons, and characters. "A word fitly spoken, how good is it! It is like apples of gold in pictures of silver." Yet caution, though it should qualify our zeal, should not quench it. We should be courageous, as well as discreet:

"And if some proper hour appear,
"I'll not be overaw'd;
"But let the scoffing sinner know
"That I can speak *for* God."

He speaks *to* God. And this is the better evidence of our sincerity. For many speak *of* God, and many *for* him, who never speak *to* him. While the world hears them, and the Church hears them, the closet does not. But the Christian's delight in God, and the duties and exigencies of his spiritual condition, will bring him often to his seat, and he will address Him much in a way of adoration, and praise, and confession, and intercession, and prayer.

If you are the subject of this grace use it, and be concerned that the words of your mouth, as well as the meditation of your heart, may be acceptable in God's sight. Beware of any return of the old malady. There is an occasional, partial, comparative dumbness, and it is brought on by sin. This stops our speech. It did so in the case of David when he had fallen by his iniquity. It not only broke his bones, and deprived him of joy, but of confidence, and filled him with fear and silence. He could neither speak, as he had done, of God, or for God, or to God. It is a sad evil, and if it be your experience, do—it is the best thing you can now do—do as he did. Take the case, and lay it before God, and say, "Open thou my mouth, and my lips shall show forth thy praise."

"Then will I teach the world thy ways;
"Sinners shall learn thy sov'reign grace;
"I'll lead them to my Savior's blood,
"And they shall praise a pard'ning God.

"O may thy love inspire my tongue!
"Salvation shall be all my song!
"And all my powers shall join to bless
"The Lord, my strength and righteousness."

MAY 28.—"Grow in grace, and in the knowledge of our Lord and Savior Jesus Christ."—2 Peter, iii, 18.

IF we consider these words as containing two injunctions, may we not view the second as prescribing the way for the accomplishment of the first? It is certain that there is a supreme excellency in the knowledge here recommended, and that he who would grow in grace, *must* grow in the knowledge of our Lord and Savior Jesus Christ.

This knowledge is supposed to be progressive. It was gradual, even in its communication to the world. Judaism was the dawn: Christianity the day. Prophets and righteous men desired to see the things that we see, and did not see them; and to hear the things that we hear, and did not hear them. There are degrees, also, in its attainment and experience. Four ways we may grow in this knowledge.

First. In its *extent*. Who has advanced near the extremities of this field? How little do the wisest know of the treasures hid in it!

"The Cross, the Manger, and the Throne, | "Are big with glories yet unknown."

Angels know much more than they did. But they still desire to look into these things. How much more should we!

Secondly. In its *certainty*. This is, and must be, the same in itself; but as to us, the degree of it depends upon the perception of evidence, and the mind may be led along from possibility to probability, and from probability to full conviction. The firmness of belief may be also strengthened by the confirmations of experience. The whole life of a Christian is a series of tests by which he tries and proves the word of God. He is, therefore, perpetually increasing in the full assurance of understanding, and has his heart established with grace.

Thirdly. In its *influence*. This implies the former, but is distinguishable from it. There cannot be practical knowledge without speculative. But who will not own that there may be speculative knowledge without practical? Who is ignorant of the difference there is between knowing things in theory, and in experience? between the apprehensions of the judgment, and the bias of the will, and the glow of the affections? Who feels, and fears, and loves, according to his belief? Alas! how often do we see and approve better things, and follow worse! How often are the clearest dictates of the understanding, and even convictions of the conscience, counteracted by our appetites and passions! We believe that we are dying creatures, and live as if we were to live here always! We own ourselves under the providence of Him who doth all things well, and we murmur and repine as if his dealings were unjust or unkind? We doubt not the Savior's power and love; and yet we cannot trust in him, and are strangers to consolation and peace!

Fourthly. In its *appropriation*. Job could say; "I know that *my* Redeemer liveth." David said, "God *is* the strength of *my* heart, and *my* portion for ever." The first Christians said, "We *know* that the Son of God is come, and hath given *us* an understanding, that we may know Him that is true; and we *are* in him that is true." Oh! who does not want more of this delightful confidence to raise him above the world, to support him in his trials, to embolden him in his profession, and to enable him to triumph over the fears of death?

O God, preserve me from delusion in a business of everlasting importance! Let me feel a thousand terrors rather than perish with a lie in my right hand. But if I am thine, save me from the uncertainties I now feel. Give me the full assurance of hope unto the end. Let me know, not only that there are exceeding great and precious promises, but that I am an heir of promise; not only that in the Lord Jesus all fullness dwells, but that I am blessed with all spiritual blessings in heavenly places in him; and say unto my soul, I am thy salvation.

MAY 29.—"Ye are the children of the Lord your God."—Deut. xiv, 1.

THE Jews were so by nation. All men are so by creation and providence. Christians are so by special grace, according to the language of inspiration: "Ye are all the children of God, by faith in Christ Jesus." As many as received him, to them gave he power to become the sons of God, even to them that believe on his name; which were born, not of blood, nor of the will of the flesh, nor of the will of man, but of God." Let us make this relation a standard by which to estimate four things.

First. The Divine goodness. Here we only follow the example of the apostle John. *He*, even he, could not comprehend it; but he admires it, and calls upon others to admire it with him: "Behold what manner of love the Father hath bestowed upon us, that we should be called the sons of God!" What manner of love! How rich! how free! how expensive! What difficulties stood in the way! Yet he removed them. How, said he, shall I put thee among the children? But he did it. Yes, he not only spared and pardoned us; he not only admitted us into his family as servants, but as sons; and for this purpose he gave his own Son for us, and his Spirit to us. "When the fullness of time was come, God sent forth his Son, made of a woman, made under the law, to redeem them that were under the law, that we might receive the adoption of sons. And because ye are sons God hath sent forth the Spirit of his Son into your hearts, crying, Abba, Father. Wherefore, thou art no more a servant, but a son; and if a son, then an heir of God, through Christ."

Secondly. The believer's dignity. Secular nobility derives all its lustre from flesh and blood; and if retraced, will be found to originate in the dust of the ground, from which Adam was taken. It has little value, unless in the fancies of men. But our relation to God confers real and durable honor; compared with which the most magnificent titles in the world are mere shadows and smoke. How did the Jews boast of having Abraham to their father! "Is it a light thing," said David, a subject, "that I should be a son-in-law to the king?" But

I think of the majesty and dominion of God! The world is his, and the fullness thereof; I behold the productions of the earth, and the wonders of the skies, and say,

"My Father made them all!"

Thirdly. The happiness of the Christian. The relation has connected with it the promise of pardon; and we daily need it, for in many things we offend all. But I will spare him, says God, as a man spareth his own son that serveth him. It gives us free access to God in prayer, and inspires us with confidence and hope of success: "If ye being evil know how to give good gifts unto your children, how much more shall your Father which is in heaven give the Holy Spirit to them that ask him!" Hence correction: "For whom the Lord loveth he chasteneth, and scourgeth every son whom he receiveth." Hence education; he does not leave the child to himself, but trains him up in the way that he should go. He who feeds the ravens will not suffer the righteous to famish. Their heavenly Father knoweth what things they have need of before they ask him, and will suffer them to want no good thing. And if children, then heirs, heirs of God, and joint heirs with Christ. Many are born to an estate which they never obtain, but here the inheritance is reserved in heaven; and they are kept by the power of God, through faith, unto salvation, on earth.

Fourthly. The duty of the saints. Are they all the children of the Lord their God? Then they ought to fear him. If I am a father, where is my fear? This will keep them from offending him. This will make them studious to please him. This will induce them to pray, "Let the words of my mouth, and the meditation of my heart, be acceptable in thy sight, O Lord, my Strength and my Redeemer."

As his children they must walk worthy of God, who hath called them unto his kingdom and glory. We have read of a Polish prince who carried the picture of his father always in his bosom; and on any particular occasion he would take it out and view it, and say, Let me do nothing unbecoming so excellent a father.

Christians, do nothing unbecoming the rank of your family, and the grandeur of your descent. Be harmless and blameless, the sons of God, without rebuke. Be followers of God, as dear children. Be ye perfect, even as your Father who is in heaven is perfect.

MAY 30.—"Ask of me."—Psalm ii, 8.

—THIS is the condition of a very important grant. Ask of me, and I shall give thee the heathen for thine inheritance, and the uttermost parts of the earth for thy possession.

Whatever appears humiliating in the condition to which the Savior submitted, let it be remembered that he entered it voluntarily and knowingly. He was aware that if the children were partakers of flesh and blood, he likewise himself must also take part of the same, and that in all things it behooved him to be made like unto his brethren. He must, therefore, not only suffer, but obey; and though he was a Son, yet learned he obedience. He must, therefore, pray. Prayer is the act of an inferior nature; and the Word was made flesh. Though rich, he became poor, and made himself of no reputation.

Many objections are made to prayer. Some of them are specious, but they are all founded in ignorance. The best way to answer them is to take our stand on the Scripture, and make our appeal. Does not God derive his character and glory from his hearing prayer? Is not his Spirit the Spirit of grace and of supplication? Is not this his command? Is not this his promise? "Ask, and it shall be given you; seek, and ye shall find." Does He dispense with this, even in the case of his Son? And can it be dispensable with regard to us? We know his determination: For all these things I will yet be inquired of by the house of Israel to do it for them. "Ask, and I shall give thee."

—But how was *he* to ask? First, when he was on the earth, he prayed like one of us. He prayed alone, and in company with his disciples; he prayed in the wilderness. and in the garden, and on the cross. "In the days of his flesh, he offered up prayers and supplications, with strong crying and tears, unto him that was able to save him from death, and was heard in that he feared." Secondly, he continued the presentation of his desire when he entered heaven. We know not whether this was done vocally, but it was done really. Thirdly, he does it relatively. Thus prayer is made for him continually. And whenever individuals, ministers, and churches, pray for the success of his cause, *He* is asking.

—And his prayer, and our praying, are founded on the same consideration, viz. his sufferings and death. The counsel of peace was between them both. It was said, that when the Father should make his soul an offering for sin, he should see his seed, and prolong his days, and the pleasure of the Lord should prosper in his hands; he should see of the travail of his soul, and should be satisfied. This was the joy set before him; and having fulfilled the awful condition on which it was suspended, he pleads for it. *He* therefore asks in his *own* name, and on his *own* behalf. And *we* ask on the *same* behalf, and in the *same* name, according to his own direction: "Whatsoever ye shall ask, believing in my name, ye shall receive." And this should encourage and embolden us. There can be no more uncertainty attending the success of our asking, than of his, for herein we are identified with him. There is no unfaithfulness with God; and he hath said, "Ask of me, and I shall give thee the heathen for thine inheritance, and the uttermost parts of the earth for thy possession." If our prayers are sincere, they must be influential; and we shall exert ourselves in the Redeemer's cause. Nor can we labor in vain. We are on the sure, the rising, the prevailing side. Merchants, heroes, politicians, may all weary themselves for very vanity. But we are at a certainty. A king shall reign and prosper. "His name shall endure for ever: his name shall be continued as long as the sun: and men shall be blessed in him: all nations shall call him blessed. Blessed be the Lord God, the God of Israel, who only doeth wondrous things. And blessed be his glorious name for ever: and let the whole earth be filled with his glory. Amen, and amen."

MAY 31.—"And it came to pass, as he sat at meat with them, he took bread, and blessed it, and brake, and gave to them."—John, xxiv, 30.

THIS was not a *sacramental* meal, as when he took bread, and blessed it, and brake it, and said, This is my body. Neither was it a *miraculous* meal, as when he took the loaves, and blessed them, and multiplied them. But an *ordinary* meal. Yet he blessed the food. And this he did always. And his example has the force of a law with all his followers; for "he that saith he abideth in him, ought himself also so to walk as he walked." Hence the command, "Whatsoever ye do, in word or deed, do all in *the name of the Lord Jesus*, *i. e.* as his disciples, who are not only to believe in him, but to *represent him.*

From his observing this practice, we may be sure that it is wise, and useful, and necessary. Sin has brought a curse upon all our enjoyments, and the blessing of God alone can take it off.

"How sweet our daily comforts prove,
"When they are season'd with his love."

But how true—

"'Tis all vain, till God has blessed."

"Man liveth not by bread alone, but by every word that proceedeth out of the mouth of God." Can he also abuse the bounties of Providence, who has implored the divine benediction upon the use of them? Can he indulge in excess? Will he not add to his faith, temperance? It is lamentable, therefore, that such a duty should ever be omitted, or performed with haste and irreverence, as if the performer was ashamed of the performance.

—Let the Savior's conduct also teach us not to confine our religion to extraordinary and sacred occasions. In all our ways let us acknowledge God. Morning and evening worship is good; but let us be in the fear of the Lord all the day long. It is well to inquire in his temple; but let us abide with God in our calling. We must remember the Sabbath, and keep it holy; but the spirit of devotion is to actuate us during the week, and to induce us, whether we eat or drink, or whatever we do, to do all to the glory of God. Tell me not what a man is in a storm—but in the calm. Not how he behaves himself in sickness—but in health. A Balaam may pray, Let me die the death of the righteous. A David prays, Unite my heart to fear thy name. There is a goodness which depends upon impulse, not principle; upon outward excitement, not upon internal disposition. There is a devotion that resembles the blaze of straw; but that which is spiritual is like the fire on the Jewish altar—kindled from above, and which never went out. It is a stream fed by a living fountain; not a sudden torrent, however wide or impetuous at the time, produced by the melting of the snow, or a summer's thunder-storm. The water, says the Savior, that I shall give him, shall be in him a well of water, springing up into everlasting life.

JUNE 1.—"I am the vine."—John, xv, 5.

MINISTERS are not to preach themselves, but Christ Jesus the Lord. But he was his own subject—he preached himself. How could he have done otherwise, concerned as he was to be useful? For,

"None but Jesus; none but Jesus,
"Can do helpless sinners good."

And *he* knew this far better than we do? And who was able to declare what he truly was, so well as himself?

—Here he calls himself the vine. A very easy and natural image. And natural images are the most preferable in divine things. Many writers and preachers love those allusions which show their learning, and which the uneducated cannot understand. Our Savior never takes his comparisons from the sciences, and seldom from the arts; but from natural scenery, which is obvious and intelligible to all.

A vine is not so remarkable in its appearance as many other trees. In loftiness, it yields to the cedar; in strength, to the oak; in sightliness, to the palm tree and the fir. The greatness of Jesus was spiritual. He had no earthly pomp and riches. Like his kingdom, he was not of this world. Hence it was said, "He shall grow up before him as a tender plant, and as a root out of a dry ground; he hath no form nor comeliness, and when we shall see him there is no beauty that we should desire him."

The vine is renowned for its fertility. One single vine, planted by the empress Lavinia, yielded one hundred and eight gallons of wine in one year. Many grapes grow on one cluster, many clusters on one branch, and many branches on one tree. How many have been saved by the Lord Jesus! In him all fullness dwells. In him we are blessed with all spiritual blessings. What clusters were brought from Eshcol, to show Israel the goodliness and fruitfulness of Canaan! And what specimens of heaven, what earnests of the inheritance, what first-fruits of the Spirit, do faith and hope bring believers from him, even while they are in the wilderness!

The nature of the produce of the vine is delightful and profitable. The fruit is sweet to the taste. The juice it yields cheers and makes glad the heart of man. Give wine to those that be of heavy hearts. It was sometimes used medicinally. The good Samaritan poured oil and wine into the wounds of the bleeding traveller. And he brings us health, and cure, and comfort, and delight, and more than angels' food; for

"Never did angels taste, above,
"Redeeming grace, and dying love."

The vine also yields shade, and it was valued for this purpose in the East. Hence we so often read in the Scripture, of sitting under the vine and the fig tree. They had walks and bowers made of these; and while the fruit refreshed them, the shelter screened them from the sun. And he is a shadow from the heat, and rescues us from the evil of every annoyance to which we are exposed. I sat, says the church, under his shadow with delight, and his fruit was sweet to my taste.

The image, therefore, is pleasing and striking, and aids us in our conceptions of him, and communion with him. Yet it teaches us as much by contrast, as by comparison. A vine is not always green. It does not always bear. It never bears twelve manner of fruits. It does not endure for ever. But all this is true of him.

The fruit of the vine, if taken too largely, will injure the partaker; but there is no danger here. While we are forbidden to be drunk with wine, wherein is excess, we are commanded to be filled with the Spirit. The produce of the vine is only for the body, and for time; but his benefits are for the soul and eternity. Many cannot obtain the advantages of the vine; but none, however poor and mean, are excluded from the participations of Christ. The image, therefore, is but an humble one, and falls far short of his glory. So does every thing that is employed to show forth his worth, his glory, or his grace.

" Nor earth, nor seas, nor sun, nor stars,
" Nor heaven, his full resemblance bears;
" His beauties we can never trace,
" Till we behold him face to face.

" Oh! let me climb these lower skies,
" Where storms and darkness never rise!
" *There* he displays his powers abroad,
" And shines, and reigns th' incarnate God!"

June 2.—" Ye are the branches."—John, xv, 5.

For whatever he is, they have a relation corresponding with it. Thus, if he is the king, they are the subjects; if he is the shepherd, they are the sheep; if he is the head, they are the members. Therefore, having said to his disciples, I am the vine, he adds, Ye are the branches.

This reminds us of their union with him. The vine and the branches are connected. The latter are even parts of the former; and it would be absurd for a person to say, I did not hurt the vine; I only injured the branches. Why persecutest thou *me?* said the Savior to Saul, who was persecuting his followers. He that touches them, touches the apple of his eye. And as he is sensible of their wrongs, so he feels every kindness shown them, and says, inasmuch as ye did it unto one of the least of these my brethren, ye did it unto me.

This gives them a character of likeness. The branches are the very same kind of wood as the vine; and the very same sap pervades them both. And they that are joined to the Lord are of one spirit. The same mind is in them which was also in Christ Jesus.

This shows their dependence. " The righteous shall flourish as a branch:" but the branch does not bear the tree, but the tree the branch. Whatever likeness there may be, in all things he has the pre-eminence. He is our life and strength. Abide, says he, in me, as the branch cannot bear fruit of itself, except it abide in the vine, no more can ye, except ye abide in me, for without me ye can do nothing.

This proclaims their usefulness. The branches are the beauty and excellency of the vine, and *by* these its vigor and fertility are displayed. He is glorified in his people. He makes them to blossom and yield fruit. He diffuses his goodness through their prayers and lives. In him is their fruit found, as to its source and support; but they bear it—they are branches, and are filled with all the fruits of righteousness, which are, by Jesus Christ, unto the glory and praise of God.

Let me learn one thing from all this. Let me accustom myself to derive spiritual reflections from all the material objects around me. A taste for natural scenery is pleasing and good in itself. But let me not approach it, as a creature, only to enjoy; or a phliosopher, only to admire; but as a Christian, also, to improve. Let sense be a handmaid to faith; and that which is seen and temporal, raise me to that which is unseen and eternal.

JUNE 3.—"Which is our hope."—1 Timothy, i, 1.

MUCH has been said in praise of hope. It has been called the mainspring of motion. The soul of enterprise. The balm of life. The soother of care. And the healer of sorrow.

We are not, however, going to speak of hope in general. We, therefore, say nothing of the hope of the worldling, which is a thing of nought. Or of the hope of the infidel, which is annihilation. Or of the hope of the Antinomian, which is a devil's dream. Or of the hope of the Pharisee, which is a spider's web. Or of the hope of the hypocrite, which is a lie in his right hand. But of *our* hope—as Christians. And what is this? Jesus Christ, says the apostle, he "is our hope." He deserves and realizes the character four ways—He is our hope substantially, meritoriously, efficiently, and exemplarily.

He is the object of our hope. There be many that say, Who will show us any good? But *any* good will not answer the wishes of a believer. His supreme aim is the—principal, the—only good—

"Sufficient in itself alone,
"And needful, were the world our own."

It is to win Christ; to be found in him; and in him to be blessed with all spiritual blessings. The Christian's hope is chiefly laid up for him in heaven. And is not He the essence of all blessedness there? The place is glorious; but what would it be without his presence? The company is attractive; but what would friends, and saints, and angels be without communion with Him? We sometimes hear it said, "Well, we are all hoping for the same heaven!" But nothing can be more false. A natural man is hoping for one kind of heaven, a spiritual man for another, and each herein follows his peculiar disposition. I cannot hope for what I do not love and desire. As a man, I may hope for a heaven that shall secure me from hell, and exempt me from all toil and trouble, and furnish me with things in which I feel pleasure. But it is only as a Christian I can long to depart to be with Christ, which is far better; and be able to say,

"'Tis heaven on earth to taste his love,
"To feel his quick'ning grace;
"And all the heaven I *hope* above,
"Is but to see his face."

—He is the ground of our hope. In proportion to the use and grandeur of a building should be the basis. Nothing can equal the vastness and value of the believer's expectation. If we are wise, therefore, we shall inquire what is to bear it up. And no other foundation can any man lay than that is laid, which is Christ. Every thing else we depend upon will prove sand. But here is rock; and he that believeth on him shall not be ashamed. View him as incarnate. Why is not our condition as hopeless as that of devils? Verily he took not on him the nature of angels, but he took on him the seed of Abraham. Because the children were partakers of flesh and blood, he likewise himself, also, took part of the same. He assumed the nature he would save; and he will save, as surely as he assumed it. View him as the gift of God; God so loved the world that he gave his Only Begotten. What can discourage us now? If our unworthiness, or the greatness of the blessing, could prove a hindrance to the divine goodness, it would have operated earlier, and he would have withholden from the guilty *this* unspeakable gift. But He that spared not his own Son, but delivered him up for us all, how shall he not with him also give us all things! But his goodness is wise goodness, just goodness. It must be as honorable to himself as it is beneficial to us; and we behold his Son set forth as a propitiation, through faith in his blood, to declare his righteousness. Sin is punished while it is pardoned. Even the law has nothing to complain of in our deliverance; it is much more glorified in our salvation than it would have been by our destruction. One died for all; and he was infinitely more than all. Do we question whether he finished the work that was given him to do; and whether it was an offering and a sacrifice to God of a sweet smelling savor; and whether he shall see of the travail of his soul and be satisfied? Behold him discharged from the grave, and ascending up on high, and receiving gifts for men, even for the rebellious, and entering into the holy place, there to appear in the presence of God for us! What can we desire more? If, while we were enemies, we were reconciled to God by the death of his Son, much more now, being reconciled, we shall be saved by his life. "Who is he that condemneth? It is Christ that died, yea, rather, that is risen again, who is even at the right hand of God, who also maketh intercession for us." Will not this suffice? He raised him up from the dead, and gave him glory, that our *faith and hope might be in God?*

—He is the author of our hope. For it is not natural to us, neither is it derived from ourselves, but he produces it in us by his Holy Spirit. Means may be used, but the excellency of the power is of him, and not of them. Hence says the apostle to those who were glorying in men, Who then is Paul, and who is Apollos, but ministers by whom ye believed, even as the Lord gave to every man? Every thing in the new world is done by the Spirit of Christ. Under a conviction of guilt enough to condemn us a thousand times over; did we find it an easy thing to hope in God at first, and believe that he was pacified toward us for all that we had done, and that we were accepted in the Beloved? Have we proved it an easy thing since to keep this hope lively and flourishing, yea, to maintain it at all? How often should we have said, My hope is perished from the Lord, and have given all our profession up, but for "the supply of the Spirit of Jesus Christ," in glorifying him afresh; according to the promise, "He shall receive of mine, and shall show it unto you."

—He is also the model of our hope. For though he is unspeakably more than our example, he is nothing less; and the higher views we have taken of him do not hinder, but, indeed, the more require our saying, that the same mind which was in him must be in us; that we must walk even as he walked; that we must pray as he prayed; fear as he feared, and hope as he hoped. And how did he hope? "I will," said he, "put my trust in Him." He was remarkable for this. It was not to quote prophecy, that his insulters, when he was on the cross, said, "He trusted in God: let him deliver him now, if he will have him; for he said, I am the Son of God." It was to reproach him for the confidence in God which they knew he had professed to exercise. It will be well if our enemies can revile us for nothing worse. David seems early to have been dedicated to God; but it was in the name of the holy child Jesus he spake, when he said, " Thou art he that took me out of the womb; thou didst make me hope when I was upon my mother's breasts. I was cast upon thee from the womb; thou art my God from my mother's belly." From his earliest infancy, from the first exercise of reason he honored him. Nor did he ever fail in his confidence in God. In every extremity he trusted in him. Even when in anguish on the cross, and dying, he cried, " *My* God, *my* God, why hast thou forsaken me?" " Father, into *thy* hands I commit my spirit." His confidence, also, was equally cheerful. He sung a hymn when he was entering the garden of Gethsemane. Though a man of sorrows and acquainted with grief, instead of murmuring, he said, " In the midst of the church will I sing praises unto thee." Thus may I bear the image of the heavenly till he shall appear, and I shall be perfectly like him, for I shall see him as he is.

JUNE 4.—**" The woman then left her water-pot."—John, iv, 28.**

THREE reasons may be assigned for this:

Perhaps she left it from kindness to our Savior and his disciples. His disciples had gone into the city to buy meat, and had just returned, and they were now going to partake of the homely fare. But for beverage they had nothing to draw with, and the well was deep. She, therefore, leaves them her vessel to enable them to draw and drink. Female kindness, and contrivance, and accommodation, are as quick as thought, and need no prompter. I admire the simplicity of early hospitality. See Rebekah and Abraham's steward: " And she said, Drink, my lord; and she hasted and let down her pitcher upon her hand, and gave him drink." Ah! ye generous hearts! who wish to do good, and feel your want of power, do what you can, and what you cannot will never be required of you. Remember the Savior's words: " Whosoever shall give to drink unto one of these little ones a cup of cold water only in the name of a disciple, verily I say unto you, he shall in no wise lose his reward."

—Perhaps she left it from indifference. She was now so impressed and occupied with infinitely greater and better things, that she forgets the very errand that brought her to the well. The feelings of new converts are peculiarly strong and lively. The eternal realities and glories that open to their view, dazzle their minds, and render them incapable of distinctly observing other objects. Considering the infirmity of our nature, it is not to be wondered at if the powers of the world to come, and the " one thing needful"—the care of the soul, should, for the time, engross all their attention, and make them too heedless of other claims. Hence, what we should censure in others. we excuse in young beginners, especially if they are suddenly awakened. I say excuse; for we never wish to justify ignorance, imprudence, and rashness. God is not the God of confusion; but says, " Let every thing be done decently, and in order." Religion is not to draw us off from our business and callings. Neither are we to leave our places and stations in life, even in pursuit of things good in themselves. When the demoniac had been dispossessed, he besought the Savior that he might be with him. But "Jesus suffered him not; but said, Return to thine own house, and show how great things God hath done for thee." And, says Paul to the Thessalonians, "Study to be quiet, and to do your own business, and to work with your own hands;" to provide things honest in the sight of all men; to maintain your families without dependence; and have to give to him that needeth; and to preserve your religion from censure. We are not, therefore, to abandon our water-pots. We are not to be careless of our worldly substance; but to preserve and use it. Witness the cautions in Scripture against suretyship, and *backing bills*, and the admonition, "Gather up the fragments that remain, that nothing be lost." Yet those who are born from above, and bound for glory, are only strangers and pilgrims upon earth: and they who have found the Pearl of Great Price, will not, and cannot, feel toward worldly things as they once did. They cannot be so anxious to gain them; so overjoyed in possessing them; so depressed in losing them. And they will be willing to forsake whatever the service of God requires them to part with, however dear or valuable. Thus Matthew, sitting at the receipt of custom, upon hearing the call, "Follow me," "arose and followed him."

—Perhaps she left it, as it would have proved a hindrance to her speed. The king's business requires haste: and in this she was now engaged; and, burning with zeal, she could not bear the thought of losing a moment in communicating the knowledge she possessed; and of saying to her neighbors, Come, see a man which told me all things that ever I did. Is not this the Christ? She knew the importance of the case; and the brevity, and uncertainty of the opportunity. It was not the gratification of their curiosity—it was their life. And if he withdrew from the well before they arrived, the day of their visitation might never return. Upon the same principles, let us get rid of every impediment, and avoid every delay, not only in gaining good for ourselves, but in doing good for others. All is hanging—upon the moment? "Whatsoever thy hand findeth to do, do it with thy might. There is no work, nor device, nor knowledge, nor wisdom, in the grave, whither thou goest."

JUNE 5.—**"Be thou their arm every morning."—Isaiah, xxxiii, 2.**

THIS is a prayer for others. And, when we repair to the throne of the heavenly grace, we should never forget our fellow Christians. But those will never pray earnestly, or even sincerely, for others, who do not pray for themselves. Every believer, therefore, includes himself in the number of those for whom he implores the blessing; "Be thou their arm every morning."

He is made sensible of his own weakness and insufficiency. He knows, he feels, and he increasingly knows and feels, his need—of an arm—a divine arm—every morning.

—For what purpose?

—He needs this arm to defend him in all his dangers, and to keep him from all evil, especially the evil of sin, that it may not grieve him.

—He needs this arm to uphold him under his burdens; whose pressure often urges him to exclaim, "Lord, I am oppressed, undertake for me."

—He needs this arm to lean on, in all his goings. What a journey lies before him! And what step can he take alone! This is the image of the church. She is represented as coming up out of the wilderness, leaning on her beloved.

And, as this arm is necessary—so it is sufficient—and it is kindly held out in the promises and invitations of the word—There, says God, "Let him take hold of my strength." And we take hold of it by faith and prayer.

—Let me then avail myself of the privilege—Be thou my arm every morning. Let me lean—and converse with thee. Let me lean—and feel thee at my side. Let me lean—and go forward without dismay or discouragement. "Because he is at my right hand, I shall not be moved. Therefore my heart is glad, and my glory rejoiceth: my flesh also shall rest in hope. For thou wilt not leave my soul in hell; neither wilt thou suffer thine Holy One to see corruption. Thou wilt show me the path of life: in thy presence is fullness of joy: at thy right hand are pleasures for evermore."

June 6.—"And walk humbly with thy God."—Micah, vi, 8.

Why not joyfully? There is a foundation laid for this. It is their privilege. It is said, they shall sing in the ways of the Lord. This is not, however, absolutely necessary. In a sense, Christians may go on without it. We have known much self-denial, and deadness to the world, and spirituality of devotion, and zeal for the glory of God, and the welfare of others, in persons who may be said to be saved by hope, rather than confidence. But with regard to humbleness of mind, this is indispensable—*always*, and in—*every* thing: and *no* progress can be made without it. So that when Luther was asked what was the first step in religion, he replied humility; and when asked what was the second and third, answered in the same way. And Peter admonishes Christians to be clothed with humility; as if he would say, This is to cover, to defend, to distinguish, to adorn all. But how is our walking humbly with God to appear?

It is to appear in connexion with divine truth. Here God is our teacher; and if, as learners, we walk humbly with him, we shall cast down imaginations and every high thing that exalteth itself against the knowledge of Christ; we shall sacrifice the pride of reason; and having ascertained that the Scriptures are the word of God, and discovered what they really contain, we shall not speculate upon their principles, but admit them on the divine authority. Nothing can be more proud and vain than to believe no more than we can comprehend, or can make appear to be credible in itself. Is not this founding our faith on knowledge, and not on testimony? Is not this trusting God like a discredited witness in court, whose deposition is regarded only as it is collaterally supported? Is this honoring his wisdom or veracity? Is this receiving with meekness the engrafted word? Is this receiving the kingdom of heaven as a little child?

—It will appear in connexion with divine ordinances. Here we walk with God as worshippers, and if we walk humbly with him, we shall have grace, whereby we may serve him acceptably, with reverence, and with godly fear. We have, indeed, in Christ, boldness and access with confidence; but it is by the faith of him: that is, by the confidence of one who feels his encouragement derived from a mediator. We may come boldly to the throne of grace: but it is to obtain *mercy* and find *grace* to help us—the boldness, therefore, can only be the boldness of the indigent and the guilty, who have nothing of their own to plead. We approach him as a father; but if I am a father, says he, where is mine honor? We have heard some address the Supreme Being with such a levity and freedom as they would not have used to a fellow creature a little above their own level in life. We should keep our feet when we go to the house of God. He is in heaven, and we upon the earth, therefore our words should be *few*.

—It will appear in connexion with his mercies. Here we walk with God as our benefactor; and if we walk humbly with him, we shall own and feel that we have no claim upon God for any thing we possess or enjoy. Am I indulged? I am not worthy of the least of all his mercies. Am I distinguished?

"Not more than others I deserve, | "Yet God hath given me more."

Am I successful? I will not ascribe it to my own skill, or the power of my own arm. I will not sacrifice to my own net, or burn incense to my own drag. The blessing of the Lord, it maketh rich, and he addeth no sorrow with it.

—It will appear with regard to our trials. Here we walk with God as our reprover and corrector; and if we walk humbly, we shall not charge him foolishly; we shall not arraign his authority, or ask, What dost Thou? We shall not resist, or expose ourselves to the reflection, Thou hast smitten them, and they have not grieved. We shall be in subjection to the Father of Spirits, and live. We shall be dumb, and open not our mouth, because He does it. Or if we speak, it will be to acknowledge that his judgments are right, and that in faithfulness he has afflicted us. "I mourn, but I do not murmur. I wonder not that my troubles are so heavy, but that they are so light. I more than deserve them all, and I need them all. I would not only bear, but kiss the rod. It is the Lord: let him do what seemeth him good."

—It will appear with regard to our conditions. Here we walk with God as our disposer and governor; and if we walk humbly we shall hold ourselves at his control; we shall be willing that he should choose our inheritance for us; we shall not lean to our own understanding, but in all our ways acknowledge him. We shall be satisfied with our own allotment, and learn, in whatsoever state we are therewith to be content. We shall abide in the callings wherein his providence has placed us, and not be eager to rise into *superior* offices, feeling our unfitness for them, and fearful of their perils; saying, "Lord, my heart is not haughty, nor mine eyes lofty; neither do I exercise myself in great matters, or in things too high for me. Surely I have behaved and quieted myself as a child that is weaned of his mother: my soul is even as a weaned child."

It will appear with regard to our qualification and ability for our work. Here we walk with God, as our helper and strength; and if we walk humbly, we shall be sensible of the insufficiency for all the purposes of the divine life; that we know not what to pray for as we ought, unless the Spirit itself helpeth our infirmities; that the preparation of the heart, and the answer of the tongue, are from the Lord; that with regard to the exercise of every grace, and the performance of every duty, as the branch cannot bear fruit of itself, except it abide in the vine, no more can we, except we abide in him; for without him we can do nothing. Did Peter walk humbly with him, when, even after the warning he had received, he leaned on his own resolution for superior constancy?

> "Beware of Peter's word,
> "Nor confidently say,
> "I never *will* deny thee, Lord;
> "But grant I never may."

Here, humility is, to fear always; and to pray, Hold thou me up, and I shall be safe.

—It will appear with regard to the whole of our recovery. Here we walk with God as a Savior, and if we walk humbly, we shall not go about to establish our own righteousness, but submit ourselves unto the righteousness which is of God, and acknowledge that we have nothing to glory in before Him. Not by works of righteousness which I had done, but according to his mercy he saved me. I look to the rock whence I was hewn, and to the hole of the pit whence I was digged. How long did he wait for me! What pains were used in vain to bring my heart to him! He was found of me when I sought him not. And how little have I attained! I am still an unprofitable servant; the sins of my holy things would condemn me, I must look only for the mercy of our Lord Jesus Christ unto eternal life. If I am called, he called me by his grace. If I have a good hope, it is a good hope through grace. "By the grace of God I am what I am." Happy this humble walker with God! God resisteth the proud, but giveth grace unto the humble.

> "All joy to the believer! He can speak—
> "Trembling, yet happy, confident, yet meek;
> "Since the dear hour that brought me to thy foot,
> "And cut up all my follies by the root,
> "I never trusted in an arm but thine,
> "Nor hop'd, but in thy righteousness divine;
> "My pray'rs and alms, imperfect and defil'd,
> "Were but the feeble efforts of a child;
> "Howe'er perform'd it was their brightest part,
> "That they proceeded from a grateful heart.
> "Cleans'd in thine own all-purifying blood,
> "Forgive their evil, and accept their good;
> "I cast them at thy feet—my only plea
> "Is what it was, dependence upon thee—
> "While struggling in the vale of tears below,
> "That never fail'd, nor shall it fail me now,
> "Angelic gratulations rend the skies;
> "Pride falls unpitied, never more to rise;
> "Humility is crown'd, and faith receives the prize."

JUNE 7.—"The Lord is our Judge."—Isaiah, xxxii, 2.

In ancient times the character of a judge was united with that of a sovereign. To deliver the award of acquittal, condemnation, or pardon, was the exclusive prerogative of Majesty. Even in our days the sentence pronounced by the appointed expositors of the law must have the fiat of the monarch before it can be fulfilled.

The word Judge is frequently in the Scripture synonymous with Ruler. But as here the Lord, as "our judge," is distinguished from the Lord, as "our lawgiver" and "our king," the term should be taken in its more peculiar meaning. And this view of God should blend with every other character he sustains; not to depress hope; but to prevent presumption; not to hinder our access to God, but to sanctify us when we come nigh him; not to inspire gloom, but to exclude from us all that carelessness and levity so inconsistent with our dependence and responsibility. "If ye call on the Father, who, without respect to persons, judgeth according to every man's work, pass the time of your sojourning here in fear."

He is our future judge. So then, says the Book, every one of us must give account of himself to God. And God will bring every work into judgment, with every secret thing. And who could bear the thought of this process without the knowledge of a Mediator! The only way to find safety in that day, is to look for the mercy of our Lord Jesus Christ unto eternal life; and to be found in him. He is our advocate with the Father, and he is the propitiation for our sins. The charges brought against us are all true, and we have nothing to offer even in our own extenuation. But we appeal to our surety, and he answers for us. Who is he that condemneth? It is Christ that died; yea, rather, is risen again; who is even at the right hand of God, who also maketh intercession for us.

He is our judge at present. And the apostle speaks of it as a privilege of the gospel dispensation, that "we are come to God, the judge of all."

Are you perplexed about the path of duty while importance is attached to every step, and yet you must move forward? Refer yourselves to his unerring counsel. Be influenced and encouraged by the command and the promise, "Trust in the Lord with all thine heart, and lean not unto thine own understanding. In all thy ways acknowledge him, and he shall direct thy paths."

Is your spiritual state doubtful to your own minds? And do you dread delusion? Present the case before Him, and say, "Search me, O God, and know my heart; try me and know my thoughts, and see if there be any wicked way in me, and lead me in the way everlasting."

Do you lie under the misapprehension of friends and the reproaches of enemies? Say, with Job, "Behold, my witness is in heaven, and my record is on high." How often did David turn from the groundless and cruel censures of men, to him who knoweth all things! "Lord, my heart is not haughty, nor mine eyes lofty, neither do I exercise myself in great matters, or in things too high for me. Surely I have behaved and quieted myself as a child that is weaned of his mother; my soul is even as a weaned child." "Let my sentence come forth from thy presence; let thine eyes behold the things that are equal." Are you reviled? Revile not again. Do you suffer? Threaten not—but commit yourselves to Him that judgeth righteously. It is pleasing to have the approbation of our fellow creatures; but there is a higher, a juster, a more merciful tribunal. It is a light thing to be judged of man's judgment. He that judgeth us is the Lord. "Therefore, judge nothing before the time, until the Lord come, who both will bring to light the hidden things of darkness, and will make manifest the counsels of the heart, and then shall every man have praise of God."

JUNE 8.—"The grace that is in Christ Jesus."—2 Timothy, ii, 1.

GRACE is connected with the whole of our recovery as sinners. It is all in all in every part of our salvation. Whether he is chosen, or redeemed, or justified, or converted, or sanctified, or preserved, or comforted, the believer will acknowledge, by the grace of God I am what I am—not I, but the grace of God which is with me.

But where is this grace to be found? The apostle tells us when he speaks of it as the resource of Timothy, both as a minister and a Christian, Thou, therefore, my son, be strong in the grace that is *in Christ Jesus.* As Mediator, he is the principle and treasury of it with regard *to us.*

It is in him exclusively. And we may as well think of finding snow on the bosom of the sun, or paradise in hell, as to think of finding, elsewhere than in him, wisdom, righteousness, sanctification, and redemption. As Pharaoh said to the famishing multitudes that cried to him for bread, "Go unto Joseph, he has all the corn;" so perishing sinners are sent to be blessed with all spiritual blessings in heavenly places in Christ. If there was only one well in the vicinity of a place, this would soon become the scene of concourse, and hither all the inhabitants would repair, or die. And to him shall the gathering of the people be. If any man thirst, said he, let him come unto me and drink. Neither is there salvation in any other; for there is none other name given under heaven among men, whereby they must be saved. And what Christian will refuse to join in the ascription, Of *his* fullness have *all* we received, and grace *for* grace?

It is in him all sufficiently. For it is not in him as water in a vessel, which, though as large as the brazen sea, would, by constant drawing, be soon drawn dry; but as water in a spring, which, though always flowing, is always as full as ever. It is not in him like light in a lamp, which, however luminous, consumes while it shines, and will soon go out in darkness; but like light in the sun, which, after shining for so many ages, is undiminished, and is as able as ever to bless the earth with his beams. There never has been a deficiency in him; and there never will—never can—for Jesus Christ is the same yesterday, to-day, and for ever.

It is in him relatively. He has it for the use and advantage of his people. Is he head over all things? It is to his body, the church. Has he power given him over all flesh? It is that he might give eternal life to as many as the Father hath given him. Is he exalted at the right hand of God? It is to be a Prince and a Savior, to give repentance unto Israel, and forgiveness of sins. Did he receive gifts? It was for men, and even for the rebellious also, that the Lord God might dwell among them. Many trustees are faithful to their office. The rich have wealth for the poor; but often the poor share very little of it, for it is either hoarded by avarice, or squandered by extravagance, and the design of the donor is subverted by the steward But here there is no danger of this. He to whom all our welfare is intrusted will be faithful, not as a servant, like Moses, but as a son over his own house. His work falls in with every disposition of his heart. He so loves the recipients of his bounty, that he even died for them, and rose again. The power and authority to bless them was the joy set before him, for which he endured the cross and despised the shame.

And it is wisely in him. Could we *see* no reason for it, we ought to believe in the propriety of his placing it in him, rather than in ourselves; for God does all things well; and we may always infer the rectitude of his conduct even from his adopting it. And when he has *told* us, too, that a particular course of action "became him," it is absurd to speculate, and profane to object. But it is easy to apprehend the wisdom of God in his pleasure that in him should all fullness dwell. It is thus infinitely secure. Adam had all in his own hand, and soon failed, and ruined his whole race. And should we act better than he? But "this man abideth ever:" and therefore the covenant, of which *he* is the head, is everlasting, ordered in all things, and *sure*. By this appointment also, there is rendered necessary a communion between Christ and Christians, equally honorable to him, and beneficial to them. Let me explain this by a simple reference. An infant, when born, if left to himself, would perish; for he is entirely unequal to his own support. But he is not abandoned. Provision is made for his nourishment. Where? In another. In whom? The one above all others interested in him—and whose relation to him—whose anguish on his behalf—whose love—will always yield him a welcome access to her breast; and the mutual action of giving and receiving will endear the babe to the mother, and the mother to the babe. It is well we cannot live independent of Christ Jesus. How much are his glory and our welfare connected with the blessed necessity of our daily and hourly intercourse with him!

JUNE 9.—"And a certain man, lame from his mother's womb, was carried, whom they laid daily at the gate of the temple which is called Beautiful, to ask alms of them that entered into the temple."—Acts, iii, 2.

WHAT an object of distress was here? Some, if they are poor, are strong and healthful; and limbs and labor are sufficient for them. And some, if they are sickly and infirm, have wealth, or relations and friends that can afford them support. But here penury and helplessness are combined. The sufferings of some are accidental, and endured for a season only; but this man's affliction entered the world with him, and upward of forty years he had endured the calamity.

What a vale of tears is this earth? To what a variety of evils are the human race exposed? Oh, could we see all!—could we see a little of the millionth part! What is a burial-ground? a field of battle? a hospital? every disordered body? but a commentary upon sin, as the text? For sin

"Brought death into the world, and all our wo."

—Can we see such a case as this, and not be thankful for our exemption and preservation? Shall we say, He deserved to be such a cripple, but I did not? Or rather, shall we not say, By the grace of God we are what we are?

Such an instance of misery is presented to try our disposition. The eye affecteth the heart, and was designed to do it; and none but a Priest or Levite will pass by on the other side. Such rights will attract the notice of the humane and the merciful, and move all his bowels of compassion, and put in requisition all his powers of relief. Job, even with regard to his prosperity, which too often makes men insensible and careless, could make this appeal: "When the ear heard me, then it blessed me; and when the eye saw me, it gave witness to me; because I delivered the poor that cried, and the fatherless, and him that had none to help him; the blessing of him that was ready to perish came upon me: and I caused the widow's heart to sing for joy." "I was eyes to the blind, and feet was I to the lame."

As the only expedient of this poor wretch was begging, so, to give him an advantage, they placed him daily at the Beautiful gate of the temple, to ask alms of them that went in. This was wise. Surely he who is going to seek mercy, will be ready to show it. Surely he who is going to pray for pardon, will not be unforgiving and implaeable. "Therefore, if thou bring thy gift to the altar, and there rememberest that thy brother hath aught against thee, leave there thy gift before the altar, and go thy way; first be reconciled to thy brother, and then come and offer thy gift." What communion hath light with darkness? What fellowship can the cruel and uncharitable have with Him who is love itself?

Piety, without benevolence, is hypocrisy. "If a man say, I love God, and hateth his brother, he is a liar: for he that loveth not his brother whom he hath seen, how can he love God whom he hath not seen? And this commandment have we from him, That he who loveth God love his brother also." The tongue of men and angels, without charity, is as sounding brass, or a tinkling cymbal. The gift of prophecy, the understanding of all mysteries and all faith, so that we could remove mountains, would be nothing without charity. How such a man, whatever be his profession, can be a partaker of divine grace, perplexed even an inspired apostle. "Whoso hath this world's good, and seeth his brother hath need, and shutteth up his bowels of compassion from him, how dwelleth the love of God in him?" How well he adds—"My little children, let us not love in word, neither in tongue; but in deed and in truth."

"And hereby we know that we are of the truth, and shall assure our hearts before him."

June 10.—"He delighteth in mercy."—Micah, vii, 18.

Causes are best discovered in their effects. We determine the nature of the spring by the quality of the streams. The tree is known by the fruits. We judge of men's principles and dispositions by their pursuits and conduct. God himself, so to speak, submits to be examined in the same way. To ascertain what he is, we have but to consider what he does. The things the Scripture testifies concerning him, are confirmed and exemplified by the facts to which it refers us. Thus, says the church: "As we have heard, so have we seen in the city of our God." Is he called, "The God of all grace?" "The Father of mercies?" Is it said, "He is rich in mercy?"

"He delighteth in mercy?" Let us pause and reflect, and we shall find the proofs and illustrations more wonderful than the assertion itself.

"What hath God wrought" to gain the confidence of our guilty and, therefore, foreboding and misgiving minds! for this is the first step in the return of a sinner to God; we can only be saved by hope. And here let us follow the example of the inspired John; what is it that arrests and enraptures his attention? "Herein is love." Where? In what? "Herein is love: not that we loved God, but that he loved us, and sent his Son to be the propitiation for our sins." Not that he would overlook the other doings of God; but here *he* saw most clearly that "God is love." God's soul delights in his own Son. yet he would seem to delight more in mercy; for when he met with him and us on Calvary, he said, *Thou* shalt die, and *they* shall live. It therefore pleased the Lord to bruise *him;* that by his stripes *we* might be healed, and through his sweet smelling sacrifice become nearer to God than if we had never sinned. And we must here take in not only the expensiveness of the act, but the character of the objects. It is the reasoning of another apostle: "Scarcely for a righteous man will one die; yet peradventure for a good man some would even dare to die. But God commendeth his love toward us, in that while we were yet sinners Christ died for us." And having made the provision, so that all things are now ready, would he endeavor to awaken our attention to it? would he send forth the ministry of reconciliation to beseech us to accept it, unless he delighted in mercy?

He delights, also, not only in the exercise of mercy *to* us, but *by* us. He, therefore, would not leave mercy to the operation of reason and religion only; but, as our Maker, he has rendered it a law of our being. By our very physical constitution, pity is an unavoidable emotion. When we see the pain and distress of a fellow creature, the eye affecteth the heart. We involuntarily feel an uneasiness, which prompts us to succor—even to relieve ourselves. As far, indeed, as this is implanted in us, it is a mere instinct. But who produced it there? Who made it natural? Who rendered it so difficult to be subdued and destroyed? but a Being who delighteth in mercy? Besides, though it be originally an instinct only, by cherishing it we render it a virtue; and by exciting and exercising it from religious motives, we turn it into a Christian grace.

And see what stress he has laid upon it in his word. How often does he enjoin it! How dreadfully has he threatened the neglect of it? And what promises has he made to the practice of it? "He shall have judgment without mercy who showed no mercy." "But blessed are the merciful, for they shall obtain mercy." He has told us, that no clearness of knowledge, no rectitude of opinion, no fervor of zeal, no constancy of attendance on ordinances, no talking of divine things, will be a compensation for charity. "Whoso hath this world's good, and seeth his brother have need, and shutteth up his bowels of compassion from him, how dwelleth the love of God in him?" And hence the pre-eminence our Savior gives it in the proceedings of the last day. "Then shall the King say unto them on his right hand, Come, ye blessed of my Father, inherit the kingdom prepared for you from the foundation of the world: for I was an hungered, and ye gave me meat: I was thirsty, and ye gave me drink I was a stranger, and ye took me in; naked, and ye clothed me; I was sick, and ye visited me: I was in prison, and ye came unto me." The language has been perverted, for men dream of merit where, above all things, we need mercy. This word "for" is here not causative, but evidential—just as we may say, the spring has come, *for* the birds sing; the singing of the birds does not cause the coming of the spring, but is the effect and proof of it. But even this distinction affords the merciless no favor; for though the practice here so noticed be not the procuring of the blessedness, it is the character of the blessed. On every ground, therefore, the man who is a stranger to it is not entitled to hope. For which reason, too, our Lord goes on to the subjects of condemnation. And who are these? Tyrants? robbers? murderers of fathers and mothers? perjured persons? No—but the slothful and the selfish—the unkind tongue—the close hand—the unfeeling heart—the unpitying eye—the foot that knew not the door of misery. "Then shall he say also unto them on the left hand, Depart from me, ye cursed, into everlasting fire, prepared for the devil and his angels: for I was an hungered, and ye gave me no meat: I was thirsty, and ye gave me no drink: I was a stranger, and ye took me not in: naked, and ye clothed me not: sick, and in prison, and ye visited me not."

Let us, therefore, not only believe and admire, but let us be followers of him who delighteth in mercy. We cannot love him unless we are concerned to please him; and we cannot please him unless we are like-minded with him. Neither can we enjoy him. Resemblance is the foundation of our communion with him. He only that dwelleth in love, dwelleth in God, and God in him. "BE YE THEREFORE MERCIFUL, EVEN AS YOUR FATHER, WHO IS IN HEAVEN, IS MERCIFUL."

JUNE 11.—"And it came to pass, that when Isaac was old, and his eyes were dim, so that he could not see, he called Esau his eldest son, and said unto him, My son: and he said unto him, Behold, here am I. And he said, Behold, now I am old, I know not the day of my death: now therefore take, I pray thee, thy weapons, thy quiver, and thy bow, and go out to the field, and take me some venison; and make me savory meat, such as I love, and bring it to me that I may eat; that my soul may bless thee before I die." Genesis, xxvii, 1—4.

IN Isaac's blindness we see one of the frequent accompaniments of age. Age is generally an aggregate of privations, diseases, and infirmities. If, by reason of strength, we reach fourscore years, the strength then becomes labor and sorrow: labor in the preserving, and sorrow in the possession.

"Our vitals, with laborious strife,
"Bear up the crazy load;
"And drag the dull remains of life
"Along the tiresome road."

A powerful reason why we should remember our Creator in the days of our youth, that we may have a resource when the evil days come, in which we shall say, I have no pleasure. What a privilege, when exercised with the loss of sight and of hearing; with trembling of limbs and sleepless nights, and fearful apprehensions, and failure of desire; to have God for the strength of our heart, and our portion for ever; and to hear him saying, "Even to your old age I am He; and even to hoar hairs will I carry you: I have made, and I will hear; even I will carry, and will deliver you."

—The reflection upon his mortality may be adopted by every individual, whatever his condition, or health, or age. All are ignorant of the time of their dissolution. For the human race dies at all periods, as well as in all circumstances; and we know not what a day may bring forth. But when Isaac says, "I know not the day of my death," he means that it was near; and that every day might be reckoned as his last. Death is not far from every one of us. But while, as the proverb says, the young may die, the old must die. And it becomes the aged to think frequently and seriously of their departure as at hand—to prepare for it—and to regard zealously the call of every present duty. It was the prayer of Moses, "So teach us to number our days, that we may apply our hearts unto wisdom." It was the profession of our Lord and Savior, "I must work the works of Him that sent me while it is day, the night cometh wherein no man can work." It was the admonition of Solomon, "Whatsoever thy hand findeth to do, do it with thy might, for there is no work, nor device, nor knowledge, nor wisdom, in the grave, whither thou goest."

Thus Isaac was roused into a concern to finish his work before he finished his course; "Now therefore take, I pray thee, thy weapons, thy quiver, and thy bow, and go out to the field, and take me some venison; and make me savory meat, such as I love, and bring it to me, that I may eat, that my soul may bless thee before I die"—not afterward. In like manner Elijah, when waiting for his ascension into heaven, said to Elisha, "Ask now what I shall do for thee, *before* I be taken up from thee"—believing his intercourse with him, and his acting for him, would then be terminated. This is a solemn, and should be a useful thought. Look at your children, your relations, your friends, your neighbors, and see in what way you can serve your generation. *Now* you can bless them by your prayers, your counsels, your example, your liberality—but all these opportunities are confined to life, and this life is a vapor, that appeareth for a little time, and then vanisheth away! Isaac did well in seizing the present moment to set his house in order before his death. But there are two things in which he was blamable.

First. He shows too great a regard for the indulgence of his appetite. It is mournful to see a good man, and especially an old man, instead of mortifying the deeds of the body, studying his sensual gratification, and making provision for the flesh, not to fulfil the wants, but the lusts thereof. Carriages are dragged as they are going down hill.

Secondly. He was more influenced by natural affection than a regard to the will of God. He wished to make Esau heir, but God had expressly declared, "the elder shall serve the younger." Isaac could not have been ignorant of this. Had he forgotten it? Or did he disregard it? Here we see his frailty. But this does not render the purpose of God of none effect. His counsel shall stand, and he will do all his pleasure. Rebekah on the other hand, was fond of Jacob; and a father has no chance against a mother, who has a favorite whom she is determined to advance: especially such a selfish.

crafty, cunning creature as was here at work. Her aim, indeed, fell in with God's design; but this concurrence arose, not from her piety, but her partiality. Her conduct was unjustifiable and sinful; for we must not do evil that good may come. She had the divine promise on the side of her preference, and she should have rested in the Lord, and waited patiently for him, and not have fretted herself in any wise to do evil. "He that believeth maketh not haste." Had she quietly committed her way unto the Lord he would have brought it to pass without those wretched consequences that afflicted the family. For God uses instruments without approving of them; and though he makes the folly and passions of men to praise him, he fails not to prove that it is an evil and bitter thing to forsake him, and to act without his fear in our hearts.

—How painful would it be to go on, and see a mother teaching her child to tell lies, and to see a son imposing on the blindness of an aged father! We have no notion that Rebekah was ever religious, and we are persuaded that Jacob was not pious at this time. We believe he was converted in his journey from Beersheba to Haran. At Bethel God met with him; and there he spake with *us*.

June 12.—"And the Lord went before them by day in a pillar of a cloud, to lead them the way; and by night in a pillar of fire to give them light, to go by day and night. He took not away the pillar of the cloud by day, nor the pillar of fire by night, from before the people."—Exodus, xiii, 21, 22.

This institution was necessary: for there was no path in the desert; and they had no maps, no pioneers, no guides. But, says God, I have not brought you out of Egypt to leave you to wander and perish in the wilderness. Behold your Conductor to the rest and the inheritance which the Lord your God giveth you. Accordingly, by this, they were to be regulated in all their journeying. As this rose, they rose; as this paused, they paused; as this turned to the right hand or to the left, they turned. It sometimes called them to leave a more endeared spot, and to stop in a less inviting scene; but they were not at liberty to cling to the one, or decline the other: the signal was instantly decisive. This pillar was obviously nothing less than a real miracle—yet how little were the observers affected by it! They sinned with this hovering prodigy over them; and even committed idolatry! We are prone to ascribe too much moral efficacy to such supernatural appearances. They soon become as unimpressive and uninfluential as the ordinary means of grace are with us.

It was a symbol of the divine presence. "The Lord was in the pillar." It was this nearness of God that insured their safety, and gave them their distinction and pre-eminence. There he was always at hand, always in view. "And," says Moses, "what nation is there so great, who hath God so nigh unto them, as the Lord our God is in all things that we call upon him for?"

But how extensively adapted was this provision to their state and exigencies! It was both a pillar of a cloud, and a pillar of fire, to lead them in the way; the one appearance was for the day, the other for the night. Fire by day would have added to the dazzling and fervidness of a burning sky—the pillar was therefore a cloud by day, and screened them like a large umbrella from the scorching rays of the sun. Cloud by night would have added to the gloom, the darkness, and the dread of danger—the pillar was therefore a fire by night, to lick up the unwholesome damps, to warm the chilling atmosphere, and to afford them a light, by which they could see to move about in their tents, and also to travel, as they often did, after the sun was set.

If this ordinance showed his wisdom and goodness, the continuance of the blessing evinced his patience—for, notwithstanding their unworthiness, and their provocations, and their various corrections, this pillar was not taken away from before the people till they reached the border of Jordan, and came to their journey's end!

He has a people for his name now. They are only strangers and pilgrims on earth, bound for a better country, that is, a heavenly. This they would never reach, if they were left to themselves. But they are not. The God of Israel is with them. They have not the same sensible proof of his presence as the Jews had. But they have real evidence of it, and it is satisfactory to their own minds. He keeps them from falling. He accommodates himself to their conditions. He is a very present help in trouble. He makes his goodness to pass before them. He leads them by his word, and his Spirit, and his providence. He has also said, I will *never* leave thee, nor forsake thee. Therefore they may boldly say, This God is our God for ever and ever: He will be our guide unto *death*.

"Thus, when our first release we gain,
"From Sin's old yoke, and Satan's chain,
"We have this desert world to pass,
"A dangerous and a tiresome place.

"He feeds and clothes us all the way;
"He guides our footsteps lest we stray;
"He guards us with a powerful hand;
"And brings us to the promised land."

June 13.—"The censers of these sinners against their own souls, let them make them broad plates for a covering of the altar."—Numbers, xvi, 38.

He had solemnly forewarned and admonished the rebels themselves before they suffered; and thus, in wrath, he remembered mercy. When Korah, Dathan, and Abiram, who headed the conspiracy, were buried alive, and their companions, the two hundred and fifty princes, men of honor, were burned with fire, he would make them beacons, and prevent others from coming into the same condemnation. Orders, therefore, were given to take up the censers in which they had dared to burn incense, and make of them broad plates to cover the altar of burnt offering—that they might "be a sign unto the children of Israel;" *i. e.* a memorial to the Levites, and the comers thereunto, of the revolt of these men, and that they were punished for invading an office which God had forbidden them.

Whence we note, that the sin which is hurtful to the transgressors, should be useful to the observers.

"These sinners against their own souls!" Yes; whenever men sin, they sin *against themselves.* Society cannot exist without laws, and laws are nothing without penalties. Connivance at the guilty, would be cruelty to the innocent. In every well-ordered government, crimes are punished. And will they, can they escape, in the empire of a Being, holy in all his ways, and righteous in all his works? What would you think of a magistrate, who bore the sword in vain, and who was not a terror to evil doers, as well as a praise to them that do well? What would you think of him, if, when you brought before him the incendiary of your house, or the murderer of your child, he should say, Oh, this does not regard me—and smile, and say, Go in peace! We dislike the word vindictive justice—there seems something malignant in it; but substitute in the room of it, the vindicatory or punitive justice of God, and we contend that this is essential to the excellency of his character, and that you could not esteem, nor even love him, without it. What regard could you have for a being who equally respected lies and truth, cruelty and kindness, a Nero and a Howard? We readily own, that when anger and wrath are ascribed to God in the Scriptures, they do not imply any thing like passion in us, but only principle. But principle they do establish! and this principle is the soul of order; adherence to rectitude; determination to punish.

And we may see this denounced in his threatenings. For his wrath is *revealed* from heaven against all unrighteousness and ungodliness of men. If this book be true, the wicked shall not stand in his sight. He hateth all workers of iniquity.

He has also confirmed and exemplified it in his conduct. Look to heaven, and see the angels sinning against themselves, and cast down to hell. See Adam and Eve driven from the garden of Eden. See the flood carrying away the world of the ungodly. See the inhabitants of the plain; and Pharaoh; and the nations of Canaan; and the Jews, though so peculiarly indulged of God. Yea, and good men —he even visits *their* transgressions with a rod; and though he *forgives* their iniquities, he takes vengeance on their inventions. See Moses and Aaron forbidden to enter the land of promise; and Eli and David so awfully judged in this life. And if these things are done in the green tree, what shall be done in the dry? and if the righteous are recompensed in the earth, how much more the sinner and the ungodly!

It would be easy to trace the injury of sin with regard to every thing of which the welfare of the sinner is compounded. His connexions ought to be dear to him. But how does he sin against these? How does the wicked child rend the heart of his parents, and bring down their gray hairs with sorrow to the grave. How does the husband, by his vices, instead of providing for those of his own house, reduce the wife he ought to love, even as himself, to indigence and wretchedness, and her hapless babes along with her. What a blessing is health. But how does he sin against this! By intemperance and sensuality he is made to possess the iniquities of his youth, which lie down with him in the dust. Envy is the rottenness of the bones. So are hatred and malice. And so are all those corroding anxieties and fears which those must feel who have no confidence in God, or hope of heaven. Reputation is desirable, as it enables us to live in the esteem of others, and valuable, as it is an instrument of usefulness—a good name, says Wisdom itself, is better than great riches. But who regards the sinner? Who confides in him? What is his friendship, or his promise? The name of the wicked shall rot. A wicked man is loathsome, and cometh to shame. We must be measured and weighed by our souls. The mind is the standard of the man. This is the seat of happiness or misery. But he that sinneth against me, says God, wrongeth his own soul. Wrongs it of peace —for there is no peace to the wicked. Wrongs it of liberty and pleasure—for he is in the *gall* of bitterness, and in the *bond* of iniquity. Wrongs it of safety—for the wrath of God abideth on him: he is condemned already.

But let not these sinners suffer in vain. They are our martyrs. They die and perish for us. Their loss should be our gain; and their destruction our salvation.

The first advantage we may derive from an observation of the sins and sufferings of others, is the confirmation of our faith. And nothing can tend more to establish our belief in the truth of the Scripture, than to take its declarations and decisions, and compare them with the documents of men's lives. The Bible tells us that the way of transgressors is hard. That they proceed from evil to evil. That a little leaven leaveneth the whole lump. That the companion of fools shall be destroyed. That the love of money is the root of all evil. And he must be blind that has not—seen this, as well as—read it.

Another benefit, is gratitude. When we see the wicked, we see what *we* should have been, but for preventing and distinguishing grace. Who made me to differ? Have I a heart of flesh, while they are insensible? Am I light in the Lord, while they are darkness? Am I walking in the way everlasting, while destruction and misery is in their paths? By the grace of God, I am what I am.

The observation should also awaken and excite zeal. Surely none so much need our compassion, as those who are destroying themselves for ever. We talk of doing good. What advantage can we procure a fellow creature like that godliness, which is profitable unto all things? What enemy can we rescue him from, like his lusts and vices? If we convert a sinner from the error of his ways, we save a soul from death, and hide a multitude of sins.

It should also serve to wean us from the present world. What a bedlam it is! what a sink of corruption! What righteous soul is not daily, hourly, vexed with the filthy conversation of the ungodly?—Thus the ear, the eye, the heart, is constantly sickened. We behold the transgressors, and are grieved. O that I had in the wilderness a lodging-place of way-faring men. O that I had wings like a dove, for then would I flee away, and be at rest—with the spirits of just men made perfect—dwelling in love, and dwelling in God!

Finally. Let us fetch from it, warnings. When Daniel, addressing Belshazzar, reminded him of his father's pride and destruction, he aggravates his guilt, by saying, "Thou knewest all this." When the apostle mentions "the sins and plagues that Israel knew," he says, "Now these things were our examples, to the intent we should not lust after evil things, as they also lusted. Neither be ye idolaters as were some of them; as it is written, The people sat down to eat and drink, and rose up to play. Neither let us commit fornication, as some of them committed, and fell in one day three and twenty thousand. Neither let us tempt Christ, as some of them also tempted, and were destroyed of serpents. Neither murmur ye, as some of them also murmured, and were destroyed of the destroyer. Now, all these things happened unto them for ensamples: and they are written for our admonition, upon whom the ends of the world are come. Wherefore, let him that thinketh he standeth take heed lest he fall."

And surely, O my soul, if the sins of others may be rendered thus profitable, I ought to be concerned to gain something from my own. Let me learn wisdom from my follies; and strength from my weakness; and standing from my falls. Let me see more of my depravity; and put on humbleness of mind; and apply to the Blood of Sprinkling; and never more trust in my own heart, but be strong in the grace that is in Christ Jesus; and be sober and vigilant; and till I am beyond the reach of evil, pray, "Hold thou me up, and I shall be safe."

June 14.—" Jesus saith unto him, Have I been so long time with you, and yet hast thou not known me, Philip?"—John, xiv, 9.

—He had been with Philip and his fellow disciples corporeally, for the Word was made flesh and dwelt among them, and they beheld his glory. But his bodily presence was confined to Judea, and few knew him after the flesh. And soon he was known so no more, for he was received up into heaven. But it is remarkable, that while on earth, he evinced that his efficiency was not dependent on his bodily presence, for he performed cures at a distance, as we see in the case of the nobleman's son, and the centurion's servant, who were healed by no application, but simply by his volition, as if to encourage the belief, that when removed hence, he could still operate here.

And if his word is to be relied upon, he is with his people now. What was his promise to his ministers? to his churches? to individuals? "Lo! I am with you alway, even unto the end of the world?" "Where two or three are gathered together in my Name, there am I in the midst of them." "If a man love me, he will keep my words, and my Father will love him, and we will come unto him, and make our abode with him." Therefore he has either given promises which he is unable to fulfill or though now in heaven, he is with his disciples on earth—with them specially, graciously, spiritually. Effects prove the existence of the cause; the operation of the workman shows his presence; and that "*his* Name is near his wondrous works declare." He has done enough *in* the Christian, to demonstrate that he is *with* him—and he hath said, I will never *leave* thee, nor *forsake* thee.

—Yet he says to Philip, "Hast thou not known me?" Philip was not entirely ignorant of him; but he knew him not sufficiently, he knew him not comparatively—he knew him not, considering how he might have known him. And is not this the case with us? Some have very little knowledge of any kind. They never guide even the common affairs of this life with discretion. They seem incapable of improvement. Even suffering does not teach them wisdom. "Experience," says Franklin, "is a dear school; yet fools will learn in no other." But many do not learn even in this.

Yet the children of this world are wiser in their generation than the children of light. We live in a land of vision; we have Sabbaths, and Bibles, and religious ordinances, and teachers; yet as to a knowledge of the peculiar truths of the Gospel, and the reality of Christian experience, numbers are as ignorant as heathens. "The light shineth in darkness, but the darkness comprehendeth it not." Must we go on? What do many Christians, real Christians, who have long had the great Teacher with them—what do even they know? What do they know of their own interest in him? Are they not unable to determine what their spiritual condition is, and to say, with Thomas, *my* Lord and *my* God? How little do they know of his salvation! How little of the glories of his person! How little of the nature of his dispensations toward them; so that they are confounded with the fresh discoveries they make of the evils of their own hearts; perplexed with their own afflictions; desponding if difficulties multiply, and they see no means or way of escape; and ready to conclude that he has shut out their prayers, because he does not immediately and sensibly answer them; all from their knowing so little of the *manner* in which he deals with his people!

Yet the defectiveness of their knowledge is very censurable, especially after *long* intimacy with him. Hence the apostle reproaches the Hebrews, "When for the time ye ought to have been teachers, ye have need that one teach you again, which be the first principles of the oracles of God." Hence our Lord said to his disciples on another occasion, "Are ye also yet without understanding?" And here again he says, "Have I been *so long* with you, and *yet* hast thou not known me, Philip?" He had scarcely been three years with them then; and he had very gradually developed himself, and kept back many things for a future communication. Yet it was a long period, considering its importance and privileges, and always having access to him with their inquiries, and hearing his discourses, and witnessing all his conduct, they ought to have gained much more than they did. But they were slow of heart, and made very little progress, as we see by their various mistakes and embarrassments. Yet what right have we to cast a stone at them? How few, how poor, how wretched, have been our attainments! And yet he has been much longer with many of us—ten—twenty—forty years—abounding too with every assistance. Four things ought to make us blush at the thought of this.

First. The necessity and value of the knowledge we have made so little proficiency in. How much depends upon it, our usefulness, our preservation from error, our peace and comfort, and our progress in the divine life; for though we may grow in knowledge without growing in grace, we cannot grow in grace without growing in knowledge. Religion does not act upon us mechanically, but morally; *i. e.* through just views and motives.

Secondly. Some have made far greater advancement in much less time, and with very inferior advantages. They set out long after, but they soon passed us on the road. They have had very little pious intercourse, and have seldom heard a Gospel sermon. Yet when we converse with them, and see them in the relations, duties, and trials of life—how much below them must we feel.

Thirdly. Our obligations and responsibility rise with our means and opportunities. What an advantage are pious relations! What a privilege is a Gospel ministry! What a precious talent is time!

Where is conscience, while we look at our improvement of all these? Where much is given much will be required.

Lastly. Our unprofitableness is the subject of divine disappointment and complaint. "What could have been done more to my vineyard that I have not done in it? Wherefore, when I looked that it should bring forth grapes, brought it forth wild grapes?" The thought of displeasing and dishonoring him is nothing to some. But shall *we* provoke, and grieve his Holy Spirit? Can we who love him, and know what he has done for us, can we be insensible to the Savior's decision? "Herein is my Father glorified, that ye bear much fruit; so shall ye be my disciples?"

What remains, but that we admire and adore the patience of Him who still bears with us, though we have so often constrained him to ask, "How long shall I be with you? how long shall I suffer you?" And let us search and try our ways, and turn again unto the Lord. Let us guard against indecision and sloth. Let us be diligent in the use of all the means of religious improvement. Let us not cease to pray that we may be "filled with the knowledge of his will, in all wisdom and spiritual understanding. That we may walk worthy of the Lord unto all pleasing, being fruitful in every good work, and increasing in the knowledge of God."

"Then shall we know, *if* we follow on to know the Lord. His going forth is prepared as the morning. And he shall come unto us as the rain, as the latter and former rain unto the earth."

June 15.—"When the Most High divided the nations their inheritance, when he separated the sons of Adam, he set the bounds of the people according to the number of the children of Israel."—Deuteronomy, xxxii, 8.

This is an important and interesting communication, and it supplies us with two facts. First. That *God* originally divided the nations their inheritance. When, after the deluge, he gave the new earth to the children of men, he did not throw it in among them, so to speak, for a kind of scramble, that each might seize what he could; but he assigned them their several portions, that the discontented might not invade the peaceful, nor the mighty prey upon the weak. God permits what he does not approve; but nothing can be more contrary to his design and pleasure, than for powerful states to invade and incorporate little ones. And the crime generally punishes itself. Such unjust and forced accessions add nothing to the safety, strength, or happiness of the acquirers, but become sources of uneasiness, corruption, and revolt; so difficult is it to suppress old attachments and patriotical instincts that are almost equal to the force of nature. Paul justifies the sentiment of Moses, "He hath made of one blood all nations of men for to dwell on all the face of the earth, and hath determined the times before appointed, and the bounds of their habitation, that they should seek the Lord, if haply they might feel after him, and find him, though he be not far from every one of us."

Secondly. In the arrangement of the limits and conditions of mankind, He had an especial reference to the future commonwealth of Israel. For they were by far the most important detachment of the human race. They were the Lord's portion, and the lot of his inheritance. They were the depositaries of revealed religion. The heirs of the righteousness which is by faith. To them pertained the adoption, and the glory, and the Covenant, and the giving of the Law, and the services of God, and the promises; theirs were the fathers, and of them, as concerning the flesh, Christ came. We cannot trace this fact perfectly for want of more materials, and we know not all the purposes of God in making and keeping the Jews a peculiar body; otherwise we should clearly see how all the dispensations of God corresponded to their privileged destination. One thing is to be observed. They were not intended to engross the divine favor, but to be the mediums and diffusers of it. They were not only to be blessed, but to be blessings. Hence their being placed in the midst of the earth, that from them knowledge might be derived, and proselytes to revealed religion might be made; and that, in the fullness of time, out of Zion might go forth the Law and the Word of the Lord from Jerusalem, and that the great Supper, as our Lord calls it, and which was designed for the whole family of Adam, might be spread in the middle of the earth, and be accessible to all.

While we here see that there is nothing like chance in the government of the world, there is what may be called a peculiar providence in particular instances. And here we cannot help thinking of our own country. No country on earth bears such a comparison with Judea in privilege and design. Its appropriation and appointment will account for its preservation, and emerging from difficulties which seemed likely to swallow it up. And when we consider what it is, and what it more than promises to be, we can find reason for its insular situation, its government, laws, and commerce; its talent, and learning, and influence, and dominion. We are a sinful people, but, as "the new wine is found in the cluster, and one saith, Destroy it not, for a blessing is in it; so, says God, will I do for my servants' sakes, that I may not destroy them all." We cannot approve of every thing we have done, especially in the West and East Indies; but we cannot be ignorant that God is overruling it for good, and has ends in view far beyond slave-holders and mercantile companies, and statesmen. We have fought, and we have conquered, but the negro is instructed, and the captive is made free, and openings are made and occupied for the spread of the Gospel.

The economies of heaven on earth have always been regulated by one end—the cause of the Messiah; and could we view things as God does, we should perceive how all the revolutions of the world, the changes of empire, the successes or defeats of haughty worms, have affected this cause, immediately or remotely, in a way of achievement or preparation, or purification, or increase; of solidity or diffusion; and that all things are going on, not only consistently with it, but conducively to it. For, says the Ruler over all, "I have sworn by myself, the word is gone out of my mouth in righteousness, and shall not return, that unto me every knee shall bow, every tongue shall swear."

And, O Christian, there is a special providence over thee. The hairs of thy head are all numbered. One thing regulates all that befalls thee, all the dark, as well as the clear—all the painful, as well as the cheerful—thy spiritual—thy everlasting welfare. "For we know that all things work together for good to them that love God, to them that are the called according to his purpose."

June 16.—" Thy loving-kindness is before mine eyes."—Psalm xxvi, 3.

And it will be well to follow David, and to keep the loving-kindness of God before *our* eyes also. And this should be done four ways.

First. As a subject of contemplation. The mind will be active, and it is our wisdom to regulate and sanctify our thoughts. Isaac went out into the field at eventide to meditate, and we may infer the nature of his reflections from his character. David said, My meditation of him shall be sweet. How precious are thy thoughts unto me, O God! How great is the sum of them! People complain of the difficulty they feel in fixing their minds; but the duty would become easier by use—and surely they can never be at a loss for a theme. Let them take his loving-kindness and set it before their eyes. Let them observe it as it appears in the promises of his word; in the history of his church; in their own experience. And let them pass from the instances of his loving-kindness to the qualities of it, and dwell upon its earliness, and fullness, and extensiveness, and seasonableness, and constancy. "Whoso is wise, and will observe these things, even they shall understand the loving-kindness of the Lord."

Secondly. As the source of encouragement. How often shall we need this! We shall feel our want of it under a sense of our guilt, and unworthiness, and continued imperfections; and nothing short of the exceeding riches of his grace, in his kindness toward us by Christ Jesus, will be able to relieve us. But this *will* relieve us, and *effectually* too. It will give us everlasting consolation, and good hope through grace, and boldness and access with confidence by the faith of him. And it will do all this without reconciling us to our sins, or even our infirmities—yea, it will make us lament our deficiencies the more, grieving that we serve him so little who loves us so much. We shall want it in our afflictions. And who can hope to escape these in a vale of tears? Now nothing is so desirable in our sufferings as to see, not only the *hand* but the *kindness* of God in them. For often they look like the effects of his wrath, and we tremble under them, and cry, "Do not condemn me. I could bear these trials, if I thought they were only the strokes of a father's rod, and sent in love." And they *are* sent in love. They are only the strokes of a Father's rod, laid hold of with reluctance, and laid aside with pleasure.

Thirdly. As an excitement to praise. It is afflicting to think how little the loving-kindness of God is acknowledged by those who are constantly partaking of it. How lamentable, says Leighton, is it, that a world, so full of God's mercy, should be so empty of his glory. Oh, says David, again and again, Oh that men would praise the Lord for his goodness, and for his wonderful works to the children of men! Were there not ten lepers cleansed? but where are the nine? Did ever Hezekiah render according to the benefits done him? And are we better than they? And whence is it that we feel so little the obligations we are under to the God of our mercies? Because the mercies of God are so little remarked and remembered by us. Nothing can impress us when it is out of our minds and thoughts. Therefore, says David, "Bless the Lord, O my soul, and forget not all his benefits." At the moment when God appears for us, we are sensible of his goodness, and speak well of his name; but like the Jews, we soon forget his works, and the wonders which he has shown us. We inscribe our afflictions upon a rock, and the characters remain—we write our mercies in the sand of the sea shore, and the first wave of trouble washes them out.

Lastly. We should keep his loving-kindness before our eyes as an example for imitation. The Scripture calls upon us to be followers of God as dear children. But in what? His moral, and not his natural perfections. We may wish to resemble him in power and independence, and to be as gods, knowing good and evil. But we are to be concerned to reverence Him, not as the greatest, but as the best of beings—to be faithful as he is faithful, to be holy as he is holy—to be patient, and forgiving, and kind, like him. "I say unto you, Love your enemies; bless them that curse you; do good to them that hate you; and pray for them which despitefully use you, and persecute you; that ye may be the children of your Father which is in heaven; for he maketh his sun to rise on the evil and on the good, and sendeth rain on the just and on the unjust." Be ye therefore merciful, even as your Father which is in heaven is merciful.

You would do well to keep in view some of your fellow creatures, who feel that it is more blessed to give than to receive. Think of a Howard, a Thornton. But in *Him* the fatherless findeth mercy. God is love. We cannot equal him. But it is our happiness to resemble. He that dwelleth in Love, dwelleth in God, and God in him. "Put on therefore, as the elect of God, holy and beloved, bowels of mercies, kindness, humbleness of mind, meekness, long suffering, forbearing one another, and forgiving one another, if any man have a quarrel against any: even as Christ forgave you, so also do ye. And above all these things, put on charity, which is the bond of perfectness."

June 17.—"The breath of our nostrils, the Anointed of the Lord, was taken in their pits, of whom we said, Under his shadow we shall live among the Heathen."—Lamentations, iv, 20.

Some commentators suppose that these words are intended to apply to the Savior. We see no ground for this. Others imagine that there may be a reference to him under the case of Zedekiah. However this may be, the passage may be used—not to prove any doctrine, but to remind us of several things pertaining to the Lord Jesus, and fully established in the Scriptures of Truth.

—Such as his office—"The anointed of the Lord." The very meaning of the word Messiah in the Old Testament, and of Christ in the New. Prophets, priests, and kings, were anointed at their consecration. He was all these; and therefore he is said to be anointed with the oil of gladness, above his fellows. Here the term imports majesty; and he is the King of glory, the King of saints, the King of nations—"With my holy oil have I anointed him."

—Such is the estimation in which he is holden by his subjects—"The breath of our nostrils." He is not so regarded by others. The world knew him not. The Jews received him not. He is now, as to the multitude, despised and rejected of men. This was the case once with his own people. They acknowledge it; and look back with shame and sorrow upon a period—and with some of them it was a long period—during which he had no form or comeliness, nor any beauty that they should desire him. But he has been revealed in them. And now he appears fairer than the children of men, and altogether lovely. Faith makes him precious. He is their righteousness and strength; their glory and joy; all their salvation and all their desire. We may be excessive in our attachment to a creature; but we can never think too highly of Him. It was Idolatry in these Jews to call their prince the breath of their nostrils; but Jesus is really and absolutely so to us. How dear! How important! How indispensable!

> "This flesh of mine might learn as soon
> "To live, yet part with all my blood;
> "To breathe when vital air is gone,
> "Or thrive and grow without my food."

—Such is their expectation from Him—"Of whom we said, Under his shadow we shall live among the Heathen." The Israelites were literally among the Heathen, surrounded as they were with the Gentile nations. This was also the case with the first Christians. Yea, they were not only encompassed by them, but intermixed with them. In one house dwelt an Idolater; in the next a worshipper of God. A Pagan and a Christian labored together in the same field, or the same manufactory. We should not undervalue the outward advantages of Christianity. How much more privileged are we, than our missionary brethren! They live under his shadow—but it is among the Heathen! While we have our sabbaths, and temples, and preachers, and our fellow Christians, with whom we take sweet counsel together. Though there are no heathens among us, nominally, and as to dispensation, yet there are some who know nothing doctrinally: and many who know nothing spiritually: many who are without God in the world, and who hate and oppose, as far as they are allowed, the religion we experience. And how often is a righteous soul vexed with the conversation of the ungodly, and constrained to sigh, "Wo is me, that I dwell in Mesech!" But whatever be the disadvantages of our condition, there is a shadow—and *his* shadow—under which we can *live!* A shadow from the heat—not the shadow of a summer cloud only; but of a great rock in a weary land: the shadow of a tree yielding, not only shade, but fruit, according to the acknowledgment of the Church—"I sat down under his shadow with great delight, and his fruit was sweet to my taste." So it is said, "They that dwell under His shadow shall return; they shall revive as the corn, and grow as the vine: the scent thereof shall be as the wine of Lebanon." His shadow means protection, and all the blessings of his empire. The reign of some rulers is like the shadow of a vulture over the bird of prey; or as a hurricane over the flooded meadow, and the stripped forest—but let the children of Zion be joyful in their King. Blessed are all they that put their trust in him.

—Such is his apprehension or suffering—"He was taken in their pits." They watched him, and persecuted him, through life. At length he was betrayed into the hands of his enemies; and they insulted nim, and crucified him, and laid him in the grave. Then his disciples said, "We trusted that it had been he which should have redeemed Israel"—"The breath of our nostrils, the Anointed of the Lord, was taken in their pits, of whom we said, Under his shadow shall we live among the Heathen."

—But here correspondence becomes contrast. No type, no image, no illustration, can do justice to him: and when examined, it will always be found to teach more by unlikeness, than by conformity. Zedekiah's subjects had their hopes disappointed and destroyed by *his* arrest: and when carried away, and imprisoned at Babylon, he could no longer defend or comfort them. But Jesus is our hope, notwithstanding his apprehension and death—yea, and in consequence of it. He is made perfect through sufferings. And thus it is that he brings many sons unto glory. When he fell into the hands of his enemies, they thought they had now completely succeeded. But their triumph was short. He fell: but in dying he overcame. And then was the judgment of this world, and then was the Prince of this world cast out. We therefore glory in his cross, because he here becomes the Author of eternal salvation. He died for us, and rose again; and because he lives, we shall live also.

—Let us, then, *live* under his shadow—securely live; nobly live; joyfully live—not only having life, but having it more abundantly.

—And let us invite others to come, and share with us. "In that day shall ye call every man his neighbor under the vine, and under the fig-tree."

JUNE 18.—"After these things Paul departed from Athens, and came to Corinth; and found a certain Jew named Aquila, born in Pontus, lately come from Italy, with his wife Priscilla; (because that Claudius had ordered all Jews to depart from Rome;) and came unto them. And because he was of the same craft, he abode with them, and wrought: for by their occupation they were tent-makers."—Acts, xviii, 1—3.

AQUILA and Priscilla were persons of great religious excellence. They are often mentioned with commendation in the Epistles, as well as in the Acts of the apostles, especially where Paul says to the Romans, "Greet Priscilla and Aquila, my helpers in Christ Jesus, who have for my life laid down their own necks; unto whom not only I give thanks, but also all the churches of the Gentiles." They were born in Pontus, they then resided in Italy, and were now in business at Corinth. Hither they had been driven by an imperial decree, and probably thought hard of the measure that banished them. But in consequence of this trial they became acquainted with Paul, and had him for their host, their friend, and companion. And what a companion must a man of his talents and grace have been! And what an advantage must they have derived from his morning and evening devotions! and his example! and his constant conversation! Surely they would acknowledge, It is good for us that we have been afflicted.

The lives of some have been very changeable, and in their removals, contrary to a disposition to enjoy a fixed and permanent dwelling, they have been ready to murmur and complain. But nothing occurs by chance; and all the ways of the Lord are mercy and truth to those that fear him. Let such remember that they know not what designs God has to accomplish by events of this nature, either with regard to themselves or their connections. Let them also reflect that this is not their rest, and view every present residence as

"Preliminary to the last retreat."

In proportion as we look after a better country, and realize it as our own, all earthly situations will be alike indifferent to us—yea, we shall find each of them none other than the house of God, and the gate of Heaven.

Paul not only lodged with them but wrought; for they were of the same occupation with himself. For though he had been educated at the feet of Gamaliel, he had been bred to the craft of tent-making. The Jews were accustomed to give their sons a calling, whatever was their condition in life, wisely considering it a prevention of idleness, a security from temptation, and a resource in accidental indigence. Hence, of their doctors, one was surnamed Rabbi, the shoemaker; another, the baker; another, the carpenter. Bicaut says, the Grand Seignior, to whom he was ambassador, was taught to make wooden spoons. Is this degrading? Seneca says, he would rather be sick, and confined to his bed, than be unemployed. Adam and Eve were placed in the garden to dress and to keep it. And our Savior declined not working at his supposed father's business. Paul, the chief of the apostles, was not ashamed of labor. But as a man of taste and learning he must have been fond of reading, and he desired Timothy to bring him his books and parchments. It seems, therefore, strange, that his friends should not have indulged him with leisure and entire freedom for his office also, by exempting him from manual toil. The workman is worthy of his hire; and this he always claimed as a *right*, contending that they who preached the Gospel should live of the Gospel; adding, also, that no man who warreth entangleth himself with the affairs of this life.

But a right is sometimes to be given up, and there is no general rule but allows of exceptions. Priscilla and Aquila were not rich, and would lament their inability to do more for their illustrious guest. And he had an independence of mind, and seeing these worthy people themselves laboring to gain a livelihood, he would not be burdensome, but pay for his accommodations. And they are mean souls who will endure to be supported by the alms, and especially the industry of others, when their own hands are sufficient for them. They who will not work should not eat. In a word, Paul knew the infancy of the cause, and was acquainted with all the circumstances of the case, and acted, we may be assured, with wisdom and prudence. Yet his conduct displayed the noblest self-denial and zeal.

There are two places in which he refers to his working. The first shows the degree in which he toiled often, after teaching, sitting up late at night. "Ye remember, brethren, our labor and travail, for we labored *night* and day, because we would not be chargeable unto you." The second tells us that his aim was not only to support himself, but to be able to succor others. "Ye yourselves know that these hands have ministered to my necessities, and to *them* that were with me." What a soul had this man! And how well could he add, "I have showed you all things, how that so laboring ye ought to support the weak, and to remember the words of the Lord Jesus, how he said, It is more blessed to give than to receive."

JUNE 19.—"**Be strong in the grace that is in Christ Jesus.**"—2 Tim. ii, 1.

WE may have this grace, and not be strong in it. The reality is one thing; the degree is another. We read of weak faith, as well as of strong faith. There are lambs in our Shepherd's fold as well as sheep; and in our Father's house there are little children as well as young men. But while there is in religion an infancy which is natural and lovely, there is also another which is unlooked-for and offensive—it is the effect of relapse. It is not of the beginning of the divine life, but of an after period the apostle speaks, when reproving the Hebrews, he says, "Ye are *become* such as have need of milk, and not of strong drink." We must not despise the day of small things. The Savior himself does not break the bruised reed, nor quench the smoking flax, but he is concerned to bring forth judgment unto victory. And while the feeble-minded are to be comforted, the slothful to be stimulated; and all are to be kept from "settling upon their lees."

Every thing shows how necessary it is to be *strong* in the grace that is in Christ Jesus. Your dangers require it. These are to be found in all the relations, offices, conditions, and circumstances of life. Your passions are not wholly mortified. There is the sin that yet dwelleth in you. The world lieth in wickedness, and you are passing through it. Your adversary, the devil, goeth about seeking whom he may devour. How much depends upon one lapse! And did not Abraham equivocate? and Moses speak unadvisedly? and Peter deny his Lord? And what says all this? but, Be strong in the grace that is in Christ Jesus.

—Your duties require it. You have a family, and with your house you are to serve the Lord. You have a calling; and in this you are to abide with God. You have the exercises of devotion, in which you are to worship God in Spirit and in truth. You have to walk by faith, and not by sight. You are to have your conversation in heaven, while every thing conspires to keep you down to earth.

—Your usefulness requires it. Your are not to live to yourselves, but to him that died for you and rose again. You are to look, not on your own things, but also on the things of others. You are to walk in wisdom toward them that are without, and endeavor to win souls. You are to do good as you have opportunity unto all men, especially unto those that are of the household of faith.

—Your trials require it. Who but must reckon upon these in a vale of tears? And if you faint in the day of adversity, your strength is small. To glorify God in the fires, and to recommend religion by its supports and comforts, when every thing else fails, demand no small share of grace.

—Your consolations require it. Consolations are not only delightful, but they are even of practical importance in religion. They enlarge the heart and enliven zeal, and embolden courage, and wean from the world. And you read of a peace that passeth all understanding! and a joy that is unspeakable and full of glory! Yet what do some of you know of these? More grace would bring more evi dence, and raise you more above your fears and depressions. If ye will not believe, surely ye shall not be established.

—Death requires it. Other events may, but this must occur. It is a melancholy day to those that have no God, and a very serious one to those who have. To think of it, to meet it, with triumph, or even with confidence, will not this call for more grace than you now possess? And what is the language of all these demands? Despond! No—but be strong in the grace that is in Christ Jesus. Without Him you can do nothing; but through his strengthening of you, you can do all things.

Rest not, therefore, in any present attainment. Like Paul, forget the things that are behind, and reach forth unto those that are before. It is to be lamented that we are easily dissatisfied where we ought to be content, and content where we ought to be dissatisfied. In temporal matters we should have our conversation without covetousness, and be content with such things as we have; but here, alas! we are avariciously anxious. And though three feet are enough for us in the cradle, and seven in the grave, nothing will hardly satisfy us between. But in *spiritual* things, with what trifling acquisitions are we contented! Yet here it is even our duty to be covetous, to be ambitious! And as before us lies an infinite fullness, and we are not straitened in our resources, let us not be straitened in our desires and expectations, but ask and receive, that our joy may be full.

JUNE 20.—**"Thou hast given me the heritage of those that fear tny name."—Psalm lxi, 5.**

So then, they that fear God have a heritage. All of them have not a heritage in the world, and they need not be ashamed to own it. They have the honor of conformity to their Lord and Savior, who had not where to lay his head. And though they have nothing, they yet possess all things. "I know thy poverty, but thou art rich." Indeed, as to temporal good, they are above others. He blesses their bread and their water; and bread and water, with the favor of God, are dainties. And a little that a righteous man hath, is better than the riches of many wicked. It is not only sweeter, but safer, and will go further. For it is true, as Philip Henry often told his family, the grace of God will make a little go a great way. And we have often seen it; and should have been amazed how some individuals, with their very slender means, could make a very decent appearance, and pay their way, and have a trifle to give to him that needeth, did we not know that the secret of the Lord was upon their tabernacle. Godliness, also, with contentment, is great gain. Contentment is a kind of self-sufficiency. It does not allow us to want what Providence denies. And who, whatever be his affluence, can be more than content? A man is satisfied with much less in a journey than he has at home. Now regeneration makes a man a stranger and a pilgrim upon earth; and then reason, as well as faith, says to him,

"Turn, pilgrim, turn; thy cares forego;
"All earth-born cares are wrong:
"Man wants but little here below;
"Nor wants that little long."

—But as to spiritual good, they may well say, The lines are fallen unto me in pleasant places; yea, I have a goodly heritage, For the

Lord is the portion of their inheritance, and of their cup. His testimonies are their heritage for ever, and they find them the rejoicing of their hearts. All the exceeding great and precious promises are theirs. And theirs is the inheritance incorruptible and undefiled, and that fadeth not away, reserved in heaven for them. Compared with this, what was the heritage of a Jew in Canaan? Of Adam in paradise? What is the heritage of a crowned worldling? of an angel in glory? Yet this is as true as it is wonderful. "This is the heritage of the servants of God, and their righteousness is of me, saith the Lord."

—For this heritage is not obtained by force, nor by purchase, nor by desert; but by bounty and grace, It is "given."

And we may know that we possess it. David speaks without any hesitation, Thou *hast* given *me* the heritage of those that fear thy name.

O that I could read my title clear. Praise waiteth for thee, O God, in Zion. I long to be able to praise thee as the health of my countenance, and my God. Say unto my soul, I am thy salvation. And show me a token for good.

--Above all, as—whatever they may doubt or fear, blessed are they that do hunger and thirst after righteousness, for they shall be filled, enable me—if I cannot say with confidence, Thou hast given me the heritage of those that fear thy name: enable me to pray, with supreme desire, "Remember me, O Lord, with the favor that thou bearest unto thy people; O visit me with thy salvation; that I may see the good of thy chosen, that I may rejoice in the gladness of thy nation, that I may glory with thine inheritance. And,

"In the world of endless ruin
"Let it never, Lord, be said,
"Here's a soul that perish'd, suing
"For the boasted Savior's aid."

June 21.—"Neither give place to the devil."—Ephesians, iv, 27.

If this admonition be connected with the words immediately preceding; "Be ye angry, and sin not; let not the sun go down upon your wrath;" the apostle intimates that sinful passion arises from the influence of the devil; and that when it prevails, we give up ourselves to his power. And can there be a truer specimen of hell, than a man in a state of fury and revenge! But there is nothing in the case that requires us to confine the address to the repulsion of wrath. The truth is, that Satan has access to us, and in various ways is always endeavoring to encroach upon us; and it must be our object to repel him. The image is familiar and striking. If an enemy was trying to enter your field, your garden, or your house—you would withstand him; for you would see, that as you yielded, he advanced. In every successful temptation, Satan gains upon us, and takes a position which we ought to have kept.

With the philosophy of this subject we have nothing to do, but only with the fact itself. The sacred writers as much support the doctrine of diabolical agency, as of divine. They make use of the same terms and phrases in the one case as in the other. Is God said to open the eyes of our understanding? Satan is said to blind the minds of them that believe not. Is God said to work in us to will and to do? Satan is the spirit that now worketh in the children of disobedience. Are Christians filled with the Spirit? Why, says Peter to Ananias, hath Satan filled thine heart? But while the fact is proved, nothing is said of the mode in which his operations are carried on. We cannot think, however, that it is always done personally and immediately. This would involve an impossibility. If he were *thus* soliciting every individual in every part of the earth at the same time, (and his work *is* always going on,) he must be omnipresent and omniscient. But he is the God of this world; and having under him all that is in the world, the lust of the flesh, the lust of the eye, and the pride of life; and having all the errors and the wickedness which *he* has introduced into our region to make use of, and such a depraved nature as ours to work upon—he has power enough to employ *mediately* for all his purposes. The bird need not be afraid of the fowler, if he keeps away from his gun and his snare; for he is not in much danger from his fingers. How is the fish taken? The angler does not wade into the water, and seize it in his hand. He does not even *see* his prey; but he reaches it, and secures it, by a baited hook at the end of his line and his rod; yet *he* catches the fish, and would do the same if his instrument was a mile long.

There are many reasons why we should not give place to the devil. One is because his designs are always bad. He may transform himself into an angel of light. And he may endeavor to introduce his evils and mischiefs under specious names, representing covetousness as laying up for the children, and pride as dignity, and revenge as a becoming spirit, and trimming in religion as prudence, and conformity to the world as winning others. Thus we are hardened through the deceitfulness of sin. But we ought not to be ignorant of Satan's devices. We read of his depths and his wiles—and God, in his word, tears off all his disguises, and shows us at once that his aim is only to ensnare, and enslave, and rob, and degrade, and wound, and destroy. He, therefore, that yields, wrongeth his own soul, and loves death.

Another is, because the more you give way, the more advantage he has over you. It will always be found much more easy to keep him out, than to let him out. When the Moors were admitted into Spain, they staid there for more than six hundred years, in spite of every groan and effort—so much harder is expulsion than exclusion.

Let us therefore avoid parleying with this enemy. He will rise in his demands with every concession. He is not to be treated with, but rejected. Let us guard against beginnings; they increase unto more ungodliness; in this down-hill course we easily proceed from evil to evil. When a person walks out in the morning clean in his apparel, he is cautious how he treads, and the first soil he contracts affects him, but the second offends less, and the fourth much less still; till he says, "it matters not now," and heedlessly dashes on. The youth is not profligate at once; but evil communications corrupt good manners. The first time he complies with a temptation, he feels a reluctance; and after the crime is committed, his conscience smites him. But a degree of this is overcome by every subsequent repetition; and the profaner of the sabbath, and the drunkard, and sensualist, go boldly on, waxing worse and worse. One sin naturally leads to another, prepares for another, pleads for another, and renders another necessary;

either by way of finish or concealment. Thus David, to hide his adultery, commits murder; and then impiously ascribes this to the providence of God: "The sword smiteth all alike!"

Another reason is, because you need not yield. You are not forced. If the devil compelled you, he would also justify you; for there can be no guilt where there is no liberty. The motives to sin can never be so great as the arguments to forbear. What can weigh for a moment against the authority of an infinite Being on whom we entirely depend? And what is any indulgence or suffering, compared with endless happiness or misery? Would God have enjoined upon us a thing that is impracticable? And is not his grace sufficient for us? And is it not attainable by us? Is not his promise true, Ask, and it shall be given you? And in the history and experience of his people in all ages, do we not see proof of this? Have not multitudes in the same condition, exposed to the same perils, feeling the same weaknesses and depravity, been more than conquerors?

Finally, resistance is the way to success, and insures it. Hence, says God, resist the devil, and he will flee from you. Can God be mistaken? Can he deceive? And does not every one know that persons slacken in any course or action in proportion as they want encouragement? For hope is the mainspring of motion. If a beggar be relieved, however slenderly or seldom, he will in extremity repair to the door again, but not if he be positively and invariably refused.

Resist, therefore, *steadfastly*, and show that you are in earnest and determined. For there is a heartless, undecided refusal, that invites renewed application, or at least does not shut the door entirely against importunity. If Satan cannot look into the heart, he is acquainted with the ways in which it shows itself, and is sure to know whether there is a latent wandering after what is professedly renounced, and so will be led to watch his opportunity, and work his means.

—But the apostle adds, Resist him steadfastly *in the faith*. There is no fighting on a quagmire. Faith furnishes the only solid, the only safe ground on which we can contend. Faith clothes us with the whole armor of God. Faith connects us with the Captain of our salvation, without whom we can do nothing, but through whose strengthening of us we can do all things.

"And Satan trembles when he sees
"The weakest saint upon his knees."

"A Friend and Helper so divine
"Doth my weak courage raise;
"He makes the glorious vict'ry mine,
"And his shall be the praise."

June 22.—"He left Judea, and departed again into Galilee. And he must needs go through Samaria."—John, iv, 3, 4.

For two reasons. Because Samaria lay in his passage, and because he had in design the conversion of this poor woman. We cannot imagine an event of such magnitude in itself, for there is joy in the presence of the angels of God over one sinner that repenteth, and attended with such consequences as this was, for it involved the salvation also of many of the Samaritans; we cannot imagine that such an event was accidental. Nothing takes place by chance in our most common affairs, and is the conversion of a soul for everlasting blessedness a casualty?

In the recovery of sinners the grace of God is equally necessary and illustrious. By grace are we saved through faith; and that not of ourselves, it is the gift of God, not of works, lest any man should boast, for we are his workmanship, created in Christ Jesus. And in the conversion Jesus here accomplished, we have an example of this grace. An example of its freeness, of its gentleness, of its power, and of its effects.

—Of its *freeness*, in selecting this wicked wretch, in spite of her unworthiness, and without her desire, and making her not only the partaker but the instrument of his goodness.

—Of its *gentleness*, in having recourse to no means of alarm, no violence. No angel appears with a drawn sword, no lightnings flash, no thunder rolls, no threatening terrifies. All is mercy, all is mildness, and he employs circumstances the most natural and suitable, to bring her to conviction, and to induce her to pray.

—Of its *power*, in the victory it gained over the corruptions of her heart. If there be a moral disorder that seems incurable, or an evil capable of resisting all reasoning and motive, it is the spirit of impurity. But behold here a new creature. She is not only pardoned but renewed, and the change wrought at once!

—Of its *effects*, she not only believes with the heart, but confesses with the mouth. She is not only enlightened but inflamed. No sooner has she gained good than she is concerned to do good. Personal religion becomes social. She cannot for a moment keep from others what she has seen and heard herself. What benevolence! What zeal! What urgency! What fortitude! "The woman then left her water-pot, and went her way into the city, and saith to the men, Come, see a man which told me all things that ever I did; is not this the Christ?" And what success, too! For they who speak from experience seldom speak in vain. "Then they went out of the city, and came unto him." Some of these might have accompanied her from curiosity, and some from the mere contagion of example; but not a few were deeply and savingly impressed. "And many of the Samaritans of that city believed on him for the saying of the woman, which testified, He told me all that ever I did. So, when the Samaritans were come unto him, they besought him that he would tarry with them; and he abode there two days."

The sight of this had so affected our Savior as, it would seem, to take away his appetite. He had been hungry as well as thirsty; and the disciples had gone away into the city to buy meat. But when they returned, and prayed him, saying, Master, eat; he said unto them, I have meat to eat that ye know not of. And when they said one to another, Hath any man brought him aught to eat? He said, "My meat is to do the will of him that sent me, and to finish his work." What a repast have I had since you left me! A poor, sinful Samaritaness has been here. And I have manifested myself to her. And under the impression she hastened to inform and invite her neighbors to come and hear me, and has prevailed! "Say not ye, there are four months, and then cometh harvest?" But see the encouragement we have to scatter the seeds of divine truth. "Lift up your eyes and look on the fields." See the woman and her company coming over yonder plain "for they are already white unto harvest." Here the success is so immediate, that "the sower and the reaper rejoice *together*." And so it is written, "Behold, the days come, saith the Lord, that the ploughman shall overtake the reaper, and the treader of grapes him that soweth seed; and the mountains shall drop sweet wine, and all the hills shall melt."

JUNE 23.—**"The Lord will give strength unto his people; the Lord will bless his people with peace."—Psalm xxix, 11.**

THE God of nature gave David a fine poetical genius. And he employed it like a good man for his own improvement, and the profit of many. It is well to take advantage of the excitement of any present feeling, and to give it a religious direction, according to the admonition of the apostle James. Is any afflicted? let him pray. Is any merry? let him sing psalms. David did this; for he was accustomed to put his sentiment into verse, on the occurrence of any interesting or significant event. Many of his psalms took their rise from a trouble or a deliverance he had just experienced. The thirty-first psalm was written at the dedication of his new house. The one hundred and fourth was a spring meditation. The eighth is a night scene. The nineteenth a morning piece. The lines before us were composed in a thunder storm.

Thunder is one of the sublimest displays of Deity. It generally produces fearfulness and terror. Caligula, the emperor, at the hearing of it, would creep into any hole or corner. But such a man should reflect, that if God has a mind to kill him, he can do it without raising nature into a storm—his breath is in his nostrils; he is crushed before the moth. "Thine eye is upon me, and I am not!" And we should do well to think of a more dreadful event; like Baxter, who, when a storm came on as he was preaching, by which the congregation was obviously disconcerted and dismayed, paused, and then said, "Men and brethren, we are assembled here to prepare for that hour, when the heavens, being on fire, shall be dissolved, and the elements shall melt with fervent heat; the earth, also, and all the works that are therein, shall be burnt up."

All greatness is comparative. David, therefore, naturally addresses "The mighty;" as much as to say to them, You are flattered and feared, but what is the greatest of you before *Him!* Think of the THUNDER, and adore. "Give unto the Lord; O ye mighty, give unto the Lord glory and strength. Give unto the Lord the glory due unto his name; worship the Lord in the beauty of holiness. The voice of the Lord is upon the waters; the God of glory thundereth; the Lord is upon many waters. The voice of the Lord is powerful, the voice of the Lord is full of majesty. The voice of the Lord breaketh the cedars; yea, the Lord breaketh the cedars of Lebanon. He maketh them also to skip like a calf; Lebanon and Sirion like a young unicorn. The voice of the Lord divideth the flames of fire. The voice of the Lord shaketh the wilderness; the Lord shaketh the wilderness of Kadesh. The voice of the Lord maketh the hinds to calve, and discovereth the forests." Here let the mind review the description, and we shall see how truly and vividly David's imagination marked and portrayed the circumstances and effects of the phenomenon.

He then leads us from the uproar of nature, to the small and still voice of *grace.* He retires with us into the sanctuary of God, *there* to testify the glory of his *goodness*, and to calm and cheer us with the assurance of his *providential* empire over all the commotions of life, and his attention to the welfare of his people: "And in his temple doth every one speak of his glory. The Lord sitteth upon the flood; yea, the Lord sitteth King for ever. The Lord will give strength unto his people; the Lord will bless his people with peace."

But this promise, you say, is made to "his people." It is, but be not afraid. Perhaps these people will not be found so unlike yourselves as you imagine. It is here implied, that they are *weak* and *distressed*, otherwise they would not want strength and peace. Both these blessings are insured.

—Are they by nature without strength, and have they from experience a growing conviction of their inability? Yet, with all this sense of weakness, have they trials to endure, duties to perform, a race to run, a warfare to accomplish? As their day, so shall their strength be. His grace is sufficient for them. Let the weak say, I am strong.

—Do they need rest and refreshing? The God of peace shall give them peace always by all means. Not worldly peace. He has no where absolutely engaged to give this—I say *absolutely;* for if it be good for them, they shall not want it; for they shall want *no* good thing. But there is a peace as far exceeding every other as the soul surpasseth the body, and the heaven the earth, and eternity time—the peace of God, which passeth all understanding, and which keeps the heart and mind through Christ Jesus. This does not depend upon outward things. In the world, says the Savior, ye shall have tribulation, but in me ye shall have peace. And hence, as when weak they are strong—so, though sorrowful, they are always rejoicing.

Yet it is only the beginning of it they have here. At death they enter into peace fully. Every enemy is then vanquished, and the din of war is heard no more. The dangerous, treacherous, raging, sickly sea, is crossed; and then are they glad, because they be quiet. So he bringeth them unto their desired haven.

June 24.—" And he departed thence, and entered into a certain man's house, named Justus, one that worshipped God, whose house joined hard to the synagogue. And Crispus, the chief ruler of the synagogue, believed on the Lord with all his house; and many of the Corinthians, hearing, believed, and were baptized."—Acts, xviii, 7, 8.

This was at Corinth. Here he continued a year and six months, assured that the Lord had much people in that city. At first he reasoned in the synagogue every Sabbath, and persuaded the Jews. But upon their opposing and rejecting him, he sought another place to teach in. It was not a building appropriated to public worship. At this time, and long after this, the Christians had no such edifices. They assembled wherever they could find an accommodation. The spot was, indeed, consecrated, not by a religious ceremony, but by the presence of God, and the service itself. The Savior himself attached no holiness to walls or ground; but said, *Where*—let it be where it will—two or three are gathered together in my name, *there* am I in the midst of them. He preached not only in the temple, and in the synagogue, but in the private dwelling, and by the way-side, and in the mountain, and on board a ship. And his apostles followed his example, and *every where* lifted up holy hands without wrath and doubting.

The house Paul now entered belonged to a worshipper of God, whose name was Justus; and it joined hard to the synagogue. The nearer the church, the proverb is, the further from God. This is founded on the observation, that what men can easily reach and enjoy, they often neglect. And who are they that come late to the sanctuary? Not those from a distance, but they who live near. Who are absent in bad weather? Those who have carriages, or can procure vehicles; not they who come on foot. Who most frequently excuse their non-attendance? The strong and healthful; not the indisposed and weak. Who sleep during the service? Not the poor and laborious, who have seldom an hour of repose—but the lazy and genteel, who never know what fatigue means.

It was a trial of principle in this man to open his house to Paul. It would create him inconvenience, and trouble, and expense; and it would draw upon him danger and reproach; as it was an open avowal of his adherence to the cause; and he knew that the sect was every where spoken against. How many professors of religion, yielding to their selfish and dastardly reasonings, would have refused. They would have said—But what will people think of me? What will my relations say? And may not my business suffer? We are never prepared for a course of godliness till we can give up every thing to God, especially our paltry reputation, and our worldly profit. Bunyan, with as much truth as genius, places all the pilgrims under the conduct of Mr. Great-Heart. It is to intimate that we shall need courage every step of the way to the shining city. Let us consult not with flesh and blood, but only with conviction: and go forth to the Savior without the camp, bearing his reproach. We shall then, not only retain peace of mind, but please Him whose loving-kindness is better than life. Did Obed-edom repent of taking in the ark? The Lord blessed his house, and all that pertained to him. Who was ever a loser by any thing he did for the cause of God? Who *can* be a loser while *He* remains true who said, Them that honor me I will honor. They shall prosper that love Zion?

What Justus did in accommodating Paul, rewarded and dignified him: and it is now told for a memorial of him. How must it have delighted him to see the good that was done under his own roof! There is joy in the presence of the angels of God over one sinner that repenteth. But here a man of some rank and influence, Crispus, the chief ruler in the synagogue, believes—nor is this all. His *house* too is added to the Lord! Yea, and *many* of the Corinthians, hearing, believe and are baptized!

Yet Paul baptized but few of them. And when he wrote his epistle to these people, he rejoiced in the fact. This has puzzled those who look upon the dispensation of the sacraments, as they are called, as by far the most honorable and sacred part of the ministerial function. And in all churches persons are allowed to preach before they are *authorized* to administer. And many reasons have been alleged, to account, consistently with this, for Paul's conduct in thanking God, that in all the time he staid here, and notwithstanding the multitude of converts, he had only baptized Crispus and Gaius, and the household of Stephanus. But the reason he himself assigns overturns an unscriptural notion and practice—He had devolved upon others the baptism of the new converts, because, says he, Jesus Christ sent me not to baptize—which outward form could be dispensed by others of inferior station and talent; but—which is by far the most important and difficult part of my office—to preach the Gospel.

JUNE 25.—" The ark of the Covenant of the Lord went before them in the three days' journey, to search out a resting-place for them."—Numbers, x, 33.

THAT is, the *Lord* did this. But the ark was the cymbal of his presence, and the seat of his residence; from which by the cloud, he regulated all their movements. Yet the expression is still metaphorical; and we must not suffer the condescension of his language to injure the glory of his perfections. He feels no perplexity. He never deliberates; never examines; never searches: for "there is nothing that is not manifest in his sight." But as men do this, and must do this, if they would avoid mistakes, and decide and act judiciously: the Lord thus intimates—that his wisdom was concerned in all their journeyings; and that his people may keep their minds in perfect peace, being stayed on him—for, as strangers and pilgrims on the earth, he careth for them—they are under his guidance—nothing befals them by chance. All their removals, and their rests; all their situations, their trials, their comforts, are chosen for them by the only wise God their Savior, who is always on the *look-out for* them—"For the eyes of the Lord run to and fro throughout the whole earth, to show himself strong in the behalf of them whose heart is perfect toward him."

He not only leads his people in the way that they should go, but is concerned to afford them *repose*, as well as direction. Thus, in his promise to Moses, he said, "My presence shall go with thee, and I will give thee rest." Thus, in the review of his goodness, he says, by Jeremiah, "The people which were left of the sword found grace in the wilderness, even Israel, when I went to cause him to rest."

Thus here he searched out for them a resting place—*in* their journey, and *after* it. To the former, Moses refers, when he says, "The Lord your God went in the way before you, to search you out a place to pitch your tents in;" before they reached Canaan, he led them into many resting places; in some of which they continued only days; in some, weeks; in some, months; and in a few, even years. It was a fine resting place when they came to Elim, where were twelve wells of water, and threescore and ten palm trees. But this was at the beginning of their journey, and designed to encourage them. They could not look for many stations like this, each however which they successfully occupied—was of the Lord's selection.

We may apply this to the temporal residences of Christians. How moveable have some of them been! But *He* has led them from one situation to another; and it should be satisfying for them to think, that he could find a better resting place for them than they could have chosen for themselves, for he perfectly knows both the place and the persons. Sometimes the lines fall to them in agreeable scenes, and he kindly exceeds their hopes. In other cases the abode is less inviting, and even trying. But they must acquiesce, without murmuring or complaining, in their Conductor's disposal, conscious that they are not worthy of the least of all his mercies, and remembering that they are not yet come unto "*the* rest and inheritance which the Lord giveth them."

—It will apply, also, to their spiritual peace and refreshment in their travels. "Thus saith the Lord, Stand ye in the ways, and see, and ask for the old paths, where is the good way, and walk therein, and ye shall find rest for your souls." There are spiritual resting places on this side heaven. In their acquaintance with his Throne, his House, his Day, his Word, the Covenant of Peace—here he affords them the shadow of a great rock in a weary land. Here he maketh his flock to rest at noon. Here they lie down in green pastures, and are fed beside the still waters.

But the principal resting place he sought out for them was at their journey's end. It was Canaan: "In the day I lifted up my hand unto them, to bring them forth of the land of Egypt, into a land that I *had espied for them*, flowing with milk and honey, which is the glory of all lands."

Yet there is a better country. And this, Christian, He is looking out for you! Whatever you now enjoy, your repose is imperfect, and interrupted. Something, aloud, or in a whisper, says, Arise, and depart hence, for this is not your rest. But there remaineth a rest for the people of God. A rest from all toil and temptation. From all sorrow and sin. A rest not only *in* God, but a rest *with* him.

> "O glorious hour! O bless'd abode!
> "I shall be near, and like my God!
> "And flesh and sin no more control
> "The sacred pleasures of my soul."

JUNE 26.—'And upon this came his disciples, and marvelled that he talked with the woman: yet no man said, What seekest thou? or, Why talkest thou with her?"—John, iv, 27.

THAT is, immediately upon the conversation, and just as he had said to her, I that speak unto thee am the Messiah.

Thus their return broke off the conference, and the woman was probably grieved to see the disciples so near at hand. Our most interesting interviews in this world, are often and soon interrupted. It is sweet to hold converse with our fellow Christians, and with ministers, and it is far sweeter still to hold communion with the Savior. There are moments in the sanctuary and the closet, when we can say,

> "While such a scene of sacred joys
> "Our raptur'd eyes and souls employs,
> "Here could we sit, and gaze away,
> "A long, an everlasting day."

But not only our sinful distractions, but our lawful connexions, and businesses, and cares, invade and disperse our enjoyments, and make us long after a state where these interruptions will be no more. Now we have visions, or, at best, but visits—then we shall be for ever with the Lord.

—The disciples were astonished, and the cause of their marvelling was, "That he talked with the woman." Had they an apprehension that she was a woman of ill character? And, like the Pharisees, did they suppose that it was incompatible with the sanctity of the Messiah to hold any intercourse with persons of infamous reputation? This is not probable. She was a stranger to them. Our Lord, indeed, knew her; but it was by his divine prerogative; and as yet he had no opportunity to speak of her to his disciples.

—It is more likely that their wonder arose from seeing him in close and friendly conversation with a woman of Samaria; for the Jews had no dealings with the Samaritans. The rancor excluded even the common civilities of life. At present his disciples seemed not aware of their Lord's design to extend favor to the Gentiles, and were but little acquainted with the nature of his kingdom, "where there is neither Jew nor Greek, bond nor free, male or female, for we are all one in Christ Jesus." Again. Women have not always been properly regarded. If they contribute to their own degradation they must blame themselves. It has often been asked, why the conversation of even wise men is, with women, always vain and trifling? We do not entirely admit the fact. If, however, there be truth in the supposition, the cause is to be found in females themselves; they must be pleased with such discourse; for men will naturally accommodate themselves to their taste, and it is their interest to do so. Let women rise, and vindicate their sex; many are now doing so; let them show that they consider themselves, and wish to be considered as rational as well as animal creatures; and as companions as well as playthings and toys, and articles of sense and dress. But at this period the sex were treated, and are so still, in the East, as a kind of beings inferior to men. Now, the disciples, knowing that Jesus never trifled in conversation, but always spoke superiorly and divinely, were amazed to find him discoursing on deep and important subjects with a poor menial woman, judged incapable of understanding them. The meanness of the persons to whom he manifested himself always scandalized flesh and blood. Have, it was asked, any of the rulers believed on him? But this people, who know not the Law, are cursed. Yet it was his *glory* that the poor had the gospel preached unto them, and that the common people heard him gladly. When he rejoiced in spirit, he said, I thank thee, O Father, Lord of heaven and earth, that thou hast hid these things from the wise and prudent, and revealed them unto babes. And his apostle follows in the same strain. "For it is written, I will destroy the wisdom of the wise, and will bring to nothing the understanding of the prudent. Where is the wise? where is the scribe? where is the disputer of this world? hath not God made foolish the wisdom of this world? But God hath chosen the foolish things of the world to confound the wise: and God hath chosen the weak things of the world to confound the things which are mighty; and base things of the world, and things that are despised, hath God chosen, yea, and things which are not, to bring to nought things that are: that no flesh should glory in his presence."

But we here see the diffidence and submission of the disciples—

"Yet no man said, What seekest thou! or, Why talkest thou with her?" Confidence in his greatness and rectitude awed them into silence. Whence we recommend two things. First, let us observe the words of Solomon, "If thou hast *thought* evil, lay thine hand upon thy *mouth.*" A good man should make conscience of the state of his mind as well as of his speech; but what we cannot always prevent in thought, we may restrain in expression. Words are worse than thoughts, they add to them; they show more of the dominion of evil; they are more injurious to others, and betray ourselves more into difficulties. In a multitude of words there wanteth not sin. Therefore let us resolve to take heed to our ways, that we sin not with our tongue. David prayed, "Set a watch, O Lord, before my mouth, keep the door of my lips."

Secondly, as the reverence of the disciples induced them not to question the propriety of our Lord's conduct, though for the present they could not understand it, so should we act toward him. He is not bound to give account of any of his matters, and he often requires us to walk by faith, and not by sight. But we know that his work is perfect, his ways are judgment. Let us never charge him foolishly, but acquiesce in the most mysterious of his dispensations, assured that he has reasons for them which at present satisfy him, and will satisfy us when they are finished and explained. What we know not now, we shall know hereafter. "Shall not the Judge of all the earth do right?" "Just and true are all thy ways, O thou King of saints."

JUNE 27.—**"Thou hast been a shadow from the heat."—Isaiah, xxv, 4.**

AND what he has been, he is—the same yesterday, to-day, and for ever.

Heat means evil—any evil, every evil, from which it is desirable to be screened. Heaven is a state, and many have reached it, where the sun does not light on them, or any heat. But it is otherwise here. Here many things affect the mind, as oppressive heat does the body, and make us pant for deliverance and repose. The wrath of God—a sense of his fiery law in the conscience—the temptations of Satan—the persecutions of wicked and unreasonable men—afflictions, public and private, personal and relative—here is the heat.

Where is the shadow? Behold me, says the Savior of sinners, behold me! Come unto me, and I will give you rest. *This* is the rest, says God, wherewith ye shall cause the weary to rest, and this is the refreshing.

But what kind of shadow is He? We read in the Scripture of the shadow of a cloud, of the shadow of a tree, of the shadow of a rock, of the shadow of a tabernacle from the heat. The shadow of the cloud in harvest is grateful, but transient. The shadow of a tree under which we sit down, is delightful; but it is limited to a small distance, and the rays frequently pierce through the boughs. The shadow of a great rock is dense and cool, but it befriends not on every side, and covers little from the vertical rays. The shadow of a tabernacle into which we may continually resort, and find not only room but entertainment, is the most complete and inviting. All these have some truth in their application to Him, but none of them can do justice to the subject. He is what they imply, but *more;* and not only more than each of them, but more than all of them combined, and more than all of them combined in their best estate; and infinitely more. He is not only *perfect*, but *divine;* and he that dwelleth in the secret place of the Most High shall abide under *the shadow of the Almighty.*

Let me leave, then, other shadows. They are all inadequate to the wants of the soul, and, in some way or other, will be sure to fail me; yea, whatever else I get under for shelter, will not only prove vanity, but vexation of spirit.

But let me make use of this shadow from the heat. He is not far off. He is accessible. He is easy to approach. And it is only by repairing to him that I can enjoy the benefit derivable from him. And while believing, I rejoice in him with joy unspeakable. Let me show my benevolence by recommending him to others. They, also, are strangers to repose. They want rest unto their souls. And he is sufficient to receive, and defend, and succor, and bless all. O happy period! when the eyes of men, as of all the tribes of Israel, shall be toward the Lord! And when in him all the families of the earth shall be blessed! The Lord hasten it in his time!

JUNE 28.—"What doest thou here, Elijah?"—1 Kings, xix, 13.

THE principle of this question was not ignorance. God well knew how, and why he came there. But he would know from Elijah himself: and therefore asks him—that being called upon to account for his conduct, he might be convinced of his folly, and be either speechless, or condemned out of his own mouth. We may view the inquiry three ways.

First, as an instance of God's moral observation of his creatures. His eyes are upon the ways of man, and he pondereth all his doings. Nothing can screen us from inspection. Elijah was in a wilderness, and alone; he had even left his servant behind him—but the eye of God followed him. And the eyes of the Lord are in every place beholding the evil and the good. And let us not imagine that he only looks after an extraordinary character, like Elijah. No one is too small and inconsiderable to be disregarded by Him. Every human being is not only his creature, but his subject, and responsible to him. The meanest slave is great in the sight of God, as possessed of a soul, and destined for eternity. God has a right to know where we are, and what we are doing; and a much greater right than a father or a master has to know this, with regard to a child or a servant: for we are absolutely his. And he is interested in observing our conduct; interested as a judge, who is to pass sentence upon our actions: and interested as a friend and benefactor, who would check us when we are going astray, or recall us when we have wandered. For,

Secondly, we may consider it as a reproof given to a good man. He ought not to have been here, hiding himself from his enemy, and begging that he might die; but should have been engaged in carrying on the cause of God in the reformation he had so nobly begun. He was therefore blamable. God does not cast him off; but he reprehends him: and as many as he loves he rebukes and chastens.

And faithful are the wounds of this Friend. And how does he administer this reproof? He had all the elements under his control; and he showed him what he *could* do: "And he said, Go forth, and stand upon the mount before the Lord. And, behold, the Lord passed by, and a great and strong wind rent the mountains, and brake in pieces the rocks, before the Lord; but the Lord was not in the wind: and after the wind, an earthquake; but the Lord was not in the earthquake: and after the earthquake, a fire: but the Lord was not in the fire: and after the fire, a still small voice. And it was so, when Elijah heard it, that he wrapped his face in his mantle, and went out, and stood in the entering in of the cave." "And, behold, there came a voice unto him, and said;" You cowardly deserter? You ungrateful, rebellious wretch? No: but—"What doest thou here, Elijah?" And this "in a still small voice"—a kind of under tone, or whisper, as if no one should hear it beside. Here was no upbraiding; nothing to inflame passion; but a kind and calm appeal to reason. How forcible, and yet tender! It is thus his gentleness makes us great. It is thus he does not break the bruised reed, or quench the smoking flax. It is thus he calls upon us to be followers of him, as dear children. If a brother be overtaken in a fault, let us not employ the earthquake, the wind, and the fire—but the still small voice. Let us take him aside. Let us tell him his fault between him and us alone. Let us restore such a one in the spirit of meekness. Reproof should never be given in a passion. It is too much, says an old writer, to expect that a sick patient will take physic, not only when it is nauseous, but boiling hot. And we know who has said, "In meekness instructing those that oppose themselves." "The wrath of man worketh not the righteousness of God."

Thirdly, as a rule by which we may judge ourselves. Let us suppose that we heard God addressing us, as he did Elijah. How should we answer him? Could we say, I hope I am where thou wouldst have me to be, and doing what thou wouldst have me to do? He *does* thus inquire. And therefore it behooves us so to act as to be able to give a satisfactory account of our conduct. Let us apply the question to our troubles. How came we in these? Have they befallen us in following after God? Or have we drawn them upon ourselves by our folly and sin? Let us apply it to our connexions. We are choosing associates. Are we walking with wise men, or are we the companions of fools? We are engaging ourselves for life. Are we marrying in the Lord, or unequally yoking ourselves with unbelievers? "What doest thou *here*, Elijah?" Let us apply it to our recreations. Are they such as conduce to the health of the body, and accord with purity of mind? Or are they amusements and dissipations which, if God should call us to account, would strike conscience dumb? Let us apply it to our stations. Are we abiding with God in our own callings? or are we acting out of our proper sphere of duty? How many have injured, if not ruined their usefulness and comfort, by improper removals, or striking their tent without the cloud? Let us apply it to our religious services. We ought to have an aim, and a very worthy one, in coming to his house. Happy they who, when they hear the inquiry, What doest thou here, Elijah? can say, Here I am—not from custom or curiosity, but to hear what God the Lord will speak, and to see his power and his glory as I have seen him in the sanctuary.

And let us remember that a false answer will be more than useless. We often assign a reason very different from the true one, to an inquiring fellow creature—and him we may deceive—but God is not mocked.

June 29.—" Then spake the Lord to Paul in the night by a vision. Be not afraid, but speak, and hold not thy peace: for I am with thee, and no man shall set on thee to hurt thee; for I have much people in this city."—Acts, xviii, 9, 10.

The Lord is a very present help in trouble; and before his people *express* their apprehensions, he foresees them, and effectually provides against them.

It is obvious Paul was now depressed and discouraged. He had nature in him as well as grace. The Christian, and even the apostle, did not destroy the man. He had genius; and not only great sensibility, but a tinge of melancholy is perhaps inseparable from this endowment. He was also the subject of bodily enervation; and was now worn down, not only by the constant preaching, but also by working manually, day and night, to support himself and relieve others. In allusion to which, he says, in his letter to these Corinthians, "I was with you in weakness, and in fear, and in much trembling." Yea, he was now, it would seem, afraid—of men—of suffering persecution—of death. Is this he that said, None of these things move me, neither count I my life dear to myself, so that I may finish my course with joy? Yes; the same. He then spoke sincerely, and according to the frame he was in. But what a change do we feel, if the Lord hides his face; or faith fails; yea, or if there be only a variation in the humors of the body, or the state of the weather.

The Lord, therefore, removes his fear by the assurance that no man should set upon him to hurt him; for "He was with him, and had much work for him to do;" so that even his destination secured him. And see how faithfully and *remarkably* this was accomplished. For though the place was so abandoned, and he had so many enemies, he continued there a year and six months, teaching the word of God among them, without any molestation. At length a storm arose, which tried his confidence in the promise; but it issued in the proof that the Savior in whom he trusted was true and righteous altogether. For all the Jews in the city made a violent insurrection against Paul, and brought him before Gallio, the deputy; but he refused to take cognizance of the affair, and drave them from the judgment seat. Upon which, provoked by his conduct, the Greeks, who had joined the Jews in this assault, fell upon Sosthenes, the chief ruler of the synagogue, and beat him in sight of the bench. But Paul, on whose account the persecution was raised, was suffered to escape uninjured, and continued his labors a considerable time longer undisturbed, and at length withdrew from the place in peace.

—Is not this enough to prove that nothing is too hard for the Lord? that he can turn the shadow of death into the morning? that our enemies, however numerous and malignant, are all under his control, and cannot move a hair's breadth beyond the length of the chain in which he holds them?

Do we not here see, that if we have his promise, we have enough to establish, strengthen, settle us, whatever our difficulties and dangers may be? Heaven and earth may pass away, but his word cannot fail. If a child in the dark feels his father's hand grasping his, and hears him say, I am with thee, fear not, he is calmed and confident. Yea, says David, though I walk through the valley of the shadow of death, I will fear no evil, for thou art with me. He hath said, I will never leave thee nor forsake thee: so that we may boldly say, The Lord is my helper, and I will not fear what man shall do unto me!

"How safe and happy are they,
"Who on their good Shepherd rely!
"He gives them out strength for their day;
"Their wants he will surely supply.
"He ravens and lions can tame—
"All creatures obey his command:
"Then let me rejoice in his name,
"And leave all my cares in his hand."

June 30.—"There is a river, the streams whereof shall make glad the City of God."—Psalm xlvi, 4.

What can this "river" be, but that blessed covenant to which David himself repaired in the time of trouble, and extolled beyond every other resource or delight—Although my house be not so with God, yet hath he made with me an everlasting covenant, ordered in all things, and sure; for this is all my salvation, and all my desire, although he make it not to grow.

And what are "the streams" of this river? but the out-goings and effects of this divine constitution—The blood of Jesus—The influences of the Holy Spirit—The doctrines and promises of the gospel—The ordinances of religion, and all the means of grace.

There are four ways in which the streams of a river would gladden the citizens. They will all apply, in a pre-eminent degree, to the case before us.

The first regards *prospect*. Nothing can be more pleasing or interesting to those who relish the simple beauties of nature, than to walk by the side of living streams; to see the fish playing and disappearing; the green weeds waving their long streamers in the water; the reeds bending and recovering themselves again; the rippling of the shallows, and the glassy reflections of the deeps; while the bushes and trees form a quivering shade on the banks. Here is enough to fix the tasteful mind, and to induce the poet to take out his pen, and the painter his pencil. What views have Christians by the side of their streams! How various! how endearing! how impressive the objects which strike and occupy their minds! "My meditation of him shall be sweet; I will rejoice in the Lord."

The second regards *traffic*. It is an unspeakable advantage to a place to be accessible by water, as it renders commerce not only practicable, but easy and extensive. The Humber was the making of Hull. The Thames has rendered London so famous. Were this stream dried up or diverted, how would the mistress of the nations be humbled and reduced! It is owing to their trade, carried on by means of their rivers, that many cities on the continent have united themselves to the ends of the earth, and acquired such distinction and wealth. And by these streams Christians obtain riches for the soul, and eternity; unsearchable riches, durable riches, with righteousness. It is by these they carry on business with the land that is very far off, the merchandise of which is better than the merchandise of silver, and the gain thereof than fine gold.

The third regards *fertility*. Imagine a dry and barren land where no water is, and think what happiness would ensue, if springs gushed forth from the sands, and meandered through meadows with grass and reeds, and rushes. Lot chose the plain country, the vale of Sodom, near Jordan, because it was watered, like the garden of the Lord. Did you never read the words of Balaam, in describing the blessedness of Israel? "As the valleys are they spread forth, as gardens by the river's side, as the trees of lign-aloes which the Lord hath planted, and as cedar trees beside the waters." What is a tree planted by the rivers of water, bringing forth in its season, and with never-withering leaves; but a Christian by these streams, growing in the divine life; adorned with the graces of the Spirit, and filled with all the fruits of righteousness which are by Jesus Christ unto the glory and praise of God?

The fourth regards *supply*. What could a city do without this precious, all-important fluid? An enemy, therefore, always endeavors to cut off the water, to compel a place the more suddenly and speedily to surrender. Hence the boast of Rabshakeh: "With the sole of my foot I have dried up all the rivers of the besieged places." This shall never be the case here. Your resources can never fail. Your relief can never be cut off. You have always access to the God of all grace. And how superior are your supplies! How free! How full! How satisfying! "Jesus answered, and said unto her, Whosoever drinketh of this water shall thirst again; but whosoever drinketh of the water that I shall give him, shall never thirst; but the water that I shall give him shall be in him, a well of water springing up into everlasting life."

Are you asking, Who will show us any good? Let the subject supply an answer. O there is—there *is* a river, the streams whereof make glad the city of God. Forsake the foolish and live, and go in the way of understanding. Leave the world and enter the Church. There—how unlike creatures, who are all vanity and vexation of spirit—there you will find a Savior full of grace and truth. Acquaint now thyself with him, and be at peace, thereby good shall come unto thee.

O my soul, am I the subject of this happiness? Let me give proof of it. Let me be a witness for God. Let me exemplify his word. Let me convince others that there is—a reality—an excellency—a blessedness in the religion of Jesus, that can set the heart at rest, and yield a joy unspeakable and full of glory.

The pleasures of which we have been speaking are the pleasures of the way. What will be those of the end!

"If such the sweetness of the *streams*,
"What must the fountain be?
"Where saints and angels draw their bliss
"Immediately from thee."

END OF VOL. I.

EXERCISES FOR THE CLOSET,

FOR

EVERY DAY IN THE YEAR.

BY WILLIAM JAY,
Author of "Christian Contemplated," "Family Sermons," "Prayers," &c. &c.

Never be without a book, in daily reading, of a direct scriptural and devotional tendency. HALE.

The testimonies of Thy grace
I set before mine eyes:
Thence *I derive my daily strength,*
And there *my comfort lies.* WATTS

VOLUME II.

STEREOTYPED AND PRINTED BY D. FANSHAW

NEW-YORK:
PUBLISHED BY EZRA COLLIER,
148 Nassau-street.
....
1838.

CONTENTS OF VOLUME II.

JULY.

AUGUST.

SEPTEMBER.

OCTOBER.

NOVEMBER.

DECEMBER.

MORNING EXERCISES

FOR THE CLOSET.

July 1.—"I beseech thee, show me thy glory."—Exod. xxxiii, 18.

This prayer was not entirely proper. It would seem that Moses desired some visible display of Deity, or some kind of representation—and so far it was refused. "He said, Thou canst not see my face; for there shall no man see me and live. Behold, there is a place by me; and thou shalt stand upon a rock: and it shall come to pass, while my glory passeth by, that I will put thee in a cleft of the rock, and will cover thee with my hand while I pass by: and I will take away mine hand, and thou shalt see my back parts—but my face shall not be seen."

Here we see the weakness of man, even physically considered. How little can we bear! When Daniel only saw an angel, he fell into a deep sleep; and John, at the sight of Him on whose bosom he had often leaned, fell at his feet as dead. Flesh and blood cannot inherit the kingdom of God, neither doth corruption inherit incorruption.

We cannot go on well till God has gained our full confidence. Let us never suppose that he denies us any thing from insufficiency to give, or from a grudging disposition; "He that spareth not his own Son, but delivereth him up for us all; how shall he not with him also freely give us all things? The very same principle that leads him to give us some things, induces him to withhold others—a regard to our safety and happiness—

"Good, when he gives, supremely good,
"Nor less when he denies;
"E'en crosses, from his sovereign hand,
"Are blessings in disguise."

Had He yielded all the wish of Moses, he would have been destroyed upon the spot. He therefore rejects what was evil, but grants what was good—"I will make all my goodness pass before thee, and I will proclaim the name of the Lord before thee; and will be gracious to whom I will be gracious, and will show mercy on whom I will show mercy." We are *morally* defective; and our infirmities appear even in our prayers—we know not what to pray for as we ought. What would be the consequence if all our desires were accomplished? It is our privilege that God is as wise as he is kind; that he knows what is really good for us; and answers us not according to our wishes, but our wants; and according to what we ourselves *should only* pray for, if we were alive to our real welfare, and always knew wherein it consists.

Thus qualified, we cannot do better than to make this prayer our own, and desire God to show us his glory. For he alone can do it efficiently. As the sun can only be seen by his own shining, so God can only be known by his own revealing—in his light we see light. But we have every encouragement we could desire, if we seek him. If any lack wisdom, let him ask of God, who giveth to all men liberally and upbraideth not, and it shall be given him. Then shall ye know, if ye follow on to know the Lord.

Let us pray, therefore, that he would show us more of his glory. More of it in his works. More of it in his ways. More of it in his dispensations and ordinances. And, above all, more of it in the face of Jesus Christ. Nor let us ever think that we do not stand in need of this. For who expressed this desire? but a man who had been indulged already beyond any of his fellow creatures! Yet, after communications the most deep and extensive; after being inspired to write Scripture; after beholding God in the burning bush; after talking with him as a man talketh with his friend—so far is he from being satisfied, that his soul is drawn forth after more; and he, even *he* cries—I beseech thee, show me thy glory. Behold another instance. Paul, after all his intimacies with the Lord Jesus for many years, thus expresses himself: "That I may know him!" But who is Moses? who is Paul? "Which things the angels desire to look into."

Yet some are so perfectly indifferent to the subject of this prayer, that *they* say unto God, Depart from us, for we desire not the knowledge of thy ways. But spiritual darkness is the forerunner and pledge of eternal. If our Gospel be hid, it is hid to them that are lost. Because they are a people of no understanding, therefore he that made them will not have mercy on them; and he that formed them will show them no favor.

July 2.—"And from thence they went to Beer; that is, the well, whereof the Lord spake unto Moses, Gather the people together, and I will give them water. Then Israel sang this song, Spring up, O well; sing ye unto it. The princes digged the well, the nobles of the people digged it, by the direction of the Lawgiver, with their staves. And from the wilderness they went to Mattanah; and from Mattanah to Nahaliel; and from Nahaliel to Bamoth."—Num. xxi, 16—19.

Beer was a pleasing station to the Jews; and it is a very instructive one to us. They here came into a dry place; but they neither rebelled nor murmured against God, or his servant Moses.

See, first, How easily the Lord can supply the wants of his people—"Gather the people together, and I will give them water." Not only is every good gift and every perfect gift from above, but all our temporal comforts come from the hand of God. We are not to look for miracles; but then we may be assured that his word can be accomplished without them: "For sooner all nature shall change than one of God's promises fail." And He has said, "Thy bread shall be given thee; and thy water shall be sure." And what he has promised, he is able also to perform. Let us not limit the Holy One of Israel. Nothing is too hard for him. He can turn the shadow of death into the morning. Jehovah-jereh! The Lord will provide. "When the poor and needy seek water, and there is none, and their tongue faileth for thirst, I the Lord will hear them, I the God of Israel will not forsake them. I will open rivers in high places, and fountains in the midst of the valleys; I will make the wilderness a pool of water, and the dry land springs of water."

Secondly. See how want endears our blessings. "Then Israel sang this song, Spring up, O well; sing ye unto it." We feel unthankful for this precious fluid, because it is so common, and we have never been deprived of it. But had we gone several days in a wilderness without it, how should we have exalted and praised God at the sight of a refreshing supply. It is thus, by their removal or suspension, we are taught the worth of our comforts. How is liberty prized and enjoyed, after bondage? and health, after sickness? and spring, after winter? and morning, after night? We become indifferent to the means of grace. By a change of residence, or by accident, or disease, we are deprived of the privileges of the sanctuary—then, ah! then we remember these things, and pour out our souls in us: for we had gone with the multitude; we went with them to the house of God, with the voice of joy and gladness, with a multitude that kept holy day.

Oh, says David, when he was faint, Oh that one would give me to drink of the water of the well that is by the gate of Bethlehem! And were we equally athirst, spiritually, how should we long for the well of salvation, and say—

"Thou of life the fountain art;
"Freely let me take of thee;
"Spring thou up within my heart;
"Rise to all eternity!"

Thirdly. His agency does not exclude or supersede our instrumentality. "The princes digged the well, the nobles of the people digged it by the direction of the Lawgiver with their staves"—God filled it; but they digged it; This was their part. This they could do—and why should God have exempted them from it? He gives the increase; but Paul must plant, and Apollos water. He furnishes the wind; but we are to spread the sails. He gives; but we gather. Prayer and diligence, dependence and activity, harmonize in the Scripture, and are only inconsistent in the crudeness of ignorant and foolish men. Paul makes divine influence not an excuse for the neglect of means, but a motive and encouragement for the use of them: "Work out your own salvation with fear and trembling; for it is God who worketh in you both to will and to do of his good pleasure."

Fourthly. However pleasing any of our present stations are, we must, if we are the Israel of God, leave them. "And from the wilderness they went to Mattanah; and from Mattanah to Nahaliel; and from Nahaliel to Bamoth." The part they left is called, indeed the wilderness; and so it was—but it was good for them to be there.

There they had witnessed proofs of the power and goodness of God, and enjoyed a time of refreshing from his presence. But they had compassed the place long enough; and, decamping from this loved scene, had to journey on in the desert. Here, also, Christians have their indulgences. But these are designed, not to induce them to tarry, but to encourage them to advance. In the midst of their enjoyments, a voice cries, Arise ye, and depart hence; for this is not your rest.

These people would have been more willing to move—because they knew they were moving toward Canaan, a better country, the end and aim of their journey; and—because they were under the direction of God, as their guide, and who would never leave them nor forsake them. So it should be with us.

JULY 3.—"Faint."—"Judges viii, 4.

WHAT war is there that has nothing to depress? nothing to animate? and that does not furnish a diversity of feelings in those who carry it on?

Christians resemble these followers of Gideon, and subduers of the Amalekites—faint, yet pursuing.

Yes—while engaged in this good fight of faith, they may be *faint*. We need not wonder at this, if we consider the enemies they have to vanquish—bodily appetites; filthiness of spirit; a depraved nature; all sin and error; the present evil world; the devil, and his angels. If we also consider the qualities of their adversaries—their number—their malignity—their power—their policy—their success: for they have cast down many mighty; yea, many strong men have been slain by them—Oh! when we think of the heroes, the statesmen, the princes, the philosophers, the divines, and all the myriads they have enslaved and destroyed, who is not ready to tremble, and exclaim, "I shall one day perish!"

There is also the length of the service. It is not for a season only, but for life. We are not allowed to receive any proposals of peace. We cannot enter into a truce—no, not even to bury the dead. Let the dead bury their dead. We are to fight on through summer and winter—by day and night—in every situation and condition. He that endureth to the end, the same only shall be saved. In conversion we throw away the scabbard; in death only we lay down the sword. While we are here, something is still to be done; something still to be avoided—in company—in solitude—in health—in sickness. And is it nothing to watch in all things! To pray without ceasing! In every thing to give thanks! To be always abounding in the work of the Lord!

There are also occasional difficulties too common to be overlooked; and it is easy to suppose a few of them. What marvel if the soldier is faint—when the road is rough and thorny—and the weather is warm and oppressive—and he hungers and thirsts for want of seasonable refreshments and supplies, which are interrupted, if not cut off—and he feels a loss of strength, occasioned by a wound from without, or an indisposition from within Is this talking parables? There is not a Christian on earth whose religious experience will not easily explain it all.

And if this, therefore, be *my* experience—let me remember that there is nothing ominous, nor even peculiar, in it. Every subject of divine grace is well acquainted with *this* heart's bitterness—

and *must* be—or much of the Scripture could not be applied to him, either in a way of description, or comfort.

—And let me be thankful that to will is present with me, though how to perform that which is good I find not. If I faint, I do not *flee*. Faint—yet PURSUING.

JULY 4.—" Yet pursuing."—Judges, viii, 4.

THE life and experience of the Christian are full of contrasts. He resembles the bush of Moses, which was seen burning, but not consumed. And his language is, Cast down, but not destroyed; sorrowful, yet always rejoicing; as dying, and, behold, we live. We are now viewing him as a soldier. In our last page we saw him faint; but we shall now find him, amidst all that is grievous, feeling no disposition to give in, or give up—yet pursuing.

—And there is much to encourage and animate him. There is something in himself, and which is nothing less than a principle of divine grace. Every thing else will decline, when it meets with its proper temptation. Natural and merely moral resources are as the morning cloud, and the early dew which soon passeth away. But we are confident of this very thing, that He which hath begun a good work in us, will perform it. That which is divine is durable and invincible. That which is born of God overcometh the world.

—There is also much to encourage him in his cause. It is a good warfare. It will bear examination. Conscience entirely approves of it. Angels applaud it. There is, therefore, nothing to make us waver, or hesitate. Every thing feeds courage. We *ought* to engage and persevere. It is the cause of truth, of righteousness, of glory—of real glory. It would be more honorable to be foiled in this cause, than to conquer in any other.

—There is also much in his leader and commander. Some chiefs have so attached and inspired their troops, that they would plunge into any enterprise, or follow them into any danger. It was said, proverbially, at Rome, that it was unbecoming a Roman soldier to fear while Cæsar was alive. It is much more unworthy a Christian soldier to fear while Christ is alive; for, because, says he, I live, ye shall live also. When Antigonus heard some of his troops rather despondingly say, How many are coming against us? he asked, But how many do you reckon *me* for? And whenever *we* think of our foes, and the Captain of our salvation, we may truly say, More are they that be with us, than they that be with them. Greater is He that is in us, than he that is in the world. Who goes before us? Who teaches our hands to war, and our fingers to fight? Who provides for us? Who renews our strength? What limits have His wisdom and power? Did He ever lose an action yet? or a single soldier?

"A friend and helper so divine,
" Doth my weak courage raise;
" He makes the glorious vict'ry mine,
" And his shall be the praise."

—And, oh! let me think of the certainty of the issue! Fear unnerves: but it would make a hero of a coward to assure him in the conflict that he should overcome. This can rarely or never be done in other contentions: for nothing is so doubtful as the result of a battle. Prudence, therefore, says, Let not him that putteth on the harness boast himself like him that putteth it off. But the Christian enters the field under peculiar advantage. However trying or lengthened the struggle may be, he fights not uncertainly—

"The weakest saint
"Shall win the day,
"Though death and hell
"Obstruct the way."

Yea, in all these things we are more than conquerors!

—For what will be the result of success? What do other victors gain? How precarious, how unsatisfying, how poor and mean, the rewards of the world's warriors, compared with the acquisitions of the good soldier of Jesus Christ! He that overcometh shall inherit all things!

"Then let my soul march boldly on,
"Press forward to the heavenly gate;
"There peace and joy eternal reign,
"And glittering robes for conq'rors wait.'

JULY 5.—"Submit yourselves to God."—James, iv, 7.

THIS is the great thing—This is the excellency, the essence, the proof, of religion. God is our Savior. Our Lawgiver. Our disposer. Under each of these characters, his people are made willing to submit to him in the day of his power. And nothing but the efficiency of divine grace can influence a man cordially to resign himself to God in either of these relations.

We must submit ourselves to God, as the Savior. Here our concern with him begins, and—must begin. For we are condemned, and the first thing is to obtain deliverance. We are diseased and dying, and the first thing we want is the physician and the remedy. When, therefore, the Jews asked our Lord, What must we do that we may work the works of God? "This," said he, "is the work of God, that ye believe on him whom he hath sent." And when the jailer asked Paul and Silas what he should do to be saved, they said unto him, "Believe on the Lord Jesus Christ." God is a sovereign, at whose mercy we absolutely lie. We have no claims upon him; and it is wonderful that he is disposed to undertake our case at all. But he requires us to submit; and will not allow us to prescribe. He will have the entire management of our case, or he will have nothing to do with it. And it might be supposed that there would be no great difficulty here. But men are not sensible of their condition and danger: and there is much in the nature and manner of this salvation that is not palatable to the pride of the human heart. No court is paid to our reason; but we are required to trust in a plan concerning which we have never been consulted; and even to become fools, that we may be wise. However decent and moral our character has been, we must be content to enter into life in the very same way with the chief of sinners. We must renounce our own righteousness, and plead for acceptance as guilty. We must depend on another for all our strength. We must acknowledge that all we have is from the exceeding riches of his grace; and be crying, to the last, "Not unto us, not unto us, O Lord, but unto thy name, give glory, for thy mercy and thy truth's sake."

But to this, every awakened and humbled sinner is brought. And his submission is not the effect of necessity only. It is accompanied with acquiescence and approbation. He sees a consistency and an excellency in it that delight him, while it relieves. And though he knows there is no other way—yet if there were a thousand, he would turn from them all, and say, God forbid that I should glory, save in the cross of our Lord Jesus Christ.

We must submit ourselves to Him, as the Lawgiver; and be willing to live, not to the lusts of men, but to the will of God. He is only the author of eternal salvation unto all them that obey him. We cannot love Him, till we hope in his mercy: nor run in the way of his commandments till we are freed from the load of guilt and terror—a burden too heavy for us to bear. But faith is followed by love: and love, by obedience. We are delivered from the hand of our enemies, says Zecharias, not to be lawless, but to serve Him, who has made us free, without fear, in holiness and righteousness, before Him, all the days of our lives. Our obligations are infinitely increased by redeeming grace and dying love. And every believer feels them, and acknowledges that he is not his own, for he is bought with a price, and bound to glorify God in his body and in his spirit, which are God's. The love of sin, as well as the love of self, is subdued in him: and he gratefully asks, "What shall I render unto the Lord for all his benefits toward me?" "Lord, what wilt thou have me to do?" He finds his yoke easy; and accounts his service to be the truest freedom. He cannot, indeed, do the things which he would, and this is his grief: but he delights in the law of God after the inward man. He would not bring down the divine commands to his deficiencies; but longs to rise to the level of their perfection. And though he is full of complaints, it is of the servant, and not of the Master—He always speaks well of *his* name: and recommends him to others.

We must also submit to him, as our disposer, and be willing that he should choose our inheritance for us. Man naturally loves independence: he wishes to be at his own control; and to have the management of events, both as they affect others and himself. Many, also, who talk much of the providence of God, are constantly striving with it. Hence they envy the successes of their fellow creatures; and are discontented and repining when things do not fall out according to their mind; and—especially under their trials, think God deals improperly with them: and so charge him foolishly, or unkindly.

But this temper is, at least, dethroned in the Christian; and he is disposed to say, "Here I am; let Him do what seemeth him good. I am ignorant and liable to be imposed upon; but he is all-wise; and by not sparing his own Son for me, he has justified the implicit confidence of my heart. Let him, therefore, determine the bounds of my habitation, and arrange all the events of my condition. If things are not such as I had wished and reckoned upon, I have no reason to complain. He has a right to do what he will with his own; and he always uses it in a way the most conducive to my welfare. How often have I desired him to undertake and act for me! And when he complies—is it for me to murmur, and dispute; or say unto Him, What doest thou?

"Lord, I would, I do submit;
"Gladly yield my all to thee:
"What thy wisdom sees most fit,
"Must be surely best for me.
"Only when the way is rough,
"And the coward flesh would start,
"Let thy presence and thy love
"Cheer and animate my heart."

July 6.—"What went ye out into the wilderness to see?"—Matt. xi, 7.

These are the words of Jesus to the multitude concerning John, to whose preaching they had repaired. "There were many of you—and persons of all ranks and conditions—and some from a great distance. What did you think of the preacher? What induced you to attend his ministry? Surely you had some reason for it—some design in it. What was it?"

May we not learn from hence that we should always have an end in view in repairing to the ordinances of religion? and be able to answer the question, *Why* we attend the preaching of the word?

This becomes us, even as men. Men ought not to act at random; or, like the inferior creatures who are led by blind impulse or instinct, without reflection or motive. They, as the Scripture says, have no understanding, and must be governed and guided by those above them. But God teaches us more than the beasts of the field, and maketh us wiser than the fowls of the air; for there is a spirit in man, and the inspiration of the Almighty giveth him understanding. And wherein is this pre-eminence to appear, but in our acting wisely, and with design?

—We rise higher, and say, that without this we cannot please God. There can be nothing religious without design. Intention is essential to moral conduct. And though a good motive cannot sanctify a bad action, a bad motive will always vitiate a good action. The Pharisees fasted, and prayed, and gave alms; but it was to be seen of men, and thus all was corrupted in its principle.

—Without an aim in our attendance, we have nothing to pray for before we go; nothing to make the subject bear upon, while we are hearing; nothing by which to examine ourselves, when we return. How can we decide whether our meeting together is for the better or the worse? whether we have failed in the opportunity, or succeeded? Success is the accomplishment of an end, and must be judged of by it.

—A man that acts without an end, never acts in earnest. It is the end that stimulates zeal; that sweetens labor; that repays every expense. What would induce a patient to the taking of medicine, or the losing of a limb, but the thought of restoring or preserving health and life?

—To finish the argument—the concern itself here should be taken in the account. In common and trivial matters we may act without motive; but in momentous ones, every kind of deliberation is wisdom. And how important is our attendance on the word of life! It regards God; and the soul; and eternity. Its consequences will remain for ever. It must furnish the most awful part of our future account. We forget these exercises; but they are all recorded in the book of God's remembrance. We have soon done with the sermon; but the sermon is not done with us, till it has judged us at the last day. What an insult is offered to God, to come before him, and, by an appearance of devotion, to call forth his attention, when, in reality, we have nothing to do with him! What a trifling is it with divine things! And what can be so dangerous as this! It impairs the conscience, and deadens moral sensibility. It renders the means of grace unimpressive by familiarity; and provokes God to withhold or withdraw the influence essential to their success.

But, admitting that we always ought to have an end in view, what OUGHT THAT END TO BE? Not curiosity and amusement. This was the case with Ezekiel's hearers. They went to his preaching as persons go to a concert.

—Not criticism and cavilling. Many are wiser than their teachers. They come to judge, not to learn, and make a man an offender for a word. Many come to our Savior to "catch him in his talk."

—Not an outward advantage. A man, by his attending the Gospel, may secure himself reputation, business, or friendship. But this is trading in divine things. And what is the hope of the hypocrite, though he hath gained, when God taketh away his soul!

—Not the quieting of conscience. Some are at ease in Zion because they hear the word of truth, though they do it not. But the Apostle tells us, they deceive their own selves; and our Lord calls them fools, because they build upon the sand.

—But the end should be—

To obtain the conversion of the soul to God. This is the very design of the ministry itself. And how many have we known, since we attended the word, who have been turned from the error of their ways, into the path of peace! Has faith come to us by hearing? Has this efficacy ever been our aim—our wish—our prayer?

It should also be, to gain all needful instruction. This was the case with many who came to hear John. The people, the publicans, and the soldiers severally said to him—"And what shall we do?" They did not inquire after the duty of others, but after their own. David went to inquire in God's temple, and said, I will hear what God the Lord will speak. The best disposition we can go in, is when we have no partialities, and can sincerely ask, Lord, what wilt thou have me to do? Not shunning to hear all the counsel of God; or counting the preacher our enemy, because he tells us the truth.

It should be, to have divine things reapplied and reimpressed. If we do not want new information, it is desirable to be reminded of forgotten truth, and to have our knowledge reduced to experience and practice. The principle of divine grace cannot be lost. But what changes do believers feel in their frames! How often do their souls cleave unto the dust! And here they obtain quickening, according to his word. And by waiting upon Him their strength is renewed.

It should be, also, to aid in upholding the public means of grace for the advantage of others. How adapted to usefulness is the institution of preaching. We may judge what a neighborhood would be without the ministry of the word, when we see what it is even with it. Here are always to be heard calls to repentance, and proclamations of pardon. Here is always furnished solace to the afflicted, and excitement to the careless.

It is lamentable that so little of this spirit is to be found in the midst of so much hearing as there is in our day. We read of a concourse of people in the Acts, occasioned by the clamor of Demetrius, of whom it is said, "Some cried one thing, and some another; for the assembly was confused; and the more part knew not wherefore they were come together." With the exception of crying out, here is a fair representation of many a religious audience. A few are informed and principled, but the mass have no aim, or an improper one.

—Yet in another view, it is pleasing to see a place filled with hearers. They are in the way, and God may meet with them. His grace is sovereign and free. Some who come with no serious design, have been convinced of all, and judged of all, and confessed that God was in the midst of them of a truth.

Yet his sovereignty is not our rule, but our resource. What he may do, is one thing; what he will do, is another. He has said, "Draw nigh to God, and he will draw nigh to you."

And though he is sometimes found of them that seek him not, he is always found of them that seek him.

July 7.—"O wretched man that I am! Who shall deliver me from the body of this death!"—Rom. vii, 24.

It is commonly supposed that here is a reference to a cruel usage sometimes practised by the tyrants of antiquity, and which is mentioned by Virgil and Cicero, and Valerius Maximus. It consisted in fastening a dead carcass to a living man. Now suppose a dead body bound to your body—its hands to your hands—its face to your face—its lips to your lips. Here is not only a burden, but an offensive one. You cannot separate yourself from your hated companion—it lies down, and rises up, and walks with you. You cannot breathe without inhaling a kind of pestilence; and "Oh!" you would say, "O how slowly the parts corrupt and fall off—O how can I longer endure it! When shall I be free! O, wretched man that I am! Who shall deliver me from the body of this death?" This is very strong. Yet it comes not up to Paul's case; for he is speaking of a wretchedness, not without him, but within.

Whatever we may think of this allusion, here is a representation of the sin that dwelleth in us—it is the body of this death, or, as it is in the margin, this body of death. It is called—*a body*, to intimate the entireness and universality of the evil; thus we call a code of laws a body of laws, and a system of divinity a body of divinity. And it is a body of—*death*, to mark its malignant effect. Gunpowder is a body of destruction: arsenic is a body of poison: sin is a body of death. It brought death into the world; it has slain all the inhabitants of the earth, and will soon slay us; it has brought upon us spiritual, as well as corporeal death; and it produces a deadness, even in the souls of believers, and hinders the operation of those vital principles which they have received from above. By this baneful influence the tendencies of the divine life in them, which are so glorious, are chilled and checked; and therefore they are frequently wandering in meditation, and stupid in reading and hearing, and insensible in prayer, and dull even in praise; so that

> "Hosannas languish on our tongues,
> "And our devotion dies."

Till, roused by reflection, they cry,

> "Dear Lord, and shall we ever live
> "At this poor dying rate?
> "Our love so faint, so cold to thee,
> "And thine to us so great."

—My soul cleaveth to the dust; quicken thou me according to thy word.

For there are remains of this evil even in the subjects of divine grace. None of them are free. In many things, says James, we offend all. In all our doings, says the church, our sins do appear. My tears, says Beveridge, require to be washed in the blood of Christ, and my repentance needs to be repented of. Those who could die for the Savior, have used the most humbling language with regard to themselves. Sometimes, says Bradford, O my God, there seems to be no difference between me and the wicked; my understanding seems as dark as theirs, and my will as perverse as theirs, and my heart as hard as theirs. Yea, says Paul, at the end of so many years of advancement, I have not attained; I am not already perfect. After this, "who can say, I have made my heart clean; I am pure from my sin?"

But observe the distress this remaining corruption occasions them. It is their chief burden and grief, O wretched man that I am! Who shall deliver me from this body of death? Paul never said any thing like this of any of his sufferings; yet he was a great sufferer—he suffered the loss of all things; he was once stoned, thrice he suffered shipwreck, he was twice beaten with rods, five times he received forty stripes save one; he was in prisons more frequent, in deaths oft. Yet, so far from groaning and complaining, he tells us he took pleasure in all this, because it was for Christ's sake. And it is a sad evidence against us, if we are more affected with our calamities than with our corruptions. We are not required to be stoics: we may feel our sufferings; but there is something we shall feel more if we are in a right state of mind, viz. an evil heart of unbelief, in departing from the living God.

The people of the world judge of Christians by their own views and feelings; and because *they* love sin, and would deem the liberty to indulge in it a privilege—they think Christians are disposed to take every advantage for the same purpose. But how shall they who are dead to sin live any longer therein? Sin is their abhorrence; and at the foot of the cross they have sworn to have indignation against it for ever. They have a new nature; and as *far* as they are sanctified, there is as perfect a contrariety between them and sin, as between darkness and light. Hence the contest within. The flesh lusteth against the Spirit, and the Spirit against the flesh: and these being contrary the one to the other, they cannot do the things that they would. And will not this be painful? If a mechanic longed to excel in his workmanship, and an enemy stood by and marred every thing before he put it out of his hand—would not this be vexatious? Would not a man in a journey of importance, and anxious above all things to speed his way, feel a hindrance that would impede him for an hour more than an idler would the loss of a day? He that delights in neatness will suffer more from a single stain than another would from wearing a filthy garment. Because their sentiments are evangelical, their enemies seem to think their feelings must be Antinomian; but though this may not be made plain to others, their doctrinal views befriend holiness, and with their mind they serve the law of God—yea, they delight in the law of God after the inward man. The goodness of God leadeth them to repentance. His love is shed abroad in their hearts, and they love him in return. They grieve to think they serve him so defectively, and have still in them so much of that which he infinitely hates. How painful to think that while they repose upon his bosom, they should often pierce it too!

In a word, while many would represent the Christian, if not an enemy to holiness and good works, yet too indifferent to their claims, he is abasing himself before God for the hidden evils of his heart; and is more affected with his sins of infirmity than his revilers are with sins of presumption. Thus you may drive a sword through the body of a dead man, and no muscle moves; while the puncture of a thorn will pain a living one all over.

JULY 8.—"But ye are washed; but ye are sanctified; but ye are justified." 1 Cor. vi, 11.

WE consider the word "washed," as a general term, comprehending a twofold cleansing—a cleansing from the guilt, and a cleansing from the pollution of sin. It would be easy to show that in the Scripture it is used in both these senses. The two added articles, therefore, are explanatory of its meaning here—Ye are washed, that is, ye are sanctified and justified.

What we wish to observe, is—that both these are found in the same subjects. Justification and sanctification should be always discriminated; but they must never be disunited. Where they are not distinguished, a religious system cannot be clear; and where they are divided, it can never be safe. Where they are not distinguished, law and gospel, free-will and free-grace, the merit of man, and the righteousness of Christ, run into a mass of confusion and disorder. And where they are divided, Pharisaic pride, or Antinomian presumption, will be sure to follow.

Be it remembered, then—That the one regards something done for us; the other, something done in us—the one is a relative, the other a personal change—the one a change in our state, the other in our nature—the one is perfect at once, the other is gradual—the one is derived from the obedience of the Savior, the other from his Spirit—the one gives us a title to heaven, the other a meetness for it.

But let us not forget their union. It is supposed that this was typified in the dying of the Lord Jesus, when from his pierced side there came forth blood and water—the one to atone, the other to purify. But not to lay too much stress on an historical incident, and which can be physically accounted for, the truth to which we allude is most expressly asserted in the word of God. "If any man be in Christ, he is a new creature: old things are passed away, behold, all things are become new." "There is no condemnation to them that are in Christ Jesus, who walk not after the flesh but after the Spirit." We need one as well as the other. And if we were not sanctified, as well as justified, we could neither serve God properly, or enjoy him. Suppose an unrenewed man pardoned, he would be no more able to see the kingdom of God than before; but would feel the company, the pleasures, and employments of the state, uncongenial and irksome. Or suppose you had a son; and you forbad him to enter a place of contagion, on pain of losing all you could leave him. He goes and is seized with the infection—he thus is not only guilty, by transgressing your command, but he is also diseased. And do you not perceive, that your forgiving him does not heal him? He wants not only the father's pardon, but the physician's aid; and in vain is he freed from the forfeiture of his estate, if he be left under the power of his disorder.

Let us therefore judge of the one, by the other; and make our election, by making our calling, sure. To be justified freely from all things; to have passed from death unto life; and never to come into condemnation again, is a privilege of infinite value—and there is a possibility of knowing that it belongs to us. But how is it to be known? Not by an audible voice from heaven, as the woman heard—"Thy sins are forgiven thee." Not by a sudden impulse, or working the mind into a persuasion which we are unable to justify. For the very thing to be determined is, whether this confidence be a good hope through grace, or a mere presumption. If the confidence itself were sufficient, the Antinomian would be surer than the Christian; but he has a lie in his right hand. The sacred writers do not consider this certainty of mind as self-proved; and regard all apprehensions of its wavering, as unbelief. They tell us to "fear, lest a promise being left us of entering into his rest, any of us should seem to come short of it." They call upon us to "examine ourselves, whether we be in the faith; and to prove our own selves." "We know," says John, "that we have passed from death unto life—because we love the brethren." "Hereby we know that he abideth in us, by the Spirit which he hath given us." This is the way, walk ye in it. What is the Spirit which he hath given you? Does it convince of sin? Does it cause you to hunger and thirst after righteousness? Does it glorify Christ?

It is true that we are justified by faith; but faith is justified by works. Has this promise been fulfilled in us? "Then will I sprinkle clean water upon you, and ye shall be clean: from all your filthiness, and from all your idols, will I cleanse you. A new heart also will I give you, and a new Spirit will I put within you; and I will take away the stony heart out of your flesh, and I will give you a heart of flesh. And I will put my Spirit within you, and cause you to walk in my statutes, and ye shall keep my judgments, and do them." As far as we are strangers to this practice, and to these dispositions, whatever our knowledge or our assurance may be, we ought to tremble. For though the grace of God finds us sinners, it does not leave us such. While it "bringeth salvation," it teacheth us "that, denying ungodliness and worldly lusts, we should live soberly, righteously, and godly in this present evil world; looking for that blessed hope, and the glorious appearing of the great God and our Savior Jesus Christ; who gave himself for us, that he might redeem us from all iniquity, and purify unto himself a peculiar people, zealous of good works."

JULY 9.—"**And it came to pass, that, as he was praying in a certain place, when he ceased, one of his disciples said unto him, Lord, teach us to pray, as John also taught his disciples.**"—Luke, xi, 1.

THOUGH "one" of the disciples said this, we have no reason to think the rest differed from him. He was the mouth for them all. When our Lord said to the twelve, will *ye* also go away? *Peter* answered—but it was in the name of his brethren, and expressed the conviction of each of them—"Lord, to whom shall *we* go? Thou hast the words of eternal life." It is very probable *he* was the speaker here; for his heart was always in his mouth But whoever the speaker was, every thing here was praiseworthy.

I admire his decorum. Some are satisfied with the moralities of conduct; but there are the proprieties too; and these are not to be overlooked. "Let every thing be done," says the Scripture, 'decently, and in order." This should be peculiarly the case in our holy assemblies. Let us guard against every thing that is unseemly, and disturbing. Let us avoid coughing as much as we can. Let us not look and stare all over the house of God. Let us not talk or whisper. Let us beware of coming in during the service. How painful and injurious is it to the preacher and worshipper to be interrupted and diverted in those sacred moments in which we ought to attend on the Lord without distraction. Observe these disciples. They surrounded our Savior while he was engaged—but with breathless silence; and did not not break in upon his devotion—but waited till he had "ceased praying."

I admire his emulation. Having heard his Master, he began to say, Well, this *is* prayer. What dignity! What wisdom! What reverence! What submission! What fervor! According to this, we have never prayed yet—Lord teach us to pray. Indeed, the more we attend on him in any thing, the less shall we think of ourselves. The beams of this sun will soon darken our tapers.

But the disciple did well. He wished to resemble what he so much admired. And thus we should always endeavor to improve by the superior endowments and excellencies of others. These should not excite envy, or yield discouragement; but excite to imitation. What others are, they are by grace; and when we see how any of our fellow Christians bear prosperity, or endure affliction, or fill up their stations, we should be anxious to follow them, even as they follow Christ.

I admire his spiritual wisdom. Some wish to resemble others in worldly possessions; or bodily qualities; or mental endowments and acquisitions. But it is better to resemble them in grace, than in any of these. Many would rule, or compose, or speak, like others; but the thing is, to *pray like them*. It is by prayer we hold communion with God. It is by this we unlock all his treasures. He that knows how to pray, has the secret of safety in prosperity, and of support in trouble. He has the art of overruling every enemy, and of turning every loss into a gain. He has the power of soothing every care; of subduing every passion: and of adding a relish to every enjoyment—the merchandise of it is better than the merchandise of silver; and the gain thereof, than much fine gold. Many things are good for me; but none so good as to draw nigh to God.

I admire his humility. He is convinced that they are not sufficient of themselves for the duty, but need divine aid. We want instruction in every thing; for the way of man is not in himself; it is not in man that walketh to direct his steps. But we peculiarly need guidance here. The Spirit helpeth *our* infirmities, says the apostle; for *we* know not what to pray for as we ought. The best of men have erred in their prayers. Take my life from me, says Elijah, in the very midst of his usefulness. I beseech Thee, says Moses, show me thy glory. You ask for death, says God, for no man can see me and live. "And James and John, the sons of Zebedee, came unto him, saying, Master, we would that thou shouldest do for us whatsoever we shall desire. And he said unto them, What would ye that I should do for you? They said unto him, Grant unto us that we may sit, one on thy right hand, and the other on thy left hand, in thy glory. But Jesus said unto them, Ye know not what ye ask: can ye drink of the cup that I drink of? and be baptized with the baptism that I am baptized with?" What would children be—how miserable—how useless—what burdens to themselves—and what plagues to others, if they had whatsoever they desired!—As to temporal blessings, it is hard to distinguish between our real, and our imaginary wants; and between what is pleasing, and what is profitable. And even as to spiritual things—we never see their beauty and glory, so as to desire them supremely, till the Lord teaches us to profit. Nor do we know of ourselves how to come before the Lord, and deal concerning them. Under a sense of guilt, and a concern to obtain acceptance, what strange expedients do we often adopt; and what a self-righteous traffic do we carry on, before we come to the blood of sprinkling, and make mention of his righteousness only. We may also err, as to our end and aim. We often ask, and receive not, because we ask amiss, that we may consume it upon our lusts.

—An easy thing to pray! Who that has made the trial, and is concerned for the result of it, but exclaims, with Elihu, "teach us what we shall say unto Him; for we cannot order our speech by reason of darkness?" Lord teach us to pray.

JULY 10.—"Thanks be unto God for his unspeakable gift."—2 Cor. ix, 15.

WE have always been accustomed to think of Christ when these words are pronounced; and we are not disposed to give up this application without necessity. And we see no such necessity—if we appeal to authority: for not to mention many of the ancients, this application is supported by many of the moderns, also; by a Henry, a Scott, a Doddridge. And we see no such necessity—if we refer to the writer of the words. Paul's mind was full of Christ; and the love of Christ constrained him: and nothing is more common in his Epistles than sudden and unlooked-for allusions to him. To which we may add, the nature of the case itself: for if the words would apply to the charity of the Corinthians, how much stronger will they apply to the Savior of sinners! And though we would do justice to every part of the Scripture, we would yet rather be followers of Coccius than Crellius, of whom, as expositors of the Bible, it was said, the one found Christ every where, the other no where.

God then (this is the meaning) so loved the world, that he *gave* his only-begotten Son, that whosoever believeth on him should not perish, but have everlasting life—and he is not only a gift, but an UNSPEAKABLE GIFT. Much has indeed been said of this gift in Christian conversation: in the sermons of ministers; in the preaching of prophets and apostles; in the Scriptures of truth, of which it is the principal, and in a sense, the only subject. But it is not in the power of words to do it justice. And we see how even inspired men labor for terms and images, when they would hold forth a little of the Savior's glory.

Here is a gift unspeakable—if we consider the greatness of his person. We consider him a man of sorrows: but he was not always so. He was born in the fulness of time: but his goings forth were from of old, from everlasting. In the beginning was the Word, and the Word was with God, and the Word was God. All things were made by Him, and without him was not any thing made that was made.

—Unspeakable—if we consider the immensity of the plenitude which he possesses, as Mediator, for our use. Some things include many more. What an unspeakable blessing is a fountain, being the source of all the refreshing streams that flow from it, and fertilize and beautify the ground! What an unspeakable blessing is the sun, that makes our day, our spring, our summer! What would the earth be without the sun! What an unspeakable blessing is life, with all its intelligence, pursuits, productions, and enjoyments! He is the fountain of living waters. He is the sun of righteousness. He is the life of the soul and eternity. He not only insures every thing else, but contains it—In him it hath pleased the Father that all fullness should dwell. In him we are blessed with all spiritual blessings in heavenly places.

—And can we think of this, and not exclaim, *Thanks* be unto God for his unspeakable gift? Nothing is so detestable as ingratitude. The very heathens condemn it. One of their philosophers said, Call a man ungrateful, and you call him every thing that is vile. The Lacedæmonians made it punishable. South compares such a wretch to the sea, that turns the sweet influences of the clouds into brine; and to the grave, which is always receiving, and never restoring. How soon we complain of a want of thankfulness in our fellow creatures toward ourselves! How soon do we abandon them, when our favors seem lost upon them!

And yet what are these favors, when, too, we are under an obligation to show them, from a community of nature, and the command of God! How few! How small! How far from being entirely pure in their motive! With how little self-denial and sacrifice attended! Herein is love! not that we loved God, but that he loved us, and sent his Son to be the propitiation for our sins.

And can this love deserve only a careless reflection of the mind? a cold acknowledgment of the lip? Ought it not to claim and consecrate the heart? Ought we not to ask every moment, What shall I render unto the Lord for all his benefits toward me? Ought we not, by the mercies of God, to present our bodies a living sacrifice?

"Were the whole realm of nature mine,
"That were a present far too small:
"Love so amazing, so divine,
"Demands my soul, my life, my all."

JULY 11.—"And he arose, and did eat and drink, and went in the strength of that meat forty days and forty nights unto Horeb, the mount of God."
1 Kings xix, 8.

HAVING, on Mount Carmel, witnessed the triumph of truth over idolatry, and destroyed Baal's prophets, and predicted the return of rain and urged the king to hasten home lest he should be impeded by the approaching torrents, "Elijah girded up his loins, and ran before Ahab to the entrance of Jezreel." Had Ahab properly regarded Elijah, he would have taken him up into his chariot, as the eunuch did Philip, and have honored him before his attendants, and conversed with him respecting the awful state of the country. But he did not cordially like him, and was happy to get rid of him as soon as possible; as Felix said unto Paul, "Go thy way for this time; when I have a convenient season I will call for thee."

But we admire the conduct of Elijah. He was not elated by the recent unparalleled honors conferred upon him, above the duty of a subject; and therefore, notwithstanding the character of

Ahab, he pays respect to him as his sovereign, and renders honor to whom honor was officially due.

—It is probable that Elijah came to Jezreel to carry on the reformation he had begun, and hoping that the late miracle would give him a powerful influence. But soon after he arrives in the suburbs, he learns the determination, not of the queen consort, but of the queen regent, (for Ahab, though King, was completely governed by a termagant wife,) to put him to death. "And Ahab told Jezebel all that Elijah had done, and withal how he had slain all the prophets with the sword. Then Jezebel sent a messenger unto Elijah, saying, So let the gods do to me, and more also, if I make not thy life as the life of one of them by to-morrow about this time." Upon this, he should have stood his ground, and have resolved to go on with his work, leaving events with God, and relying upon that providence and grace which had so signally appeared for him. He should have replied, as Chrysostom did, when Eudoxia, the empress, threatened him, "Go tell her that I fear nothing but sin;" or as Bazil did, when Valerius, the Arian emperor, sent him word that he would put him to death: "I would that he would; I shall only get to heaven the sooner;" or as Luther did, when they would have dissuaded him from going to Worms: "I would go, if there were as many devils there as there are tiles upon the houses;" or the prince of Conde did to the French king, when he proposed to him, going to mass, or perpetual banishment, or death: "As to the first of these, by the grace of God I never will; and as to the other two, I leave the choice of either to your majesty."

But where is the faith that never staggers through unbelief? the hand that never hangs down? the knee that never trembles? We are amazed at the magnanimity of Elijah before, in reproving Ahab to his face, opposing single-handed all the followers of Baal, and slaying Jezebel's four hundred and fifty chaplains! But what is man! He cannot stand longer than God holds him, or walk further than God leads him. This same hero now turns pale, and flees for his life! "And when he saw that, he arose, and went for his life, and came to Beersheba, which belongeth to Judah, and left his servant there?" And why did he leave him? Was it from tenderness, wishing to save him from the perils to which he himself was exposed? Or was it the more perfectly to conceal movements, as one could be more easily hid than more? Or did he wish for unrestrained, unwitnessed intercourse with God? There are seasons and places, in which we wish no eye to see, no ear to hear—but God to be all in all. Abraham left his young men below, when he ascended to worship God. And Jesus said to Peter, James, and John, in the garden, Tarry ye here, while I go and pray yonder.

However this was, "he went a day's journey into the wilderness, and came and sat down under a juniper tree;" and, fatigued with journeying and hunger, and harassed with forebodings, and despairing of further success in his exertions, he asked to resign, not only his office, but his life: He requested for himself that he might die; and said, It is enough: now, O lord, take away my life; for I am not better than my fathers"—*i. e.* I am not fitter to bear their trials, or discharge their duties, than they were. Why then should I remain, when they are removed? I have done and suffered my share. This was the language of nature, not of grace. Children grow fretful as they grow sleepy. Paul longed to depart to be with Christ, which was far better; yet he was willing to abide in the flesh, because it was needful for others. While we are ready to go, we must also be willing to stay, if God has any thing for us to do, or to suffer. To be impatient for retreat, especially as soon as we meet with disappointment, is unmanly and sinful!

Though Elijah was forward to die, it was a peevish haste, and evinced that he was in a very improper frame for the event. But God remembered that he was dust, compassionated his weakness, and appeared for him, even in a strait of his own producing—not dealing with him after his desert. "And as he lay and slept under a juniper-tree, behold, then an angel touched him, and said unto him, Arise and eat. And he looked, and, behold, there was a cake baken on the coals, and a cruise of water at his head; and he did eat and drink, and laid him down again." Before, he had fed him by ravens; now, he supplies him by one of those heavenly messengers who are all ministering spirits unto the heirs of salvation. The office seemed beneath one of these glorious beings. But he was as much pleased to bring a meal to this weary traveller, as he would have been had he received orders to manage the affairs of an empire. Angels have no partialities. They consider not the *nature* of the command, but only the *Author*. May his will be done on earth, as it is done in heaven.

—But what *was* the meal? A cake of bread and a cruise of water? Nature is content with little, and grace with less. How many disorders arise from excess! A voracious appetite is a judgment; a delicate one is an infirmity: a dainty one is a disgrace. Ministers, above all men, should not be given to appetite, or be fond of dainty meals. And those who entertain them should not insult them by the nature and the degree of their preparations. Did our Savior require much serving? Did not he reprove Martha for being cumbered about many things When an angel was the guest, Abraham brought him forth a cake, baked on the hearth, with butter and milk. And when an angel, who had the command of every store, catered for the greatest and best man of the age—it was a cake of bread and a cruise of water.

—"But the angel of the Lord came again the second time, and touched him, and said, Arise, and eat; because the journey is too great for thee." God's caring for his people is not only relieving, but prospective. He foresees what they will need, and prepares them for difficulties and duties which they had not reckoned upon. He strengthens the shoulder when the burden is going to be increased. And when he gives them an additional supply of faith, hope, peace, and joy, little, perhaps, do they imagine what trials they are to endure, or what steps they are to take, in the strength of it!

—But how was Elijah fitted for his journey! Surely the sustenance derived from this meal was miraculous. But it shows us what his power can do; and teaches us that man liveth, not by bread alone, but by every word that proceedeth out of the mouth of God. "And he arose, and did eat and drink, and went in the strength of that meat forty days and forty nights, unto Horeb, the mount of God." And why did he choose to repair hither? Would no other place have afforded him an equally safe retreat? Was he actuated by curiosity, or piety? Here was much to strike his mind, and to aid his faith and devotion. Here, would he say, Israel encamped! Here fell the manna! Here moved, and here stood, the fiery cloudy pillar! On the top of this hill God spake all the words of his law! And *there* God spake with Moses, face to face! How much is connected with some spots! "And Jacob awoke—and said, How dreadful is this place! This is none other but the house of God, and this is the gate of heaven."

"JULY 12.—"I die daily."—1 Cor. xv, 31.

WE need not confine the meaning, but take the expression in all its latitude of import. In what sense could not Paul make this acknowledgment? In what sense is it not possible, or proper for us to make it?

First. He died daily, because he professed to preach the Gospel, in constant hazard of life. "In labors," says he, "more abundant, in stripes above measure, in prisons more frequent, in deaths oft. Of the Jews five times received I forty stripes save one. Thrice was I beaten with rods, once was I stoned, thrice I suffered shipwreck, a night and a day I have been in the deep; in journeyings often, in perils of waters, in perils of robbers, in perils by mine own countrymen, in perils by the heathen, in perils in the city, in perils in the wilderness, in perils in the sea, in perils among false brethren; in weariness and painfulness, in watchings often, in hunger and thirst, in fastings often, in cold and nakedness." Well might *he* affirm, "I die daily." But in this sense, you say, the words are not applicable to us. It is true, from many of his dangers you are secure. Your religion is not exposing you to the loss of your life, or even of your liberty, or your substance. But do not even *you* die daily? Are you not in jeopardy every hour? Are you not surrounded by wicked and unreasonable men, whose vices and passions would destroy you, without the restraining providence of God? Are you not liable to a thousand accidents? Do not

"Dangers stand thick through all the ground,
"To push us to the tomb?
"And fierce diseases wait around,
"To hurry mortals home!"

What a frail thing is the human body! How strange that such a curious machine, composed of such a multitude of delicate organs, should continue so long in force and operation! Know you not that the heart beats seconds; and that sixty movements of the blood take place every minute—so that sixty times every minute the question is asked, whether we are to live or die! We die daily!

Secondly. Paul could say this, as death was actually invading him daily. And this is the case with us. We are mortal, not only in destination, but state. We decay while we receive sustenance. We talk of dying! But is this a future thing? Have we not always been dying? Why

"The moment we begin to live, | "We all begin to die."

We talk of dying! Why many of us are half dead already, and some much more. Many of our connexions are dead; many of our comforts; many of our hopes. We have buried many of our opportunities; and days and years—and every year, and every day, brings us near the *entire* end of the whole. It is absurd to confine dying to the act of separation between soul and body—this is only the finishing stroke. We die daily.

Thirdly. Paul, by a moral decease, died daily. So should we. To die to an object, according to the Scripture, is to have no more connexion with it, or attachment to it. Thus the apostle says to the Romans, "Reckon ye yourselves to be dead indeed unto sin." "How shall we, who are dead to sin, live any longer therein?" And this moral dying is frequently expressed by the word crucifixion, in allusion to the mode of it; and to remind us also of the cause, as well as the example. Hence it is said, "Our old man is crucified with him, that the body of sin might be destroyed, that henceforth we should not serve sin; for he that is dead is" thus "freed from sin. Now if we be dead with Christ, we believe that we shall also live with him." Thus the Christian dies daily, by a course of mortification to sin, and the world, and the impression of things seen and temporal, and the power of temptation. "For they that are Christ's have crucified the flesh, with its affections and lusts."

Fourthly. Paul died daily by a readiness for his dissolution, whenever it should take place. And the man who is like-minded will feel a concern to be prepared to die—in a good state, and—in good frame—to die safely—to die cheerfully—to die glorifying God—and having an *abundant* entrance into the everlasting kingdom of our Lord and Savior. And this must commence with the apostle's desire, "To win Christ, and be found in him." Nothing can be done to purpose, in our preparation for eternity, till we have said, "Into thine hand I commit my spirit; thou hast redeemed me, O Lord God of truth." The voice from heaven only pronounces those blessed who "die in the Lord"—in a state of union and communion with him—having his righteousness to give them a title to, and his grace to give them a meetness for, the inheritance of the saints in light.

But we should be concerned, not only to be habitually, but actually ready to die. That is, to be in a waiting posture; having our loins girded, and our lamps burning; keeping our consciences clear and calm; drawing off our affections from earth; that, when the summons comes, we may be willing to depart, and not be constrained to plead for protraction, "O spare me a little, that I may recover strength before I go hence, and be no more." In the history of Charles V., emperor of Germany, we are told, that he resigned the reigns of government, and retired into a convent in Spain. There he resolved to celebrate his own obsequies. For this purpose, he ordered his tomb to be erected in the chapel of the monastery of St. Justus. Thither, at the proper season, all his domestics were ordered to march in funeral procession, carrying in their hands black tapers. The emperor followed in his shroud. Arrived at the place, he was laid in his coffin. The service of the dead was performed: and when the ceremonies were ended, the doors were closed, the attendants dismissed, and he was left alone. After remaining some time in the grave, he arose, and repaired to his apartment, filled with all those awful reflections which the solemnity was adapted to inspire. Now we do not recommend the practice of such a gloomy and abject superstition. But you may sanctify the expedient, at least, in thought. You may anticipate an event that must befall you. And Oh that you were wise, that you understood this, that you would consider your latter end! Oh that you would remember, that the service you perform for others will certainly be required for yourselves! Oh that when you see man going to his long home, and the mourners going about the streets, you would say, "I also am accomplishing, as an hireling, my day; and in a little time, my neighbors, friends, and relations shall seek me—and I shall not be!" —Would it be improper or useless for you, in imagination, to suppose yourselves—entering your sick chamber—stretched upon a bed of languishing—dying—wrapped up in your winding sheet —laid in your coffin—friends, for the last time, touching your cold cheek with their lips or the back of their hand—the lid screwed down—and your remains borne through the mutes at the door—and accompanied to the grave—and left there—while the spirit had returned to God, who gave it. In endeavoring to realize this condition, I ask, How would the world appear? What would you think of the censure or praise of men? What of many of your pursuits? Would not this check the levity of the mind, and the pride of life? Would not, also, this contemplation break the force of surprise?

"Familiar thoughts can slope the way to death."

—But if we think not of the subject, the event will be a sudden precipice.

—The sum of human wisdom is, to keep us from surprise in any thing—the sum of divine wisdom is, to keep us from surprise in death. We know not how soon the event may come, nor in what manner it may befall us. It may not wait the close of threescore years and ten; and it may not announce its approach by the common warnings of sickness. If we have not learned this truth already from our observations of mortality—neither should we be persuaded though one rose from the dead.

July 13.—"I will yet for this be inquired of by the house of Israel, to do it for them."—Ezek. xxxvi, 37.

That is, what he had been promising, and notwithstanding the freeness and certainty of the engagement. Such is the revealed "will" of God. And his will is law, and law from which there lies no appeal. Nothing, therefore, can dispense with the obligation of prayer. But let us look at this fact.

As we have no claims upon God, and all he does for us must be from pure mercy and grace, no one can deny that he has *a right* to determine the way in which his favors shall be conferred. Nor can it be questioned that he is the most *competent judge* in this case. For his understanding is infinite; he knows himself and his relations; and he knows us and our welfare, perfectly.

But let us not suppose that he acts arbitrarily, though he may act sovereignly. And let us remember, too, that his acting sovereignly does not consist in his acting without reasons, but in his being governed by reasons which are often far above, out of our sight.

His wisdom and his goodness are to be seen here, as plainly as his authority. Some vainly ask, Where is the propriety of prayer?. Can prayer be necessary to inform a Being, perfect in knowledge? Or to excite a Being, always ready to do good? Or to induce a Being with whom there is no variableness, to change his measures? But the question is beside the mark. What is not necessary as to God, may be necessary as to *us*. Religion is founded, not in *his* wants, but in *ours*. Does not something of this kind obtain among all ranks and conditions of our fellow creatures? All-parental as you are, do you always dispense with your child's asking for what he wants? As a master, though willing to forgive, do you not deem it needful to require the servant that has offended you to confess his fault, and implore pardon?

How many are the advantages arising from God's requiring us to ask, that we may have; and seek, that we may find! The exercise of prayer keeps alive a sense of our indigence and dependence. Every time I go to God in prayer, I am reminded—that I am ignorant, and that he is wise; that I am weak, and that he is powerful; that I am guilty and miserable, and that he is merciful and gracious; that I am nothing, and that he is all in all.

—Prayer, by bringing us into the presence of God, will impress us with his excellencies; and the intercourse we have with him will lead us to admire, and fear, and love, and resemble him. For we soon catch the spirit, and take off the manners of those with whom we are intimate, especially if they are above us, and we much esteem them. It is said that those who are about the court, have an air and address peculiar to themselves, and that it is difficult, if not impossible, for another to assume it. A man who is much at the throne of grace, will betray it in a manner of feeling, speaking, and acting, that a religious pretender can never exemplify.

—Hereby, too, the blessing is more endeared, and enhanced. We never much regard what we acquire without application or effort. The effort is a kind of price; and we judge of the commodity by the cost. That which *blesses* us is what relieves our *wants;* fulfils our *desire;* accomplishes our *hope;* crowns our *sacrifices.* God's blessings are not bestowed upon those who are incapable of feeling their value—they would *then* yield neither pleasure to the receiver, nor praise to the Giver. His way, therefore, is to make us sensible of our need; to show us the importance and excellency of the favors; and to draw forth our souls after them. Then we are in his way. Then we can plead his promise. For blessed are they that do hunger and thirst after righteousness, for they shall be filled.

JULY 14.—"My peace I give unto you."—John xiv, 27.

PEACE sometimes signifies a confluence of temporal good things. But this is not the meaning of it here. Our Savior himself was poor, and a man of sorrows. And he said to his disciples, In the world ye shall have tribulation. Yet at the same time they were to have peace in him. This peace, therefore, must have been something which trouble could not hinder or injure. It must have been a spiritual privilege—composure of mind; especially—for here is the source of the greatest perplexity and disquietude; the calm of conscience, arising from a hope of our acceptance in the beloved. Before it can be enjoyed, the awful breach between God and us must be healed; and the blessed partaker of it be able to say, Thou wast angry with me; but thine anger is turned away, and thou comfortest me. For there must be a sense or apprehension of God's favor, which is life. I may be pardoned; but if I am ignorant of my forgiveness, my anxieties and uneasiness will remain. But when He says to my soul, I am thy salvation, then being justified by faith, I have peace with God—not only peace with him above, but peace with him within—a peace that passeth all understanding.

For who can adequately conceive the value of this donation? We need not descend into the depths of hell, to inquire what the miserable victims of despair would give for a moment's enjoyment of it. Let those speak who have been convinced of sin, who have felt a wounded spirit, and, expecting to fall into the hand of the living God, have exclaimed, What must I do to be saved! What were the feelings of the man slayer, with the avenger of blood at his heels! And what was the change he experienced, as soon as he had entered the appointed asylum, and could turn round and face the foe! Say ye—for ye have realized the blessed transition—ye who have fled for refuge to lay hold of the hope set before you.

"'Tis a young heav'n on earthly ground, | "And glory in the bud."

It is a cluster of the grapes of Eshcol. It weans from the world. It enlivens duty. It smooths the rugged path of adversity. It turns a dying chamber into the House of God, and the gate of Heaven.

But the Savior calls it his peace—"*My* peace I give unto you." It would be a low sense of this, though a true one, that he came and preached it. It was his in an infinitely more expensive way. He procured it for us. He came not to tell the way to heaven, but to be the way—not to show us how to make our peace with God, but to make it; and he did make it—we were reconciled unto God by the death of his Son. The chastisement of our peace was upon him, and by his stripes we are healed—he made peace by the blood of his cross. And he applies it by the agency of his Holy Spirit; enabling us to believe, and enter into rest; and maintaining our hope in all the changes of life, and under a continued sense of our unworthiness and guilt. Nor is it more his by derivation than distinction. Many have peace; but how unlike his! There is the peace of the sinner. This is of Satanic origin. The strong man armed keepeth his palace and his goods in peace. But this peace is worse than war. It is not founded in conviction, but ignorance. It cannot endure thought. It is unworthy of the name of peace—there is no peace, saith my God, to the wicked. How can a man retire, and go to sleep, when, if he dies before the morning, (and how easily may his bed become his grave!) God is under an oath to damn him? He denies it, or forgets. There is the peace of the self-righteous Pharisee; and the peace of the Evangelical hypocrite; both of which will prove as the spider's web, and as the giving up of the ghost. There is the peace of the worldling, who, in the calm of his fireside or evening's walk, musing on his abundance, says, O my soul, thou hast much goods laid up for many years; take thine ease; eat, drink, and be merry. But he may, that very night, have his soul required of him; and then whose are those things which he has provided? What is it to be at ease in our circumstances, and to enjoy peace with our neighbors, and in our families, while we are at war with God, and his wrath abideth on us!

—But this man shall be the peace, when the Assyrian cometh into the land! Look to him. Repair to him. "He healeth the broken in heart, and bindeth up all their wounds." While you neglect Him, you may seek peace, but you will never find it. But he cries—oh! hear him—"Come unto me, all ye that labor and are heavy laden, and I will give you rest." And is not this the very thing you want? Rest? Rest unto your souls? Believe him. Try his word. "Lo this, we have searched it, so it is; hear it, and know thou it for thy good."

JULY 15.—"And it came to pass, that when Jesus had finished these parables, he departed thence. And when he was come into his own country, he taught them in their synagogue, insomuch that they were astonished, and said, Whence hath this man this wisdom, and these mighty works? Is not this the carpenter's son? is not his mother called Mary? and his brethren, James, and Joses, and Simon, and Judas? and his sisters, are they not all with us? Whence then hath this man all these things? And they were offended in him. But Jesus said unto them, A prophet is not without honor, save in his own country, and in his own house. And he did not many mighty works there, because of their unbelief."—Matt. xiii, 53—58.

—His own country here means, not Bethlehem, where he was born, but Nazareth, where he had been brought up—a poor and despised place; so that it was proverbially asked, "Can any good thing come out of Nazareth?" Yet there was He found, who is the King of Glory!

Here he taught in their synagogues. *What* he taught is not recorded. But we may determine the substance of it from his addresses on other occasions, and from the end which he always kept in view—"to seek and to save that which was lost." Of his *manner* of teaching, we cannot form an adequate conception. It was all his own. "Grace was poured into his lips." Even those who derived no saving advantage from it—even his enemies—said, "Never man spake like this man."

Accordingly, the people here were astonished. Wonder has its place in religion; and there is every thing in the Gospel to call it forth. But many emotions of this kind are not powerful enough to produce any decisive result; and the subjects of them behold, and wonder, and perish. Thus it was here. They acknowledge his works to be mighty works, that is, miraculous; but are offended with his want of education, having been at no university, at the feet of no Gamaliel; never having learned letters. And also because he was not a man of birth and rank, but had relations in common life, and was himself engaged in manual employment. See how the god of this world blinds the minds of them that believe not. Who can stand before envy and prejudice? If he had the wisdom, and did the works—both which they admitted—it was the more commendable, and the more marvellous, that he was so pre-eminent without any ordinary helps, and the more likely was he to be divinely inspired. There seemed no other way of accounting for the prodigy. And this seems to strike them. But men do not value things according to their real excellence. And when there is not a cordial liking to any subject, every circumstance which would otherwise befriend is converted into objections.

In answer to their offence, our Savior remarks, "A prophet is not without honor, save in his own country, and in his own house." Usefulness depends upon acceptance, and acceptance upon esteem. Hence a bishop is to have a good report of them that are without; and hearers are commanded not only to receive such, but to hold them in reputation. But those who have been above a man in condition, do not like to come down and listen to him as an instructer and reprover; and those who have been upon a level with him, have been too familiar to feel veneration toward him. Many things, though quite consistent with sanctity, yet breed not that reverence and respect which attach to a man that comes to us, so to speak, from a kind of distance, and is only seen through the medium of his sacred office. The case here stated is not universally and absolutely true. But it is so generally and comparatively; and even our Savior himself was not an exception to it. After this, some of his servants need not be astonished at the treatment they experience. Neither should they fret and complain. They must take human nature as it is, and accommodate themselves prudently, as much as they can innocently, to the actual state of society. This governed the Master; and he assigns it as the reason why he preferred laboring elsewhere: "He said unto them, Ye will surely say unto me this proverb, Physician, heal thyself: whatsoever we have heard done in Capernaum, do also here in thy country. And he said, Verily I say unto you, No prophet is accepted in his own country."

But what a conclusion is here! "And he did not many mighty works there, because of their unbelief." *Some* he did. Mark says, he laid his hands on a few sick folk, and healed them. But what was the prevention of more? He generally required faith in his miraculous exertions. Hence the expressions—Be it unto thee according to thy faith. Believest thou that I am able to do this? If thou canst believe, all things are possible to him that believeth. There were, indeed, some cases in which he wrought without this; at least, without the faith of the individual; though even then faith was found in those who applied on his behalf, or who brought him to Jesus.

But faith is always necessary in spiritual operations. He can produce faith within us; but he cannot carry on his works of grace without it. If he could, it would be in contradiction to his word; and by a blind, positive, physical force, without their knowledge, feeling, wishes, or designs. But this is not his way. He does every thing by faith. We are saved through faith. Hence the importance of believing. The first, the chief concern, is to get faith. Talk not of the sufficiency and excellency of the remedy—it cannot heal us unless it be applied; and it can only be applied by faith. The Gospel is the power of God to salvation—but it is only to every one that believeth.

There is something infinitely evil in unbelief, if we only consider what it *prevents*. It stands, and it is the only thing that does stand, between a sinner and the relief of the Gospel. Let him believe, and he is saved. He that hath the Son, hath life; and he that believeth, hath the Son. As to others, the wrath of God abideth on them; for nothing else can withdraw them from under it. The Jews could not enter into Canaan because of their unbelief. It equally bars heaven against us. But what mighty works attend faith! By faith we are justified. By faith we are sanctified. We stand, we walk, we live by faith.

And Oh, what an injurious bar to a Christian himself is unbelief! How much does it hinder him from achieving in a way of duty, and realizing in a way of privilege! What keeps him so weak and wavering? Unbelief. "Surely if ye will not believe, ye shall not be established." If we depend on our frames and feelings, we draw from a summer brook, instead of the well of living waters. Pleasing experiences are cordials; but faith is the soul's food. Faith in the promise would immediately tranquilize us, as it did Paul in the storm: "Be of good cheer; for I believe God, that it shall be as it was told me." What keeps a Christian so poor in consolation? Unbelief. "Filled with all joy and peace in believing." "Believing, we rejoice with joy unspeakable and full of glory."

Who would not, then, by faith let loose all the sources of divine mercy and grace? Who would not cry out, with tears, "Lord, I believe; help thou mine unbelief?"

JULY 16.—"Call to remembrance the former days."—Heb. x, 32.

THIS will soon convince us that there is nothing new under the sun, and keep us from saying, "What is the cause that the former days were better than these?" In many respects we have the advantage. In knowledge, and civilization, and liberty, and trade, and the conveniences and comforts of life, and above all in spiritual privileges, we far surpass our predecessors.

If we look back to the period of Judaism, we shall have reason to say, "Blessed are our eyes, for they see; and our ears, for they hear; for many prophets and righteous men desired to see the things that we see, and did not see them, and to hear the things that we hear, and did not hear them." They had the type, we have the reality; they had the promise, we have the accomplishment; they had the dawn, we have the day—God having provided some better thing for us, that they without us should not be made perfect.

If we look back to the period previous to the entrance of the Gospel into our own country—what were our ancestors? Naked, painted savages in the woods; oppressed by cruel rites; enslaved by idolatry: being without Christ; strangers to the commonwealth of Israel; having no hope, and without God in the world.

We were called Christians long before the Reformation. But look at the period prior to that auspicious event. In what a state of mental degradation were we—religion, superstition—the service performed in an unknown tongue—the Scriptures kept from the common people—and nothing suffered to peep or mutter but as priestcraft allowed!

And when men began to know the words of life, and to serve God in spirit and in truth, what interdictions were they under; and to what fines, imprisonments, tortures, and deaths, were they exposed by the spirit of persecution—Popish, and—even Protestant! Remember the former times, in which your forefathers endured a great fight of affliction for conscience' sake. Think how they would have rejoiced to see a day, in which we sit under our own vine and fig-tree, and none can make us afraid; and the Gospel is spreading far and wide; and individuals, and churches, and communities combine to make manifest the savor of the Redeemer's knowledge in every place. Christians should judge by a rule of their own; and deem those the best times in which the best cause flourishes most. We therefore live in the most preferable era the world ever yet witnessed.

But it is well for us also to remember the earlier periods of our own personal history and experience—our days of religious nothingness, when we never called upon his name, and had no fear of God before our eyes. What feelings does the review of these days require!

But other days, better days, blessed days, followed after we knew God, or rather were known of him. *He* remembered these. "Go and cry in the ears of Jerusalem, saying, Thus saith the Lord, I remember thee, the kindness of thy youth, the love of thine espousals, when thou wentest after me in the wilderness, in a land that was not sown. Israel was holiness unto the Lord, and the first-fruits of his increase." And shall *we* forget them? Can we forget them?

"How sweet their memory still!"

In one respect, the review must be humbling. For how little has our practice corresponded with our profession, or our proficiency with our advantages! Yea, instead of advancing, have not we stood still, or rather gone back? We read of "the first ways of David." They were, alas! his best. The king of Israel never equaled the shepherd of Bethlehem. When at ease in Zion, his soul prospered much less than when he was hunted like a partridge upon the mountains. And have *we* never sighed, "Oh that it was with me as in months past!" Here is the charge: "I have somewhat against thee, because thou has left thy first love." Let us not deny it, but remember from whence we are fallen, and repent, and do our first works.

Are we in trouble? Do we see no way for our escape? Does God seem to have forgotten to be gracious? Let us remember the years of the right hand of the Most High. His love, and power, and truth, are still the same. And because he has been my help, therefore in the shadow of his wing will I rejoice

---

JULY 17.—"Ye have an unction from the Holy One."—1 John, ii, 20.

WHO is this Holy One? Unquestionably the Lord Jesus. It was one of the names by which he was known in the days of his flesh. The devils knew him by it, and said, We know thee who thou art, The Holy One of God. Ye denied, said Peter and John to the Jews, the Holy One and the Just. He was so called from the innocency of his life, the purity of his nature, and the eminency of his perfections; and therefore in a sense applicable to no mere creature. God is often called the Holy One, in the Old Testament; and, alluding to the very place where holiness is thrice ascribed to him by the seraphim, the evangelist affirms, "This said Isaiah, when he saw his glory, and spake of him." He is relatively, as well as personally, holy; and evangelically, as well as legally. He is as holy in his Gospel as in his law. He is as holy in his dispensations as in his ordinances. He is holy in all his ways, and righteous in all his works. He came by water, as well as blood; and gave himself for us, to redeem us from all iniquity, and to purify unto himself a peculiar people, zealous of good works. And though he will bring millions from the depraved race of Adam to glory, he will bring them all there, not having spot, or wrinkle, or any such thing.

And what is this unction from Him? John was a Jew, and well knew that oil, unction, anointing—it is all the same thing—was used to consecrate—to beautify—to refresh and delight. The word, therefore, is used here for the influence of the Holy Spirit. And this is derived from the Lord Jesus. This was typified in the case of Aaron, when the oil was poured upon his head, and went down to the skirts of his garments. So, here, the unction descends from the head of the church to the lowest members of the body. Hence it is so often called the Spirit of Christ. It comes to us through his mediation, and comes to us from his possession. For it was not, as Mr. Howe observes, the design and effect of the sufferings and death of Christ, that the Spirit should be given immediately to any individuals; but that the whole dispensation should be lodged in his hands, and the administration be the honor of his office. He received gifts for men, and this was the chief of them. Being by the right hand of God exalted, says Peter, and having received of the Father the promise of the Spirit, *he* hath shed forth this which ye now see and hear. He therefore said to his disciples, "It is expedient for you that I go away; for if I go not away, the Comforter will not come unto you; but if I depart, I will send him unto you." "And he shall not speak of himself; but whatsoever he shall hear, that shall he speak; and he will show you things to come. He shall glorify me; for he shall receive of mine, and shall show it unto you."

Thus it pleased the Father that in him should all fullness dwell. And of his fullness, says every saved, every sanctified sinner, have all we received, and grace for grace.

Have we this unction from the Holy One? If any man have not the Spirit of Christ, he is none of his. Destitute of this, our religion will be a form of godliness, without the power; practice, without principle; duty without delight—a task—weariness—vanity. We can only know that He abideth in us, by the Spirit which he hath given us.

—If strangers to the benefit, let us seek it. We know to whom we are to apply. He is able, he is willing, to give us the supply of his own Spirit. How encouraging to address ourselves to one who loved us, and gave himself for us—who says, If any man thirst, let him come unto me and drink—who never sent one suppliant empty away—who never will—never can—for he cannot deny himself.

Let us cherish this unction. It is what the apostle means, when he says,, "Grieve not the Holy Spirit of God, by which ye are sealed to the day of redemption." Not only does gratitude require this, because of what the Spirit has already done for you, but a concern for your own welfare. What can you do without his aids and comforts? In consequence of his sin, David feared the entire loss of his agency; and therefore cried, Cast me not away from thy presence, and take not thy Holy Spirit from me. Yea, he had suffered the loss of the consolation and support which he alone can give: *Restore* unto me the joy of thy salvation, and uphold me with thy free Spirit.

Let us diffuse this unction. Let us make manifest the savor of the Redeemer's knowledge, in every place; in every condition; in every company. Let it so abound in our conduct, temper, and discourse, that we may be distinguished and recommended by it. So that all may take knowledge of us that we have been with Jesus.

July 18.—"God, who is rich in mercy."—Ephesians, ii, 4.

In a thousand things God entirely eludes our research. In every thing he surpasses our comprehension. But we know that he is merciful—we are sure that he is rich in mercy. And we cannot be too thankful that the eminence of an attribute so essential to our happiness and hope is not obscurely revealed, but so plainly and fully made known in the works of his hands, the dispensations of his providence, the promises of his word, the provisions of his house, and the Son of his love.

For who does not need this assurance? The self-righteous Pharisee, who thanks God that he is not as other men are—he does not require it. And the proud pretender, who is free from all sin—he does not require it—he formerly required it, but he has now attained, he is now already perfect. But there are four classes of characters to whom it must be like life from the dead.

First. The victims of affliction. These are not rarely to be met with in this vale of tears. To such we would say, We ask you not what your distresses are; but if oppressed, say, Lord undertake for me. Cast thy burden upon the Lord, and he shall sustain thee. Repair not, under the pressure of wo to the rope, or the bowl of intoxication, or the dissipations of the world—this is like Saul's going to the witch of Endor; but go to the throne of the heavenly grace, imploring the pity of the God of all comfort. He does not afflict willingly, nor grieve the children of men. It is your welfare that has called forth this seeming severity. He knows your frame. He remembereth that you are dust. He lays upon you no more than he will enable you to bear. He will not always chide: neither will he keep his anger for ever. When the benevolent end of the dispensation is answered, he will readily lay aside the rod, and say, "Is Ephraim my dear son? is he a pleasant child? For since I spake against him, I do earnestly remember him still: therefore my bowels are troubled for him; I will surely have mercy upon him, saith the Lord. Set thee up waymarks, make thee high heaps; set thine heart toward the highway, even the way which thou wentest: turn again, O virgin of Israel, turn again to these thy cities." For He is rich in mercy.

Secondly. Convinced penitents. They were formerly always extenuating their guilt; now they are dwelling only upon the aggravations of it. Lately they seemed unsusceptible of alarm; but now they refuse to be comforted. Such is their unworthiness!—the number and greatness of their sins! They are cast out of his sight! And there is only for *them* a certain fearful looking for of judgment and fiery indignation! But Oh! awakened sinner, there is hope in Israel concerning this thing. There is everlasting consolation, and good hope through *grace*. With the Lord there is mercy, and with him is plenteous redemption. Judge not of Him by a human standard. Who is a God like unto Him? View him not through the medium of your own feelings. Believe his own word, wherein he assures you that he is ready to forgive; that he will abundantly pardon. Believe his oath, wherein he swears by himself, "As I live, saith the Lord, I desire not the death of him that dieth; wherefore turn, and live ye."

"Raise thy downcast eyes, and see
"What forms his throne surround;
"They, though sinners once, like me,
"Have full salvation found."

—He is rich in mercy.

Thirdly. Desponding backsliders. These, after walking in the way everlasting, have fallen by their iniquity, and perhaps feel more anguish of mind than when they were first led to repentance. They say, and they say justly, "No one has sinned with such enhancement as I have done. I have sinned against the dearest relations, and under the highest obligations, and against the greatest advantages. I have sinned, after being made to know what an evil and bitter thing it is; and also after tasting that the Lord is gracious. My sin has been more injurious in its effects than that of others; it has more dishonored religion, and grieved the Holy Spirit of God." All this they ought to feel; yet must not *they* forget that He is rich in mercy. It is this belief that will break the heart most, and make it sorrow after a godly sort. It is this alone that will lead them forward, with weeping and supplications, saying, Lord, take away all iniquity: create in me a clean heart, O God, and renew a right spirit within me. And He —will He refuse to reply, "I will heal their backsliding, I will love them freely; for mine anger is turned away from him?"

"Return, ye wandering souls, return,
"And seek his tender breast;
"Call back the memory of those days,
"When there you found your rest.

"Behold, great God, we come to thee,
"Though blushes veil our face;
"Constrain'd our last retreat to seek
"In thy much injur'd grace."

Fourthly. Persevering believers. These have holden on their way, and, having obtained help of God, continue to this day. They ought, therefore, to feel thankful. But it becomes them, also, to be humble. Indeed, the more they advance in the divine life, the more will they be dissatisfied with themselves. They will be deeply affected with a sense of their unprofitableness, and numberless infirmities. If their outward conduct has been fair to men, they know how little their heart has been right with God. They know the sins of their holy things would be enough to condemn them, if God should bring them into judgment with him. Their language, therefore, still is, God be merciful to me, a sinner. This is their only relief—living and—dying—He is rich in mercy.

JULY 19.—"As the appearance of the bow that is in the cloud in the day of rain, so was the appearance of the brightness round about. This was the appearance of the likeness of the glory of the Lord."—Ezekiel, i, 28.

THERE is always ground for the prophet's complaint, "Seeing many things, they *observe* not." How often do even objects peculiarly designed and adapted to excite and impress, fail to strike, or at least to awaken any proper attention. This is the case with the rainbow. Children wonder at the novelty, grandeur, and construction of the figure, but seldom ask a question about it. The common people, who are much abroad in the field, rarely give it a gaze, and never connect a thought with it, but as it may be supposed, by the time of its exhibition, to intimate the state of the weather. And what does the philosopher better? In the pride of science, he despises the vulgar; but, though able to explain the mediate cause of the phenomenon, he never looks after any thing the Scripture says concerning it. But who is, *here*, not only a naturalist, but a moralist? And not only a moralist, but a Christian? A Christian in the field, as well as in the temple making that which is seen and temporal the means of communion with that which is unseen and eternal.

The rainbow may be viewed three ways. First. Physically. Thus it is, in the sky, a semicircle of various colors, which appears in showery weather. It is gendered by the sun-beams, on a cloud. When there is a moist and dark cloud opposite the sun, and disposed to receive and reflect his rays, the bow is seen; and never without this concurrence.

Secondly. Federally. The first time we read of it in the Book of Genesis is in this covenant relation. "I do set my bow in the cloud, and it shall be for a token of a covenant between me and the earth. And it shall come to pass, when I bring a cloud over the earth, that the bow shall be seen in the cloud: and I will remember my covenant which is between me and you, and every living creature of all flesh: and the waters shall no more become a flood to destroy all flesh." It was in being before. But now it was made a divinely constituted sign, or token. Thus it should lead us to think of the holiness and justice of God, in the destruction of the old world: and also of his forbearance and goodness, in engaging not to destroy it in like manner: and in affording a sensible assurance of it. The appearance may be, in some measure, viewed as even typical of the event. The bow was early the principal weapon of war; and soon became the emblem of it. David says, "He hath bent his bow, and made ready his arrows upon the string, to shoot at the persecutors." But here is a bow without arrows, and without a string! When a man uses the bow in a hostile manner, the ends are toward himself; and the back is toward the enemy. But here the bow is reversed—the back is toward heaven; and the ends toward the earth. And therefore if it had arrows upon the string, they must be discharged upward, not downward—the earth is safe, and has nothing to fear from it. If this should be thought more curious than wise, yet the bow thus viewed, if not a type, is a proof and a pledge. It says, the flood is gone—never to return! And here we feel a perfect certainty. However long or violently the rain falls, we are not alarmed. We look to the bow in the cloud; and are sure, that, "while the earth remaineth, seedtime and harvest, and cold and heat, and summer and winter, and day and night, shall not cease." And why do we not feel equally sure with regard to another interposition?

For thirdly. The bow is to be viewed evangelically. "For a small moment have I forsaken thee; but with great mercies will I gather thee. In a little wrath I hid my face from thee for a moment; but with everlasting kindness will I have mercy on thee, saith the Lord thy Redeemer. For this is as the waters of Noah unto me: for as I have sworn that the waters of Noah should no more go over the earth; so have I sworn that I would not be wroth with thee, nor rebuke thee. For the mountains shall depart, and the hills shall be removed: but my kindness shall not depart from thee, neither shall the covenant of my peace be removed, saith the Lord that hath mercy on thee." Here we find God doing in a nobler case, what he did after the deluge. Here we find him—with a better, an everlasting covenant, ordered in all things and sure. And to render the allusion similar, and to afford strong consolation to those who are fleeing for refuge to lay hold of the hope set before them; we have his oath, accompanied with a sign, or token, that should subdue every apprehension. Where? What is it? "Upon the likeness of the throne," says Ezekiel, "was the likeness as *the appearance of a man above upon it.*" We know to whom this refers. "And I saw as the color of amber, as the appearance of fire round about within it; from the appearance of his loins even upward, and from the appearance of his loins even downward, I saw as it were the appearance of fire, and it had brightness round about. As the appearance of *the bow that is in the cloud in the day of rain*, so was the appearance of the brightness round about—*This was the appearance of the brightness of the glory of the Lord.*" An emblem of his glory, both as to his person, and importance. Who can help admiring the rainbow? It is one of the most beautiful appearances in nature. How various the colors! Yet the celestial tints are united; and though distinct, melt into each other, to make one astonishing whole. And his name is wonderful. What a combination of excellencies is found in him—"He is altogether lovely."

"All human beauties, all divine,
"In our Beloved meet and shine."

All the charms of nature; all the attractions of all creatures in earth and in heaven; are blended in him, and infinitely surpassed —"For how great is his goodness; and how great is his beauty!"

It also reminds us of his importance. He insures us safety—covenant safety. We are justified by his blood, and saved from wrath through him. He is the hope—the consolation of Israel. He that believeth on him shall not—cannot perish; but have everlasting life.

Let us look to him, and be comforted, against every adverse threatening. Afflictions cannot overwhelm us. The Law cannot curse us. Enemies cannot injure us. "Nay, in all these things we are more than conquerors through him that loved us. For I am persuaded, that neither death, nor life, nor angels, nor principalities, nor powers, nor things present, nor things to come, nor height, nor depth, nor any other creature, shall be able to separate us from the love of God, which is in Christ Jesus our Lord."

JULY 20.—"They took knowledge of them that they had been with Jesus." Acts, iv, 13.

THIS recognition is explained two ways. Some take it literally, as referring to the persons of the Apostles. These, their arraigners remembered, when they looked at them, for they had seen them before in company with him. And this, it is more than probable, was the case. For some of this very council attended his examination on the night of his apprehension. Yea, he was examined in the very house of this Caiaphas—and we are assured, that, Peter on the occasion, went into the High Priest's palace to see the end. Jesus, also, had openly taught in the Temple, when, more than once, some of these men were present, disputing with him; and he was always accompanied by his disciples—No wonder, therefore that Peter and John were recognized by them. But others take it in allusion to their qualities, behavior, and mode of speaking; connecting it particularly with the former words. And "when they saw the boldness of Peter and John, and perceived that they were unlearned and ignorant men, they marvelled—and they took knowledge of them that they had been with Jesus:" remarking that they were of the same party; or, as we should say, of the same stamp. So the sentence has been commonly understood. And three remarks may be made upon it.

First. Some have been with Jesus. Peter and John had been, as to his bodily presence, with him, for several years, in public and in private; going out and coming in with him—and who is not ready to envy them such intercourse? But he was received up into glory: and they who had known him after the flesh, knew him so no more. Yet he has promised his people his spiritual presence, to the end of the world. And thus though now invisible, he is yet accessible. Hereafter they will be for ever with the Lord. But this heaven begins on earth. They were naturally without Christ; though not as to dispensation, yet as to experience. But their religion began with an introduction to *him*—they were made sensible of their need of him. They sought him; and they found him. They had much to do with him then; and they have had much to do with him ever since. And they only go on well in religion as they are able to say, "When I awake, I am still with thee"—"I am continually with thee." They are with him—and in his word—in his House—at his Table—with him in the closet—in the field—

"Where'er they seek him he is found, | "And every place is holy ground."

They are with him, as pupils are with their teacher—as servants are with their master; waiting upon him all the day—as followers with their leader; willing to follow him whithersoever he goeth—as soldiers with their commander, fighting the good fight of faith; For "they that be with him, are called, and chosen, and faithful;" and "he that is not with him, is against him."

Secondly. It is expected, that they who are with him should resemble him. It is proverbially said, Tell me a man's company, and I will tell you his character. And it is well known, that like not only attracts, but begets like.

Hence the importance we attach to the choice of associates. Hence we say to the unmarried—Be not unequally yoked together with unbelievers. Hence, to the young—He that walketh with wise men shall be wise; but a companion of fools shall be destroyed. If we enter the house of mourning, we instantly catch the sympathy. The heart softens. The countenance contracts. The eye melts—How different are our sensations in the circle of festivity and mirth! It is said, that those who live at Court have a manner of their own, which others cannot successfully put on.

All association, however limited, produces some influence. But the conformity will be in proportion—to the degree of the intima-macy—and the constancy of the intercourse—and the love we have to the individual—and the veneration we feel for his greatness. Now all these will apply supremely to the Christian's acquaintance with Christ. And therefore the resemblance must be the greater—especially when we add to all this—That it is the duty, and the main business of his religion, to imitate him—For he that saith, he abideth in him, ought himself also so to walk as he walked. And if any man have not the Spirit of Christ, he is none of his.

Thirdly. This conformity will not be overlooked. The Christian himself may be not sensible of it; for the more progress he makes in the divine life, the more humble will he be. Moses was not aware of the brilliancy of his face when he came down from *being with God;* and was surprised to see the people dazzled at the glory of his countenance. And Paul said, I have not attained, I am not already perfect. But God will take knowledge of it—Angels will take knowledge of it—Ministers will take knowledge of it—His fellow Christians will take knowledge of it—The world will take knowledge of it—His profiting will appear unto all men. And though the wicked cannot be pleased with it; yet they are aware of what, by their profession, Christians ought to be; and their consistency will enthrone them in their conviction, and put to silence their ignorance; and may constrain them to glorify God in the day of visitation.

If persons are seen firm in principle; fearless in duty; zealous in the cause of God; yet humble and lowly; and gentle and tender; and patient in suffering; and ready to forgive—no one need to be told with whom *they* have been.

So, if you are proud, and vain, and worldly-minded, and avaricious, and revengeful, and censorious, and unkind, we do not require you to tell us with whom you are most intimate. And though we do not believe in witchcraft, we know that you have a familiar spirit—and we know who and what he is. And "glory not, and lie not, against the truth. This wisdom descendeth not from above, but is earthly, sensual, devilish. For where envying and strife is, there is confusion and every evil work. But the wisdom that is from above is first pure, then peaceable, gentle, and easy to be entreated; full of mercy and good fruits; without partiality, and without hypocrisy. And the fruit of righteousness is sown in peace of them that make peace."

JULY 21.—"O taste and see that the Lord is good."—Psalm xxxiv, 8.

THAT God is good is too obvious to be denied: though, alas! we are so little affected with it. He is good to all, and his tender mercies are over all his works. He openeth his hand, and satisfieth the desire of every living thing. As to *ourselves*, he made us, and why did he not make us reptiles? He placed us so high in the scale of beings, and furnished for our reception a world filled with his bounty and beauty. He gives the sweet interchange of hill, and vale, and wood and lawn. He makes the outgoings of the morning and evening to rejoice; and, in the succession and produce of the seasons, crowns the year with his goodness. He not only provides for our support, but for our comfort. He not only feeds and clothes, but feasts and adorns us. All our senses might have been so many inlets of pain, but they are the avenues of a thousand pleasures: and we are furnished with the most delightful colors, and sounds, and perfumes, and relishes. Our food might have been rendered distasteful; but he has made it pleasant, and connected gratification with the most necessary act of life; so that no one eats from a sense of duty, or to avoid death; but for pleasure.

Distinguished from this general kindness of God, there is, however, a peculiar goodness; and which regards us, as *sinners*. It is called, in the Scriptures, mercy and grace. It led Him to remember us in our low estate, and to make provision for our salvation from every effect of the fall. He spared not his own Son. He was delivered for our offences, and raised again for our own justification. And in him all things are now ready for our acceptance. And, unworthy as we are, we may obtain all spiritual blessings in heavenly places, and—for ever. Herein is love! And this favor which he bears unto his people, and which regards the soul and eternity; this good-will of Him that dwelt in the bush—This is what we are supremely to seek after.

But what is the best way to know this goodness! David does not say, Hear, and know; read and know; believe, and know; but *taste* and *see* that the Lord is good. That is, apply to him for yourselves, instead of relying on the authority of others; as in a case of disputed relish you determine not by testimony, but taste. In other words it means experience. Experience is knowledge derived from experiment, in contradistinction from theory. Since the mighty mind of Bacon beat down hypothesis, and introduced the inductive system, philosophy has reasoned from facts, and experimental philosophy has been much applauded. Why then should we ridicule experimental religion? Is there no standard in divinity to which we can appeal? Is there no test to be applied to the truth of pious pretensions? Are there no facts to bear out or to contradict what the Scripture says of sin? of repentance? of hope? and of peace and joy in believing?

Some, and, in our day, many, know divine things in a way of speculation. But they are not under their operation; they feel not the powers of the world to come. And these are the most unlikely characters to be wrought upon. They are familiar with the truths of the Gospel; they admit all the preacher advances; they acknowledge all he proves: but it has no influence over the heart and life. They believe in hell but make no attempt to flee from the wrath to come. They believe in heaven, but do not set their affection on things above. They believe in the value of the soul, and that its redemption ceaseth for ever, and yet neglect the only opportunity to embrace the things that belong to their peace. They go through the Bible; but its threatenings do not alarm, and its promises do not allure them. They resist every motive. They have been wooed and awed a thousand times in vain. They say;

and approve better things, and follow worse. They are not happy, and contrive to be miserable. They are in the jaws of death, and yet are at ease in Zion. What paradoxes! What contradictions are you! Of what worth is *your* knowledge! To know a refuge, and never enter it! To know a remedy, and never apply it! To know good, and never partake of it! This will not only leave you to perish, but deprive you of excuse, and aggravate your sin and condemnation. Like Uriah, with his fatal letter, you carry information that will place you in the front of the battle. Be not satisfied, therefore, till you know these things to purpose; which can only be, by your knowing them experimentally.

Then your heart will be established with grace; and you will be so confirmed in the truth, that you will not be led away by the error of the wicked, to fall from your own steadfastness.

Then you will desire greater degrees of it; and, having tasted that the Lord is gracious, your prayer will be, "Lord, evermore give us this bread."

Then you will be excited and qualified to address others; for you will speak from the heart, and recommend a tried remedy—a remedy that has effectually cured yourselves. "Lo this, we have searched it, so it is; hear it, and know thou it for thy good."

JULY 22.—" To him that overcometh."—Rev. iii, 21.

THERE are seven addresses of this kind, closing the seven epistles, which John was to write, and send to the churches which were in Asia: to Ephesus and Smyrna, and Pergamos, and Thyatira, and Sardis, and Philadelphia, and Laodicea. Overlooking what is peculiar in each of them, let us notice what is common to all. Four things are so.

First. All of them regard a particular character. It is a successful soldier. Him that *overcometh*. This reminds us of the nature of the Christian's life. It is a warfare. It was such, unquestionably, in the apostles' days. We read of their wrestling with principalities and powers; of their fighting the good fight of faith; of their resisting unto blood. If it be said, "The language is figurative," we allow it. But it must, or we are trifled with, imply realities. And what are these? If it be said, "Religion is not the same thing now as it was then," we ask, When was it changed? And by whom? And what *is* it at present? What would be thought of a preacher, who should come forward in public, and say, A religious life was a difficult thing once, but it is a very easy one now. The first Christians were required, in order to be the disciples of Christ, to deny themselves, and take up their cross, and follow him in the regeneration; but all this is dispensed with now! He may prophesy falsely—and the people may love to have it so: but what will be done in the end thereof? If, therefore, you think yourselves in the way everlasting, without knowing any thing of this spiritual warfare, you are in a pitiable condition—and pertain to the strong man armed, who keeps *his* palace and goods in peace.

Secondly. All of them are attached to an individual—not to *them* that conquer, but to—*him* that overcometh. As much as to say, Each is perceived by me in the crowd; and if all in church should prove corrupt, and one only maintain his fidelity—faint, yet pursuing—let *him* not be ashamed, or afraid. *He* shall be confessed before my Father, and the holy angels. For *him* that honors me I will honor.

Thirdly. All of them contain the *assurance of some reward* of grace. The food of paradise—a crown of life—the hidden manna, and the white stone—the morning star—white raiment—a pillar in the temple of God—a seat with the Savior on his throne. But these who can describe or comprehend? They are yet to be revealed. But we know enough to animate us in the conflict, and to convince us that godliness is profitable unto all things.

Fourthly. All represent the *Lord Jesus as the Author and Bestower* of every honor and indulgence. *I* will make: *I* will give; *I* will grant—says he, who procured all for us—and in whom all fullness dwells. The joy set before him, for which he endured the cross, and despised the shame, was the gratification of his benevolence, in receiving gifts for men. And he shall see of the travail of his soul, and shall be satisfied. He saves them spiritually now. And he shall raise up their bodies at the last day. And he shall say to those on his right hand, Come, ye blessed, of my Father, inherit the kingdom prepared for you from the foundation of the world.

He shall come to be glorified *in* his saints, and to be admired *in* all of them that believe. Amen.

JULY 23.—"**For thou, Lord, art good, and ready to forgive, and plenteous in mercy unto all them that call upon thee.**"—Psalms, lxxxvi, 5.

THE first word "for," shows that the text contains a reason for something; and it was this, as we see by the preceding verse—"Unto thee, O Lord, do I lift up my soul." We learn from it of what importance it is to place and keep the Supreme Being before the eye of the mind, in an amiable and inviting character, when we have to do with him. Tell me not there is danger in such representations—they may gender presumption. They may. Every thing is liable to abuse. But for this we are not answerable. We are saved by hope. By withdrawing his confidence in God, man fell; and he can only be restored by replacing it in him. The first step of a sinner, in returning to God, must result from this trust. Accordingly, the design of revelation is to produce and support it. "For whatsoever things were written aforetime, were written for our learning, that we, through patience and comfort of the Scriptures, might have hope." The same is said of the mediation of Christ: "By him we believe in God, who raised him up from the dead, and gave him glory, that our faith and hope might be in God." More are destroyed by despair than by presumption. When once a man says, There is no hope, he becomes abandoned; and the despondence he feels is the strongest link in the chain that binds him to an unconverted state. Let there be, therefore, always a refuge open, and into which a sinner, when he looks back, and wishes to enter, may return. Tell him yet there is room. Tell him that God is good, and ready to forgive, and plenteous in mercy unto all them that call upon him.

And from hence let me also learn, that—when we have no comfort arising from personal assurance, there is encouragement enough in the general views which the Scripture gives us of God, to induce us to wait on the Lord, and keep his way. David does not here say, I will lift up my soul to Him; for he is *my* God, and he has given me the heritage of them that fear his name; but he looks to his goodness, and readiness to forgive, and the plenteousness and impartiality of his mercy—these considerations do not require me to ascertain, before I come to him, that I am a saint; but tell me to come, as a sinner; and assure me, that he will in no wise cast me out. When I know not that I *have* grace, how delightful is it to know that it is attainable; and to hear a voice, saying, Whosoever will, let him take of the water of life freely! Thus Mr. Scott said, when dying, that those Scriptures refreshed and comforted him most which were not limited to a particular class, but open to all.

Yet, however good, and forgiving, and merciful, He is—this is nothing to those who refuse or neglect to—"call upon him." Such blessed assurances are not intended to make us careless; but to excite and animate our applications to him. Prayer is the way in which he who has a right to determine, and who cannot err, has chosen for our obtaining his favors—Yet I will be inquired of. Ask, and ye shall have. Seek, and ye shall find.

Those, therefore, that live without payer, are shut out from the blessedness. But this is not all. They incur, also, the curse, which results from the contempt of his grace. There is no aggravation of misery like the consciousness of patience exhausted, kindness abused, opportunity lost. But lost entirely by our own fault! Lost for ever! *This* conviction will be the food of the worm that never dies, and the fuel of the fire that can never be quenched.

July 24.—"Prove me now."—Malachi, iii, 10.

There is nothing of which men are more tenacious than the honor of their veracity. How offended do they feel, if we seem to suspect the truth of their word, by requiring a pledge or voucher before we can venture upon it. If a king were to address his subjects in a way of privilege, and they should say—We must try thy faithfulness before we can trust it—he would consider himself insulted, and, in wrath, have nothing to do with them. God is veracity itself; and magnifies his word above all his name. And he might justly say to us—Such are my declarations—dishonor me not, by requiring any confirmation—I am entitled to implicit credence, and if ye will not believe, surely ye shall not be established. But he knoweth our frame; and he knoweth the absolute importance of our confidence in him—and therefore he allows us to acquire it in our own way, and seems more concerned for our satisfaction than for his own glory.

And yet hereby he glorifies himself too; for by this method he not only shows his kindness and condescension in accommodating himself to our infirmities, but obtains a sensible and satisfactory conviction in favor of his truth. In addition to testimony, we are furnished with experience. What we have read and heard, we have brought to trial—and have demonstrated ourselves. So that we do not merely believe. There must be, indeed, a degree of faith to induce us to make the trial—but when we have made it, and made it successfully, the proof increases the confidence of faith—and he that *thus* believeth hath the witness in himself.

Hence, when God invites us to prove him, it is not sinful to do it—yea, it would be sinful to refuse. We see this in the case of Ahaz. "Moreover, the Lord spake again unto Ahaz, saying, Ask thee a sign of the Lord thy God; ask it either in the depth, or in the height above. And Ahaz said, I will not ask, neither will I tempt the Lord." He did not decline it from confidence in God, or from humility—but from desperation or indifference. "Not I—it is useless." Isaiah so understood it, as appears from his answer and complaint: "And he said, Hear ye now, O house of David; it is a small thing for you to weary men, but will ye weary my God also?" When He allows a privilege, it becomes us gratefully to use it: we reflect upon his kindness and wisdom if we do not. Some, like Gallio, care for none of these things. They do not think religion or revelation worthy of proof. Hume said he had never read through the New Testament in his life! As much as to say, It is nothing to me, whether these things be true or false. I will take no pains to ascertain whether we have souls as well as bodies; whether another world succeeds this; whether, after death, there be a judgment, or a heaven, or a hell!

There is, indeed, a censurable proving of God; and it is more than once charged upon the Jews of old. It was founded in unbelief, and led them to dare his judgments. Thus Pharaoh, and thus Adam and Eve, tried his word, in his threatenings. This is always wrong. First, because, if the trial proves the denunciation true, the proof is useless; for it is derived from the infliction of the evil itself: we are convinced by being punished. And, secondly, we cannot put the menaces of God to the test, but by criminal conduct. It is only by sinning, that we *can* try whether what he has threatened against sin will be accomplished—as the practice is the condition on which the penalty is suspended. But it is otherwise with the promises of God—if we find them true, we are saved and happy: and we can only seek the proof of their truth, in what is good and improving; in praying, in obedience, in the use of the means which God has ordained.

Let us then prove him—and see whether his word will come to pass or not. Let us prove him with regard to the freeness of his mercy. For he hath said, "Come and let us reason together: though your sins were as scarlet, they shall be white as snow; though they were like red crimson, they shall be as wool." "Let the wicked forsake his way, and the unrighteous man his thoughts; and let him return unto the Lord, and he will have mercy upon him; and to our God, for he will abundantly pardon. For my thoughts are not your thoughts, neither are your ways my ways, saith the Lord." Let us prove him with regard to the efficacy of his grace. For he hath said, "My grace is sufficient for thee, for my strength is made perfect in weakness." Let us prove him with regard to the care of his providence. For he hath said, "There is no want to them that fear him." "He careth for you." "The hairs of your head are all numbered." Let us prove him with regard to the advantage of benevolence. For he hath said, "God is not unrighteous to forget your work and labor of love, which ye have showed toward his name, in that ye have ministered to the saints, and do minister." Let us prove him in regard to the blessedness of his service. For he hath said, "Godliness is profitable unto all things, having promise of the life that now is, and of that which is to come." "Verily I say unto you, There is no man, that hath left house, or parents, or brethren, or wife, or children, for the kingdom of God's sake, who shall not receive manifold more in this present life, and in the world to come life everlasting."

By how many millions *has* all this been proved! Yes; his word has been a tried word, and it has never failed in the trial, and never will.

Let us make the trial for ourselves, and set to our seal that God is true. Thus we shall become his witnesses to others, and be able to say, "O taste and see that the Lord is good; blessed is the man that trusteth in him."

JULY 25.—"For Moses truly said unto the fathers, A prophet shall the Lord your God raise up unto you of your brethren, like unto me; him shall ye hear in all things whatsoever he shall say unto you. And it shall come to pass, that every soul which will not hear that prophet shall be destroyed from among the people."—Acts, iii, 22, 23,

THERE was a remarkable resemblance between Moses and the Messiah, which it would be easy to trace. But the likeness here spoken of regards his office. Moses was a prophet, a peculiar prophet, a pre-eminent prophet. He introduced and established the whole of the Jewish dispensation with miracles, wonders, and signs. He was the mediator between God and the people. Other prophets received divine communications through various mediums; but he received every thing from God immediately. "If there be a prophet among you, I the Lord will make myself known unto him in a vision, and will speak unto him in a dream. My servant Moses is not so, who is faithful in all my house—with him will I speak, mouth to mouth, even apparently, and not in dark speeches; and the similitude of the Lord shall he behold." But, if "the law was given by Moses, grace and truth came by Jesus Christ." "No man hath seen God at any time; the only begotten Son, who is in the bosom of the Father, he hath declared him." Yea, in all things he has the pre-eminence. Moses was faithful as a servant; but Christ as a Son over his own house. The commission of Moses was confined to one nation; but Christ is not only the glory of his people Israel, but a light to lighten the Gentiles—the light of the world.

Every office the Savior sustains requires a corresponding disposition in those to whom he is sent. As he is a prophet, we are commanded to "hear him." It cannot mean a mere hearing. Then many would be safe who are condemned already. But it includes our believing his instructions with a faith unfeigned, and our cordial submission to them; or, as the apostle expresses it, our obeying from the heart the form of doctrine delivered us. Blessed are they that hear the word of God and "keep it." If he commands us to lay up treasure in heaven, and we mind earthly things, if he tells us to deny ourselves, and take up our cross, and follow him, and we live to the lusts of men—if he says, Look unto me, and be ye saved, and we go about to establish our own righteousness—we do not hear him, but despise and reject him. He that hath his commandments, and *keepeth* them, he it is that loveth him—and he it is that heareth him.

We are not only to hear him, but to hear him "in all things whatsoever he shall say unto us." Some dislike the mysterious parts of Christianity; some the humiliating; some the practical. But the only inquiry of a true disciple is, "Lord, what wilt thou have me to do?" He will not dictate; he will not object; he will not prefer—but say, "I esteem all thy commandments concerning all things to be right, and I hate every false way." The test of real obedience is, to "do all things without murmurings and disputings."

Nothwithstanding our duty and our responsibility, it is here supposed that some "will not hear this prophet." This is a sad intimation, and we might wonder at the fact. But the depravity of human nature will account for it, and all history confirms it. Some ridicule and oppose. Many never attend the means of grace. Numbers have only "a form of knowledge;" and others, only "a form of godliness," while denying the power thereof.

And to what are they exposed? "It shall come to pass that every soul that will not hear that prophet shall be destroyed from among the people." Mark the impartiality of the sentence, "every soul." The refusers may be many; and they may differ from each other. But though each may turn to his own way, all are going astray. There is only one path of life, but there are many avenues to death. And it matters not what our particular character is, whether profligate or formalist, Pharisee or hypocrite—*he* that believeth not shall be damned—and without holiness *no* man shall see the Lord. See the nature of the doom, "shall be cut off." This is not correction, but excision; not, however, annihilation—this would be a privilege. They shall seek death but they shall not find it. In vain will they ask the rocks to fall on them, and the mountains to cover them. The penalty is not the loss of their being, but of their happiness and of their hope; the destruction of body and soul for ever. Observe the dreadfulness of the aggravation, "from among the people." They are intermixed now, and some of them very peculiarly. They attend in the same sanctuary; they live under the same roof; they are united by the ties of friendship and of blood. But their privileged situation and condition only evinced and increased their depravity. "Let favor be showed to the wicked, yet will he not learn righteousness; in the land of uprightness will he deal unjustly; and will not behold the majesty of the Lord." Their present advantages, therefore, will afford them no security. Neither will they be able to retain them. The wicked shall not stand in the judgment, nor sinners in the congregation of the righteous. But severed from the just, they will be led forth with the workers of iniquity; and carry away with them into the place of torment only the remembrance and the guilt of all they neglected and abused here.

See, then, that ye refuse not him that speaketh; for if they escaped not who refused him that spake on earth, how much more shall not we escape, if we TURN AWAY FROM HIM THAT SPEAKETH FROM HEAVEN?"

JULY 26.—" The kingdom of heaven is like unto treasure hid in a field; the which, when a man hath found, he hideth, and for joy thereof goeth and selleth all that he hath, and buyeth that field."—Matt. xiii, 44.

How well may the Savior call the Gospel a treasure! The tongue of an angel could not describe its value and preciousness. It meets and relieves every want of the soul. It blesses us with all spiritual blessings. It is the true riches; unsearchable riches —durable riches. It profits in the day of wrath. It delivers from death. It ennobles in the world to come.

A man may *find* a treasure hid in a field, by accident, or by search. There is nothing casual in the salvation of a sinner, as to God; but as to *himself*, the event may be wholly undesigned, and unlooked for. He may have been seeking, but not for this object; like Saul, who was searching when Samuel met him; but it was for his father's asses, and not for the kingdom. Thus the Lord is found of them that sought *him* not; and asked not for him. Matthew was sitting at the receipt of custom when the Savior said, Follow me. Saul was in a journey of iniquity, when the Savior appeared to him in the way, and called him by his grace. Some have gone to the house of God, from mere custom, or curiosity, or a design to ridicule; but have returned to pray, and have said, what wilt thou have me to do? But, says Henry, though he is sometimes found of them that seek him not, he is always found of them that seek him. This was the case with Cornelius. He was a devout man, and feared God, with all his house; praying and giving alms always, *when* Peter was sent to tell him words by which he was to be saved. Nathanael had retired beneath the fig-tree, to read and reflect, and pray, when the Savior took knowledge of him, and said, Thou shalt see greater things than these. And there are those now, who are awakened, rather than enlightened: they feel their spiritual wants, and are using the means of grace. And whatever ignorance or legality mixes with their efforts, they are in the search, and shall find. He who has touched the heart, and turned it from the world, will fulfil the desire of them that fear him; he also will hear their cry, and will save them. Then shall we know, if we follow on to know, the Lord.

The *emotions* of the finder are naturally portrayed. First, when he hath found the treasure he hideth it. When we are anxious to secure a thing, we conceal it. The way therefore is here used for the end; and hiding refers not to secrecy, but safety. The allusion is to that holy jealousy recommended by the apostle, when he says—Let us therefore fear, lest a promise being left us of entering into his rest, any of us should seem to come short of it; looking diligently, lest any man fail of the grace of God. To that trembling at God's word—when we are more affected with the inviting, than with the awful parts. To that solicitude to obtain which always genders apprehension. Oh! how shall I make all this my own! Oh! if I should miss, or lose! What must I do to be saved?

Secondly. He feels joy thereof. Not that firm and glorious joy which arises in the established Christian, from a consciousness of possession, and who can say, I know that my Redeemer liveth: but the joy that results from discovery of the reality, the excellency, the suitableness, the all-sufficiency, the attainableness of the blessing; and is called, Rejoicing in hope. The patient, with the disease yet oppressing him, cannot feel at ease; but he is gladdened, even on the brink of the grave, when he hears of the arrival of a physician, bringing with him a remedy that was never applied in vain.

Thirdly. He goeth—for now it is impossible for him, like many, to sit still—and selleth all that he hath, and buyeth the field. That is—he is fully determined to submit to the cost of procuring it, whatever it may be. We can offer no equivalency for the possession: nor is this the meaning of the word so often employed in this connexion. In *this* way, were we to buy, it would be without money, and without price. But the meaning is simply *exchange;* as, in buying, we part with something to gain something. Hereby, we show our estimation; for what stronger proof can we give of our valuation of an object, than parting with all we have for the sake of it? And the case here is such, that we *must* make a choice, and a sacrifice, to evince our preference, and attain our desire. Some things must be absolutely given up. Some, conditionally. And all, as to supreme regard and dependence. Are we willing, then, to part with our sins? All our sins? Even our bosom lusts? The right hand? The right eye? Are we willing to part with our own wisdom? not leaning to our own understanding, but receiving the kingdom of God as little children, and becoming fools that we may be wise? Are we willing to part with self-righteousness? not with the practice of obedience, morality, and good works; but only the substitution of them in the room of the Savior, and reliance on them for our acceptance before God, and the pleading them as a title to heaven—instead of saying, In the Lord have I righteousness and strength? Are we willing to part with the world? The promises of superiors? The applause of companions? The smiles of friends? The ties of the dearest relations? For "he that loveth father or mother more than me, is not worthy of me."

This is a hard saying. But every thing requires sacrifice, and every thing in proportion to the importance of the attainment. And we are more than indemnified, for all we suffer or lose. "Verily I say unto you, there is no man, that hath left house, or parents, or brethren, or wife, or children, for the kingdom of God's sake, who shall not receive manifold more in this present time, and in the world to come life everlasting."

JULY 27.—"This grace wherein we stand."—Romans, v, 2.

WHAT is this state? And what is this standing? The state is a state of *grace;* and means, the privileged condition in which all Christians are found, though they were by nature children of wrath, even as others. It is expressed by our apostle, in the preceding words—Being justified by faith, we have peace with God, through our Lord Jesus Christ; by whom also we have access by faith into *this* grace.

It may well be called this grace; for it only flows from, and only proclaims, the exceeding riches of his grace in his kindness toward us, by Christ Jesus. How dreadful it is to have God for our adversary! He, in whom we live! He who is about our path, and our lying down! He, on whose side all creatures rise up, and range themselves! He whose look is death, and whose frown is Hell! What were our alarms, when we began to discover our danger, and conscience induced to cry, "What must I do to be saved?" And when we saw the storm was passing off; when we were told that the dreadful breach was made up; when we believed that God was pacified toward us for all that we had done—what were our feelings then, but life from the dead? And in that day we said, "O Lord I will praise thee; thou wast angry with me, thine anger is turned away, and thou comfortest me."

But we may be reconciled to another, so as to be forgiven, and not be admitted into the intimacies of friendship. After Absalom was, through the intercession of Joab, allowed to return to Jerusalem, two years elapsed before he was allowed to see the king's face. But God favors us with the most familiar intercourse and communion. We come boldly to the Throne of Grace; and in every thing, by prayer and supplication, make known our requests. We dwell in his house. We eat at his table. We walk with God. We lean on his arm, and on his bosom. He honors us with his confidence, and trusts us with his secrets. He allows us to put him in remembrance, and plead with him; and say—can his condescension go further? Concerning the work of my hands, command ye me. This grace takes in, also, approbation and complacency. He takes pleasure in them that fear him. He rests in his love. He joys over them with singing. They are his children, his bride, his jewels, his glory. And as their persons, so their services are accepted in the Beloved. Poor as they are, he smiles upon them. Their prayer is his delight; and their alms are the odour of a sweet smell. He views their motive, and passes by their mistakes. He regards their wish and design; and says, in their failures, "It is well that it was in thy heart."

Hence follows sympathy and compassion. What is done to

them, he resents as a personal injury: for he that toucheth them, toucheth the apple of his eye. In all their affliction, he is afflicted. And though he corrects them, it is for their profit. He takes the rod with reluctance, and he lays it aside with pleasure. He cannot withstand their yielding and tears. Is Ephraim my dear son; is he a pleasant child? For since I spake against him, I do earnestly remember him still.

" So fathers their young sons chastise,
" With gentle hand and melting eyes;
" The children weep beneath the smart,
" And move the pity of the heart."

In *this* grace, they *stand.* Standing, here, intends firmness, stability, permanence. This is sometimes opposed to condemnation—If Thou, Lord, shouldest mark iniquity, O Lord, who shall *stand?* To which we may answer—No one that appeals to his own obedience; but every one that is found in Christ: for there is no condemnation to them that are in him. For *who* is he that condemneth? It is Christ that died, yea, rather, that is risen again; who is even at the right hand of God, who also maketh intercession for us. Hence, without presumption, they may exclaim,

" Bold shall I *stand* in that great day,
" For who aught to my charge shall lay?
" While, through his blood, absolved I am,
" From sin's tremendous curse and shame!"

Sometimes it is also opposed to defeat. Take to you the whole armor of God—that ye may *stand* in the evil day; and, having done all, may *stand.* And of this, they may be assured; for whatever disproportion there is between them and their enemies, the *worm* Jacob shall thrash the *mountains.* Some warriors have barely overcome; another such victory would have almost ruined them; but a Christian, having vanquished all his adversaries, stands with his feet on their necks; and is ready to engage as many more—Yea, in all these things we are more than conquerors, through him that loved us.

The more privileged any condition is, the more anxieties does it awaken. It is easy, therefore, to imagine what a Christian must feel, if he apprehended any uncertainty as to the state he is in. But that state is as safe as it is blessed. "For I am persuaded, that neither death, nor life, nor angels, nor principalities, nor powers, nor things to come, nor height, nor depth, nor any other creature, shall be able to separate us from the love of God, which is in Christ Jesus our Lord."

" Arise, my soul, my joyful powers,
" And triumph in my God:
" Awake, my voice, and loud proclaim,
" His *glorious* grace abroad.
" He raised me from the deeps of sin,
" The gates of gaping hell;
" And fixed my standing more secure
" Than 'twas before I fell."

JULY 28.—"Let the heart of them rejoice that seek the Lord."—1 Chronicles, xvi, 10.

—AND yet many believe, or pretend to believe, that religion is a joyless thing!

The *heart* has very little, if any, share in other enjoyments. These delights only gratify the appetites, and strike the senses, and charm the imagination. But where is the heart? Even in laughter the *heart* is sorrowful; and the end of that mirth is heaviness. In religion the heart finds relief, repose, satisfaction, joy.

Yes, "the heart of those who are fully assured of their condition; who have already attained, or have far advanced in the divine life." Nay—says the prophet—Let the heart of them rejoice that *seek* the Lord. And there are three reasons for this.

First. Because it is an evidence of grace. They may draw a conclusion against themselves, and refuse to be comforted; but no man can seek to know, and enjoy, and serve, and resemble God, from mere nature. Actions may not indicate the state of the mind; but desires spring from it. We may be forced to do; but we cannot be compelled to prefer, and to choose.

Secondly. Because their success is sure. This is the case in no other pursuit. In the fields of worldly labor we may spend our strength for nought, and in vain. A rival may bear off from us a prize, which we have long been chasing, and at the very moment we are seizing it. The cup of enjoyment, filled with eager hope, is often dashed to the ground from the very lip that touches it. But their heart *shall* live that seek God. He that goeth forth and weepeth, bearing precious seed, shall *doubtless* return again with rejoicing, bringing his sheaves with him. Blessed are they that do hunger and thirst after righteousness, for they shall be filled. Is their unfaithfulness with God? Did he ever say to the seed of Jacob, Seek ye me in vain!

Thirdly. Because, when they *have* found, their aim and their wish in seeking are fully answered. All they can desire is treasured up in Him: and they that seek the Lord, shall not want *any* good thing. As to success in other cases, the wise man tells us, All is vanity and vexation of spirit—vexation, if we miss; and vanity, if we gain. To one of these alternatives we are inevitably subjected. We must be disappointed, either in acquiring them—and this is often the case, or in possessing them—and this is always the case.

"In vain we seek a heav'n below the sky;
"The world has false, but flattering charms:
"Its distant joys show big in our esteem,
"But lessen still, as they draw near the eye:
"In our embrace the visions die,
"And when we grasp the airy forms,
"We lose the pleasing dream."

But while every thing earthly falls short of hope, it is not possible to form an expectation adequate to the riches of the glory of the inheritance in the saints. What is it to have God himself for our portion and exceeding joy! To be blessed with all spiritual blessings in heavenly places in Christ! To realize a happiness that solitude increases, that trouble improves, that death perfects! As it is written, Eye hath not seen, nor ear heard, nor have entered into the heart of man the things which God hath prepared for them that love him.

While thus the heart of them that seek him should rejoice, the heart of others should be induced to seek him. At present he is not far from any one of you. He is even inviting you to seek him. But, yet a little while, and if you seek him, it will be too late. Therefore, seek ye the Lord while he may be found; and call ye upon him while he is near.

JULY 29.—" To whom he showed himself alive after his passion."—Acts, i, 3.

How much will eternity reveal to our astonished minds ! and in reference to a thousand things, we may safely follow the advice of the Poet—

" Wait the great teacher, Death ; and God adore."

The Scripture is given to establish our faith, and comfort our hearts, and sanctify our lives ; but not to amuse us, and to gratify our curiosity. Our Savior rose from the dead, and ascended into heaven : but between these events there elapsed a considerable portion of time. During these intervening weeks, where was he ? And how employed ? One thing only we know—that he frequently showed himself to his disciples. The fact cannot be questioned.

But what purposes were these intermediate appearances intended to answer ? The Lord does not always give an account of any of his matters ; and we ought to be peculiarly cautious in assigning reasons for *his* conduct, who says, " My ways are not your ways, and my thoughts are not your thoughts." We cannot however, err in remarking,

—That they were the accomplishment of his word. He had said, " Ye now have sorrow ; but I will see you again, and your hearts shall rejoice ; and your joy no man taketh from you." " I will not leave you comfortless, I will come to you. Yet a little while, and the world seeth me no more ; but ye see me." Now though these declarations extend to his final coming to judgment, and his advent in the gifts and graces of the Holy Ghost ; yet they more immediately ensure his manifestation of himself between his resurrection and his glory. And if the disciples understood it not at the time, the meaning would be explained by the verification. And they would see how well they might in every other case rely upon his promise.

—They were also to convince them how fully he had forgiven them, and thus gain the confidence of their hearts. For they had behaved very unworthily. After all he had done for them, and their own professions of attachment, when the hour of trial came, they all forsook him and fled. How much he felt their defection, we learn from his complaint, " I looked for some to take pity, and there was none ; and for comforters, and I found none." And their own consciences upbraided and condemned them for their vileness. And therefore had he gone away to heaven, and they had not seen him, they would have feared his resentment and displeasure—but he appeared to them again and again ; and always with kindness in his looks, and peace on his lips ; and at last, laying his hands on them, he was taken up to heaven in the very act of blessing them—thus telling them that he had the same heart as ever, and was more than pacified toward them after all that they had done.

—They were also to evince the certainty of his resurrection. The importance of this event rendered it necessary that it should be placed beyond the possibility of all reasonable doubt. The disciples were not eagerly credulous of the fact, but slow of heart to believe : and their diffidence has been overruled to confirm our faith. For they required and obtained every kind and degree of proof. And these deponents were many. And were eye and ear witnesses. And even handled the word of Life. And did eat and drink with him. And for a length of time. And in cases of a most peculiar nature. *They* could not be mistaken; and *we* cannot be deceived. He is risen indeed, and therefore he is the Son of God; and we are not in our sins, and the dead in Christ are not perished; and because he lives we shall live also.

—They were also to impart information on subjects not touched, or only hinted at before: because the disciples were not able to bear them; and the proper hour was not yet come. And therefore the sacred historian says, that he not only showed himself alive after his passion, by many infallible proofs, being seen of them forty days, but also *spake* to them of things pertaining to the kingdom of God. And this led them to think so differently of this kingdom from what they had done before, and to wait by prayer for its coming in righteousness, peace, and joy in the Holy Ghost.

But when he said, I am no more in this world; and, also, Lo! I am with you always, even unto the end of the world: and when he said, "He that hath my commandments, and keepeth them, he it is that loveth me; and he that loveth me shall be loved of my Father, and I will love him, and will manifest myself to him." Surely he intended a manifestation beyond his appearance, between his grave and his glory. And this we ourselves may hope to claim. But how is it that he will manifest himself unto us, and not unto the world? We disclaim all pretensions to personal manifestations. Some have contended for these; and, like Colonel Gardiner, have believed that they corporally saw him. But surely this was mistaking a lively impression on the mind for a reality. The case speaks for itself. Being embodied, he *could* render himself visible; but then it would be a true representation; we should see him as he *is*. And accordingly Saul saw him, when he appeared to him in his way to Damascus, with a body glorious above the brightness of the sun. But these good people always see him as he is not—they always see him bleeding on the cross—but he is not there—he dieth no more, death hath no more dominion over him. We need no sensible appearance.

—But there is a spiritual manifestation absolutely necessary Paul experienced this, or the outward vision would have been of little avail: "It pleased God," says he, "to reveal his Son in me." And our Savior himself said, He that seeth the Son, and believeth on him, hath everlasting life. It is a perception, by faith, of his glory, so as to induce us to love him, and trust in him, and follow him.

—There are also special manifestations of himself (we mean as to clearness and enjoyment) occasionally experienced by his people; and which excite them to exclaim, "This is none other but the House of God, and this is the Gate of Heaven." These are not their food, but cordials. They are regulated by their condition and exigencies. But though they are limited, as to number and degree, they are most desirable and valuable. They make us better acquainted with heaven, than all the descriptions in the world. And they make us long after a state—in which his servants shall serve Him; and they shall see his face—"And so shall they be for ever with the Lord."

JULY 30.—"This is now the third time that Jesus showed himself to his disciples after that he was risen from the dead."—John, xxi, 14.

NOT the third time in succession—for he had appeared before this to the women, and to Cephas, and to James, and to the two disciples going to Emmaus. But third time in kind; *i. e.*, the third time when the disciples were together.

—"And on this wise showed he himself." The *place* was, "the sea of Tiberias," called, also, the lake of Gennesserat, and the lake of Galilee. We should like to visit this sea, whose surface and whose shores so often felt the presence, and witnessed the miracles of the Son of God.

—The favored *party* were "Simon Peter, and Thomas, called Didymus"—he had lost much by his absence before, but now he keeps close to his brethren—"and Nathanael, of Cana in Galilee" —we thought well of him from the beginning; for though at first he had some infirmities, he was open to conviction, and loved retirement; and he who saw him under the fig-tree assured him that he should see greater things than these—"and the sons of Zebedee," John and James—"and two other of his disciples"—who are not named. But it may be asked, How came the disciples here, seeing when he rose from the dead they were (unless, perhaps, Nathanael) at Jerusalem? The Savior had said, "The hour cometh, and now is, when ye shall be scattered every one to his own;" and it is said, "Then the disciples went away again unto their own home." This was the effect of fear. But though fear made them flee, yet their repairing down into Galilee was enjoined them by the angel who appeared to Mary Magdalene and the other Mary. And Jesus himself had said, before his death, "After I am risen, I will go before you into Galilee." They believed his word; and obeyed, and he was faithful that had promised.

—But how did he find them *engaged?* "Simon Peter," who had a house of his own, and perhaps had retained the implements of his business, "saith unto them, I go a fishing. They say unto him, We also go with thee." This was not, as some imagine, blamable; as if they ought to have remained fasting and praying; or as if this exertion was the effect of their despondency, with regard to his appearance, and his care to provide for them. We are persuaded they acted commendably. It showed their humility—that, though advanced, they were not elated, nor ashamed of their former engagement; and their wish—not to be burdensome to any, if they could supply their own wants, and with quietness work, and eat their own bread; and also their diligence— in redeeming their time, and not waiting for him in idleness. And he appeared to them, though not engaged in a religious exercise, but in a secular, honest calling; as the angels had appeared to the shepherds, when keeping their flocks by night. And if he came to any of us, by death, how much better would it be for him to find us active, in fulfilling the duties of a useful station, than telling our beads, or kneeling before a skull, or a crucifix, in a cell! When Elijah was consciously waiting for the chariot that was to carry him to heaven, what did he? Retire to fast and pray? No; but he continued talking with his pupil and successor, for his improvement—determined to be useful to the last, and to live as long as he breathed. And blessed is that servant, whom his Lord, when he cometh, shall find so doing.

—But "that night they caught nothing." Though, in an ordinary way, the hand of the diligent maketh rich, yet this rule has its exceptions; and these should be sufficient to teach us that the blessing of the Lord, *it* maketh rich; and that, except the Lord build the house, they labor in vain that build it. The race is not always to the swift, nor the battle to the strong. Men, and even good men, may for a while be baffled in their efforts—to teach them the lesson of dependence upon Providence; and to keep them, when success cometh, from sacrificing to their own net, and burning incense to their own drag, as if by these their portion had been made plenteous.

—He loves to astonish, as well as relieve his people: he therefore often delays his appearance, till our hopelessness has prepared us for the display of his glory to the greatest advantage. Weeping may endure for a night; but joy cometh in the morning. "When the morning was come, Jesus stood on the shore." But they knew not that it was Jesus—supposing him to be some common person, waiting their coming ashore, to purchase what they had caught. And this was the meaning of the question, "Children, have ye any meat?" *i. e.* Have you succeeded in fishing? And have you any provision to dispose of? Upon their answering No, he showed his omniscience. He saw where a shoal was approaching the boat, and ordered them to cast the net on the right side of the ship—assuring them that they should find. They did so—and who ever lost by obeying? So signal was their success, that they were not able to draw the net for the multitude of fishes!

—Thus good men sometimes see their affairs, after many a fruitless struggle, taking a favorable turn, and every thing succeeding beyond their expectation. At evening tide it shall be light. "It is vain for you to rise up early, to sit up late, to eat the bread of sorrows: for so he giveth his beloved sleep." We shall look at this narrative again.

JULY 31.—"And on this wise showed he himself."—John, xxi, 1.

—WE have traced this appearance down to the moment when the disciples ascertained who he was. John recognized him first, reminded, as it would appear, by a former miracle of the same kind, and on the performance of which Peter had exclaimed, Depart from me, for I am a sinful man, O Lord. Yet Peter was not at present struck with the recollection himself. But no sooner does John say to him, "It is the Lord," than the ship can hold him no longer; but, girding himself with his fisher's coat, he plunges into the sea to reach him! What rashness! What zeal! How perfectly in character does this man always appear! He was fervent, but acted by feeling rather than reflection. He had a warm heart. The Lord had lately turned and looked upon him in the judgment hall, and he went out and wept bitterly. He had had much forgiven, and he loved much. The Savior had more than pardoned his late sad conduct; and had sent a message to him distinctly: "Go, tell my disciples, and Peter!" And how could he love Him enough? And love is strong as death. Many waters cannot quench love, neither can the floods drown it.

—The rest of the disciples followed slowly, but surely, dragging the net. Had all done like Peter, the fish had been abandoned, and the vessel left to be drifted and injured. While we admire some, we must not condemn others. The dispositions and the duties of men are various; and while some perform splendid ac tions, and excite notice, others go ploddingly on in the sober discharge of their common calling—but they also have the testimony that they please God.

—What did they find when they came to land? "A fire of coals, and fish laid thereon, and bread." This was to show that he cared for them; that they should be furnished, not only with grace sufficient for them, but with food convenient for them; and that verily they should be fed. He had reminded them of this on a former occasion. When he sent them forth on their missionary excursion unprovided, they had misgivings how they were to be supplied—though they were ashamed to make known their fears. But he who employed them was bound to maintain them—and when they returned, he said, "When I sent you forth without purse and scrip, lacked ye any thing? And they said, Nothing." "O fear the Lord, all ye his saints; for there is no want to them that fear him! The young lions may lack, and suffer hunger; but they that seek the Lord shall not want for any good thing." You serve a kind Master, and the world is his, and the fullness thereof—Jehovah-jireh! But we read, "Thou shalt eat the labor of thine hand; and nothing has such a peculiar relish as what is gained by the blessing of God upon our own endeavors. He therefore also said unto them, "Bring of the fish which ye have now caught. Simon Peter went up, and drew the net to land full of great fishes, a hundred and fifty and three; and for all there were so many, yet was not the net broken." And thus, while they must have marvelled and adored at what was nothing less than a miracle, they were not only supplied for their immediate use, but the sale of the capture would pay their expenses back to Jerusalem, and while waiting there for the promise of the Father.

—Filled with reverence and awe, they seemed reserved, and disposed to keep back. He therefore invited them; "*Come* and dine. And none of his disciples durst ask him, Who art thou? knowing that it was the Lord." But still keeping back, "Jesus then *cometh*" to them, "and taketh bread, and giveth them, and fish likewise." The meat was ordinary, and coarsely dressed; but it was wholesome, and the appetite of labor made it welcome. We do not live to eat, but eat to live. Nature wants little, and grace less. Luther often dined upon a herring, and Junius on an egg. If it be, as is said, beneath a philosopher to be nice and finical in his food, how much more is it so in a Christian! in a minister! Jesus censured Martha, and commended Mary. The table he spreads for us is frugal and simple. It is the world, the flesh, the devil; disease and death bring in the rest. No mention is made of his blessing the repast, but there is no doubt but he did. It was his constant usage—to teach us to be religious in our common actions; and that man liveth, not by bread alone, but by every word that proceedeth out of the mouth of God.

But did he actually partake of the provision himself? What says Peter? "He showed him openly; not to all the people, but unto witnesses chosen before of God, even to us who did eat and drink *with him* after he arose from the dead." Did he rise with the same body that died? "Behold," said he, "my hands and my feet, and see that it is I myself. Handle me and see; a spirit hath not flesh and bones, as ye see me have." Did his body undergo any change before his ascension? Will things in a future state be possible that are not necessary? We know but in part. And the sacred writers prophesy but in part.

—But "Blessed is he that shall eat bread in the kingdom of God." Let me be one of the number to whom he shall say, "Ye are they which have continued with me in my temptations. And I appoint unto you a kingdom, as my Father hath appointed unto me; that ye may eat and drink at my table in my kingdom, and sit on thrones, judging the twelve tribes of Israel."

AUGUST 1.—"So when they had dined"—John, xxi, 18.

—THEY did not, we presume, continue long at table. Table, indeed, they had none. The place was the sea-side The viands bread and fish. The fare dressed and served coarsely. Yet part of it was miraculously provided before they landed; and part of it supplied from the wonderful capture they had just made. Here were seven apostles—and the Lord of angels. Who, then, would not have been at the homely meal? who, having any piety, or any wisdom, would not have preferred the entertainment—thus dignified—however humble—to the sumptuous feast of Belshazzar, or Ahasuerus? Where there is much provision for the flesh, there is little repast for the mind. And this is commonly found *after* the meal. It has often been lamented that the best part of society should be expected to withdraw as soon as dinner is ended; but females may be assured, that with few exceptions, they sustain no loss by their removal.

—But here, when they had dined, discourse followed, which has been deemed worthy the page of inspiration, and was written for our learning and admonition. It commenced with an inquiry. "Jesus saith to Simon Peter, Simon, son of Jonas, lovest thou me more than these? He saith unto him, Yea, Lord; thou knowest that I love thee. He saith unto him, Feed my lambs. He saith to him again, the second time, Simon, son of Jonas, lovest thou me? He saith unto him, Yea, Lord; thou knowest that I love thee. He saith unto him, Feed my sheep. He saith unto him the third time, Simon, son of Jonas, lovest thou me? Peter was grieved because he said to him the third time, Lovest thou me? And he said unto him, Lord thou knowest all things; thou knowest that I love thee. Jesus said unto him, Feed my sheep."

The question was put to Peter because of his late conduct. Instead, therefore, of showing any pre-eminence in him, it implied his fall, and tended to his humiliation. This, and this alone, was the reason why our Lord thus freely, yet tenderly, addressed *him* in the presence of his brethren. It was necessary both for *his* sake, and for *their* sakes.

The question was first put comparatively—Lovest thou me *more than these?* There is something ambiguous and equivocal in the expression. Did our Lord, by *these*, refer to the fish, the nets, the boat, his present occupation and profit? Doddridge says this is a forced and frigid sense. But this does not appear. By this calling, Peter had gained his subsistence—he might naturally be attached to it—and feel a degree of reluctance at leaving it, without any other means of support in view—and, as our Lord would be freely served, he inquires whether Peter was willing to resign all —and go a-fishing no more—and be wholly engaged in his service. Or did he point to the rest of the disciples when he said, Lovest thou me more than *these?—i. e.* more than these thy brethren love me? To this, Whitby objects; because it would be impossible for Peter to answer such an inquiry, as he could not know the hearts of others, and compare them with his own. But the question refers not to Peter's *knowledge*, but to his *opinion*. He had already expressed a degree of self-preference, as well as self-confidence, when he said, "Though all should be offended because of thee, yet will I never be offended"—and he had now *done* more than the other disciples, in swimming to shore, to reach him first. "Am I, then," says Jesus, "to suppose that thou lovest me more than *these?*" Peter's reply shows his improvement: "I have done with judging others—and I say nothing of the *degree* of my love—but thou knowest the *reality*."

—It was *thrice* renewed. Thrice is used as a kind of perfect number. In Peter's vision, the thing was done thrice, to render it the more observable. There is little doubt, however, that our Savior alluded to the repetition of his offence—and the forewarning he had received: "Before the cock crow twice, thou shalt deny me *thrice*."

—Peter, when asked the question the third time, was *grieved*. This grief was not anger at the Savior's conduct; but pain to think that he had rendered his love to so dear a Master suspicious; and fear also—as he knew he never spoke in vain—that there was a cause for this additional inquiry, and that it intimated an apprehension of some fresh peril. This sensibility showed a good frame of mind.

—To *all* the inquiries he replies, without a moment's hesitation, and addresses himself, in *each* instance, to the Savior's own knowledge, with an additional force in the *last* appeal: "Lord, thou knowest all things: thou knowest that I love thee. I do not say I shall never yield to temptation again—Lord preserve me! And I wonder not that those who can only judge from the outward appearance, think unfavorably of me, after all that I have done. But thou seest the heart." We ought to stand clear with men; but it is a peculiar satisfaction, when we are misjudged of our fellow-creatures, to know that our witness is in heaven, and our record is on high.

—After every answer, our Lord commands him to feed his lambs, and his sheep. Here, again, a desperate cause wants to find a proof of Peter's supremacy. But he is not told to lord it over all the other *shepherds*, but to do the work of a *pastor* himself—the very same thing which Peter, too, enjoins upon others: "Feed the flock of God that is among you." Yea, instead of his being exalted above his brethren, he is again reproved and abased. *They* had not forfeited their charge; but he had; and it was necessary to renew it. And therefore, now he is re-converted, he is re-commissioned. If a servant had offended and forfeited his place, it would not be enough for the master to say, I forgive thee, but I can no more trust thee or employ thee. Nothing would be deemed a full restoration, but re-employment.

Two things may be observed here. First, the difference there is among the Lord's people. There are not only sheep, but lambs. These mean new converts and weak believers. These are not to be disregarded. *He* does not despise the day of small things, and he tells those who are strong to bear the infirmities of the weak. Secondly, see what the Lord requires, as the principle of his service. "If you love me, Peter, feed my lambs, feed my sheep—I wish you to do nothing for me, unless you do it from love. This alone will render your work your delight, and carry you through all its difficulties. Love is strong as death." And while he requires the love as the principle of the service, he requires the service as the proof of the love. "You cannot show your love to me personally; show it relatively. I have a cause—endeavor to promote it. I have followers—aid them: and inasmuch as ye do it unto one of the least of these my brethren, ye shall do it unto me."

Ah! this love, O my soul, is the grand thing! Without it, whatever be my religious pretensions, I am nothing. Let me put my name in the place of Peter's, and suppose the Lord Jesus asking me this question, Dost *thou* love me?

"Lord, it is my chief complaint,
"That my love is weak and faint;
"Yet I love thee, and adore;
"O for grace to love thee more!"

August 2.—"Verily, verily, I say unto thee, When thou wast young thou girdedst thyself, and walkedst whither thou wouldest; but when thou shalt be old, thou shalt stretch forth thine hands, and another shall gird thee and carry thee whither thou wouldest not. This spake he, signifying by what death he should glorify God.—John, xxi, 18, 19.

—This was another part of his discourse, "when they had dined." He had enjoined Peter his doing work, and now he appoints him his suffering work. In such a world as this, doing well and bearing ill are commonly connected; in the first days of Christianity they were inseparable.

The representation may be applied to the difference there is between youth and age. The glory of young men is their strength. They can gird themselves, and go with ease, and speed whither they would. And let them use well their powers and opportunities. Let them be active and useful, and prepared for the future. Other days will come, and when they shall be old, they shall stretch forth their hands, and another shall gird them, and carry them whither they would not. They will be helpless and dependent. People long for age—but what is it, but longing for days in which we have no pleasure; when we shall be dim-sighted, and hard of hearing, and tremblings will come upon us; and the grasshopper will be a burden, and desire fail! These are the effects of the state--if by reason of strength our years are three-score and ten, yet is our strength labor and sorrow. Let us secure succor against such a period. It is said, an old man has no friend but his money. But if we are kind, and live not to ourselves, we shall not want those who will rock the cradle of our age. And, above all, God will be our comfort and strength; and bear and carry us; and gently take us to himself; where our youth shall be renewed like the eagle's, and mortality swallowed up of life.

But our Lord, we are assured, designed to intimate that, after Peter had served him as an apostle, he was to honor him as a martyr, "signifying by what death he should glorify God." Thus,

First. Our Lord foresaw Peter's sufferings, and the manner in which he was to finish his course. And he foresees all that shall befall each of us. We know not what a day may bring forth. But nothing is left to chance. No event will turn up that is new to him, and for which he has not provided.

Secondly. Peter was not to die till he should be old. Very good and useful men have been removed in the midst of life—and this is one of the most mysterious dispensations of providence. But this is not always the case. Religion conduces to health and longevity. Many of God's most eminent servants have "filled their days," and come to the grave in a good old age, like a shock of corn fully ripe, in its season. And the hoary head is a crown of glory, when it is found in the way of righteousness. Such a man is not only a kind of physical wonder—that he should have been preserved so long with such a feeble frame, and exposed to so many outward dangers—but a moral wonder, that, with such a heart, and in such a world, he should have held on his way, and kept his garments clean, and been without offence. He is a monument to the glory of divine grace.

Thirdly. He was to die by crucifixion. This is the meaning of his stretching forth his hands, and being girded and carried whither he would not"—*i. e.* his arms would be extended on a cross, and he would be bound, to be led to a death of violence, not agreeable to his feelings, and at which nature would revolt. For religion does not divest us of humanity; an aversion to pain is not inconsistent with submission to the will of God; we may love the result of death, and shudder at the passage. Paul wished not to be unclothed, but clothed upon; and Jesus himself, with strong cryings and tears, said, Father, if it be possible, let this cup pass from me. Peter would, and would not; there was nature in him, as well as grace. And while the spirit would be willing, the flesh would be weak. We see this related of some of the martyrs. Latimer, in one of his letters in prison, says to his friend, "Oh! pray for me! I sometimes shudder, and could creep into a mouse-hole; and then the Lord visits me again with his comforts; and thus, by his coming and going, shows me my infirmity." Ridley, at the stake, said to the smith that was driving in the staple, "Knock it in hard, my good fellow, for the flesh may have its freaks." And when they were leading Rawlins along to the flames, chancing to see his wife and children among the crowd, he burst into a flood of tears; and, striking his breast, he exclaimed, "Ah! flesh, you would have your way; but I tell thee, by the grace of God, thou shalt not gain the victory."

Lastly. His death was to issue in divine glory. Persecution has always been overruled to advance the cause it aimed to destroy. The wrath of man has praised God. The blood of the martyrs has been the seed of the churches. The death of such men has been honorable to the truth and grace of the Gospel. It has awakened attention, and induced inquiry; and, by displaying the temper and supports of the sufferers, such impressions have been made upon the spectators, that, before the ashes were extinguished, others were ready to be baptized for the dead.

We are not martyrs. But we are often called to suffer; and we may glorify God in the fires. There is only one way into the world; but there are many ways out. By which of these we are to pass we know not. But we may glorify God by the death we shall die—if we are enabled to exercise faith, patience, and penitence; if the joy of the Lord is our strength; and we can, from experience, recommend his service.

For this, we should be concerned. And, but for this, we presume many would desire to die "softly, suddenly, and alone." Yet what they should choose, they wot not. They, therefore, leave all with their heavenly Father—only praying, that Christ may be magnified in their body, whether it be by life or by death.

August 3.—"And when he had spoken this, he saith unto him, Follow me. Then Peter, turning about, seeth the disciple whom Jesus loved, following, which also leaned on his breast at supper, and said, Lord, which is he that betrayeth thee? Peter seeing him, saith to Jesus, Lord, and what shall this man do? Jesus saith unto him, If I will that he tarry till I come, what is that to thee? Follow thou me.—John, xxi, 19—22.

—This is another part of the discourse when they had dined. It is the reproof of Peter, who, though recovered from his fall, and recommissioned to his office, was not faultless. Who can understand his errors?

—The case was this. As soon as our Lord had tried Peter's love, and predicted his death, he said unto him, "Follow me." This is to be taken literally: for though it might be intended as a symbol, yet he now arose from his seat, and, walking away from the company, he told Peter to come after him—probably wishing to have some communication with him apart. Peter obeyed. But John, seeing this, and fearing that our Lord was departing, and would take Peter along with him, could not remain where he was—and so he followed them, silent and anxious, and perhaps weeping. Peter turning around, sees him; and asks, "Lord, and what shall this man do?" It is probable this arose partly from an affectionate concern for his companion; and, considering the peculiar friendship there was between them, we might have considered the question as excusable, if not even laudable.

But we are sure it was wrong in the motive. Peter, instead of being satisfied with a knowledge of his own duty and destiny, and praying to be able to perform the one, and endure the other, wishes to pry into John's future circumstances—to know what was to become of him; whether he also should suffer; and what death he should die. This, in the view of him who reproved not according to the hearing of the ear, involved it in an improper curiosity—a principle, when indulged always the most unprofitable in itself, and often the most rude in its exercise, and injurious in its effects. Our Lord always discouraged it; and therefore he here rebukes Peter in these memorable words—"If I will that he tarry till I come, what is that to thee? Follow thou me—" as I have commanded thee. How many things engage our time and attention, which do not concern us! How often do we turn from what is plain and important; and perplex and amuse ourselves with what is too distant to reach; too deep for us to fathom; too complicated for us to unravel; or too trifling to merit regard! When poring over the future state of the heathen, and the destiny of idiots, and the decrees of God, and the union of forknowledge and free agency, and the fulfilment of prophecy, is not the Savior asking, "What is that to thee? Follow thou me!" "The secret things belong unto the Lord our God; but those things which are revealed belong unto us, and to our children for ever, that we may do all the words of this Law."

Our present knowledge is proportioned to our present state. More information upon certain subjects would now injure, rather than improve, by multiplying our diversions and drawing us more off from the one thing needful. We are now in a state of action and preparation. Let us leave the knowledge that is too wonderful for us. A day-laborer will gain more of it in a moment after he enters heaven, than any philosopher or divine can acquire by the toil of a whole life. Let us wait the great teacher, Death, and God adore—Shall not the Judge of all the earth do right!

But what have we to *do?* FOLLOW THOU ME. Lord help me to follow thee, as thy disciple and thy servant—immediately, without delay—freely, without constraint—fully, without reserve—and constantly, without change, or—a shadow of turning!

AUGUST 4.—"Then went this saying abroad among the brethren, that that disciple should not die; yet Jesus said not unto him, He shall not die; but if I will that he tarry till I come, what is that to thee?"—John, xxi, 23.

WHAT did he mean by his coming to John? It may be understood three ways.

—Of his coming by a natural death; and he was the only apostle who did not suffer a violent end.

—Of his coming to destroy Jerusalem; and he survived that event.

—Of his coming at the last day; in which case he answers Peter, by the supposition of miracle, "What if I choose that he should continue on earth till I come to judge the world?" In this sense it was taken.

But observe how it was mis-reported. Jesus only supposed a case, and it was turned into an assertion. He only said, what *if* I will that he tarry till I come; and it was circulated that he *should* so tarry—and the saying went abroad among the brethren that he should not die. Who has not heard the absurd story of the wandering Jew? Whether any now believe such a delusion, we know not; but we see what influence the notion had in the early ages. Beza mentions an imposter in his time, at Paris, who gave out that he was the deathless John, and was burnt at Toulouse.

—But see how ready people are to credit things strange and wonderful—O that they were equally ready to receive the witness of God!

How many mistakes have arisen from deviating by little and little from the language of revelation. Many errors might be prevented, and many ratified, if we could bring the parties to the very words the Holy Ghost useth. Let us distinguish between divine truth, and men's explanations of it. Let us not take up with the statements of Calvin, or Arminius, or any other reporter, while we can go to the Scripture itself. "To the Law and to the testimony: if they speak not according to his word, it is because there is no light in them."

But let us make a moral use of this misrepresentation, and learn the importance of accuracy in our statements. It is owing to the neglect of this that there is so much *circumstantial falsehood:* we refer to the relations of facts, true in substance, but false in circumstances. Some seldom or never apprehend things distinctly; and how can they report them accurately! Some have memories that rarely retain perfectly what they hear. Some are careless, and mind not morally what they say. Some are full of eagerness and feeling: and love to excite—and for this purpose they have to enlarge and enhance. From one cause or another, many who would shrink back from a direct lie, occasion deception by those omissions or additions which can give an erroneous turn or effect to the case spoken of. By this means what aid is given to slander, and what injury is often done to character, where there is no risk on the one side, and no redress on the other!

Look at the text, and see what consequences may result from the substitution of a *shall*, for an *if;* and always make conscience of your speech. Distinguish things that differ. What you know as probable, state as probable; and state as certain, only what you know to be certain. As a good remedy for this, and every other evil of the tongue—Let us be swift to hear, but slow to speak—Let us remember, that in the multitude of words, there wanteth not sin—Let us believe, that by our words we are to be justified or condemned—Let us keep our hearts with all diligence; for out of them are the issues of life—and let us pray—Set a watch, O Lord, before my mouth, keep the door of my lips.

August 5.—"Put ye in the sickle for the harvest is ripe."—Joel, iii, 13.

The season renders the language interesting; and we may consider the words, literally, as an address to husbandmen.

The husbandman waiteth for the precious fruits of the earth, and hath long patience for it, until he receive the early and the latter rain. He casts the seed into the ground, where it seems lost. For a while, he sees nothing to reward his labor and expense: for that which he soweth is not quickened except it die. But it soon rises from the dead: and he perceives the blade, gently rising through the earth. Then comes winter. The wind howls over it; the frost bends and binds it; the snow covers and oppresses it—but it weathers all. The spring arrives. The stalk shoots up; and the ear appears, and the full corn in the ear. The crop ripens; and the golden harvest waves its treasures; and calls for the reaper to fill his hand, and he that bindeth sheaves, his bosom. The husbandman may think little or nothing of God—unless he wants fine weather; but it is *He* that worketh all in all: and whatever interventions there may be, *He* is the first cause: "And it shall come to pass in that day, I will hear, saith the Lord, I will hear the heavens, and they shall hear the earth; and the earth shall hear the corn, and the wine, and the oil; and they shall hear Jezreel."

And herein we see the power of God. The spectators wondered when five loaves were multiplied into a sufficiency for more than five thousand consumers. Why are not we struck, when we see the grain in the earth annually increasing thirty, sixty, an hundred fold? It is the commonness of the effect that prevents our astonishment. The only difference in the cases is, that in one instance, the operation is sudden; in the other, it is slow; but this magnifies the agency, instead of detracting from it.

—And here we see the truth of God. When Noah and his family left the Ark, and saw the new world, every appearance of cloud awakened their fears; and God, to tranquilize them, said, "I will not again smite any more every thing living, as I have done. While the earth remaineth, seed time and harvest, and cold and heat, and summer and winter, and day and night, shall not cease." And every time the sickle is put in, he tells us that he is a faithful God, and that we may always rely upon his word.

—Here we behold his goodness. For whom does he thus constantly and plenteously provide; but an unworthy, guilty, ungrateful world; who will overlook his kindness and abuse his benefits, and turn his gifts into weapons of rebellion against him! Were he to deal with them after their desert, or reward them according to their iniquities, the heavens over us would be brass, and the earth, iron; the grain would perish in wetness, or be burnt up with drought; and we should have cleanness of teeth in all our dwellings; and while the children cried for bread, the mother would have none to give them.

—Here we also trace the wisdom of God. For though all things are of God, he does not encourage sloth. Our avidity is as necessary as our dependence. Though there is a part we cannot do, there is a part we can do—and if this be neglected, God will do nothing. We cannot furnish the soil; but we must manure it. We cannot produce the seed; but we must sow it. We cannot ripen the field; but we must reap it. "What Thou givest them, that they gather."

Let us be thankful that another of these pleasing and instructive periods has arrived. And while we see the valleys standing thick with corn, and hear the little hills rejoicing on every side; let us pray for the appointed weeks of harvest.

—And remembering another, and an infinitely more important opportunity, may we give all diligence, while it continues to secure its blessings; lest, in the anguish of disappointment, and the remorse of despair, we are forced to exclaim; "The harvest is past, the summer is ended, and we are not SAVED." "Behold now is the accepted time; behold now is the day of salvation." Put ye in the sickle; for the harvest is ripe.

AUGUST 6.—"**Put ye in the sickle; for the harvest is ripe.**"—**Joel, iii, 13.**

WE have taken these words literally; let us now view them metaphorically. We have heard them addressed to the husbandman; let us now consider them as addressed—to spiritual instructors—to public judgments—to the messengers of death—to the angels of God at the last day—Put ye in the sickle; for the harvest is ripe.

First, as addressed by God to the ministers of his word. That we are allowed such an application, is obvious. Our Lord said, "The harvest is truly plenteous, but the laborers are few; pray ye therefore the Lord of the harvest, that he would send forth laborers into his harvest." By harvest he intends means of usefulness and opportunities; and by laborers, those whose office is to endeavor to make use of them. So again; "Say not ye, There are yet four months and then cometh harvest; Behold, I say unto you, Lift up your eyes, and look on the fields; for they are white already to harvest." Here he refers to the season of doing good to the Samaritans, which he was now improving; for, in consequence of the testimony of the woman, many of them were eager to hear, and were coming over the plain. The case is, when the grain is ripe, if it be not gathered in, it is liable to perish. The season for saving it is short and uncertain. Men, therefore, forego care, and endure fatigue to secure it. But what is the safety of the grain, to the salvation of souls! How many are destroying, for lack of knowledge! But the period is favorable for informing them. We have religious freedom; and our exertions are unimpeded. None makes us afraid. We have the Scriptures in full circulation. The rising generation are taught to read. Religious parties excite and emulate each other. Prejudices are wearing away. Persons are willing to hear. And not preachers only, but parents, masters, neighbors, Christians at large—all in doing good, have the finest opportunities, if they will seize them; and the loudest calls, if they will obey them—But the space for all this, will not, cannot continue—Therefore, "whatsoever thy hand findeth to do, do it with thy might; for there is no work, nor device, nor knowledge, nor wisdom, in the grave, whither thou goest."

Secondly, as addressed to public judgments. Thus we are principally to understand the passage before us. The people spoken of were ripe for ruin—God therefore calls for the executioners of his wrath to cut them down. Thus it was with the people of Canaan, when their iniquity was full; and Joshua and his army were the reapers. Thus it was with the Jews themselves: and Nebuchadnezzar was called in to punish them: and afterwards the Romans, to destroy them. Thus it has been with many nations since. And thus it has been with many a community, even in our own times. The work was soon done; for the reapers were the Lord's, and the fields were fully ripe. Are we in danger? We have reason for apprehension, if we estimate our condition by our guilt, and our guilt by our privileges. Let us not be high-minded, but fear. God can never be at a loss for instruments. He can mingle a perverse spirit in the midst of us. He can take wisdom from the prudent, and courage from the brave. Hearts, events, elements, all are his. He has a controversy with us; and, by menacing dispensations, seems to say aloud, Cut it down; why cumbereth it the ground? But these threatenings are mercifully conditional. "At what instant I shall speak concerning a nation, and concerning a kingdom, to pluck up, and to pull down, and to destroy it; if that nation, against whom I have pronounced, turn from their evil, I will repent of the evil that I thought to do unto them." May we hear, and fear, and turn unto the Lord—and he will leave a blessing behind him, that we perish not.

Thirdly, as addressed to the messengers of death—accidents, diseases, whatever can bring us to the grave. This regards us individually. Whatever be the destiny of the nations, we know our own destiny; old or young, rich or poor, it is appointed unto us once to die. This is the way of all the earth. But when are people ripe for this removal hence?

It is certain that sin ripens the transgressor for hell. But *when* he is ripe, it is not easy to decide. The most grossly and openly vicious are not always the most guilty before God. We see a profligate wretch, and deem him ripe for ruin, and wonder *he* is not cut down—when, perhaps, though not immoral, we ourselves are much more criminal in the sight of Him who judgeth righteously. He, perhaps, never had our advantages, and was pressed by severer temptations than we ever were. If asked, therefore, *when* a man is ripe for destruction, we acknowledge we cannot determine. But it must be wise to beware, and to keep from every approximation to such a dreadful state. Surely when a man is insensible under the word, and incorrigible under the rebukes of Providence, and his conscience ceases to reprove, and he can turn divine things into ridicule, he must be, as the apostle says, "nigh unto cursing."

—Holiness ripens the saint for glory. But here, again, *when* he is matured and made meet for it, we cannot ascertain. Actions strike us; but some have few opportunities for exertion, and yet they have much of the life of God in their souls. We should think favorably of a man, in proportion as he was dissatisfied with himself; and esteemed the Lord Jesus; and relied upon him; and was anxious to resemble him; and acknowledged God in all his ways. However, the Lord knoweth them that are his, and them that are not his; and he chooses the most proper time to remove them—the wheat for the barn, and the chaff for the burning. But the end of all things is at hand. And,

Fourthly, God thus addresses his angels at the last day. When this mandate will be given is uncertain. But we are sure of the event, as we are ignorant of the period. And then shall the Son of man come in the clouds of heaven, with power and great glory. Then cometh the end. Then all will be ripe. His purposes will be accomplished. His promisings and threatenings will be verified. Time itself will be no longer. The earth will be cleared of all the produce; and the very fields in which it grew will be destroyed. "The field is the world; the good seed are the children of the kingdom; but the tares the children of the wicked one; the enemy that sowed them is the devil; the harvest is the end of the world; and the reapers are the angels. As, therefore, the tares are gathered and burned in the fire, so shall it be in the end of this world. The Son of man shall send forth his angels, and they shall gather out of his kingdom all things that offend, and them which do iniquity, and shall cast them into a furnace of fire; there shall be wailing and gnashing of teeth. Then shall the righteous shine forth as the sun in the kingdom of their Father. Who hath ears to hear, let him hear." Let him hear *this*. How many things are continually said! And how are we to judge of them? One says, this is excellent; another, this is all-important. But if you would know what is the *real* value of these things, bring them to *the standard*—bring them to the *great day!* How do they abide this trial?

"Wherefore, beloved, seeing that ye look for such things, be diligent, that ye may be found of him in peace, without spot, and blameless." If you say, "All this is far off; and many things must be previously accomplished:" remember you cannot say this of death. There is but a step between you and death. How soon, therefore, may all the prophecies be fulfilled, and the world be at an end with you! And as death leaves you, judgment will find you. Many who once heard the warnings, are now in possession of the facts. Could we ask them—now they have entered the eternal world by death, and are waiting for the judgment to come—Is there one of them that would not bear his testimony to the importance of every sabbath, and every sermon, with which you are favored? Is there one of them that would say, "While I was living, the preacher was too close, and too alarming?" Rather would he not say, "Why was he not more in earnest? And Oh! wretch that I was, to disregard his voice—and come into this place of torment!" It is all over with them. But it is not too late for you. Seek ye the Lord while he may be found and call ye upon him while he is near.

August 7.—" For the kingdom of God is not in word, but in power."—1 Corinthians, iv, 20.

Let us not abuse, but improve this important decision. It may be abused in two instances:

First. When it leads us to undervalue the outward institutions of piety, and the ordinary means of grace. Some would so refine religion as to make it unsuited to human beings. We have bodies, as well as souls, and we are required to glorify God in the one, as well as in the other. Our devotion is indeed nothing unless we " lift up our hearts with our hands ;" bodily exercise need not be excluded in order to our worshipping in spirit and in truth. There may be the form of godliness, without the power; but while we are here, the power cannot be displayed or maintained without the form. Enthusiasts may tell us they never had so much religion as since they have given up what are called its ordinances; for now every day is a sabbath, and every place a temple, and every voice a preacher. But they are not to be believed. Even all the private and practical duties of life are more fully and regularly discharged by those who wait upon God in his appointments. It is a dangerous delusion that leads people to the neglect of those means of grace which God, who knoweth our frame, has enjoined us to use, and to the use of which he hath promised his blessing. In the New Jerusalem, John saw " no temple there;" but the experience of every Christian leads him, while he is here, to love the habitation of God's house, and to acknowledge that it is good for him to be there. The streams that will be needless when we reach the fountain-head, are valuable in the way. Our present aliments will be unnecessary hereafter; but what pretender would be so ethereal as to dispense with them now?

Secondly. When we are heedless of regulating the energy of our religion by the rule of the word. It is desirable to enlist the feelings on the side of truth and excellence. Impulse is useful, and even necessary to exertion and success; but, in proportion to its force, it requires guidance, if not restraint. It is good to be always zealously affected in a good thing; but, without knowledge, zeal may, even in a good cause, carry us astray; so that our good may be evil spoken of, and even produce evil. Something must be allowed for persons wanting in judgment; and for young converts, especially if they have been suddenly awakened. The novelty and the vividness of their views and impressions of eternal things may occasion some mistakes and improprieties in harmonizing religion properly with secular and relative life. But what we excuse we are not to command. If one duty defrauds or kills another, it is a robber or a murderer. The wise man tells us every thing is beautiful in its season: and Paul enjoins us to do every thing decently and in order. But, under the sanction of such an authority as our text, we have known religious servants who have risen above their masters, and lectured and reproved them; we have known men who have left their callings, and rushed into offices for which they were not designed; we have known females, who, instead of being keepers at home, have neglected their husbands and children, to gad about after favorite preachers; we have known orthodox professors, who have broken out into every kind of rudeness and rancor, under a notion of being faithful and valiant for the truth. Disputants have contended earnestly for the faith, with pens dipped in gall, and tongues set on fire of hell: persecutors have killed others to do God service; and the priest with the crucifix, has urged the dragoon not to do the work of the Lord deceitfully, or keep back his sword from shedding blood!

The decision may be improved by applying it in two cases. First, in judging ourselves. And here the leaning should be to the side of severity. Let us be satisfied with nothing short of the real power of religion. Whatever we depend upon, while we are strangers to this, will be more than useless—it will issue in the most dreadful disappointment. It is better to err on the side of caution than of self-security. According to our Savior, the delusion accompanies some to the very door of heaven; they knock, with confidence that they shall be admitted; and are surprised and confounded when they hear from within, I know you not, whence ye are. Do not place your religion in attending on divine ordinances; or in a mere belief of the truth; or in some outward reformation; or in some particular course of duty, to which you may have inducements that render it easy. Search and try your ways. See whether you have given God your whole heart, and can sacrifice every bosom lust. See whether your religion has any thing in it above the efficiency of natural principles—whether it is flesh or spirit—whether you are under the law, or under grace. Examine yourselves. If believers—Does your faith work by love? And do you love in word and in tongue, or in deed and in truth? If penitents—Have you said with Ephraim, what have I any more to do with idols? If worshippers—Do you only draw nigh to Him with the mouth, and honor Him with your lips, while your heart is far from Him? If hearers—Has the Gospel come to you, not in word only, but in power, and in the Holy Ghost, and in much assurance?

Secondly. In judging others. And here the leaning should be to candor. We should beware how we deny this power to a fellow professor, without just evidence. It is always a difficult thing to decide the degree of another's religion. Men differ exceedingly, even in their natural temperament. How sanguine is one! How phlegmatical is another! Some are constitutionally bold and forward; others are equally timid and retreating. Is it to be supposed that all these will show their piety precisely in the same manner? We often ascribe to religious ardor what is the effect of a liveliness and volubility of temper. Hence, when we meet with an individual who is always speaking on religious topics, we are apt to consider him a zealous soul, and to suppose that all his talkativeness results from pious principle. Whereas, it is more than probable, if we followed him through life, we should find him as eager on secular occasions as on religion. On the other hand, when we meet with a man who shrinks from notice, and is backward to speak of divine things, and especially of his own experience, we frequently set him down as one who is not fervent in Spirit, serving the Lord. But may not this man be very much the same in all other cases? And if so, should we not do him injustice by judging of his state in religion by the slowness of his speech, and the hesitation of his temper, and the tardiness of his conduct, which constitute a caret in his whole life? Judge not after the outward appearance, but judge righteous judgment.

Again. If you have reason to conclude that a fellow Christian has this divine reality, let it satisfy you. Love and esteem him, though he differs from your opinions, and walks not with you in the outward order of the Gospel. What is the chaff to the wheat? I love those Scriptures which inspire us with zeal, not to make proselytes to a party, but converts to the Savior—which tend to unite the truly pious to each other, and embattle them against the common foe—which diminish those inferior things that bigots are always magnifying, and attach supreme importance to those that infinitely deserve it. "For the kingdom of God is not in word, but in power." "For the kingdom of God is not meat and drink; but righteousness, and peace, and joy in the Holy Ghost." "For in Christ Jesus neither circumcision availeth any thing, nor uncircumcision, but a new creature. And as many as walk according to this rule, peace be on them, and mercy, upon the Israel of God."

AUGUST 8.—"Lord, teach us to pray."—Luke, xi, 1.

THIS was the language of one of his disciples, as soon as he had heard *him* pray in a certain place. He did not interrupt our Lord in the exercise; but when he had ceased, he said, wishing to resemble him, "Lord, teach us to pray."

It was well in him, not only to attach importance to prayer, and to feel his own ignorance and insufficiency in the performance, but to address one who is always able and willing to hear and help us. None teaches like Him. Four ways he teaches to pray

First. By his word. A form or model—why not both?—was immediately given these disciples—"He said unto them, When ye pray, say, Our Father which art in Heaven, Hallowed be thy name. Thy kingdom come. Thy will be done, as in heaven, so in earth. Give us day by day our daily bread. And forgive us our sins, for we also forgive every one that is indebted to us. And lead us not into temptation: but deliver us from evil." The Scripture at large has many instructions how we are to pray. In one place we are told to pray without ceasing—In another, to come boldly to the throne of Grace—In another, to let our words be few—In another, to ask in faith, nothing wavering—In another, to ask in the name of Jesus—"If ye shall ask any thing in my name, I will do it."

Secondly. By his example. Whoever lives without prayer, he did not. His example has the force of a law; and "he that saith he abideth in him, ought himself also to walk even as he walked. As to place—he prayed in the Wilderness, and he prayed in the Garden. As to time—we read of his rising up early in the morning to pray; and praying in the evening; and continuing all night in prayer. As to observation—he prayed privately, alone, and with his disciples, and in public. As to cases—he prayed when he was baptized; and has taught us to sanctify all ordinances and duties by prayer. When going to send forth his Apostles, he prayed, to teach us to engage in no enterprise, relying on our own wisdom and strength. When he was transfigured, he prayed to teach us how to escape the snares of glory and greatness. With strong crying and tears he made supplication, when he was sore amazed and very heavy, to teach us, if afflicted, to pray. To teach us to love our enemies, when they pierced his hands and feet, he prayed, "Father, forgive them, for they know not what they are doing." And teach us how to finish our course, he dies, praying—"Into Thy hands I commit my spirit."

Thirdly. By his providence. Ah! Christians, this may explain many a dispensation that has made you tremble and grieve. "I will go, and return to my place, till they acknowledge their offence, and seek my face: in their affliction, they will seek me early." That is—I will teach them to pray. What did Absalom, when he wished for an interview with Joab, who, when sent for, refused to come? Go, said he to his servant, and set his corn on fire—and then he will soon come. And so it fell out. And speedily and eagerly approaching him, Why hast thou done this? says Joab. Absalom replies—Not because I designed to injure thee; but I wanted to converse with thee; and my messengers were refused. So when you are lifeless in prayer, and backward in the exercise, and disregard the invitation, "Seek ye my face;" some fiery trial consumes or threatens some of your possessions or comforts; and, alarmed and perplexed, then you anxiously say unto God, "Do not condemn me; show me wherefore Thou contendest with me." You then also want succor and consolation; and therefore pray, "Let thy loving kindness be for my comfort, according to thy word unto thy servant." How many of the prayers of God's people in the Scripture were, both in their reality and excellency too, the offspring of those measures by which the Lord not only chastened, but taught them.

Fourthly. By his Spirit. What means "praying in the Holy Ghost," but praying by his influence? Why is he called "The Spirit of grace and supplication?" Is it not because he brings us upon our knees, and keeps us instant in prayer? If any man have not the Spirit of Christ, he is none of his: and this Spirit awakens the conscience, and makes us sensible of our needy and perishing condition: and shows us the glory, as well as the absolute importance of Divine blessings; and causes us to hunger and thirst after righteousness; and leads us into all the truth connected with our relief; and through the blood of the cross inspiring hope and confidence, enables us to cry, Abba, Father.

Nor is it only in the beginning of a devotional life that this assistance is required: "Likewise the Spirit also helpeth our infirmities," says the Apostle: "for we know not what we should pray for as we ought: but the Spirit itself maketh intercession for us with groanings which cannot be uttered." And where is the

Christian who would not often have given over the exercise, under a sense of his imperfections and weaknesses, but for the hope of the supply of the Spirit of Jesus Christ; and the promise, "If ye then being evil, know how to give good gifts unto your children, how much more shall your heavenly Father give the Holy Spirit to them that ask him?" This has revived him again; and, out of weakness he has been made strong, and delighted himself in the Almighty.

Happy they who, by the great Teacher, are thus taught to pray. You may be ignorant of many things; but you know the way to the throne of grace. You may have little learning; but you can speak the language of Canaan. You may be unnoticed of your fellow creatures; but your fellowship is with the Father, and with his Son Jesus Christ. And a life of prayer will soon be followed by an eternity of praise.

But how awful the condition of those, who never express this desire—Lord, teach us to pray! Can the love or the fear of God dwell in you? Can you dispense with the blessings of salvation? Or do you think that God, who has said, "For all these things will I be inquired of," will deny himself? Well, *another* instructer will soon teach you to pray—a dying hcur—a judgment day—but in vain! "Then shall they call upon me, but I will not answer: they shall seek me early, but they shall not find me."

AUGUST 9.—"Give glory to the Lord your God before he cause darkness." Jeremiah, xiii, 16.

THE removal of the Gospel is darkness. The Gospel will never be removed from the world; but it may be withdrawn from a particular place or people. It is the very thing denounced; "I will remove thy candlestick out of his place, except thou repent." And this has been done. The Jews are an eminent example. The Kingdom of God was taken from them. And when we consider the miracles, the institutions, the privileges, by which they were distinguished, and see how they were all laid waste; well may the apostle say, Behold the severity of God—and if he spared not the natural branches, take heed lest he also spare not thee. Where now are the seven Churches in Asia? Where is the famous Church of Rome, whose faith was spoken of throughout the whole world? At present, you have the inestimable benefit. Be not as the swine, who knows not the value of the pearl, and therefore tramples it under foot. What wonder, if the manna should be taken away, when you despise it as light food? The Scriptures may be continued, and the preaching of the Gospel be removed: and thus the word may be precious, because there is no open vision. What a blessing to see our teachers; and to hear a word behind us, saying, This is the way; walk ye in it! Faith cometh by hearing. And what if the Lord should send a famine in the land—not a famine of bread, nor a thirst for water; but of hearing the words of the Lord—and we should run to and fro to seek the word of the Lord—and shall not find it? Give glory to the Lord your God before he cause darkness.

Impenitence is darkness. A man may be surrounded with food; yet he dies, if he cannot use and digest it, as much as if he were in want of the aliment. The means of grace may remain, and we become incapable of deriving benefit from them. It is an awful fact, that God punishes one sinner by another, and judiciously blinds those who provoke him. Because they like not to retain him in their knowledge, he gives them up to a reprobate mind. Because they receive not the love of the truth, that they may be saved, he sends them strong delusion to believe a lie. They are joined to idols; and he lets them alone. They delight in error; and they find it. They seek objections to the faith once delivered to the saints; and they are overcome by them. They trifle with the Gospel; and, at length, they cannot seriously regard it, or feel any impression under it: and thus is fulfilled the prophecy of Esaias, which saith, By hearing ye shall hear, and shall not understand; and seeing ye shall see, and shall not perceive. Give glory to the Lord your God, before he cause darkness.

—Public calamity is darkness. Was not the Babylonish bondage darkness to the Jews; when their country, the glory of all lands, was desolated; and they carried away captives, and oppressed as slaves, and insulted as a proverb and a by-word? And would not national distress be darkness to us? Some effects of this, we have experienced: but how inconsiderable have they yet been, compared with the sufferings of other countries, or our own deserts! And is there no danger of greater? If God has a controversy with us, it is in vain to argue—we must submit. If he is provoked, and determined to punish, vain is the authority of rulers, the wisdom of statesmen, and the courage of warriors. "But he has a people among us." He has—and he will take care of his own; but he can secure them and destroy others. Or even they themselves may help forward, or even occasion calamity—for no sins offend him like theirs; and they may be chastened of the Lord, that they may not be *condemned* with the world. When the ship sailed from Joppa, there was only one good man on board; and the storm was for his sake; and the sea could only be calmed by his being cast into it. Give glory to the Lord your God before he cause darkness.

The loss of reason is darkness. And how soon may the understanding be eclipsed! How easily may the slender and mysterious basis on which intellect rests, be destroyed! See Nebuchadnezzar, eating grass like an ox. See the Philosopher, moping in drivelling idiocy. Religion can only operate through the medium of thought; and, therefore, while you have your mental powers, employ them—lest darkness come upon you.

—The loss of health is darkness. Is it nothing to be made to possess months of vanity? or to have wearisome nights appointed us? to be chastened, also, with pain upon our bed, and the multitude of our bones with strong pain; so that our life abhorreth bread, and our soul, dainty meat; and our bones, that were not seen, stick out? Yet, on this season, many suspend an attention to the concerns of religion. When thought is broken to pieces, and every avenue to the soul is occupied with the anguish of disease, and the anxieties of recovery; surely sufficient for that day is the evil thereof. Use your health while you have it, lest darkness come upon you. The same applies to age. Then desire fails; the grasshopper is a burden; light and hearing, and memory, and judgment, decline. Remember, therefore, says Solomon, now thy Creator in the days of thy youth, while the evil days come not, nor the years draw nigh, when thou shalt say, I have no pleasure in them.

—Death is darkness. Then you must give up your employments, however interesting; your possessions, however valued; your connexions, however endeared; your religious advantages, however important—and, stripped and silent, retire into the gloom of the grave. This darkness is certain. It cannot be remote. It may be close at hand. There may be but a step between me and death, "before I go whence I shall not return, even to the land of darkness, and the shadow of death: a land of darkness, as darkness itself; and of the shadow of death without any order, and where the light is as darkness."

—Hell is darkness—outer darkness; where there is weeping, and wailing, and gnashing of teeth. The dreadfulness of this state, it is impossible either to describe or imagine. But we know, that it is possible to escape it. We also know that the present is the only opportunity. Behold, *now* is the accepted time; *now* is the day of salvation. Give glory to the Lord your God, before he cause darkness.

Blessed be God, for his long suffering goodness, and his warning mercy. He might justly have spared his words, and come instantly to blows. But he speaks before he strikes: and he threatens, that he may not destroy. May the kind alarm awaken our fear; and may our fear produce flight; and may we flee for refuge to the hope set before us, even Jesus, who delivers from the wrath to come.

August 10.—"He must increase, but I must decrease."—John, iii, 30.

This was spoken of the Redeemer, by his forerunner John. And it is not to be considered as the language of complaint, or sullen acquiescence—as if he would say, "I dislike it; but it is unavoidable. It is my grief; and I must bear it." No. It was as agreeable in his feelings, as it was firm in his belief. And it showed a fine and a noble soul in this man. The spirit that is in us lusteth to envy. We love something distinguishing, and therefore exclusive. We wish to rise, even by the depression of others. It is trying, even to a good man, to withdraw, and see a successor filling his place better than himself, and, as the honors he has worn are transferred to another, to say, "He must increase, but I must decrease." It is not an easy thing to go down well; or for a setting star to exult in a rising sun.

But it was thus with John. He knew his rank, and approved of his place. He was the servant, not the master. The friend, not the bridegroom. The church was not married to him. "He that hath the bride is the bridegroom: but the friend of the bridegroom, which standeth and heareth him, rejoiceth greatly because of the bridegroom's voice. This my joy therefore is fulfilled, He must increase, but I must decrease."

What does he mean by this increase? Not an increase in his temporal condition. As he had been poor, so he was to continue. Many of his professed followers seek great things to themselves: but we may judge of his estimation of them by his choice: for they were all within his reach. But though he had a kingdom, it was not of this world. Nor is it by any kind of earthly distinction and indulgence that he has characterized Christians, or raised their hope. He has nowhere engaged to make them rich in this world's good, but only rich in faith. He has nowhere told them that they shall be free from trouble, but only that in him they shall have peace.

The increase partly regards his personal ministry. Both John and Jesus were preachers and leaders. John's "course" was ending; but Jesus was only commencing his public work. John was going to lose his disciples, and Jesus to gain them, and become a much more famous minister, by miracles, and clearness, and grandeur of doctrine, and the permanency of his success. Indeed, we have no reason to believe that John ever preached after this. The end of his mission was answered. He was a voice; and, having made his proclamation, he was silenced. He was the morning star; and, having ushered the Sun of Righteousness in, he disappeared. He was the forerunner, to introduce the Messiah; but the Messiah was now come and verified, and acknowledged.

But it was the same as saying, Christianity must increase. Christianity was small at first; but it was to resemble the shining light, which begins with the dawn, but becomes perfect day. Or to be like the mustard seed, which, however diminutive, grows the greatest amongst herbs, and becomes a tree, so that the birds of the air come and lodge in the branches thereof. Or the portion of leaven, which, hid in the meal, continues to diffuse itself till the whole be leavened. His doctrine was possessed only by himself for a time. He then communicated the secret to twelve, then to seventy. His followers, after this, were not numerous, and they consisted chiefly of the common people; for it was scornfully asked "Have any of the rulers believed on him?" After various trials, the number of disciples in Jerusalem, previously to the descent of the Spirit, were about one hundred and twenty. Then three thousand were added in one day—and the Lord added to the church daily such as should be saved. Thus mightily grew the word of God, and prevailed. It soon spread beyond the bounds of Judea, and reached the ends of the Roman world—the heralds of thanking God, who always caused them to triumph in Christ, and made manifest the savor of his knowledge by them in every place. How much has his cause done since! And how is it expanding now! But a vaster increase is yet to take place. His glory shall be revealed, and all flesh shall see it together. For now shall he be great to the ends of the earth. Such is the language of the Scripture, and nothing has yet taken place sufficient to fulfill it. It is therefore before us. We know that heathenism, and Mahomedanism, and Popery, shall be destroyed. And we know that the Jews shall look on him whom they have pierced—and if the casting them away was the reconciling of the world, what shall the receiving of them be, but life from the dead?

—And there is no uncertainty here—it *must* be. The mouth of the Lord hath spoken it. His death insures it. He has power over all flesh to accomplish it. Let those who love him, and are laboring to advance his cause, rejoice, and be encouraged—they *cannot* fail. "His name shall endure for ever; his name shall be continued as long as the sun; and men shall be blessed in him; all nations shall call him blessed. Blessed be the Lord God, the God of Israel, who only doth wondrous things. And blessed be his glorious name for ever; and let the whole earth be filled with his glory. Amen, and amen."

AUGUST 11.—"Wherefore, my beloved, as ye have always obeyed, not as in my presence only, but now much more in my absence."—Phil. ii, 12.

"THAT which is unsavory cannot be eaten without salt." And therefore, to render it palatable, we season it. When we are going to reprove a fault, or enforce a duty, we should, as much as possible, commend; for praise opens the mind, and prepares for the reception of rebuke or admonition. This wisdom the apostle here displays. There was nothing in him like flattery; but, to introduce his most solemn charge, that they would work out their own salvation with fear and trembling, he applauds these Philippians for four things.

First. Their *obedience*. Belief, knowledge, profession, talk, every thing is vain without this. The Gospel was made known for the obedience of faith—and these Philippians had "obeyed."

Secondly. The *constancy* of their practice. Lot's wife, at the angel's command, left Sodom; but "she looked back." The Galatians "did run well; but were hindered:" "they began in the Spirit, and ended in the flesh." The goodness of Ephraim and Judah was like a morning cloud, and as the early dew that passeth away—but these Philippians had "always" obeyed.

Thirdly. The *increase* of their diligence and zeal. They had "much more" obeyed. They not only held on their way but waxed stronger and stronger; not only continued, but always abounded in the work of the Lord. Nothing is more desirable or pleasing than to see this progression. It is like the shining light, that shineth more and more unto the perfect day. It is like the springing of the earth, first the blade, then the ear, and after that the full corn in the ear.

Fourthly. The *progress* of their improvement under disadvantages. They had much more obeyed "in his absence" than in his presence When he was no longer with them as a witness to observe, as an example to excite, as a preacher to watch and to warn, to address and to animate. Some attend the word and worship of God from the influence of a friend, or the authority of a father or a master. Jehoash followed the Lord all the days of

Jehoiada, the high priest, who brought him up; but as soon as this eminent servant of God was dead, the young prince became an idolater, and even slew a prophet of the Lord. There are many who regard the eye of man more than the eye of God. It is well when our devotion springs from inward principle, and does not depend upon outward excitement; when we not only forsake, but abhor that which is evil; and not only follow, but cleave to that which is good. There is scarcely an individual, perhaps, that does not sometimes pray. But does he delight himself in the Almighty? Will he always call upon God? There are few but are afflicted or alarmed into occasional piety. But are we the same in health as in sickness? In the house as in the temple? On the week as on the Sabbath?

What an immense loss must the Philippians have sustained in Paul's absence from them! Yet they obeyed much more in his absence than in his presence. Surely this shows that when he left them, God did not leave them. It teaches us that God does not depend upon instruments, though he is pleased to make use of them. It proves that, by his own Spirit, he can make up for the want of any creature advantage. When, by persecution, the church has been deprived of their pastors; or, by accident or disease, Christians have been destitute of the public ordinances of religion; they have seen his power and his glory *as* they have seen him in the sanctuary. The streams were gone, but the fountain was near. And where the providence of God has denied the usual means of grace, we have known the sufferers to prosper in the divine life, even more than those who have enjoyed an affluence of privileges.

"I cannot bear *thine* absence Lord—
"My *life* expires if *thou* depart:
"Be thou, my heart, still near my God,
"And thou, my God, be near my heart."

AUGUST 12.—"Sing unto the Lord, O ye saints of his, and give thanks at the remembrance of his holiness."—Psalm, xxx, 4.

It would be perfectly useless to call upon *others* to do this in their present state.

"None but the soul that feels his grace
"*Can* triumph in his holiness."

Since the fall, this attribute, which renders God so amiable in himself, and which draws forth the highest praises of heaven, makes him unlovely to an apostate creature. There is nothing the sinner thinks of with so much dislike as a perfection that justifies all his fears, and opposes all his inclinations and pursuits. What an enemy the world naturally is to the holiness of God, may be seen in the practice of the heathens. Among all the heroes they deified, they advanced none for those qualities which approach the most nearly to it; but frequently for passions the most remote from it; and at best, only for some physical power, valued or useful in the concerns of this life. Esculapius was deified for his skill in curing diseases. Bacchus for the use of the grape. Vulcan for his operations in fire. Hercules for his destroying monsters: and so of the rest. But not one of them all was advanced to this honor for the virtue of holiness—as if this property was beneath their notice in the formation of a deity; or they loved a god better that had nothing to do with it.

It was upon this principle that they who are now saints "would" once themselves "have none of Him;" and really said unto God, "Depart from us; we desire not the knowledge of thy ways." Hence, if they loved the Sabbath, it was a day of leisure and recreation; not as "the holy of the Lord, and honorable." Hence they disliked his people, as renewed, because they were images of this pure original.

What a blessed evidence is it in their favor, that they can now glory in his holy name, and sing and give thanks at the remembrance of his holiness! But such is the change they have experienced, that they *do* contemplate him with pleasure as holy in all his ways, and righteous in all his works. It is a relief, a satisfaction to their minds, in every perplexity in nature or providence, that the Judge of all the earth must do right. They delight in the law of God, which is holy, just, and good, after the inward man. The gospel appears to their minds glorious, because "therein is the righteousness of God revealed from faith to faith; that he might be just and the justifier of him which believeth in Jesus." This attribute now smiles upon them. They have a vast interest and hope in it. As holy, they can depend upon his truth, and are assured of the fulfilment of his word. They know that He, who has said, I will abundantly pardon: I will never leave thee, nor forsake thee, is a God that cannot lie. Yes, says the Christian, since He who loves me is purity itself, and his influence is almighty, he will sprinkle clean water upon me, and I shall be clean. He will destroy in me the sin which he infinitely hates. He will make me a partaker of his holiness, and render me meet for the inheritance of the saints in light.

But without this love to holiness we cannot see the kingdom of God. We are, both by Scripture and by the nature of the case, excluded for ever from his presence, which could only make us miserable. What fellowship hath light with darkness? What communion hath righteousness with unrighteousness?

Some talk of the less amiable views of the Supreme Being—yea, of the darker side of the Deity. I wonder what side this is. The Book tells me: and—I believe it—I feel it, that "God is light, and in him is no darkness at all." Therefore, thus saith the Lord; "Let not the wise man glory in his wisdom, neither let the mighty man glory in his might; let not the rich man glory in his riches; but let him that glorieth glory in this, that he understandeth and knoweth me, that I am the Lord which exercise loving kindness, judgment, and righteousness in the earth; for in these things I delight, saith the Lord."

AUGUST 13.—"And David said, Is there yet any that is left of the house of Saul, that I may show him kindness, for Jonathan's sake?"—2 Sam. ix, 1.

LET me not pass by this without remark.

—*See the low state of Saul's house!* He had a very numerous family, sufficient to have replenished a country; and yet it was now so reduced, dispersed, concealed, or unknown, that it was necessary to inquire whether any remains of it were left. So God setteth the solitary in families. Some houses, distinguished for their wealth and nobility, fall into indigence and obscurity; while others are completely terminated, their last branch having withered in the dust. "Their inward thought is, that their houses shall continue for ever, and their dwelling places to all generations; they call their lands after their own names. Nevertheless, man being in honor, abideth not; he is like the beasts that perish." "Be not thou afraid when one is made rich, when the glory of his house is increased." Vanity of vanities! saith the preacher—all is vanity!

—*See a fine instance of the forgiveness of injuries.*—Saul had been David's sworn foe, and had pursued him to the last with remorseless malignity. Yet while he was alive, David never took an advantage to injure him, when he had him completely in his power. And when he died, he mourned over him, and eulogized him far beyond his desert. And, years after, he inquires whether any of his family was left—not to cut them off, lest they should disturb his government—or to punish the sins of the father upon the children. Thus Athaliah arose, and destroyed all the seed royal: and Abimelech would leave none remaining of his father's house, and slew his brethren, the sons of Jerubbaal, being threescore and ten persons, upon one stone. And the same barbarous exterminations have always been practised in the east. But David asks if any is left, to "show him kindness." Let us learn from hence not to avenge ourselves, but rather to give place unto wrath. A greater than David has said, "Love your enemies; bless them that curse you." And he perfectly exemplified his own command: "When he was reviled, he reviled not again; when he suffered, he threatened not," but prayed, "Father, forgive them, for they know not what they do."

We have here a *proof of real and refined affection*—that I may show him kindness "for Jonathan's sake." Jonathan had been his bosom friend, and his open and generous conduct had justly endeared him to David. We love steadiness of attachment. Thy own friend and thy father's friend forsake not. A friend is born for adversity, and loveth at all times; and his regard will extend beyond the individual, to his connexions and offspring. God himself acts upon this principle, and tells us that the children of his servant shall continue, and that the generation of the upright shall be blessed. "I have been young," says David, "and now am old; yet have I not seen the righteous forsaken, nor his seed begging bread." And shall not we act upon the same principle in another case? Who remembered us in our low estate? Who, when rich, for our sakes became poor? and died, that we might live? He was received up into glory, and is no more in the world. But are there none left of his family who stand in need of our assistance? Let us pity and relieve them. Whatever we do unto one of the least of all these, he will esteem as done unto himself.

—It was *honorable in David not to wait to be addressed, but to endeavor to search out the object.* We are to advise liberal things, and not only to seize, but to seek opportunities of doing good. The most needy and deserving are generally the least clamorous; and, like the stricken deer, retire and bleed alone. And such we must seek after. We should not wait for the enforcement of claims, if conscience tells us they are due. Yet some, we fear, would never pay a debt, if they thought the creditor had forgotten it. But justice is the rule of our duty.

—We can go no further in our praise of David. Surely his kindness loses somewhat of its excellency in its lateness. Mephibosheth was five years old when David ascended the throne; and was now married and had a son. Thus a considerable number of years must have elapsed since God had delivered him out of all his adversity. He therefore (though better late than never) should have made this inquiry much earlier. What shall we say to this? We ought to make the best of every thing, especially in the conduct of great and good men. But none of them are faultless. And the sacred writers always show their impartiality. They always record things just as they occurred, regardless of consequences—their only aim is truth. It has been said, in exculpation of David, That he was so much engaged in war, and pressed with such a multiplicity of engagements! There was a truth in this: but it does not entirely excuse him. He had entered into covenant with Jonathan; and should immediately have shown his seed "the kindness of God;" that is, the kindness which he had sworn in his presence to exercise. Let us take heed that indulgence does not harden the heart: and when we prosper, let us watch and pray, lest we enter into temptation. The prosperity of fools destroys them; and the prosperity of wise men commonly injures them. As people rise in the world, they get bad memories. The Chief Butler did not remember Joseph, but forgot him: Lord, what is man!

In all things Jesus has the pre-eminence. He remembered us as soon as he came into his kingdom. And, though passed into the heavens, he is touched with the feeling of our infirmities.

August 14.—"And David said unto him, Fear not; for I will surely show thee kindness, for Jonathan thy father's sake, and will restore thee all the land of Saul thy father; and thou shalt eat bread at my table continually. And he bowed himself, and said, What is thy servant, that thou shouldest look upon such a dead dog as I am?"—2 Samuel, ix, 7, 8.

David had inquired whether there was any left of the house of Saul, that he might show him kindness for Jonathan's sake. Upon which Ziba, an old retainer in Saul's family, said unto the king, "Jonathan hath yet a son, which is lame on his feet." This lameness was occasioned by an accident, in consequence of the battle of Gilboa, by which his grandfather and his father were both slain. The nurse, not only from the terror such an event naturally inspires, but also from knowing that Mephibosheth was now the heir apparent to the throne, and that the victors would eagerly seek to apprehend him, to secure and conceal her precious charge, took him up and fled; but fell and crippled him for life. To how many perils are children exposed in their rearing; and how thankful should we feel to the providence of God, if we have escaped them. Yet, instead of pitying Mephibosheth, we ought rather to congratulate him on this affliction. In the earlier stages of society, corporeal accomplishments were much rated; and had not Mephibosheth been thus disfigured and dismemberd, the adherents of Saul's house would probably, as he was the next heir, have proclaimed *him* instead of his uncle Ishbosheth; and then it is most likely he would have been murdered as *he* was. Who knows what is good for man in this vain life? And who knows what is evil? How often have we deprecated things for which we have afterwards been thankful! How much do we owe to the disappointments of life! What dangers have ill health, or reduced substance, prevented!

"Ye fearful saints, fresh courage take!
"The clouds ye so much dread
"Are big with mercy, and shall break
"In blessings on your head."

—"And the king said, Where is he? And Ziba said, Behold, he is in the house of Machir, the son of Ammiel, in Lo-debar." Here, probably, resided in obscurity his mother's relations: and here he himself was forgotten, like a dead man out of mind. Machir, with whom he dwelt, seems to have been a noble, generous man, who took charge of Mephibosheth from pity of one born to honor, and the son of so excellent a father; and not from any disaffection to David. Yea, we afterward find him equally kind to David; and furnishing him with every refreshment when he was driven an exile into his neighborhood, by the rebellion of Absalom. And may not David's kindness to Mephibosheth at this time, have induced Machir the more promptly and extensively to exert himself in favor of David in his subsequent distress? If so, it says, "Give a portion to seven, and also to eight; for thou knowest not what evil shall be upon the earth." The aid we impart to-day, we may want to-morrow. Blessed are the merciful, for they shall obtain mercy.

The king sent and fetched him. And observe his introduction at court. When he was come unto David, he fell on his face, and did reverence. David had done the very same to this cripple's father a few years before, bowing himself three times to the earth. What changes take place in the conditions of men. David had too reflective a mind not to think of this. He had probably never seen Mephibosheth before, though he was born about the time of his intimacy with his beloved father. The first thing I suppose he would look for in his features, would be the image of Jonathan. David had too much sensibility not to be impressed with the affecting scene. Feeling is always brief in expression. He utters only one word: but the manner in which he pronounced it said every thing. And David said, MEPHIBOSHETH! It was the language of surprise, tenderness, and endearment.

—But why was he afraid of David? It is not probable that he apprehended any danger from him. But he had been living in the country, and in privacy, from a child. And it is no unusual thing for a stranger to be intimidated at the presence of a very superior and extraordinary man. Madame de Stael, though accustomed to the highest society, and endued with such powers of address and conversation, says she was breathless in the company of the late emperor of France; and could never rise above this prostration of mind. But David was a greater man, and as great a warrior, considering the age in which he lived. Seeing the depression of his countenance, and his tremor;

—David said to him, "Fear not, for I will surely show thee kindness, for Jonathan's sake;" and gave him the assurance of two things. First—Upon the suppression of Ishbosheth's faction, Saul's estate had been confiscated to the crown—this he promises to give him with all its future revenues. And secondly—He assigns him a residence in his palace, and a constant access to himself: I will restore thee all the land of Saul thy father; and thou shalt eat bread at my table continually.

—And how did Mephibosheth receive these honors? He was not one of those who take every favor as a debt, and imagine their friends are only doing their duty, and very imperfectly, too, perhaps, in every kindness they show them—But he exclaims, "What is thy servant, that thou shouldest look upon such a dead dog as I am?" A dog is fitter to be under the table, than at the side of it; and a dead dog is fitter for the ditch, than the palace. It was a strong, proverbial expression, used to signify how mean, and base, and unworthy, and unqualified, he deemed himself. But if *he* received these benefits from David with so much thankfulness and humility, how ought *we* to feel under those blessings which God bestows upon us? And here let me ask three questions.

And, first—not to dwell on the ordinary bounties of his providence; Has he not remembered us in our low estate? Has he not sought and saved our souls? Has he not restored our forfeited inheritance? Has he not given us a name and a place in his house, that we may eat and drink at his table, in his kingdom?

Secondly. And are not the blessings He has conferred upon us infinitely greater than those Mephibosheth received from David? It might seem an immense thing to a worldly mind, to be fetched out of distant obscurity; and enriched with a royal demesne; and allowed to live at a splendid court. But Mephibosheth, perhaps, was not even so happy as before: and for whatever purposes he valued his elevation, he soon left it, and found that he had set his eyes on that which is not. But we are blessed with all spiritual blessings in heavenly places in Christ. Our dignities and enjoyments yield the most perfect satisfaction. And they will endure for ever.

Thirdly. And how much less reason had we to look for such favors from God, than Mephibosheth had to expect such bestowments from David? He was David's fellow creature, and had a claim founded in the community of nature. He was the son of an intimate friend, to whom he was under obligation. He was always a relation, being the child of his brother-in-law. Though a sufferer, he was innocent, and had always conducted himself properly toward David.

—But, Lord, what is man, that thou art mindful of him; or the son of man that thou visitest him? We were strangers—enemies by wicked works—unworthy of the least of all his mercies deserving that his wrath should come upon us as the children of disobedience! What then ought to be our self abasement? our gratitude? But where are they? Are they urging us to exclaim, Not unto us, O Lord, not unto us! By thy grace we are what we are! Are they inducing us to utter abundantly the memory of his great goodness; and recommend him all the day long to others? Are they constraining us, by his mercies, to present our bodies a living sacrifice, holy and acceptable, which is our reasonable service?

AUGUST 15.—"**Praise waiteth for thee, O God, in Zion: and unto thee shall the vow be performed.**"—**Psalm lxv, 1.**

HERE we have the church's praise, and the church's vow—the suspension of the one; and the fulfillment of the other.

In general, God waits for our praise. And how slow and reluctant are we in rendering it! And how seldom, at last, do we render, according to the benefit done unto us! But here praise waits in Zion for him. The meaning is, that the deliverance or blessing which they were in need of had not arrived; but they were looking for it—They had their harp in their hand, ready to strike up a song of thanksgiving; but delay kept them silent; praise waited, therefore, because the church waited.

And this is no unusual thing, first, as to their spiritual experience. They wish to be able to view him as the strength of their heart, and their portion for ever; and to claim all the exceeding great and precious promises as their own. But they are doubtful and uncertain; yea, they often exclude themselves from all part and lot in the matter. Now we cannot praise him for what we think he has not done for us, or given to us; but only for what he has. If, therefore, he has forgiven, and accepted us, the acknowledgment of the blessing requires the knowledge of it. Yet how many are in a state of anxiety, waiting for the Lord more than they that watch for the morning; and praying, Say unto my soul, I am thy salvation! And,

Secondly, as to providential dispensations. How long was it, even after David had been anointed by Samuel, before he was established on the throne! How long did Joseph wait, with every prospect growing darker, before his prophetic dreams were accomplished! And so Abraham, "after he had patiently endured, obtained the promise." God keeps back, till self-despair and the failure of creature confidence have spread a dark ground, on which his glory *must* be seen. He loves to surprise, as well as relieve. He will convince us, in future difficulties, that he is able to do for us exceedingly abundantly above all we can ask or think. Therefore at eventide it is light: and he turneth the shadow of death into the morning.

Here, however, let it be observed, that Christians cannot be ever entirely silent. They have always much to praise God for. Whatever be their present condition—it might have been much worse—yea, in every thing they are to give thanks. Nor will they be silent long. The vision is only for an appointed time.

Yet a little while, and he that shall come, will come, and will not tarry. And they need not be silent at all if they have faith in God: for faith can see the certainty of the thing before it takes place; and cause us always to triumph in Christ, while yet the warfare is not actually accomplished.

If hope deferred maketh the heart sick, when it cometh it is a tree of life. Therefore says the church, "Unto thee shall the vow be performed." The vow means their solemn engagement to praise Him when the deliverance or blessing arrived. "If He appears to my joy, I will give him the glory that is due unto his name—witness my vow." We are not fond of vows: they often ensnare the soul, and give the enemy an advantage over us. And Christians, as they advance in self-knowledge, are commonly more disposed to pray *to* God, than to stipulate *with* him. It is a useful hint which Cowper gives us—

"Beware of Peter's word;
"Nor confidently say,
"I never *will* deny the Lord,
"But, grant I never may."

Yet vows in some cases may be useful. They may prove as a kind of fence to the field, or hem to the garment. They may serve to remind us, when we forget; and to humble us, when we fail. But two things should be always observed. The first is, that they be formed in an entire dependence upon divine grace. "By Thee only will we make mention of thy name." "Through God we shall do valiantly."

"Man's wisdom is to seek
"In God his strength alone;
"And e en an angel would be weak,
"That trusted in his own."

The second is, that when we have made them, we should be concerned to fulfill them. "When thou vowest a vow unto God, defer not to pay it; for he hath no pleasure in fools; pay that which thou hast vowed. Better is it that thou shouldest not vow, than that thou shouldest vow and not pay." Yet how often have men bound themselves when they were in danger, sickness, and affliction; and, forgetting or violating their vow, have turned again to folly! Even Jacob, after all his solemn covenanting with God, in the prospect of his journey, was awfully remiss upon his return; till, divinely rebuked, he said, "Let us arise and go up to Bethel; and I will make there an altar unto God, who answered me in my distress, and, was with me in the way which I went." Hannah was more exemplary. She had vowed, that if her prayer was answered, she would give her son to the Lord as long as he lived. The surrender was painful: but as soon as she had weaned him she took him to Shiloh, and brought him to Eli: "And she said, Oh, my lord! as thy soul liveth, my lord, I am the woman that stood by thee here, praying unto the Lord. For this child I prayed; and the Lord hath given me my petition which I asked of him; therefore also I have lent him to the Lord; as long as he liveth he shall be lent to the Lord." "Well done thou good and faithful servant."

August 16.— Notwithstanding, lest we should offend them, go thou to the sea, and cast a hook, and take up the fish that first cometh up; and when thou hast opened his mouth, thou shalt find a piece of money; that take, and give unto them for me and thee."—Matthew, xvii, 27.

How well was it foretold that his name should be called, Wonderful!

What a surprising combination of attributes was displayed in him! Observe the case before us. Here, while we behold his penury and dependence—so that he did not possess wherewithal to pay the Temple-tribute, we perceive his omniscience—so that in Peter's house he could pierce the waters of the sea, and discern a particular fish, and see what was in its body—and announce a piece of money there—and the very coin by *name*. Surely the darkness hideth not from him; but the night shineth as the day. "Neither is there any creature that is not manifest in his sight; but all things are naked and opened unto the eyes of Him with whom we have to do."

He who saw the *stater* in this fish, sees what money we are in the possession of—and how we acquired it—and the way in which we are using it. He sees whether we are needlessly hoarding, or wastefully expending it. He sees whether we are making it our hope and confidence, or valuing it only as an instrument of lawful enjoyment, and of pious and benevolent use. He sees the responsibilities of the owner; and knows how he will feel when he shall be called to leave it; and when he will be required to give an account of it.

Here we also behold his power and dominion. He is Lord of all. The beasts of the field obey him. At his bidding not a dog moves his tongue in the departure of the Israelites: and, at his command, the dumb ass, speaks with man's voice, and rebukes the madness of the Prophet. The fowls of the air obey him—at his order, the ravens bring Elijah bread and meat in the morning and evening. The fishes of the sea obey him—at his command, a great fish swallows the disobedient, and disembarks the penitent Jonah—and, here, a fish at his requirement goes and takes up from the bottom of the sea a stater, and then goes and bites at Peter's hook, with this in his maw! "All things are put under his feet: all sheep and oxen; yea, the beasts of the field; the fowls of the air, and the fish of the sea, and whatsoever passeth through the paths of the sea."

Could any thing be better adapted to encourage the confidence of the disciples in the kindness and all-sufficiency of his providence, when he was sending them forth, as sheep among wolves, and without any known supplies to live upon? He commissioned the Seventy to go in pairs through the whole country; but he sent them forth without purse, or scrip, or shoes. And they had, it would seem, many uneasy and distracting thoughts at the time.

They did not, indeed express them; but our Lord was aware of them, and remembered them. And when he came back, he brings them to their own recollection; "How came you to think that I who employed you, should not provide for you? Did you doubt my inclination, or my ability? When I sent you forth without purse and scrip, lacked ye any thing? And they said, Nothing, Lord."

Are you called to leave behind you those who seem to hang on your care? Hear this Savior at your dying bed, saying, "Leave thy fatherless children, I will preserve them alive; and let thy widow trust in me." "O fear the Lord, all ye his saints; for there is no want to them that fear him. The young lions do lack and suffer hunger; but they that seek the Lord shall not want any good thing."

AUGUST 17.—" Ye know all things."—1 John, ii, 20.

THE reason, or the cause, is previously given—" We have an unction from the Holy One." This unction means the Spirit of grace and truth. This the Savior possessed personally; he " was anointed with the Holy Ghost and with power;" and had the Spirit without measure. And, as Mediator, for the suffering of death, he received all the fullness of it for the supply of his people. They therefore derive it from him; and it is not only sanctifying, but illuminating; it leads them " into all truth;" and " they know all things." This is a bold expression; but the extensiveness of it must be taken with four distinctions.

First. It means only things *religious*. It does not intend to intimate that every Christian is familiar with the secrets of Nature; the resources of trade; the mysteries of government; the structure of language; and a thousand other things. With regard to these, he may be far surpassed by the people of the world. Not that religion stupefies its possessor—yea, it is favorable to the acquisition of knowledge generally, by rousing and employing the mind, and thereby improving it—but it is distinguishable from learning and science; and makes us acquainted with " the things which accompany salvation."

Secondly. It means things not only religious, but *revealed*. " The secret things belong unto the Lord our God; but those things which are revealed belong unto us, and to our children for ever, that we may do all the works of this law:" a passage which should never be forgotten. It would draw some persons a little further from the decrees of God, and a little nearer to his commands. The sacred writers prophesy but in part. Had every thing been revealed in the Scripture, the world could not have contained the books that would have been written; and our attention would have been so divided that the one thing needful would have been forgotten. There are numberless subjects upon which a busy and curious mind would speculate, concerning which the word is silent. But where God says nothing, we are not to be wise above what is written. If men will conjecture, let them conjecture without devouring much of their time, or injuring their temper; and without censoriousness, self-conceit, and positiveness—He that hath a dream, let him tell a dream. What is the chaff to the wheat? When our Savior had foretold the duty and destination of Peter, and Peter, not satisfied with this, asked concerning John, "Lord, and what shall this man do?" instead of answering him, he reproved his impatient and presumptuous curiosity; "What if I will that he tarry till I come; what is that to thee? Follow thou me."

Thirdly. It not only means things revealed, but revealed things of *importance*. Every thing, even in the Scripture, is not equally momentous and interesting. Some things are hard to be understood; but then it is not necessary to be able to understand them. Yet such things as these are not without their use, if they make us humble, by showing us the limits of the human understanding, and lead us, while we adore *here*, to study elsewhere. How many things are there in the geography, the chronology, the natural philosophy of the Scriptures, in which we may be safely unversed? A man may be able to number his days so as to apply his heart unto wisdom, without knowing when Antichrist will be destroyed. He may not know what creature Behemoth was, or where Ophir was; and yet he may know what is life eternal, and the way to it he may know. The Jews had the fiery cloudy pillar, not to examine, but to follow. They knew no more of its essence at the end of forty years, than at the beginning; but it had led them, by a right way, to the city of habitation. There are things which concern the Lord Jesus, and to know these is the excellency of knowledge. These will make us wise unto salvation. These are things that are ornamental to a Christian—and these are not to be undervalued; but others are essential to his very being. Some things conduce to our comfort; but others even involve our safety. It is desirable, but not equally necessary, that a Christian should be informed in all these truths.

Fourthly. With regard to things of importance, it only means a *comparative* knowledge of these, in our present state. Of the God of grace as well as of the God of nature, we are compelled to say, "How small a portion is known of him!" What one truth is there that we can trace back completely to its rise, or follow to its last outfall? We read of things which angels desire to look into; of a peace which passeth all understanding; of a joy unspeakable. The love of Christ passeth knowledge.

"The cross, the manger, and the throne,
"Are big with glories yet unknown."

More we cannot concede. If Christians are comparatively ignorant, they are comparatively wise. They are children of the light, and of the day. They have an understanding given them to know Him that is true. Not that they are endued with a new physical faculty; but they have another kind of knowledge—and it is as superior as it is peculiar. There is as much difference between their present and their former knowledge, as between the shining of the glow-worm and the vital lustre of the sun. They have a *heart* to know. They see divine things, not only in their reality, but in their *beauty* and *excellency;* and, while this gives them a firmer conviction of their certainty than they had before, so it gains their affection to them, and brings them under their influence. Thus, with them, the darkness is past, and the true light now shineth. They walk in the light, as He is in the light. The secret of the Lord is with them, and he shows them his covenant. "The natural man receiveth not the things of the Spirit of God; for they are foolishness unto him; neither can he know them, because they are spiritually discerned. But he that is spiritual *judgeth all things*."

Thus another reproach is rolled away. Christians are not only considered as slaves; as cowards; as the victims of gloom and melancholy; but are often despised, or pitied, as fools. Yet are they the wisest people in the world. Their religion, from first to last, is wisdom. And it is justified of all her children.

AUGUST 18.—"**My voice thou shalt hear in the morning, O Lord, Ps. v. 3.**

AUTHORS have found the morning the best time for study and composition—hence it has been called the friend of the muses. It would be easy to prove that it is equally a friend to the graces and the duties—it is the finest season for reflection and devotion. David found it so, and therefore resolves, "My voice shalt thou hear in the morning, O Lord." What voice? The voice of praise, and the voice of prayer—the one excited by looking back, the other by looking forward.

—How much is there in the morning to call forth the voice of thanksgiving! Let us think of the season we have just passed through. How many houseless creatures this night have had no place where to lay their heads! How many victims of accident and disease have been full of tossing to and fro, until the dawning of the day; their beds have not comforted them, nor their couch eased their complaint! How many have been deprived of repose while attending their neighbors, friends, and relations, in sickness and sorrow! How many, since the last setting sun, have entered an awful eternity! How many, this night, have been cut off in their sins! Many have been terrified, robbed, injured, murdered, by wicked and unreasonable men! How many have been consumed by fire, or drowned with water! How many, this night, have been engaged in works of darkness; and who, if any knew them, would be in the terrors of the shadow of death! How many have risen this morning to pass the day in anguish! How many to suffer want! How many who have all things richly to enjoy, have risen only to live another day without God in the world! They lie down and rise up like the beasts that perish: God is not in all their thoughts. And is it otherwise with us? What shall we render unto the Lord for all his benefits toward us? Bless the Lord, O my soul, and all that is within me, bless his holy name. O magnify the Lord with me, and let us exalt his name together.

—And with how many of these merciful nights have we been favored! Hence, perhaps, we have been so little affected with the goodness of God in them. How strange! that what increases the greatness of our obligation should diminish the sense of it! Yet it is by the interruption, the suspension, the want of our comforts, we are made to learn the value of them. Let us guard against this perverseness of ingratitude; and remember that if our mercies are common, they must be numerous, and so increase the claims to our praise.

—And shall our gratitude evaporate in a mere morning acknowledgment? Shall we not, by the mercies of God, dedicate ourselves to his service, and be in his fear all the day long?

And when we think of the day before us, how much is there to awaken concern! And what is *our* concern, without the attention of God? He shall, therefore, in the morning hear, not only the voice of praise, but the voice of prayer.

Who is to guide me through the day upon which I have entered? How much depends upon one mistake in my movements? And how easily may I go astray? The way of man is not in himself; it is not in man that walketh to direct his steps. "Cause me to hear thy loving kindness in the morning, for in Thee do I trust; cause me to know the way wherein I should walk, for I lift up my soul unto Thee."

Who is to guard me through the day? And I am much more exposed when awake, than when asleep. My soul is more exposed—more exposed to sin—and sin is the greatest evil. And what am I, to resist a corrupt heart, a wicked world, and all the powers of darkness? "Hold Thou me up, and I shall be safe. Be Thou my arm every morning; my salvation also in the time of trouble."

Who is to help me through the day? I have many duties to discharge. I am to live soberly, righteously, and godly. I am to walk in wisdom toward those that are without: I am to speak the truth in love: I am to adorn the doctrine of God my Savior in all things. "Lord, without thee I can do nothing. Let thy grace be sufficient for me; and thy strength made perfect in weakness."

Who is to give me success in the business of the day? I know I ought not to be idle, but to be diligently and prudently employed in my lawful calling. Means are mine; but how much more is necessary than my wisdom and anxiety. "The blessing of the Lord it maketh rich; and he addeth no sorrow with it." "Except the Lord build the house, they labor in vain that build it; except the Lord keep the city, the watchman waketh but in vain. It is in vain for me to rise up early, to sit up late, to eat the bread of sorrows: for so he giveth his beloved sleep."

Who is to prepare me for the events of the day? And I know not what the day may bring forth. Perhaps I may receive the most unwelcome intelligence. Perhaps I may sustain losses in property. Perhaps I may meet with mortification from my fellow creatures, and be tried with disappointments in friends. My child may this day fall sick. The desire of mine eyes may be taken away with a stroke. There may be but a step between me and death. It is wonderful we live a day through. "May I know how to be abased, or how to abound. If in the world I have tribulation, in the Savior may I have peace. So teach me to number my days that I may apply my heart unto wisdom—That whether I live, I may live unto the Lord; or whether I die, I may die unto the Lord: so that, living and dying, I may be the Lord's."

AUGUST 19.—"I am married unto you."—Jeremiah, iii, 14.

MARRIAGE is the nearest and most intimate of all human relations. It is surpassed only by the union between soul and body. Here are two persons meeting together, who perhaps never saw or heard of each other some time before; yet, coming under the power of this ordinance, are united in a connexion that exceeds the claims of nature, and the wife becomes dearer than the dearest parent. "Therefore shall a man leave his father and his mother, and shall cleave to his wife; and they shall be one flesh."

—Thus, Christians, though once strangers, and far off, become the people of God, a people nigh unto him; yea, one with him, in a perpetual covenant that shall not be forgotten—and He is not ashamed to own the relation, "I am married unto you." What is supremely and essentially included in this relation, when properly established?

—In such a marriage there is mutual love. This love regards the person, and not the endowments. And such a love there is between God and his people. It commenced on his side much earlier than on their's; and his love to them produced their love to him. For love begets love: and we love him, because he first loved us. Yet the love *is* mutual—and he says, "I love them that love me."

The same may be said of mutual choice. In a proper marriage, the parties freely elect each other. God has chosen his people; and they have chosen him: for, though once averse to him, as their Lord and portion, they are made willing in the day of his power; and this power is not violence, but influence—the influence of wisdom and goodness. He works in them to will and to do of his good pleasure. He draws them, and they run after him; and they can all say from the heart, "Whom have I in heaven, but Thee? and there is none upon earth that I desire beside Thee."

In this connexion, there is also confidence and communication. Where this is wanting, the spirit of it is materially injured; and the relation is very defectively maintained. It is readily allowed, that the woman should not carry on designs concealed from the husband; but is not every thing here reciprocal? And is he justified in treating her with reserve and silence? Yet there are many wives, who have had no intimation of the state of their husband's affairs, till they have found themselves plunged into a condition overwhelming them with surprise, as well as calamity. The secret of the Lord is with them that fear him; and he will show them his covenant. And they, in all their ways, acknowledge him. They pour out their hearts before him; they hide nothing from him.

There is, also, in this alliance, fellowship and community of goods. However poor or mean the wife was before, she is now raised to a participation of the husband's rank and affluence: and however free and independent he was before, the husband now shares in all the condition of the wife. And thus the believer dedicates himself to God, with all he is and has. He feels his cause his own; he deplores its reproaches, and rejoices in its success. And God gives himself, with all he is and has, to the believer. In all his afflictions, He is afflicted: and he that toucheth him, toucheth the apple of His eye.

Finally. There is complacency and delight. As the bridegroom rejoiceth over the bride, so shall thy God rejoice over thee.

He will rejoice over thee with joy; he will rest in his love; he will rejoice over thee with singing.

How wonderful is this! and yet how true!

How blessed are the people who are in such a case!

Art thou in this happy, this glorious condition? All hail! Thy maker is thy husband. There was joy in the presence of the angels of God the hour thou gavest thy consent to the proposals of the Gospel.

Art thou willing to be united to him? His ministers invite and woo thee. Come—for all things are now ready. Resemble not Israel, who would have none of him; and so were given up to their own heart's lust. Behold, now is the accepted time: behold, now is the day of salvation.

AUGUST 20.—"His going forth is prepared as the morning; and he shall come unto us as the rain, as the latter and former rain unto the earth."
Hosea, vi, 3.

"HIS going forth," and "his coming," mean his displays and communications, on the behalf of those who earnestly and perseveringly seek after him, according to the words immediately preceding, "Then shall we know, if we follow on to know, the Lord." *This* contains the *assurance* of their success. But here is added the *illustration* of it. It consists of two images equally beautiful and encouraging.

The first derived from the morning; "His going forth is prepared as the morning." When the morning is not yet come, we fully rely upon it: we know it is coming: we know it is secured in the appointment of providence, and the arrangements of nature. It never yet failed; and it never will, as long as the world endures. And does not the God of all grace express the immutability of his counsel by the certainty of this very allusion? "Thus saith the Lord, If ye can break my covenant of the day, and my covenant of the night; and that there shall not be day or night in their season; then may also my covenant be broken with David, my servant." What can hinder the approach, and the rising of the sun? And his going forth is prepared as *surely* as the morning.

—And as *luminously* too. The morning drives away the darkness, and shines upon our path; so that we see where we are, and how to move. "If a man walk in the day, he stumbleth not, because he seeth the light of this world. But if a man walk in the night, he stumbleth, because there is no light in him." The Lord will come, and manifest himself to his people. He will show them his covenant. He will lead them into all truth. And, with regard to doctrine, and experience, and practice, and also their interest in the divine favor, he will make darkness light before them, and crooked things straight: these things will he do unto them, and not forsake them.

It is also as *delightsome* as the morning. The night is a season of gloom, as it is a period of confinement, and danger, and fear, and anxiety. Paul's mariners, in the storm cast four anchors, and wished for the day. David refers to travellers and sentinels, who watch for the morning, as the image of his waiting for the Lord. Some nights are less cheerless than others; but, at best, they have only the moon and stars—the sun is wanting—he alone can make the morning: and when he comes, the birds sing, the lambs play, and man partakes of the cheerfulness that spreads all around. "Truly the light is sweet: and a pleasant thing it is for the eyes to behold the sun." Creatures are pleasing; but none of them can supply the place of God. He is our sun, as well as our shield; and the language of the gracious heart is, Oh! when wilt thou come unto me? Thou alone canst put my fears to flight, and inspire me with joy unspeakable and full of glory."

But the morning comes not all at once, but *gradually*. What a difference is there between the first glimmerings of the dawn and the splendor of noon! So the path of the just is as the shining light, that shineth more and more unto the perfect day.

The second is derived from the rain—"He shall come unto us as the rain; as the latter and the former rain unto the earth." God asks, "Can any of the vanities of the Gentiles send rain?" He claims the production as his own divine prerogative, and justly wonders that we do not notice it more than we do. "Neither say they in their heart, Let us now fear the Lord our God, that giveth rain; both the former and the latter in his season." In Judea the rain was less frequent, and more periodical than with us. It peculiarly fell after autumn and spring, that is, just after seed-time, and just before reaping—the former to soften the ground, and quicken the grain, and aid the springing thereof; the latter, to fill the corn in the ear, and hasten its maturity.

What would nature be without rain? We are equally dependent on the grace of God. But, under the influences of his word and Spirit, we revive and grow as the corn. These influences are always needful; but it is pressing the metaphor to observe, that there are two seasons when they are peculiarly experienced? The one is connected with the beginning of the divine life—this may be called the former rain. The other with the close of it—this may be called the lattter rain. The one is to enliven. The other to confirm. To the "former" many can look back, and ask—

"Where is the blessedness I knew
"When first I saw the Lord?
"Where is that soul-refreshing view
"Of Jesus and his word?"

—Others are longing for the "latter." Their salvation is nearer than when they believed. But they do not yet feel as they wished. They want more faith, more hope, more consolation—more of all the fullness of God. Let the last showers descend; and the appointed weeks of harvest come; and the produce be brought home, with "shoutings, Grace, grace, unto it!"

August 21.—"Therefore, his sisters sent unto him, saying, Lord, behold he whom thou lovest is sick."—John, xi, 3.

These words furnish several sources of remark and instruction.

The first regards the *love* of Jesus. In his love to Lazarus there was something peculiar, and something common. He loved him with a partial, and he loved him with a divine affection. To know Christ after the flesh is a privilege which has long since ceased; and to be loved by him under the advantage of his humanity, was a favor restricted to a few. But there is, however, another sense in which, as he loved Lazarus, so he loves us; and though we share not in the partial regard of the friend, we are the subjects of the divine regard of the Savior. This love commenced from no excellency in us, like the love of creatures. It took knowledge of us, as sinners. It began before the foundation of the world. It led him to espouse our cause, and brought him under an engagement to suffer and die for us. His people remember this love more than wine. It passeth knowledge.

The second regards the *affliction* of Lazarus. He "was sick." Sickness is one of the common calamities of life; and it is one of the most painful and trying. Yet Lazarus was exercised with it, though he was loved of Jesus. This explains the nature of his love, and shows us that it does not exempt its subjects from affliction. It is not the foolish fondness of a father, who, when correction was necessary, spares the child for his crying. He that thus "spareth the rod, hateth his son: but he that loveth him, chastens him betimes." Could we now see, as we shall hereafter, the principle, the design, the alleviations, the advantages of the afflictions of the righteous, we should perceive that they are not only compatible with divine love, but the fruit, the proof of it. "Whom the Lord loveth he chasteneth, and scourgeth every son whom he receiveth. If ye endure chastening, God dealeth with you as with sons: for what son is he whom the father chasteneth not?"

The third regards the *mission* of the sisters. "Therefore the sisters *sent* unto Jesus." Their affliction led to this application. To induce us to send to him is the design of our trials; for we are too forgetful of him in ease and prosperity. "In their affliction they will seek me early." What can we do without him, then? Therefore, says the Teacher, as well as the Chastiser, "Call upon me in the day of trouble." And what a solace! what a relief! what a source of support, sanctification, and deliverance, is prayer! John's disciples, therefore, when their master was beheaded, not only took up the body, and buried it, but "went and told Jesus." "I will say unto God," was the resolve of Job, "do not condemn me; show me wherefore thou contendest with me." "And," says David, "From the end of the earth will I cry unto Thee when my heart is overwhelmed: lead me to the rock that is higher than I." Thus it has been with all who have *heard* the rod. They all have said, "A glorious high throne from the beginning has been the place of our sanctuary."

—Therefore his *sisters* sent unto him. It is pleasing when in our natural relations, we have spiritual friends who will carry our cases, and spread them before the Lord. Many, in their sickness, have connexions about them who are kind and attentive; but they never speak a word to them of their souls; and never administer to them the cordials of the gospel, though they often apply self-righteous opiates to stupefy conscience. They send for the physician and the lawyer, but do not address the Savior for them. But some, like Lazarus, have those who will bear them upon their minds, and call in the aid of the Hope of Israel, the Savior thereof, in the time of trouble. And what an encouragement and comfort is this to those who are scarcely able to lift a thought to God for themselves: whose broken and distracted petitions seem unworthy of notice; and who know that the prayer of the righteous availeth much.

The fourth is, the *message* they conveyed to him, "Saying, Lord, behold, he whom thou lovest is sick." From hence we may learn two things. First. The Lord's love gives us encouragement in prayer, and furnishes us with our most prevailing plea in dealing with him. They do not say, he whom *we* love—though this was true. Nor he who loves *thee*—though this was true: but he, whom *thou* lovest. How wise, how expressive was this. As much as to say, "Hast thou not deigned to regard him already? Has not thy kindness for him raised our confidence in thee, and our expectation from thee? Will not others turn their eyes toward thee, and see whether thy friendship is like the friendship of the world, which leaves its dependents in the hour of necessity and distress? "A true friend loveth at all times: but is born for adversity." We read of pleading with God: and filling our mouths with arguments: but our most suitable and successful ones must be derived from himself, and especially from his own goodness. "I plead nothing of my own—not even my love to thee:

'Yet I love Thee, and adore: | 'Oh for grace to love thee more!'

But my love to thee is weak and cold; and whatever it be it is the effect of thy love to me. I was once a stranger, and an enemy, and should have remained so still, hadst not thou found a way into my heart. But thou hast redeemed me by thy blood. Thou hast called me by thy grace. Thou hast opened my blind eyes, and turned my feet into the path of peace. And after all this love, wilt thou cast me off? Couldest thou not have destroyed me. without showing me such things as these?"

Secondly. It is better for us, when we seek the Lord for temporal things, to refer our own suit to his own good pleasure. I admire the manner in which these pious women addressed him. They do not prescribe—they hardly petition—they particularize nothing. They do not say, Lord, come to this house—come immediately—remove his malady—what will become of us, if Lazarus should die? But they state the case, and leave it: "Lord, behold, he whom thou lovest is sick." When therefore, we have to pray for deliverance from some trouble, or the acquisition of some outward favor, let us do it with modesty and reserve. For these blessings are promised not absolutely but conditionally; that is, if they are good for us: and in the very same way they are to be implored. We must not desire them, if they would be hurtful; and they may be injurious: and God perfectly knows whether this would be the result of success and indulgence. Had the Jews prayed in this manner, for flesh, he would not have given them their heart's desire, and sent leanness into their souls. What we extort as it were, from God, by restless importunity, turns the blessing into a curse. The feverish and inflamed state of the mind renders the gratification of the craving dangerous.

We cannot be too earnest with God about spiritual blessings; but as to every thing of a temporal nature, temperance of mind becomes us; and, in resignation at his feet, we must endeavor to say, "Here I am; let him do what seemeth good."

"Assure me of thy wondrous love,
"Immeasurably kind:
"And, Lord, to thine unerring will
"Be every wish resigned."

AUGUST 22.—"The word of Christ."—Colossians, iii, 16.

So the Scriptures are called, because he is the author, and because he is the subject of their contents. They are not only derived from the inspiration of his Spirit, but they are full of his person, and character, and sufferings, and glory. There is nothing, perhaps, admitted into them, but has some relation to him. We cannot, in any instances, trace this connexion at present: but we shall see more of it when, in the church, the light of the moon shall be as the light of the sun, and the light of the sun shall be sevenfold, as the light of seven days. And, perhaps, to explore it perfectly, will be a part of the blessedness and employment of heaven. But when our Lord urged his hearers to search the Scriptures, he said, "They are they that testify of me." And going to Emmaus with the two disciples, "he expounded unto them, in *all* the Scriptures, the things concerning himself."

We may divide the Scriptures into six parts.

There is the *historical* part. He is the substance of this. In Adam, we see him the head and representative of his people. In Noah, as the restorer of a new world. In Isaac, as a victim laid on the altar. In Joseph, as a sufferer and a savior. In Moses, as a lawgiver. In Aaron, as a high priest. In Joshua, as a leader and commander. In Solomon, as the prince of peace. In Jonah, as buried and rising from the grave.

There is the *ceremonial* part. Of this he is the substance. He is the body of all its shadows, the reality of all its types. He is the rock whose streams followed the Israel of God. He is the manna, the bread, that came down from heaven. In the city of refuge, we behold him as our security from avenging justice. And in every bleeding sacrifice as the atonement for our sins.

There is the *prophetical* part. Here he is all in all. "To him gave *all* the prophets witness." "The testimony of Jesus is the *Spirit* of prophecy."

There is the *promissory* part—And how large and glorious a portion of it is filled with exceeding great and precious promises! And what blessing can we need, that is not furnished under the pledge of a God that cannot lie? "But all the promises of God in him, are yea; and in him amen, to the glory of God by us."

There is the *practical* part. To be a Christian is to live not to ourselves, but to him that died for us, and rose again. Of good works, his example is the rule; his love is the motive; his Spirit is the author. He is the altar on which all our sacrifices are to be offered. Prayer is asking in his name. We are to love our wives, even as he loved the church, and gave himself for it.

There is the *doctrinal* part. And what is the great mystery of godliness? "God was manifest in the flesh, justified in the Spirit, seen of angels, preached unto the Gentiles, believed on in the world, received up into glory." Every doctrine of the Gospel, as treated by the inspired authors, leads to him. If we are justified, it is by his righteousness. If we are sanctified, it is by his Spirit. If the glory of God shines forth, it is in the face of Jesus Christ. Providence is, all power given unto him in heaven and in the earth. The whole of Christianity is called, "The truth as it is in Jesus."

Take him out of the Bible, and you take the sun out of our world; and the soul out of the body; and what is left?

It is this that so powerfully endears the sacred volume to every real Christian—It is the word of One, he supremely loves, and feels infinitely necessary to all his comfort, and all his hope. Of him, he can never read or hear enough.

O my soul! let this word of Christ dwell in thee, richly, in all wisdom. And never forget the admonition of kindness, as well as authority. "Bind it continually upon thine heart, and tie it about thy neck. When thou goest it shall lead thee; when thou sleepest, it shall keep thee; and when thou awakest, it shall talk with thee."

AUGUST 23.—"Wait on the Lord, and keep his way, and he shall exalt thee to inherit the land; when the wicked are cut off, thou shalt see it."
Psalm xxxvii, 34.

HERE is a twofold admonition.

First. "Wait on the Lord." "I hope I do so." But are you *sure* of this? Is there any thing in your religious exercises that really deserves the name of waiting on God? For persons may read without attention, and hear without faith, and sing without praise, and pray without desire. They may draw nigh to him with the mouth, and honor him with the lip, while the heart is far from him. But God is a Spirit; and they that worship him must worship him in Spirit and in truth. "I hope I do thus wait on Him." But do you thus wait on him *sufficiently?* First. In his sanctuary? Secondly. In the family? Thirdly. In the closet? Fourthly. In all your concerns; like David, who said, "On thee do I wait all the day, Lord!"

Secondly. "And keep his way." This is beautifully connected with the former. Wait—and work. Wait—and walk. Get grace—and exercise it. Persevere in the use of means, if present comfort be withholden. Neither give up the course in which you are engaged—nor turn aside—nor stand still—nor look back—nor seem to come short; though superiors frown—and companions reproach—and iniquity abounds—and the love of many waxes cold—and numbers walk no more with him. In all opposition, and through every discouragement, let your soul follow hard after God. Thus did Job; and therefore he could say, "My foot hath held his steps; his way have I kept, and not declined. Neither have I gone back from the commandment of his lips: I have esteemed the words of his mouth more than my necessary food." So it was also with the church. "Our heart is not turned back, neither have our steps declined from thy way; though thou hast sore broken us in the place of dragons, and covered us with the shadow of death." We have enough to animate us to hold on—"After two days will he revive us: in the third day will he raise us up, and we shall live in his sight. Then shall we know if we follow on to know the Lord. His going forth is prepared as the morning; and he shall come unto us as the rain, as the latter and former rain unto the earth."

Here is a twofold promise.

First. "He shall exalt thee to inherit the land." God is the source of all elevation and honor. He raised the Jews to the possession of Canaan, the glory of all lands. But he dignifies Christians with a title to a better, even a heavenly country; where, "with kings, are they upon the throne." But He advances them here, as well as hereafter. For he is "the glory of their strength, and in his favor their horn is exalted," and not only with regard to spiritual, but temporal things. For "the meek shall inherit the earth." Not that all of them are rich and great in the world. So far from it, they are commonly a poor and afflicted people. Not that every thing is actually in their possession, or that they have a civil right to it—dominion is not founded in grace: but security is; peace is; contentment is; happiness is. As to covenant interest and enjoyment, and improvement, "all things are theirs."

Secondly. "When the wicked are cut off, thou shalt see it." And they will be cut off. They are often cut off, even in life, from their places, and riches, and prospects. At death they are cut off from all their possessions and comforts: for, poor as their portion here is,

"'Tis all the happiness they know."

Yea, they are then cut off from all the means of grace, and the hopes of mercy. In the last day they will be cut off from "the resurrection of life; and before the assembled world, they will hear the Judge irreversibly excluding them from himself, the source of all happiness. "*Depart*, ye cursed, into everlasting fire, prepared for the devil and his angels."

Dreadful as the ruin is, there is nothing in it to alarm the *praying and persevering* believer. He will have no share in it. The vengeance that falls and crushes the foe, will not—cannot touch the friend. He will only be a spectator; and strange as it may now seem, the sight will not affect his happiness. But is it necessary to go further; and represent it as a source of pleasure and delight? Surely it is enough that he will see it, and adore the mercy that graciously saved *him;* and acquiesce in the justice that righteously condemns others.

As the saint will only see the destruction of the sinner, so the wicked will see the salvation of the righteous, and not partake of it. But to see such a blessedness; to see what was once within his own reach, and is now enjoyed by others—this must be a source of the keenest anguish. Such was the display of plenty to the interdicted nobleman at the gate of Samaria: "Behold, thou shalt see it with thine eyes; but thou shalt not eat thereof." And we know who has said, "There shall be weeping and gnashing of teeth, when ye shall see Abraham, and Isaac, and Jacob, and all the prophets, in the kingdom of God, and you yourselves thrust out."

August 24.—"Smite the Shepherd, and the sheep shall be scattered; and I will turn mine hand upon the little ones."—Zech. xiii, 7.

—We know who this Shepherd was. God speaks of him, in the former part of the verse, as "his fellow;" and calls him "his Shepherd." He was God's Shepherd, because he appointed him to take the charge of his church, and to perform, on their behalf, all the duties implied in the pastoral office. Hence it was foretold of him, "He shall feed his flock like a shepherd; he shall gather the lambs with his arm, and carry them in his bosom, and shall gently lead those that are with young." This character the Savior applied to himself, with an attribute of distinction; "I am the good Shepherd." Paul styles him, "That great Shepherd of the sheep." Peter calls him, "The chief Shepherd;" and, "The Shepherd and Bishop of souls." Let the language of my heart be, "Tell me, O Thou whom my soul loveth, where thou feedest, where thou makest thy flock to rest at noon."

"'Tis there, with the lambs of thy flock,
"There only, I covet to rest;
"To lie at the foot of the Rock,
"Or rise to be hid in thy breast.

"'Tis there I would always abide,
"Nor ever a moment depart;
"Preserv'd evermore at thy side,
"Eternally hid in thine heart."

—He was to be "smitten." Every one that enters this vale of tears is a sufferer. But he was "a man of sorrows;" and could say, "Behold, and see if there be any sorrow like unto my sorrow, which is done unto me, wherewith the *Lord* hath afflicted me in the day of his fierce anger." For, though he suffered from devils, who had their hour and power of darkness: and though he suffered from men—for, against him, both Herod and Pontius Pilate, with the Gentiles, and the people of Israel, were gathered together—yet it was only to do whatsoever *his* hand and *his* counsel determined before to be done. It pleased the Lord to bruise him: he put him to grief. When therefore, the Jews esteemed him stricken, smitten of God, and afflicted, they were right in the fact, but mistaken in the cause. They supposed he suffered for guilt; and so he did—but the guilt was not his own. "He was wounded for our transgressions; he was bruised for our iniquities: the chastisement of our peace was upon him; and with his stripes we are healed." Here let me contemplate the evil of sin, in the sufferings of this divine victim. And here let me dwell on that love, which passeth knowledge, that led him, all innocent as he was, voluntarily to become a sacrifice on our behalf; and to suffer, the just for the unjust, that he might bring us unto God. The glory of the Gospel; the hope of the sinner; the triumph of the believer—all lies here—"It is Christ that died."

—It was a sad thing that his own disciples should abandon him, at the very moment he was going to die for them, and after all their professions of determined adherence to him. But when the Shepherd was smitten, "the sheep were scattered." In this desertion, an emblem was furnished of his all-sufficiency for his work, and of the entire meritoriousness of his passion, without addition or co-operation from any creature. He trod the winepress *alone;* and, of the people, there was *none* with him. *By himself* he purged our sins. But, in this dereliction, he was not taken by surprise; for he had previously said, "Behold, the hour cometh, yea, is now come, that ye shall be scattered every man to his own, and shall leave me alone." Yet how much he felt it, may be inferred from his lamentation and complaint: "I looked for some to take pity, but there was none; and for comforters, but I found none." Let not his people count it a strange thing, if they are betrayed or forsaken—It should remind them of the fellowship of his sufferings.

But behold an instance of forgiving mercy and renewing grace; "And I will turn mine hand upon the little ones." His disciples were little in the eyes of the world; and less in their own. They were few in number, and poor in condition. They were weak in faith and fortitude—and were now dismayed, and desponding. But he did not give them over unto death. He knew their frame; he remembered that they were dust. As soon as ever he was risen from the dead, he appeared to them—not clothed in terror; but saying, "Peace be unto you." He exerted again the powerful influence of his Holy Spirit; and renewed them again unto repentance; and established their faith and hope; and gave them enlarged views, and fresh courage, so that they were ready to suffer and to die for his name.

Surely,

"His heart is made of tenderness, | "His bowels melt with love."

A bruised reed will he not break; and smoking flax will he not quench, till he send forth judgment unto victory. And in his name shall the Gentiles trust.

AUGUST 25.—"O Thou that heareth prayer! unto thee shall all flesh come."—Psalm lxv, 2.

We have no claims upon God; and are not worthy of the least of all his mercies. It is therefore surprising that he should hear prayer at all. But he glories in it; and by nothing is he so much distinguished. He derives his fame, his character from it—"O Thou that hearest prayer!"

And we need not wonder at this, when we consider—How *constantly* he has heard prayer; even ever since men began to call upon the name of the Lord. And how *many* prayers he has heard. If we are to pray without ceasing, the prayers of one individual will be very numerous. What, then, is the aggregate multitude that has been offered by all the millions that ever sought his face? And how *largely* he answers prayer—giving grace and glory, and withholding no good thing pertaining to life and godliness. And how *readily* he answers prayer: "Before they call," says he, "I will answer; and while they are yet speaking, I will hear." And how *certainly* he hears prayer. We have his promises, which are firmer than the earth and the heavens. It may not be easy to ascertain when, or how, he answers us, as the God of our salvation: but this we know, that he cannot deny us, without denying himself. He cannot lie—and he has said, "Ask, and it shall be given you; seek, and ye shall find; knock, and it shall be opened unto you; for every one that asketh, receiveth; and he that seeketh, findeth; and to him that knocketh, it shall be opened."

—What should be the influence of this glorious truth? "Unto Thee shall all flesh come." If these words had stood separately, we should have taken them as affirming, that all flesh would come to him at the last day to be judged. But the reference is not to God on the judgment-seat, but on the mercy-seat; and it is well that we can kneel at the latter, before we stand at the former. The meaning is, that men shall seek to him in *prayer;* and not some, but *many;* not many, but *all.* Surely here is nothing less than a prophecy of the calling of the Gentiles. Not only shall the seed of Jacob, his chosen, seek unto him; but those also that were strangers to the commonwealth of Israel, and without God in the world, crying only unto idols that could not save. The Jews in latter times, were carnal, and selfish, and averse to the extension of their privileges: but the more ancient and spiritual of their nation rejoiced in the prospect of it; and they had intimations from the beginning, that the Gentiles, also, should be fellow-heirs, and of the same body, and partakers of the promise of Christ, by the Gospel. "All nations whom thou hast made, shall come and worship before thee." "My house shall be called the house of prayer for all people."

If the practice here insured is to result from the character here expressed, the character must be known. For "how can they call upon him, in whom they have not believed? And how can they believe on him, of whom they have not heard?" Accordingly it is said, "From the rising of the sun, even unto the going down of the same, my name shall be great among the Gentiles; and in every place incense shall be offered unto my name, and a pure offering."

And, to notice this more personally, we see of what importance it is to entertain encouraging views of God. Confidence in his mercy and grace will alone draw us into his presence. And therefore the ground of this confidence must be firm and obvious.

Much advantage, also, upon this principle, must result from reviews of our own experience of his goodness. All success is animating, especially in prayer. "Because he hath inclined his ear unto me, therefore will I call upon him as long as I live."

—Let *me* come to him among all those that are coming. And immediately. For there is a time when he will not hear prayer. "Then shall they call upon me, but I will not answer; they shall seek me early, but they shall not find me."

AUGUST 26.—"Yea, I will betroth thee unto me in righteousness, and in judgment, and in loving-kindness, and in mercies."—Hosea, ii, 19.

IN the covenant of grace, there is God's part, and there is our part. But God—or it would never be accomplished—undertakes for the latter, as well as the former—He engages to do all that is necessary *for* his people, and *in* them.

Here is the *nature* of the connexion he will establish with them; "I will *betroth* thee unto me." And the *manner* of it—"In *righteousness*, and in *judgment*, and in *loving-kindness*, and in *mercies*."

First. I will do it, says he—in *righteousness*—And no wonder, seeing he is holy in all his ways, and righteous in all his works. But the soul that sinneth, it shall die. Righteousness, therefore, seems to require that he should punish them, rather than admit them into his favor. Ah, awakened souls want to see a way in which God is just, as well as the justifier. And he has provided for this; and he tells us in the gospel, that, though sin is pardoned, it is also condemned; and that, though the transgressor escapes, the curse falls upon another, who, by bearing it himself, redeems us from it, and is the end of the law for righteousness to every one that believeth. The law, therefore, instead of being injured, is magnified and made honorable; and even more than it would have been by the destruction of the sinner. In the sinner's destruction, justice would have been always satisfying, but never satisfied. Whereas the satisfaction was now completed at once, "by the one offering up of himself." Then, also, justice would only have been displayed passively—but now it is displayed actively too. Then, it would have been displayed only in them —but now, it is also displayed by them. Then, they would have hated, and cursed it for ever—now, they love it, and delight to extol it. For righteousness here is not to be taken only for the way in which he makes the guilty just, but the way in which he makes the depraved holy. This comes from the same gracious agency; and is equally necessary with the former; as he could not admit them to communion with himself while in a state of sin—For, "how can two walk together except they be agreed?" And, "what fellowship hath righteousness with unrighteousness?"

Secondly. In *judgment*. The heathens placed Mercury, the god of wisdom, by the side of Venus, the goddess of marriage: and for good reason; since there is nothing in which judgment is so needful—yet few things are entered upon with so little discretion and reflection. Hence the wretched consequences that ensue. For what can be expected from those hasty and thoughtless matches, in which, adaptation, age, temper, and even piety, are all overlooked? But God knows what he does, and why he does it. He has reasons, which justify the measure to his own infinite understanding. Hence salvation is called his counsel; in which also he is said to abound toward us in all wisdom and prudence. And this is true, not only as to the contriving and procuring of it, but also as to the applying. The place, the time, the manner, the means of their conversion, will all evince, when known, that his work is perfect, and his ways judgment. We see but little of this now. Yet there are openings into it which carry the mind away in contemplation and surprise; and which assures much more remains for our discovery and rapture in the world of light. This applies also to his people, as well as to God. Their choosing him and consenting to his gracious proposals, will bear examination. It is wisdom: and wisdom which is justified of all her children. The world may censure; but they are able to give a reason of the hope that is in them. The spiritual judgeth all things, though he himself is judged of no man.

Thirdly. In *loving kindness.* Without this, it were better for persons never to come together. The parties mutually need it; and need it daily. They should be filled with tenderness, to bear and sympathize with each other; and the law of kindness should rule in their looks, words, and actions. This is seldom wanting on the female side. Their love is not only more pure and disinterested, but more fervent and undeclining, and better prepared to endure privation and sacrifices. Men are fond of power and authority; and therefore they are commanded—not to govern them—this they will do readily enough; but to love their wives, and not be bitter against them. God says to his church: "You shall find me full of tenderness and compassion. I know your frame, and remember that you are dust. I will pity your infirmities, and spare you. If I afflict, it shall not be willingly. If I chide, I will not contend for ever. I will look to the heart, and judge you according to your meaning, and your desires." It would seem strange to apply the exercise of this quality to *them*, as well as to Him. Kindness towards God seems too low an expression; but he himself has sanctioned it—"I remember thee, the kindness oi thy youth, and the love of thine espousals, when thou wentest after me in the wilderness, in a land that was not sown." Every thing they do for Him, he takes kind at their hand: and their ingenious disposition will make them fearful of grieving his Holy Spirit; and anxious to walk "worthy of him unto all pleasing."

Fourthly. In *mercies.* This is distinguishable from the former. *That* was the effect; *this* shows the cause—and it is mentioned, in addition to loving-kindness, to remind us that all we possess, or expect, springs solely from the free and undeserved grace of God—and also to meet those discouragements to which we are always liable, from a sense of our unworthiness and ill-deservings. There is not a just man on earth that liveth, and sinneth not. In many things we offend all. What humiliations must a Christian feel, when he reviews even his sabbaths, and holy communions! and when he compares his proficiency with his obligations and advantages! But God will not cast away his people; but have mercy upon them according to the *multitude* of his *tender* mercies. This is children's bread; and the children of God will not, cannot abuse it—yea, the more they are persuaded of this truth, the more holy and cheerful, and vigorous they will be in duty. Grass that grows in orchards, and under trees, is of a sour quality: it wants the sun. Fruits that grow in the sun are richer and riper than those which grow in the shade. The best frame we can be in, is to be upholden by a free spirit, and to act under a full sense of our divine privileges. Let us therefore sing of the mercy of the Lord for ever, and if he ever *seems* to have forgotten to be gracious, let us plead with him, and say, "Where is thy zeal, and thy strength, the sounding of thy bowels, and of thy mercies toward me? Are they restrained?" Here again the import includes, not only that we receive mercy, but exercise it—not toward Him personally—this is impossible—and he needs it not. But his creatures need it; his people need it. And what is done to them he will consider as done to himself. And what is so just and proper, as that they who are forgiven, should forgive? And that they who live by mercy, should be merciful?

AUGUST 27.—"—Heirs—."—Titus, iii, 6.

If we properly observe those who are Christians indeed, we shall find in them a peculiarity that distinguishes them from, and an importance that ranks them above all other creatures. What an assemblage of qualities, excellencies, and advantages must they possess, to do any thing like justice to the various and numberless representations by which they are held forth to our view and admiration in the Scriptures of Truth! Let me contemplate them under the character of *Heirs.*

As such, we may consider them *in the grandeur of their estate.* A man may be an heir to a cottage, or a large domain, or even a throne. But what is the inheritance of Christians! In one place they are called "heirs, according to promise"—in another, "heirs of the grace of life"—in another, "heirs, according to the hope of eternal life"—in another, "heirs of Salvation"—in another, "heirs of the kingdom, which the Lord hath promised to them that love him." Paul prays that the Ephesians may be enlightened to know it; and speaks of "the hope of their calling," and "the riches of the glory of his inheritance in the saints." The inheritance of the worldling, who has his portion in this life; the inheritance of the Jew, in Canaan; the inheritance of Adam, in Paradise; the inheritance of angels, in heaven; all come far short of the believer's expectation. At present, it cannot be fully either described or conceived—it is a glory to be revealed—it doth not yet appear what we shall be.

We may consider them in the *solidity of their title.* No person ever had a claim to an estate so clear and decisive as the Christian has to his inheritance. He may not, indeed, be certain of it in his own mind. There is a difference between a right, and the perception of it. An heir, by reason of his tender age, or infirmity, or disorder, may be unconscious of what awaits him. And Christians may be ignorant and fearful. They may condemn them selves, when God has justified them freely from all things; and they may conclude that they have no part nor lot in the matter, while yet their title is as valid as the word and oath of God can make it—it is also perfectly inseparable from the birth that makes them new creatures, for they are born of God, and, "if children, then heirs, and joint heirs with Jesus Christ;" and, being one with him, their heirship is as undeniable as his.

We may view them, also, in the *certainty of their possession.* An heir who has had the clearest and fullest title to an estate, has yet never enjoyed it. To take possession of it, perhaps he had to cross the sea, and was wrecked. Or he travelled by land, and was murdered. Or, in reaching maturity, he fell a prey to one of the many diseases to which humanity is liable. Or, if he was preserved, the estate was destroyed: for there is no place of security on earth. Or, if the estate was not destroyed, it was *usurped*, and by fraud and villany, alienated from its lawful owner. How many figure away, only in the rights of others! But what shall hinder the Christian from realizing his hope? His inheritance is incorruptible and undefiled, and fadeth not away, reserved in heaven for him, where danger never comes. And the heir is as safe as the estate; being "kept by the power of God, through faith, unto salvation."

But observe these heirs in the circumstances of their *minority* For there is a period of non-age: and "the heir, as long as he is a child, differeth nothing from a servant, though he be Lord of all; but is under tutors and governors until the time appointed of the father." Before this season arrives, he must submit to many restraints, not pleasant to his feelings, and the reasons of which he cannot fully appreciate. Yea, there may be cases in which he may even be constrained to borrow from a domestic or neighbor, who has none of his expectancy. And Christians must not reckon that their present indulgences will equal their future reversions. They are now under a course of discipline, in which they must exercise self denial, and appear less favored than many around them. But they rejoice in hope, and not only so, but, as the heir has something more from his estate than the prospect of it; as he has education and attendance, becoming his rank; and remittances, to enable him to live, answerable to his destination: so Christians have new supplies from their riches in glory, and are training up, under a divine teacher, for the sublime spheres they are to fill; and their ministering spirits do always behold the face of our heavenly Father.

And what is *the deportment that becomes these heirs?* It ought to be ennobled. Holiness is the true dignity of the soul, and sin, its vilest degradation. They are, therefore, to "have no fellowship with the unfruitful works of darkness; but rather reprove them." And, oh! the infinite delicacy of the Gospel! they are to "abstain from the very appearance of evil." It ought to be humble and grateful. They were, by nature, only children of wrath. If their relation is glorious, it is derived entirely from grace. There were difficulties in the way of their adoption, which God alone could remove. "But I said, How shall I put thee among the children, and give thee a pleasant land, a goodly heritage?" But he removed these obstacles by the sacrifice of his own Son, and the renovation of his own Spirit; and, poor and vile as they were, he raised up the poor out of the dust, and lifted the needy from the dunghill, to set them with princes, even the princes of his people. It ought to be very cheerful and happy.

"A hope so much divine, | "May trials well endure."

But so inferior are natural things to spiritual, that, when the one are applied to the illustration of the other, they teach us as much by contrast as by comparison—what, then *is the differ-*

ence between these and earthly heirs! In other cases, the inheritance is diminished by the number of co-heirs. But here, the multitude of partakers, instead of injuring, increases the blessedness of each possessor. In other cases, the father dies before the child inherits. Here, the father never dies. In other cases, the heir, by dying, loses his inheritance. Here, he gains it by dying—it is then he comes of age. In other cases, an estate passes from hand to hand. Here, is no succession—it is our heritage for ever. "This is the heritage of the servants of the Lord; and their righteousness is of me, saith the Lord."

August 28.—"Iniquities prevail against me—as for our transgressions, thou shalt purge them away."—Psalm lxv, 3.

This is the language of complaint and of triumph. It was uttered by a Jew; but every Christian can make it his own. For, as in water, face answereth to face, so the heart of man to man, in every age, and under every dispensation.

As to the complaint, there are two ways in which iniquities may prevail against the Christian. The first is in the growing sense of his guilt. This may be occasioned by afflictions, which bring our sins to remembrance; or by any thing which increases self-knowledge; for this must always show us more of our unworthiness and depravity. Suppose a man in a dungeon, abounding with noxious reptiles. While all is dark there, he sees none of them; but as the light increases, he sees more of them—the light seems to bring them, and to multiply them; but it only discovers what was there before. Some pray that God would show them all the corruptions of their heart; but this would probably drive them into distraction or despair. They could not bear the whole disclosure, especially at first; and therefore they are made sensible of them by little and little.

The second is in the power of their acting. This prevalence cannot be entire; for sin shall not have dominion over them; but it may be occasional and partial. An enemy may make a temporary irruption, and do injury, though he may be soon expelled again. In a war, checks and discomfitures are not incompatible with general and final success, as we see in the history of the Romans. The Israelites were repulsed at Ai; but they returned to the assault with more caution and wisdom, and succeeded. And thus, whatever advantages the foe may gain *against* Christians, the God of peace will bruise Satan under their feet shortly. David does not say, Iniquities prevail *with* me, but *against* me. As to many, they prevail with them, *They* drink in iniquity, as the ox drinketh in water. *They* draw iniquity with cords of vanity, and sin as it were with a cart rope. But a Christian is made willing in the day of God's power, and therefore can say, "To will is present with me, but how to perform that which is good I find not. When I *would* do good, evil is present with me." Ahab is said to have sold himself to work wickedness. But it is otherwise with a poor slave in Africa. He is kidnapped, or taken by force, and disposed of to some demon-trafficker in flesh and blood. He resists and weeps—but they prevail *against* him. And, says Paul,

I do not sell myself, but I am sold under sin. So then it is no more I that do it, but sin that dwelleth in me. O wretched man that I am, who shall deliver me! Poison in a serpent never produces sickness; but it does in a man; because it is natural to the one, but not to the other. Sin does not distress the sinner; but it offends, beyond every thing else, the renewed mind.

The words are broken and abrupt; but when the church adds, "As for our transgressions, thou shalt purge them away," they are, assuredly, the triumph of faith, after a plunge of distress, and a pause of thoughtfulness. There are two ways, according to the Scripture, in which God purges our transgressions; and they always go together. The one is by pardoning mercy. Thus David prays—"Purge me with hyssop, and I shall be clean; wash me, and I shall be whiter than snow. Hide thy face from my sins, and blot out all mine iniquities." Thus the blood of Jesus Christ cleanseth us from all sin. And they that believe on him are justified from all things.

The other is by sanctifying grace. "I will sprinkle clean water upon you, and ye shall be clean; from all your filthiness, and from all your idols will I cleanse you." And this is as much the work of God as the former. He subdues our iniquities, as well as forgives them. He not only ordains peace for us, but works all our works in us.

The Christian is *persuaded* of this gracious deliverance, and therefore expresses himself with confidence. And a foundation is laid for this confidence; and such a firm and scriptural foundation, as that he may feel himself perfectly safe in the midst of danger; and, under the deepest sense of his desert, joy in God, through our Lord Jesus Christ, by whom he has now received the atonement; and, with regard to all the conflicts of in-dwelling sin, take courage, and sing— "I shall not die, but live, and declare the works of the Lord."

"My spirit holds perpetual war,
"And wrestles and complains;
"But views the happy moment near
"That shall dissolve its chains.

"Cheerful in death I close my eyes,
"To part with every lust;
"And charge my flesh, whene'er it rise,
"To leave them in the dust."

AUGUST 29.—"So then they which be of faith are blessed with faithful Abraham."—Galatians, iii, 9.

THE outward distinctions of life awaken the envy of some, and gender discontents in others. And yet how little depends upon them! All that is essential to the real welfare and chief happiness of man, lies open to all who choose to avail themselves of it. All cannot become scholars; but all may be made wise unto salvation. All cannot acquire wealth; but all may gain the unsearchable riches of Christ. All cannot walk upon the high places of the earth; but all may be great in the sight of the Lord. Abraham, the founder of the Jewish nation, was considered the most dignified and indulged of the human race; yet every Christian, however poor and despised, stands related to this extraordinary character, and is blessed with him. "If ye be Christ's, then are ye Abraham's seed, and heirs, according to his promise." "They which are of faith, the same are the children of Abraham." "So then they which be of faith are blessed with faithful Abraham." And how was he blessed?

He was *justified*. And blessed are they whose iniquities are forgiven, and whose sins are covered: blessed is the man to whom the Lord will not impute sin. For him there is no wrath to come, no sitting in death, no curse in affliction. But came this blessedness upon Abraham only? "What saith the scripture? Abraham believed God, and it was counted unto him for righteousness. Now it was not written for his sake alone, that it was imputed to him, but for us also, to whom it shall be imputed, if we believe on him that raised up Jesus our Lord from the dead; who was delivered for our offences, and was raised again for our justification." So then they that be of faith are blessed with faithful Abraham. And are all authorized to say, "Therefore being justified by faith, we have peace with God through our Lord Jesus Christ."

—Abraham was called the *friend of God*—and was called so by God himself. "But thou, Israel, art my servant, Jacob whom I have chosen, the seed of Abraham, my friend." If Eusebius held it such a privilege to be the friend of Pamphilus: If Lord Brookes so gloried in the distinction, as to have it inscribed upon his tomb—

"Here lies the friend of Sir Philip Sidney,"

what was the honor of Abraham, in being acknowedged the friend of God? Yet such honor have all the saints. They are not only pardoned, but admitted to intimacy. They walk with God. His secret is with them; and he shows them his covenant. In all their afflictions, he is afflicted. He loveth at all times; and will never leave or forsake them. "So then they which be of faith are blessed with faithful Abraham."

—Abraham, also, was blessed with *usefulness*. "I will bless thee," says God, "and make thee a blessing." This was done, not only in the descent of the Messiah from him, in whom all the families of the earth were to be blessed eventually, but by his prayers, and instructions, and example, and exertions, and influence, wherever he came. Thus also are all believers blessed. Not one of them is useless. They are disposed to do good; and their desire is gratified. They are qualified to do good; and as stewards of the manifold grace of God, they serve their generation by his will. They are the salt of the earth, to preserve; the light of the world, to inform; and a dew from the Lord, and as showers upon the grass, to cool and refresh, and revive, and fertilize; "I will save you, and ye shall be a blessing."

—Abraham was *divinely protected:* and God said to him, "I am thy shield." "I will bless him that blesseth thee; and I will curse him that curseth thee." He preserved him in his going out and coming in. He covered his head in the day of battle, when he rescued his kinsman, Lot. He suffered no man to do him wrong: yea, he reproved kings for his sake, saying, Touch not mine anointed, and do my prophet no harm. And thus, though many rise up against believers, and they feel themselves to be perfect weakness, their defence is of God, who saveth the upright in heart. He is their refuge and strength; a very present and all-sufficient help in trouble. They are kept by the power of God, through faith unto salvation; therefore they need not fear what their enemies can do unto them.

Abraham had not only a divine protection, but an *infinite portion:* "I am," says God, not only "thy shield," but "thy exceeding great reward!" This necessarily includes what God was to do for him beyond the grave. It could not have been fulfilled in this life. When we find him, a few years after this assurance, sickening and dying, and laid in the cave of Machpelah, we are constrained to ask, Is this the reward, the great, the exceeding great reward, consisting, so to speak, of God himself? Ages after this, God said to Moses, at the bush I *am*—not I was—but, I *am* the God of Abraham, of Isaac, and of Jacob. The relation, therefore, remained; for, "He is not the God of the dead, but of the living." They were then living, as to their spirits; and would as certainly live, as to their bodies, in the resurrection, as if it had already taken place. Hence the reasoning of the apostle; "By faith he sojourned in the land of promise, as in a strange country, dwelling in tabernacles with Isaac and Jacob, the heirs with him of the same promise: for he looked for a city that hath foundations, whose builder and maker is God." "And truly, if they had been mindful of that country from whence they came out, they might have had opportunity to have returned. But now they desire a better country, that is, a heavenly: wherefore God is not ashamed to be called their God: for he hath prepared for them a city." Our Savior also allowed him to be in glory; and even represented heaven by a union and intimacy with him: "The beggar died, and was carried by angels into Abraham's bosom." Well, and nothing less than this is the glad and glorious destination of every believer. For they that be of faith are blessed with faithful Abraham.

The grand inquiry therefore is—"Dost thou believe on the Son of God?" For we have access only by *faith* into this grace, wherein we stand, and rejoice in hope of the glory of God.

For they that are not of his faith are cursed with—the faithless nobleman, to whom it was denounced, "Thou shalt see it with thine eyes, but thou shalt not taste of it." And with the faithless Jews, whose carcasses fell in the wilderness; and who "could not enter in because of unbelief." And "with hypocrites and unbelievers, where there is weeping, and wailing, and gnashing of teeth."

AUGUST 30.—"Pass the time of your sojourning here in fear."
1 Peter, 1, 17

FROM these words, I might consider the nature of the Christian life—which is a *sojourning here:* and also—the *time* appointed for it. But let me rather reflect upon the *manner* in which I am to pass the one, in accomplishing the other. "Pass the time of your sojourning here *in fear.*" This cannot intend every kind of fear, without making the Scripture inconsistent with itself: for how often does it forbid fear!

We must not, therefore, give way to apprehensions of any

thing we may suffer from our fellow creatures, in following the path of duty. Here we should boldly say, "The Lord is my helper; I will not fear what man can do unto me." "Fear not," says the Savior—mentioning the extremest case—"Fear not them that kill the body, and after that have no more that they can do." And this, Paul exemplified: "None of these things move me; neither count I my life dear unto myself, so that I might finish my course with joy." When Peter and John were threatened, if they spake any more in the name of Jesus, they replied, We have nothing to do with consequences: we cannot but speak the things which we have seen and heard: we ought to obey God rather than man: and he has commanded us to preach the gospel to every creature. So should it be with us. We are not, indeed, to run into sufferings for our religion; but we can never go on well in divine things till we are delivered from the fear of man that bringeth a snare. What is it but this, that produces so many concealments, and defections, and inconsistencies, in those who know what is right, and are incited by their convictions, but have not courage enough to resolve and proceed? Perfect love casteth out this fear; and is strong as death.

We are equally to shun a distrustfulness of God's word. This fear is at once the most dishonorable to God, and injurious to our own souls. It robs us of comfort, and lays open the mind, to temptation; as we see in Abraham, who, in a moment of unbelief prevaricated, and debased and exposed himself in Gerar. Having the assurance of God in any case, we should feel no uncertainty as to the result—it must be accomplished—we have something firmer than the earth and the heavens to rely upon. But we may fear, not—whether we shall perish in the way everlasting; but whether we are in it. Not—whether the promise will fail; but whether we are the heirs of promise; as the apostle even admonishes—"Let us therefore fear, lest a promise being left us of entering into his rest, any of us should seem to come short of it." This is a case too important to be taken for granted. The consequences of mistake are remediless; and the possibility, yea, the probability of it, is great. It will, therefore, be better to err on the side of solicitude, than of security.

A servile fear, too, is not to be cherished. This may, indeed, precede something better: but if our fear of God begins, with the Judge, it must end with the father. It argues a very low degree of religion, when a man can only be held to duty, like the slave, by the dread of the lash. We have not, says the Apostle, received the Spirit of bondage again to fear; but the Spirit of adoption. The slave is converted into the child; and God spareth him as a man spareth his own son that serveth him.

But there is a proper and all-important fear, which God has engaged to put into the hearts of his people, that they may not depart from him—It is a fear of respect, and esteem, and gratitude. It regards not only God's greatness, but his goodness. There is, therefore, nothing irksome in it. It is compatible with consolation and joy: and the first Christians walked in the fear of the Lord, and in the comfort of the Holy Ghost. It is, in reality, the same with affection—the love which an inferior bears to a superior—the love of a dutiful child to a parent; or of a good servant to a master; or of a thankful dependant to a benefactor. This shows itself much in a way of reverence, and obedience, and attention. Hence, the more I love God, the more I shall fear him: the more I shall dread to offend him; the more I shall study to please him; the more I shall ask, "Lord, what wilt thou have me to do?" the more I shall pray. "Let the words of my mouth, and the meditation of my heart, be acceptable in thy sight, O Lord, my strength, and my Redeemer."

There is, also, a fear of caution, in which it becomes us to live. This regards sin. Sin is the greatest evil to which we can be exposed. And we may see enough in the case of David to make even a good man stand in dread of it. For though God put away his sin, as to its future penalty, yet it was ever before him in the sufferings it occasioned. The sword never departed from his house. He was filled with dread of divine abandonment. He was deprived of his peace and joy. His bones were broken: and his tongue was struck dumb. And a holy God will always cause the backslidings, even of his own people, to reprove them, and make them know that it is an evil and a bitter thing to sin against him. He will becloud their hope, and destroy their comfort, and perhaps quarter troubles upon them for life. Reputation, which is the produce of years, may be ruined in a moment: and the effect of a thousand good actions may be lost, by one evil deed. He who has befriended religion, may cause the way of truth to be evil spoken of, and become a judgment upon the whole neighborhood in which he dwells.

And are we in danger of this? Read the Scriptures. See the falls of good men; and men eminently good. Have not we a subtle and active enemy always at hand? Have we not a wicked world without us? and an evil heart within us? Owing to our remaining depravity, are we not liable to be ensnared by every thing we come in contact with, however harmless in itself? If we *think* caution unnecessary, we have the *greatest* need of it: for "pride goeth before destruction, and a haughty spirit before a fall." Wherefore, let him that thinketh he standeth, take heed, lest he fall. Be not high minded, but fear.

If we would maintain this frame of mind, let us walk circumspectly; not as fools but as wise. Let us not be anxious to rise in the world, and gain the affluence which will require a moral miracle to preserve us. "He that makes haste to be rich, shall not be innocent." "They that will be rich, fall into temptation, and a snare, and into many foolish and hurtful lusts, which drown men in destruction and perdition. For the love of money is the root of all evil; which while some coveted after, they have erred from the faith, and pierced themselves through with many sorrows."

—Let us keep our mouth with a bridle. In a multitude of words there wanteth not sin.

—Let us not run into perils, uncalled of God. We are only authorized to look for his protection when we are brought into them in the discharge of duty. And, while we watch, let us also constantly pray, "Hold thou me up, and I shall be safe" "BLESSED IS THE MAN THAT FEARETH ALWAY."

AUGUST 31.—"I will betroth thee unto me for ever.' —Hosea, ii, 19.

How well is it said of Christians, "Ye who sometimes were far off, are made nigh by the blood of Christ." They are not only pardoned, but employed in his service. They are not only reconciled, but admitted into friendship and intimacy. Yea, they are not only friends and favorites, but they are his bride—"I will betroth thee unto me;" and observe the permanency of the relation, "I will betroth thee unto me for ever."

"Permanency," says the poet, "adds bliss to bliss." How is every possession and enjoyment without it, impaired in value! Yea, the more important any acquisition be, and the more necessary we feel to our happiness, the more alive are we to apprehension of danger: the more averse are we to absence; the more painful is separation; the more intolerable is the thought of loss.

Yet, to whatever we are attached here, do we not set our "hearts on that which is not?" It is said that the Jews, in their nuptial ceremony, always threw a glass upon the ground, to signify, that the union then forming was as frail as the emblem was brittle. Without the figure, if we are wise, there is enough to remind us of the fact: and well does the apostle reason, when he says, "Brethren the time is short: it remains, therefore, that they who have wives be as though they had none."

We take each other, "till death do us part." And the relation is terminated by death—not the death of both—but the death of either. What then is the tenure of the treasure? What is our life? It is even as a vapor that appeareth for a little time, and then vanisheth away. Has God given you a companion in the days of your vanity? Rejoice; but rejoice with trembling. Perhaps, already the wife has been called to give up "the guide of her youth:" or the husband "the desire of his eyes;" with whom they once took sweet counsel together, and walked to the house of God in company!

But Christians can never be in a widowed state. They can never lose their defence, their glory, their joy. There is nothing precarious in the transactions of God with his people. "I know that what ever God doeth, it shall be for ever; nothing can be put to it, and nothing can be taken from it." How delightful in a world of changes to know that *He* changeth not, and therefore that we shall not be consumed. Every thing seems reeling around me, and sinking beneath my feet: but I have hold of something firmer than the heavens and the earth—the word, the oath of eternal faithfulness and truth. "For the mountains shall depart, and the hills shall be removed: but my kindness shall not depart from thee, neither shall the covenant of my peace be removed, saith the Lord that hath mercy on thee." "I will make an everlasting covenant with them, that I will not turn away from them, to do them good; but I will put my fear in their hearts, that they shall not depart from me." I have had many a persuasion which has failed me, because, though the confidence was strong, the foundation was weak. But here the full assurance of faith can never do justice to the certainty of the event. "For I am persuaded, that neither death, nor life, nor angels, nor principalities, nor powers, nor things present, nor things to come, nor height, nor depth, nor any other creature, shall be able to separate us from the love of God, which is in Christ Jesus our Lord."

SEPTEMBER 1.—"The word of life."—Philippians, ii, 16.

THIS is a representation of the Gospel; and it well deserves our notice. All life is valuable; but there are several kinds of it, rising above each other. There is vegetable life—this is superior to mere matter; as a tree is more excellent than a stone. There is animal life—this is superior to vegetable; as a bird excels a tree. There is rational life—this is superior to animal; as a man excels a bird: for man was made a little lower than the angels. There is a spirit in man, and the inspiration of the Almighty giveth him understanding. Yet there is a life superior to rational—it is called the life of God; a life from which we are naturally alienated; but to which all subjects of divine grace are restored by the Savior, who came, not only that we might have life, but have it more abundantly. It will be completed in heaven but it is begun here. The case is this. Man, by transgression, is dead in *state;* for cursed is every one that continueth not in all things written in the book of the law to do them. He is also dead in *disposition*—or, as the apostle expresses it, dead in trespasses and sins. But the Christian is passed from death unto life. He is no longer exposed to condemnation, for he is justified by faith, and has peace with God. And he is no longer under the power of moral death; for he is quickened and made to walk in newness of life. "I compare," says he, "my present with my former experience. I was once dead to divine things, for they no more impressed me than sensible things affect a dead corpse. But now, for the very same reason, I hope I am alive; for these very things do affect me, do interest me, do excite in me hope and fear. I am susceptible of spiritual joy and sorrow. I live, for I breathe the breath of prayer. I feel the pulse of sacred passions—I love, and I hate. I have appetite—for I hunger and thirst after righteousness. I walk, and I work—and though all my efforts betray weakness, they evince life."

But what will this life be, when there shall be no more death—when the body shall partake of the immortality of the soul—when both shall be glorified together—in a perpetual duration of knowledge, purity, friendship, riches, and glory. This is life eternal!

Now the Gospel is called the word of this life; and it has four relations to it: A relation of discovery—for it reveals the reality and excellency of this life; the way in which it is obtained; the source from which it flows; and every particle of information we have concerning it. A relation of conveyance—for it communicates; it produces this life. A relation of support—for it is the means, not only of begetting this life, but of maintaining and increasing it. Therefore, it is considered as its food; adapted to all stages of its being—milk, if we are babes; strong meat if we are men. A relation of order—it is the rule by which this life is governed, as to doctrine, worship, experience, exertion. To this rule all our religion must be brought; and as many as walk according to this rule, peace be on them, and mercy, and upon the Israel of God.

SEPTEMBER 2.—"Holding forth the word of life."—Philippians, ii, 16.

THE apostles did this supernaturally. They received their commission immediately from God; and were preserved from all mistakes in delivering his counsel; and could work miracles in confirmation and defence of it. Ministers do this officially. They pretend to no original communications from God, no new discoveries—they derive what they publish from the Scriptures; and they call upon you to prove whether these things are so. Yet their preaching is a divine ordinance—a work which an angel might covet; the simple design of which is to hold forth the word of life.

But there are many ways of doing this, common to all Christians, and they are the persons the apostle here addresses. They may hold it forth by their profession. This is not to be considered as a substitute for experience, but as flowing from it. Experience is a secret thing between God and their own souls; but their religion is to be visible as well as real. They that are in darkness are to show themselves; and we are to confess with the mouth, as well as to believe with the heart, unto salvation. They may hold it forth by example. And this must evince the sincerity, and conduce to the efficacy, of your profession. You are required to walk worthy of the vocation wherewith you are called; and to constrain others, by your good works which they behold, to glorify God in the day of visitation. Nothing is so eloquent as the silence of a holy, consistent, and lovely life. Actions speak louder than words; and by these you can cause the way of truth to be evil spoken of, or adorn the doctrine of God our Savior in all things. It is thus *all* can be "holders forth," whatever be their condition, and without leaving their place and station. This is the way in which servants are to preach to their masters and mistresses, and children to their parents. Indeed, with regard to all of us,

"*Thus* shall we best proclaim aloud
"The honors of our Savior God;
"When the salvation reigns within,
"And grace subdues the power of sin."

This is not, however, to hinder express exertions. By these, when the life is in accordance with them, much may be often done. There are few so situated and limited as not to have some opportunities and influences by which they may be useful, and in a much greater degree than they are aware of, if they will seize them with simplicity, and diligence, and prayer. The talents of men are various, but the servant who has only one will be condemned if he wraps it up in a napkin. When we can do little individually, we can do something by joining with others, and recommending and aiding those institutions which aim at the diffusion of the cause of Christ. We cannot translate the Scriptures into other tongues, but we can circulate them. We are not at liberty to go abroad ourselves; but we can be fellow-helpers to the truth, by contributing to missions. Silver and gold we have none; but we can apply to those who have. We are not donors; but we can be collectors.

What should induce us to hold forth the word of life? Interest. The regard we pay to the Gospel will bless our souls; for, like its Author, it says, Them that honor me, I will honor. We seldom labor in vain in this work; but if our efforts should prove successless, in some way or other they will return into our own bosom. The most respected, and the most happy Christians, are the unselfish, the active, the fervent in spirit, serving the Lord.

Benevolence. The Gospel is not only wonderful, but all-important. It is the Gospel of our salvation. It is the bread, the water of life. For dying souls it is the only remedy. It has done more already for even the public welfare of nations than all the civil institutions of men; and by this alone will the wilderness and solitary place be made glad, and the desert rejoice and blossom as the rose.

Piety. It is thus God's perfections are displayed. It is thus his enemies are to be diminished, and his subjects increased. It is thus his kingdom comes. And what claims has he not upon us for our service? Whose are we? Who bought us with a price?

Our relation in the church. Why have we joined ourselves to a religious society, and placed ourselves under the ministry of the word? Is it only to commune together in privilege, or also to co-operate together in usefulness? Holding forth the word of life, says the text—That I may rejoice in the day of Christ, that I have not run in vain, nor labored in vain.

SEPTEMBER 3.—"Speak, Lord; for thy servant heareth."—1 Samuel, iii, 9.

THIS shows a temper of mind which we should feel on every occasion. But what does He say to us now we are leaving home for a season; and shall in a peculiar sense be for a while strangers and pilgrims on earth?

He requires us, in this excursion, to look to our motives. Surely sin is out of the question. What a dreadful thing it would be to go from home to get opportunities to commit iniquity, without danger of observation and discovery! To such it might well be said, This journey shall not be to thine honor. But the object is lawful, if it be business; if it be friendship; if it be relative affection; if it be health; if it be recreation, within proper bounds, and with a view to prepare for future application.

He requires us to move in a dependence on his providence. The way of man is not in himself; it is not in man that walketh to direct his steps. In his hand, our breath is; in his, are all our ways. There are many who live without God in the world. James describes the presumption of such an individual in the thought of a journey, and a project—"Go to now, ye that say,

To-day or to-morrow we will go into such a city, and continue there a year, and buy and sell, and get gain: whereas ye know not what shall be on the morrow. For what is your life? It is even a vapor that appeareth for a little time, and then vanisheth away. For that ye ought to say, if the Lord will, we shall live, and do this or that. But now ye rejoice in your boastings: all such rejoicing is evil." Paul speaks of a prosperous journey, by the will of God. Nothing can be done without his permission and blessing. He can set every thing against us, or make every thing conduce to our profit. He can spread a gloom over the fairest scenes of nature; or he can comfort us on every side. The elements are his. He preserveth man and beast. Let us remember our entire reliance upon him; and hear him at this moment saying, "Commit thy way unto the Lord; trust also in him, and he shall bring it to pass."

He requires, that wherever we go, we should maintain the consistency of our character. This does not forbid the exercise of prudence. We are even commanded to be wise as serpents, as well as harmless as doves; and walk circumspectly, not as fools, but as wise: and especially to walk in wisdom toward them that are without. But this does not require the surrender of principle, or even the concealment of it. We are not to be ashamed of the Savior, and of his words; but confess him before men. If we become all things to all men, it must be in things sinless and indifferent. If we please our neighbor, it must be for his good to edification. If we yield, and "trim our way," an act unbecoming our profession, we shall not only lose the benefit of reproving, convincing, and impressing others, by a practical testimony, but procure for ourselves contempt, instead of esteem. For those who understand not our experience, can comprehend our duty; and those who do not admire piety, despise inconsistency.

He, therefore, requires us to seize and seek opportunities of usefulness. All cannot act in the same way. Our stations and abilities differ: and we are not to suffer our good to be evil spoken of. But let us beware of indecision and excuse. "He that observeth the wind shall not sow; and he that regardeth the clouds shall not reap." Who may not be a blessing in every place in which he is found? Who can tell the influence, immediate or remote, of a proper and lovely example? of a word fitly spoken? of a book lent, or a tract given? of a *wise* and *moral* distribution of alms? "In the morning sow thy seed, and in the evening withhold not thy hand; for thou knowest not whether it shall prosper, either this or that, or whether they shall be alike good." Let us never think any of our possessions or endowments our own. They are talents; and, "as every man hath received the gift, even so let us minister the same one to another, as good stewards of the manifold grace of God." Many of our opportunities are already gone, and they are gone for ever. How many remain, we know not; but they are few and uncertain. Let us awake, and resemble him who went about doing good; and who said, "I must work the works of him that sent me while it is day; the night cometh when no man can work."

He requires that we should not be careless and inattentive observers of his works. The works of the Lord are great, in number and in quality; and are sought out of all them that have pleasure therein. And I will, says God, that thou magnify his works which men behold. We can see them every where; but, as we move from one place to another, we perceive them in a greater variety. And when from an inland situation we reach the watery world, we behold his wonders in the deep. The sea is his, and he made it; and, with all its immensity, holds it in the hollow of his hand. What wisdom do we recognise in the salineness of the fluid; and in the ebbing and flowing of the tide? What power appears in raising, and in calming the billows; and in giving to the sea his decree, that the waters should not pass his commandment; saying, Hitherto shalt thou come, and no further; and here shall thy proud waves be stayed! And we should observe his works, not only as objects of curiosity and wonder, but as excitements to admiration and praise. We should regard them not as naturalists and philosophers, but with the views and feelings of Christians.

He requires that we should find in all we see, confirmations of our faith in his word. The Scripture tells us of the flood by which the ungodly world was destroyed and the earth convulsed and torn—And what indications of this awful catastrophe do we often meet with! The Scripture tells us, that though God made man upright, he sought out many inventions, and that we are gone astray: there is none righteous, no not one—And where can we go and not discern this? "While the earth remaineth, seedtime and harvest, and cold and heat, and summer and winter, and day and night, shall not cease." And in the succession of the seasons, we see this pledge redeemed. He is good to all, and his tender mercies are over all his works—and we have but to open our eyes, and we see him opening his hand, and satisfying the desires of every living thing.

He requires, that in our progress and our return, we should be thankful. And how much is there to awaken our gratitude? That we have not only been supplied and supported, but have had so many agreeable prospects and entertainments, and changes—that we have been preserved in our going out and our coming in—that we have been secured from wicked and unreasonable men—that no accident has spilt our life upon the ground, or bruised a limb of our body—that our property has been secured, as well as our persons and health—that no plague has come nigh our dwelling—and that we know also that our tabernacle is in peace! Bless the Lord, O our souls; and all that is within us, bless his holy name!

He requires that we should realize life itself as only a journey, and think of getting home. We are but strangers and sojourners here, as were all our fathers. There is none abiding. "Lord, make me to know mine end, and the measure of my days, what it is; that I may know how frail I am." "So teach us to number our days, that we may apply our hearts unto wisdom."

SEPTEMBER 4.—"Peace I leave with you."—John, xiv, 27.

WE know whose words these are—And who was ever so qualified and authorized to speak of peace as he? He is called the Prince of Peace. His ministers are the messengers of peace. His word is the Gospel of peace. His way is the path of peace. An angel announced peace at his birth; and he himself bequeathed peace at his death—"Peace I leave with you."

For we may consider the words, so to speak, as a part of his last will and testament. Lands, and houses, and goods, and silver, and gold, he had none to leave. But such as he had he disposed of in a manner following. That is to say; his soul to God—Father, into thy hand I commit my spirit. His body to the envy and malice of his enemies—to be buffeted, and scourged, and crucified. His wearing apparel, to the soldiers—who divided his garments among them, and for his vesture cast lots. His widowed mother, to the care of John—who, from that hour, took her unto his own home. But what have his disciples all this time? Has he forgotten them? No—"Peace I leave with you."

But why does he bestow it upon them in a way of legacy? First; to make it the dearer. They would thus prize this boon—It was the remembrance of their dying Lord and Savior. Any thing left us by a dying friend, if it be only a book, or ring, is esteemed and valued. Secondly; to render it the surer. If it be but a man's testament, yet if it be confirmed, no man can disannul it. But here every thing concurs to establish confidence. The will is written, witnessed, and sealed. And the testator dies: for a testament is of no force while the testator liveth. And the executor is true and honest, and will see all punctually fulfilled—this is the Holy Ghost, which is to glorify him, by taking of his, and showing it unto them.

This bestowment was much more than they deserved. They had always been dull scholars; and sadly repaid the labors he had expended upon them. They had been very defective servants; and, only a few hours before, had been disputing among themselves which of them should be the greatest. And now, as his suffering drew near, instead of showing themselves his sympathizing friends, they were all going to forsake him, and flee—yet loving his own who were in the world, he loved them unto the end.

"Happy disciples, to be thus remembered, honored, and enriched?" You are ready to exclaim, "how we envy you!" But these words were not confined to them. They were personally to enjoy the privilege; and they are immediately addressed—But, in receiving this assurance, they stood as the representatives of all his people, to the end of time. And you, even you, if you love and follow him, are as much included in the bequeathment as if you were mentioned by name. Witness his following intercession: "Neither pray I for these alone; but for them also which shall believe on me through their word, that they all may be one, as thou, Father, art in me, and I in thee, that they also may be one in us, that the world may believe that thou hast sent me: and the glory which thou gavest me I have given them that they may be one, even as we are one."

SEPTEMBER 5.—"I will strengthen them in the Lord."—Zech. x, 12.

THIS is the very assurance our hearts want, as we think of ourselves, and survey the duties and trials of the Christian life. And we cannot two confidently rely on the accomplishment of it, for it comes from the lips of faithfulness and truth. But we may err as to the manner in which it is to be fulfilled, and therefore our expectation is to be regulated and qualified accordingly.

Let us observe, then, that the fulfilment of the promise, as long as we are here, will not exempt us from all cause of complaint. It will keep us in our work, but not cause us to cease from our labor. It secures us assistance in our conflict; but the war lasts for life. However strong our faith, and firm our hope, and long-suffering, unto all joyfulness, our patience, we shall still be sensible, and the more sensible too, of resistance, deficiency, defilement; and still acknowledge that, when we would do good, evil is present with us—and groan, "O wretched man that I am! who shall deliver me from the body of this death?"

This impartation of strength will also be seasonable, and proportioned to the exigencies of our condition: "As thy days. so shall thy strength be." What we are to look for is, not grace for imaginary purposes, but for real; not grace for future difficulties, but present; or, as the apostle has it, grace to "help in time of need." It does not, therefore, follow, that what is formidable in the prospect, may be so in the event. You may fear death while living, and not fear it at last. "Is this," said Dr. Goodwin, "is *this* dying? Is this the enemy that dismayed me so long—now appearing so harmless—and even pleasant?"

These supplies of strength are to be sought after and expected in God's own way—that is, in the use of the means which he has ordained. So his word deals with our hope. "Draw nigh to God, and he will draw nigh to you." "Blessed is the man that heareth me, watching daily at my gates, and waiting at the posts of my doors." "He giveth power to the faint; and to them that have no might he increaseth strength. Even the youths shall faint and be weary, and the young men shall utterly fall; but they that wait upon the Lord shall renew their strength: they shall mount up with wings as eagles: they shall run, and not be weary, and they shall walk, and not faint."

And have I not found it so? In the day when I cried, has he not answered me, and strengthened me with strength in my soul? Have not I kneeled down with a contracted, and risen up with an enlarged heart? When I have read his word, hath he not thereby quickened me? Have I not found him, in his palaces, for a refuge! Has he not sent me help from the sanctuary, and strengthened me out of Zion?

—How foolish, then, to avoid religious exercises when I am not in a proper, and spiritual, and lively frame! *The means of grace* are surely then the most necessary—as fire is the more needful when we are cold, and excitement when we are dull.

It is only a part of the truth that we are to pray *with* the Spirit—we are also to pray *for* it. Witness the language of the Savior: "If ye then, being evil, know how to give good gifts unto your children, how much more shall your heavenly Father give the Holy Spirit to them that ask him?" Witness the example of the church: "Awake, O north wind, and come thou south, Blow upon thy garden, that the spices thereof may flow out."

SEPTEMBER 6.—"He found him in a desert land, and in the waste howling wilderness; he led him about, he instructed him, he kept him as the apple of his eye."—Deut. xxxii, 10.

AND will not this apply, O Christian! to thee, as well as to Israel?

Will not the *finding?* He found them in a desert land, in a waste howling wilderness. And where did he find you? What was your natural state? What was the world lying in wickedness? What was the earth, as filled, from the effects of sin, with vanity and vexation of spirit? There he found you, not you him. To his name give glory, for the mercy and the truth's sake. You indeed find him—but how? "I am found of them that sought me not—I am sought of them that asked not for me." You did choose him—but as the cause or consequence of his choice. Hear his own language: "Ye have not chosen me, but I have chosen you, and ordained you, that you should go and bring forth fruit, and that your fruit should remain." Who can refuse to acknowledge, We love him, because he first loved us?

—Will not the *leading?* He led them about. There was no road, and much depended upon their movements. He therefore became their conductor—and we know how he did this. It was by a fiery cloudy pillar. As this advanced, they removed. As this turned to the right or the left, they turned also. As this paused, they remained. Thus they were freed from all anxiety. The distance they had to go was not great in itself. Jacob's sons, with their asses, soon passed and repassed between Egypt and Canaan. And the Israelites quickly reached Kadesh-barnea, which was not far from Jordan; but they were turned back. And if you consult a map, and observe all their winding marches, you will see the propriety of the expression, He led them about. And has he not thus led you? You knew the way of man is not in himself. You cried unto the Lord, and said, Lead me in thy truth, and guide me; for thou art the God of my salvation; on thee do I wait all the day. And he said, I will lead thee and guide thee, and instruct thee with mine eye. And has he ever abandoned you? What mistakes has he prevented! How often has he hedged up your path, to keep you from going astray! From how many embarrassments, the effect of your acting without him, has he extricated you! He always led you in the right way; but it has often been a trying one, and such as you could not have foreseen or conjectured. In your temporal affairs he has perhaps checked you, and turned you back—you have had life to begin again, and to seek other openings and labors. And as to your spiritual experience, instead of gaining more of the assurance of hope, doubts and fears have invaded you; and instead of victory over your enemies, you have been led to see and feel more of the evil of your hearts—while you have often asked, If I am his, why am I thus? Yet all this has fulfilled the promise, "I will bring the blind by a way that they know not; I will lead them in paths that they have not known; I will make darkness light before them, and crooked things straight. These things will I do unto them, and not forsake them."

—Will not the *teaching*? He instructed them. They had the finest opportunities in the world to learn, cut off as they were from intercourse with surrounding nations, and alone, with God as their preceptor. When at Horeb, they sat down at his feet, and received of his words. He gave them laws and ordinances. He sent them Moses, and Aaron, and Miriam. He taught them much by events, pleasing and painful. He showed them in example the evil of sin, the happiness of obedience—yea, he gave them his good Spirit, says Nehemiah, to instruct them. And has he not instructed you? If you have been unprofitable learners, the fault has been your own. You have had every thing favorable in your situation; a thousand resources of information have opened around you; you have the Scriptures, the preaching of the word, Christian intercourse, and that Spirit which is to teach you all things. Every thing that has befallen you has read you lessons. Some things you *must* have learned—that this is not your rest—the folly of trusting in your own hearts—the greatness of your unworthiness—and that it is of the Lord's mercies that you are not consumed.

—Will not the *protection*? He kept them as the apple of his eye—the tenderest part of the tenderest member. Did the serpents bite them? He provided a remedy and healed them. Did enemies assail them? It was not with impunity. He reproved kings for their sakes, saying, touch not mine anointed, and do my prophets no harm. Amalek Sihon, king of the Amorites, and Og king of Bashan, found, to their peril, that he made their cause his own. Did Balaam use divination and enchantment? He owned there was no enchantment against Jacob, nor divination against Israel; he cursed them, but the curse was turned into a blessing. In travelling, were they exposed to the sun? The Lord was their shade on their right hand. He preserved them in their going out and in their coming in—they were a people saved of the Lord. Who has kindly, tenderly, constantly kept you? Have you had no enemies? And why have you not been a prey to their teeth? Why has not your heart turned back, nor your steps declined from his ways? *He* has holden you up. You have been kept by the power of God through faith unto salvation.

This is what he has done for you.

—What have you done for him?

—What are you doing?

—What do you resolve to do?

SEPTEMBER 7.—"The word of the Lord, that came unto Hosea, the son of Beeri, in the days of Uzziah, Jotham, Ahaz, and Hezekiah, kings of Judah, and in the days of Jeroboam, the son of Joash, king of Israel."—Hosea, i, 1.

WE are not informed whether he had been trained up for the holy office, or been called in a manner sudden and unlooked for. Some of the prophets were taken at once from following their common occupations; as we see in the instances of Elisha and Amos. Others were taken—and this was more generally the case—from the schools of the prophets; where, by retirement, and prayer, and meditation, and instruction, they were gradually prepared to minister in holy things. Thus God both sanctified the use of means, and showed that he was not confined to them. It is the same now. Some of the most pious, eminent, and useful ministers the churches have ever possessed, have been educated for the purpose; and we ought to be thankful for such institutions; and on these, for our spiritual supplies, we must *principally* depend. But we must not limit the Holy One of Israel. He will sometimes take a man out of our rules, and give him acceptance and success. And we must receive a Bunyan, as well as an Owen. When will persons allow God to work in his own way? and learn that, because one thing is right, another need not be wrong? But Hosea was *divinely commissioned*—"The word of the Lord came unto him." "For the prophecy came not in old time by the will of man, but holy men of God spake as they were moved by the Holy Ghost." And they could *demand* attention, in the name of Him who sent them—"Thus saith the Lord."

—His *descent* is also remarked. He was "the son of Beeri." The Jews have a rule, that the prophet whose father is named, was the son of a prophet. But this does not always hold. Nothing is recorded of Beeri. Yet it is reasonably concluded, that unless he had been a man of some distinction, and from whom Hosea derived honor, he would not have been mentioned. And this he might have been, without possessing worldly rank and riches. The righteous is more excellent than his neighbor. He is happily and nobly descended who springs from those who are great in the sight of the Lord. He may well exult, and say—

"My boast is not, that I deduce my birth
"From loins enthron'd, and rulers of the earth;
"But higher far my proud pretensions rise—
"The son of parents pass'd into the skies!"

Let us so live, that our children may derive from us advantage and respect.

But the principal thing is, the *time* of his ministrations—"In the days of Uzziah, Jotham, Ahaz, and Hezekiah, kings of Judah; and in the days of Jeroboam, the son of Joash, king of Israel." Now if he prophesied only from the end of Jeroboam's reign, the son of *Joash*, to the beginning of Hezekiah's, it would have been near seventy years. But he prophesied *in* the reign of both. And if we allow him a few years in each of these, and reckon up the length of the reigns between—his ministry must have been little short of eighty years; and it was probably even more. And five things may be observed from hence.

First. How very little we have of his prophecyings. Twelve short chapters, read in much less time than a modern sermon, include all that has been perpetuated of far the longest ministry on record. Some labor for posterity; and leave behind them works which will render them a blessing to future ages. Others are called more to serve their own generation, by the will of God; and are preachers, rather than writers. How useful was Whitefield, as a preacher! while his few writings have had little circulation, and rather serve to excite wonder that he was so powerful in another capacity. How useful has Hervey been, as a writer! while his preaching was without excitement, and scarcely distinguished by any effect. Some, like Doddridge, have excelled, both in the pulpit and from the press. Every servant of God has his peculiar gifts, and his apprcpriate sphere—"Even so, Father, for so it seemeth good in thy sight."

Secondly. He must have begun his ministry very young. Paul forbids the ordination of a novice, lest he should be lifted up with pride. Talent is not all that is necessary for the sacred office. How necessary is the knowledge that is derived from experience! and the confidence that grows out of the trial of character! Thirty was the age for entering on the Levitical service. And not earlier than this period did John and Jesus thus commence their public ministry. But "the word of God is not bound." Timothy was young: so young that Paul was obliged to say, "Let no man despise thy youth." Samuel was employed, while yet a child. Jeremiah was consecrated from the womb. And this was nearly the case with Hosea. What a privilege, what an honor, to be early dedicated to the service of God! "I remember thee, the kindness of thy youth."

Thirdly. He must have been very old before he retired from labor. Some do not design early enough, but stand about in the way of usefulness—The excellent Cornelius Winter often prayed to be preserved from this error. Indeed, few can set well, and say of a successor, with proper feelings, "I must decrease, but he must increase." Others resign too soon. They would retire upon a pension, before they are disabled in a holy war. A minister may want the sprightliness and vigor of youth, and yet have the ripeness and richness of age; and the fruit may drop without much hard shaking. Some nobly fall at their post—sword in hand—faithful unto death—and, with the crown of life obtain the commendation, "Thou hast labored, and hast not fainted."

Fourthly. He must have passed through a vast variety of condition. He lived in the reign of one good king, and of four bad ones. He saw peace, and much war. He saw plenty, and more than once, scarceness and famine. He saw a few partial revivals of religion; but witnessed general and constant wickedness. How many of his relations, friends, and pious connexions, had fallen! How lonely must he have felt! How changed his views! How convinced must he have been, that all below is vanity and vexation of spirit! while yet, God was the strength of his heart, and his portion for ever. How much he knew of what was doing in other countries we cannot determine. But within the compass of his ministry lived Lycurgus, the famous Lacedæmonian legislator; and Hesiod, the Greek poet; and Rome was begun to be built.

Finally. A man of God may labor long, and do very little good. The people he addressed not only continued wicked but waxed worse and worse: and the captivity he had threatened, he lived to see commenced. He certainly saw a part of Israel carried away captive, by Tiglath Pileser; and probably the entire destruction of the kingdom of the ten tribes, by Salmanezer. This must have been very painful. But it did not slacken his efforts. We are not answerable for our success. If we lose our labor, we shall not lose our reward. A greater than all said, "I have labored in vain, I have spent my strength for nought, and in vain; yet surely my judgment is with the Lord, and my work with my God."

SEPTEMBER 8.—"Despisest thou the riches of his goodness, and forbearance, and long-suffering?"—Romans, ii, 4.

ONE of the ways in which God addresses us, in his word, is expostulation. To expostulate is to accuse before an open rupture. It is the lingering of friendship, offended indeed, but unwilling to abandon its object without further trial. It is anger blended with kindness: it is chiding, accompanied with entreaty. This is a very pleasing view of the Supreme Being, and induces us to exclaim, Lord, what is man that *thou* art mindful of him; or the son of man that thou visitest him? By the transgression of his law, we reduced ourselves to ruin. He remembered us in our low estate, and provided for our deliverance. The blessing was placed before us, and within our reach—But we disregard it, and contemn the Savior as well as the Ruler. Thus we deserve that his wrath should come upon us. Yet, before he pronounces sentence, he sends for us into his presence; and reasons with us—that being unable to defend our conduct, we may acknowledge, by our silence, that we have acted a part that leaves us without excuse, and without hope—"Despisest thou the riches of his goodness, and forbearance, and long-suffering?"

God is good to all; and the apostle speaks of "the richness of his goodness." These riches appear in numberless displays. But he adds—"and forbearance, and long-suffering;" to induce us to consider the latter, as the proof of the former.

To see then the riches of his goodness, let us contemplate his forbearance and long-suffering. Every thing in God enhances his patience. His *greatness* enhances it. We are more affected with an affront from an equal, than from a superior; and more from an inferior, than from an equal. How does the master resent an offence from his slave! or a king from a subject? But all comparison fails between God and us. He is the maker of all things, and all nations before him are as nothing. This is the being insulted. And who is the offender? A grovelling worm upon a dunghill—and yet he bears with us—His *wisdom* enhances it. We cannot be affected with affronts of which we are ignorant. How would some be enraged if they knew only what is *said* of them by some of their "dear five hundred friends;" how they turn them into ridicule before they have well left their house; and what freedoms they take with their character, and their conduct, in almost every company. But none of our offences are secret from God. He hears all—sees all—and knows perfectly every imagination of the thoughts of our heart—And yet he bears with us. His *holiness* enhances it. If we do not think and feel a thing to be an affront, there is no virtue, for there is no difficulty in enduring it. The trial is when it touches us to the quick, in some most valued interest. But sin is exceeding sinful. By nothing does God deem himself so dishonored. He is of purer eyes than to behold iniquity. It is the abominable thing which his soul hates—and yet he bears with us. His power enhances it. Why do we put up with a thousand wrongs? We know them and feel them; but we reluctantly submit, because we have no way to punish them. Why are not sinners destroyed? Moses, when he had provoked the Egyptians, saved himself by flight. But whither can we go from God's presence, or flee from his Spirit? Some, when they have provoked resentment, have defied it, and successfully too. But who ever hardened himself against God, and prospered? His look is death—And yet he bears with us. His *bounty* enhances it. We complain peculiarly of an injury, or an insult, from one who is much indebted to us. From another, we say, we could have borne; but he is viler than the brute; for the ox knoweth his owner, and the ass his master's crib. But we are under infinite obligations to the God we provoke. In him we have lived, and moved, and had our being. His table has fed us; his wardrobe has clothed us; his sun has warmed us. And this is not all. His kindness continues, notwithstanding all our ingratitude. And he not only spares us, but in every way indulges us. He waits to be gracious, and is exalted to have mercy upon us.

Yet are these riches of his goodness "despised." Despised by *inconsideration*. We treat them as unworthy of our notice. They do not occupy our thoughts or our speech. Despised by disobedience. We resist their design, which is to lead us to repentance. God calls, but we will not answer. He knocks, but we refuse to open—Who is the Lord, that we should obey his voice? Despised by *perversion*. We turn them into instruments of rebellion: and make them the very means of increasing our impenitency. If we thought God would strike us into hell the next sin we committed, it would not be committed; but since he is too kind to do this, we offend him. We are evil because he is good. "Because sentence against an evil work is not executed speedily, therefore the heart of the sons of men is fully set in them to do evil."

How *unreasonable* is this! How *vile* is this contempt! How *shameful!* If an individual was to behave toward a fellow creature, as men are continually acting toward the blessed God, no one could notice him but with astonishment and disgrace. Yet we talk of the dignity of human nature! or contend that it is but slightly injured by the fall!

—And how *dangerous!* How *ruinous* is this contempt! It is true, God is merciful and gracious; but he will by no means spare the guilty. If we reject the Gospel, the law takes hold of us—yea, we have to deal with the Gospel, too—and shall find it to be the savor of *death unto death.*

SEPTEMBER 9.—"They joy before thee, according to the joy in harvest." Isaiah, ix, 3.

THREE circumstances are here mentioned. They *joy.* They joy *before thee.* They joy before thee, *according to the joy in harvest.* Each of these will supply an interesting and useful meditation.

THEY JOY.

Among the many mistakes entertained concerning religion, no one is more common than the notion, that it prescribes a forced, gloomy, melancholy course; engaged in which we must bid adieu to every thing like pleasure. And nothing can be more injurious than this notion: for men will naturally turn from religion, while they view it as the enemy of their happiness. But nothing is so unfounded and false as this opinion. Let us take it to three tribunals.

Let us bring it to the bar of *reason.* It must be allowed that God is able to make us happy or miserable. And, if so—is it likely that he will suffer those who hate and oppose him to be happy? and those who love and try to please him to be miserable? What a notion of the supreme Being would this imply! And what could equally blaspheme his character? And has a hope that my sins are pardoned, that God is my Father, that providence is my guide, that death is my friend, and that heaven is my portion, a tendency to inspire me with sadness or with joy? And which is most adapted to make me wretched or comfortable within? Malice, or benevolence? Passion, or meekness? Pride, or humility? Envy, or complacency? Anxiety, or confidence? Distant things do not sufficiently impress us. We need something immediate. Our propensity to present gratification is powerful. And must not religion meet this state of feeling, and provide for it? Thirsty as man is, if there be no pure stream at hand, will he not kneel down to the filthy puddle? What is to preserve us from being drawn away by the allurements and dissipations of the world, but our having something better to satisfy our hearts at home, and to keep us from roving? What can sustain us in our trials, and animate us in our duties, if destitute of present consolation? The joy of the Lord is our strength. We shall soon decline a course in which we feel no interest or delight. And if we are strangers to holy pleasure, how can we impress others in favor of religion? It is by singing at their work, that his servants praise their master; and prove that his yoke is easy, and his burden light.

Let us take it to the bar of *Scripture.* Read the Bible all through for this purpose. Take its commands—What are these? "Rejoice in the Lord, and be glad, ye righteous; and shout aloud for joy, and all ye that are upright in heart." "Rejoice evermore." "Rejoice in the Lord always; and again I say, rejoice." Take its promises—What are these? "Blessed is the people that know the joyful sound: they shall walk, O Lord, in the light of thy countenance. In thy name shall they rejoice all the day; and in thy righteousness they shall be exalted." "The ransomed of the

Lord shall return, and come to Zion, with songs." "They shall go out with joy, and be led forth with peace: the mountains and the hills shall break forth before them into singing, and all the trees of the field shall clap their hands." Take its representation: What are these? Go back to the beginning of the Gospel. The first churches walked not only in the fear of the Lord, but "in the comfort of the Holy Ghost." Peter, addressing Christians at large, says, "In whom believing, ye rejoice with joy unspeakable and full of glory." If *we* libel Christianity, and cause the way of truth to be evil spoken of, they honored it. What hindered their joy? Losses did not—"They took joyfully the spoiling of their goods." Persecutions did not—"They received the word in much affliction, with joy of the Holy Ghost." Guilt did not—They joyed in God through our Lord Jesus Christ, by whom they received the atonement. Death did not—They longed to depart to be with Christ, which was far better. Eternity did not—They were looking for that blessed hope, and hastening unto the coming of the day of God. Joy was then considered an essential part of genuine religion. The circumcision not only worshipped God in the Spirit, and had no confidence in the flesh; but also rejoiced in Christ Jesus. And the apostle would as soon have excluded from it, righteous conduct, and a peaceable temper, as spiritual joy: for, says he, "the kingdom of God is not meat and drink; but righteousness, and peace, and joy in the Holy Ghost."

Let us bring it to the bar of *experience*. Experience signifies knowledge derived from experiment, in opposition to theory and hypothesis. And experimental philosophy has been of late years, much extolled. And why should not experimental religion be equally recommended? Is there no standard in spiritual things, to which we can appeal? And is there no way of subjecting the truth and importance of their claims to trial? Many are indeed too careless, and too prejudiced to pursue the process. But some have examined, and reduced the subjects to decision. And they, and they only, are the persons to whom you should repair in a case of this kind. They have this advantage over you. You have never tried their principles; but they have tried yours. You have never walked in their ways: but they have walked in yours; and know, as well as you, that they are not pleasantness and peace. And after trying your resources, and finding them to be vanity and vexation of spirit, they have tried the Savior's promises, and have found them to be full of grace and truth. At first, they could only be swayed by faith; but now they have the witness in themselves. They know, for they have applied to him, that he is a suitable, a willing, a mighty Savior. They know they were strangers to peace, till they were reconciled to God, by the death of his Son—but they have come to the blood of sprinkling. They know that once they were ignorantly asking, Who will show us any good? but they have found the fountain of life; and can say, It is good for me to draw nigh to God. *They*, therefore, ought to be heard. They can speak with confidence and earnestness; for they speak from experience—and this is their language; "Lo this, we have searched it, so it is; hear it, and know thou it for thy good."

"That which we have seen and heard declared we unto you, that ye also may have fellowship with us; and truly our fellowship is with the Father, and with his Son Jesus Christ."

Let us listen no longer to a report as false as it is evil. It is a good land which the Lord our God giveth us. Let no man's heart fail him.

SEPTEMBER 10.—"They joy before thee, according to the joy in harvest." Isaiah, ix, 3.

THEY joy—BEFORE THEE. This shows

The *sincerity* of this joy. All men are in view of God; and they are always before him: but the wicked and worldly never *joy* before *him*. *Their* joy is all show and profession: it may deceive their fellow creatures; but it cannot impose on God. He sees through all the hypocrisy of *their* happiness; he knows, that in the midst of their sufficiency, they are in straits; and that they sigh and groan, though others do not hear them, over all their successes and indulgencies. Their joy is for company, not retirement. They cannot partake of it, till they forget God. One thought of Him damps all their pleasure. Therefore they say unto God, Depart from us, we desire not the knowledge of thy ways. And hence, they dislike conscience, God's deputy and secretary. They cannot relish their enjoyments till they have sent him out of the way, or lulled him to sleep, or stupified him with an opiate, or silenced him with a bribe; one look, one word from conscience, will be enough to spoil all their delights. They never taste one drop of real joy. There is no peace, saith God, to the wicked. But the Christian's joy will bear the gaze of God. It lives and flourishes in his presence. And so far is he from shrinking back from the eye of his heavenly Father, that the thought of being near him, with him, before him, affords him relief and satisfaction. He can say, with Asaph, "Nevertheless I am continually with thee: thou hast holden me by my right hand. Thou shalt guide me with thy counsel, and afterward receive me to glory. Whom have I in heaven but thee? and there is none upon earth that I desire beside thee. My flesh and my heart faileth; but God is the strength of my heart, and my portion for ever."

This reminds us of the *secrecy* of this joy—It is before him—and often he alone discerns it. Strangers intermeddle not with it. And the world knows it not. Seeing Christians often poor, and afflicted, and despised, they are at a loss to conceive how *they* can be joyful. They are therefore men wondered at. Their fellow creatures can see their burdens—these are often plain enough: but they see not their supports; and how, underneath them, are the everlasting arms; or they would not wonder that they do not sink. They see their losses and trials; but their communion with God, and the comforts of the Holy Ghost, are invisible. Neither are the subjects of this joy disposed to divulge it to all. They are, indeed, ready to say to them that fear God, Come, and I will tell *you* what he hath done for my soul: but, were they to communicate their feelings to others, they would not, could not, under stand them. It would be worse than speaking of the pleasure of literature to a clown; or of the pleasure of melody and harmony to a man who has no ear for music. The joy also does not operate and discover itself like common mirth. It is not the froth that swims and shows on the surface. It lies deep. It is not noise, but composure. It is the calm of the mind; the content of the heart; the sunshine of the soul; a peace that passeth all understanding. A man, if joyful, does not joy like a child. "True joy is a serious thing." But God sees his people, even when sorrowful, yet always rejoicing either in possession, hope, or desire. He sees them turning aside from the world, to refresh and exhilarate their spirits alone with himself: and hears them (when no other hears them) saying, "How precious are thy thoughts unto me, O God! how great is the sum of them! If I should count them, they are more in number than the sand: when I awake, I am still with thee."

"Be earth, with all her scenes, withdrawn;
"Let noise and vanity begone:
"In secret silence of the mind,
"My heaven, and there my God I find."

They joy before Him—and this also reminds us of the *medium* of this joy; not indeed exclusively, but pre-eminetly so. It is connected with the worship and ordinances of God. And the allusion is to the three annual solemnities of the Jews when they went to appear *before the Lord* in Zion. For there he was considered as residing. There was his house—his table—his attendants. This, said he, is my rest for ever; here will I dwell, for I have desired it. Hence, says David, when shall I come, and appear before God? These services were called feasts. There were songs to be sung in the way to them. The people went with the voice of joy and gladness to keep holy day. And when they arrived, they were required "to rejoice before him." Is God less present in our assemblies, than in those of the Jews? Has he not said, "In all places where I record my name, I will come unto thee, and I will bless thee?" And many can set to their seal that God is true. They know he is there, waiting to be gracious, and exalted to have mercy. They have found him there, and conversed with him, as a man talketh with his friend. They have seen his power, and his glory, in the Sanctuary, and have there tasted that the Lord is gracious. Hence they hail the Sabbath, as the day of holy convocation, with delight. They are glad when the summons comes, to go into the house of the Lord. They come before his presence with thanksgivings; and as they approach their pleasant things, can say—

"The sorrows of the mind,
"Be banished from this place:
"Religion never was designed
"To make our pleasure less."

Yes, they who mourn; and are these comforted—they who come burdened with guilt; and are these set free—they who come in the midst of trouble, and find him in his palaces for a refuge—they who come cold and languid, and are quickened according to his word: these know the truth of his promise, "I will bring them to my holy mountain, and make them joyful in my house of prayer." And they know the meaning of the declaration, "They joy BEFORE THEE."

"Though pinched with poverty at home;
"With sharp afflictions daily fed:
"It makes amends, if they can come
"To God's own house for heavenly bread.

"With joy they hasten to the place
"Where they their Savior oft have met;
"And while they feast upon his grace,
"Their burdens and their griefs forget."

SEPTEMBER 11.—"They joy before Thee, according to the joy in harvest."—Isaiah, ix, 3.

THEY joy before Him—ACCORDING TO THE JOY OF HARVEST. And what is this joy?

It is a joy connected with *exertion*. Reaping is no easy thing. But this is not all. There is manuring, and ploughing, and sowing, and harrowing, and weeding. All these are previously necessary to the joy of harvest. The husbandman does not eat the bread of idleness. His labor fills his hands. Every season has demands upon him: and the end of one work is the beginning of another. Indeed, nothing valuable is to be obtained without diligence and difficulty: yea, it would not be valuable, or prized, if it were acquired priceless and painless. And are not we to exercise ourselves unto godliness? And is it nothing to worship God in Spirit and in truth? And to watch in all things? And to pray without ceasing? And to keep the heart with all diligence? "But the grace of God does all this *for* us." It does. But it is equally true, that it does all this *by* us, too. God does not believe and repent; but enables us to believe and repent. We run the race that is set before us, and fight the good fight of faith—though in Him is all our help found.

This joy requires *patience*. The husbandman soweth in hope; but the accomplishment is future. Weeks and months, and many dreary weeks and months, intervene, before his wishes can be fulfilled. Yet he is not foolish enough to suppose that he has labored in vain, because he cannot reap as soon as he has sown; or childishly eager enough to cut down the grain green, to hasten the harvest. But what does he? "The husbandman waiteth for the precious fruit of the earth, and hath long patience for it, until he receive the early and latter rain." And so Abraham, after he had patiently endured, received the promise. Christians, also, are required to wait. And let them remember that in due time they shall reap, if they faint not. And they have not long to wait. Their salvation is nearer than when they believed. Yet a little while—a few more rising and descending suns, and it shall be said, "Put ye in the sickle; for the harvest is ripe." In the mean time the process is hourly advancing to maturity; and the end shall prove that every thing is most beautiful and most profitable in its season. "It is good for a man both to hope, and quietly wait for the salvation of the Lord."

This joy is not free from *anxieties*. When the seed is first thrown into the ground, it seems lost; and when it revives from a kind of death, and springs up, it has to encounter the frosts of winter, the changing and blights of spring, the lengthened dryness or wetness of summer. And when the period has arrived for securing the precious treasure, solicitude is more alive and alert. The husbandman often rises, and looks at the sky. Ten times in the day he examines the glass. He goes about with a heavy heart, and a depressed countenance, and often forebodes the worst; and it is not till he has safely housed the whole, that he can give up himself to satisfaction and delight. But how will this apply to Christians? Is there any thing precarious in the purpose and promise of God? No. But it is otherwise with their apprehensions. Their eternal prospects awaken all their concern; and they have a thousand doubts and fears concerning their safety and success. Am I an heir? Is this repentance toward God, and faith toward our Lord Jesus Christ? Can these wandering thoughts and imperfect desires be prayer? What if, after all, I should fail of the grace of God, and come short of the glory to be revealed?

But this joy is *great.* When the harvest is come, every face betrays pleasure. The very toil seems delight. They that pass by say, "We bless you in the name of the Lord." "He that soweth, and he that reapeth, now rejoice together." Pennant tells us, in his Travels, that in parts of Scotland he sometimes saw large numbers reaping to the sound of a musician behind them, playing on the bagpipe, and thus enlivening the scene, and softening the work. And David says, "They that sow in tears shall reap in joy," or, as it is in the margin, reap singing. And he adds, "He that goeth forth, weeping, bearing precious seed, shall, doubtless, return again with rejoicing, bringing his sheaves with him." And who has not heard the shoutings of the rustics, as the last loaded wain returned from the field, covered with green boughs? And who has not witnessed the rude mirth of harvest-home? But if "the poor laborers sing," think of the owner! Now his anxieties are dispelled! now his patience is rewarded! ow his exertion and expense are abundantly repaid—his garner is full, affording all manner of store; and he hails, in his possession, the means of indulgence, improvement and wealth! Yet, what is this joy, compared with the Christian's! The one is for the body; and the other for the soul. One is for time; the other is for eternity. One is common to the wicked and the righteous; the other is peculiar to the subjects of divine grace. The one may gender intemperance and sin; the other sanctifies, while it contents.

Let me learn, then, to improve the works of creation to pious purposes; and make nature a handmaid to grace.

And let me be thankful for the harvest with which we have so recently been favored. He has again "prepared of his goodness for the poor." All, indeed, are concerned. "The king is served by the labor of the field:" but kings have many ways of living that poor people have not. We do not think of palaces or mansions, so much as of the dwellings of the poor, when we view the waving fields. He has not only given us plenty, but afforded us the appointed weeks of harvest. "O that men would praise the Lord for his goodness, and for his wonderful works to the children of men! For he satisfieth the longing soul, and filleth the hungry soul with goodness."

Yet man liveth not by bread alone, but by every word that proceedeth out of the mouth of God. Let me therefore labor, not for the meat that perisheth, but for that meat which endureth unto everlasting life. All spiritual blessings, in heavenly places, are provided and presented. But the season for securing them is limited, short, and uncertain. Now is the accepted time; now is the day of salvation. And how many, in consequence of neglect, have exclaimed, at a dying hour—THE HARVEST IS PAST; THE SUMMER IS ENDED—AND WE ARE NOT SAVED!

SEPTEMBER 12.—"**Yea, he loved the people.**"—**Deuteronomy, xxxiii, 3.**

THERE can be no doubt of this, with regard to Israel. They were often reminded of it, and as often told *why* he set his love upon them. The reason was not their greatness; for they were the fewest of all people. Nor their goodness; for they were a stiff-necked people; but because the Lord had a favor toward them. Hence he chose them, and redeemed them, and provided for them, and distinguished them by miracles and privileges. "To them pertained the adoption, and the glory, and the covenants, and the giving of the law, and the service of God, and the promises." "He dealt not so with any nation."

But has he less appeared to thee, O Christian! saying, Yea, I have loved thee with an everlasting love, and with loving-kindness have I drawn thee? Here is the source of your salvation. However wide, and however far it flows, here the river rises; and take what stream of it you please, it will lead you up to this spring-head, the free and undeserved favor of God. "Yea, he loved the people."

But his love to his people, so to speak, is of three kinds.

—A love of *benevolence*—which consists in wishing and designing them good.

—A love of *beneficence*—consisting in doing them good. This appears in a thousand instances. But the principal one of all is, his remembering them in their low estate, and sending his only begotten Son into the world, that they might live through him. *Herein*, therefore, says the apostle John, is *love;* not that we loved God, but that he loved us, and sent his Son to be the propitiation for our sins. It was necessary to find a way in which his goodness could reach us, consistently with his nature as a holy Being, his claims as a lawgiver, and his honor as a governor. And this medium of our salvation does not, therefore, detract from the original of it; for if he required a sacrifice, he furnished one, and it was the *Lamb of God*. And therefore, the apostle says, Being justified *freely* by his grace, through the redemption which is in Christ Jesus.

—A love of *complacency*. The love of benevolence, and the love of beneficence, regarded them as unworthy and as miserable: but the love of complacency regards them as new creatures. He cannot take pleasure in them while they are destitute of his image, and enemies to him by wicked works. What fellowship hath righteousness with unrighteousness? And what communion hath light with darkness? But he prepares them for his delighting in them, and holding intercourse with them. He saves them by the washing of regeneration, and the renewing of the Holy Ghost. Then he takes pleasure in them that fear him, in them that hope in his mercy. Does a man take pleasure in his inheritance? In the wife of his bosom? In the children of his affection? In the work of his hands? They are all this, and more than all, to the God of all grace. He puts their tears into his bottle—Are they not in his book? Their prayer is his delight. Their alms are the odour of a sweet smell. He corresponds with them. Visits them. Takes up his abode with them. He rejoices over them with joy. He rests in his love. He joys over them with singing.

What can I wish for more? Suppose men reproach? Since I have been precious in his sight, I have been honorable; and he has loved me. Let them curse; but bless Thou. One smile of thine is better than life; and will more than balance a universe of frowns.

Let my portion, and the portion of mine, be—"The good will of Him that dwelt in the bush."

SEPTEMBER 13.—"And he said, Lord God, whereby shall I know that I shall inherit it?"—Gen. xv, 8.

WHY had not God that very moment promised it? And was not his word sufficient? They, surely, have never made the trial, who imagine that it is an easy thing to believe. To confide in a Being invisible, and whom we have so deeply offended, and to hang our everlasting hope upon his naked truth, requires the exertion of the power that raised up Christ from the dead. Who never feels in him the working of an evil heart of unbelief? Our Lord upbraided his own Apostles with their unbelief. And even the father of the faithful deserves something more than God's engagement to give him the land of Canaan—Whereby shall I know that I shall inherit it?

Yet God pardoned his servant in this thing; and stooped to his weakness; and yielded him what he required. And Abraham was satisfied with the sign and the seal.

There is a better country, even a heavenly. The possession of it is an object worthy of all our concern. And they who love it, and seek it supremely, cannot leave their claim undecided and uncertain: and therefore their language will be, "say unto my soul, I am thy salvation;" "Give me a token for good;" "Whereby shall I know that I shall inherit it?" Why you have the promise of God, who cannot lie! Yes: and this infallibly insures it, to all those to whom it belongs—But who are the heirs of promise? Away with dreams, and visions, and sounds in the air, and impulses, and accidental occurrences of passages of Scripture. We have surer evidence. We have unerring proofs, furnished by God himself. Search his word with diligence and prayer. *There* you will find, not the names, indeed, of the heirs of eternal life, but their characters—their qualities—their taste—their choice—their way—their aim.

Let me fix on one of these vouchers, only—It is a preparation for it. Where this is found, the title can never be absent. The apostle therefore gives "thanks to the Father, who hath made us meet to partake of the inheritance of the saints in light." In another place he says, "He hath wrought us for the self same thing." And he does nothing in vain. If he has, by the agency of his Holy Spirit, fitted you in the temper of your soul, for the world of glory, you may be assured that he designs you for it. If you bear the image of the heavenly, you will partake of their condition. If you have the dawn of that blessed state, you will have the day. Grace is of the same nature with glory—they differ only in the degree. Is heaven not only the high but the holy place in which entereth nothing that defileth? And do you hunger and thirst after righteousness? Does the blessedness consist in adoring the Lamb that was slain; and in being like him; and in seeing him as he is? And are you now glorifying only in his cross; and following him in the regeneration; and praying that you may know him in the power of his resurrection, and the fellowship of his sufferings? Will the distinctions in life, now al lowable and necessary, be done away; and only those remain which arise from character? And are you valuing persons, not according to their outward circumstances, but their real, their moral, their spiritual worth? As no inquiry will be made there, *where* we have worshipped, but *how;* nor to what denomination we pertained, but whether we were Jews inwardly—can you now pray, from the heart, "Grace be with *all* them that love our Lord Jesus Christ in sincerity?" Can you now say, "*Whosoever* shall do the will of my Father who is in heaven, the same is my brother, and sister, and mother?" Then heaven is already begun; and therefore insured; for we are confident of this very thing, that he which hath begun a good work in you, will *perform it until the day of Jesus Christ.* If you can take the representations of the employments and enjoyments of heaven given us in the Scripture, and can *desire* these things, and *hope* for these things, and find your *liberty* and *happiness* in them, you have the earnest of the inheritance, and are sealed by the Holy Spirit of God, unto the day of redemption. Let me not, then, O my soul! be faithless, but believing; and rejoice in hope of the glory of God.

'When I can read my title clear
"To mansions in the skies,
"I bid farewell to every fear,
"And wipe my weeping eyes."

SEPTEMBER 14.—"Lean not unto thine own understanding."—Prov. iii, 5.

THE understanding is a natural faculty, by which man is distinguished from inanimate creatures, and also from the animal world. The sun, the moon, the sea, and rivers, are impressed by laws, of which they know nothing; and follow their destiny, wholly unconscious of the operations they perform. The beasts of the field, and the fowls of the air, have an instinct which often surprises us. But, while it is exact as far as it goes, it is exceedingly limited; it admits of no variety or progression. These beings are no wiser now than when they went to Noah for shelter, and to Adam for names—But there is a spirit in man; and the inspiration of the Almighty giveth him understanding. By means of this endowment, he can look backward and forward. He can examine and judge. He can survey principles in their abstraction; and duties in their circumstances; and actions in their moral bearings. He can refuse the evil, and choose the good against present feelings, and imposing appearances.

This faculty, from the lowest degree of reason to the highest reach of intellect, is the gift of God, the Father of lights; and should be cultivated by us, as men and as Christians. We should rejoice that we live in a country and in an age so favorable to all kinds of information. It is a sad reproach to many, that in the midst of knowledge they are found so ignorant as they are—it must be the result of dissipation or sloth.

But though we are to prize, and improve, and make use of our understanding, we are not to *lean* to it. Yet, if we were not prone to this, the caution would be needless. There is nothing of which men are so proud as their knowledge. There are more than a few who would rather be charged with a want of principle than a want of understanding; and would rather pass for knaves than fools. This regard seems, indeed, to be a kind of equalizer of the human race: and the only thing with which all are satisfied, and in which they feel an ineffable complacency, is their *own* understanding. They lean to their *own* understanding in preference to the understanding of others; whom yet, if asked, they would consider as very superior to themselves, both in capacity and experience. They may, indeed, consult with an adviser; but it is in hope of finding a confirmation of their own opinion: and should his judgment differ from theirs, they would feel little difficulty in resolving by which to abide. We frequently see this in those who are just entering the world, and so much need a guide to escape those early mistakes that may affect the whole of their future life. Whatever quickness of perception they may possess, they surely must be destitute of that practical wisdom that grows out of observation and trial—Yet, how little do "the younger submit themselves to the elder!" Men carry this disposition even into the things of God. They regard their own reason more than his word; and are reluctant to believe what they cannot comprehend. We are told that Alphonsus the royal astronomer, having apprehended some seeming irregularities among the heavenly bodies, was daring enough to say, "Had I been by the Creator when he made the world, I would have given him some good advice." We justly shudder at his profaneness—and yet, who has not fallen into a similar error? Who has not found fault with God, in his manner of governing the world, the church, the family, the individual! Who has not been ready to direct the Spirit of the Lord; and, being his counseller, to teach him?

To preserve us from this tendency, let us remember how limited our own understanding is; how many objects there are entirely beyond its reach; and that there is nothing with which it is perfectly acquainted. Let us also reflect, how much we are impressed by appearances; and how different these often are from the realities of things. "Who knoweth what is good for a man in this life; and the days of his vain life, which he spendeth as a shadow? What should we be at this hour, if things had always been according to our mind and wishes? Let us look back, and see how frequently we have erred, both in our hopes and fears. We now clearly see, that what we so eagerly desired would have proved our injury or ruin; and that what we are so anxious to escape has conduced to our best welfare: so that we can say, "It is good for me that I have been afflicted."

We are very incompetent to judge for ourselves, because we know not the influence other and untried events will exert upon us. To these, we go forward with our present views and feelings, not aware that new scenes will produce new views and feelings; and we may unfold secrets in our character of which we have no conceptions, and which may fill us, not only with surprise, but dismay. Thus, when Elisha predicted with tears, the atrocities he would commit, Hazael shuddered at the thought, and sincerely exclaimed, "What! is thy servant a dog, that he should do this thing?" the man of God only answered, "The Lord hath showed me that thou shalt be king over Syria," and his elevation transformed him from the man into the monster which he had execrated! And if by leaning to our own understanding, we take one wrong step, what consequences, immediate or remote, personal or relative, may arise from it! See this in David. I shall now perish, said he, one day, by the hand of Saul: "there is nothing better for me than that I should speedily escape into the land of the Philistines." The oracle, had he consulted it, would not have told him so. In truth, it was the worst measure he could have devised, as it tended to alienate the affections of his countrymen, to justify the reproaches of his enemies, to deprive himself of the means of grace, to put himself out of the Divine protection, and to lay him under obligations to a benefactor he could not oblige, without betraying the cause of God. Accordingly, he was soon drawn into a scandalous equivocation with Achish, and was ordered to go and fight against his own people Israel. And when he was released from this embarrassment, and went back, he found that, in his absence, his residence and property had been destroyed, and his family been carried away captives. "O Lord, I know that the way of man is not in himself: it is not in man that walketh to direct his steps." Lot leaned to his own understanding, and chose the landvale of Sodom, which was well-watered like the Garden of the Lord. By this movement, he separated himself from intercourse with his pious uncle. He was taken captive by the confederate kings. He was strangely induced to reside in the town itself; and dwelling among them, in seeing and hearing, vexed his righteous soul from day to day, with their unlawful deeds. At length, he was burnt out of house and home. His wife, for looking back, became a pillar of salt; so that he never after could go or look that way. His daughters damned by the vices of the place—But we dare not go on—Trust in the Lord with all thine heart—Lean not to thy own understanding—In all thy ways acknowledge HIM, and HE shall direct thy paths.

SEPTEMBER 15.—"Lord, what wilt thou have me do?"—Acts, ix, 6.

THIS is a very marvellous question, considering from whom it came. For the inquirer, till now, had hated the Name of Jesus: and was at this very time actually engaged in the persecution of his followers. What would he have thought, if some one could have told him, that in a few hours, in a few moments, he would be a worshipper at the feet of the Nazarene! But so it was: and he, trembling and astonished, said, Lord, what wilt thou have me to do?

Let us never despair. The chief of sinners are within his reach. He has a mighty arm; strong is his hand, and high is his right hand. What changes has his grace already accomplished; and what changes must it accomplish still, if the promise be fulfilled, "Instead of the thorn shall come up the fir tree, and instead of the brier shall come up the myrtle tree; and it shall be to the Lord for a name, for an everlasting sign, that shall not be cut off." But let us make this inquiry our own. It is every way worthy of our adoption.

It is personal in its aim—Lord, what wilt thou have *me* to do? Many seem more anxious to reprove others, than to know their own faults; and are busily employed in pulling the mote out of their brother's eye, while a beam is in their own. Some are always reading and hearing for others. And we have known persons applying, in a sermon, to some fellow-worshipper, things, every one else in the assembly would deem most proper for themselves. But we should think of ourselves in divine things; and bring home every truth to our business and bosoms, whether it encourages or censures—praying, Search *me*, O God, and know my heart; try *me*, and know my thoughts; and see if there be any evil way in me, and lead me in the way everlasting. When our Lord had informed Peter of his duty and destiny, Peter saw John coming toward him, and asked, Lord, and what shall *this* man do? But our Savior said, What is that to thee? follow thou me.

It is practical in its subject—What wilt thou have me to *do*?—Not to know, to hear, to believe, to talk of. Religion, indeed, extends to every thing: but every thing is not essential to it. But practice is. If ye know these things, happy are ye if you do them. Faith without works, is dead, being alone. Though a man say, he hath faith, and hath not works; can faith save him? Every part of the truth, as it is in Jesus, has a bearing upon the heart, and the life, of the receiver; and is according to godliness.

It is impartial in its desire—Lord, *what* wilt thou have me to do? I do not prescribe. I do not select. I do not prefer. Thy pleasure, alone, I ask to know, and am resolved to follow—Speak, Lord, for thy servant heareth. True obedience is compatible with defects; but not with partialities. If a man regards some things, and not others, in religion; those he regards, he regards from some other motive than the will of God: for *this* would lead him to regard the one as well as the other; seeing they are all enjoined by the very same authority. He that offends in one point, is guilty of all; not in the act, but in the principle *i. e.* he violates the authority of the whole. For he that saith, Forsake not the assembling of yourselves together, said also, Enter into thy closet. If, therefore, you engage in public worship, and never retire for devotion, you are an offender. He that said, Do not commit adultery, said also, Do not kill: now if thou commit no adultery, yet, if thou kill, thou art become a transgressor of the law. We never can truly obey, therefore, unless we can say, with David, I esteem all thy commandments concerning all things to be right; and I hate every false way.

SEPTEMBER 16.—"Lord what wilt thou have me to do?"—Acts, ix, 6.

BEFORE we yield ourselves to any one, we should have full confidence in him; and the confidence should be founded on knowledge. To no fellow creature can we wholly resign ourselves, either of right or with safety; for he has no title to us, so we know not what his depravity may require of us. We owe duties to our fellow creatures; and to many of them we must say, What wilt *thou* have me to do? Yet we must obey *them* only "in the Lord." But his authority is supreme. He has infinite claims to my implicit homage.

Five principles demand and more than justify the absolute surrender of myself to Him—saying, Lord, what wilt thou have me to do?

First. The righteousness and excellency of his requirements. Each of his prohibitions only says, Do thyself no harm. Each of his injunctions is an order to be wise, and rich, and noble, and happy. While following him, my understanding never blushes; my conscience never reproaches me. I can give a reason for my obedience, as well as my hope. His will is always a reasonable service—His work is honorable and glorious.

Secondly. The relations in which he stands to his people. He is their Husband—He is their Father—He is their Master—He is their Sovereign—He is their Maker—from whom they have derived all they have and are. And surely, in each of these, it becomes them to ask, "Lord, what wilt *thou* have me to do?"

Thirdly. His greatness. This is unsearchable. He is Lord of all. All the angels of God worship him. All things were created by him, and for him: and he is before all things; and by him all things consist. His greatness is necessary to the illustration of his goodness, and crowns it with glory and honor. What condescension is there, where there is no dignity? But he was in the form of God, and took upon him the form of a servant—there was the stoop! He was rich, and for our sakes, became poor. There was the grace! Greatness alone produces, not attachment, but dread and aversion. But, while *he* has all power in heaven and in earth, he is full of grace and truth—

"His heart is made of tenderness; | "His bowels melt with love."

Therefore, fourthly, the obligations he has laid us under by his kindness. What are the obligations any of our fellow creatures have laid us under? What have they done for us? suffered for us? How few, how inconsiderable, how unexpensive, how unattended with any thing like sacrifice and self-denial, have their acts of favor been! But he, without our desert, and against the greatest demerit, remembered us in our low estate; and, in his love and pity, redeemed us. And how? He was made a curse for us. He bore our sins in his own body on the tree. By his stripes we are healed. Where does he stand? how does he appear? when he says, "My son, give me thy heart?"

"See from his head, his hands, his feet,
"Sorrow and love flow mingled down:
"Did e'er such love and sorrow meet,
"Or thorns compose so rich a crown?"

And can we wonder at the result?

"Were the whole realm of nature mine,
"That were a present far too small;
"Love so amazing, so divine,
"Demands my soul, my life, my all."

No legal process ever produced this surrender. The display of terror and mere authority never made one cordial convert to any cause. Would you be induced to love another, by his commanding you to do so, and threatening you, if you do not? No; but by a display of love—love begets love. And we love Him, because he first loved us—at the Cross we are effectually wooed and won—there we are drawn, and there we are bound with cords of a man and the bands of love.

Lastly. His engagement to reward our devotedness to him. Christians are not mercenary; but they cannot serve him for nought. The recompense must be of grace, and not of works—so much the better is it for their hope: for if it is to be measured and judged of now, not according to their doings, but his own abundant mercy, which is to be displayed in it. Hence will he say at last, with regard to those poor performances over which they have blushed and wept, "Well done, good and faithful servant; enter thou into the joy of thy Lord." But he is not unrighteous to forget their work of faith and labor of love, now. *In* keeping his commandments, there is great reward. Great peace have they that love his law; and nothing shall offend them. He is the best of masters. He furnishes them with ability for their work. He lays no more upon his servants than he enables them to bear. He will comfort them in affliction. He will not cast them off in old age. He will remember the kindness of their youth. When heart and flesh fail, he will be the strength of their heart, and their portion for ever. And at death, receive them to himself: that where he is, there they may be also. Sinners talk of the pleasures of sin; but they never commend them at last. The people of the world boast of its amusements and delights, but they never speak well of it at parting. In every season, in every condition, however trying, the Christian can say, Thou hast dealt well with thy servant, O Lord.

"Then Peter said, Lo, we have left all, and followed thee. And he said unto them, Verily I say unto you, There is no man that hath left house, or parents, or brethren, or wife, or children, for the kingdom of God's sake, who shall not receive manifold more in this present time, and in the world to come life everlasting."

September 17.—"Notwithstanding, lest we should offend them go thou to the sea, and cast a hook, and take up the fish that first cometh up; and when thou hast opened his mouth, thou shalt find a piece of money: that take, and give unto them for me and thee."—*Matthew*, xvii, 27.

In the midst of this supernatural scene, a sanction is thus given by our Savior to the use of means. The supply was, in its source, preparation, and announcement, miraculous; yet Peter, who is to receive it as a favor, is to procure it by his instrumentality. The peculiar nature of the instance only renders it the more conclusive; for if our Lord would not dispense with the use of means in an extraordinary case, surely he will not dispense with it in an ordinary one. Some good, but not very wise people, seem to think that instrumentality detracts from the divine glory; and that God is honored more by acting *im*-mediately. But instrumentality supposes and requires agency; and the means themselves are always the Lord's own, and he gives them their success. His producing an effect by various concurrences and co-operations, displays more of his perfections, and gives more opportunity to observe them, than his causing a result by an instant volition.

Here was something which Peter could do, and something which he could not do. He could not replenish the fish with the money, or make it swim in the direction of his bait; but he could procure the bait, and throw in the hook, and in the most likely place; and stand, and watch. Why does not the Lord dispense with all this, and cause the fish to spring on shore, and appear at once upon Peter's table? Because he would not sanction indolence. Because he would render even his miracles moral, as well as marvellous. Because his exertions were not a mere parade of power, but a display of wisdom and goodness—meeting indigence, relieving weakness, confirming faith: but not encouraging folly and presumption—teaching us to trust—but forbidding us to tempt him.

In like manner, there is always something which we cannot do; and something which we can do—but the evil is, that we commonly derive from the former, excuses for our neglect of the latter; and so God's agency becomes a reason for our inactivity, instead of exciting our diligence—perfectly contrary to the meaning of the apostle, when he says, "Work out your salvation with fear and trembling, *for* it is God which worketh in you to will and to do of his good pleasure." In natural things we are wiser. Can the husbandman produce an ear of corn? He knows it is perfectly impossible. But he can manure, and plough, and sow; and in the use of these he expects the divine efficiency—but *never* in the *neglect* of them. No man can quicken his own soul. But there are means which are designed and adapted to serve us; and we can pray, "Come, thou north wind, and blow, thou south." It is thus that religion possesses the evidence of analogy; and in the God of grace we see the God of nature. He feeds the fowls of the air, not by putting it into their mouths, but by furnishing provision; and giving them wings, and eyes, and feet, and beaks, to find and make it their own—"That thou givest them, they gather." And *thus* "he satisfies the desire of every living thing." He could warm us without the fire, and sustain us without food—but we know what would be the consequence were we to disregard these, under a notion of honoring him by a dependence on *his agency*.

Though the effect here was beyond the means, yet there was an *adaptation* in them. Peter was a fisherman; and he is employed in his own line; and his fishing was not only the condition of the result, but the medium—and *conduced* to it. And in general we may observe, that while the insufficiency of the means serves to display the power of God, the suitableness of them shows his wisdom. And such a suitableness there is. A pen cannot write, without a hand to use it; yet there is an adaptation in the instrument to the work, which is not the case with a hammer. Some seem to use the means of grace only as tests of their submission to the divine appointment—not as things which have a real tendency even in themselves to do them good. They expect the divine blessing *in* them, but not *by* them—*i. e.* not as an effect resulting *from* them under the divine influence—as if, in the use of them, they were planting and watering pebbles, which by an almighty exertion, *could* be made to yield produce—instead of using them as a man sows wheat, and looks for wheat to arise from it—not without God, but by God, in his own way. Faith cometh *by* hearing; and hearing *tends* to produce it, by informing and convincing the mind. The same may be said of a religious education, in forming the moral and pious character of the child.

Peter did well not to disobey, or reason, but to follow implicitly the divine order; fully expecting success. And he was not—could not be—disappointed. And thus let us act without murmuring or disputing. Let us use the means which he has prescribed, not only swayed by his authority, but relying on his promise—that none of those that wait for him shall be ashamed.

SEPTEMBER 18.—"I have sent forth thy prisoners out of the pit wherein is no water."—Zech. ix, 11.

PERSONS may be prisoners, as felons, as robbers, as debtors, as captives taken in war. The character of the subjects of divine grace, by nature, involved all these.

A pit wherein there is no water, is a situation expressive of destitution, wretchedness, and danger. There the victim has nothing to relieve his wants; nothing to quench his raging thirst. He cannot live in it; he cannot escape from it—he is ready to perish. Such was Joseph's pit, and Jeremiah's dungeon. In such a condition the Lord finds his people.

But he does not leave them there. He always produces a change in their favor. If they are in darkness he calls them into his marvellous light. If they are far off, he brings them nigh. If they are prisoners in a pit wherein there is no water—he sends them out of it. In his love and pity he redeems them, and makes them free indeed.

The work is entirely his own; and the principle cannot be mistaken. How unworthy were they of his notice! How great the evil from which they have been rescued! How infinite the blessedness resulting from it. And after such a deliverance as this, shall they again break his commandments? A soul redeemed, demands a life of praise. Let my people go, that they may serve me. What has he sent them out of their bondage to do? but to go and tell sinners such as they themselves once were, that with the Lord there is mercy, and with him plenteous redemption! but to show forth his praise; and acknowledge by the grace of God they are what they are? but to walk in newness of life: to run in the way of his commandments: to return and come to Zion with songs and everlasting joy upon their heads?

And can this be a task? Did Zechariah think so when he sung and prayed—"That he would grant unto us, that we being delivered out of the hand of our enemies, might serve him without fear; in holiness, and righteousness before him all the days of our lives?"

September 19.—"Then shall we know, if we follow on to know the Lord." Hosea, vi, 3.

Whether we consider these words as an excitation and an encouragement addressed by the godly to each other, or to their own souls, they remind us of an important aim; a necessary duty; and an assured privilege.

—The *aim* is "to know the Lord." For the soul to be without knowledge it is not good. All the operations of the Spirit are begun and carried on in the renewing of the mind. Nothing can be moral or religious in our dispositions and actions, that is not founded in knowledge; because it must be destitute of principle and motive; and the Lord looketh at the heart. Real repentance must arise from proper views of the evil of sin, in connexion with the cross of Christ—"They shall look upon him whom they pierced, and shall mourn for him." Even faith is impossible, without knowledge—"For how can they believe in him of whom they have not heard?" But what says the Savior? "This is life eternal, that they know Thee, the only true God; and Jesus Christ, whom thou hast sent." This declaration not only decides the importance of this knowledge, but also the nature of it. It is not a philosophical knowledge of God, as an almighty being, the maker and upholder of all things; or even a knowledge of him as holy in all his ways, and righteous in all his works. Such views of him alone, must, on the mind of a sinner, gender dread and aversion. The grand thing in the restoration of a fallen and guilty creature, is to know that he is reconcilable; that he is willing, even now, to become our friend; and has already given undeniable proof that he is waiting to be gracious, and is exalted to have mercy upon him. And all this is only to be seen in the Only Begotten of the Father, who has declared him. God in nature, is God above me: God in providence, is God beyond me;

God in law, is God against me; but God in Christ, is God for me, and with me. Neither is this knowledge of him, a merely speculative acquaintance with him; such as men may possess, who behold, and wonder, and perish. There is a great difference between the decisions of the judgment, and the bias of the will; between the convictions of the conscience, and the submission and acquiescence of the heart—"With the heart man believeth unto righteousness"—"I will give them a heart to know me"—"He hath shined in our heart, to give us the light of the knowledge of the glory of God in the face of Jesus Christ."

Connected with this there is a necessary *duty*. It is "to follow on" to know the Lord.

—This takes in the practice of what we already know. To what purpose would it be for God to afford the light they have? It would only increase their sin and their condemnation. "Whosoever hath, to him shall be given, and he shall have more abundance; but whosoever hath not, from him shall be taken away even that he hath." And we see this constantly exemplified. When men love not to retain God in their knowledge, it is their interest to see things less clearly; and so they part with one truth after another, as it becomes troublesome; till God gives them up to strong delusion to believe a lie. While those who do his will, know of the doctrine; advancing toward the light, they get more into its shining; and as far as they have already attained, walking by the same rule, and minding the same thing, if in any thing else they be otherwise minded, God reveals even this unto them.

—It also includes diligence in the use of appointed means: such as reading the scriptures, and hearing the word preached, and meditation, and "walking with wise men," and above all, prayer to the Father of lights, according to the promise, "If any of you lack wisdom, let him ask of God, that giveth to all men liberally, and upbraideth not; and it shall be given him." "If thou criest after knowledge, and liftest up thy voice for understanding; if thou seekest her as silver, and searchest for her as for hid treasures; then shalt thou understand the fear of the Lord, and find the knowledge of God."

—It must also mean perseverance in this course. "Blessed is the man that heareth me, watching daily at my gates, waiting at the posts of my doors." Here is not only watching, but waiting. Some run well; and are hindered. But we are to run with patience the race that is set before us; and by patient continuance in well doing, to seek for glory, honor, and immortality.

—Nor shall this be in *vain*. "Then shall we know, if we follow on to know the Lord." The privilege is as *sure* as the word of God, confirmed by his faithfulness, and all history, and all experience, can make it. And if probability will actuate a man to engage in an enterprise, and continue in a series of exertions and sacrifices, how much more should actual certainty! Let, therefore, this full assurance of hope excite and influence us in two cases.

The first is with regard to ourselves. The way of the Lord is strength to the upright. Keep his way; and your path shall be as the shining light, that shineth more and more unto the perfect day. Your perplexities shall be solved; your doubts removed; your fears subdued. Crooked things shall be made straight, and rough places plain. You shall know more of him in his word, providence, and grace: and more of him as the strength of your heart, and your portion for ever.

The second regards others. Be not impatient if they cannot embrace all your religious views at once; and are amazed at some parts of your experience. In grace, as well as in nature, there must be infancy before manhood. Though now their acquaintance with divine things be small, and they only see men as trees walking, the Enlightener will put his hand a second time to the work, and they shall see clearly. If their heart be broken off from sin and the world; and they are asking the way to Zion, with their faces thitherward—they shall not err therein. "Who hath despised the day of small things?"

SEPTEMBER 20.—"In him is no sin."—1 John, iii, 5.

—No sin original. David said, I was shapen in iniquity, and in sin did my mother conceive me. The same may be said by every individual of the human race. Our Savior was truly a man—But to secure him, in the participation of our nature from pollution, behold a new thing in the earth! He is made only of woman; a virgin conceives and bears a son; and that holy thing which is born of her, is called the Son of God. His people are holy by renovation; he was so by nature. Even when sanctified, they feel within them a conflict; the flesh and the spirit oppose each other, and they cannot do the things that they would. But he had no warfare of this kind. He could not say, I find then a law, that, when I would do good, evil was present with me. All his senses, and appetites, and passions, moved in obedience to reason, and in unison with the will of God.

Hence there was in him no sin actual. In proof of this the testimony of his friends may be deemed partial, though they had the best opportunities of knowing him: and they all gloried in the avowal, that he did no sin, neither was guile found in his mouth. But hear the multitude—He hath done all things well. Hear the dying thief—This man hath done nothing amiss. Hear Pilate who judicially examined him—I find no fault in this man: I am pure from the blood of that just man. Hear Judas, the domestic spy, after three years of intimacy with him—I have betrayed innocent blood. No one ever had more keen or malicious observers, especially in the Pharisees, whom he had exasperated to fury, by laying open their pious wickedness to the people. But he challenged every adversary—Which of you convinceth me of sin? If there be any thing in us susceptible of evil influence, Satan will be sure to find it; for he has a bait suited to every disposition—but the Prince of this world came and had nothing in him. He struck the sparks, but there was no tinder. Events, whether prosperous or painful, are severe trials; and if there be mud at the bottom, the waves will cast up mire and dirt—But he was in all points tempted like as we are, yet without sin. He was made under the

the law; and this law is so spiritual, that the holiest of men, when they have compared themselves with it, have always prayed, Enter not into judgment with thy servant, O Lord; for in thy sight no flesh living shall be justified. But even this law had nothing to complain of in him; it found, in principle and in practice, all the obedience it required. And how was he viewed by him who is greater than the heart, and knoweth all things! He always did the things that pleased the Father.

—The fact, therefore, is undeniable. But whence this exception? How came this one man alone to have no sin in him, while, as to the myriads of the human race beside, they are all gone out of the way; there is none righteous, no, not one! It can only be accounted for upon the admission that he was the Lord from heaven; the Holy one of God; the Word made flesh; the only begotten of the Father—full of grace and truth; who received not the Spirit by measure; in whom dwelt all the fullness of the Godhead bodily.

This is not an unimportant decision. The innocency of his character affects the credibility of his mission and his doctrine. A being in whom was no sin could not have been a deceiver; but he constantly declared that he came forth from God; that he came to seek and to save that which was lost; that he would cast out none that came to him. Lord, I believe, help thou mine unbelief.

It serves to evince the *nature* of his suffering and death. He had no sin of his own, and therefore if he died not for the sins of others, he died without any reference to sin at all. And where is the God of judgment? That be far from him to slay the righteous with the wicked. No one ever suffered under his government absolutely innocent; but either as personally or relatively guilty; bearing his own desert, or the desert of others. But in him was no sin—yet he was esteemed stricken, smitten of God, and afflicted. And so he was—" But he was wounded for our transgressions, he was bruised for our iniquities; the chastisement of our peace was upon him, and with his stripes we are healed."

But without this, he could not have been qualified for his work. He had *immediately* to approach Infinite Purity. His sacrifice would not have been accepted, unless he had offered himself without spot to God. Such a High Priest became us, who was harmless, holy, undefiled, and separate from sinners, and who needed not to suffer for his own sins, dying only for those of others.

—What a character is here! others are lovely, but he is altogether lovely. And see what humanity can become, and will become, in all his followers. For they are predestinated to be conformed to him. The spirits of just men will be made perfect; and though they will be re-embodied, their bodies will have no seed of corruption in them: for they also will not be derived, but produced. They could not have full communion with him, without complete likeness to him—But this we know, that when he shall appear, we shall be like him for we shall see him as he is. "And every man that hath this hope in him purifieth himself, even as he is pure."

September 21.—"My presence shall go with thee, and I will give thee rest."—Exodus, xxxiii, 14.

This exceeding great and precious promise belongs to the Christian, as well as to Moses. What is he authorised to expect from it? My presence shall go with thee *to guide thee*, and I will give thee rest *from perplexity.* How miserable would a man be in travelling, if his journey were important, and yet he was ignorant of the way, and every moment liable to err! In this case nothing could relieve him so much as a guide who was willing to go with him, and able to show him the course he should always take. And his satisfaction would be in proportion to the confidence he reposed in the disposition and capacity of his leader. Nothing can equal the importance of the journey we are taking; life or death, salvation or perdition, depends upon the issue; and "the way of man is not in himself; it is not in man that walketh to direct his steps." If left to himself, he will err at every step, and in the greatness of his folly go for ever astray. The Christian feels this, and therefore prays, "Lead me in thy truth, and guide me, for thou art the God of my salvation; on thee do I wait all the day." And does God disregard his cry? "Thus saith the Lord, thy Redeemer, the Holy One of Israel, I am the Lord thy God which teacheth thee to profit; which leadeth thee by the way that thou shouldest go." This extends to doctrine, to experience, to all his temporal concerns. He is not indeed to look for miracles, but he is under the conduct of God: and he has given no promise but can be, and shall be fulfilled. When the Jews were marching to Canaan, they had a pathless desert to go through: but they were free from all perplexity, because they had a fiery, cloudy pillar, to regulate all their movements. We have the same. For "this God is our God for ever and ever: he will be our guide even unto death."

My presence shall go with thee, *to guard thee*, and I will give thee rest *from apprehension.* A Christian has not only a pilgrimage, but a warfare to accomplish. No sooner has he set his face Zion-ward, than he has reason to exclaim, "Lord, how are they increased that trouble me! Many there be which rise up against me; many there be that say of my soul, There is no help for him in God." And what wonder if, while without are fightings, within are fears? And how is he to rise above them? He knows that, if left to himself, he must perish long before he reaches that better country. But he is not alone. There is One at his right hand, who says, "Abide with me; for he that seeketh thy life, seeketh my life; but with me thou shalt be in safeguard." At the sound of this, his mind is relieved, his confidence rises, and he sings, "The Lord is my light and my salvation; whom shall I fear? The Lord is the strength of my life! of whom shall I be afraid?"

"A Friend and Helper so divine
"Does my weak courage raise;
"He makes the glorious vict'ry mine,
"And his shall be the praise."

My presence shall go with thee, *to provide for thee*, and I will give thee rest *from anxiety.* The manna was not to be hoarded, but gathered daily: and we are to feel our constant dependence upon God for the supply of the Spirit of Jesus Christ. And is this trying? Could we wish it to be otherwise?

"Though in ourselves we have no stock,
"The Lord is nigh to save:
"The door flies open when we knock,
"And 'tis but ask and have."

"They that wait upon the Lord shall renew their strength." "My grace is sufficient for thee." What more can we desire? When we have trusted in God for the soul, it might be imagined easy to trust in him for the body. But temporal things are sensible, and near, and pressing; and some cases would be enough to awaken all their forebodings; but he has said, "I will never leave thee, nor forsake thee." "Fear the Lord, ye his saints; for there is no want to them that fear him. The young lions do lack and suffer hunger; but they that seek the Lord shall not want any good thing." Jehovah-jireh! The Lord will provide.

My presence shall go with thee, *to comfort thee*, and I will give thee rest *from sorrow*. However you may be stripped, you shall not be destitute of consolation; though the fig tree shall not blossom, nor fruit be in the vine—you shall rejoice in the Lord, and joy in the God of your salvation. His presence is a substitute for any creature; it more than repairs every loss. Some leave us from rottenness of principle; some from infirmity, rather than depravity. Death abridges our circles. Who can look back over a few years, and not exclaim, "Lover and friend hast thou put far from me, and mine acquaintance into darkness?" Yet if the lamps be extinguished, the sun continues. If the streams fail, we have the fountain. Are the consolations of God small with thee? In the multitude of thy thoughts within thee, do not his comforts delight thy soul?

But there is an event that must take place. Oh! when I shall gather up my feet into the bed, and turn my face to the wall—then, all creatures withdrawn, and flesh and heart failing—Oh! what can support me in the prospect, and, above all, in the reality? Be of good courage. He who is with thee in the wilderness, will be with thee at the swellings of Jordan, and open a way through the flood, and give thee a dry shod passage over, into the land flowing with milk and honey. He who has been with thee in life, will be still more with thee in death. And therefore you may boldly say, with one before you, "Yea, though I walk through the valley of the shadow of death, I will fear no evil, for thou art with me; thy rod and thy staff, they comfort me."

From this hour let me never forget this blessed promise. "My presence shall go with thee; and I will give thee rest." Let me believe it with a faith unfeigned. Let me ascertain my title to it. Let me plead it before the throne of grace. Let me apply it in my perplexities, and apprehensions, and anxieties, and sorrows. Let me bind it about my neck, and write it upon the table of my heart—that when I go, it may lead me; when I sleep, it shall keep me; and when I awake, it may talk with me. Amen.

SEPTEMBER 22.—"Thy Maker is thine husband."—Isaiah, liv, 5.

THE relation in which God stands to us must be all-important. If we are his people, he is related to us, not only as the God of nature and providence, but as the God of grace. This spiritual connexion is held forth under various forms—none of which is more common, simple, or well known, than the marriage union.

The marriage union is honorable in all. It is exemplified in the larger part of the human race. It was established in paradise, where it was not good for man to be alone; and in commendation of it our Savior wrought his first miracle. But applied to God and us, it is a metaphor; and therefore to be soberly explained. For while we are not to overlook the wisdom and kindness of the Holy Ghost in meeting our weakness of apprehension, we are not to press every circumstance of the comparison into an article of allusion. The relation into which God enters with his people, is analogous to that which subsists between the husband and the wife. This could be easily explained and understood.

But let us take the reality of the connexion itself to show us three things. First. The condescension and goodness of God. Nothing will bear a comparison with it. Consider what He is; his independence, his greatness, and his glory. And view them in their unworthiness, lowness, vileness. How wonderful that *He* should thus magnify *them*—and set his heart upon them! They had neither birth, nor relations, nor wealth, nor wisdom, to recommend them. It cannot, indeed, be denied that they are distinguished by all these attributes now: but this is the consequence of the relation, and not the cause of it. "*Since* thou hast been precious in my sight, thou hast been honorable, and I have loved thee."

Secondly. The privilege of believers. Blessed are the people who are in such a case; yea, happy is the people whose God is the Lord. They have one, in the nearest of all relations to them, who is love itself; and will bear with their infirmities, and in all their afflictions be afflicted—who is infinitely wise, and knows their frame, and will never mistake their welfare—who is almighty, and able to defend them from every danger, and to make all things work together for their good—who is faithfulness and truth, and will never leave them nor forsake them—who lives for ever, and renders the union eternal and indissolvable.

Thirdly. Their duty. They must mind their husband's concerns. They must regard properly his relations. They must obey him—the wife promises this in marriage; and the apostle enjoins it: Wives, submit yourselves unto your own husbands. He extends it to every thing; but this must be qualified with one condition—every thing reasonable and righteous. Vashti refused Ahasuerus, when he sent for her to come and exhibit herself before a company of intoxicated lords and officers, in violation of all decency, and the laws of veiled concealment in which women then lived; and we justify her disobedience. But, with regard to us, the will of God is absolute, not only because he has a propriety in us which one creature can never have in another, but because all his commandments are right. The wife is required to reverence her husband. This must be a hard saying in some cases, seeing there are sometimes so few materials to excite veneration in the *head* of the wife—But this should have been thought of before; and persons should not voluntarily contract relations, the duties of which they cannot perform, and dare not neglect. But God's excellencies are infinite. It is delightful to give him the glory that is due to his holy name. The wife, also, must be faithful to her husband: "She is for him, and not for another." And we are only the Lord's. There is such a thing as spiritual adultery; to avoid which we are to keep ourselves from idols. Milton's wife departed home again; but she returned and humbled herself, and was re-admitted to favor. But here is the duty of the church—"Hearken, O daughter, and consider, and incline thine ear; forget also thine own people, and thy father's house; so shall the King greatly desire thy beauty; for he is thy Lord; and worship thou him.'

September 23.—"I beseech Euodias, and beseech Syntyche, that they be of the same mind in the Lord. And I entreat thee also, true yoke-fellow, help those women which labored with me in the Gospel, with Clement also, and with other my fellow-laborers, whose names are in the book of life. Rejoice in the Lord alway; and again I say, Rejoice."—Philippians, iv, 2—4.

The apostle much valued and commended the Philippian converts. He here calls them—his "brethren;" his "dearly beloved;" "and longed for;" his "joy and crown." Many people *distress* and *disgrace* their ministers; but these yielded Paul both comfort and honor. He does not, however, deem them above the need of exhortation; yet, though he might have been bold to enjoin what was convenient, for love's sake he beseeches and entreats. The subject is threefold.

First. Unanimity and concord. This regards a particular instance of disagreement in the church. "I beseech Euodias, and beseech Syntyche, that they be of the same mind in the Lord." Here were two women, obviously of some note, who were at variance. We are not informed whether the ground of difference was civil or religious. Perhaps it was owing to a tale bearer; for a tale bearer separateth true friends. Perhaps it was a mere trifle in the outset. In our mistakes, prejudices, passions, and infirmities, the enemy of souls always finds materials for exciting dislike and contention. Perhaps they were both to blame—this is commonly the case; and therefore the Scripture says, forgiving *one another*. The feelings of females are quick; and their imaginations too often give importance to a real or supposed offence. And two such individuals at variance, may draw in others, form parties, and embroil a whole church. When this is the case, their own edification is at an end; and from others is driven that union of soul which is necessary to give efficacy to social prayer, when we meet together in one place, with one accord, waiting for the promise of the Father. The apostle, therefore, would not that Euodias and Syntyche should oppose, or keep shy of each other; but composing their difference, keep the peace, and live in love. The Savior is the Lamb of God; and if we have the mind that was in him, we shall display "the meekness and gentleness of Jesus Christ." The Holy Ghost descended upon the Head, and enters his followers, as a dove: and

"The Spirit, like a peaceful dove,
"Flies from the realms of noise and strife;
'Why should we vex and grieve his love,
"Who seals our souls for heavenly life?"

—We read in ecclesiastical history of two Christians who had quarrelled in the morning; but in the evening one of them sent a note to the other—"Brother, the sun is going down"—referring to the apostle's words, "Let not the sun go down upon your wrath"—and the hint produced reconciliation. When President Edwards had preached one of his first sermons after the remarkable outpouring of the Spirit upon his labors, he observed two families, when the congregation had withdrawn, remaining, as if by joint consent.—Upon approaching them, he found they had, to that day, been in a state of variance; but owing to the influence they were now under, they could not depart from the House of God till they were reconciled.

—Secondly. Mutual assistance. "And I entreat thee, also, true yoke-fellow, help those women which labored with me in the Gospel, with Clement also, and with other my fellow laborers, whose names are in the book of life." Some have imagined that those woman here alluded to were Euodias and Syntyche. If it were so, we should learn that persons who have been betrayed into improper temper and conduct in a partial instance, may yet have been worthy and useful characters; and they are not to be rejected, but restored, in the spirit of meekness. But such a limitation is unnecessary. Whoever these females were, they had co-operated with Paul and his associates in the ministry—not in public preaching, for this our apostle had expressly forbidden; but in various offices suited to their sex and condition; by their devotion, and example, and conversation; by their privately instructing the ignorant; by their bringing up children; washing the saints' feet: attending benevolent institutions; ministering to the wants of the apostles. All who wish to be useful, may be employed without violating any of the decorums of life, or quitting their proper stations. On their behalf, Paul addresses his "true yoke-fellow." It is absurd to suppose this means, as some have thought, Paul's wife. For it seems more than probable that he never was married: and the gender of the adjective here used, is masculine. Was it the jailor? He had been one of the apostle's first converts at Philippi; and had much assisted him in the Gospel. Or was it Epaphroditus? But he was not at this time at Philippi. Perhaps it was one of the bishops or deacons mentioned in the beginning of the Epistle; with whom Paul had been peculiarly connected in travelling, and preaching. Whoever he was, he was to help those females who had been so serviceable to Paul, and Clement, and their comrades: by his prayers and consolations, and every kind of attention their personal or relative, temporal or spiritual, circumstances would require. How honorable was it to be thus distinguished and recommended by the apostle! Who was ever a loser by any thing he did for the cause of the Redeemer? He that watereth shall be watered also. God is not unrighteous to forget the work of faith and labor of love. Wheresoever the Gospel is preached, that which these women did shall be told for a memorial of them.

Thirdly. Constant joy—"Rejoice in the Lord alway: and again I say, rejoice." Rejoicing is a pleasing exercise; but it is not so easy a one. In a vale of tears; in an enemy's country; without, fightings; within, fears; pressed down with a sense of unworthiness; burdened with infirmities; wearied with a body of sin and death: what wonder if we hang our harp on the willows? or, at least, that we cannot always sing the Lord's song? Yet we are enjoined to rejoice "always." We are. But how? In what? In whom? In the world? In creatures? In ourselves? Then would it indeed be impracticable. But it is "in the Lord." And in him there is enough at all times, and in every condition, to encourage and delight. We are empty, but in him all fullness dwells. In him is all the wisdom, pardon, righteousness, strength, and hope, we need. His grace is sufficient for us—He is AN INFINITE RESOURCE.

Therefore says the apostle—I have not spoken thoughtlessly—I know what I have said; and why I have said it—I know that the thing is possible—And I know, also, that it is proper—that nothing becomes a Christian more: and that by nothing can he be more useful—I therefore repeat it—AND AGAIN I SAY REJOICE.

SEPTEMBER 24.—"He that saith he abideth in him, ought himself also so to walk, even as he walked."—1 John, ii, 6.

THE state here spoken of, is *abiding in* Christ. A man's *saying* he is thus in him, is done two ways. The one is to himself—and so it is belief. The other is to his fellow-creatures—and so it is profession. The rule of such a man's life, is the example of Christ—*walking as he walked.* And to this he is under an obligation to conform—He *ought* to walk even as he walked. The obligation is fourfold.

First. He ought to walk even as he walked, from a principle of *evidence.* Deception in religious concerns is not only possible, but common; and the consequences, if the delusion continues, will be dreadful Hence we should be anxious to know whether our hope is any thing better than presumption; or our safety is any thing more than self-security. If from self-confidence, we contemn such solicitude, let us remember that the Sacred Writers command us not to be high minded, but fear; and to examine and prove, whether we be in the faith. There are, indeed, many proofs of a gracious state; and there are some of a more experimental nature to which we do well to take heed: but none of them can afford us relief, if they are unaccompanied by an imitation of Christ. "Why call ye me Lord, Lord, and do not the things which I say?" "If any man have not the spirit of Christ, he is none of his." "He that is joined to the Lord is of one Spirit." "If any man be in Christ, he is a new creature."

Secondly; he ought to walk even as he walked, from a principle of *consistency*. The relations and conditions in which we are found determine the propriety of our conduct. When we know what a man is, we conclude what it becomes him to do. A steward is expected to be found faithful; and dishonesty draws upon him censure and condemnation from all. Every one is sensible that a king and a bishop should not act like common men; but that a dignified and sacred line of conduct is required by their rank and office. Christians are kings and priests unto God; and therefore they must walk worthy of the vocation wherewith they are called. The man who advances peculiar and superior claims to any thing, has no reason, no right to complain, if he be judged by his pretensions. He who wishes to pass as a Christian, avows himself related to Christ; and by his doctrine and character he must be tried: he ranks himself above the world, and challenges the inquiry, What do ye more than others?

Thirdly. He ought to walk even as he walked, from a principle of *usefulness*. He will thus put to silence the ignorance of foolish men. He will wipe off the reproach attached to the Gospel. He will adorn the doctrine of God our Savior in all things. He will be the means, by his good works which they behold, of inducing those that are without, to enter the way everlasting. No one can imagine the influence and efficiency of a life entirely Christian. It is a blessing to the whole neighborhood in which it is displayed. It is like a dew from the Lord, and as showers upon the grass. But by an unworthy and unbecoming conduct, a professor of religion can destroy much good. He causes the way of truth to be evil spoken of. He hardens transgressors. He perplexes the weak. He grieves the strong. He opposes and discourages all those who are laboring to win souls. Wo to the world, because of offences? And wo to that man by whom the offence cometh!

Fourthly. He ought to walk even as He walked, from a principle of *gratitude*. We feel and acknowledge the kindnesses shown us by our fellow-creatures; and, in consequence of it, we endeavor to meet their wishes, and to avoid whatever pains or displeases them: for actions speak louder than words. What has not Christ done for us? See his condescension, when, in the form of God, he took upon him the form of a servant. See his grace, when he was rich, and for our sakes he becomes poor. See him in the manger, and in the garden. See him upon the cross, dying: and upon the throne reigning for us, and making all things work together for our good. And surely we shall feel that a peculiar, a supreme love to him become us. And how are we to show it? Shall we ever grieve his Holy Spirit? Shall we not ask, Lord, what wilt thou have me to do? Shall we not pray, "Let the words of my mouth, and the meditation of my heart, be acceptable in thy sight, O Lord, my strength and my Redeemer?" He that hath my commandments and keepeth them, he it is that loveth me. He that offereth praise, glorifieth me; and to him that ordereth his conversation aright, will I show the salvation of God. Upon which, Philip Henry observes, Thanksgiving is well, but thanksliving is better.

If we walk like him now, we shall walk like him hereafter. It is his own promise—"Thou hast a few names even in Sardis, which have not defiled their garments; and they shall walk with me in white; for they are worthy."

SEPTEMBER 25.—"I will hasten my escape from the windy storm and tempest."—Psalm lv, 8.

SUCH was the language of David—And it may be the language of any other good man in the depth of distress. But is it allowable and proper? There is no perfection here; and there is nothing concerning which we should indulge more tenderness of censure, than hasty expressions, uttered under the pressure of pain or grief. Perhaps it was to prevent our severity here, that the cases of Job and Jeremiah are recorded, both of whom, though eminent in piety, cursed the day of their birth. The Scripture is not harsh upon them; and it is observable, that when James refers to one of these bitterly complaining sufferers, he only says, "Ye have heard of the patience of Job." They who have never been in a state of peculiar distress, know little of the feelings of human nature under it. But there are others who can respond to the invitation of sympathy, "Pity me, pity me, O ye my friends, for the hand of God hath touched me!" And the Father of mercies knows our frame, and remembers that we are dust. We are not required to choose suffering for its own sake; or to be indifferent to ease and deliverance. Our Savior himself had not that fortitude which mocks at pain; but that which he deeply felt, and yet submitted. With strong cryings and tears he prayed, "Father, if it be possible, let this cup pass from me: nevertheless, not my will, but thine be done."

But what allows of excuse, truth does not require us to commend. It was his infirmity that induced David to long for death to hasten his escape from the stormy wind and tempest: and an old writer tells us, it would have been more honorable for him to have asked for the strength of an ox, to bear his trials, than for the wings of a dove, to flee from them. Is not such language unworthy and ungrateful? Should we overlook and forget all our comforts? *Have* not these been great and numerous? And did we *then* long to flee away? Yea, *are* they not many and various, even *now*? And shall we only dwell on the dark side? Let us examine again; and let truth and thankfulness stand by the while. And may they not *yet* be many and great? Afflictions are not immutable dispensations. What changes often take place, to the surprise, as well as joy, of desponding sufferers?

"The Lord can change the darkest skies:
"Can give us day for night:
"Make drops of sacred sorrow rise
"To rivers of delight."

And is there not unbelief in the case? You are afraid of all your sorrows; and not only of their continuance and increase, but of their influence and effects. You dread lest you should not bear them properly, so as to glorify God; but sink in the day of adversity, and—sin too. Yet, O thou of little faith! wherefore dost thou doubt? Is not he *able* to preserve, and support, and comfort thee? And has he not *engaged* to do it? Has he not said, I will never leave thee, nor forsake thee? "When thou passest through the waters, I will be with thee; and through the rivers, they shall not overflow thee; when thou walkest through the fire, thou shalt not be burnt: neither shall the flame kindle upon thee." And has not his conduct always accorded with this assurance, both with regard to others, and with regard to yourselves?

"Did ever trouble yet befall,
"And He refuse to hear thy call?
"And has he not His promise past,
"That thou shalt overcome at last?"

More than once you have been appalled in the prospect of a trial; but when the evil day came, there came with it mercy and grace to help in time of need. Perhaps you even gloried in tribulation—and you would not refuse to pass through some of those distressing exercises again, to enjoy the same peace and comfort.

Is there not much ignorance and inconsideration in this impatience? How do you know that it is better to escape from these troubles than to bear them? Not one of them has befallen you by chance; and may you not infer the righteousness of them all, from their very Author? Is not his work perfect, and his ways judgment? He doth all things well. Does he detain you in distress because he does not love you? Yea, he loved you with an everlasting love, and withheld not his own Son from you. You may therefore entirely confide in him, assured that if he does not release you, it is because he waits to be gracious; and also equally assured, that blessed are all they that wait for him—for it is good for a man, not only to hope, but quietly wait for the salvation of the Lord.

First. Your own welfare may require the process. The Savior was made perfect through suffering; and the character of every Christian is more formed and improved from his afflictions, than his enjoyments. What would some of you have lost, had you fled away before such a trying dispensation enriched your faith and hope! How much of your happiness in heaven will arise from a review of your present conflicts on earth! The very trial of your faith is precious; and the crown of life is promised, not to him that *escapes*, but to him that *endureth* temptation. Afflictions are heavenly agents, and work out for you a far more exceeding and eternal weight of glory.

Secondly. The welfare of others may require it also. We are detained here to be useful; and we are often most useful in our trials. Nothing strikes like facts. The passive graces are the most impressive. They are better than a thousand sermons—better, to arrest the careless, to instruct the ignorant, to encourage the timid, to comfort the desponding. It was well Bunyan did not escape from the prison at Bedford, or we should not have had his Pilgrim's Progress and his Holy War. Paul was a prisoner, and knew that to depart and be with Christ was far better; nevertheless, because it was more needful for the Philippians, he was willing to abide in the flesh, and acquiesced in the adjournment of his deliverance and bliss. And here you also may be wanted. Perhaps you have a venerable mother, and are required to rock the cradle of her age, who rocked the cradle of your infancy. Perhaps you are a parent, and a rising family is dependent on your care, instructed by your wisdom, edified by your example. We are all placed in circumstances where we may prove a blessing; and this is our only opportunity. We may glorify God in heaven; but not in the same way as now—not by submission, patience, and self-denial. This is an advantage we have above the glorified. They cannot exercise candor, and forgive injuries, and relieve distress, and save souls. Life is ours, as well as death. Therefore, all the days of our appointed time let us wait, till our change comes.

SEPTEMBER 26.—" And he brought him to Jesus."—John, i, 42.

THESE are few words; but they are very instructive and improving. We may ask three questions.

To whom was he brought? " He brought him to *Jesus.*" To whom should he have been brought, but unto him? He had the words of eternal life. In vain would he have been brought to the princes of the world; to the philosophers of antiquity; to the moralists of the age; to the scribes and Pharisees; to Moses; to the law. Moses wrote of him; and the law was a school master to bring men to Christ, that they might be justified by the faith of Christ, and not by the deeds of the law. To him, says Isaiah, shall men come. To him, said the dying Jacob, shall the gathering of the people be. There alone they can find the wisdom they need; the pardon they need; the peace they need; the strength they need. In him they are blessed with all spiritual blessings in heavenly places—neither is there salvation in any other.

Who was brought? It was Simon Peter—" He brought *him* to Jesus." He is a character frequently and largely noticed in the sacred history. For, in consequence of this introduction, he became, not only a disciple of Jesus, but a preacher of the Gospel, and an apostle; and, from the low occupation of a fisherman, he was made a fisher of men; and, by one cast of his net, he gained three thousand souls. Let us endeavor to bring men to the Savior, remembering that we know not what he will do, not only in them, but for them, and by them. While he saves them, he may also employ and dignify them. However unlikely they at present appear, we may by-and-by observe them, with joyful surprise, and adoring gratitude, not only as Christians, but as ministers in his church, and extensively serving their generation according to the will of God. *Whatever* condition they may fill, or office they may discharge, they will be, must be useful. Like their father Abraham, they will be not only blessed, but blessings. In converting one, we do good to many. Who ever went to heaven alone?

We may also ask—*who* brought him? It was Andrew—" *He* brought him to Jesus." Andrew had been for some little time with Jesus himself; and he immediately evinces the influence of the intercourse on his own mind, by his concern to bring others to the same Savior. And there is nothing peculiar in this? They who have seen his glory, will be sure to proclaim his worth. They that have tasted that the Lord is gracious themselves, will be always constrained to invite others—*O taste and see that the Lord is good: blessed is the man that trusteth in him.* And they always speak of him best who speak from experience.

Andrew was not only acquainted with Jesus, but he was also related to Peter. *He first findeth his own brother Simon, and saith unto him—We have found the Messias.* The expression intimates that he also prevailed upon others, but that he *began* with him. His finding him *first*, might have been accidental; but it is much more probable that it was by design. He thought, and he thought justly, that his own brother had, though not an exclusive, yet a prior claim to his attention, and therefore, while many lead their friends and relations, their own flesh and blood, into the haunts of dissipation, the counsel of the ungodly, the way of sinners, the seat of the scornful, and so bring them to the Devil; Andrew instantly performed toward Simon, his own brother, a brother's part—And he brought him to Jesus.

Let us not forget this. We are to disregard none of our fellow-creatures; but surely those who are connected with us by the ties of friendship and of nature, have the first right to our solicitude. How is it possible for us to think of them, and not exclaim with Esther, in the dread of a more tremendous perdition—How can I bear to see the destruction of my kindred? In endeavoring to do good to these, we have also greater opportunities and advantages, by reason of our influence, and ease of access. Let, then, Grace sanctify and engage in her service, all the force and endearment of natural affection. Let the pious sister pray for, and plead with an irreligious brother. Let the godly wife strive to save her own husband. Let the husband allure to accompany him, the desire of his eyes. And oh! let parents awaken, and blend their anxieties and efforts, to bring to Jesus their children. When Moses lifted up the serpent in the wilderness, all the wounded were to obtain cure by looking. But children were bitten, as well as men and women. Had we been there, we should have seen many a father leading along his little daughter to a place of vision; and many a mother, pressing near with her infant son in her arm, and pointing his eyes to catch the shining remedy. So has the Son of Man been lifted up, that whosoever believeth on him should not perish, but have everlasting life—and the young need him; and the sooner they are brought to him the better. The sooner will they be prevented from injuring society: the sooner will they enter on a course of usefulness, during which they will scatter a thousand blessings. If we do good to an old man, it is all-important to himself; but then it goes off with him. Whereas, the good communicated to a child, is not only valuable personally but relatively. It descends from him, and is spread by him, as he rises up and multiplies in life: and the result of the whole cannot be estimated.

And if we bring them to him, will he reject or despise them?

Let his command determine this—"Feed my lambs." Let his conduct decide it—"And they brought young children to him that he should touch them. And his disciples rebuked those that brought them. But when Jesus saw it, he was much displeased, and said unto them; Suffer the little children to come unto me, and forbid them not; for of such is the kingdom of God. And he took them up in his arms, put his hands upon them, and blessed them."

Let those that *have* children, and let those that *are* children, think of this, and be encouraged.

"A flower, when offered in the bud, | "Is no vain sacrifice."

Another flower thus offered, can never arrive at perfection. It must wither and die. But this flower shall live and blossom as a rose. The Redeemer will put it into his bosom; and the fragrance shall spread through the Church below, and Temple above.

SEPTEMBER 27.—"And he brought him to Jesus."—John, i, 42.

WHAT Andrew here did with Simon, we are to do with our fellow creatures—We are to bring them to *Jesus*.

But can men be brought to him *now?* Did he not say, I am no more in the world? How happy were they who lived when he was on earth! They could repair to him in every trouble, and tell him every distress. Ye benevolent neighbors! you could carry the paralytic, and place him beneath the very eye of Mercy. You anxious father! you could go to him, and say, "Sir, come down ere my child die." You, Martha and Mary, as soon as Lazarus was afflicted, you could send to him, saying, "Lord, behold, he whom thou lovest is sick." And cannot you, my dear readers, cannot you apprise him of your desire or your grief? Have not you, at your disposal, a messenger, that you can dispatch to him in a moment, in the twinkling of an eye? "While they call, I will answer; and when they speak, I will hear." And has he not said, Lo! I am with you always, even unto the end of the world? and wherever two or three are gathered together in my name, there am I in the midst of you? If these words be true, he can be, he must be, he is, with his ministers and people now. Though no longer visible, he is accessible. We may apprehend him as to his essential presence, by which he fills heaven and earth. We may apprehend him also, as to his peculiar presence, by which he is nigh to them that are of a broken heart, and saveth such as be of a contrite spirit. He is to be found in the Scriptures. In his House. At his Table. On his Throne. In the garden and the field—

"Where'er we seek him he is found, | "And every place is holy ground"

But can *we* bring souls to him? Not efficiently. This is the work of God only. "No man can come unto me, except the Father hath sent me draw him." And the sooner we are convinced of this, the better. We shall then make all our attempts in dependence on the agency of his Spirit: and thus honoring him, he will honor us. But we may do this instrumentally. For God makes use of means: and he employs *men;* and employs them not only to do good to their fellow creatures temporally, but spiritually—Not only to relieve their bodies, but to save their souls. And various and many are the ways in which we may thus bring men to Jesus. We may do it by intercession: for he hears prayers for others, as well as for ourselves. We may do it by the influence of example. Nothing speaks so loud as the silent eloquence of a holy, consistent, and lovely life. By this, wives may win their husbands without the word; and servants may adorn the doctrine of God our Savior in all things. By this, *all* may be useful. All cannot be learned; all cannot be rich; but all may be exemplary. We may do it by instruction. Thus Andrew brought Peter—We have found, says he, the Messias. And thus the woman of Samaria brought her neighbors, saying, Come, see a man that told me all that ever I did; is not this the Christ? By a word fitly spoken—a letter—an invitation to hear the Gospel—the commendation of a good book—the diffusion of the Bible—the sending forth missionaries—the supporting of ministers, whose office it is to turn men from darkness to light. By all these, and many more, we may be the means of introducing souls to Jesus.

But *why* should we be concerned to bring them? Four things should make us alive to this work. First. To feel a concern for it, is an evidence of grace. There cannot be a better. Indeed, every other evidence is fallacious without this: and this is always to be found in a real Christian. For however he may walk in darkness, as to a knowledge of his own interest in divine things, and draw the conclusion that he has no part nor lot in the matter; he never is insensible and indifferent to the success of the Gospel and the salvation of souls. This makes the eye sparkle upon whose lid hangs the shadow of death. Secondly. To attempt it is a duty. A duty that cannot be declined, without the greatest guilt. A duty arising from the relation in which we stand to our fellow-men, as bone of our bone, and flesh of our flesh. A duty enforced by the will of God, clearly made known in the injunction, As we have opportunity, let us do good unto all men—for what good can equal this? Thirdly. To accomplish it, is the most glorious enterprise. What is the rescue of a whole nation from civil bondage, compared with the deliverance of one soul from the power of darkness, and translating it into the kingdom of God's dear Son! Can a trifle throw heaven into ecstacy! But there is joy in the presence of the angels of God over one sinner that repenteth. The work, therefore, is its own motive; its success is its own recompense. And so the apostle deemed it; "If a man err from the truth, and one convert him, let him know that he which converteth a sinner from the error of his ways, shall save a soul from death, and shall hide a multitude of sins." Fourthly. To fail in it is no disgrace. Yea, failure here is infinitely more honorable than success in any other enterprise. But wise and good efforts are never in vain. If they are useless as to the direct object, they do good collaterally. If they relieve not the beneficiary, they bless the benefactor. His prayers and endeavors return not void into his own bosom. We are a sweet savor of Christ, not only in them that are saved, but in them that also perish. The promise is not made to success—for *this* does not belong to us; but to exertion. "Be thou faithful unto death, and I will give thee a crown of life."

But while we endeavor to bring others to Jesus, let us see to it that we have come to him ourselves. It is awful to think of being the instruments of his grace, while we are not the subjects—

"Great King of grace! my heart subdue;
"I would be led in triumph too:
"A willing captive to my Lord,
"And sing the victories of his word."

SEPTEMBER 28.—"The precious sons of Zion, comparable to fine gold, how are they esteemed as earthen pitchers the work of the hands of the potter?"—Lamentations, iv, 2.

SUCH is the difference between the judgment of God and the spirit of the world, concerning the precious sons of Zion. In the estimation of God, (and his judgment is always according to truth,) they are comparable to gold, yea, fine gold. And they are so for their rareness, and their purity, and their value, and their durability, and for their bearing the severest probation, and, instead of being injured by the trial, deriving improvement, and lustre, and usefulness from it.

But, as that which is highly esteemed among men is abomination in the sight of God; so that which is approved and commended of God is undervalued and despised by men. The world, therefore, knoweth them not. It knew *Him* not. Their Lord and Savior was despised and rejected by them. And they, as his followers, are esteemed as earthen pitchers, the work of the hands of the potter. They judge only from sense and outward appearances; and Christians are often poor and afflicted. They see the outside of the tabernacle; and this is covered with goats' skins, and badgers' skins, dyed red: but they never enter the holy place, nor approach Him who sitteth between the cherubims. They are sensual, not having the Spirit; and spiritual things are spiritually discerned. They do not feel their need of blessings which constitute the happiness and glory of the children of God, and therefore prize not the possessors of them. Yea, the carnal mind is enmity against God, and causes them to dislike every thing that bears his impression and likeness.

Yet even these despisers shall behold, and wonder, and perish. When the delusions of time shall give place to the unveiled realities of eternity, they will be compelled to exclaim, *We* fools counted their lives madness, and their end to be without honor. How are they numbered with the saints, and their lot is among the children of God! Yea, even now there are moments, when, if we could witness the workings of conviction, we should hear many a Balaam admiring, and praying—How goodly are thy tents, O Jacob! and thy tabernacles, O Israel! Let me die the death of the righteous, and let my last end be like his!

Christians should not be uneasy and impatient under the mistakes and reproaches of their adversaries. It is a light thing to be judged of man's judgment—He that judgeth them is the Lord.

Their praise is not of man but of God. They should know that this is not their day. Their day is coming. It will be the manifestation of the sons of God. Yea, conscious of what, by the grace of God they are, they should learn in whatsoever state they are, therewith to be content. In every thing they should give thanks. Their souls should make their boast in the Lord. They should never scruple to extol and recommend their privileges and excellencies. That which we have heard and seen, says the apostle John, declare we unto you, that ye also may have fellowship with us. And is this desirable? And truly our fellowship is with the Father, and with his son Jesus Christ.

Who is on the Lord's side? O my soul! art thou? Dost thou love and admire those whom God approves and honors? Canst thou call the saints that are in the earth, The excellent? and say, In them is all my delight? Moses chose rather to suffer affliction with the people of God, than to enjoy the pleasures of sin for a season; and esteemed the reproach of Christ greater riches than the treasures of Egypt.

"Oh! may I see thy tribes rejoice,
"And aid their triumphs with my voice:
"This is my glory, Lord, to be
"Join'd to thy saints, and near to Thee."

SEPTEMBER 29.—"Arise ye, and depart; for this is not your rest."
Micah, ii, 10.

ONE of the old divines, in his pastoral admonitions to his people, exhorts them—not to look for that in the Law, which can only be found in the Gospel—not to look for that in themselves, which is only to be found in Christ—not to look for that in the creature which is only to be found in the Creator—and not to look for that on earth, which is only to be found in heaven.

The present is not our rest—It was not designed to be our rest—It is not fit to be our rest—And if we are Christians, we have relinquished it as our rest, and have chosen another. Yet who does not need this exhortation? Our souls naturally cleave unto the dust. Many, Like Reuben and Gad, prefer an inheritance on this side of Jordan. And even the godly themselves, who have not their portion in this life; but have said, As for me I will behold thy face in righteousness, I shall be satisfied when I awake with thy likeness; even these need to have their pure minds stirred up, by way of remembrance. "My people," says God, "have forgotten their resting place."

He, therefore, who takes pleasure in the prosperity of his servants, sends them this message, "Arise ye, and depart, for this is not your rest." And there are five messengers by which he sends it.

The first, is his word. And we should read and hear it for this very purpose. It meets us in our complaint and inquiry, "Who will show us any good?" and says, "Acquaint now thyself with *Him*, and be at peace; thereby good shall come unto thee." It forbids us to lay up treasures on earth. It commands us to seek those things that are above. It denounces the curse and misery of making flesh our arm. It proclaims the grandeur of the soul: and sets before us what alone is worthy of it. It leads us into all truth; and places us at the foot of the cross, by which the world is crucified unto us, and we unto the world; and then we are enabled to say—

"Farewell, world! thy gold is dross,
"Now I see the Savior's Cross:
"Jesus died, to set me free
"From the law, and sin, and *thee*."

The second, is affliction. God speaks by the rod, as well as by the word. While he chastens us with his hand, he teaches us out of his law. Has he not, by events, plainly addressed us, "Ye have dwelt long enough in this mountain; turn ye, and take your journey?" Has he not by repeated frustrations of our hope, plainly said to us, "Let it suffice thee: speak no more to me of this matter?" Perhaps our purposes have been broken off, even the thoughts of our hearts; or we have been made to possess months of vanity; or lover and friend has been removed far from us, and amidst the wreck of every thing dear to us, a voice, though we knew not at first that it came from Heaven, said, "What hast thou here? and what dost thou here?" And if we are so much attached to the world, with all our losses and distresses, what should we have been without them? If the pilgrim be ever seduced from his way, it is by flowers and prospects; if ever he sits down and sings himself asleep, it is in a pleasing scene, and in fine weather—not when the sky is dark and stormy, and the road is rough and miry—for then, by contrast, the thought of home becomes dearer; and he feels an excitement to quicken his pace.

The third, is worldly success. This, in some respects, may convince us more of the insufficiency and emptiness of every thing here, than even our deprivations. When a man is disappointed *in* attaining his object, he may still imagine that there *is* happiness in what he misses; and that he is miserable because he misses it. But when he has gained the prize, he is convinced that the dissatisfaction he feels arises from the nature of the thing itself. We long for certain acquisitions, with all the fondness of hope; and feel no apprehension, unless on the side of failure. We cannot believe, from the acknowledgments of others, that these things will belie expectation, and still leave a void within. But when we have made the trial ourselves—when we have formed the connexion, filled the office, gained the fortune, we desired—and in the midst of our sufficiency, we are in straights, we sigh over our indulgences themselves; and enjoyment, as well as affliction, cries, All is vanity and vexation of spirit—Arise, and depart; for this is not your rest.

The fourth, is the earnests and foretastes of a better world. And such Christians are favored with, in the comforts of the Holy Ghost; in accesses to the throne of Grace; in the power and glory of God which they see in the sanctuary; and in those sacred moments of divine communion, alone, when they can say

"While such a scene of sacred joys
"Our raptur'd eyes and soul employs,
"Here we could sit and gaze away
"A long, an everlasting day."

And these not only call, but allure and win the heart, away. When the clusters of grapes were brought to the Israel of God in the wilderness, they said, in very intelligible language—What does your present condition supply like this? See what grows in the land that is before you. Taste; and go up and possess it.

The last, is death. Every apprehension and approach of this cries—"It is high time to awake out of sleep, for now is your salvation nearer than when you believed." But it orders us to depart really, as well as morally. Thus God indeed sends, by it, not only to his people, but for them. And it seems surprising that they should ever be ready to turn away from the messenger. A child at school welcomes every messenger from home to him; but he desires most the messenger that comes for him. Joseph sends to Jacob, and for him, at once; and his father not only heard the words, but saw the wagons—"Oh! these are really to carry me to him—I shall soon see my son—and die in peace."

Such a messenger, Christian, is death to you. Come, says God, you have toiled long enough—you have feared long enough—you have groaned long enough—your warfare is accomplished—enter the rest which the Lord your God giveth you—come; for all things are now ready.

Yes; you will soon hear the voice saying--O Israel! you must this day go over Jordan. And why should you be unwilling to exchange the desert for the land flowing with milk and honey? Is not this the purpose of your travels? the end of your desires? the completion of your hopes?

"But the swelling river rolls between." Fear not. The ark of the covenant will go before you, and divide the waves; and you shall pass over dry-shod. And then let the streams reunite, and continue to flow on—you will not wish them to reopen for your return. What is misery to others is joy to you—"I shall go the way whence I shall not return."

SEPTEMBER 30.—"If then I be a father, where is mine honor?"—Mal. i, 6.

WE admire the Scripture mode of allusion and comparison. Its images are taken from the most obvious and simple things; and while they illustrate the spiritual subjects to which they are applied, they also impart moral lessons. While they enjoin the duties we owe to God, they remind us of those we owe to our fellow creatures: and the child is instructed and reproved, by the address which informs and admonishes the Christian.

In the words before us, here is, first, a principle supposed—Indeed it is expressed in the foregoing sentence: "A son honoreth his father." It is a dictate of nature, of custom, of observance in all ages and countries. The child, as soon as he can reason, finds himself under the control of a superior, at once dear and venerable; to whom he is obliged, and on whom he is dependent: he asks of him information; he looks to him for provision; he confides in his care and wisdom; he obeys his orders, and submits to his discipline. If stricken, he does not reproach, or think of striking again. What says Solomon? "The eye that mocketh at his father, and despiseth to obey his mother, the ravens of the valley shall pluck it out, and the young eagles shall eat it." A modern writer has made free to turn these words into ridicule, by ranking them with those senseless bugbears by which nurses often terrify children. But if the ignorance of infidels, with regard to every thing scriptural, was not extreme, he might have known that under the Jewish law, filial disobedience was a capital offence. "For every one that curseth his father or his mother shall be surely put to death: he hath cursed his father or his mother; his blood shall be upon him." And Moses mentions also the mode. "If a man have a stubborn and rebellious son, which will not obey the voice of his father, or the voice of his mother, and that, when they have chastened him, will not hearken unto them: then shall his father and his mother lay hold on him, and bring him out unto the elders of his city, and unto the gate of his place; and they shall say unto the elders of his city, This our son is stubborn and rebellious, he will not obey our voice; he is a glutton; and a drunkard. And all the men of his city shall stone him with stones, that he die: so shalt thou put evil away from among you; and all Israel shall hear, and fear." Hence, what is threatened, might have been literally accomplished. But when we consider how figuratively the Easterns expressed themselves, we may admit the reality of an awful penalty on the transgressor, without pleading for the literal execution. We have a remarkable instance of filial honor in the regard the Rechabites paid to the authority of their father. "They said, we will drink no wine: for Jonadab the son of Rechab our father, commanded us, saying, Ye shall drink no wine, neither ye, nor your sons, for ever: neither shall ye build house, nor sow seed, nor plant vineyard, nor have any; but all your days ye shall dwell in tents: that ye may live many days in the land where ye be strangers. Thus have we obeyed the voice of Jonadab the son of Rechab our father in all that he charged us, to drink no wine all our days, we, our wives, our sons, nor our daughters: nor to build houses for us to dwell in: neither have we vineyard, nor field, nor seed: but we have dwelt in tents, and have obeyed, and have done according to all that Jonadab our father commanded us." It is lamentable to think how little of this obedience is to be found in children now. Yet there is far less piety in the world, than morality.

Here is, secondly, an obligation inferred—it is, that if other fathers are to be honored, we are much more bound to honor God. For he is a Father far above the truth of the relation in all other cases. We have had fathers; but they were fathers of our flesh—but he is the Father of our spirits. They were fathers only subordinately, and neither the sex, or the form, or the talents of the child resulted from their choice—but he is supremely, efficiently, absolutely our Father—he made us—and endued us with all our powers—and from him must spring all our hopes.

And, therefore, not only is the reality of the relation found in him, but the perfection too. He always acts the part of—a wise and good Father—completely—divinely. Other fathers often chastise their children for their own pleasure; but He for our profit. They may be implacable; but He is ready to forgive. They may neglect to educate or provide; but He teaches us to profit, and suffers us to want no good thing.

The duty also is enforced by the eminence of his character, and the grandeur of his condition. His understanding is infinite. His power is almighty. His dominion is everlasting. He is Lord of all. "It is he that sitteth upon the circle of the earth, and the inhabitants thereof are as grasshoppers; that stretcheth out the heavens as a curtain, and spreadeth them out as a tent to dwell in; that bringeth the princes to nothing: he maketh the judges of the earth as vanity." To this consideration he himself appeals, in the close of this chapter. "But cursed be the deceiver, which hath in his flock a male, and voweth, and sacrificeth unto the Lord a corrupt thing; for I am a great King, saith the Lord of hosts, and my name is dreadful among the Heathen."

Thirdly. Here is a complaint alleged. "If I am a Father, where is mine honor?" And has he no ground for this inquiry? Men often complain without cause. They are unreasonable in their demands and expectations. They may be mistaken with regard to the nature and design of many actions, because they judge after outward appearance. But God's claims are unlimited. He sees motives. He looketh to the heart. He takes our meaning. And passing by our mistakes and infirmities, accepts and commends our aims and endeavors. And yet he complains. And how deeply deserved! and how extensively applicable is the charge he brings! See the generality of mankind—have they any concern to please him? Take the professors of his religion—what do they more than others? Take even the subjects of his grace—even in them, where is the honor? Is it here? in constantly asking, Lord, what wilt thou have me to do? Is it here? in meekly submitting to his rebukes? Is it here? in speaking well of his name, and recommending him to others?

Let us make the deficiencies and sins of others a mirror in which to behold our own. Do I meet with ingratitude in a fellow creature, that I have relieved? Let it soften my resentment, and keep me from resolving to do no more for him. Let me inquire how *I* have behaved toward my heavenly Benefactor. Do I reflect on an undutiful child, and perhaps justly too? Yet let me ask whether my heavenly Father has not much more reason to condemn me—if *thou*, Lord, shouldest mark iniquity, O Lord, *who* should stand!

How necessary is it for us to fall down at his footstool; and pray, Enter not into judgment with thy servant, O Lord; for in thy sight shall no flesh living be justified!

What a blessing is the Gospel, that assures us, with the Lord there is mercy, and that his grace is sufficient for us!

But O let this make us the more concerned to honor him—and to be harmless and blameless; the children of God—without rebuke!

October 1.—"Wo unto you that desire the day of the Lord! To what end is it for you? The day of the Lord is darkness and not light."

Amos, v, 18.

We may apply this to the day of death. How often do men, when in trouble and disappointment, express a wish that God would now take away their life from them, supposing that it is better for them to die than to live! We cannot, indeed, be always sure of the sincerity of their desire; and they may not be sure of it themselves. Under the pressure of present feeling, they may imagine that death would be welcome; when, perhaps, if it actually appeared, they would decline his aid. And if they *would* not, they *ought*. For *their* fleeing from trouble is as if a man did flee from a lion, and a bear met him; or went into the house, and leaned his hand on the wall, and a serpent bit him.

Let me, then, beg these sons of sorrow to inquire, whether the event they long for will be a real remedy for their complaints. Are they sure that death will be annihilation? perfectly sure that there is nothing beyond the grave? Can they prove that there is no future state, and that in this state there is no misery, but happiness only? Judas hanged himself. And what then? He went to his own place; which was far worse than his former condition, even under all the horrors of remorse.

If the Scripture be true, *all* are not happy at death. Yea, *none* are then happy without a title to heaven, and a meetness for it. And have *you* this title? Where is it? What is it? "He that believeth on the Son, hath everlasting life; and he that believeth not the Son, shall not see life, but the wrath of God abideth on him." Have you this meetness? What is it? Do you love holiness? Without this, *could* you be happy in a holy place? in a holy state? in holy company? in holy engagements? in holy enjoyments? Is the Redeemer precious to your souls? and do you delight in him? Without this, *could* you be happy, to be for ever in his presence, and hearing for ever his praise? *Could* a man, without an ear or taste for music, be happy, by being removed into a world of melody and harmony? Need you be told, that happiness does not arise from the excellency of the object, but from its adaptation to our disposition? That nothing can make us happy, but what relieves our *wants*? fulfills our *desires*? and satisfies our *hope*? Without holiness, therefore, *no* man *can* see the Lord.

How absurd, then, is it to wish to leave this world for another, before you are sure the exchange will be for your advantage! For your advantage it cannot be, if you die unpardoned and unrenewed. Blessed are the dead that die *in the Lord*. But out of him you are out of the city of refuge, and the avenger of blood is upon you. Out of Him, you are out of the ark, and in the midst of the deluge. No; the day of *your* death is not better than the day of your birth. Whatever your privations, and losses, and distresses here may be, they are only the beginnings of sorrow, and all you suffer from them is only as a drop to the ocean, compared with the damnation of hell. And, once gone from time, there is no return. As the tree falleth, so it lies.

Instead, therefore, of wishing this only and all-important season ended, you should be thankful that it is prolonged, if it be continued even in a vale of tears; and account that the long suffering of God is your salvation, for he is not willing that any should perish.

Remember, also, that these disappointments and sorrows, which make you so impatient, may prove the greatest blessing, and the valley of Achor be given you for a door of hope. For God does not afflict willingly, nor grieve the children of men. He renders earth desolate, to induce you to seek a better country. He strikes away every human prop, and puts failure and vexation into every worldly scheme, that you may turn from idols to the Supreme Good.

"What should I wait or wish for, then,
"From creatures, earth, and dust?
"They make our expectations vain,
"And disappoint our trust.

"Now I forbid my carnal hope,
"My fond desires recall;
"I give my mortal interest up,
"And make my God my all."

—Away, then, with every thought of the rope or river. Say, "I will arise, and go unto my Father." He is in sight, waiting to receive thee graciously, and to love thee freely. Repair to the throne of the heavenly grace. You cannot spread your sorrows *there* in vain. If tempted to despair, try his word. No one ever trusted, and was confounded. Cry, "Lord, I am oppressed; undertake for me." "Come," says the Reliever of every burden, "Come unto me, *all* ye that labor and are heavy laden, and I will give you rest."

The Athenian said, "I should have been lost, if I had not been lost." What made the prodigal think of home, but want? Where did Manasseh find his father's God, but in affliction? We often feel for those who have been reduced, and say, They have seen *better* days; but if in their prosperity they forgot God that made them, and lightly esteemed the Rock of their salvation, and in their adversity have thrown themselves into his arms; these, these are the *best* days they ever saw, and they will draw forth their praise for ever. This, my suffering friend, may be your case, and will be, if you seek unto God, and unto God commit your cause. He can, he will turn the shadow of death into the morning, and you shall join the multitude who are saying, IT IS GOOD FOR ME THAT I HAVE BEEN AFFLICTED.

OCTOBER 2.—"I will hear what God the Lord will speak."—Psalm lxxxv, 8.

AND surely if *He* speaks, in whatever way he expresses himself, it becomes us to hear, and to hear immediately. To-day, if ye will hear his voice, harden not your hearts. Let us not, therefore, "be unwise, but understanding what the will of the Lord is." There are four cases in which we should adopt this resolution.

First. I will hear what God the Lord will speak as to *doctrinal truth.* If error were harmless, we should not be commanded to "buy the truth, and sell it not;" to "prove all things, and to hold fast that which is good." It is of unspeakable importance to have proper sentiments on all religious subjects. But concerning all these subjects different opinions prevail, and it is certain that all these opinions cannot be true. Hence persons are often perplexed, especially at the beginning of the Christian life. What, in this case, are we to do? One cries, Lo! here is Christ; and another, Lo! there. Be it so. We are not left without witness. It would be sad and dangerous had we no rule to go by; no standard to which we can appeal. But we have such an advantage. And in things of moment it is plain and obvious. And it is accessible—it is in our possession. It is the testimony of God recorded in the Scriptures. I will, therefore, make no system of divinity, drawn up by fallible creatures like myself, my oracle, but enter at once the temple of Revelation, and inquire there. I will call no man master upon earth; one is my master, even Christ; and all besides are only brethren. I need not ask what Arminius or Calvin speaks—they themselves are to be judged out of this Book; and what they deliver is no further binding upon me than as *they* can say, "Thus saith the Lord." "To the law and to the testimony: if they speak not according to this word, it is because there is no light in them." "I will hear what God the Lord will speak." In this inspired volume I have the judgment of God himself upon every subject with which it is necessary for me to be acquainted. And I will go to it; not with a previous bias, but open to conviction; not to dictate, but to learn; not full, but to be filled. I will not be influenced to embrace a doctrine, because it is easy of comprehension; or to reject it, because it is mysterious. It is infinitely reasonable to believe *whatever* God speaks; and my only concern is to ascertain what he *has* spoken.

Secondly. I will hear what God the Lord will speak, as to my *movements in life*. How ignorant and short sighted are we! How liable to mistake! How incapable of distinguishing between appearances and realities; and of deciding what will be good or evil for us! Surely we have erred and suffered enough already, to convince us that "the way of man is not in himself." How much depends on one wrong step, as it regards our comfort, usefulness, and reputation! Even when the iniquity is pardoned, the natural consequences may be long left to operate. They cannot often be remedied; and so repentance is quartered upon the offender all his days. How frequently has this been exemplified in irreligious marriages; and changes of residence and business, through fancy, pride, or avarice; or even good, but mistaken motives! A Christian, therefore, should take every step of importance—and what step may not be important? feeling a responsibility that makes him tremble; and an anxiety that urges him to seek council from above—"I will hear what God the Lord will speak"—and regulate my marches by the cloud. But while I wait upon God, I must also wait for him: and integrity and uprightness are to preserve me while I do so. For He tells me, that if a man sets up idols in his heart, and comes to inquire of him, he will answer him, but "according to his idols." And this is done, not only by a penal influence, but by natural effect; for every thing will be colored according to the passion through which I view it. If therefore I do not consult God sincerely, it would be better for me not to do it at all; for it can only dishonor him, and delude myself. But if I go in simplicity, and say, "Lord, what wilt thou have me to do?" I come within the reach of the promise, "In all thy ways acknowledge him, and he shall direct thy paths."

Thirdly. I will hear what God the Lord will speak, as to the *dispensations of his providence*. Nothing is more trying than what an old divine calls "a dumb affliction:" so that when we put our ear to it, we can seem to hear nothing, as to what it implies, or intends. Varying the metaphor a little, Job was in such a state of ignorance and perplexity: "Behold, I go forward, but he is not there; and backward, but I cannot perceive him; on the left hand, where he doth work, but I cannot behold him: he hideth himself on the right hand, that I cannot see him." In such a condition, it affords relief to be able to add: "but *he* knoweth the way that I take." Yet duty requires that *we* should have some knowledge of it ourselves. A natural man is only concerned to escape from trouble: but the Christian is anxious to have it sanctified and improved. He is commanded to bear the rod. While God chastens, he teaches. I must therefore be in a learning frame of mind. I must say unto God, "Show me wherefore thou contendest with me"—"I will hear what, by this event, God the Lord will speak."

Fourthly. I will hear what He will say also, *in answer to prayer.* Here is a thing, I fear, generally disregarded. How many petitions are never thought of after they have been delivered? We knock at the door, and go away, and never even look back to see whether it be opened unto us. Can we expect that God will attend to those prayers which we contemn ourselves? Are such addresses any thing better than a mockery of the Supreme Being?

Let us therefore hear what he says in reply to our requests. Is it not pleasing to know that we are not forsaken nor forgotten of our best friend? To be able to rectify a gloomy conclusion? To reason from the past to the future? And like a beggar to derive encouragement from success? "For I said in my haste, I am cut off from before thine eyes; nevertheless thou heardest the voice of my supplications, when I cried unto thee." "I cried unto him with my mouth, and he was extolled with my tongue. If I regard iniquity in my heart the Lord will not hear me: but verily God hath heard me; he hath attended to the voice of my prayer. Blessed be God, which hath not turned away my prayer, nor his mercy from me." "I love the Lord, because he hath heard my voice, and my supplications. Because he hath inclined his ear unto me, therefore will I call upon him as long as I live."

OCTOBER 3.—"Let your moderation be known unto all men. The Lord is at hand."—Philippians, iv, 5.

—WHAT moderation? Moderation with regard to your appetites. Some make a God of their belly, and glory in their shame. Many indulge in eating and drinking, beyond the demands of bodily refreshment, or the allowances of health. Your moderation, with regard to your passions. You are to be angry, and sin not. The sun must not go down upon your wrath. The fear, the joy, the love, the grief, allowable in themselves, may become excessive in the degree. Your moderation with regard to the distinctions of life. These are to differ from "the pride of life"—in apparel, in furniture, in servants. Your moderation, in professional pursuits, and the cares of trade—diligent in business, but not "entangling yourselves in the affairs of this life;" content with sober and solid gain; and not by hazard and speculations, making haste to be rich. Your moderation, in the exaction of rights; whether pecuniary—in declining the rigor of the law, for debt; or personal—in waiving the claims of authority and preference, as Abraham did in the case of Lot. Your moderation in your opinions and zeal. Many things in religion are of far less importance than others, even if true—But as to the truth of them, this is not easily ascertained; and we see men of equal talent and piety on each side of the question. The truth generally lies in the middle; and he is commonly nearest to it who is abused by both the opposite parties.

And what a reason is there to enforce this admonition! "The Lord is at hand." The word signifies nigh, either as to place or time. If we take it as to place—it refers to his presence—I am a God at hand, and not afar off. He is about our path and our lying down, and is acquainted with all our ways. Thus he is always nigh to see and observe, to aid or oppose, to bless or to punish.

"O may these thoughts possess my breast,
"Where'er I rove, where'er I rest:
"Nor let my weaker passions dare
"Consent to sin—for God is there!"

—If we take it as to time—it refers to his coming—"The coming of the Lord drawing near." This is true, not only as to the certainty of the event, and the confidence of faith; but as to his real approach. If the Lord was at hand when Paul wrote this Epistle, how much more now two thousand years have rolled away! But he comes by death—and this, as to consequences, is the same to us as his coming to judgment. And there is but a step between us and death.

—If a multitude of people were assembled together, and behaved tumultuously, and the king was coming along the road—"The king is at hand," would instantly reduce them to order and silence; and every eye would be turned toward *him*. If a number of criminals, forgetful of their condition, were improperly amusing themselves, or striving together, and a signal told them the judge was entering the town to try them—what an effect would this instantly have upon their mind and their conduct! But what is your case? He is not only your Sovereign but your Judge—and, "behold, the Judge STANDETH BEFORE THE DOOR!"

How lamentable is it, that to enforce what is wise and just, and good, in itself, we should need such motives—and that these motives, after all, should have so little influence over us! That we should be constantly reminded of such a Being—led back to the grace of his first coming—and forward, to the glory of his second coming—and think, and feel, and speak, and act, and live, as we do! "So teach us to number our days, that we may apply our hearts unto wisdom."

OCTOBER 4.—"The path of the just is as the shining light, that shineth more and more unto the perfect day."—Proverbs, iv, 18.

WHAT does this fine image imply? What does it express? Solomon traces the resemblance between the path of the just and the rising light, in three articles. Each *shines*. Each shines *more and more*. Each shines more and more *unto the perfect day*.

The rising light *shines*. It is the very nature of it to do so. It thus shows itself, and renders other things visible: for whatsoever doth make manifest is light. Without this, the works of the field, and the human face divine, would be all a blank—but the shining of the light lays open their beauties, and fills us with admiration and praise. Thus the Christian's path breaks out of obscurity; the darkness is past; and the true light shineth. His religion is not only real, but apparent. And as it need not, and should not be hid; so it will not, and cannot be hid. Its operation will evince its existence. Its principles will display themselves in its practice. There will be the work of faith, and the labor of love, and the patience of hope, and the fruit of the Spirit. Pity will get into the eye. Meekness will smile in the features. The law of kindness will dwell upon the tongue. The hand, ready to communicate, will unawares slide into the pocket —they that were in darkness will show themselves; and, in a thousand ways, their light will shine before men.

But the *shining* of the rising light is noble and glorious. It is one of the most splendid appearances in nature. The rising sun is as a bridegroom coming out of his chamber—we hardly wonder the poor heathen, in the absence of revelation, should worship it—the lustre is often too powerful for the naked eye. And how was it with Moses, after communion with God? His face shone so that the Israelites could not steadfastly behold the glory of his countenance. He was not aware of it himself, till, seeing the people dazzled he was obliged to take a veil. And the humility of the Christian may keep him from perceiving his own excellencies: but others will take knowledge of them; and his profiting will appear unto all men. And nothing is so impressive and influential as the life of a Christian, when he walks worthy of the vocation wherewith he is called. It was not necessary for the first believers at Jerusalem to lay down rules to exclude improper characters from their communion—their purity, their dignity, their majesty, repelled them—"And of the rest durst no man join himself to them; but all the people magnified them."

—Yet the *shining* of the rising light is not mere lustre. It is a source of usefulness, as well as of admiration. It warms and enlivens. It fertilizes the gardens and the fields. It makes the valleys to stand thick with corn, and the little hills to rejoice on every side. And so Jesus went about doing good. And so Christians are blessings in all the places wherein they move. Let us make this image our model in our endeavors to serve our generation. The sun says nothing—it does good without noise—it shines unasked, constantly, impartially—it rises on the evil, as well as on the good—so may we be merciful.

But the shining light shines *more and more.*—So does the path of the just. His religion is a gradual and progressive thing. We therefore read of growing in grace, and in the knowledge of our Lord and Savior. Of the Thessalonians, it is said, Their faith grew exceedingly; and the love of every one of them toward each other abounded. As far as we are stationary in our attainments, we are censured and condemned by the image. But to derive comfort from it, it is not necessary that we should be every thing at once. Nothing in nature reaches its perfection suddenly. The babe proceeds, by slow degrees, into the man. The blade precedes the full corn in the ear. Let us not despise the day of small things. What was the oak once, but an acorn? What is the dawn, to the noon?

But the shining light shines more and more *unto the perfect day.* The allusion is not taken from a meteor, that blazes for a moment, and then disappears. Nor from the morning cloud and early dew, that soon passeth away: but from the rising sun, that always attains its end, and completes what it begins—rising upward—and shining—onward till it is day—perfect day.

When did the sun ever make a dawn, and not carry it into full day? Who can drive him back or stop his course? If it had enemies, and they cursed its beams, the rage would be as vain as unreasonable—"He rejoiceth as a strong man to run a race. His going forth is from the end of the heaven, and his circuit unto the ends of it: and there is nothing hid from the heat thereof." So shall it be with all those who are set in motion for eternity by divine grace. "They that love Him shall be as the sun when he goeth forth in his might." There is no enchantment or divination against them. In all opposition they shall be more than conquerors. He who is the author, shall also be the finisher of their faith. They shall soon lose all their infirmities. They shall emerge into perfect knowledge, holiness, and joy—And "then shall the righteous shine forth as the sun in the kingdom of their Father. HE THAT HATH EARS TO HEAR, LET HIM HEAR."

But who can help recalling the beautiful lines of Dr. Watts, which, though written for the infant mind, are worthy the perusal of angels?

"How fine has the day been, how bright was the sun,
"How lovely and joyful the course that he run;
"Though he rose in a mist when his race he begun,
"And there followed some droppings of rain!
"But now the fair traveller's come to the west,
"His rays are all gold, and his beauties are best;
"He paints the sky gay, as he sinks to his rest,
"And foretells a bright rising again.

"Just such is the Christian—his course he begins,
"Like the sun in a mist, while he mourns for his sins,
"And melts into tears; then he breaks out and shines,
"And travels his heavenly way:
"But when he comes nearer to finish his race,
"Like a fine setting sun, he looks richer in grace,
"And gives a sure hope, at the end of his days,
"Of rising in brighter array."

OCTOBER 5.—"Who is gone into heaven."—1 Peter, iii, 22.

—MANY had gone there before. Abel was the first that entered: and it is encouraging to think, that the first victim of death was a partaker of glory—human nature being found in heaven, before it was seen in hell. How long he was alone there, we know not. But others soon followed: and our Savior must have found there a multitude which no man could number.

But though many had gone into heaven before, none of them had gone in the same way and manner with himself. Others had entered without their bodies; but he had entered incarnately. Two had indeed entered embodied; but they did not take their bodies from the grave. Enoch and Elias died not, but were only changed. Jesus died and was buried; and passed to glory from the tomb. Others entered heaven by mere favor, presenting no claim from their worthiness and obedience; but he entered by merit—He deserved all the glory he obtained—It was no more than the reward of his doing and suffering. Others entered as private individuals; and their entering did not insure the entrance of others—not even of their friends and relations. Religion is a personal thing: and it could not be inferred, that because the husband or the father was glorified, the wife or child would follow. But he entered as a public character, as the head and representative of his people: and because he lives, they shall live also. Hence says the apostle, "He hath quickened us altogether with Christ, and raised us up and made us sit together with him in the heavenly places."

It is expedient for us, therefore, that he went away; and as Joseph's going from the prison to the palace was not only his own advancement, but the salvation of his father's house, so Jesus is gone into heaven, not only to be crowned with glory and honor, but to execute the remainder of his mediatorial work, on behalf of the redeemed. "For if, when we were enemies, we were reconciled to God by the death of his Son; much more, being reconciled, we shall be saved by his life." But did he not say, when he expired, "It is finished?" He did—and it *was* finished—and nothing could be *added* to it. But what was finished? The procuring of salvation only—not the application of it. The former was done upon the cross; the latter is done upon the throne. What he suffered to acquire, he is exalted to bestow. He is exalted to be a Prince and Savior; to give repentance unto Israel, and forgiveness of sins.

Even in his priestly character, it behooved him not only to suffer, but to enter into his glory. The apostle therefore says, If he were on earth, he could not be a priest; because he could then only have fulfilled one part of the office. For the high priest not only offered the sacrifice, but entered the holy place—and sprinkled the blood upon the mercy-seat and burned incense—and made intercession for the people. Jesus therefore, after dying for us, entered into heaven itself, there to appear in the presence of God for us. By his own blood he entered in once into the holy place, having obtained eternal redemption for us—"Wherefore he is able also to save them to the uttermost that come unto God by him, seeing he ever liveth to make intercession for them."

Here he fought, and overcame; but the Conqueror must have his triumph—displaying his spoils, and enriching the multitude. He therefore ascended on high, leading captivity captive, and received gifts for men, even for the rebellious also, that the Lord God might dwell among them. "And he gave some, apostles; and some, prophets; and some, evangelists; and some pastors and teachers; for the perfecting of the saints, for the work of the ministry, for the edifying of the body of Christ."

He was a prophet, by his own preaching. But how local, and confined, and successless, was his personal ministry! The work was to be done by another ministry. Corporally, he was to withdraw: "But," said he, "the Comforter, which is the Holy Ghost, whom the Father will send in my name, he shall teach you all things, and bring all things to your remembrance, whatsoever I have said unto you." "I have yet many things to say unto you, but ye cannot bear them now. Howbeit, when he, the Spirit of truth, is come, he will guide you into all truth: for he shall not speak of himself; but whatsoever he shall hear, that shall he speak; and he will show you things to come." Thus *he* considered his personal presence and agency far inferior to the dispensation of the Spirit. And yet some are looking for his bodily advent again, as if this was to effect what the Holy Ghost could not accomplish. What purpose is to be executed in the spread of the Gospel; or the conversion of souls? or glorification of the Church? to which the energy of the Spirit is not adequate? Not by might, not by power, but by my Spirit, saith the Lord. Were he here in his body, he would be confined to one place at a time, and many would envy the honor of seeing him in vain. But in his Spirit, he can be everywhere, and enjoyed of all.

October 6.—"I am a stranger with Thee, and a sojourner, as all my fathers were."—Psalm xxxix, 12.

So life was viewed and felt by David. He was very superior to many of his ancestors. He had wealth, and power, and honor, and reigned the greatest monarch of the east. But no condition can make the heir of immortality a citizen here. Others are strangers and sojourners, as to the transitoriness of their continuance in this world, and the certainty of their removal from it; but not as to their disposition—they mind earthly things; and would be glad to live here always. But the child of God is, in principle, what he is in fact; and in experience, what he is in destination. He is also born from above and bound for glory. And though he is detained here in a foreign land for a while, for the discharge and the management of certain duties and interests; yet he thinks, even while thus engaged, of leaving it, in due time, for his own country—where his best relations reside—where lies his inheritance—and where he is to dwell for ever.

"There is my house, my portion fair;
"My kindred and my friends are there,
"And my abiding home:
"For me my elder brethren stay,
"And angels beckon me away,
"And Jesus bids me come."

Am I a stranger and a sojourner with God? Let me realize, let me exemplify the condition. Let me look for the treatment such characters commonly meet with. Like widows and orphans, they are often imposed upon, and wronged, and injured. They are turned into ridicule and reproach, because of their speech, their dress, their manner, and usages. And Christians are a peculiar people. They are men wondered at. The Savior tells them not to marvel, if the world hates them, for they are not of the world even as he is not of the world. This treatment is, in reality, a privilege, rather than a matter of complaint. It is when I am admired and caressed, and I find every thing agreeable in my circumstances; it is then I feel something of the *settler*. But the disadvantages of my state make me think of home; and induce me to arise, and depart hence, because this is not my rest.

And surely, if any of my own nation be near me, I shall be intimate with them. We all know the heart of strangers. We all feel the same preferences. The same hope inspires us. The same end unites us. And we shall speak often one to another; and contrast our present with our future condition; and inquire when we heard from home, and when we think of departing for it—and thus beguile the hours, and relieve the absence.

And let me not be entangled in the affairs of this life. Let me keep myself as detached as possible from things which do not concern me. Let me not embarrass myself, as an intermeddler and busy-body, in other men's matters. But study to be quiet, and to do my own business. And pray for the peace of the country through which I am passing. And be thankful for every advantage I enjoy in my temporary exile.

And let my affection be set on things that are above, and my conversation be always in heaven. Let me not be impatient for home; but prizing it; and longing for it; and judging of myself by my relation to it. Who has not joined in the proverbial sentiment, "Home is home, however homely?" We read of some Swiss soldiers on foreign service, who were so affected with a song that vividly recalled to mind their native valleys, and the houses in which they were born, that the officers were obliged to forbid the use of it. But, Oh! my Father's house! Here, toil; there, rest. Here, trouble; there, joy and gladness. Here, darkness; there, light. Here, sin; there, spotless purity. Here, the tents of Meshech and Kedar; there, the spirits of just men made perfect, and the innumerable company of angels, and the Lord of all. "With such views," says Dr. Goodwin, "let who will be miserable, I will not—I cannot."

OCTOBER 7.—**"I will feed my flock, and I will cause them to lie down, saith the Lord God."—Ezekiel, xxxiv, 15.**

THIS is spoken of the subjects of divine grace.

Individually considered, they are called sheep, to remind us of their personal qualities; their weakness, meekness, gentleness, harmlessness, patience, and submission. Some, in their affliction, toss like a wild bull in a net. Lay hold of a swine, and the neighborhood is alarmed. But observe the fleecy sufferer. She indeed palpitates. And the Christian may palpitate—and tremble—and be ready to faint; but his very manner silently says, I know, O Lord, that thy judgments are right, and that thou in faithfulness hast afflicted me. Let thy loving-kindness be for my comfort, according to thy word unto thy servant.

—*Distinctively* considered, they are not all sheep. Many of them are lambs. But these are sheep in nature and degree; and are equally dear to the Shepherd, with the older parts of his charge. Yea, he gathers the lambs with his arm, and carries them in his bosom; and gently leads those that are with young, or have young, as the margin is, and leads them thus because of the lambs. Lowth renders it, "The nursing ewes he will gently lead." And we are persuaded that the force of this tender image applies to the lambs, and not to the mothers. If the latter were driven on fast, the former could not keep up with them, especially in rough ground; and thus losing their maternal supplies, would droop and perish.

—*Collectively*, they are a flock. And *one* flock only, according to our Savior's words, "One fold and one Shepherd." Whatever differences there are among them, they are only the differences of sheep, and of lambs. What difficulty is there in believing this? Essential sameness is not destroyed by circumstantial distinction Unity is not incompatible with variety. Many branches make but one tree: many members but one body. Bigots would banish harmony from the church of God: for there can be no harmony where all the sounds are the same. God promised that he would give his people one heart and one way. And our Lord prayed that his followers might be one. Have this prayer and this promise been fulfilled? We dare not suppose the contrary; but if they have, we may see what kind of *oneness* was intended. Not a oneness of opinion; not a sameness in forms of worship, and modes of discipline—for these never have been found—but a oneness, a sameness consistent with the variations that have obtained among them. A unity of spirit. A community of principles. A fellowship of privileges—all being redeemed by the same blood, justified by the same righteousness, renewed by the same grace, and joint heirs of the same glory. "There is neither Jew nor Greek, there is neither bond nor free, there is neither male nor female; for ye are all one in Christ Jesus."

And is this flock ever forsaken or forgotten by Him? "I will feed my flock, and I will cause them to lie down, saith the Lord God." But tell me, O thou whom my soul loveth, *where* thou *feedest; where* thou makest thy flock to *rest at noon*. For why should I be as one that turneth aside by the flocks of thy companions?

"Fain would I feed among *thy* sheep; | "Among them rest, among them sleep."

What says David? "The Lord is my shepherd; I shall not want. He maketh me to lie down in green pastures; he leadeth me beside the still water."

This is grace. What is glory? What said the angel to John? "They shall hunger no more, neither thirst any more; neither shall the sun light on them, nor any heat. For the Lamb, which is in the midst of the throne, shall feed them, and shall lead them unto living fountains of waters; and God shall wipe away all tears from their eyes."

There is another flock in the world. This consists of goats They also have a shepherd. It is the devil: and they are taken captive by him at his will. He has also under shepherds to do his work; and to him they are amenable; and what a reward will he render them! But his flock, his direful flock—what food, what repose have they! What in time, or eternity! The way of transgressors is hard. The end of these things is death—the second death. And if any of them should be intermixed with the flock of Christ, and escape detection here—"before Him shall be gathered all nations; and he shall separate them one from another, as a shepherd divideth his sheep from the goats; and he shall set the sheep on his right hand, but the goats on the left." "And these shall go away into everlasting punishment; but the righteous into life eternal."

OCTOBER 8.—"But in every thing, by prayer and supplication, with thanksgiving, let your requests be made known unto God."—Philippians, iv, 6.

THIS is a simple and pleasing account of prayer. It is the making of our requests known unto God. He, indeed, knows them perfectly before we express them. But he will know them from us, that we may be properly affected with our own wants, and prepared for the display of his goodness and grace. And the apostle reminds us of three things very worthy of our attention, with regard to prayer.

First. It is the prevention and cure of care. "Be careful for nothing—*but* in every thing, by prayer and supplication, with thanksgiving let your requests be made known unto God." All feel anxiety to be rid of a galling load. But the question is, how are we to disencumber ourselves of the burden? All acknowledge the disorder, and many remedies have been prescribed by way of remedy; but if some of them touch the paroxysm of the complaint, none of them reach the root of the malady. The commonness of the case, the brevity of time, the usefulness of giving way to solicitude, and the injurious effects of it; all these are true and proper—but they do not go far enough. The fact is, if *we* are not to be careful, some one must care for us. And the thing is—and nothing less than this can tranquilize the mind—to be under the management of Him, who loves us better than we love ourselves, knows unerringly what is good for us, and is able to make every thing conduce to our welfare—"Casting all our care on Him; for he careth for us." And this is done by prayer. Hezekiah took the letter, and went and spread it before the Lord. Hannah poured out her heart before God, and her countenance was no more sad. In whatever has befallen or foreboded him, every believer has made the trial, and been able to say, with Asaph, "But it is good for me to draw near to God."

Secondly. It is to be very extensively, yea, universally performed. Not in some things, or in many things—but in *every* thing, by prayer and supplication, we are to make known our requests unto God. Some only pray when God's chastening hand is upon them. In their affliction they seek him early. And this, as far as it goes, is not to be censured. Many, like Manasseh, have first sought God in trouble. Prayer is peculiarly seasonable in distress. But though prayer may commence in affliction, it is not to cease with it, or be confined to it. Prayer is equally needful to preserve and sanctify us in prosperity. It is not praying on extraordinary occasions, but on common ones, that evinces a pious frame of mind. Do we delight ourselves in the Almighty? Do we always call upon God? In all thy ways, says Solomon, acknowledge Him. It is thus alone we give God the glory of his universal providence; not thinking with the Assyrians, that he is the God of the hills only, but also of the valleys; and that a sparrow falleth not to the ground, without our heavenly Father; and that the very hairs of our head are all numbered. Some imagine that many things are too little to be the subject of prayer. A distinction is indeed to be made between the particularity and minuteness of *private* and *public* prayer—But let us remember, that we are not to consider any thing too little for our prayer that God does not deem beneath his notice: and, also, that it is difficult, if not impossible for us, in many cases, to ascertain what is little; as events the most important often hinge on circumstances apparently the most trivial. Joseph's going to inquire after the welfare of his brethren on the plain, seemed a slight thing. Yet he, that morning, took leave of his father for more than twenty-one years; and went a way by which he never returned. Saul sought his father's asses—a thing that seemed devoid of consequence; but perhaps he is now in hell, owing to it, for then began his prosperity, which destroyed him—then Samuel met him, and anointed him king over Israel. You go out, not knowing what a day may bring forth, as to your happiness or misery—Before the evening, you may meet accidentally with a connexion that shall prove a source of joy or suffering through life. "Why this is enough to make one live and move in constant trembling." This is not the design of it—but it *is* designed to induce you—in every thing to commit your way and your works unto the Lord.

Thirdly. It is to be always attended with a pleasing companion. But in every thing, by prayer and supplication, *with thanksgiving*, let your requests be made known unto God. And does not this imply, that we can never approach God without having cause for gratitude? Hence it is said, in every thing give thanks. Whatever be our condition, we have much more to be grateful for, than to complain of—Complain! What can ever justify this? Why should a living man complain, a man, for the punishment of his sin? Let our losses and afflictions be what they may, He has not dealt with us after our desert, nor rewarded us according to our iniquity. Yea, the trials themselves are the effects of love, and designed to work together for our highest welfare.

—And does it not teach us, that whenever we go to God to ask for fresh favors, we should be sure to acknowledge the reception of former ones? How seldom is this the case! How much selfishness is there even in our devotion! How much more of them is occupied in petition than in praise! Urged by our necessities, we go, and call upon God in prayer! but when we have succeeded, we forget to return to give him the glory that is due unto his holy name. Were there not ten cleansed? But where are the nine? Where is even Hezekiah? He rendered not according to the benefit done him.

OCTOBER 9.—"I did know thee in the Wilderness, in the land of great drought."—Hosea, xiii, 5.

THIS "Wilderness" means the vast desert in which the Jews wandered for forty years, between Egypt and Canaan. It is characterized by one attribute—"A land of great drought." And this was enough to render it trying. But it was in every respect formidable and repulsive. Witness the language of Jeremiah: "Neither said they, Where is the Lord that brought us up out of the land of Egypt, that led us through the Wilderness: through a land of deserts, and of pits; through a land of drought, and of the shadow of death; through a land that no man passed through, and where no man dwelt."

But *here* God says, "I knew thee." It cannot mean a mere acquaintance with their condition and circumstances; for what can be hid from *Him?* But it intends two things.

First. He knew them there, so as to provide for them. Thus it marks his goodness; and forms a contrast with the conduct of many of our fellow creatures. A friend is born for adversity: and to him that is afflicted, pity *should* be showed from his friend. But, alas! this is rarely exemplified. They who were intimate enough with their connexions before, scarcely know them when they are in distress. The flower which, when fresh and fragrant, was put into the bosom, is, when withered and dry, thrown away. The garden, which, while yielding every kind of gratification, is constantly visited, is deserted in winter. But it is otherwise with God. Though he never leaves his people, he has peculiarly promised to be with them in trouble. And David acknowledged this: "Thou hast known my soul in adversities." And has he not known our souls in the same state? Has he not been better to us than our fears; and proved himself "a very present help in trouble?" So it was with Israel—he found them in a desert land, in a waste howling wilderness; and though the situation afforded them no supplies, he allowed them to want no good thing. He led them by a pillar of cloud by day, and a pillar of fire by night—healed the bitter waters of Marah—fetched them honey out of the rock, and oil out of the flinty rock—rained down manna upon them—suffered not their raiment to wax old upon them, nor their foot to swell in travelling—vanquished their enemies—gave them ordinances—and sent his Holy Spirit to instruct them—so that Moses well said, "Happy art thou, O Israel; who is like unto thee, O people saved of the Lord!"

Secondly. He knew them there, so as to approve of them, and acknowledge them. It is undeniable that the word *know* has this meaning, when it is said, "The Lord knoweth the way of the righteous." "If any man love God, the same is known of him." "Know them that labor among you." But *did* God *thus* know them in the wilderness? Not absolutely, but comparatively. They followed him out of Egypt and not one lingered behind. At the Red Sea they sang his praise. At Sinai they cheerfully and unreservedly acceded to his covenant. And though they were guilty of many perversenesses and rebellions, yet they never wholly relinquished his worship and established idolatry and wickedness by a law, as they afterwards did in Canaan. While we dwell on imperfections, God loves to make the best of things. Sarah spake unadvisedly with her lips; but she uttered one good thing—she called Abraham, Lord; and this only is mentioned. Job cursed the day of his birth: but when James refers to him, we hear only of the patience of Job. And observe God's *gracious* testimony concerning Israel at this period: "Go, and cry in the ears of Jerusalem, saying, Thus saith the Lord, I remember thee, the kindness of thy youth, the love of thine espousals, when thou wentest after me in the wilderness, in a land that was not sown. Israel was holiness unto the Lord, and the first fruits of his increase: all that devour him shall offend; evil shall come upon them, saith the Lord."

Adversity will not, of itself, secure godliness. Persons may be reduced, and not humbled; they may be afflicted, and God not know them in their distress. Yet, in general, if you observe others, and review your own experience, you will find times of affliction have been more friendly to religion than seasons of ease and prosperity.

First. When has God known your conscience most wakeful, and your heart most watchful against sin? Before I was afflicted, says David, I went astray; but now have I kept my word.

Secondly. When has God known your souls most weaned from the world, and willing to leave it? When all was agreeable and inviting? or when every thing conspired to tell you, that this is not your rest?

Thirdly. When has he known you value most the communion of saints; the means of grace; the preaching of the word? When did your eye bedew your Bible? When pressing the sacred volume to your bosom, did you say, Unless thy laws had been my delight, I should have perished in mine affliction?

Fourthly. When has he known you most frequently and earnestly addressing the throne of his Grace? In their affliction they will seek me early. In the day of my trouble I sought the Lord. Even the Savior himself, being in an agony, prayed more earnestly. "O my people," says he here, "you and I were better acquainted in the wilderness, when you were in a low condition; and left to my immediate care; and you lived daily by faith. Then you made me many a visit—but now we seldom meet." Such is the effect of indulgence under fullness. He therefore immediately adds, "According to their pasture, so they were filled; they were filled, and their heart was exalted; therefore have they forgotten me."

OCTOBER 10.—"And the children of Israel took their journeys out of the wilderness of Sinai; and the cloud rested in the wilderness of Paran."
Numbers, x, 12.

If the Jews, as the apostle assures us, were our ensamples, in nothing do they more represent the experience of Christians than in their progress from Egypt to Canaan.

—They had now continued many months in the wilderness of

Sinai, where the law was given, and all the ordinances of divine worship were established. There they had committed idolatry and provoked the Most High to anger; and there he proved himself the just God and the Savior. He forgave their iniquities, but took vengeance on their inventions. They were now to enter the wilderness of Paran, a vast desert of nine days' journey; and where the greater part of their subsequent stations were fixed. "And the children of Israel took their journeys out of the wilderness of Sinai; and the cloud rested in the wilderness of Paran." *Thus they only marched from one wilderness into another.* And is not this the case with all our changes in this world? Let us look at a few of them; and we shall see, that whatever they may promise—as to satisfaction and happiness—they leave us much the same as they find us.

It is not so when we pass from one *period* to another? Every age has been full of complaints; and here it is remarkakle, instead of supposed improvement, the inquiry has always been, "What is the cause that the former days were better than these?" We end one year with a kind of gloom, and hail the arrival of another; but the months are found the same with those which had previously passed away. The winter is not without cold, nor the summer without heat. We feel in our early days the confinement of shool, and the restraints of a father's house; we long to be at our own disposal, and to enter life for ourselves. But where is the man that has not exclaimed, "O that I was in the days of my youth!" Much is said of an agreeable and peaceable old age. Who does not desire many days, that he may see good? yet is their strength labor and sorrow. Another girds, and leads us whither we would not. In vain we look around for our early and endeared connexions—lover and friend is put far from us, and our acquaintance into darkness. The days are come in which we may say, "I have no pleasure in them." "All that cometh is vanity."

Is it not the same when we pass from one *residence* to another? There are few but have known local changes; and some, by a train of events, have been led to pitch their tents in situations the most remote from all their former expectations. Sometimes a removal is not at our own option. In other cases it seems very inviting and desirable. It may have preferable claims. But still it is a removal *in* the wilderness, and not *out* of it. To Abraham, God said, "Get thee out of thy country, and from thy father's house, into a land that I will tell thee of:" and this was the land of *Promise.* Yet even there he shared in the troubles of his nephew, Lot—went for years without an heir to his wealth—was tried in offering up his son Isaac—and buried his Sarah out of sight, in the cave of Machpelah. There, by faith, he sojourned as in a strange country, dwelling in tabernacles—not at home but looking for a city which had foundations, whose builder and maker is God.

Is it not the same when we go from one *condition* to another? Many deem it a fine thing to pass from obscurity to splendor—forgetful that distinction and fame will draw forth envy, and excite evil speaking, and deprive us of the sweets of retirement and leisure. David rose from a shepherd's cottage to the grandeur of a palace—and then sighed, "O that I had wings like a dove; for then would I fly away and be at rest." How wise was the Shunamite! When Elisha offered to speak for her to the king; "I dwell," said she, "among mine own people." Some deem it a great thing to rise from indigence to wealth. By their eagerness to acquire it, all seem to think, if they could have affluence, they should want nothing. But does a man's life consist in the abundance of the things which he possesseth? His desires increase with his means; and in the midst of his sufficiency he is in straits. The same may be said in passing from activity to leisure. "Oh!" says one, "when I have acquired so much, and can withdraw from the world, where I have been so tried, I *shall* be happy." But to withdraw from the world is not so easy. Habits form a second nature. Few are qualified, either to improve or to enjoy solitude. No kind or degree of exertion is so much at variance with happiness, as having nothing to do. Ennui is an insect that preys upon all bodies at rest.

"And *Satan* finds some mischief still, | "For idle hands to do."

He found David alone: and Eve alone. It is the will of nature and Providence that we should pass from individual into social life; and Solomon says, He that findeth a wife, findeth a good thing, and obtaineth favor of the Lord. And the conjugal condition, wisely and piously entered, in a general way, admits of more happiness than any other. But it may produce the keenest anguish. At best, it cannot yield pure and unalloyed felicity—our affections become sources of anxiety and fear—we share the pains, as well as the pleasures, of those who are one with us—and every delightful tie is mortal. How impatient are some to enter the parental relation! Lo! children are a heritage of the Lord, and the fruit of the womb is his reward. But the Proverb truly calls them, certain cares, and uncertain comforts. How often do the father and mother mourn over undutifulness, depravity, an early grave. Childhood and youth are vanity.

"This is a very gloomy view of things;" but is it not a true one? a Scriptural one? And if so, should it not check presumption and vain confidence? Should it not inspire sober and moderate expectation, with regard to every earthly scene—in those who are just entering life? or those who are on the verge of any change in it?

Is there, however, nothing to encourage and comfort under such a dispensation? Much every way. Such a state of things is not *casual*—"And the children of Israel took their journeys out of the wilderness of Sinai; and the cloud rested in the wilderness of Paran." Therefore, though they removed from one desert into another, it was under the Lord's guidance and conduct. He determines the bounds of our habitation, and administers all our comforts and our crosses. Such a state of things we are not *unapprised of*; and therefore, if we go on, buoyed up with hopes which must issue in disappointment, the fault is our own; as all history, observation, experience, and Scripture tell us enough to prevent it. Such a state, too, is not *peculiar* to us—it has been known by all our brethren who were before us in the world, and will be realized by all those who come after us. Nor is it our *final* state. Another is discovered and promised. There remaineth a rest for the people of God; a better, even a heavenly country—a few more stages, and we shall remove to the glory of all lands—no thorns there, no dangers there—after all our movements in the wilderness, we shall move out of it: and the days of our mourning will be ended. Neither is it an *unmixed* state. If this earth is not heaven, it is not hell: if we are not in Canaan, the Desert we are in is not like Egypt, from whence we came out. Like the Jews, we have many advantages and comforts, though the place itself yields us nothing. We have the fiery cloudy pillar; and water from the rock; and the manna; and Moses, Aaron, and Miriam; and the grapes from Eshcol; and God, who is nigh unto us in all that we call upon him for. Yea, the very difficulties, mortifications, and distresses of the state are *useful*. They try us, and humble us, and do us good with regard to our latter end. But for these, how unwilling should we be to go. How vain would the admonition be, "Arise, and depart;" unless it were enforced with the conviction, "This is not our rest."

Let this, therefore, keep us from the murmurings of discontent, and the forebodings of despondency. Though serious, let us not be gloomy. And while free from delusive hopes, let us not yield to unbelieving fears—but thank God, and take courage.

OCTOBER 11.—**" And he led them out as far as Bethany; and he lifted his hands, and blessed them. And it came to pass, while he blessed them, he was parted from them, and carried up into heaven."—Luke, xxiv, 50, 51.**

—FROM another Scripture, it would seem that he ascended from Mount Olivet. But there is no contradiction here. The same eminence is intended—on the one side of it, in the garden of Gethsemane, he suffered; on the opposite side, stretching down to Bethany, he was received up into glory. And we see the latter was some considerable distance from the former: for, of the attendants at his ascent, it is said, "Then returned they unto Jerusalem from the mount called Olivet, which is from Jerusalem a Sabbath-day's journey."

Thither he seems to have led his disciples, and for the sake of abstraction and privacy; for he had said before his death, "The world seeth me no more." They had seen him and believed not. To what purpose should other proofs be displayed before those on whose minds all his miracles had made no impression? And here was a sufficient number to attest the fact: and reason cannot question the competency of these witnesses, either as to capacity or sincerity.

But how wonderful and pleasing is the manner in which he took his leave! His disciples had often tried him. They had always betrayed great imperfections; and, after their professions of attachment to him, as soon as he was apprehended, they all forsook him, and fled. He might well have cast them off, but he loved them even unto the end. He might have forgiven them;

and yet have left them unseen—or silently—or with a frown—or with a rebuke—and this would almost have broken their hearts: but "he lifted up his hands, and blessed them!" Thus proclaiming the most cordial forgiveness; thus assuring them, that they might rely on his remembering them when he was come into his kingdom.

Dr. Priestly is much perplexed about his present residence and employment. It would appear, he says, from some intimations in the Epistles, as if he still had occasionally something to do with the church; but what this is we cannot conjecture. And there is no doubt, says he, but he is now somewhere on earth: for what relation can he have to any other planet? But we are assured that, while he blessed his disciples, he was parted from them, "and carried up into *heaven*." Where this is, we are not informed: but it is obviously a place; for he was clothed in a body like our own; and, corporeally, he cannot be every where. But wherever he *thus* is, there is heaven. And this accords with his own language—"I go to prepare a *place* for you." And though heaven is to be considered *more* as a state than a place; and though even now our happiness does not depend essentially upon local situations, yet these have their importance—And what beautiful and enchanting places have we seen, and heard of, and imagined! But "eye hath not seen, nor ear heard, neither have entered into the heart of man, the things which God hath prepared for them that love him." What a residence was Eden, before the fall of the first Adam! But this fell infinitely short of the excellency of the abode of the second Adam, the Lord from heaven—

Oh! the delights, the heavenly joys,
"The glories of the place,
"Where Jesus sheds the brightest beams
"Of his o'erflowing grace!"

Well, let us think of him where he now is, and inquire what is our duty with regard to him. Hear Paul: "Seeing then that we have a great high priest, that is passed into the heavens, Jesus the Son of God, let us hold fast our profession." We need not be afraid to own him—for he is able to take care of us, however we may be exposed. We need not be ashamed to avow him—for he has every thing to induce us to glory in him. Some comparative excuse might be made for Peter. When he denied him, he was a prisoner at the bar, and going to be crucified as a malefactor. But where is he when we deny him? In the midst of the throne—crowned with glory and honor—the Lord of all.

Let us follow him in our thoughts and affections. Why seek we the living among the dead. He is not *here*. He is in heaven; and where our treasure is, there should our hearts be also. Let us therefore have our conversation in heaven, and seek those things that are above, where Christ sitteth at the right hand of God. There, some of us have much to interest us now. We seem more related to another world than this—and, reflecting upon our losses, we sigh and say, "What do I *here?* and what have I *here?*" How many among the blessed can we reckon up, who we feel are drawing us after them! But here is the principal attraction.

"Jesus, my all. to heaven is gone:
"He whom I fix my hopes upon:
"His track I see, and I'll pursue
"The narrow path till him I view."

And let us rejoice in the expectation of being for ever with him. "Which hope we have as an anchor to the soul, both sure and steadfast, and which entereth into that within the vail; whither the forerunner is for us entered, even Jesus." The anchor that holds the ship is cast out of it; and our hope must go out of ourselves. The anchor lays hold of something invisible; and our hope enters heaven. Yet it would find nothing as the ground of its grasp *there*, if *he* was not there. But he *is* there—and there for *us*—and *his* being there, insures *ours*. He is the forerunner of the whole company; and said he, as he entered, "I am come; and all my people are coming." Unless we are there also, he would be disappointed—for he prayed, Father, I will that they whom thou hast given me be with me where I am, to behold my glory. He would be unfaithful—for he said, "Where I am, there shall also my servants be." He would be imperfect—for he is the bridegroom, and they are the bride; he is the head, and they are the members of his body.

O blessed confidence? let me feel thy influence in every duty and in every trial. Henry, after a sweet representation of the place, exclaims, "If this be heaven, O that I was there!" How matchlessly simple and affecting does Bunyan end his story of Christian and Hopeful, after they had passed the river, and approached the Shining City, the object of all their solicitude!—"Now, just as the gates were opened to let in the men, I looked in after them, and beheld the city shone like the sun: the streets, also were paved with gold; and in them walked many men, with crowns on their heads, palms in their hands, and golden harps to sing praises withal. There were also of them that had wings, and they answered one another, without intermission, saying, 'Holy, holy, holy, is the Lord.' And after that, they shut up the gates; WHICH WHEN I HAD SEEN, I WISHED MYSELF AMONG THEM."

OCTOBER 12.—"I am the good Shepherd."—John, x, 14.

To prove, or rather to exemplify his goodness, let us consider his sheep in three periods and conditions, and observe his conduct toward them in each.

First. See them in their *natural* state. Thus they were fallen and guilty creatures, in want and danger, and ready to perish. Here his goodness appeared in undertaking their cause, and engaging to be their Shepherd. For nothing but goodness could have induced him to do this. He was under no power or authority to constrain him. He was influenced by no application or desire in the subjects of his pity. And he was not ignorant of what the interposition would cost him. He knew that if he would be their shepherd, he must bleed and die. What says the church? "All we, like sheep, have gone astray; we have turned every one to his own way; and the Lord hath laid on him the iniquity of us all." What says he himself? The good shepherd giveth his life for the sheep." And all this he suffered, not complainingly, but with inexpressible alacrity and pleasure. I delight to do thy will. How am I straitened till it be accomplished! Nor was this all.

After he had redeemed them by his blood, he had to search and find them, and bring them from their wanderings into his fold. Hear his own representation. He goeth after that which is lost in the wilderness until he find it. Well, and when he has traversed the desert, weary, and wounded by the thorns and briars, and has found it, what does he? Does he complain of his privations, fatigues, and sufferings? No; he layeth it on his shoulder REJOICING; and when he cometh home, he calleth together his friends and neighbors, saying unto them, Rejoice *with me;* for I have found the sheep which was lost.

Secondly. View them in their *restored* estate. Here his goodness appears in making such ample and rich provision for them. For he does not bring them into barrenness. They shall not want. I will feed them in a good pasture. It appears in affording them repose, as well as food. For they want rest, as well as supplies, especially at noon. And, says he, I will not only feed my flock, but cause them to lie down. He maketh them to lie down in green pastures. It appears in recalling them when wandering. He restoreth my soul, says David. It appears in defending them. They shall never perish, says the shepherd, neither shall any pluck them out of his hand. It appears in accommodating himself so kindly and tenderly to their age and weakness. "He shall feed his flock like a shepherd; he shall gather the lambs with his arm, and carry them in his bosom, and shall gently lead those that are with young."

Thirdly. See them in their *final* state. Here he does much for them; and they are often deeply affected with it, especially when they consider where he found them, and what they once were. But when they took him in his promises they see that he intends to do infinitely more. How great is the goodness which he has laid up for them that fear him! Earth is too narrow to contain it. Time is too short to display it. It doth not yet appear what they shall be. There is a land of pure delight; a better, a heavenly country, prepared to receive them. There is, indeed, a dark valley to pass before they can enter it. But it is safe—and short—and their Shepherd is with them there, and his rod and his staff will comfort them. And when they are over, "they shall hunger no more, neither thirst any more; neither shall the sun light on them, nor any heat. For the Lamb which is in the midst of the throne, shall feed them, and shall lead them unto living fountains of waters; and God shall wipe away all tears from their eyes." Blessed Jesus! how well hast thou said, "I am the good Shepherd!"

Oh! let those that belong to him, love him, and honor him with their confidence. Trust in him at all times, ye people. Resign to him all your interests. It is enough that he careth for you. You know his aim. And you know that all his ways are mercy and truth.

But are we a part of his charge? Are we sheep? Are we lambs? How may I know this? They are marked—marked in the *ear*—and marked in the *foot*. My sheep *hear* my voice—and they *follow* me.

OCTOBER 13.—"And I will spare them, as a man spareth his own son that serveth him."—Malachi, iii, 17.

If a man spares any one, it will surely be his own son. The very relation pleads for him. Even a faulty child is a child still, and is not easily turned out of doors, like a servant. Absalom had risen in rebellion against his father; and David was compelled to fight with his own son—But Oh! said he, on the eve of the battle, deal gently, for my sake, with the young man, even with Absalom! Who can imagine his feelings while thinking of the action! With what hope and fear was his parental bosom fluttering when the messenger arrived with the result! Who does not seem to hear his very heartstrings break, as he goes up into the chamber, weeping, "O my son Absalom, my son, my son Absalom! would God I had died for thee, O Absalom, my son, my son?" But when a son is dutiful, and the father sees that he desires, and aims, and endeavors to please him! Now this is the image God here employs, to raise our confidence the more. I will spare them, as a man spareth his own son that serveth him. In the same strain is our Savior's tender appeal: "If ye then, being evil, know how to give good gifts unto your children, how much more shall your Father which is in heaven give good things to them that ask him?" God's own children who serve him, need sparing mercy. It is exercised toward them four ways.

First. He spares them as to exemption. This has often been seen in times of public and general calamity. Does the flood come and sweep away the world of the ungodly? An ark is provided for the saving of Noah and his house. Are the cities of the plain destroyed? Lot is sent forth out of the overthrow. Darkness that might be felt enveloped the Egyptians; but the Israelites had light in all their dwellings. When the executioners were approaching Jerusalem, Set a mark, said God, upon the foreheads of the men that sigh and that cry for the abominations that are done in the midst of the land. Some of his servants are taken away from the evil to come. Pious connexions removed by death, are often spared the sight of relative troubles, under which, perhaps, they would have sunk. Many a pious youth, like Abijah, has come to an early grave in peace, and been housed from storms after. The heathens said, They whom the gods love, die young. How often has he spared us—spared our lives, our senses, our limbs, our substance, our relations and friends—with regard to all of which we must gratefully acknowledge, It is of the Lord's mercies that we are not consumed.

—Secondly. He spares them as to correction. As his word tells us, "He that spareth the rod hateth his son?" He will not himself refuse to strike when it is needful. Whom the Lord loveth, he therefore chasteneth. But how? What is the prayer of his people? O Lord, correct me, but with judgment: not in thine anger, lest thou bring me to nothing. And he hears them, and spares them as to the degree of the affliction. "In measure, when it shooteth forth, thou wilt debate with it: he stayeth his rough wind in the day of the east wind." They are afflicted, but they have alleviations. It might have been much worse; it is so with others. One comfort is gone; but many remain. Cast down, but not destroyed. "Like as a father pitieth his children, so the Lord pitieth them that fear him. For he knoweth our frame; he remembereth that we are dust." For the same holds with regard to continuance—he will not always chide, neither will he keep his anger for ever. "I will not contend for ever, neither will I be always wroth: for the spirit should fail before me, and the souls which I have made." See an instance of this sparing goodness expressed with incomparable tenderness with regard to Ephraim. "Is Ephraim my dear son? Is he a pleasant child? For since I spake against him, I do earnestly remember him still. Therefore my bowels are troubled for him: I will surely have mercy upon him, saith the Lord."

Thirdly. He spares them as to exertion. He considers their strength, and will not require of some what he ordains for others. A father, in his family, would not impose upon an infant the service he would lay upon the young man. To some, in Thyatira, the Lord said, I will put upon you none other burden. The children are tender, says Jacob, and the flocks and herds with young are with me; and if men should over-drive them one day, all the flock would die. How much does this remind us of another, of whom it is said, "He shall feed his flock like a shepherd; he shall gather the lambs with his arm, and carry them in his bosom, and shall gently lead those that are with young. When our Savior was blamed for not enjoining fastings on his disciples, he replied, "No man putteth a piece of new cloth unto an old garment; for that which is put in to fill it up taketh from the garment, and the rent is made worse. Neither do men put new wine into old bottles; else the bottles break, and the wine runneth out, and the bottles perish: but they put new wine into new bottles, and both are preserved." There is, says Henry, in well-doing an over-doing, and such over-doing as may prove undoing. Many religious people are blamable here. They expect too much to be given up before persons have realized the comforts of the Holy Ghost. They want to effect every thing at a stroke. They forget their own ignorance and slowness when God began to deal with them. They forget Him who does not despise the day of small things: and who said to his followers, I have yet many things to say unto you, but ye cannot hear them now.

Fourthly. He spares them as to acceptance. Their best actions are imperfect. Their holiest duties are defiled. Their obedience needs pardon. To whom does not this apply? Nehemiah had done much for the cause of God; but does he appeal to justice to reward him? No; but to mercy, to forgive him: "Remember me, O my God, concerning this also, and spare me according to the greatness of thy mercy." Paul, after extolling Onesiphorus so highly, prays that even he may find mercy of the Lord in that day. I am looking, says the great John Howe, dying, for eternal life: not as a profitable servant, but as a pardoned sinner. Where is the Christian, however distinguished his attainments, who, even in looking over his sabbaths, and his communions at the Lord's table, and every alms-deed he ever performed, is not constrained to pray, "Enter not into judgment with thy servant, O Lord; for in thy sight shall no flesh living be justified?" Well; he will spare you, as to your deficiencies in duty. He takes the design. He regards the motive. He looketh at the heart. He will pardon what is yours; and reward what is his own. For he views you and your services through the mediation of his dear Son, in whom he is well pleased. Ah! he spared not him, that he might spare you. If we sin, we have an Advocate with the Father, Jesus Christ the righteous; and he is the propitiation for our sins. And as God said to Job's friends, so he says to us. "My servant shall pray for you, and him will I accept; lest I deal with you according to your folly."

—Never forget the goodness and kindness of God. He is your Father—and he will spare you.

But spare not yourselves. Mind no labor or expense in his cause. Deny yourselves, and take up your cross, and follow him fully—follow him whithersoever he goeth.

October 14.—"According to their pasture, so were they filled; they were filled, and their heart was exalted; therefore have they forgotten me."
Hosea, xiii, 6.

In this and the former verse, God places Israel before us in two situations and conditions—The Wilderness, and Canaan. He reminds us of his knowledge of them in the former; and of their disregarding him in the latter. He commended them in their low estate; but had to complain of them in their prosperity; "I did know thee in the wilderness, in the land of great drought." But delivered from the privations and hardships of the desert, they entered the Land of promise—the glory of all lands—a land of wheat and barley—a land of vineyards, and fig-trees, and pomegranates—a land wherein there was no scarceness—a land flowing with milk and honey. And what was the consequence?

First. Selfish indulgence—"*According* to their pasture, *so* were they *filled*." And was this sinful? We plead for no monkish austerities. "Every creature of God is good, and nothing to be refused, if it be received with thanksgiving; for it is sanctified by the word of God and prayer." He "giveth us richly all things to enjoy." But the enjoyment of Christians differs from the excess of the sensual. We are not to feast ourselves without fear. We are not to make provision for the flesh, to fulfill the lusts thereof. We are not to throw the reins on the neck of appetite: and feed ourselves to the full. The mistake of many is, that they suppose every thing is their own. They are only stewards of the manifold grace of God. They think they may sleep as much as they like; dress as much as they like; consume as much as they like: but the Scripture is our rule, and not our own inclination. There is the cause of God, and of the poor, to be thought of, as well as our own gratification. The first lesson in the school of Christ, is self-denial—Where, in the lives of some, does this ever appear? Temperance is one of the graces of the Spirit—And does this consist only in avoiding the grossness of drunkenness and gluttony ? No; but in not "*filling* ourselves *according* to our pasture."

Secondly. Pride—"They were filled, and their *heart was exalted.*" This was the case even with Hezekiah: even *he* rendered not according to the benefits done him; for "his heart was lifted up." And, by charging them that are rich in this world not to be high-minded," nor to "trust in uncertain riches," the apostle shows the tendency there always is in worldly success, to gender vanity and false confidence. Hence it is said, "Pride compasseth them about as a chain; violence covereth them as a garment." They even think more highly of their understanding—as if their wisdom grew with their wealth. They speak with authority; and answer roughly.

Thirdly. Unmindfulness of God—"Therefore have they forgotten me." And how common is it for men, in the midst of their sufficiency, to lose the sense of their obligations to God, and dependence upon him, and need of him. Hence Agar prayed against being rich; "lest I should be full, and deny thee, and say, who is the Lord?" Hence the caution to the Jews, at their taking possession of all the good things in Canaan: "Then beware lest thou forget the Lord which brought thee forth out of the land of Egypt, from the house of bondage." But, alas! the admonition was unavailable. "Jeshurun waxed fat, and kicked. Thou art waxen fat, thou art grown thick, thou art covered with fatness: then he forsook God which made him, and lightly esteemed the Rock of his salvation."

This gives us a very humbling view of our human nature. It is possible for us to consider it so innocent, so amiable, so noble, as some would represent it to be? View it, not as it appears in the dregs of society, but as it is seen in common and reputable life, and in what are called, "the better sort" of people. See men able to bear nothing without abuse—evil, because God is good—drawn from him by the very things which should lead to him—ungrateful, in proportion as they should love and praise him—and even converting his gifts into weapons of rebellion against him! Lord, what is man!

Let the fact arouse us to caution and circumspection, if Providence smiles upon us, and we are placed in easy and agreeable circumstances. Yea, let us not only watch, but pray, lest we enter into temptation. Let us seek that grace which can alone enable us to manage a full estate properly, so as to elude its snares, and discharge its duties. Then we shall see, that what is impossible to men is possible to God. It was said of Vespasian, that he was even the better man for being an emperor. So there are some, whose prosperity, instead of destroying them, displays and increases their excellency; and they are not only rich in temporal things, but rich in faith, and rich in good works. These instances, however, are rare.

—And the perils of the condition should check our eagerness after worldly influence and ease. Why do we envy those that rise? Because we attach an undue value and importance to their acquisitions. "Be not thou afraid when one is made rich, when the glory of his house is increased; for when he dieth he shall carry nothing away; his glory shall not descend after him." These possessions are not only transient, but unsatisfying; and vexatious; and corrupting. Yet, regardless of the testimony of Scripture, and all history and experience, how many, even professors of religion, crave and pursue them as if they were the supreme good. But seekest thou great things unto thyself? seek them not.—Bring your mind unto your condition; for you never will be able to bring your condition to your mind. Your desires will enlarge with your indulgence; as fuel adds to the fierceness of the flame. Therefore let your conversation be without covetousness, and be content with such things as ye have; for He hath said, I will never leave thee nor forsake thee.

Learn also resignation under afflictive dispensations, either in crossing your schemes, or in reducing your resources. "Because they have no changes, therefore they fear not God." It was said of Moab, "Moab hath been at ease from his youth, and he hath settled on his lees, and hath not been emptied from vessel to vessel, neither hath he gone into captivity; therefore his taste remained of him, and his scent is not changed." The Prodigal was more favored—a famine drove him home. Manasseh was mercifully ruined—in his affliction he sought the Lord God of his father, and he was found of him. And he gives you the valley of Achor for a door of hope. Do not think hardly of him, under whose discipline you now are. He knew your danger, and interposed to prevent it. He has hedged up your way with thorns, but it is to keep you from following lying vanities, and forsaking your own mercies. He tries you, but it is for your profit. He sees what you can bear. And he who loved you, so as to give his own Son for you, will suffer you to want no good thing.

October 15.—"And the Lord said unto me, I have heard the voice of the words of this people, which they have spoken unto thee; they have well said all that they have spoken."—Deuteronomy, v, 28.

Thus He expressly mentions his having *heard* what they had *said* to Moses. It is equally true that he hears all we say; and has heard all we have ever said. This is a solemn thought; especially as he has heard all our words, not as an unconcerned auditor, but as a witness and a judge. How many of them have we forgotten! But they are all in the book of his remembrance. And, says the faithful Witness, "For every idle word that men shall speak, they shall give account thereof in the day of judgment. For by thy words thou shalt be justified, and by thy words thou shalt be condemned."

Here, the words which God had heard were the words of religious avowal—"Speak thou unto us all that the Lord our God shall speak unto thee; and *we will hear it, and do it.*" And he has heard all our religious resolutions and engagements. First. Our more private ones; when we have been impressed alone—with regard to such a temper, that we would watch against it—with regard to such a temptation, that we would pray for grace to resist it—with regard to our time, that we would redeem it—with regard to our substance, that we would honor the Lord with it. And, secondly, with regard to our more public and solemn ones; when we joined ourselves to his people, and went to his table; and, over the memorials of dying love, said, "Henceforth, by thee only will I make mention of thy name."

"Here, in thy house, I leave my vow,
"And thy rich grace record;
"Witness, ye saints, who hear me now,
"If I forsake the Lord."

I have heard, says he, the voice of the words of this people. And adds, with approbation, containing in it complaint, "They have well *said* all that they have *spoken*." But talking and doing are two things; and even, with regard to ourselves, one of them goes a very little way without the other. Yea, it rather offends—it adds insult to injury. We scorn a flattering profession, contradicted by actions. Actions, we say, speak louder than words. What is lip service in religion! Judas gave our Lord the lip—called him Master—and kissed him—and betrayed. Ezekiel's hearers extolled his preaching, and brought others to admire him; but their hearts went after their covetousness. They heard his words, but did them not. So David testifies of these Jews, "When he slew them, then they sought him; and they returned, and inquired early after God. Nevertheless, they did flatter him with their mouth, and they lied unto him with their tongues. For their heart was not right with him, neither were they steadfast in his covenant." And so here. They spoke well in expressing their readiness to hear and do. But God, who knew them better than they knew themselves, immediately exclaimed, "O that there was such a heart in them."

—Speech is one of the most uncertain criterions by which we can judge of character, either as to the reality or degree of religion. From education, reading, and hearing, persons may easily learn to talk well. They may even surpass others, who are far better than themselves; as an empty vessel, when touched, sounds louder than a full one; and as a shallow brook is more noisy than a deep river. Some speak little, especially concerning themselves, from a fear of deception, and a concern lest they should appear to others above what they really are. Baxter, in his life of Judge Hale, says, For a time, I feared he was wanting in experimental religion, as he seldom spoke of his own spiritual views and feelings. But upon acquaintance I found I was mistaken. He had heard from many in his times so much hypocrisy and fanaticism that he was urged toward the extreme of silence. And it is the better extreme of the two. Christians feed on the hidden manna, and have a white stone, with a new name in it, which no man readeth save he that receiveth it. Would it not be better for some to talk less of their high confidence, and their wonderful ecstacies, before those who are weak in faith and comfort, and who are in danger of being depressed by comparison? How assuredly do some speak of the time when they were "enlightened," or "converted," as if they could ascertain the period of the second birth as exactly as that of the first! Might it not, sometimes at least, be better to speak of the fact with less decision? and always to consider the work not so much done as doing? or to pray that it might be done—as David did—"Create in me a clean heart, O God, and renew a right spirit within me?"

To how many individuals will the words before us apply! Here is a champion for the truth. He has defended its purity and importance. He has contended earnestly and, as far as argument and evidence goes, wisely, for the faith once delivered to the saints. He has well *said* all that he has *spoken.* But where is the spirit of truth? the meekness of wisdom? the mind of Christ? Every page of controversy ought to have at the top, "The wrath of man worketh not the righteousness of God:" and at the bottom, "If any man have not the spirit of Christ, he is none of his." Another has entered the sanctuary of God, and, in language equally beautiful and true, has acknowledged, We have erred and strayed from thy ways like lost sheep—we have followed too much the devices and desires of our own hearts—there is no health in us. And he has well *said* all that he has *spoken.* But where is the broken heart, and the contrite spirit? How often, after these confessions, is the sermon, founded upon them, disliked, and the preacher of it condemned! Here is a third. He has gone to his brethren in distress, and justified the ways of God to man. But does he justify God's dealings with himself in trouble? He has well *said* all that he has *spoken;* but he reminds us of the language of Eliphaz to Job: "Behold, thou hast instructed many, and thou hast strengthened the weak hands. Thy words have upholden him that was falling, and thou hast strengthened the feeble knees. But now it is come upon thee, and thou faintest: it toucheth thee, and thou art troubled."

But men may mistake themselves, when they do not mean to deceive others. They are often, at the time, as sincere as they are earnest. The young, the afflicted in the hour of distress, the sick, and the dying, express many things which are as true as they are good, according to their present feelings. But they do not distinguish between impulse and disposition, between outward excitement and inward principle. Hazael, at the prediction of his cruelties, ignorant of the change that power would produce in him, really execrated the character he became. Peter was presuming, but not false, when he said, Though all shall be offended because of thee, yet will I never be offended. The disciples supposed themselves established in the faith, beyond the danger of temptation to forsake him, when they said, "Now we believe." But Jesus answered them, O that there was such a heart in you! "Do ye now believe? Behold the hour cometh, yea, is now come, that ye shall be scattered, every man to his own, and shall leave me alone: and yet I am not alone, because the Father is with me."

October 16.—"And there are also many other things which Jesus did, the which, if they should be written every one, I suppose that even the world itself could not contain the books that should be written. Amen."
John, xxi, 25.

This is the language of the writer of this Gospel, in concluding his narrative. After all that he had brought forward, much more remained behind. He had composed a memoir, rather than a history: and only furnished a few specimens of a subject, boundless in itself.

Yet the expression he employs in asserting this, may seem to many surprising, if not confounding. There are two ways of solving the difficulty. First. The language is a figure; a strong hyperbole. This was very common in the east. Indeed, it is frequent with writers and speakers in all countries. Even in our familiar discourse we often, without being aware of it, express ourselves as remotely from truth, if *absolutely* considered—"I am tired to death." "I have no strength left." "Every body knows it." Such a thing is—"provided at the shortest notice"—which would be a moment. But no deception is intended: and no danger of mistake follows.

—Yet, secondly, though, this meets the difficulty, some have also a little altered the rendering, and read—not, the world would not *contain*; but would not *receive*, the books that would be written. So Doddridge and others. This is allowable in criticism; but let us observe the justness of the inference. If all the particulars of his birth, and infancy, and youth, and manhood; if all the occurrences of his private and public life; if all his actions, his miracles, his speeches, his prayers, with all their relative circumstances; if all these had been recorded—instead of a book, we must have had books; and books so large, and many, that the design must have been counteracted. For then there were no books; but were in manuscript. And who would have had leisure to transcribe them? Who would have taken the trouble? If they were purchased from transcribers, who would have endured the expense? They could only have been the property of the very rich. And when they had become their own, who could have had time to read them? Who could have remembered them all? How multiplied would have been the difficulties requiring expla nation! All these would have been with men, reasons or excuses for not procuring; or not perusing; or not understanding them.

Therefore, each of the inspired lives of our Savior himself, is not so long as many a sermon; and the four put together are far shorter than the published account of many a modern, insignificant character. But let us not complain or lament, that the whole is so compendious and brief. It is not a defect, but an excellency. The wisdom and goodness of God appear in it. It meets the more, our situations, engagements, and capacities. More would only have perplexed us, or multiplied our diversions.

—And let us remember also, that we do not want the aid of traditional supplement, or human additions to the Scriptures of truth. Though short, they are sufficient. They leave nothing obscure as to our duty, or welfare—they are able to make us wise unto salvation, through faith that is in Christ Jesus.

--And may we not suppose that it will be a part of our engagement and blessedness in heaven, to derive from those acquainted with them, or from the Savior himself, the knowledge of a thousand things concerning his eventful history, of which we are now ignorant.

—Above all, let us rejoice in what has been furnished. Let us rejoice that it is so divinely proved—and that it has been preserved uncorrupted down to our own time—and that we have it in our own language—and are allowed, and able, to read it. And let us keep the *end* of the whole in view, and never be satisfied till it be accomplished in our experience. "And many other signs truly did Jesus in the presence of his disciples, which are not written in this book: but these are written, that ye might believe that Jesus is the Christ, the son of God; and that, believing, ye might have life through his name."

OCTOBER 17.—"It is high time to wake out of sleep."—Romans, xiii, 11.

THESE words regard Christians themselves. This is undeniable, from the motive subjoined—"For now is our salvation nearer than when we believed." Are *believers*, then, asleep? Not in the sense they once were—this would be impossible. But there are found, even in them, some remains of their former depravity. Though the good work is begun in them, it is far from being accomplished. While the bridegroom tarried, even the wise virgins slumbered and slept. Yes, Christians, alas! are often in a drowsy state; and oftener in a drowsy frame. This is sadly reproachful. What! drowsy, in examining themselves whether they be in the faith? Drowsy, in praising the God of their salvation? Drowsy, in seeking mercy and grace, to help them in time of need? Drowsy, in serving their generation, by the will of God? Are they not the disciples of Jesus? Did he ever speak an idle word? Did he ever lose a useful moment? "I must work," said he, "the works of Him that sent me while it is day; the night cometh when no man can work."

Yet, if the address be proper for Christians, how much more necessary is it for those who are entirely regardless of the things that belong to their peace! Surely for them "it is high time to awake out of sleep."

—If we consider how long they have been sleeping. We ought to lament that we have lost any of our precious hours and opportunities. However short it may have been, the time past of our life should more than suffice, wherein we have lived to the will of man. What, then, should those feel who have sacrificed the whole of their youth? Perhaps the vigor of mature age? Perhaps have grown gray in the service of sin and the world? The later we begin, the more zealous should we be to redeem the advantages we have lost; and to overtake those who were wise enough to set off early. When Cæsar, in Spain, met with a statue of Alexander, he wept at the thought that this illustrious conqueror had achieved so much before *he* had even begun. High time,

—If we consider that the day is arrived, and the sun is risen so high. "The night is far spent, the day is at hand; let us therefore cast off the works of darkness, and let us put on the armor of light." We can say more than the Apostle. The night is spent. The day is *fully come*. And we are all the children of the light, and the children of the day: we are not of the night, nor of darkness—*Therefore* let us not sleep as do others. They that sleep, sleep in the night. Look into nature. The sun ariseth—and man goeth forth unto his work and to his labor until the evening. The sun shines, not for us to sleep by its lustre, but discharge the duties of our stations. And why is the Gospel given us? Why is our duty so plainly made known, but that we may follow it? And why are blessings of divine grace so clearly set before us, but that we may seek them. Our obligations always increase with our advantages. To him that knoweth to do good, and doeth it not, to him it is sin. And the servant that knew his lord's will, and prepared not himself, shall be beaten with many stripes; for where much is given much will be required. High time,

—If we consider the business they have to do. I am doing, said Nehemiah to some who would have interrupted him—I cannot come down to you; I am doing a great work. How much more may a Christian say this! He has an enterprise connected with the soul, and God, and eternity. Some things are desirable, and some are useful; but this is absolutely indispensable—

"Sufficient in itself alone; | "And needful, were the world our own."

Neglect in many a concern is injurious; but here it is ruinous—of every thing—and for ever. High time,

—If we consider the nature of the season in which this difficult and all-important work is to be accomplished. It is short: and there is but a step between us and death. It is uncertain in its continuance: and may be terminated every moment by some of those numberless dangers, internal and external, to which we are exposed. And once gone, it can never be renewed. No place will be found for repentance, though we seek it carefully with tears. High time,

—If we consider the danger they are in. If a man was sleeping in a house, and the fire was seen, not only to be kindled, but raging over his apartment; or approaching rapidly to his door or ready to catch the very curtains of his bed; who would not find it high time for him to awake, and escape for his life? This is but a weak representation of the danger of sinners. They are condemned already. The wrath of God abideth on them. They are nigh unto cursing. Their end is to be burned. Their destruction is not only insured, but begun. And we are required to save with fear, pulling them out of the fire. High time to awake out of sleep,

—If we consider, that all beside are awake. God is awake—Angels are awake—Glorified saints are awake—Brutes are awake—The children of this generation are awake—Devils are awake—Death is awake—Damnation is awake—Their damnation slumbereth not. It is high time to awake out of sleep!

—Is it not too late? Have I not reason to fear that I have passed the bounds of Divine patience? that the Lord hath shut to the door? that in resentment of my neglects and provocations, he hath given me over to a reprobate mind? that he hath poured upon me the spirit of slumber? And hence it is that I hear so often with indifference, and that nothing affects me now as it once did.

—Yet may I not hope that his long suffering will yet be my salvation? that he has spared me so long to afford space for repentance? that the seriousness of this retirement is another call of mercy? that the uneasiness, the dread, the desire I now feel, are a token for good? the lingering of pity still cries, How shall I give thee up?—Lord, save—I perish!

OCTOBER 18.—"He will speak peace unto his people, and to his saints; but let them not turn again to folly."—Psalm lxxxv, 8.

How encouraging is expectation! "He will speak peace unto his people, and to his saints."

Mark the blessing itself—*Peace.* It does not mean outward ease and prosperity. He nowhere engages to speak this: but spiritual comfort; the composure of the conscience; the satisfaction of the heart: by which the "*soul* shall dwell at ease;" the effect of confidence in God: "Thou wilt keep him in perfect peace whose mind is stayed on thee, because he trusteth in thee." How relieving is it, under a sense of guilt, to believe in the blood that cleanseth from all sin! How soothing is it, in the various changes of life, to be assured that all things shall work together for our good! How confirming is it, in the prospect of every duty, to know that his strength shall be made perfect in weakness! This is the rest wherewith we are to cause the weary to rest; and this is the refreshing.

Observe the author of the communication—*He* will speak peace. And unless *He* speaks it, it will be spoken in vain. Friends may address us; but they will be found miserable comforters. Ministers may attempt to bind up the broken heart; but they will prove physicians of no value. Ordinances may be regarded; but they will be wells without water, and clouds without rain. But "when He giveth quietness, then who can make trouble?" We can only implore, or announce peace: but His word produces, conveys it. He commandeth the blessing, even life evermore. Nothing is beyond the reach of Him who turneth the shadow of death into the morning.

Observe the heirs of the privilege—He will speak peace to his *people,* and to his *saints.* These are not different characters, but different representations of the same persons; and the one explanatory of the other. He has a people for his name: and if we ask, who they are, we are told they are saints; that is, they are holy ones. They are not perfectly holy; but they are really so. The principles of sanctification, of which they are the partakers, will soon gain the entire possession of them; but even now they have the ascendency in them. Their love of holiness is evinced even with regard to their remaining corruptions. These are their burden and distress, and for these they abhor themselves. They long, above all things, to walk so as to please God; and constantly pray, Create in me a clean heart, O God, and renew a right spirit within Me. And what have others to do with peace? "There is no peace, saith my God, unto the wicked."

Mark also the certainty of the assurance—He *will* speak peace unto his people, and to his saints. Every thing tends to confirm it. His name: He is the God of peace. His thoughts: they are the thoughts of peace. The mediation of the Son of his love: He made peace by the blood of his Cross. His dealings with us: Had he a mind to kill us, he would not have shown us such things as these. The truth of his word: The Scripture cannot be broken. But when will he do this? He will speak peace to his people, and to his saints: partially through life: specially in affliction: pre-eminently in death: and completely in heaven.

And how reasonable is the caution, "But let them not turn again unto folly."

—Here we see the character of sin: it is folly. Such the God of truth pronounces it to be now. Such, every transgressor will acknowledge it to be at last. Should not this be enough to deter us from it: that it perfectly befools us? and will fill us with everlasting shame and contempt?

—Here we are reminded, that the people of God, though saints now, were once chargeable with it. The command not to *turn again* to folly, proves this. Their being *made to differ*, supposes former sameness. They were by nature children of wrath, even as others; and they are willing to own it: and it does them no hurt to look to the rock whence they were hewn, and to the hole of the pit whence they were digged.

—We are also taught that they are still in danger, and need warning. A haughty spirit goes before a fall: and therefore they who are offended with admonition, or deem themselves above it, show how much *they* stand in need of it. Let him that thinketh he standeth, take heed lest he fall. We are always exposed to a subtle and invisible enemy; we live in a wicked world, and carry within us an evil heart. The best, in an hour of temptation, have turned again to folly.

—But against this we should feel ourselves peculiarly concerned to guard, *when* God has appeared for us, and spoken peace to our souls. We should be alike ungrateful and infatuated were we not —ungrateful: for the more he does for us, the more anxious should we be lest we offend and grieve his Holy Spirit—infatuated: for having known the evil of sin, and the bitterness of repentance, and the joy of God's salvation; shall we again cause him to hide his face from us? and wrong our own souls? For the backslider in heart shall be filled with his own ways; He will speak peace to his own people, and to his saints—BUT LET THEM NOT TURN AGAIN TO FOLLY.

OCTOBER 19.—"Seeing many things, but thou observest not."—Is. xlii. 20.

THIS charge is as applicable to us as it was to the Jews. Nothing is more common than the want of wise and proper *observation.* The objects and events adapted to excite it, and which would also reward it, are various and numberless. And some of them daily and hourly strike our senses; yet they engage none of our notice and attention as rational and moral beings. From an immense multitude, let us select two of these occurrences, by way of example—The birth, and the death, of our fellow creatures.

How little attention is excited by the birth of a child. It may perhaps, if it takes place in respectable life, be announced in the paper—inquiries may be made concerning its sex and form—it may be viewed and embraced by the friends who call ceremoniously on the mother who has been delivered. But what moral or religious reflection is ever indulged by those who are informed of the event? or even by the parents themselves? The interesting sufferer herself may be pleased with the congratulations paid her; and forget her anguish for joy that a man is born into the world; and feel a lively gratitude for the mercy she has experienced: but no one thought may arise in the mind respecting the all-important result, in the production of a new being: and such a being, too! Yet the birth of a child can scarcely be deemed less than a miracle of Nature and Providence. That child is a piece of Divine workmanship, fearfully and wonderfully made; and as fearfully and wonderfully preserved and endowed. When the Creator made it, he did a far greater thing than when he made the sun. The sun is a mass of unintelligent matter. It sees not its own light. It feels not its own heat, and is not destined to shine and burn for ever: But there is a spirit in that child; and the inspiration of the Almighty giveth him understanding. He is a moral being. He is the subject of reason and conscience. These principles are not yet developed, but they are lodged in him. They are in him, as the flower is in the seed; and the oak in the acorn. He is an heir of immortality; and though his existence began yesterday, it will never end. He will hear the heavens pass away with a great noise, and see the elements melt with fervent heat. He will stand before the judgment seat of Christ, and go away into everlasting punishment, or into life eternal.

He is also to be viewed relatively, as well as personally. And what an awful interest does he acquire from the evil he may occasion, as well as suffer! And from the good he may produce, as well as experience! He may prove a viper in the bosom that feeds him, a disgrace to his family, a curse to the nation. Many may be vitiated by his example, and led into hell by his influence. One sinner destroyeth much good. Or he may make a glad father, and prove a blessing to the neighborhood, and serve his generation by the will of God, and levy a tax of gratitude on future ages. Who that had seen Isaac Watts in the arms of his mother, sitting at the door of the prison in which his father was suffering for conscience sake, could have divined that this precious babe was the sweet Psalmist of the Christian Israel; and that the little hand that stroked her cheek was ordained to hold the pen that should instruct and edify the world to the end of time! Had we heard when the babe wept, and looked into the ark of bulrushes, we should have seen the scholar, learned in all the wisdom of Egypt—the scourge of Pharaoh, the deliverer of the Hebrews, the king in Jeshurun, the lawgiver, and the prophet of the Lord, with whom he spake face to face. What says the Lord of all? "Despise not one of these little ones; for I say unto you, that in heaven their angels do always behold the face of my heavenly Father."

Let us pass to the second article, Death. This is perpetually taking place around us: yet how little it is noticed, it was long ago remarked by Eliphaz: "They are destroyed from morning to evening: they perish for ever without any regarding it." This indifference is one of the most astonishing things in a world of wonders, especially when taken in connexion with those consequences, that, in general belief, are supposed to result from it. If a tower fell, if a mountain was swallowed up by an earthquake, we should notice it, and make it a subject of conversation for days and weeks—Yet, what is this, compared with the removal of a fellow creature, detached from all union with visible nature, excluded from every thing that once pleased or engaged him below the sun, severed from all his endeared connexions, his flesh seeing corruption, while his soul has entered into an entirely new state of existence, in immediate and perceptible communion with the Lord of all! Death is the most serious and momentous event that can befall the children of men. For it is not the extinction of being, but only the termination of one mode of it, and the commencement of another; the transition from time to eternity, from a course of action to the sentence of retribution. When the dust returns to the dust, whence it was, the spirit returns to God, who gave it; and then the divine fiat runs, "He that is unjust, let him be unjust still; and he that is filthy, let him be filthy still; and he that is righteous, let him be righteous still; and he that is holy, let him be holy still."

And yet who considers it? When the bell tolls, we hardly ask whose doom it announces. When we see a funeral in the street, we scarcely look toward it, unless it be accompanied with the pomp of mortality. We see new names on the doors of the houses; but we pass without thinking that the places which once knew the owners, know them no more for ever. A neighbor dies, and, from civility, we attend the burial, and lend him our last assistance; but return into the busy or trifling concerns of life as careless as before. Death enters our own dwelling; we feel deeply; but we reflect slightly. We mourn our loss, but the heart is not made better: we miss them for a time; but we soon furnish substitutes, or grow insensible to the want of them. When every duty the utmost decorum can exact, or the most perfect affection dictate, is discharged toward the deceased: where is the concern of the living to derive from the decease itself the spiritual profit which it is designed to yield? Where is the earnestness of the prayer, "So teach us to number our days, that we may apply our heart unto wisdom?"

Every death—the death of the young, and the death of the old; the death of the rich, and the death of the poor; the death of the saint, and the death of the sinner—has something not only serious, but appropriate to impart. But to the generality of mankind each of them says nothing—or speaks in vain.

Much of this disregard is from the frequency of the occurrence. Nothing seems to affect us strongly, but what is sudden or rare. The most important object, and the most interesting events, when they become familiar, awaken neither wonder nor attention. Yet, if we cannot regulate our impressions, we can govern our ideas; we can apply our thoughts to any subject we please; and we should not suffer what is so full of instruction to pass without just reflection. We cannot be always thinking of death; but we should never be so absent from a proper condition of mind as not to be easily recalled to the improvement of an event which must soon happen to all, and for which we may prepare, though we cannot prevent.

It is not only the commonness of the subject, but our aversion to it, that keeps us from attending to it. It is, above all things, irksome to flesh and blood: we, therefore, are always endeavoring to put the evil day far away. But since we cannot put it off, let us pray for that *grace* which will turn the enemy into a friend, and the curse into a blessing. Then, to die, will be gain: and we may live rejoicing in hope of the glory of God.

"If there be any virtue, and if there be any praise, think on these things."

OCTOBER 20.—"**Thine eyes shall see the King in his beauty.**"—Is. xxxiii, 17.

—YET what was the sight of Hezekiah, released from his affliction, and appearing cheerfully in his royal robes, to his subjects, after the destruction of the Assyrian army, compared with another sight! "But we see Jesus, who, for the suffering of death, was crowned with glory and honor." Some, in the days of his flesh, with their bodily eyes, beheld his glory. And perhaps we are ready to envy them the privilege. But this sight of him was not accompanied with salvation. "Ye also," said he, "have seen me, and believed not;" and to those who were then before him, he complained, "Ye will not come unto me, that ye might have life."

On the other hand, there is a substitute for this sight of him, and it is infinitely more available. And he is the subject of it who sees him, not with the eye of the body, but with the eye of the mind; not with the eye of sense, but with the eye of faith. "He that seeth the Son, and believeth on him, hath everlasting life." There is spiritual perception of him, as much distinguished from common knowledge as the taste of a thing is from the report of it. Thus the apostle says, "It pleased God to reveal his Son in me:" and, speaking of all Christians, as well as of himself, he adds, He "hath shined in our hearts, to give the light of the knowledge of the glory of God in the face of Jesus Christ."

The sight of the Savior will be evinced by certain effects. Self will be lowered. What can he think of his own excellencies who has been at the court above, and seen the King in his beauty? Self-admiration and self-dependence will then be at an end. "The proud looks shall be humbled, and the lofty looks shall be laid low; and the Lord alone shall be exalted in that day." So it was with Job: "Now mine eye seeth thee; wherefore I abhor myself, repenting in dust and ashes." So it was with Isaiah; Wo is me, for I am undone; for I am a man of unclean lips, and I dwell among a people of unclean lips: for mine eyes have seen the King, the Lord of hosts." The world will fade away, and lose its charms. The Sun of Righteousness will shine it out; as the luminaries of the night disappear in the effulgence of day. Attachment will result from it. Love enters by the eye. And faith is the same to the soul as this sense is to the body: therefore, to them "that believe, he is precious." He "dwells in the heart of faith." There will also necessarily arise a desire after more acquaintance and intercourse with him. Thus Paul, not because he was ignorant of him, but because he knew him, said, "That I may know him." There will also be an earnest desire to recommend him to others. As soon as Andrew knew him, he found his brother Simon, and brought him to Jesus. So did Philip his friend Nathaniel. And so did the woman of Samaria her fellow citizens.

This sight of him is a very distinguished privilege: and as it is said of his immediate followers, "Then were the disciples glad when they saw the Lord;" so we, believing, rejoice with joy unspeakable, and full of glory. There is enough in him, perceptible to the view of faith, to induce us to rejoice in the Lord *always.* But how delightful is the sight of him in the hour of conviction! A drowning man, seeing a deliverer in a boat, hastening to his assistance—a debtor, on his way to prison, seeing a surety at hand, to undertake for him—a man dying of hunger, seeing the most delicious food—never saw what I saw, when, sensible of my state and danger, and feeling myself ready to perish, my heart revived at the view of such a Savior—in his suitableness to my condition—in his all-sufficiency for my relief—and I was enabled to hope in his mercy.

—How delightful is the sight of him in the hour of desertion! If he withdraws from me, it is not to show his sovereignty, but to correct for sin: and when he hides his face I am troubled. Then creatures are all miserable comforters. Then sigh, O that it was with me as in months past! Then I pray, Restore unto me the joy of thy salvation. But when he appears, and smiles again, it is more than the joys of morning after a darksome night: or of spring, after the dreariness of winter. How delightful is the sight of him in the hour of trouble! It is then, when our purposes are broken off, even the thoughts of our hearts; when enemies oppose; when friends fail or betray; when health declines; it is then we look toward Him, who is the consolation of Israel, and say, "This same shall comfort us:" "This man shall be the peace, when the Assyrian cometh into the land." How delightful is the sight of him in the hour of death! It loosened Simeon from all below, and made him more than willing to depart—wishing, now he had seen him, to defile, to vex his eyes with nothing else. And how many have since said,

"Jesus the vision of thy face
"Hath overpowering charms;
"Scarce shall I feel death's cold embrace,
"If Christ be in my arms.

"Then, while ye hear my heart-strings break
"How sweet my minutes roll!
"A mortal paleness on my cheek,
"And glory in my soul!"

Such are the influence and the blessedness of a sight of him, by faith, here. But what is heaven? "His servants shall serve him; and they shall see his face." "Father, I will that they whom thou hast given me, be with me where I am to behold my glory." But how superior will that sight be to all our present apprehensions of him! It will be clear. It will be ceaseless. It will be uninterrupted. It will be perfect. It will be immediate. Whatever we have read or heard of him before, we shall then exclaim, with the queen of Sheba at the sight of Solomon, "The half was not told me!"

"'Tis pleasant to believe thy grace,
"But we would rather see;
"We would be absent from the flesh,
"And present, Lord, with thee."

OCTOBER 21.—"O that there were such a heart in them, that they would fear me, and keep all my commandments, always, that it might be well with them, and with their children for ever."—Deuteronomy, v, 29.

HERE we see the character of real religion. The seat of it is the *heart*—The principle of it is the *fear of God*—the expression of it is *keeping* His *commandments; all* of them; and *always.*

We have also the benefit resulting from it. The good is personal—that it might be well with *them.* And relative—and with their *children.* And durable—for *ever.*

But how lovely does God appear in the concern he here expresses! "O that there were such a heart in them, that they would fear me, and keep all my commandments always, that it might be well with them, and their children, for ever!" It is the language of complaint. It is as much as to say, "But I do not find it so." Is He then disappointed? Not as to fact—for he knows all things. But he is, as to right. Surely He may justly expect from us an attention to his voice, and the improvement of the means and advantages with which we are favored. And when he meets with nothing of this, he has reason to complain—And this is the meaning when he says, "What more could have been done for my vineyard, and I have not done it? Wherefore when I looked that it should bring forth grapes, brought it forth wild grapes?" "These three years I came seeking fruit, and finding none."

—It is the expression of desire. We are aware that when the Scripture ascribes human attributes and feelings to God, they must be understood according to the perfection of his nature. They cannot mean precisely the same in him they do in us. Yet there is always a *truth* which is the basis of all such metaphorical representations. And a slavish adherence to systematic divinity has much injured some of the finest passages of Revelation; and which were intended to be felt, rather than criticised. Let it not therefore be objected, that "our God is in the heavens, he hath done whatsoever he pleaseth;" and asked, "Who hath resisted his will?" for this is his own language, "O that there was such a heart in them!" "O that thou hadst hearkened to my commandments; then had thy peace been as a river, and thy righteousness like the waves of the sea!" "How often would I have gathered thee as a hen gathereth her chickens under her wing, and ye would not!" Yes, these are his own words—the expressions of a God that cannot lie. This affords me every encouragement I want. Unworthy as I am, I see that he does not abandon me. He is willing to save me. He is waiting to be gracious; and exalted to have mercy upon me. What is the inability of men to harmonize such declarations, and some other parts of their creed, to the oath of the living God—"As I live, saith the Lord, I have no pleasure in the death of him that dieth: wherefore, turn and live ye."

—It is the dictate of parental solicitude. It is the voice, not of a severe legislator or judge, but of a Father; a Father who spared not his own son, but delivered him up for us all; a Father who does not afflict willingly, nor grieve the children of men; a Father who says of the refractory child, "How shall I give thee up, Ephraim? how shall I deliver thee, Israel? how shall I make thee as Admah? how shall I set thee as Zeboim? mine heart is turned within me, my repentings are kindled together;" a Father who says of the relenting, self-bemoaning child, "Is Ephraim my dear son? is he a pleasant child? for since I spake against him, I do earnestly remember him still: therefore my bowels are troubled for him; I will surely have mercy upon him, saith the Lord." How often does he assume this relation, in order to deprive his greatness of terror; and to render it our encouragement and our confidence! And not only has he said, "Like a father pitieth his children, so the Lord pitieth them that fear him:" but he has taken for an image of his tenderness the heart of a mother—and surely all that is paternal indwells there: "As one whom his mother comforteth so will I comfort you." "Can a woman forget her sucking child, that she should not have compassion on the son of her womb? She may." Ah! ye mothers, your affection is ice; your heart is iron, compared with his! "yet will I not forget thee."

—Surely, "he that loveth not, knoweth not God—for God is love." *Can* this encourage us to sin? *Can* we grieve *his* Holy Spirit? *Can* we hear *him* saying in *vain*, "O do not that abominable thing which I hate?" "Or despisest thou the riches of his goodness, and forbearance, and long suffering; not knowing that the goodness of God leadeth thee to repentance: but, after, thy hardness and impenitent heart, treasurest up unto thyself wrath against the day of wrath, and revelation of the righteous judgment of God?"

October 22.—"I am come that they might have life."—John, x, 10.

Though men have differed in their definitions of life, they have all agreed in their estimation of it. Even the father of lies spake truth when he said, Skin for skin, yea, all that a man hath will he give for his life. Yet what is this life which we so highly prize? nourish with so much care? and to preserve which, we are ready to make every kind of sacrifice? What is it in duration? "A vapor that appeareth for a little time, and then vanisheth away." What is it in dignity? "We spend our years as a tale that is told." What is it in enjoyment? Hear Jacob—"Few, and full of evils, have been the days of the years of my pilgrimage." "But his was, perhaps, a peculiar case." What says Job? "*Man*, that is born of a woman, is of few days, and full of trouble" "But he expressed himself under depression and gloom."

What then says Solomon, who withheld his heart from no joy? "All is vanity and vexation of spirit." But here is a life that deserves the name; a life, spiritual in its nature; endless in its continuance; consisting not of an immortality of being only, but of blessedness; commencing in grace, completed in glory; and emphatically called, The Life of God. Of this life, the Lord Jesus here speaks; "I am come that they might have life."

—He came to *procure it for us.* The blessing comes every way free to us—but it cost him dear. If we live, he must die. "The bread," said he, "which I give, is my flesh, which I shall give for the life of the world." Princes have often sacrificed the lives of their subjects to their own: yea, and where their own have not been in danger, they have offered thousands of victims on the altar of their vanity or revenge—but the Prince of Peace gave his life a ransom for many. He was poor. He was a man of sorrows. You see him agonizing in the garden; and hear him exclaiming on the cross, "My God! my God! why hast thou forsaken me?" Why is all this? Is he guilty? "In him was no sin." Yet he was esteemed stricken, smitten of God, and afflicted. And so he was—but "he was wounded for our transgressions; he was bruised for our iniquities: the chastisement of our peace was upon him, and by his stripes we are healed." "One died for all.'

—He came to *announce it to us.* We can derive no benefit from him, without a dependence upon him; an application to him; a connexion with him. But all this requires the knowledge of him: and therefore says God, "By his knowledge shall my righteous servant justify many; for he shall bear their iniquities." It is true, we are justified by faith—but "how can we believe in him, of whom we have not heard? and how can we hear, without a preacher?" He therefore "came and preached Peace." "I am come," said he, "a light into the world, that whosoever believeth on me should not walk in darkness, but have the light of life." He proclaimed the nature of his life; the source of it; the medium of it; the certainty of it; the present enjoyment of it. His disciples, therefore, well said, To whom should we go, but unto thee? thou hast the words of eternal life. And these words he dispensed, not only by his personal ministry, but by the instrumentality of others. What the Apostles did, he did; because he sent them, and qualified them: he inspired them, and commanded them to preach the Gospel to every creature, and also to record it, for the use of all future ages; so that we can read what they delivered.

—He came to *produce it in us.* "The Son quickeneth whom he will." He received, in consequence of his death, the whole dispensation of the Holy Ghost; and hence it is called, "The Spirit of Christ." And this Spirit is, as the Apostle calls it, the Spirit of life in Christ Jesus, which makes us free from the law of sin and death. Nothing less than this can insure the result. It is above the efficiency of education; of example; of moral suasion; and of all the means of grace—without the grace of the means. The gospel cannot accomplish it, if it comes in word only —it is the Spirit that giveth life. The servant of the Lord is like

Gehazi: he went and laid the staff upon the child, but no life appeared till his master himself came. Who, then, is Paul? and who is Apollos? but ministers by whom ye believed, even as the Lord gave to every man? And they who were once dead in trespasses and sins, but are now walking in newness of life, will acknowledge that he quickened them; and will readily give him the glory that is due to his holy name.

—In this blessed business, therefore, he is all in all—he came that we might have life—came to procure it for us, as our Priest—to announce it as our Prophet—to produce it, as our King. To obtain it, by his blood. To publish it by his Gospel. To bestow it by his Spirit. He is therefore called, as well he may, this life itself in the abstract—when he who is our life shall appear, we shall also appear with him in glory.

But how many neglect him, and compel him to complain, Ye will not come unto me that ye might have life! Hence the heinousness of their guilt, and the dreadfulness of their condemnation. Whatever difficulties attend this truth—in connexion with any other, they attach only to the explanation; not to the fact itself. Nothing can be clearer, from the Scripture, than that they who thus perish will destroy themselves, and be treated as spiritual suicides.

But if we desire this life, can we suppose the Savior will refuse us, when we go to him for—the very purpose—for which he came? Did he ever refuse any? Can he refuse any? He cannot. He has bound himself, "HIM THAT COMETH UNTO ME, I WILL IN NO WISE CAST OUT."

OCTOBER 23.—"**And that they might have it more abundantly.**"—**John, x, 10.**

THUS he not only informs us of the design of his advent; "I am come that they might have life;" but, like himself, adds the extensiveness of it, "and that they might have it more abundantly." This may be exemplified in three comparisons.

—We have life more abundantly than *Adam*. His life, before the Fall, was a noble life; but it is surpassed by the Christian's. This is firmer as to its tenure. The life of innocency was precarious. It was suspended on the fallible will of man. The stock was in Adam's own hands: and he failed, and ruined all his posterity. But this life can never be destroyed. The Head of the new Covenant ever liveth; and because he lives, his people shall live also; I give unto them eternal life, and they shall never perish. It is richer as to its quality. The first man is of the earth, earthy; the second man is the Lord from heaven. As is the earthy, such are they also that are earthy: and as is the heavenly, such are they also that are heavenly. It is not the primeval body of Adam which is to be the model in our resurrection, but the glorious body of the Savior. We are to bear the image of the heavenly. Had Adam remained innocent, though he would never have died, yet must he have experienced a change before he could have been capable of enjoying the blessedness which the poorest Christian expects: for flesh and blood cannot inherit the kingdom of God. After a proper trial of his obedience, he would have been removed to a higher state: but even then he must have been a stranger to many interesting feelings and delightful enjoyments, arising from all the operations of divine grace in our recovery from the depths of the Fall, to the glories of heaven. Eden was not equal to the Paradise above. The creation of man is excelled by his redemption. The righteousness of a perfect creature is far below the righteousness of God, in which we are not justified, but "exalted."

—We have life more abundantly than the *Jewish Church.* They derived their life from the same source with us; and it was essentially the same source with ours: but we have it more plenteously as to knowledge, liberty, and enjoyment. We are fully justified in considering our spiritual advantages as very superior to their privileges, by our Savior himself, who said to his disciples, "Blessed are your eyes, for they see: and your ears for they hear. For verily I say unto you, That many prophets and righteous men have desired to see those things which ye see, and have not seen them; and to hear those things which ye hear, and have not heard them." They had the types and shadows; we have the very image of the thing. They saw the Messiah afar off, and under a veil; he is with us, and we behold him with open face. They had the first-fruits; we have the whole vintage. They had the dawn; we have the full day—God having provided some better thing for us, that they without us should not be made perfect. They, from their comparative darkness, were inspired with more disquiet; they received the spirit of bondage to fear; we receive the Spirit of adoption, whereby we cry Abba, Father. The way into the holiest was not then made manifest; the people never entered where God dwelt between the Cherubim; the high Priest only went in; and he only once a year. But we have all boldness to enter into the holiest by the blood of Jesus: and may draw near in full assurance of faith. They came to a material mountain, and that burned with fire, and unto blackness and darkness, and the sound of a trumpet, and the voice of words; which voice they that heard entreated that the word should not be spoken to them any more. "But we are come unto mount Sion, and unto the city of the living God, the heavenly Jerusalem, and to an innumerable company of angels, to the general assembly and Church of the first-born, which are written in heaven, and to God the Judge of all, and to the spirits of just men made perfect, and to Jesus the mediator of the new covenant, and to the blood of sprinkling, that speaketh better things than that of Abel."

—We have life more abundantly than we had it *ourselves before.* Vital religion, though imperfect, is growing and progressive. Under the influences of the Holy Spirit, we go from strength to strength in our course, and are renewed day by day in our experience. There is life in an acorn, but the oak has it more abundantly. There is wheat in the blade, but how much more in the full corn in the ear! What a difference between Sir Isaac Newton when a babe on his mother's knee, and a philosopher measuring the distances of the planets! "Why a man can but live." Indeed do you sometimes say, I am all languor; I have no life in me? At other times you are all vigor and alacrity. How you live then! What a difference between a man confined in a hospital, and a man at large, able to fill and enjoy his station. A man may be alive, and be blind, and deaf, and lame, and able to eat nothing with a relish. Some real Christians are little better than this—they are—this is all—just alive! But they are to be suspected who only are anxious to know that they have the reality of divine grace, while they are regardless of increase in the divine ,ife. More is desirable, more is attainable. He came not only that we might have life—but have it more abundantly.

Wherefore pray, "that he would grant you, according to the riches of his glory, to be strengthened with might by his Spirit in the inner man; that Christ may dwell in your hearts by faith; that ye, being rooted and grounded in love, may be able to comprehend with all saints what is the breadth, and length, and depth, and height; and to know the love of Christ, which passeth knowledge, that ye might be filled with all the fullness of God."

OCTOBER 24.—"**And I will give him the morning star.**"—**Revelations, ii. 28.**

If we found any difficulty in determining the subject of this promise, we could refer to the Speaker's own declaration, in another part of this Book—"I am the root and offspring of David, the bright and the morning star." Here we see the advantage of comparing one passage of Scripture with another. What is general in one is particularized in another; and what is darker in one is clearer in another.

Does he then promise *himself*—I will give him the morning star? Yes. He is the guide and the way: the teacher and the lesson: the priest and the sacrifice: the giver and the gift. He is all in all. By promising himself, he would teach us to look for happiness in himself, and not in the creature. He also knew that nothing else could satisfy the minds of his people, who would be sure to say,

"Without thy grace and thyself,
"I were a wretch undone."

"Give what thou canst—without thee, we are poor;
"And with thee, rich, take what thou wilt away."

And thus also he would encourage their expectations: for what will he withhold, if he gives himself? Therefore, because he could promise no greater, he promised himself. The bestowment of heaven would have been less than the bestowment of himself: for heaven is, so to speak, but a part of him. He that buildeth the house hath more honor than the house.

But has he not already given himself to his people? And yet he speaks as if the donation was future—I *will* give him the morning star. Yes; as soon as they believed on him they received him, and had the privilege of becoming the sons of God. But as to their knowledge, experience, and enjoyment; he communicates himselt to them by degrees. The apostle therefore says, after many years of communion with him, That I *may* win Christ, and be found in him: that I *may* know him. The promise *must* be principally accomplished hereafter. We *could* not receive him in all his fullness now. Our place, our condition, our powers, forbid. Flesh and blood cannot inherit the kingdom of God.

—But let me survey the image—I will give him the *morning star*. The morning star, to our view, is the most beautiful and luminous. It is distinguished by its sparkling brightness. Many resemble Christ; but in all things he has the pre-eminence. Prophets, priests, and kings, have been anointed, as well as he; but he was anointed with the oil of gladness above his fellows. O how great is his beauty: He is fairer than the children of men; fairer than the children of God; fairer than the sons of God who shouted for joy at the creation—Yea, he is altogether lovely.

But the thing is, that this luminary is the harbinger of day: therefore it is called the day star; and the morning star. The truth of the image, therefore, is to assure us, that to those who see Christ, and believe on him, there is a glorious season drawing on. The night of ignorance, and error, and sin, and sorrow, with them, is rapidly terminating. Weeping may endure for the night; but joy cometh in the morning. Look—look, Christians! There is the shining pledge. It never failed yet—It cannot deceive. Now is your salvation nearer than when you believed. The NIGHT is far spent, the DAY is at hand. And then your sun shall no more go down.

Let this promise put me and keep me in a proper frame of mind. Let it raise me above the world. Let it teach me, in whatsoever state I am, therewith to be content. Let it induce me to rejoice evermore; yea, in every thing to give thanks. To the upright there ariseth *light* in the darkness. If in the world I have tribulation, in him I have peace. Many things are denied me; but I can dispense with them, since he is mine. Why should I envy others? They succeed, they gain, they have. But *I* have the morning star.

"What others value, I resign:
'Lord, 'tis enough that THOU art mine:
"I shall behold thy blissful face,
"And stand, complete, in righteousness!"

OCTOBER 25.—"I am the door; by me if any man enter in, he shall be saved, and shall go in and out, and find pasture."—John, x, 9.

A DOOR is a very familiar and striking representation of the Lord Jesus. It seems hardly necessary to remark, that it must be a metaphor. Yet the papists, from taking literally what is spoken in a similar instance, have introduced the monstrous doctrine of transubstantiation. Because, when he took the bread and the wine, our Savior said, This *is* my body, and this *is* my blood; they believe that the disciples received his very body and blood; and that every communicant does the same now, when the priest has consecrated the elements: and, say they, we only take him at his word—nothing can be plainer. Upon the same principle, we may say he is timber and nails: for he says—what can be clearer? I am the door. But can any man of common sense—can a child suppose, that he means any thing more than that a door is an image of him?

—And the design of the allusion is obvious. A door is the medium of passage—And Jesus stands between God and us. He is the mediator of the new covenant. God comes to us through him: and all his blessings are conveyed to us by him. And we approach God through him. I am the way, said he—No man cometh unto the Father, but by me. And as with regard to our persons, we come unto God by him; so, with regard to our services, we offer up spiritual sacrifices, acceptable to God by Jesus Christ. And with regard to both, we have boldness and access, with confidence, by the faith of him.

—But how is the person described, who derives benefit from him? He makes use of him for this purpose—"*By* me if any man *enter* in." This supposes a spiritual concern. Many are careless about their souls. They have never been convinced of sin: never induced from an apprehension of their danger, to cry, What must I do to be saved? They are men of the world; and all their anxieties are confined within the narrow bound of time and sense. Others, if in a degree awakened, are not enlightened. Their concern is erroneously directed—for there is a way which seemeth right unto a man; but it ends in death. There is a refuge that cannot abide the storm. There is a hope that is like the spider's web—as curiously wrought, and as easily destroyed. The case is this. There is salvation in none other than in Him, who was delivered for our offences, and was raised again for our justification. In the Lord alone have we righteousness and strength. To him therefore must men come. And to him the Christian *does* come. He knows, not only that there is no salvation for him out of Christ, but that there is no salvation in him, without a dependence upon him, and an application to him. He knows that, as a medicine never taken can never cure; and as food never eaten can never nourish, so an unapplied Savior is no Savior to him. He therefore makes use of Christ for every end he is revealed to answer. He builds upon him, as a foundation. As a way, he walks in him. As a door, by him he enters in.

—And what are the advantages he obtains when admitted? *Safety*—"He shall be saved." Saved from the curse of the law, and the wrath to come—Saved from the roaring lion who goeth about seeking whom he may devour—Saved from the King of Terrors—Saved from a world lying in wickedness—Saved from an evil heart of unbelief, in departing from the living God—Saved in the Lord, with an everlasting salvation. *Liberty*—"He shall go in and out." A man is free in his own house. He goes in and out at his pleasure—and when he goes out, he is not shut out like a stranger; and when he goes in, he is not shut in like a criminal. This, too, is the privilege of sheep under the care of a good shepherd. They go in—but if they could not go out, the fold would be a prison. They therefore, at night, go in for protection; and in the morning, go out for food. The expression, therefore, is used in the Scripture as significant of freedom: and the meaning is, that what is done for the Christian's safety does not compromise his liberty. He knows the truth; and the truth makes him free: and he is free indeed—free, to go wherever he pleases in Immanuel's land—free, to partake of all the privileges of the sons of God. *Plenty*—"And find pasture." Ah! said one of them, realizing this, "The Lord is my shepherd; I shall not want. He maketh me to lie down in green pastures: he leadeth me beside the still waters." So Isaiah—"They shall feed in the ways"—the ways of his commandments, ordinances, and dispensations—"and their pasture shall be in all high places"—where they cannot be hid; but where they may seem unlikely to find supplies; as elevations, especially in warm countries, are commonly barren—but he feels them, while he lifts them up, for ever. Religion raises them; but not into regions of empty speculation—for it is added, "They shall not hunger nor thirst: neither shall the heat nor sun smite them, for he that hath mercy on them shall lead them, even by the springs of water shall he guide them."

OCTOBER 26.—"O Jerusalem! wash thine heart from wickedness, that thou mayest be saved."—Jeremiah, iv, 14.

THOUGH these words are addressed to Jerusalem: by a principle of the fairest reasoning they extend to every individual who needs the same purification and deliverance. And who does not?—Yea, the circumstance strengthens the argument. Jerusalem was called the Holy City; the City of the living God: there stood his temple; there were his servants to make known his will; they had Moses and the prophets. If *they* stood in need of such an address, is it needless for us? With all their unbelief and ingratitude, disobedience and perverseness, they were fair specimens of the human race. In Adam, all died; and from him we derive a mortal, and therefore a depraved nature—What is *man*, that *he* should be clean, or he that is born of a woman, that he should be righteous? All, therefore need pardoning mercy, and sanctifying grace—All need to be saved by the washing of regeneration, and the renewing of the Holy Ghost. But here are two difficulties.

First. God himself is represented as concerned for the success of the measure; "O Jerusalem! wash thine heart from wickedness, that thou mayest be saved." This interjection, with us, often implies weakness and grief, as well as desire. We must therefore take care how we apply such expressions to God, lest we degrade the perfections of his nature. He speaks to us after the manner of men: but his condescension must not rob him of his glory. Yet his language is not devoid of truth. However metaphorical it may be, there is in it a reality that more than justifies it. To which we may add, that even grief and weaknesss had better be ascribed to God than insincerity. Let us be assured of this, that he means what he says. While he hates our sins, he loves our souls, and is not willing that any should perish, but that all should come to repentance. He is not only the righteous Governor, but the kind Father. This is the lovely character under which he delights to display himself. Hence his expostulation with himself, "How shall I give thee up, Ephraim? How shall I deliver thee, Israel? How shall I make thee as Admah? How shall I set thee as Zeboim? Mine heart is turned within me, my repentings are kindled together." Hence the oath he has taken—"As I live, saith the Lord, I have no pleasure in the death of him that dieth: wherefore turn and live ye." Hence the sacrifice of the cross—"He that spared not his own Son, but delivered him up for us all, how shall he not with him also freely give us all things?" Hence all the means he is incessantly employing to awaken and engage our attention to the things that belong to our peace. Hence he has established the ministry of reconciliation, and sends forth his servants to beseech us, in his name, to be reconciled unto God.

Secondly. The work is considered as of our own achieving; and *we* are called upon to cleanse our hearts from wickedness. It would be a contradiction of the whole Bible, were we to be regarded as the authors. But we are the instruments. God not only worketh in us, but by us. And hence, though all is of grace, yet *we* "will and do." *We* believe and repent, and hold on our way, and wax stronger and stronger. It would be an abuse of the language to infer from it that we have power to do this naturally, or of ourselves—yet the address would be absurd, had we not the ability in some other way. God has the right to command, though we have lost the power to obey; but this is not the ground of the injunction. If in him our help was not found, he would not thus speak to us. But it is. His grace is sufficient for us. Every thing necessary for our deliverance from sin is provided and prevented in the Gospel: and we must have recourse to it in the use of the means which he has ordained. The address, therefore, is not like a command to a man to flee—a thing unnatural; and which he cannot enable himself to do: but like a command to a man, who was ready to perish for want, to take and eat. Though he has nothing of his own, he has shown him at hand every kind of supply, and he is welcome to partake of it. Or, like a command to a sick man to be cured: he cannot indeed heal himself, but he has one near him who is able and willing to heal him, and asks, Wilt thou be made whole? And to this remedy he is to submit. All such commands are designed to make us sensible of our wants and weakness, and to bring us upon our knees. *Then* every thing is possible. Forgiveness and sanctification are attainable—are certain. And having this hope in us, we purify ourselves even as he is pure. Having these promises, we cleanse ourselves from all filthiness of flesh and spirit, perfecting holiness in the fear of God. Let the work itself furnish our next meditation.

OCTOBER 27.—**"O Jerusalem! wash thine heart from thy wickedness, that thou mayest be saved."—*Jeremiah* iv, 14.**

THE words remind us that sin is of a defiling nature. It is therefore held forth by every kind of uncleanness—by wounds, and bruises, and putrifying sores; by leprosy and plague; by mire and dirt; by the rottenness and corruption of the grave. It defiles every thing it touches. In consequence of it, the whole creation groaneth; and all our eyes behold is doomed to perish, like the house of the leper, under the law, because of the infection of the inhabitant. "O do not," says God, "the abominable thing I hate."

"My soul loathed them." How great must that evil be which can induce the Creator to loathe the work of his own hands! The Father of all to loathe his very offspring! And even the "God of love, the very essence of mercy, to say to them at last, "Depart, ye cursed, into everlasting fire, prepared for the devil and his angels!" O my soul, does not sin appear to thee, as it does to Him—exceeding sinful?

Secondly. That the purification we need extends to the heart: "Wash thine heart from wickedness." The reason is, because this is the very seat of the pollution. Some, who know their lives are open to censure, will yet plead for the goodness of their hearts. But a good heart will always produce a good life, as naturally as a good tree yieldeth good fruit. Others contend that our corruption is not innate, but acquired; derived, not from within, but from without. Yet says the faithful and true Witness, "From *within*, out of the *heart* of men proceed evil thoughts, adulteries, fornications, murders, thefts, covetousness, wickedness, deceit, lasciviousness, an evil eye, blasphemy, pride, foolishness: all these evil things come from within, and defile the man. Hence,

"No outward forms can make us clean, | "The leprosy lies deep within."

And we must be pure in heart. How is this to be ascertained? By our deliverance from the *love* of sin. The love of sin defiles even more than the practice. But every man that is renewed in the spirit of his mind not only avoids sin, but hates it. He feels it to be his burden and his grief. And, while any of the abomination continues adherent to him, he exclaims, O wretched man that I am! who shall deliver me from the body of this death!

Thirdly. This purification is connected with salvation, "Wash thine heart from wickedness, that thou mayest be saved." It is *necessary* to salvation. Without holiness no man shall see the Lord. If I wash thee not, thou hast no part with me. The unrighteous shall not inherit the kingdom of God. Indeed, in such a state, and with such a disposition, the enjoyment of heaven is as impossible as the attainment. The exclusion, therefore, is not arbitrary, but unavoidable.—It will *certainly terminate* in salvation. This is not fully implied in the declaration, but it is made the matter of express promise: "Let the wicked forsake his way, and the unrighteous man his thoughts, and let him return unto the Lord, and he will have mercy upon him, and to our God, for he will abundantly pardon." It is a *part of salvation*. The man who has experienced it is not only an heir, but a subject of the blessedness. He has, not indeed the perfection of the thing, but he has more than the title and the pledge—he has the beginning. Being made free from sin, and become the servant of God, he has his fruit unto holiness, and the end everlasting life.

OCTOBER 28.--"If any man love God, the same is known of him." --1 Cor. viii, 3.

THERE is nothing so mortifying to men as inattention and neglect. Many would rather be hated than neglected. The one implies that they are deemed something; the other shows that they are considered as beneath notice. The one rouses, the other annihilates. Hence we are anxious to be known of our fellow creatures, especially those who are placed above us—and can take us by the hand—and raise us up—and put us forward in life. Yet, as men of low degree are vanity, so men of high degree are a lie. After all our servile attentions and compliances, we are never sure of gaining their regard. And what could even their zeal do for us in our most important interests? O let us turn our anxiety another way. Let us sanctify it. Let us make it the medium of our happiness. Let us be concerned to please God. Then we shall be sure to succeed, and success will be every thing. For in his favor is life. "If any man love God, the same is known of him."

This knowledge being spoken of as the highest privilege, it must intend much more than a mere acquaintance with the subjects of it: for thus all are known of him.

The least thing intended is *discernment*. The Lord knows their condition. Knows all their walking through this great wilderness. Knows all their trials. Knows the pressure of every burden they bear. Knows their frame; and remembers that they are dust. He perceives all their dangers: their enemies may plot against them, but they do it unconsciously in the sight of their Father and Friend. And, as to their persons, the Lord knoweth them that are his. He never overlooks them in the crowd. If there was only one of them in a village, or city, or nation, he would have his eye upon him. However misrepresented and reproached, he recognizes them as upright before him. However obscure their condition, he views them as the excellent of the earth. However little their faith, he watches the tears with which they cry, Lord, I believe; help thou mine unbelief. However encompassed with infirmities which sometimes perplex others, he who knows what is the mind of the Spirit, knoweth that they love him. We can only judge of motives by actions. But God judges of actions by motives. He seeth the heart; in consequence of which, in estimating the services of his people, he admits into the amount, not only all they do, but all they design to do, and wish to do, when they are hindered; and accepts them according to what they have, and not according to what they have not. Even this is a source of satisfaction to the Christian.

—But this knowledge, also, takes in *approbation*. The Lord knoweth the way of the righteous. So he does the way of the ungodly. But the meaning is, he approves it; he commends it. The Lord taketh pleasure in them that fear him, in them that hope in his mercy. He regards them with complacency, as the work of his own hands. He esteems them as his jewels, his bride, his offspring. Their prayer is his delight; their alms, the odor of a sweet smell. Approbation must be valued according to the condition and character of the being from whom it comes. It would be a reproach to pass for the favorite of Satan. The first Christians would also have deemed the friendship of the world no recommendation; for they were satisfied to say, "The world knoweth us not; for it knew him not." A great personage reflects a lustre upon a near object; a person would be ambitious to be seen intimate with the king. And to live in the affections of the wise and good, says a fine writer, is like breathing in an eastern spice grove. What a dignity is it, then, to walk with God! What a blessedness to hear *him* say, "Since thou wast precious in my sight, thou hast been honorable, and I have loved thee!" And what shall be done for the man whom the King of kings delighteth to honor?

—For this knowledge is acknowledgment. The apostle, admonishing the Thessalonians, says, "Know them that labor among you, and over you in the Lord"—that is, own them with respect, and verbally and practically treat them as their office requires. Thus God claims his people. He owns them in the dispensations of his providence, and in the agency of his grace. He signalizes them in life. He does it often more peculiarly in death, so that his saints are joyful in glory, and shout aloud upon their beds, and induce their very enemies to exclaim, Let me die the death of the righteous, and let my last end be like his! But, above all, they shall be mine, saith the Lord, in that day, when I make up my jewels. He will confess them before the assembled earth and heavens, and place them nearer the throne than angels.

Of what importance, then, is the love of God! And how carefully should we inquire whether it be shed abroad in our hearts! If *any* man love Him, the same is known of him—But *no* other. Nothing can be a substitute for this affection. Without it our knowledge, our gifts, our faith itself, are vain. If we have any thing like devotion, it is formality. If we have peace, it is delusion. If we have safety, it is a refuge of lies. And though we may go to the very door of heaven, and knock, and say, Lord, Lord, open unto us—he will profess, "I never knew you—Depart."

"Let me love thee more and more—
"If I love at all I pray;
"If I have not loved before,
"Help me to begin to-day."

OCTOBER 29.—"In the day of my trouble I will call upon thee."—Psalm lxxxvi, 7.

THIS was the language of David. David was a king, and a saint. He was pre-eminently great and good—yet neither does his rank or his godliness exempt him from trouble. But it is well to see what such a man does when trouble cometh upon him. And here we have his resolution: "In the day of my trouble I will call upon thee."

This was the wisest thing he could do; and it is the best thing we can do. For, first, Prayer is enjoined upon us in trouble. The will of God is our rule. And who can be ignorant of his command? Who has not read, "Is any afflicted? Let him pray."

Secondly. Prayer is the design of trouble. He does not afflict willingly, or grieve the children of men. He has an end worthy his wisdom and his goodness, to answer by every trial. It is to bring us to himself—and to bring us nearer to himself. It is to quicken us to pray more frequently, more earnestly; "I will go and return to my place, till they acknowledge their offence and seek my face—In their affliction they will seek me early."

Thirdly. Prayer is the evidence that trouble is sanctified. It is a great thing not to lose a trial. It is never neutral in its effect. It always injures, or improves. It is worse than nothing when it sends us to the creature, either in a way of accusation or relief. But when we turn to Him that smiteth us; and acknowledge that his judgments are right, and cast ourselves at his feet, resolved, if we perish, *there* to die—we need not say, with Job, "I am afraid of all my sorrows," but confess, with David, "It is good for me that I have been afflicted."

Fourthly. Prayer is the solace of trouble. There is some relief in tears, and therefore Nature is provided with them. It eases and soothes the bursting heart, to pour our grief into the ear of a friend, who, having rejoiced when we rejoiced, will weep when we weep. But oh! how good is it to draw near to God! How delightful is it, like Job, to pour out our tears unto him, and resemble the child that sobs himself asleep in his mother's arms, and on his mother's breast! "A glorious high throne from the beginning," says the church, "has been the place of our sanctuary." A temple that no evil enters; an asylum that no enemy invades. There the wicked cease from troubling, and there the weary are at rest.

Fifthly. Prayer is the medium of our deliverance from trouble. For this release we are allowed to be concerned. But we must seek it from God. And in doing this, we have not only his power to encourage us, and nothing is too hard for him—He can turn the shadow of death into the morning: but his goodness and love; and like as a father pitieth his children, so the Lord pitieth them that fear him. Yes, more: we have his faithfulness and truth; that we shall not, cannot, seek him in vain. He has engaged to appear to our joy; not indeed in our time and way, but in his own. He has bound himself, and put the bond into our hand: and we can produce it; and plead it; and be surer of the fulfillment, than the continuance of heaven and earth. For heaven and earth shall pass away, but his word shall not pass. And here it is, "Call upon me in the day of trouble, and I will deliver thee, and thou shalt glorify me." "Because he hath set his love upon me, therefore will I deliver him: I will set him on high, because he hath known my name. He shall call upon me, and I will answer him: I will be with him in trouble; I will deliver him and honor him."

OCTOBER 30.—"Messiah the Prince."—Daniel, ix, 25.

THIS is not the only character of the Messiah. But we must connect it with every representation we have of him, that his glory may not be injured by his condescension; nor his authority diminished by his kindness. Is he exalted at the right hand of God. It is to be "a Prince," as well as "a Savior." Is he a Priest? He is "a Priest upon his throne."

How is this Prince designated?

He is "the Prince of the *kings of the earth*." They often think little of him; and imagining themselves their own, say, Who is lord over us? But wherein they deal proudly, he is above them. They are all raised by his power, and controllable by his will; and subservient to his designs: and amenable to his tribunal. Hence his avowal—"By me kings reign, and princes decree justice. By me princes rule, and nobles, even all the judges of the earth. Hence the admonition, "Be wise now therefore, O ye kings; be instructed ye judges of the earth. Serve the Lord with fear, and rejoice with trembling. Kiss the Son, lest he be angry, and ye perish from the way, when his wrath is kindled but a little. Blessed are all they that put their trust in him."

He is "the Prince of *Peace*." He came to mediate between heaven and earth: and we are reconciled unto God by the death of his Son. Men talk of making their peace with God. If our tears, or works, or alms, could have availed for this purpose, the world would never have witnessed the sufferings of Christ. But he made peace by the blood of his Cross. One died for all—And he was more than all. The value of his sacrifice was infinite: and every end that could have been answered by the destruction of a world of sinners, has been equally and better answered by the death of the Savior. Nothing will effectually satisfy an awakened conscience but what satisfied the justice of God. Yet, surely *this* will suffice! When, therefore, it is apprehended and applied by faith, we enter into rest; and feel a peace within which passeth all understanding. By his grace, too, he reconciles us to our duty, and to our condition. He frees us from those anxieties and fears which an idolatrous regard to creatures excites; and enables us to be careful for nothing, by casting all our care upon him, who careth for us. Also, by subduing our pride and selfishness, by which alone come contentions; and inspiring us with love—the bond of perfectness; we live in harmony with our fellow creatures. Yea, we are in league with the stones of the field; and the beasts of the field are at peace with us.

He is "the Prince of *Life*." Other princes, however powerful, are mortal: and this is a reason why we should not put our trust in them. Their breath goeth forth, they return to their dust; in that very day their thoughts perish. But Jesus liveth for ever: and because he lives, his people live also. Other princes, while they are living themselves, cannot impart life to others—though, alas! they often take it away; and sacrifice thousands of their subjects to their own lusts. But Jesus had not only life in himself, but came that we might have life; and have it more abundantly. He procured, and communicates, and sustains a life superior to that of Adam in Paradise, and of angels in glory. This is the promise that God hath promised us, even *eternal* life. And *this* life is *in* his Son. He therefore that hath the Son hath life; and he that hath not the Son hath not life.

He has other designations; and all come short of his praise. But these are sufficient to show how safe and how happy all they are who have become his subjects. It was a fine compliment that Hiram paid Solomon, when he said, "Surely, because the Lord loved Israel, therefore made he thee king over them." How much more has God shown his goodness to his people, in setting this King upon his holy hill of Zion! Let the children of Zion be joyful in their King. Let them make their boast in the Lord; and in his righteousness be exalted.

Let them also be concerned to approve themselves wise, and good, and loyal subjects, to the best of Princes: so that instead of disgracing him, they may be to him for a name and a praise among all those who shall hear of so great a people.

But wo to those who reject his sceptre. As for these mine enemies who would not that I should reign over them, bring them forth, and slay them before me.

OCTOBER 31.—"Prayer shall be made for him continually."—Psalm lxxii, 15.

WE are not only to pray; but to pray without ceasing. We are not only to pray for ourselves, but for others. We are to pray for kings, and all that are in authority—for ministers—for all saints—for even our enemies, who despitefully use us, and persecute us—and what may seem strange—we are to pray for Jesus Christ. "Prayers also shall be made for him continually."

Is prayer then necessary for *him?* Is he not above the reach of danger, pain, and want? Yes. He who once had not where to lay his head, has all power in heaven and in earth; and he dieth no more; death hath no more dominion over him. The meaning, therefore, cannot be, that prayer should be continually made for him personally; but relatively. Owing to the interest he has in certain objects; what is done for them, is done for himself; and so he esteems it. We therefore pray for him, when we pray for his ministers; his ordinances; his Gospel; his Church—in a word, his CAUSE. David, therefore, exemplifying what he had foretold, immediately breaks forth, and says, "And blessed be his glorious Name for ever: and let the whole earth be filled with his glory. Amen, and amen. The prayers of David, the son of Jesse, are ended."

But *what* could we pray for on his behalf? Our prayer should vary with the state of his cause; but we should always bear four things upon our minds. First. The degree of its resources; that there be always a sufficiency of suitable and able instruments to carry on the work—to this the Savior himself directs us: "The harvest truly is great; but the laborers are few: pray ye therefore the Lord of the harvest, that he would send forth laborers into his harvest." Secondly. The freedom of its administration; that whatever opposes or hinders its progress may be removed. "Pray for us," says the Apostle, "that the word of the Lord may have free course and be glorified." Thirdly. The diffusion of its principles; that they may become general and universal; spreading through every family, neighborhood, and province, and realm. So prayed of old even the pious Jew: "That thy way may be known on earth; thy saving health among all nations. Let the people praise thee, O God; yea, let all the people praise thee." Fourthly. The increase of its glory, as well as its extent; that it may abound more in wisdom, purity, spirituality, charity, and zeal: that the light of the moon may be as the light of the sun;

and the light of the sun be sevenfold as the light of seven days: that for brass, he would bring gold; and for iron, silver; and for wood, brass; and for stones, iron. Thus, they that make mention of the Lord are to "give him no rest"—not only until he "establish"—but "make Jerusalem *a praise* in the whole earth."

But *why* should we be concerned to pray for Him? Consistency requires it. We are the professors of Christ. We profess to be his servants—but can we be wise and good servants, if we are neglectful of our Master's affairs? We profess to be his subjects—but can we be his loyal subjects, if we are indifferent to the glory of our Sovereign? We profess to be his friends—but can we have true and faithful friends, unless we make his interests our own; mourn over his dishonor, and rejoice in his prosperity? Benevolence requires it. The Gospel is the greatest of all blessings to the children of men. Wherever it enters, the wilderness and the solitary place is made glad, and the desert rejoices and blossoms as the rose. It is the power of God to salvation to every one that believeth; and where it does not save the soul, it yields a thousand advantages to the community. Who would not wish *him* success? *His* career is the march of truth, and righteousness, and peace. *He* makes the widow's heart to sing for joy. In *him* the fatherless findeth mercy.

"Blessings abound where'er He reigns,
"The pris'ner leaps to lose his chains:
"The weary find eternal rest;
"And all the sons of want are blest."

Gratitude requires it. How much do we owe him! When we consider what he has done, is doing, and will do for us: all we are, and all we have, appear to be his by a thousand claims; and nothing can equal our vileness, if we are not led hourly to ask, What shall I render unto the Lord for all his benefits? Lord, what wilt thou have me to do?

But what reason have we to conclude that these prayers for him will be *heard?* Much every way. The prayers, indeed, even of good men, are not always answered. Sometimes they know not what they ask. And when they implore what would prove evil, God's wisdom and kindness lead him to refuse. But whatsoever we ask according to his will, he heareth us. And has he not commanded us to pray, that his kingdom may come? Has he not promised it? Is not the grand condition fulfilled—"When thou shalt make his soul an offering for sin, he shall see his seed, he shall prolong his days, and the pleasure of the Lord shall prosper in his hands?" Can his death be unavailable? Can the engagements of the everlasting covenant be made void? We *cannot* pray for him in vain.

—But what is necessary to evince that our praying for him is *sincere?* For there is much prayer that is a mere mockery of God. Out of their own mouths many will be condemned hereafter; and they would feel themselves condemned already, were it not that the heart is deceitful above all things, as well as desperately wicked. A man prays to redeem his time, and to have his conversation in heaven, and goes and sits in the play-house for the answer. A father prays for the salvation of his child; and does all in his power to leave him affluent, and surrounded with temptations that render his conversion a miracle. A third prays to be damned; for he prays, "forgive us our trespasses, as we forgive them that trespass against us:" and he is implacable. When a man sincerely desires a thing, in proportion as he desires it, he will seek after it, and use all the means placed within his reach to obtain it. When, therefore, a person professes a great concern for a thing, and neglects whatever is necessary to it, we make no scruple to tax him with folly and falsehood. Let us do, in religious matters, what we do in other cases—let us judge of our faith, by our practice; and of our hearts, by our lives.

What then, you say, must we do to prove that our prayers in the cause of Christianity are sincere? Do! Some of you should come forward and offer to go forth as missionaries. What hinders? Nothing in your condition; nothing in your connexions; Nothing but the love of ease, and the fear of suffering, and the want of the *spirit* of the prayer—"Arise, O Lord, and plead thine own cause." Do! Live for him. All cannot go abroad; but all have a sphere in which they may be useful. They may hold forth the word of life, by their temper and conversation. Do! Employ all your influence with others, provoking them to love and to good works. Do! Give according to your opportunity and ability—exercising self-denial, to enlarge your ability. Read the whole verse of our text—"And he shall live: and to him shall be given of the gold of Sheba; prayer also shall be made for him continually; and daily shall he be praised."

NOVEMBER 1.—"How readest thou?"—Luke, x, 26.

It is well to be able to read. Thousands are not; and so cannot thus agreeably fill up their leisure moments, nor improve their minds by the written communications of others. But whatever a thing be in itself, the use we are to make of it, is to determine whether it be, to us, good or evil, a blessing or a curse.

Some will lament for ever, that they were taught to read. They never improved so great a talent. Yea, they perverted and abused it; reading books which undermined their principles, defiled their imaginations, and demoralized their lives. But others are thankful for such an attainment. It has afforded them not only gratification and profit, but spiritual improvement and consolation. One, in reading, has been converted from the error of his ways. Another has been guided in his experimental and practical doubts and difficulties. A third has been revived while walking in the midst of trouble.

—And if this has been the case while reading other books, how much more while reading the Scriptures of truth! This volume you are bound, above all other books, to read. It is your duty; it is your privilege—But how readest thou? How ought you to read it?

—First. You ought to read it, as the dictates of Inspiration. You do not, perhaps, deny or question this; but you ought, actually and frequently, to impress the mind with it, that when you open these pages, you may say, "I will hear what God the Lord will speak." "Speak, Lord, for thy servant heareth." The Apostle admonishes the Hebrews not to turn away from Him that speaketh from heaven. He does not say, who *spake*—but who *speaketh*. The address is to be considered as immediate. It is so to us, as well as to those who originally heard it. Had it been just written it could have had no more authority, and have been no more deserving of attention than now. How much depends upon this advice! For as we receive the word, so shall we be affected by it. If we regard it as false, it will produce no result. If as human, it will influence as human. But if divine, it will operate divinely. Hence, says the Apostle to the Thessalonians, "For this cause also thank we God without ceasing; because, when ye received the word of God which ye heard of us, ye received it not as the word of men, but as it is in truth, the word of God, which effectually worketh also in you that believe."

Secondly. Let him that readeth understand. The eunuch, returning from Jerusalem in his chariot, was reading; and reading even the Prophecies of Isaiah; but Philip said to him, "Understandest thou what thou readest?" To know the meaning of the Scriptures, it is a good thing to read on, till we come to the end of a paragraph or subject, regardless of the divisions in chapters and verses. These breaks are useful, and they are generally made in their proper places, but not always, in consequence of which the sense is injured or darkened by the writer's closing before he has finished: or commencing sometimes in the middle of the argument. Neither should he lay too much stress on a particular word or phrase; but be guided by the natural current of the passage; and endeavor always to apprehend what is the present design of the sacred writer. Here good common sense will often do more than the learned affectations of expositors, who frequently elude the solution of a difficult text, and throw doubts into a clear one. While we ought to avail ourselves of every assistance from the labors of others; and above all, to exercise our own minds; we must be humble in our inquiries, and feel and acknowledge our need of divine guidance, to lead us into all truth. "Open thou mine eyes, that I may see wondrous things out of thy laws;" so prayed David—and so must we. "If any of you lack wisdom, let him ask of God, that giveth to all men liberally, and upbraideth not, and it shall be given him." Thus the wayfaring man, though a fool, shall not err: and without this, the scholar and the genius will for ever go astray. The great impediment to divine knowledge is *the state of the heart:* and as soon as we are made deeply sensible of our need of what the Gospel is designed to afford, and willing to be saved in the Lord's own way, and to walk so as to please him, every thing opens easily and delightfully; and the path of the just is as the shining light, that shineth more and more unto the perfect day. But this can only be obtained from "the *Spirit* of truth."

Thirdly. We should read with a view of self-application. Instead of thinking of others—which is too frequently the case—we should think of ourselves; inquiring how it bears upon our character and condition; and how, as Lord Bacon says, it comes home to our own business and bosoms. If I read a threatening, "O my soul, do I stand exposed to this danger?" If I read a promise, "May I claim this blessing?" If I read a reproof or a commendation, "Am I censured by the one, or encouraged by the other?" "Lord, what wilt thou have *me* to do?"

Fourthly. We should read with a determination to reduce what we read to experience and practice. The design of all the instruction contained in the Scripture is, to bear upon the conscience and the life. The doctrine is not only according to grace, but according to godliness. If ye know these things, happy are ye if ye do them. This is the way to increase with all the increase of God. To him that hath shall be given, and he shall have more abundantly. If a man do his will, he shall know of his doctrine. We may apply to reading what the apostle James has said of hearing: "But be ye doers of the word, and not readers only, deceiving your own selves. For if any be a *reader* of the word, and not a doer, he is like unto a man beholding his natural face in a glass: for he beholdeth himself, and goeth his way, and straightway forgetteth what manner of man he was. But whoso looketh into the perfect law of liberty, and continueth therein, he being not a forgetful *reader*, but a doer of the work, this man shall be blessed in his *deed*.'

NOVEMBER 2.—"His time in the flesh."—1 Peter, iv, 2.

"FLESH" is not to be taken here morally, but physically. It is not here used to signify our corruption, but our present existence: as when Paul says, The life that I now live "in the flesh," I live by the faith of the Son of God. It intends, therefore, our life while *in the body*. For we shall not be *in* it always—a period is approaching, when the dust shall return to the earth as it was, and the spirit shall return unto God who gave it.

Our "time" in the flesh varies in circumstances, with regard to individuals. But it has four general characters, applicable to all the human race.

First. Our time in the flesh is chequered. The young may look forward and view life in the fascinations of hope; and the aged may look back, and more congenially dwell on the gloomy than on the cheerful; and the same man, in the hour of present impression, may feel himself too much elated, or too much depressed with his condition—but the truth is the same. It is neither a paradisical nor a wilderness scene. It is neither entirely dark nor light, but intermingled sunshine and shade. Who ever found life so smooth as to have no roughness? And who ever had sickness without ease, or sorrow without comfort? And who is now authorized to say, To-morrow shall be as this day, and much more abundant; or, Mine eye shall no more see good?

Secondly. It is short. And short, not only as to eternity and the ages of men before the flood, but absolutely short. The general duration is threescore years and ten. But much of this is nothing to the superior purposes of our being. We do not mean business: this may not only be rendered consistent with religion, but is made, by a Christian who abides with God in his calling, a part of it. But there is the weakness of infancy, and the childhood of age. There are the deductions of *needful* sleep, and allowed recreation, and unavoidable intercourse. It is often also cut short. How few reach seventy! and those who do, commonly look in vain to find any of the associates of their youth or maturity. Every thing expressive of brevity is seized by the sacred writers to hold forth the brevity of our time in the flesh—a flower; a flood; a tale; a dream; a vapor; a ship before the wind; an eagle pouncing on his prey. There is but a step between us and death.

Thirdly. It is uncertain. How can it be otherwise, when we consider the diseases and accidents to which we are continually exposed; and the feebleness of our frame; and the number and delicacy of the organs of which the body is composed? Sixty times every minute, as our pulse tells us, the question is asked, whether we shall live or die. The fool in the Gospel said, I have much goods laid up for many years; soul, take thine ease, eat, drink, and be merry; but that very night his soul was required of him. Persons just ready to enter connected life, have been called from marriage rites to attend funeral solemnities. The owners have been just ready to take possession of a new mansion, but have been carried to their long home. And the traveller, starting for his journey, has gone the way of all the earth.

But fourthly. It is important; yea, all-important, by reason of its relation to another, and an eternal state. It is not only an introduction to this state, but a preparation for it. It is influentially connected with it, as the sowing with the harvest. Our thoughts, words, and actions, are the seed; and whatsoever a man soweth, that shall he also reap. The present is the only season of obtaining justification and renovation: a title to heaven, and a meetness for it. *Now* is the accepted time; now is the day of salvation.

The same will apply to our doing good. Our time in the flesh is the only season in which we can glorify God and serve our generation. What a treasure then is life! And how concerned should we be to work while it is day, seeing the night cometh, wherein no man can work! In this one article the saints below are more privileged than the saints above: and we are persuaded, that those who have entered their rest would be willing, were it the pleasure of God, to come down and re-enter this vale of tears, to have the opportunities of usefulness we enjoy—who can be candid toward those who differ from us; forgive injuries; visit and relieve the afflicted; spread the Gospel; teach the ignorant; save souls from death, and hide a multitude of sins. "Whatsoever thy hand findeth to do, do it with thy might; for there is no work, nor device, nor knowledge in the grave whither thou goest."

NOVEMBER 3.—"As sorrowful, yet always rejoicing."—2 Corinthians, vi, 10.

THIS is the duty, this is the privilege of the Christian. Whether he considers and feels himself in a state of exile—or warfare—or perplexity—or penury—or varying experience—or misapprehension from others; if "sorrowful," he may, and he ought to be able to say, "Yet always rejoicing."

Though dwelling with strangers around,
And foreign and weary the land,
I homeward to Zion am bound—
The day of release is at hand.
Then, Mesech and Kedar, farewell,
To enter my welcome abode;
With friends and with angels to dwell,
With Jesus, my Savior and God!

Though hourly summoned to arms,
And legions against me combine,
I'm calm in the midst of alarms:
My weapons and cause are divine.
A Captain almighty I own,
And banner'd by faith in his name,
I shout ere the battle is won—
I more than a conqueror AM!

Perplexings though often I feel,
And mazy the paths that I tread,
My God has been leading me still,
And still he has promised to lead.
The crooked shall all be made straight,
The darkness shall beam into light;
I have but a moment to wait,
And faith shall be turned into sight.

If small my allotment below,
I will not at others repine;
Their joy is the gilding of wo,
Their wealth they must quickly resign.
Though poor, how much richer am I!
In want, I have all I desire;
My treasures the soul can supply,
And last when the stars shall expire!

If, weeping and fearing, I pass,
Through changes, in state and in frame;
Yet constant in power and grace,
My Savior is always the same.
No shadow of turning he knows,
Whose bliss is the fountain of mine;
And while his eternity flows,
My happiness cannot decline.

How little the multitude know,
Or knowing, how little they prize
The spring whence my joys ever flow,
Or source of my bitterest sighs!
But both the dear secret reveal,
That Jesus hath soften'd this heart;
And soon all my joys will fulfil,
And lull the last sigh from my heart.

NOVEMBER 4.—"Jesus saith unto him, I will come and heal him."—Matthew viii, 7.

WE may consider these words as

—An answer to prayer. And let us observe *whose* prayer it was. He never said to the seed of Jacob, Seek *ye* me in vain. But this centurion was an alien from the commonwealth of Israel; a Roman; a Gentile. Yet *he* is immediately heard. For whosoever shall call upon the name of the Lord, shall be saved: for there is no difference between the Jew and the Greek; for the same Lord over all is rich unto all that call upon him. Whoever I am, let me therefore apply, animated by the assurance, "Him that cometh unto me, I will in no wise cast out". Let us observe, also, *what* prayer it was. It was not a prayer for the petitioner himself: but for another. As he never refused any who addressed him on their own behalf; so he never refused any that addressed him on the account of others. Let this teach and encourage us to pray for others. Let friends pray for friends; and parents for their children; and masters and mistresses for their servants. We are even commanded to pray for all men.

—We may consider the words as an instance of condescension. He was fairer than the children of men; higher than the kings of the earth; and all the angels of God worshipped him: yet no sooner is his goodness implored, than, in a moment, he is ready to go and stand by the side of the pallet of a poor sick slave!—I will come and heal him. The master was very humane and compassionate, or he would not have taken the trouble to send to our Lord, on the behalf of one considered so much below him. What is a slave to many an owner? No more than a beast of burden. David found an Egyptian in the field, who had eaten no bread nor drunk any water for three days and three nights: "And David said unto him, to whom belongest thou? and whence art thou? And he said, I am a young man of Egypt, servant to an Amalekite; and my master left me, because three days agone I fell sick" A wretch! How unlike him was this centurion! But he, even *he*, is surprised, and scarcely knows how to accept of the Savior's offer. Yea, he deems it a condescension to *himself*—even *I* am not worthy that *thou* shouldest come under *my* roof. And shall not *we* condescend to men of low estate? "Did not He that made me in the womb, make him, and did not one fashion us in the womb?"

—We may consider the words as a display of power. I will come and attend him—would be the language of a friend. I will come and pray with him—would be the language of a minister. I will come and examine his case, and see if I can afford him relief—would be the language of the physician. But Jesus speaks like himself—I will come and heal him. He knew his own sufficiency. And the centurion knew it. It was the principle of his reasoning—"Though I am not the commander in chief, but a subordinate officer, yet it is not necessary even for me to go to a place in order to act—my *word* is enough, I say to one of my soldiers, Go, and he goeth; to another, Come, and he cometh; and to my servant, Do this, and he doeth it. How much more, O Lord! are all creatures and events under thy control! Thy word runneth very swiftly; and neither disease nor death can withstand it." So our Savior understood him. He therefore admired him, and said, I have not found so great faith, no, not in Israel. And we should have the same strong confidence in his ability—That he is mighty to save—able to save to the uttermost, them that come unto God by him. For

—We may consider the words as affording an emblem of the salvation of the sinner. Whatever some may think of human nature, we are fallen creatures—we are spiritually diseased—and there is no health in us—and we are ready to perish—and are incapable of recovering ourselves. And

"The help of men and angels joined,
"Can never reach our case;
"Nor can we hope relief to find,
"But in his boundless grace."

But he says, Lo! I come. I will come and heal him. It was the design of his coming in the flesh. The Son of man is come to seek and to save that which was lost. It is the purpose of his coming now in the agency of his grace. I will bring them, says he, health and cure. He heals them, meritoriously, by his stripes; efficiently, by his Spirit; instrumentally, by his word, ordinances, and providences. The recovery, indeed, he is pleased to carry on by degrees. He could by one application, yea, by one volition, remove all their complaints; but it does not comport with his wisdom. His people, therefore, continue his patients; and are no more than convalescents all through life. But if slow, the recovery is sure. Nothing can elude his skill, or baffle his remedy. When dying, they may say, with Baxter, "Almost well;" and when they enter Immanuel's land, there the inhabitant shall no more say, I am sick.

NOVEMBER 5.—"This God is our God for ever and ever."—Ps. xlviii, 14.

THIS is the language of a proprietary in God. And it is founded in truth. In the covenant of grace, established not with them, but with the surety, he has, so to speak, made over himself to his people, saying—I will be thy God. I am thine, and all that I have—my perfections, my relations, my works, my word, my ordinances, my dispensations—I am thy salvation—to thee I am all and in all. Hence there is no propriety like this, not only for the value of it, but the reality too. Justly speaking, nothing else *is* our *own*. Our time is not our own. Our wealth is not our own. Our children are not our own. Our bodies, our souls, are not our own—But God *is* our own—And God, even our *own* God, shall bless us.

It is the language of an assured proprietary—This God is *our* God. The relation may be known and claimed. And with what a repetition does David express it! "I will love thee, O Lord, *my* strength. The Lord is *my* rock, and *my* fortress, and *my* deliverer: *my* God, *my* strength, in whom I will trust; *my* buckler and the horn of *my* salvation, and *my* high tower." Here are no less, in a few words, than eight appropriations. And how desirable is it to be able to ascertain and express our own interest in all his engagements!

"When I can say, my God is mine,
"When I can feel thy glories shine,
"I tread the world beneath my feet,
"And all that earth calls good and great."

Then I am satisfied with his goodness. But can the thing be made out?—and how? They mistake, who suppose this relation results from our choosing Him, and giving ourselves to him. We do this, indeed; but it is by his grace. And, in us, this is the effect and not the cause. But as it is the effect, it is therefore the evidence. And in this way we are to trace back the stream to the fountain; making our calling, and thereby our election, sure. If we have chosen Him, we may be assured he has chosen us; and if we love him, we may be assured he loves us: for one is the consequence of the other—We love Him, because he first loved us.

It is the language of a permanent proprietary—This our God is our God *for ever and ever*. Without this, the blessedness would make us miserable: for the dearer and greater a treasure is, the more alive we are to anxiety and fear; and nothing but the assurance of its safety can enable us cordially to enjoy it. No confidence is so well founded as the Christian's. Every other possession is precarious; every other relation is breaking up. But he may, he can say, "I am persuaded that neither death, nor life, nor angels, nor principalities, nor powers, nor things present, nor things to come, nor height, nor depth, nor any other creature, shall be able to separate us from the love of God which is in Christ Jesus our Lord."

It is the language of an exulting proprietary. Boasting is excluded by the law of faith. But what boasting? All glorying in ourselves, but not in God. "My soul," says David, "shall make her boast in the Lord: the humble shall hear thereof, and be glad." So the Church boasts and proclaims the Savior—"*This* is my beloved, and *this* is my friend, O ye daughters of Jerusa lem"—What is yours? So here—*This* God is our God for ever and for ever—What is yours, O ye sons of men?

Their rock is not as our rock; our enemies themselves being judges.

NOVEMBER 6.—"There is a God in heaven, that revealeth secrets."—Daniel, ii, 28.

DANIEL was perhaps the most blameless character recorded in the Scriptures. Of course *He* is excepted from the comparison, who was "fairer than the children of men." Neither do we mean to intimate that he was sinless. He had an evil heart to lament before God; but, with regard to his conduct before men, as a professor of religion, nothing is laid to his charge. And what an honor was it to be spoken of, while living—and while young, too, by a prophet—in company with Noah and Job—as one of those who were most likely to have power with God, as intercessors!

Here we see his humility. The king said unto him, "Art thou able to make known unto me the dream which I have seen, and the interpretation thereof?" Daniel answered in the presence of the king, and said, "The secret which the king hath commanded, cannot the wise men, the astrologers, the magicians, the soothsayers, show unto the king. But there is a God in heaven that revealeth secrets." Why does he mention this, but because he would prevent the commendation of himself! and that the only wise God might have the glory that was due unto his holy name? And thus another fine character, jealous of the divine honor, said to his sovereign, "It is not in me. God shall give Pharaoh an answer of peace." The most eminent of all characters in the Christian church also said, "By the grace of God I am what I am: and his grace which was bestowed upon me was not in vain; but I labored more abundantly than they all: yet, not I, but the grace of God which was with me." Contrast with these, two of the most famous of the Heathen philosophers and moralists: one of whom said, "That we have riches, is of the gods; but that we have wisdom, is of ourselves." And the other, "A good man is, in one respect, above the gods themselves; for they are good by the necessity of nature; but he is good by choice!"

But what is the praise that Daniel transfers from himself to God? The revelation of secrets. Men are fond of secrets. With regard to themselves, they are always wishful to pry into futurity. Almanacs must therefore have something to feed this humor, or would not sell half their number. Mistresses, as well as servant maids; the old, as well as the young; would show their palms to the fortune-teller, were it not for the fear of ridicule. Were the witch of Endor alive, many would repair to her, and, like Saul, consult the devil himself at second-hand. People, too, are fond of being intrusted with secrets concerning others. But they should not. The very injunction of silence, excites propensity to transgress: and the breach of confidence, when known, often produces disgrace and strife. Envy makes us inquisitive, with regard to rivals; fear, with regard to enemies; and love, with regard to friends. It was curiosity, operating in a way of attachment, that led Peter to inquire after the destination of John—"Lord, and what shall this man do?" But the Lord did not even encourage *this*—"What is that to thee? Follow thou me."

The secret things belong unto God; things that are revealed, are for us, and for our children. Concerning many things he is silent; and where he says nothing, we are not be wise above what is written.

—But He *can* reveal secrets. His understanding is infinite. Hell is naked before him, and destruction hath no covering. "Neither is there any creature that is not manifest in his sight; but all things are naked and open unto the eyes of Him with whom we have to do."

—He *has* revealed secrets. He enabled Daniel to explain the import of Nebuchadnezzar's dream, and foretell the succession of the four monarchies. He showed Moses what the Jews would be at this very hour. What a divine prerogative was prophecy! We may conjecture, but we really know not what a day may bring forth. We may argue from causes to effects; but the existence and operation of the causes themselves depend upon the will of another. We may infer from probabilities; but the natural tendencies of things are liable to accidental derangements—and the race is not always to the swift, nor the battle to the strong. Besides, as to the predictions of Scripture, many of them regarded things so remote, that what *immediatcly* preceded them could not possibly be discerned. And others regarded events the most unlikely to take place of all occurrences in the world. And yet, when we look into history, we see how it accords with these announcements. How can we account for this, but by admitting that prophecy came not in old time by the will of man, but holy men of God spake as they were moved by the Holy Ghost?

—He *does* reveal secrets. How many now living has he called out of darkness into his marvellous light! Not that he has communicated to their minds things new in themselves—but they were new to them. The sun had been shining; but they had been in the dark, because they were blind. All the doctrine was in the Bible before; but he now leads them into all truth, and shows them not only the reality of divine things, but their importance and glory. Give a man a taste for a book of music, or science of any kind, and he will see a thousand things entirely new to him, though he possessed the work before. So "the natural man receiveth not the things of the Spirit of God; for they are foolishness unto him; neither can he know them, because they are spiritually discerned: but the spiritual judgeth all things." So the secret of the Lord is with them that fear him; and he shows them his covenant, as to their interest in its engagements and provisions. And what a discovery is this! How anxious will every awakened mind be to possess it!

"O! tell me that my worthless name
"Is graven on thy hands;
"Show me some promise in thy book
Where my salvation stands."

Say unto my soul, I am thy salvation. And what is the promise? "I will give him to eat of the hidden manna; and will give him a white stone, and in the stone a new name written, which no man knoweth, saving he that receiveth it." He also shows them the secrets of his providence, as well as of his grace. They know what he is doing, and what he will do. They know that he is fulfilling his own word, and making all things to work together for their good. They know that "behind a frowning providence he hides a smiling face;" and that even when he slays them, they have reason to trust in him. "Who is wise, and he shall understand these things; prudent, and he shall know them. For the ways of the Lord are right, and the just shall walk in them: but the transgressors shall fall therein."

—He *will* reveal secrets. Yes; there is "a day, in the which," says the apostle, "God will judge the secrets of men by Jesus Christ, according to my Gospel." Then will be developed, dreadful secrets. Then many, who had a name here, will be disowned. They had honored Him with their lips, and gained the notice of their fellow-creatures; but their hearts had been far from Him. And what is the hope of the hypocrite, though he hath gained, when God taketh away his soul? Pleasing secrets. Then they who are now deemed the enemies of the cross of Christ, will be found to have been its friends. Then they who are now considered as indifferent to holiness and good works, will appear to have mourned for sin, and prayed for purity. Then the tear dropped upon the Bible in the closet, the private act of charity, the frequent intercession for others, will be displayed and commended. He will bring to light the hidden things of darkness, and make manifest the counsels of the heart; and then shall every man have praise of God. Divine secrets. He will show why he permitted the entrance of moral evil; delayed so long the coming of his Son; suffered his Gospel to be so impeded, and his church to be so afflicted; and more than justify all his ways to men. What is now perplexing, will be made plain. What now seems disorderly, will be arranged. What now seems jarring, will be harmonized. What now seems defective, will be complete. And then, not as now, from faith, but from sight, the acknowledgment will be made, "He is the Rock; his work is perfect; for all his ways are judgment: a God of truth, and without iniquity: just and right is he." To many these mysteries are already explained. When shall we have an inheritance with the saints in light?

NOVEMBER 7.—"For neither did his brethren believe in him."—John vii, 5.

How is this charge to be understood? Two distinctions or limitations are necessary. First. It cannot be taken literally as to the name—"his brethren." Even those who very properly reject the notion of her perpetual virginity, do not suppose that these were really the children of Mary, our Lord's mother. The question which divides the ancients and the moderns turns upon this; whether they were the offspring of Joseph, by a former marriage; or whether they were born of Salome, Mary's sister, and so were our Lord's cousins-german. The latter is the more probable conclusion. Among the Jews, kinsmen in various degrees were called brethren. Abraham and Lot were uncle and nephew; yet says the former to the latter, "We are brethren." The meaning therefore is, that our Lord's more near and remote kindred did not believe on him. But secondly, this cannot be taken universally, as to the fact. For three of his brethren, at least, were found in the number of his apostles—Simon, and Jude, and James the less, who is expressly the Lord's brother. The Scripture does not gratify our curiosity; we know but little of Mary's or Joseph's relations; they seem to have been numerous; and the language before us must intimate that not only some, but comparatively many of them, had not real faith in him.

This is a very surprising announcement: but it is very instructive. Does it not favor the truth of Christianity? Had all our Lord's relations recommended and followed him, his cause might have looked human and suspicious. We know what advantage Mahomet derived from the attachment and employment of his kindred. But here every appearance of family contrivance is excluded; and we see that our Lord did not act by rules of carnal policy: his kingdom was not of this world; his Gospel was left to its own evidence and energy, and derived no assistance from the auxiliaries of error, superstition, or idolatry.

We see also what evidence may be resisted, and what means may be rendered ineffectual, by the depravity of human nature. These men had attended his preaching, and he spake as man never spake: they had often heard his conversation. They had received many instructions, reproofs, and encouragements from him, in a manner the most adapted to insure success. They had gone up with him to the festivals, and had seen his devotion. Some of them were present when he turned the water into wine. They had seen him open the eyes of the blind. Yes, these very men, "his brethren, therefore said unto him, Depart hence, and go into Judea, that thy disciples also may see the works that thou doest. For there is no man that doeth any thing in secret, and he himself seeketh to be known openly. If thou do these things, show thyself to the world." As his relations, they must have known the circumstances of his birth; the appearance of the angel to the shepherds; the journey of the wise men; the prophecying of Simeon and Anna: the testimony of John; the descent of the Holy Ghost in his baptism; his holy and heavenly life—Nevertheless, such were their prejudices and worldly dispositions, that they did not believe on him. It was not *evidence* they wanted; nor is it a want of evidence that induces persons to reject him now. The source of infidelity is not intellectual, but moral. Were it not criminal, it would not be punishable. But this is the condemnation, that light has come into the world; but men love darkness rather than light, because their deeds are evil. We think some means *must* be irresistible—but we forget that the heart is deceitful above all things, and desperately wicked. Neither will they be persuaded, though one rose from the dead.

And from hence we need not wonder if inferior characters are unsuccessful in their pious attempts. Ministers may be faithful and zealous, and yet be constrained to complain, "Who hath believed our report?" Masters may be wise and good; yet what a servant had Elisha, in Gehazi! Parents should do every thing in their power for the spiritual welfare of their children; and, in a general way, they may hope for success; but let them not wonder if, in some instances, even their tears, and examples, and entreaties, are in vain!

Let those who have irreligious relations think of Jesus. He was in this point tempted as they are. He can sympathize with them. He remembers the feelings of his heart, when even his own kindred turned away from him.

Hence none will be saved from mere relationship. Let none say, therefore, within themselves, We have Abraham to our father. The parable tells us of one in hell, who called Abraham father; and was refused by him the least gratification. It is a mercy to have pious connexions; but religion is a personal thing, and if we refuse to tread in their steps, the blessing will turn into a curse: and there will be weeping and gnashing of teeth, when we shall see Abraham, Isaac, and Jacob in the kingdom of God, and we ourselves shut out.

Finally. It is better to be of the spiritual kindred of Jesus, than of his family according to the flesh. When, therefore, the woman exclaimed, "Blessed is the womb that bare thee, and the paps which thou hast sucked;" he himself replied, "Yea, rather blessed are they that hear the word of God, and keep it." "The spiritual relation to him can never be dissolved: and it will insure every thing essential to our safety, honor, wealth, power, and happiness for ever. As the natural relation to him was not saving, so it was necessarily confined to few. But this lies open to all. "Then one said unto him, Behold, thy mother and thy brethren stand without, desiring to speak with thee. But he answered and said unto him that told, Who is my mother? and who are my brethren? And he stretched forth his hand toward his disciples, and said, Behold my mother and my brethren! For whosoever shall do the will of my Father which is in heaven, the same is my brother, and sister, and mother."

November 8.—"And when the Pharisees saw it, they said unto his disciples, Why eateth your Master with Publicans and sinners?"—Matt. ix, 11.

This is connected with a concise narrative of the conversion of the writer of this Gospel. For the account *of* himself is furnished *by* himself. It is a delicate thing for a man to write concerning himself, but the sacred authors are above all suspicion. They are always faithful and impartial, and their only aim is truth. Though Matthew here speaks of himself, the reference here was unavoidable, and he only introduces the servant, for the sake of the Master.

The case was this. After leaving the privacy of Nazareth, our Lord came and dwelt in Capernaum. This town, as it was situated on the Lake of Galilee, gave him an opportunity to pass easily in the fishing boats of his followers to any part of the adjoining country. "And as Jesus passed forth from thence, he saw a man sitting at the receipt of custom:" that is, he was receiving the tolls from the goods landed and embarked on the quay. As Luke tells us he made a great feast and bade many, it is probable he was possessed of considerable property; and, from the common character of Publicans, we might be tempted to conclude that it was the produce of illegal exaction. But it would be invidious to draw such an inference. Even a Publican was not necessarily wicked: and the consciousness Zaccheus had of freedom from extortion, is obvious from his appeal; "And if I have taken any thing from any man by false accusation, I restore him fourfold." It is even the duty of official agents to be exact and full in lawful demands. We will therefore take it for granted that Matthew was rightfully engaged when our Savior took knowledge of him; and as divine favor has been shown toward many others recorded in the Scripture, while filling up the duties of their station, we learn that diligence in our calling is acceptable to God, as well as approved of men. The angel of the Lord appeared to the shepherds while keeping their flocks by night, and announced the birth of the Messiah. Saul was seeking his father's asses when Samuel met him, and anointed him king over Israel. While drawing water at the well, Rebecca and Rachel, and Zipporah, found each a husband. The woman of Samaria found the Savior of the world.

Here it may be asked, Was our Lord's thus meeting with Matthew, the effect of chance, or of design? To this question we boldly answer—Of design. There is nothing accidental in the conversion of a sinner. If a man be saved, and called with a holy calling in time, it is according to God's purpose and grace given him in Jesus Christ before the world began.

—"And he saith to him, Follow me. And he arose and followed him." He hath a mighty voice. He upholds all things by the word of his power. By the same word he made them all: he spake, and it was done; he commanded, and it stood fast: he said, Let there be light, and there was light. So it was in the old creation; and in the new, he calleth things which are not, and they appear. As the address was instantaneous, so the obedience was immediate. What a change did the call produce in the soul of this man! How did it enlighten his mind, and inflame his heart! Doubtless his head was filled with worldly cares; but this voice, like a charm, dispossesses him. The meanness of our Savior's appearance, and the lowness of his attendants, weigh nothing with him. He was now in prosperity; he was to leave a gainful office, and perhaps saw before him only reproach and persecution: but he is satisfied, and would rather be a poor minister of Christ, than a rich officer of Cæsar. In a case of such magnitude, it might be supposed that he would have required some time to consider and examine matters. But, like Paul, he confers not with flesh and blood. The king's business requires haste. True obedience is always prompt and unreserved—He immediately followed him. O blessed Jesus, may thy call to us be so effectual, that *when* thou sayest, "Seek ye my face," our hearts may answer, "Thy face, Lord, we seek." And at thy bidding may we arise, and forsaking every carnal pursuit and worldly attachment, follow the Lamb whithersover he goeth!

Though Matthew formally surrendered his office, and all its concerns, we have no reason to believe that he sacrificed his effects; rather, we are persuaded that he carefully secured them, to be properly used and applied. Whatever we possess at the time of our calling, may be consecrated to the Redeemer, and advantageously employed in his service and the cause of benevolence. And when the heart is open, the hand and the house cannot be shut. Matthew therefore makes an entertainment for our Lord, and "behold, many publicans and sinners came and sat down with him and his disciples." These persons had formerly visited Matthew, partly for business, and partly for pleasure: now they came, invited by him with the hope of their deriving benefit from our Savior's conversation. "Who knows," says he, "but the voice that has reached my heart, may also call them by his grace?" How invariably is such a disposition found in every subject of divine grace! Come with us, said Moses to Hobab, and we will do thee good; for the Lord hath spoken good concerning Israel. O taste and see, says David, that the Lord is good: blessed is the man that trusteth in him. Come and see him, said the woman of Samaria to her neighbors. In the same spirit Matthew makes a feast, to which he calls his old friends and companions And our Savior gave them the cheerful, though not the sinful meeting: teaching us thereby not to be repulsive in our manners, nor refuse social intercourse. Of two things, however, we should be careful—To design good as our Savior did, when we enter company—and also to remember the difference there is between him and us. He had no corruption within, for temptation to operate upon; while we are easily receptive of corrupt impressions, and must always watch and pray, lest we enter into temptation.

—But the Pharisees, (pious souls!) when they saw this, were scandalized. Yet as Satan always loves to get over the hedge where the fence is the lowest; and as he assailed Eve apart from her husband; so they from fear, do not express their dissatisfaction to our Lord himself; but "said unto his disciples, Why eateth your Master with Publicans and sinners?" What did they mean? It was the tradition of the elders, that the sanctified and devout should never be seen in company with the wicked. Affecting superior sanctity, they acted upon this principle themselves, and said, "Stand by thyself; come not near to me; I am holier than thou." And they here insinuate, that if Jesus was what he professed to be, he would shun such characters as he was now with. And they seem even to feel a concern for his honor. All this was a mere pretence, supported by malice and envy. They were strangers to every feeling of piety or benevolence. They strained at a gnat, and swallowed a camel. They made long prayers for a pretence, and devoured widows' houses. They were wolves in sheep's clothing: sepulchres painted without, and full of rottenness within.

If we are Israelites indeed, in whom there is no guile, we shall be severe toward ourselves, and candid toward others. We shall see more evil in our own hearts, than we can ever see in the conduct of our fellow creatures: and though in proportion as we are pure and heavenly, we *must* feel whatever is contrary thereto—we shall bewail it before God, rather than complain of it to men. And never shall we, when the character is fair, and the life blameless, go a motive-hunting, and indulge in the vileness of suspicion. Let us not judge, that we be not judged. Let us remember, that he who knows what is man, represents censoriousness as the offspring and proof of hypocrisy. "Why beholdest thou the mote that is in thy brother's eye, but considerest not the beam that is in thine own eye? Or how wilt thou say to thy brother, Let me pull out the mote out of thine eye; and, behold a beam is in thine own eye? Thou hypocrite! first cast out the beam out of thine own eye, and then shalt thou see clearly to cast out the mote out of thy brother's eye." O for more of that charity, that "thinketh no evil; that rejoiceth not in iniquity, but rejoiceth in the truth—beareth all things, believeth all things, hopeth all things, endureth all things!"

November 9.—"But when Jesus heard that, he said unto them, They that be whole need not a physician, but they that are sick."—Matthew, ix, 12.

To perceive the force of these words, we must remember the design of them. They are in justification of our Lord's conduct. Matthew, having been called by his grace to follow him, made an entertainment, to which he invited his former friends and companions; hoping that they might derive advantage from the intercourse. But when the Pharisees saw it, they were offended, and said to his disciples, "Why eateth your Master with Publicans and sinners?" Though the murmur was not addressed to *himself*, it *concerned* himself: and he was acquainted with it: and though the complainers were undeserving of his notice—and he was under no obligation to vindicate what he was doing—he said, "I am about my proper business. I have not mistaken the objects of my attention. I came to seek and to save that which was lost. I could now have been enjoying the company of angels in heaven. My mixing, on such an occasion, with publicans and sinners, is not agreeable in itself—but I entered the world as a physician: and where should a physician be, but among the disordered and dying? They that be whole need not a physician, but they that are sick."

The vindication insinuates the real condition of mankind. They are diseased. We refer to their moral maladies. The soul has its disorders, as well as the body—and the disorders of the soul are worse than those of the body: they vitiate a nobler part; they expose to a greater danger. The consequence of the one is only temporal death; the result of the other is death eternal. These maladies are the effects of the fall; and they may be seen in the errors of the judgment—the rebellion of the will—the pollution of the conscience—the sensuality of the affections—the debasement and violence of the passions. We are sometimes blamed for degrading human nature. But we do not undervalue it, as the workmanship of God; or as to its physical and intellectual powers: but only as to its moral state and propensities. And here, not only the language of the liturgy, but all Scripture, and history, and observation, and experience, proclaim, that "there is no health in us."

It also gives an implied character of himself. He is every thing that fallen, perishing creatures can need; and he stands in the same relation to them as a physician to his patients. "I am the Lord that healeth thee," is a proclamation that well becomes his lips. Job disclaimed his friends as "physicians of no value." But this can never be applied to the Lord Jesus. In all things, in this office, he has the pre-eminence. Yea, he not only stands without comparison, but alone—there is salvation in none other. But he heals every complaint. No case, however difficult, baffles his skill; or however desperate, resists the power of his applications. He is always at home; always acccessible; always delighted to attend. He only requires our submission to his management. He cures, without money and without price.

It also describes those who disregard, and those who value him. They who reject him are "the whole." None are *really* whole: for there is none righteous; no, not one. But they are so, as to apprehension and experience. And such have always been awfully numerous. Such was Paul, "while alive without the law once." Such was the Pharisee that went up into the temple to pray. Such were all the Pharisees, who trusted in themselves that they were righteous, and despised others. Such were the Laodiceans, who said, We are all rich, and increased with goods, and have need of nothing. Such were Solomon's generation, who were pure in their own eyes, and not washed from their filthiness. Such, also, are they who, though they make no pretensions to self righteousness, are satisfied with themselves—the careless, the worldly, who live without one serious thought of their souls and eternity. Yea, such, too, are they who receive the charge in theory, and acknowledge it as they do any other Bible sentiment, but there rest—not impressed with the truth, so as to urge them to the Savior—and so he will profit them nothing.

—They who value him are "the sick." They are sensible of their malady. They have a clear and deep conviction of their guilt, and depravity, and helplessness. They are thrown into the consternation persons would feel if they discovered they had taken the plague. They feel pain. They forebode death. They exclaim, What must I do to be saved! They no longer relish their former pursuits and pleasures. They loathe sin, and can never be reconciled to it again. Their cure engages all their solicitude. And, finding that there is a Savior, and a great one, they are soon at his feet, crying, "Heal my soul; for I have sinned against thee." How infinitely desirable and delightful does the Physician now appear? Who but He? They cheerfully put themselves under his care. They implicitly follow his orders. Their motto is, "If by any means." Their inquiry, "Lord, what wilt thou have me do?" With what eagerness do they inquire after symptoms of cure! With what pleasure do they perceive and feel signs of returning health! "I bless God I have a little appetite for the bread of life—I have a little strength for spiritual exercises. Perfect that which concerneth me. Thy mercy, O Lord, endureth for ever. Forsake not the work of thine own hands."

NOVEMBER 10.—"**I am the resurrection and the life.**"—**John, xi, 25.**

THERE is a spiritual resurrection and life, which all the subjects of divine grace derive from him. But here the sense is determined by the connexion. "Thy brother," said he to Martha, "shall rise again." But as he did not specify the time, she feared to apply the assurance to her present distress, or supposed that the consolation was to be drawn from the general resurrection. "Martha said unto him, I know that he shall rise again in the resurrection at the last day." To excite her immediate hope, he reminds her of his own character and resources, and says, "*I* am the resurrection and the life." There must be a very peculiar relation between him and the resurrection to life, to justify the strength of this language. It may be exemplified in various illustrations.

He is the resurrection and the life, as he is the announcer of the doctrine. For it is a truth of pure revelation. Reason could never have discovered it. The men of wisdom at Athens, the stoical and the epicurean philosophers, however widely they differed from each other, agreed in deriding this sentiment, and deemed Paul a babbler for preaching it. How inexplicable the re-union and reanimation of our scattered dust! Where now are the bodies that trod the earth before the flood! But even these bodies, through whatever changes they have passed, shall be restored and revived! Even Adam and Eve in their flesh shall see God, and be clothed in higher perfection than Eden ever knew! But *who* abolished death, and brought life and immortality to light through the Gospel? It is true that David, and even Job, rejoiced in the expectation of this glorious event; and many allusions and expressions in the Old Testament show, that the Jewish church not only believed in a future state, but in the redemption of the body from the grave. But the book in which they are contained is called "the word of Christ," and the Spirit that testifieth these things is called "the Spirit of Christ." For as the sun scatters some light before his rising, so the Savior commenced his discoveries before his incarnation; he rejoiced in the habitable parts of the earth, and his delights were with the sons of men. But by-and-by he came in person, and preached the kingdom of heaven. How simple and sublime were his discourses! And with what an awful motive did he commend his doctrine to every man's conscience in the sight of God! He drew back the veil that hid the future, and presented the elements on fire, the opening tombs, and the dead rising to meet their judge. "Marvel not at this: for the hour is coming, in the which all that are in the graves shall hear his voice, and shall come forth; they that have done good, unto the resurrection of life; and they that have done evil, unto the resurrection of damnation." He also ordered his apostles to go forth and publish, and also record it; and they did so, the Lord working with them, and confirming their word with signs following.

He is the resurrection and the life, as he affords the pledge. Under each of the three distinguishing periods of the world, the body, as well as the soul, had been received up into glory. Before the flood, Enoch was translated that he should not see death; and he was not, for God took him. The law beheld Elijah elevated to heaven in a chariot of fire. In the days of the gospel, Jesus Christ passed through the regions of the dead, and reached the crown he now wears. And there is a union between him and his people, as between the head and the members; and because he lives, they shall live also. Yea, says the apostle, "God, who is rich in mercy, for his great love wherewith he loved us, even when we were dead in sins, hath quickened us together with Christ, (by grace ye are saved,) and hath raised us up together, and made us sit together in heavenly places in Christ Jesus."

He is the resurrection and the life, as he procures the privilege. To him we meritoriously owe all the blessings we possess. In the Lord we have righteousness and strength. And are we raised from the dead? "Since by man came death, by man came also the resurrection of the dead. As in Adam all die, even so in Christ shall all be made alive. But every man in his own order: Christ the first fruits; afterward they that are Christ's at his coming." He has redeemed our whole nature; and the body being ransomed, as well as the spirit, by no less a price than his own blood, shall be equally claimed, and renewed, and glorified.

" This living hope we owe
" To Jesus' dying love;
" We would adore his grace below,
" And sing his power above."

He is the resurrection and the life, as he is the pattern. For we shall rise, not like Adam, but like him. "The first man is of the earth, earthy: the second man is the Lord from heaven. As is the earthy, such are they also that are earthy; and as is the heavenly, such are they also that are heavenly. And as we have borne the image of the earthy, we shall also bear the image of the heavenly." In his rising from the dead, we see the model of our own resurrection; and the grandeur of our destiny. We imagine, says Paul, whatever is admirable and splendid in his glorified humanity; and we look for nothing less in ourselves; "We look for the Savior, the Lord Jesus Christ, who shall change our vile body, that it may be fashioned like unto his glorious body, according to the working whereby he is able even to subdue all things unto himself." At present the body is vile; not as the workmanship of God, but as defiled by sin, as degraded by disease, and especially as the spoil of worms, and in the corruption of the grave. What a hindrance! what a burden! what a loathsomeness is the body of this death? But then, by a change the most marvellous, it will have the same excellencies as the body of God. "So also is the resurrection of the dead. It is sown in corruption; it is raised in incorruption: it is sown in dishonor; it is raised in glory: it is sown in weakness; it is raised in power: it is sown a natural body; it is raised a spiritual body. There is a natural body, and there is a spiritual body."

He is the resurrection and the life, as he achieves the work. Hence he said to his hearers, "This is the will of Him that sent me, that every one which seeth the Son, and believeth on him, may have everlasting life: and I will raise him up at the last day." What a power will this require! But nothing is too hard for him. His almighty fiat will, in a moment, in the twinkling of an eye, pervade the depths of the sea; penetrate the recesses of the earth; and gather the remnants of death, and give them organization and life, and sight, and voice, for ever!

Happy they who are the children of the resurrection; and who will be able to welcome the restorer of all things—Lo! this is our God, we have waited for him; we will be glad to rejoice in his salvation.

For though, as an event, the resurrection will be universal; as a privilege, it will be limited. Every eye will see him. But how many will wail because of him! "And the kings of the earth, and the great men, and the rich men, and the chief captains, and the mighty men, and every bondman, and every freeman, shall hide themselves in the dens and in the rocks of the mountains; and shall say to the mountains and rocks, Fall on us, and hide us from the face of Him that sitteth on the throne, and from the wrath of the Lamb: for the great day of his wrath is come; and who shall be able to stand?"

NOVEMBER 11.—"I rejoice in thy salvation."—1 Samuel, ii, 1.

THESE are the words of Hannah, a very pious and highly accomplished female, to whom the Jews were much indebted for one of their best public characters. For Samuel was given in answer to her prayers; he was trained and formed by her instructions; and he was early dedicated to God, at the expense of her self-denial. She also edified her own generation, and she continues to edify ours, by her composition. "And Hannah prayed, and said, My heart rejoiceth in the Lord; mine horn is exalted in the Lord; my mouth is enlarged over mine enemies, because I REJOICE IN THY SALVATION." Let us notice this part of her song, and let us take the subject in the highest sense of which it is susceptible. For there are many salvations which God accomplishes; but there is one that excelleth in glory, and to which the term is pre-eminently, if not exclusively, applied. In this salvation every believer rejoices.

He rejoices in the discovery of it. He is pained indeed to think that as yet multitudes of his fellow creatures have never heard of it; and he prays that his way may be made known on earth, his saving health among all nations. But he is grateful that to him is the word of this salvation sent. There was a time, indeed, when he treated it with indifference; but when he began to see and feel his perishing condition, and to exclaim, with the jailer, What must I do to be saved? he received this intelligence as Hagar did the angel's kindness, when he opened her eyes and showed her a well: or as the Grecians heard the Roman consul's proclamation of liberty, when they cried for hours, Soter, Soter—Savior, Savior!

He rejoices in the properties of this salvation. In the freeness of it—that it requires no qualifications, no conditions, and is without money, and without price. In the purity of it, that it not only contains pardoning mercy, but sanctifying grace; and is designed to save him from his sins, which he now feels to be his worst enemies. In the perpetuity of it—that He who begins a good work will perform it until the day of Jesus Christ; that he who believes *hath* everlasting life, and shall *never* come into condemnation. In the extensiveness of it—that Jesus gave himself a ransom for all, to be testified in due time; and that this salvation is prepared before the face of all people, a light to lighten the gentiles, and the glory of his people Israel.

He rejoices in the hope of it. This hope admits of various degrees, and the joy will be influenced by them. The lowest degree of it may serve to keep the mind from despair, as a weak bough will sustain a man drowning, till a firmer support comes to his relief. But there is a lively hope; there is an abounding in hope; there is the full assurance of hope—this will fill us with joy unspeakable, and full of glory. Thousands rejoice in hope who will never obtain possession of the object of it. But the hope of Christians maketh not ashamed, because the love of God is shed abroad in the heart by the Holy Ghost which is given unto them.

He rejoices in the experience of it. For he not only apprehends it as a desirable and future good, but he has a present actual participation of it. He feels the influence of it in his conscience, in his heart, in his life. If a man be not saved on this side the grave, he will never be saved on the other. "We," says the apostle, "who have believed, do enter into rest." And "Blessed," says David, "*is* the people that know the joyful sound: they shall walk, O Lord, in the light of thy countenance; in thy name shall they rejoice all the day: and in thy righteousness shall they be exalted."

He rejoices in the completion of it. For, though now he is enlightened, yet it is with the illumination of the dawn, not of the day. Though now he is sanctified, he is renewed but in part. Though justified and adopted, he does not always know his condition, and never enjoys all the privileges of it. He has the earnests, but not the inheritance; a few of the grapes of Eshcol, but not the vineyards of Canaan. But when that which is perfect shall come, then that which is in part shall be done away. In pursuit of which, he can say, with David, "Thou wilt not leave my soul in hell; neither wilt thou suffer thine Holy One to see corruption. Thou wilt show me the path of life: in thy presence is *fullness* of joy; at thy right hand there are pleasures for evermore. "As for me, I will behold thy face in righteousness: I shall be *satisfied*, when I awake, with thy likeness."

And yet the enemy of souls tells the young, that religion is an utter enemy to enjoyment! yet the world supposes that Zion is the metropolis of gloom and sadness. But "as well the singers, as the players on instruments, are *there*." And they who have made the trial, know that her ways are ways of pleasantness, and all her paths are peace. And the God of truth has said, "Behold, my servants shall sing for joy of heart; but ye shall cry for sorrow of heart, and shall howl for vexation of spirit." Christians have a thousand things to rejoice in; but this is the chief, *the salvation of God.* And there is enough in *this* to inspire joy in the midst of every loss and trial. "Although the fig-tree shall not blossom, neither shall fruit be in the vines; the labor of the olive shall fail, and the fields shall yield no meat; the flock shall be cut off from the fold, and there shall be no herd in the stalls; yet I will rejoice in the Lord, I will joy in the God of my salvation.

NOVEMBER 12.—" So the Lord alone did lead him, and there was no strange God with him."—Deuteronomy, xxxii, 12.

CONSISTENCY is a quality which a writer finds it no easy thing to maintain, when he brings forward a character. The higher, and the more peculiar, and the more original the character be, the more is the difficulty increased. But when God is introduced, the difficulty becomes supreme. For "to whom will ye liken me, or shall I be equal?" saith the Holy One. From their knowledge of the general principles of their nature, which are the same in all, men may, with tolerable accuracy, speak of men; and describe how an individual would act in a given relation or condition. But for men to speak of God, and so represent him in all his attributes and actions, as that nothing shall fall short of an infinitely perfect Being, is what never would have been accomplished without inspiration. But we find this in the Scriptures; because holy men of God wrote as they were moved by the Holy Ghost. And hence, though the sacred writers bring God forth in every page, we may almost say, in every sentence, he always appears in character, that is, in character with himself.

One thing, however, must be admitted—and it is by no means inconsistent with this—that, in the revelation with which we have been favored, God has conformed himself to our modes of apprehension and expression. But this was necessary to render him at once intelligible and impressive. This therefore shows us, not only his wisdom, but condescension—and dignity is never degraded by condescension. Thus he speaks unto us, as unto children, with whom imitation is every thing; and levies a tax upon all the world of nature, to furnish images of himself.

There is no relation he so commonly assumes as the parental. Nor need we wonder at this, when we consider—that there is combined in it every thing at once venerable and endearing—that it appeals to the present sympathies of the heart—and aids our devotion by means even of our very instincts. And observe how he assumes it. Sometimes he takes the affection of the father; and we read, "Like as a father pitieth his children, so the Lord pitieth them that fear him." "I will spare them as a man spareth his own son that serveth him." Sometimes he appropriates the tenderness of the mother; and we read, "As one whom his mother comforteth, so will he comfort you." At other times he descends lower, and borrows from the animal, and especially the feathered tribes: and we read, "He shall cover thee with his feathers: and under his wings shalt thou trust." "How often would I have gathered thee, as a hen gathereth her chickens under her wings, and ye would not." As an eagle stirreth up her nest, fluttereth over her young, spreadeth abroad her wings, taketh them, beareth them on her wings, so the Lord alone did lead him, and there was no strange god with him."

Observe a divine agency—*the Lord led him.* The allusion is to the Jews; and the meaning is, that God conducted them in their journeyings to Canaan. They were very numerous; but the aggregate of them all was to him like an infant. "I took them by the hand to lead them out of Egypt." "He led them by the right way, that they might go to a city of habitation." "He led them about, he instructed them, he kept them as the apple of his eye."

See, also, the exclusive application of this work. "The Lord *alone* did lead him, and there was no strange god with him." The idols of the heathen were acknowledged to be limited in their powers. None of them could do every thing—there were therefore lords many, and gods many. There was a god for every exigency: a god for the sea—a god for the winds—a god for the field—a god for the garden—a god for marriage—and a god for war—and so of the rest. But, said the church, "Our God is in the heavens; he hath done whatsoever he pleased." And he himself said, "O Israel! the Lord thy God is one Lord." *He* wrought out every deliverance for them. *He* conferred every blessing upon them—and, having done the work without any helper, he deserved all the praise, and assigns this as the reason why they should not divide their regards between him and any other. "*I* removed his shoulder from the burden: his hands were delivered from the pots. Thou calledst in trouble, and *I* delivered thee; *I* answered thee in the secret place of thunder; *I* proved thee at the waters of Meribah. Selah. Hear, O my people, and I will testify unto thee: O, Israel, if thou wilt hearken unto me—there shall no strange god be in thee, neither shalt thou worship any strange god."

Here is also a resemblance of the manner in which it was performed. "*So* the Lord alone did lead him, and there was no strange god with him." How? "As an eagle stirreth up her nest, fluttereth over her young, spreadeth abroad her wings, taketh them, beareth them on her wings."

All this is not to be confined to the Jews. There is also a spiritual Israel, whom they were intended to prefigure; the circumcision, who worship God in the Spirit, and rejoice in Christ Jesus, and have no confidence in the flesh. And such a people he now has for his name; and he is leading them; leading them alone, without any one to divide with him the work, or share with him the glory. And how does he this? Let us not torture the image, but let us improve it. Three things are here ascribed to the mother eagle—not in providing for her young; for this is not the subject in question—but in educating them; in teaching them to fly. She stirreth up her nest. She fluttereth over her young. She spreadeth abroad her wings, and taketh them, and beareth them on her wings. And all this is applicable to God, in his dealing with us, and preparing to seek those things that are above.

NOVEMBER 13.—"As an eagle stirreth up her nest."—Deut. xxxii, 11.

—SHE sees the eaglets nestling, blinking and dozing, and she wishes them to fly. Arise, says she—but they refuse. She then stirs up the nest—shakes it; turns out the inside: separates, scatters the parts. That is she either destroys the nest, or makes it so uncomfortable that the young ones move out upon the neighboring boughs, where they are in a posture for flight. God does the same with us—He stirs up our nest.

First. As to our outward condition in the world. This was the case with the Jews. Egypt had been their abode, where, in the infancy of their state, they were lodged like birds in a nest; and though it was an impure one, and much straitened and confined them, they evinced no care to leave it. And it is easy to see, that if they had been well treated, and enjoyed the smiles of the government, and the former advantages of Goshen, Moses might have called long enough before they would have come out. But there arose another king, that knew not Joseph, who evil entreated them, and made their lives bitter by reason of cruel bondage. Their burdens were intolerable; their tasks impracticable; their complaints were turned into insults; their daughters were for slaves, and their sons for slaughter. And now they sigh for deliverance, and are willing to go forth, even into a wilderness, at the divine call. Thus God stirred up their nest. Manasseh was the son of good Hezekiah: but every pious principle of his education had been corrupted by power, wealth, and pleasure. He became proverbial for wickedness, and would have gone on till he had filled up the measure of his iniquity. But God stirred up his nest. "And when he was in affliction, he besought the Lord his God, and humbled himself greatly before the God of his fathers, and prayed unto him: and he was intreated of him, and heard his supplication, and brought him again to Jerusalem into his kingdom. Then Manasseh knew that the Lord he was God." What brought the prodigal to his senses, and made him think of home? A mighty famine in the land—he began to be in want. How many now living can say, "It is good for me that I have been afflicted: before I was afflicted I went astray, but now have I kept thy word!" *You* had health: but sickness invaded your frame; and you have been made to possess months of vanity, and have had wearisome nights appointed for you. *You* prospered in business: but your purposes were broken off; your schemes failed; you were put back in life, and compelled to begin the world afresh. *You* had a wife of your bosom: but the Lord took away the desire of your eyes with a stroke. *You* had a favorite child on whom you placed many a flattering expectation; but at an early grave you sighed, "Thou destroyest the hope of man"—and now, at your meals, you see David's seat is empty—and you often retire, and sigh, "Childhood and youth are vanity." And what is all this, but his stirring up your nest, and, by a sad, but salutary necessity, constraining you to turn from time to eternity from the creature to Himself, the supreme good? And what a mercy if you can *now* say—

> " *Now* to the shining realms above,
> " I stretch my hands, and glance mine eyes:
> " O for the pinions of a dove,
> " To bear me to the upper skies!
>
> " There, from the bosom of my God,
> " Oceans of endless pleasures roll:
> " *There* would I fix my last abode,
> " And drown the sorrows of the soul."

Secondly. As to our self-righteous confidence and security. We have naturally a good opinion of ourselves; and the enemy of souls loves to cherish it. He therefore keeps his palace and his goods in peace. He dreads a stir in the conscience. He knows that we must be humbled before we are exalted; wounded, before we can be healed; and be emptied of self, before we can be filled with all the fullness of God. This state of mind must therefore be disturbed and destroyed before any thing like genuine religion can commence. And what does God? By the conviction of sin, like a general at the head of an army, he enters the soul—and the man no more says, Peace, peace—his hopes are fled—he is reduced to self-despair—and his only cry is, " What must I do to be saved?" His worldly friends are alarmed for him; but they who know what is the way of the Spirit, rejoice—not that he is made sorry, but that he now sorrows after a godly sort. And the subject of the change himself may mistake the nature and design of the operation, and conclude that he is going to be destroyed. But if the Lord had a mind to kill him he would not have shown him such things as these. Thus it was with Paul. See how his nest was feathered with self-righteousness; and see how it was stirred up—" I was alive without the law once: but when the commandment came, sin revived, and I died." " For I through the law am dead to the law, that I might iive unto God."

Thirdly. As to our departure from life. We are not to remain here always; and it is no little difficulty to break up our attachment to the present state, and to make us willing to leave it. But see how this is done. After a number of years, we have a feeling persuasion that this is not our rest; that creatures are broken reeds: that the earth is a vale of tears; that the world is vanity and vexation of spirit; and having looked through every scene here, we wish for another and a nobler region of existence. Then, too, our powers begin to fail us. Pains and infirmities grow upon us. Our decaying senses shuts us out by degrees from former objects and pursuits. The days are come wherein we have no pleasure. Hearing fails. They that look out of the window are darkened. Fear is in the way. The grasshopper is a burden.

> " Our vitals, with laborious strife,
> " Bear up the crazy load;
> " And drag the dull remains of life
> " Along the tiresome road."

—And when we look around, where now are the relations and friends that once rendered life delightful? Lover and friend he has put far from us, and our acquaintance into darkness. We seem more and better related to another world than this. We feel the drawings of those who are gone—"What have I here? and what do I here?" and now the hope of usefulness ceases to detain us. How can I glorify God, or serve my generation? Why should I remain a cumberer of the ground, when so many fine and fruitful trees are cut down? And now we become better acquainted with the heavenly world we have more nearly approached—O what darkness here! and what sunshine there! What bondage here! and what liberty there! There no law in the members warring against the law of the mind. There no complaint. When I would do good, evil is present with me. Is not this worth dying for? Then the earnest and foretastes of the glory to which we are going render every thing else comparatively insipid; and the grapes of Eshcol makes us long for the vineyards of Canaan. And thus the Lord stirs up the nest of life itself, and gets the heir of immortality upon the perch for his departure—where he is able to say,

"There is a house not made with hands,
"Eternal and on high:
"And here my spirit waiting stands,
"Till God shall bid it fly."

NOVEMBER 14.—"Fluttereth over her young."—Deuteronomy, xxxii, 11.

—THIS she does to excite and teach them by her own example. And God does the same with regard to us. The eye does much more than the ear. The advantage derivable from example is universally allowed. It not only aids in the illustration of a subject, but also in the impression and influence of it; as it helps the memory, strikes the fancy, reproves indolence, encourages hope, and fires zeal. Wise teachers will therefore always teach as much as possible by example.

—How sad is the state of those who are destitute of this advantage in religion! And there are those to be found who have scarcely an instance of godliness within their reach. We pity the son who has indeed a father who instructs him, and by his own example too—but it is to swear; to profane the Sabbath; to despise the house of God. We pity the daughter who has indeed a mother who leads her, and by her own example too—but it is to idolize her person; to read novels and romances—not the words of eternal life; to repair to places of dissipation—not to the throne of the heavenly grace. Is there an individual perusing this page, who is stationed in a neighborhood or a family, where he can find no one with whom he can unite in any religious exercise; who moves on alone; and even perhaps, through reproach and opposition? Let him remember, that this may not be the case always. If he walks in wisdom toward them that are without, his endeavors in time may be available; and his prayers be heard; and though he has been denied the advantage of *having* an example, he may have the honor of *becoming* one, and of leading others in the way everlasting.

—But there a few places now, in which there are not some instances of Divine grace, sufficient to condemn the world, and to encourage those whose faces are Zionward. Some, perhaps, have many godly persons around them—and they see how superior these are to other men. How content! How grateful! How supported in trouble! How hopeful in death! Some have pious friends and relations. You have, perhaps, a sister, who often intreats you. Or a wife, who endeavors to win you. Or a father, who says, My son, if thine heart be wise, my heart shall rejoice, even mine. Or a mother, who weeps over you, and exclaims, What, my son! and the son of my womb! and the son of my vows! And what is all this, but God teaching and exciting you? And if you can read, you have an additional advantage. How many excellent lives have been published! How many fine characters are portrayed in the Scriptures! And, by the perusal of all these, you bring a cloud of witnesses and examples before you. And when you see them in the exercise and display of whatsoever is lovely and of good report, do you not see God in all this, like the eagle fluttering over her young?

But look at him in his more personal conduct. See how he not only teaches and excites by his word, but by his own example. Does he command us to be merciful? He is merciful; rich in mercy—he delighteth in mercy. Does he enjoin us to give? He daily loadeth us with his benefits. He gives us richly all things to enjoy. He spared not his own Son. Does he require us to forgive? He is ready to pardon. He abundantly pardons; "Love your enemies," says he; "bless them that curse you, do good to them that hate you, and pray for them which despitefully use you and persecute you; that ye may be the children of your Father which is in heaven: for he maketh his sun to rise on the evil and on the good, and sendeth rain on the just and on the unjust." "Be ye therefore perfect, even as your Father which is in heaven is perfect." This is not an optional thing with us—we *must* resemble him; and are only religious, in proportion as we are like him, and are one spirit with him.

To render his example the more engaging, we were going to say, he humanized it. And God was manifest in the flesh. And this rendered his example, not only the more attractive, but the more suitable, and even complete. For it is obvious that he could not have been our example, and have gone before us, in the exercise of any of those graces, or the performance of any of those duties, which imply dependence, submission, and suffering, unless he had became incarnate. The Word, therefore, was made flesh, and dwelt among us. Divine goodness walked up and down the earth, for three-and-thirty-years in human form. Here was visible the Image of the invisible God. The sovereign comes down, and goes before his subjects, to excite and allure them—See, says he: I obey, to teach you to obey—I suffer, to teach you how to suffer—I die, to make you fearless of death. "Be ye therefore followers of God, as dear children; and walk in love, as Christ also loved us, and hath given himself for us an offering and a sacrifice to God for a sweet-smelling savor."

Let ministers learn from hence to be parental, rather than magisterial; and to do more by influence than authority—"Neither as being lords over God's heritage; but being ensamples to the flock." This is what Paul enjoined on his son Timothy: "Be thou an example to the believers, in word, in conversation, in charity, in spirit, in faith, in purity." And what was his own practice? "As ye know how we exhorted, and comforted, and charged every one of you, as a father doth his children." "We were gentle among you, even as a nurse cherisheth her children. So being affectionately desirous of you, we were willing to have imparted unto you, not the gospel of God only, but also our own souls, because ye were dear unto us."

And let parents remember this image. Do, as well as teach. Be amiable. Render your religion inviting. Let your children *see* it rather than hear it. Come near them—attach them—draw them.

> "And as the bird each fond endearment tries,
> "To tempt her new-fledged offspring to the skies;
> "Employ each art; reprove each dull delay!
> "Allure to brighter worlds, and lead the way."

NOVEMBER 15.—"Spreadeth abroad her wings, taketh them, beareth them on her wings."—Deuteronomy, xxxii, 11.

THIS is to aid, and also to secure them. When they mount her back, they are little aware of her design; but away she sails with them, and sometimes she shakes them off. Then they must fly themselves; but she follows after—She hovers near them; and when their pinions flag, and they are unable to keep longer on the wing, with surprising speed and skill she darts, and places herself underneath them; and thus receiving their whole weight, she prevents their fall, succors their weakness, and refreshes them for another flight. The Lord never entirely leaves his people—and it is well he does not: for without him, they can do nothing. He does, however, in a degree, leave them, to make them more sensible of their weakness, and induce them to rely more upon himself; but not so as to hazard their safety. Thus the mother, when her infant, beginning to walk, is too venturesome, leaves him alone—not to go over a plank across a river, but in the room with her, and upon the carpet, where the fall will alarm and caution—not kill, or fracture him—and she soon takes him up, and presses him to her bosom and her lips. God has himself (how much more we need to teach and affect us!) employed another tender image. When young and feeble, the day perhaps warm, and the ground rough, the little lambs are unable to keep pace with the flock, and would be left panting and bleating behind: but the Shepherd of Israel gathers them with his arms, and carries them in his bosom.

Many are not convinced of their weakness, because they have never made, in earnest, a trial of their strength. But when a man begins to apply himself to the purposes of the divine life, he feels how unable he is to do any thing as of himself: and he would never be induced to take one step, effectually, in a religious course, without such an assurance as the Gospel presents. Possibility, probability, is not enough; he must hear the voice that cries, "My grace *is* sufficient for thee; for my strength is made perfect in weakness." And he does hear this. And, though much is required and expected of him, he sees all the means necessary to the end. He sees a cause more than adequate to the effect. It is a great thing to be a Christian: but "OUR SUFFICIENCY IS OF GOD."

He has said, "I will strengthen them in the Lord;" and "as thy day, so shall thy strength be." He aids them by his providence. And by communion with each other. And in the ordinances of religion. Ministers are "helpers of their joy." His word quickens them. His statutes help them. In the holy assemblies, and at the table of their dying Lord, while they wait upon him, he renews their strength; and they mount up with wings, as eagles; and they run, and are not weary; and walk, and not faint. But all these are only the means—the Holy Spirit is the agent. Not by might, nor by power, but by my Spirit, saith the Lord. Our dependence upon Him is entire. We pray in the Spirit; we live, we walk in the Spirit. He leads us into all truth. He seals us unto the day of redemption. But for his influence, who would not every moment despond and sink?

But the eagle, by taking and bearing her young on her wings, not only sustains and supports them, but protects and secures them. Is an anemy in sight? She soars with them above his reach. Does the archer discharge his arrows from below? They must pierce through her body before they can touch them. "The path of life is above to the wise, to depart from hell beneath." And God is the refuge, as well as the strength of his people. And to each of them, he says what David said to Abiathar, when he fled to him from the slaughter of Saul, "Abide with me; fear not: for he that seeketh thy life, seeketh my life; but with me thou shalt be in safeguard." When they can realize this, their soul dwells at ease. .This is sometimes their privilege—it ought to be always their experience. Their security is always the same: but Paul was *persuaded* of it—"I am *persuaded*," says he, "that neither death, nor life, nor angels, nor principalities, nor powers, nor things present, nor things to come, nor height, nor depth, nor any other creature, shall be able to separate us from the love of God, which is in Christ Jesus our Lord."

NOVEMBER 16.—"Thy hidden ones."—Psalm lxxxiii, 3.

THIS representation of God's people is worthy our notice. It may be taken two ways.

First. As referring to their safety. We often hide, only to preserve. This is the meaning of the word in the parable, with regard to the discovery of the treasure in the field, "which, when a man hath found, he *hideth* it." His aim is not to conceal, but to secure: and the cause is put for the effect. Thus God's people are hidden. He hid Noah in the ark, and the waters that drowned the world could not *find* him. When his judgments were coming over the land, "Come, my people," said He, "enter thou into thy chambers, and shut thy doors about thee; hide thee also for a little season, until the indignation be overpast." Hence the promise, "Thou shalt hide them in the secret of thy presence from the pride of man; thou shalt keep them secretly in a pavilion from the strife of tongues." Hence the confidence expressed by David,

"In the time of trouble he shall hide me in his pavilion: in the secret of his tabernacle shall he hide me; he shall set me upon a rock." The Savior could say, "In the shadow of his hand hath he hid me." And, "All the saints are in his hand." They are kept by the power of God, through faith, unto salvation. For He himself is their "refuge," their "hiding-place." They are his hidden ones.

Secondly. As intimating their concealment. This is not absolute; but it holds in various respects and degrees. It is true with regard to the nature of their spiritual life. Our life, says the apostle, is hid with Christ, in God; and that he refers to its invisibleness, rather than to its safety, is obvious from the words following: "When he who is our life shall *appear*, *we* also shall *appear* with him in glory." The source, principles, and actings of this life, are unintelligible to natural men; neither can they know them, because they are spiritually discerned. The heart of the believer only feels his own bitterness, and a stranger intermeddleth not with his joy. The manna upon which he feeds is hidden manna. And no one knoweth the new name in the white stone given him but the receiver. His grief is too deep to be noisy. He sitteth alone, and keeps silence. The stricken deer leaves the herd. Other warriors appeal to the senses, and get fame; but his conflicts are carried on within, visible to God only; and his laurels are all future. Others may give alms to be seen of men; but his left hand is not to know what his right hand doeth.

They are sometimes hidden by persecution. For though this does not prevent their being Christians, it hinders them from appearing as such, especially by secluding them from their social and public assemblies. This is not our case. Our teachers are not put into a corner. We can go to the house of God in company. We can feed in the ways; and our pasture is in all high places. But call to remembrance the former times, when they wandered in deserts, and in mountains, and dens, and caves of the earth; or were confined in prisons; or prayed and preached under the cover of night. But they were dear to God—they were *his* hidden ones.

—They are sometimes hidden by the obscurity of their stations. Not many of the wise, and mighty, and noble, are called: but when they *are* called, they are also exhibited. They are like cities set on hills, which cannot be hid. A little religion in high life goes a great way, and is much talked of, because it is so often a strange thing. But God hath chosen the poor of this world; and they are often rich in faith. Yet how is their moral wealth to be known? How few opportunities have they for religious display or exertion! There may be the principle of benevolence where there is no ability to give; and the Lord seeth the heart. But men can only judge from actions. Many who are great in the sight of the Lord, are living in cottages and hovels, and are scarcely known, unless to a few neighbors equally obscure.

—They are sometimes hidden by their disposition. They are reserved, and shrink back from notice. They are timid and self-diffident. This restrains them in religious conversation, especially as it regards their own experience. This keeps them from making a profession of religion, and joining a Christian church. Joseph of Arimathea was a disciple of Jesus, but secretly, for fear of the Jews. And Nicodemus, from the same cause, came to Jesus by night. They had difficulties in their situations, from which others were free. They ought to have overcome them; and so they did at last; but it was a day of small things with them at first. Others are circumstanced and tried in a similar way; and we must be patient toward all men.

They are sometimes hidden by their infirmities. We would not plead for sin; but grace may be found along with many imperfections. The possessors have what is essential to religion in them; but not what is ornamantal, and lovely, and of good report. —The same also will apply to errors. Here, again, we are far from undervaluing divine truth. It is a good thing that the heart be established with grace. But it is impossible for us to say how much ignorance, and how many mistakes may be found, even in the Israelite indeed, in whom is no guile. How little did Peter know of the most important of all subjects, when our Savior pronounced him blessed: and said he was a partaker of divine illumination! We extend this even to congregations and communities. There may be individuals in them, wiser than their teachers; and no strangers to communion with the God of all grace. Who can entertain too bad an opinion of popery? Yet we find a Nicol, a Pascal, a Fenelon, in that most corrupt church. Where may not God have his hidden ones? Let us not judge of the real number of his people, by things that do appear. It is not only candor, but truth, that tells us we may enlarge our hopes; while we ought to pray always, "The Lord add to his people, how many soever they be, a hundredfold." "Wot ye not what the Scripture said of Elias? how he maketh intercession to God against Israel, saying, Lord, they have killed thy prophets, and digged down thine altars; and I am left alone, and they seek my life. But what saith the answer of God unto him? I have reserved to myself seven thousand men, who have not bowed the knee to the image of Baal."

NOVEMBER 17.—"His seed shall endure for ever."—Psalm lxxxix, 36.

DAVID was peculiarly related to the Messiah. He wrote, as a poet, and a prophet, much concerning him. He yielded the most varied and complete type of him ever exhibited. He was at once his Lord and his Son. Hence the name of the former is often applied to the latter; and what is spoken of the one, is often to be extended to the other—and *must* be so applied, to do any thing like justice to the force of the language. And in this cause we are more than justified, by numerous appropriations of men in the New Testament, who spake as they were moved by the Holy Ghost.

Upon this principle, the words before us insure the perpetuation of his people. "His seed shall continue for ever." We shall say nothing of their number; though if we were asked the question, Are there few that shall be saved?" we could boldly answer, No!

Ignorance and bigotry have always diminished them; but they shall be found, when gathered together, a countless multitude.

But why are they called his *seed?* Because they derive their being, as new creatures, from him. "Every one that doeth righteousness, is born of him." In such a relation, we look for resemblance. This, indeed, is not invariably the case with regard to children. Some of them have little of the father's likeness, either in features or in temper. But all Christians resemble Christ. They bear the image of the heavenly; and if any man have not the Spirit of Christ, he is none of his. The relation infers duty. It does away, indeed, with all servileness; but not with service. "A seed shall serve him." "And I will spare them," says he, "as a man spareth his own son that serveth him." "A son honoreth his father." Every Christian, therefore, will ask, "Lord, what wilt thou have me to do?" The relation confers honor. His seed are descended from One who is higher than the kings of the earth; in whom are hid all the treasures of wisdom and knowledge; and whose holiness and goodness are infinite. Such honor have all his saints. But what a privilege does it bespeak! There is an amazing instinct in the brute creation toward their young. It seems to transform the very nature of some of them. The timid sheep, and the fearful bird, become bold and daring on behalf of their young. As to man, if *he* were not to provide for his own, he would be contemned by all around him: and were he a pretender to religion, he would be considered as denying the faith, and be deemed worse than an infidel. Will the Lord Jesus neglect his offspring? Will he suffer them to want any good thing? Will he not educate them? Chastise them? Resent every injury that is done them? Acknowledge and defend them?

But observe, not only their relation to him, but their perpetuity—"They shall continue for ever." They die, as well as others—they often die earlier. But, consistently with this obvious and undeniable fact, they shall continue for ever, in three senses. First. In the succession of their race to the end of the world. It will never be cut off. The church in danger! *What* church! "Upon this rock," says he "I will build *my* church; and the gates of hell shall not prevail against it." Yea, his people shall continue to increase in number and excellency. We shall leave the world better than we entered it: and so will our *children*—till Jerusalem shall be established, and be made a praise in the whole earth. Secondly. In their religious character to the end of life. If left to themselves, we could not be sure of their persevering to the end of a day or an hour. But they are kept by the power of God, through faith, unto salvation. He upholdeth them with his hand. They shall hold on their way. In their dangers they shall be more than conquerors. Thirdly. In their glorified state, through eternal ages. The world passeth away, and the lusts thereof; but he that doeth the will of God, abideth for ever. All other greatness is only for life; frequently is not so long; but at death, it *ends.* But *then,* the Christian's greatness—I will not say begins; for it began the moment he prayed—but then it continues—increases—and is perfected. Death only affects one part of him: the body is dead, because of sin; but the spirit is life, because of righteousness—and even the body shall be revived, and improved—and made like the Savior's own glorious body—and be as immortal as the soul. Every thing here is variable, fading, perishing—

> "All, all on earth, is shadow; all beyond,
> "Is substance—the reverse is Folly's creed—
> "How solid all, where change shall be no more!"

—Where we shall have not only endless existence, but endless existence beatified. Where, if we have treasure, moth and rust will not corrupt, nor thieves break through and steal. Where, if we have a house, it will not be a house made with hands, but eternal in the heavens. Where, if we have friendship, we shall part no more. Where, we shall be FOR EVER WITH THE LORD.

NOVEMBER 18.—"Open thy mouth wide."—Psalm lxxxi, 10,

THOUGH we cannot find out God perfectly in his essence or his works, we are not left in total ignorance concerning him. We have all the information our duty and our consolation require. Though he be a God that hideth himself, yet he is the God of Israel, the Savior. He has been pleased to reveal himself as the hearer of prayer. Yea, more—as exciting it—as encouraging it—as concerned for the enlargement of our desires in the performance of it. "Open thy mouth wide."

This is no easy thing, with the consciousness we feel, as sinners. But, to aid us herein, let us consider his greatness and all-sufficiency. We should expect more from a prince than from a pauper. Many have benevolence without resources—and in vain we address them. They may grieve to deny us, but they cannot relieve. When the woman cried, "Help, O king!" he said, "Whence should I help thee?" But we kneel before One, whose greatness is unsearchable—who is Lord of all. His giving a world would be less than our giving a crumb of bread. When Alexander had bestowed a very valuable present on a poor man, his modesty would have declined it. "It is too much," said he, "for *me* to receive." "But," said the emperor, "it is not too much for me to give." God gives like himself, and he is to be addressed in character with himself. We believe in God, the Father Almighty, Maker of heaven and earth. Is it comfort we want? He is the God of all comfort. Is it deliverance? Nothing is too hard for the Lord. Is it renovation? He can make all things new—He is able to do for us exceeding abundantly above all we ask or think, according to the power that worketh in us.

Let us consider his goodness. Nothing tends to contract us more than a sense of unworthiness. We ought to feel this—but we ought not to be discouraged by it; since he is the God of all grace, the Father of mercies; since he is rich in mercy, and delighteth in mercy. We are not to judge of Him by a human standard. It is an injury to us, when we are applying to him, to think of the benevolence of the most generous of our fellow creatures—so far short do they come of his glory. "My thoughts are not your thoughts, neither are your ways my ways, saith the Lord. For as the heavens are higher than the earth, so are my ways higher than your ways, and my thoughts than your thoughts." And the reference here is to his thoughts and ways of mercy, and especially pardoning mercy.

—Let us remember, also, the medium through which we implore his favors. We have boldnesss and access with confidence, by the faith of him: we have boldness to enter into the holiest, by the blood of Jesus; having such a High Priest over the house of God, we draw near in full assurance of faith. In saving and glorifying us, through the Son of his love, we do not ask God to deny his truth, or dishonor his name, or trample upon his law—yea, he magnifies his law in doing it. He declares his righteousness. While he redeems Jacob, he glorifies himself in Israel: and glory to God in the highest, is combined with peace on earth, and good will toward men. Let us think of this: and ask and receive, that our joy may be full. Whatsoever, said he, ye shall ask the Father in my name, he will do it.

—Review, also, the manner in which he has answered the prayers of his people. Has he ever refused? Has he ever given sparingly? Jacob asked for bread to eat, and raiment to put on, and a return in peace to his father's house: and, lo: he becomes two bands! Solomon asked for a wise and understanding heart: and he obtained not only this, but life, and riches, and honor! Abraham left off asking before God left off giving. Why did he stop at ten? Had not God complied with every preceding proposal, without the least reluctance! But Abraham was ashamed—he had not courage to go on.

—But is it not sufficient that he has commanded it? Having his authority, you cannot be chargeable with presumption, if you ask much. Yea, if you do not, you will be guilty of rebellion. How did he punish the guests who refused the invitation to the feast, "Come, for all things are now ready!"

—Here is also an express assurance—a promise, not only that we shall receive, but be filled. Open thy mouth wide, and "I will fill it." He will supply *all* our need from his riches in glory. He will bless us with *all* spiritual blessings in heavenly places in Christ.

Where is the Christain who lives up to his duty?—to his privilege? For God not only answers prayer really, but proportionably. He says, "Be it unto thee even as thou wilt."

Let not him, therefore, who prays rarely and coldly, think to succeed like the frequent and fervent petitioner. Honor God, and God will honor you. He does not despise the day of small things; but the hand of the diligent maketh rich."

NOVEMBER 19.—"Dost thou believe on the Son of God?"—John, ix, 35.

THIS question was addressed to a man that had been blind. Some are blind by accident, and some by disease; but this man was born blind. He had never seen even the face of her who bore him, and who, as she fed him at her breast, would often look upon him, and weep over her orbless boy. Blindness is always a sufficient affliction in itself; but here it is probable, penury was added to it. Like others of the same class of sufferers mentioned in the Gospels, he seems to have sat by the way-side, begging. Many had passed him without notice: but Jesus had compassion on him. Some had given him alms—which was all he implored; but Jesus gave him eyes, and did for him beyond all that he could ask or think. The cure was notorious. The common people acknowledged it; and they brought the man to the Pharisees, supposing *they* would be equally ready to confess it too. But see how the plainest truth can be perplexed or doubted, when it comes before those whose interest it is to deny or conceal it. First they admit the fact; but turn it against our Savior, because he had done it on the Sabbath day. This did not satisfy the people, who justly remarked, that, had he violated the Sabbath hereby, he would have been a transgressor, and God would not have thus honored a sinner. Then they pretend to question the fact itself. They set aside the man's own testimony, and call in his parents. His parents affirm that he was their son, and that he had been born blind; but, fearing lest they should be put out of the synagogue, they affect to be ignorant of the mode of his cure. How stubborn is truth! How hard is it to suppress evidence! The attempt is like trying to keep fire under ashes out in the wind—it is much if some sparks do not escape. Again they call in the man himself; and, after an artless relation, which they could not resist, and an involuntary address, which they could not endure, "they cast him out"—that is, they drove him from their presence, and excommunicated him as a member of the Jewish synagogue. Informed of this, Jesus sought, and found him—and said unto him, "Dost thou believe on the Son of God?"

There are many foolish and useless questions asked by every individual. In the company of some persons, we are in a perfect inquisition: we are tortured with inquiries concerning every body and every thing. It would be well if many professors of religion were aware that they are accountable, not only for their time, but their tongues; and would remember the language our Savior, "By thy words thou shalt be justified, and by thy words thou shalt be condemned." Many of the inquiries in the theological world, which have engrossed so much attention, and injured so much temper, have turned on subjects too deep to be fathomed, or too trifling to merit regard. When Peter, wishing to know his designs concerning John, asked, "Lord, and what shall this man do?" he replied, "What is that to thee? Follow thou me." A man in the road asked, "Lord, are there few that shall be saved?" But Jesus "answered and said unto them"—for he would not notice the trifler himself; but said unto *them* that were about him—"Strive to enter in at the straight gate; for I say unto you, that many shall seek to enter in, and shall not be able." If it be said, This was no answer to the question itself, we reply that it *was* an answer, and the only *proper* answer—an answer, by way of *rebuke*—an answer, informing *them*, and informing *us*—that "the secret things belong unto God; but things that are revealed are for us, and for our children"—and that, whatever be the number of the saved, we may be included in it, if we earnestly and immediately seek it.

But the question before us is founded in importance. We may infer this from the character of the inquirer: he never trifled, never spoke an idle word. And we may infer it also, from the nature of the case itself. For what can be so important as faith in Christ? It is the principle of all religion. It is the only medium through which we can enjoy the blessings of the Gospel. Do we live? We "live by the faith of the Son of God." Do we walk? "We walk by faith." Do we stand? "By faith we stand." Do we conquer? "This is the victory that overcometh the world, even our faith." There is no justification without it, "Being justified by faith." There is no sanctification without it, "Sanctified by faith, that is in me." There is no consolation without it, "In whom, believing, we rejoice with joy unspeakable and full of glory." In a word, there is no salvation without it; "Believe on the Lord Jesus Christ, and thou shalt be saved. The same things, therefore, in the Scripture, which are ascribed to Christ, are also ascribed by faith. The reason is, because it is only by faith we can make use of Christ, for all the purposes which he is appointed to accomplish. It is only by faith we can receive him as the gift of God: enter him, as the refuge; apply him, as the balm of Gilead; and feed upon him as the bread of life.

And unless we believe on him, we not only incur the greatest loss we can incur, but we contract the greatest guilt we can contract. We disobey the express command of God; his dearest command; the command which involves all his glory in the highest. For "This is his commandment, that we should believe on the name of his Son Jesus Christ." We make him a liar. We throw unspeakable contempt upon his wisdom and goodness. He has, at an infinite expense, provided a Savior, and brought him near, and pressed us to avail ourselves of him. And how can we contemn God so much as by making light of it, and rejecting it? "He that believeth not shall be damned." "He that despised Moses' law died without mercy under two or three witnesses: of how much sorer punishment, suppose ye, shall he be thought worthy, who hath trodden under foot the Son of God, and hath counted the blood of the covenant, wherewith he was sanctified, an unholy thing, and hath done despite unto the Spirit of grace?"

What, then, can be so momentous as this question, "Dost thou believe on the Son of God?" And yet many never give it a serious thought. They can live on year after year, without ever once inquiring, "Am I a believer, or an unbeliever?" though their everlasting all depends upon it—though now is the accepted time, now is the day of salvation—though their breath is in their nostrils, and they know that their only opportunity is as uncertain as it is short. Oh! the deceitfulness of sin! Oh! the madness of sinners! Oh! the influence of the god of this world, who blindeth the hearts of them that believe not, lest the light of the glorious Gospel of Christ, who is the image of the invisible God, should shine unto them.

NOVEMBER 20.—"Did I not see them in the garden with him?"—John, xviii, 26.

WHILE within my garden roving,
And my senses all are fed;
Rising from these lov'd attractions,
I'm to nobler subjects led:
Other Gardens
Here, in musings, oft I tread.

First, I enter *Eden's* garden,
Yielding pain, and profit too:
Adam here, while sinless standing,
Nought of fear, or sorrow knew:
But what changes
Did from his offence ensue!

Then with hope and joy reviving,
To *Gethsemane* I go!
And approach, in that dread garden,
Jesus bearing all my wo:
From his anguish
All my ease and safety flow.

In the Garden *where they laid him*,
With the Marys, there I sit;
Weeping, till I see him rising,
And embrace his pierced feet:
King of Terrors,
Now I can thy frowning meet!

In the *Church*, the *Savior's* garden—
Trees, and plants, and flowers I see;
Guarded, water'd, train'd, and cherish'd,
Blooming immortality!
All, O Calvary!
All derived *alone* from thee.

But, above all gardens precious,
See *the Heavenly Paradise*;
There the Tree of Life is bearing;
There the springs of glory rise:
And the richness
Ev'ry want and wish supplies.

There the foot no thorn e'er pierces,
There the heart ne'er heaves a sigh,
There in white we walk with Jesus;
All our loved connexions by
And, to reach it,
'Tis a privilege to die!

NOVEMBER 21.—"Now Elisha was fallen sick of his sickness whereof he died. And Joash the king of Israel came down unto him, and wept over his face, and said, O my father! my father! the chariot of Israel, and the horsemen thereof!"—2 Kings, xiii, 14.

ELIJAH was spared the common doom of mortality, and was taken to heaven in a chariot and horses of fire, without dying. But Elisha, who had honored God so much longer, goes the way of all the earth. Why was this difference? Even so, Father; for so it seemed good in thy sight.

But he does not die of natural infirmity. Neither does he die suddenly. He had fallen sick. This mode of dissolution was less desirable, with regard to comfort; but it was more favorable to usefulness. It afforded him opportunity for glorifying God, and instructing and impressing his attendants. And "the chamber where the good man meets his fate," has often been to others, as well as to the dying individual himself, the house of God and the gate of heaven. We are therefore glad to find Joash, the king of Israel, with Elisha in this situation. Such a scene is generally very uninviting to persons in the upper ranks of life. They love not, in the midst of flattery and dissipation, to be reminded of the days of darkness. But "it is better to go to the house of mourning than to go to the house of feasting; for that is the end of all men; and the living will lay it to his heart. The heart of the wise is in the house of mourning; but the heart of fools is in the house of mirth. Sorrow is better than laughter; for by the sadness of the countenance the heart is made better," more serious, and more soft.

But who was this Joash? "He did that which was evil in the sight of the Lord. He departed not from all the sins of Jeroboam, the son of Nebat, who made Israel sin: but he walked therein." Who would have looked for such a man here? Yet see the trouble he takes. He does not send to inquire after the dying prophet, but personally visits him. See his condescension and humility, in entering "a little chamber on the wall, with a bed, and a table, and a stool, and a candlestick." See his tenderness, in hanging over the expiring saint, and weeping. See his knowledge of the value and importance of Elisha—"Ah! what shall I do, and what will my people do, when thou art gone? My father! my father! the chariot of Israel, and the horsemen thereof!" How much like a pious man does Joash now appear! How little can we judge of men by particular conditions, events, and feelings? Who has not had powerful convictions? Who has not often exclaimed, Let me die the death of the righteous, and let my last end be like his. Who has not, like Felix, trembled under the preaching of righteousness, temperance, and judgment to come? Of whom has it not, in some period, been said, as it was of the young man in the Gospel, Thou art not far from the kingdom of God.

—What brings Joash here now? He had disregarded and despised Elisha before. But Elisha is now *going*. "How mercies brighten as they take their flight!" How an undutiful child prizes a parent, when he is following him to the grave! How many would listen to the voice of the preacher, when he can hear him no more! Even the Jews, who so often would have stoned Moses, mourned for him many days—and sincerely too. Who would have thought that all these fine impressions would have worn off? But Joash leaves the dying room, and the honored prophet, and enters ordinary life, and straightway forgetteth what manner of man he was; enters the tempting scenes of greatness; and his iniquities, like the wind, take him away! And who would have thought, that after the wreck of all his worldly substance; or the loss of Joseph and Benjamin; or the taking away of the wife of his bosom with a stroke; or the awfulness of a disease that led him down to the gates of death, and induced him to cry, Oh! spare me a little longer! who would have imagined, that after such lessons, any man could turn again to folly, and walk more eagerly according to the course of this world! "O Ephraim!" says God, "what shall I do unto thee? O Judah! what shall I do unto thee? for your goodness is as a morning cloud, and as the early dew it goeth away."

The devotion of natural men depends upon external excitements. They pour out a prayer when God's chastening hand is upon them; but they do not delight themselves in the Almighty—they do not always call upon God. The summer-brook may, by a storm, be swelled into a flood; but having no permanent source, it soon rolls off, and the bed is dry. A Christian's devotion may be aided by outward helps; but it does not depend upon them. His practice flows from principle: and he exemplifies the promise, "The water that I will give him, shall be in him a well of water, springing up into everlasting life." And "he only that endureth to the end, the same shall be saved."

November 22.—"And the man of God was wroth with him, and said, Thou shouldest have smitten five or six times, then hadst thou smitten Syria till thou hadst consumed it; whereas now thou shalt smite Syria but thrice."—2 Kings, xiii, 19.

Elisha was now on his dying bed; and being visited by Joash, the king of Israel, who was deeply affected with the interview, he gave him two orders, the one to shoot, and the other to smite. Both these were doubtless delivered under a prophetic impulse; and, though they seem strange to us, they were well understood by the parties.

—"And Elisha said unto him, Take bow and arrows. And he took unto him bow and arrows. And he said to the king of Israel, Put thine hand upon the bow. And he put his hand upon it, and Elisha put his hand upon the king's hands. And he said, Open the window eastward. And he opened it. Then Elisha said shoot. And he shot. And he said, The arrow of the Lord's deliverance, and the arrow of deliverance from Syria; for thou shalt smite the Syrians in Aphek, till thou have consumed them." The Romans were accustomed to declare war against an enemy by shooting an arrow into their territory.. Alexander also did this when he entered Persia. This order, therefore, was an intimation of war. Accordingly, it was discharged "eastward;" that is, toward Syria. But the man of God arose and stood behind him, while he held the bow—and put his left hand upon the king's left hand, and his right hand upon the king's right hand. For what purpose? Elisha was the representative of God, in whose name he now spake; and he thus teaches the king—that though he should use means, he should not depend upon them—that the excellency of the power was not of the weapons, but of God—and that, if his bow abode in strength, the arms of his hands were made strong by the hands of the mighty God of Jacob. It is therefore called the arrow of the *Lord's* deliverance, and by which the Syrians were to be vanquished in Aphek.

And is it not so with us? When we work, God must work with us. If his hand be not with us for good, what is our prudence, our resolution, our energy! "Not by might, nor by power; but by my Spirit, saith the Lord." Thus the apostles went forth, preaching: and "the hand of the Lord was with them; and many believed and turned unto the Lord."

Again, he said, "Take the arrows. And he took them. And he said unto the king of Israel, Smite upon the ground. And he smote thrice, and stayed. And the man of God was wroth with him, and said, Thou shouldest have smitten five or six times—then hadst thou smitten Syria till thou hadst consumed it; whereas now thou shalt smite Syria but thrice." Joash was conscious that the action was a sign, or he could not have been blamable. The action, therefore, betrayed remissness, and lukewarmness; it was expressive of his disposition, and it indicated the event. He therefore showed that he was not willing to push the war to a complete issue; he was only for injuring and enfeebling the enemy he *might* and *ought* to have *destroyed*. And so the prophet viewed it. He saw that he was half-hearted, and would not improve his advantages. He should have resembled David, who could say, "I have pursued mine enemies, and overtaken them; neither did I turn again till they were consumed. I have wounded them that they are not able to rise: they are fallen under my feet. Then did I beat them small as the dust before the wind: I did cast them out as the dirt in the streets." But Joash was more disposed to imitate Ahab, who, when Benhadad was delivered into his hands, suffered him to escape, and to recover his power and means of annoying again—in consequence of which, God said, "Because thou hast let go out of thy hand a man whom I appointed to utter destruction, therefore thy life shall go for his life, and thy people for his people."

Elisha, therefore, was offended with Joash. And was it not enough in such a case to grieve a man of God, burning with holy zeal for his cause? And is it not grievous to God's ministers now, when *we* are not strong in the grace that is in Christ Jesus? We have his promises and invitations: and we have the experience of his people, living and dying—all showing us how willing he is to help, and to make us more than conquerors. But, alas! we are satisfied with *little*—not in temporal things—where contentment is a virtue; but in spiritual things—where moderation is a crime.

Say not, Why, O why did not Joash continue smiting till the prophet said, "Enough?" Are you not chargeable with the very same offence? Are not you satisfied with slightly wounding your spiritual enemies, instead of breathing after an entire victory over them? Are not you disposed to live on a little corner of your estate, when there remains yet very much land to be possessed?

—Look at your desires! Are they not formal and few? Do you hunger and thirst after righteousness? Do your souls break for the longings they have unto God's judgments at all times? Do you open your mouth wide, that God may fill it? Do you pray, that, according to the riches of his glory, he would strengthen you with might by his Spirit in the inner man? that you may know the love of Christ, which passeth knowledge? that you may be filled with all the fullness of God?

—Look at your expectations! Are they not few and faint? Is your hope a lively hope? Is it vigorous enough to counteract the impressions of the world? Do you abound in hope? Does it bear any proportion to the exceeding great and precious promises?

—Look at your exertions! Are they not few and languid? An occasional retirement—a hasty performance of private devotion—a formal service at the family altar—a forgetful hearing of the word—without early rising—without self-denial—without taking up your cross—without *laboring* for the meat that endureth unto everlasting life—without *striving* to enter in at the straight gate—without *fighting* the good fight of faith—and taking the kingdom of heaven by force. O this vile moderation! This guilty relaxation! This smiting thrice only, instead of going forward, and deeming nothing done while any thing remains to do!

Wherefore, "giving all diligence, add to your faith, virtue; and to virtue, knowledge; and to knowledge, temperance; and to tem perance, patience; and to patience, godliness; and to godliness brotherly kindness; and to brotherly kindness, charity. For if these things be in you and abound, they make you that ye shall neither be barren nor unfruitful in the knowledge of our Lord Jesus Christ. But he that lacketh these things is blind, and cannot see afar off, and hath forgotten that he was purged from his old sins. Wherefore the rather, brethren, give diligence to make your calling and election sure; for if ye do these things ye shall never fall: for so an entrance shall be ministered unto you abundantly into the everlasting kingdom of our Lord and Savior Jesus Christ.

November 23.—"And Elisha died. And they buried him. And the bands of the Moabites invaded the land at the coming in of the year. And it came to pass, as they were burying a man, that, behold they spied a band of men: and they cast the man into the sepulchre; and when the man was let down, and touched the bones of Elisha, he revived, and stood up on his feet."—2 Kings, xiii, 20, 21.

Here we see the Moabites did not come in a large army, but in particular bands, to pillage and alarm: and it shows us in how undefended a state, at this period, the country must have been. But what has this to do with the death and burial of Elisha? The one is mentioned in connexion with the other, and has a reference to the exclamation the king made in his dying chamber, "O my father! my father! the chariot of Israel, and the horseman thereof." And see—would the historian say—see how soon this began to be exemplified! Does this cause seem inadequate to the effect? Who has not observed the importance of individuality? When Goliath came forward challenging, all the army of Israel fled. What a terror was Samson to the Philistines! They could do nothing till they could get rid of him. There are persons who are the life, the soul of a party or a community. What enterprises for the glory of God, and the spread of the Gospel, have originated from one Christian! The death of a minister has been the signal for the division and dispersion of a congregation raised by his talents and zeal. "I know," says Paul, "that, after my departing, shall grievous wolves enter in among you, not sparing the flock. Also of your own selves, shall men arise, speaking perverse things, to draw away disciples after them."

What is there peculiar here? the intimation of the historian is constantly and variously held forth in the Scripture at large. There we see the regard God pays to his people. "Thus saith the Lord, As the new wine is found in the cluster, and one saith, Destroy it not, for a blessing is in it: so will I do for my servants' sakes, that I may not destroy them all."

"Oft have our fathers told,
"Our eyes have often seen,
"How well our God secures the fold,
"Where his own sheep have been."

The ungrateful world despises them. But how much do even *they* owe to the presence and the prayers of the saints! For them blessings have been obtained or continued. They have withholden or removed judgments. They have been the "healers of the breach, the restorers of paths to dwell in." Shall not we then love them? and pray for their increase?

But here was a thing very accidental, as to the persons employed. They were a funeral party, and were going to carry the corpse further; but, seeing a number of their invaders, and wishing to make a timely escape, they hastened to lay it in the grave of Elisha, which happened to be at hand. But how wonderful was the result! "When the man was let down, and touched the bones of Elisha, he revived, and stood up on his feet!" Here the papists come (and to what other place can they come so well?) to find something to favor the doctrine of relics. Which of their churches is not furnished with the supposed remains of saints? Some of these saints, too, would have made tolerable demons. But, allowing them to have been real saints—what profit is there in their bones when they go down to the grave? The virtue here was not in the bones of Elisha, but in the power of God. And what a stupendous miracle was it! "Surely, had not the people been blind and impenitent, they must have been brought to repentance." So we think—but who said, "If they hear not Moses and the prophets, neither would they be persuaded though one rose from the dead?" Whether there were, as yet, any Sadducees in Israel, we know not. If there were, we here see a proof and an instance that the dead can be reanimated—and it matters not, as to the miracle of the fact, whether it took place two days after death, or two thousand years. God alone could have done it. And why should it be thought a thing incredible that *God* should raise the dead? *His* power is Almighty: and we see what changes and revivals it is continually producing in nature. But, with us the subject admits of no doubt. We believe (the Lord prepare us for it!) "that there will be a resurrection of the dead, both of the just and unjust."

The fathers—where are they? and the prophets—do they live for ever? No. The dearest, the greatest, the most useful, of his servants, die. But "precious in the sight of the Lord, is the death of his saints." We are losers; but to them, to die is gain. They are privileged in it. They are privileged by it. And it is desirable to be near them, living, dying and dead; in time, and in eternity. "Gather not my soul with sinners." I would "take hold of the skirt of him that is a Jew, saying, I will go with you, for I have heard that God is with you"—"Entreat me not to leave thee, or to return from following after thee: for whither thou goest, I will go, and where thou lodgest, I will lodge; thy people shall be my people, and thy God my God. Where thou diest will I die, and there will I be buried; the Lord do so to me, and more also, if aught but death part thee and me."

God can honor his servants, not only before they are in their graves, but after they are in them. The memory of the just is blessed, and useful, too. Yes, you may be the means of awakening and enlivening persons after your death—not by quickening their mortal bodies; but their souls which were dead in trespasses and sins; not by your bones, but by your examples, which shall still operate; by your instructions, which shall still speak—by the prayers you offered; by the books you gave; by the minister you educated; by the place of worship you built, while you were yet living.

—Every thing should lead us to the Savior. How much any of the Jews, of this time, knew of the Messiah, we cannot ascertain. But *we* know, that because he died, we shall live—we know, that if we are planted together in the likeness of his death, we shall be also in the likeness of his resurrection. He made the grave his own, by residence and consecration—Behold the place where the Lord lay! Into this grave we must descend—but we shall arise from it, not only living, but immortal: not, like this man, to die again, but to die no more; death having no more dominion over us. "Thy dead men shall live; together with my dead body shall they rise. Awake and sing, ye that dwell in dust; for thy dew is as the dew of herbs, and the earth shall cast out the dead."

NOVEMBER 24.—"The righteous shall flourish."—Psalm xcii, 12.

PROSPERITY in the divine life is the Christian's duty—and therefore he is commanded to grow in grace, and in the knowledge of our Lord and Savior. It is his desire—and hence he prays, Strengthen, O God, that which thou hast wrought for us. It is his privilege—and thus it is provided for, and secured by Divine promise—"The righteous shall hold on his way, and he that hath clean hands shall wax stronger and stronger." Thus David here tells us, that "the righteous shall flourish." And he tells us—

How he shall flourish—"He shall flourish like the palm tree: he shall grow like a cedar in Lebanon." Of the wicked he had said just before, "When the wicked spring as the grass, and when all the workers of iniquity do flourish; it is that they shall be destroyed for ever." They flourish as the *grass*, which to-day is, and to-morrow is cast into the oven. What a contrast with the worthlessness, the weakness, transitoriness, and destiny of grass, in a warm country too—are the palm tree, and the cedar in Lebanon! They are evergreens. How beautifully, how firmly, how largely they grow! How strong and lofty is the cedar! How upright, and majestic, and tall, the palm tree—The palm also bears fruit—dates, like bunches of grapes. It sometimes yields a hundred weight at once.

He tells us *where* he shall flourish—"Those that be planted in the house of the Lord shall flourish in the courts of our God." The allusion is striking. It compares the house of God to a garden, or fine well-watered soil, favorable to the life, and verdure, and fertility, of the trees fixed there. The reason is, that in the sanctuary we have the communion of saints. *There* our fellowship is with the Father, and with his Son Jesus Christ. *There* are dispensed the ordinances of religion, and the word of truth. *There* God commandeth the blessing, even life for evermore. "Blessed is the man that heareth me, watching daily at my gates, waiting at the posts of my doors." They that wait upon the Lord renew their strength. Hence, from their own experience, as well from the word of promise, they are increasingly induced to say with David—"I will dwell in the house of the Lord for ever."

He also tells us *when* he shall flourish—"They shall still bring forth fruit in old age." This is to show the permanency of their principles—and to distinguish them from natural productions—

'The plants of grace shall ever live;
'Nature decays, but grace must thrive:
"Time, that doth all things else impair,
"Still makes them flourish strong and fair."

The believer does not escape all the effects of years. The eye may grow dim; the ear become dull of hearing. But as the outward man perisheth, the inward man is renewed day by day. The young Christian is lovely, like a tree in the blossoms of spring: the aged Christian is valuable, like a tree in autumn bending with ripe fruit. We therefore look for something superior in old disciples. More deadness to the world, the vanity of which they have had more opportunities to see—more meekness of wisdom—more disposition to make sacrifices for the sake of peace—more maturity of judgment in divine things—more confidence in God—more richness of experience.

He also tells us *why* he shall flourish—"They shall be fat and flourishing, to show that the Lord is upright." We might rather have supposed, that it was necessary to show that *they* were upright. But, by the grace of God they are what they are—not they, but the grace of God which is in them. From him is their fruit found. Their preservation and fertility, therefore, are to the praise and glory of God: and as what he does for them, he had *engaged* to do; it displays his truth, as well as his mercy, and proves that he is upright. This cleaving also to him with purpose of heart, and not turning away from him, whatever temptations the world presents—shows that they have found him to be, what he had given himself out to be, and what they had taken him to be. Had he deceived or disappointed them, they would have forsaken him. But he has always dealt with them—he has surpassed their hopes. They therefore love their Master and his work—and are willing to follow him to prison or to death—to show that he is upright.

David, therefore, attests this from his own experience—"Let every one speak as he finds. I cannot but magnify his name; and recommend him to those who want a dependence that will not, cannot, give way. I have tried him; and tried him much, and long. I never served him for nought. I never called upon him in vain. I never trusted in him and was confounded—HE IS MY ROCK, AND THERE IS NO UNRIGHTEOUSNESS IN HIM."

NOVEMBER 25.—"Dost thou believe on the Son of God?"—John, ix, 35.

THE question concerns us, as well as the man who had been restored to sight. And it admits of solution. Indeed, the inquiry would be absurd, if an answer were possible. Some very mistaken notions are entertained of divine influence. One thing is undeniable. The grace of God, in renewing us, engages and employs us: so that we are not like wood and stone, under the operation of the saw and the chisel, merely passive, insensible, unconscious. God does not work upon us, but in us; and in us, to *will* and to *do* of his good pleasure. He is the author of repentance, by enabling *us* to exercise repentance. And cannot a man know whether he repents of any course or action in which he has been engaged? He is the giver of faith, as he teaches and aids *us* to believe. This faith, therefore, does not act in us like a charm; nor is it a mysterious, unintelligible thing, of which we can give no account. We are always to be ready to give a reason of the hope that is in us.

How then is an answer to be returned? Let us away with accidental occurrences, and dreams, and sudden impulses, and repair to the Scriptures at once; and, by their decisions, examine ourselves, whether we be in the faith, and prove our own selves. Three evidences may be adduced of our believing on the Son of God. First. Much anxiousness and uneasiness concerning it, in distinction from the temper of those who can readily and easily take it for granted. This is not the disposition of awakened souls: they find how hard it is to abound and rejoice in hope. This results from the importance and dearness of the object. It is not true, as it is often said, that it is easy to believe what we wish. Yea, in proportion as we love and value a thing, we become the more apprehensive, and require every kind of proof and assurance concerning its safety. And here the case is interesting and beyond all comparison. It is to ascertain my claims to everlasting life! What if I should be mistaken! And my heart is deceitful above all things, as well as desperately wicked! And I learn, from the word of truth, that many are imposed upon to their remediless ruin! And what if I am informed, but not enlightened! convinced, but not converted! almost, but not altogether a Christian! No wonder, in such a case, solicitudes often revive; and the prayer be daily made—"Say unto my soul, I am thy salvation." Let me not be ashamed of my hope. These doubts and fears are a token for good, and may be compared to smoke, which indeed is not fire, but proves its existence; and is never found where it is not.

Secondly. The estimation in which we hold the Savior. Hence, says the apostle, "To you, therefore, that believe, he is precious." He does not say how precious—this would have been impossible. But faith makes him more precious to the soul than sight is to the eye, or melody to the ear, or food to the hungry, or health and life to the sick and the dying. Oh! says the believer, when I see him, as he is revealed in the word; when I see in him all I want; when I see how he becomes my Savior; that, when he was rich, for my sake he became poor; and died, that I might live; when I know that he is remembering me still, now he is come into his kingdom, appearing in the presence of God for me; and making all things to work together for my good, how can I but exclaim, Thou art fairer than the children of men! His name must be as ointment poured forth—His cause must lie near my heart—I must dedicate myself to his service. I must hourly ask, Lord, what wilt thou have me to do?

"My God! and can an humble child,
"That loves thee with a flame so high,
"Be ever from thy face exiled,
"Without the pity of thine eye?

"Impossible—for thy own hands
"Have tied my heart so fast to thee—
"And, in thy Book the promise stands—
"That where thou art, thy friends must be."

Thirdly. A life of obedience. Without this, an Orthodox creed, clear knowledge, high confidence, much talking of divine things, great zeal for a party, will all in vain be called in to denominate you believers in Christ. Nothing can be more certain, than that as a man is not wise who calls himself so, while all his conduct proclaims him a fool; and as *he* is not a benefactor who never gives—unless, indeed, words, so *he* is not a believer who thinks and professes himself to be such, but he who acts and lives as such. We read of the work of faith. Where is this? By faith Noah built an ark. By faith Abraham left his own country, and his father's house. Read the eleventh chapter of the Epistle to the Hebrews, and see whether faith is a mere notion, or a vital principle. "As the body without the spirit is dead, so faith without works is dead also." "What doth it profit, my brethren, though a man say he hath faith, and hath not works? Can such faith save him?" Therefore, says James, "Show me thy faith without thy works"—show me a sun that never shines; a fire that never burns; a fountain that never flows, "and I will show thee my faith by my works." I will show thee the spring in the streams: the cause, in the effects; the principle, in the practice. Though faith can alone justify the soul: works can alone justify faith, and prove it to be of the operation of God.

NOVEMBER 26.—"My people—have forgotten their resting place."—Jeremiah, 1, 6.

God has provided every creature he has made with some convenient good, in the possession of which it reposes. Natural bodies have their proper places, toward which they are carried, and declare, by resting in them, that they are where they ought to be. Sensitive beings are led toward sensitive, and animal beings toward animal indulgence, as agreeable to their nature; and they look no farther. But God himself is the resting place of man: and it has justly been remarked, that herein lies man's excellency, that he alone, of all creatures in this lower world, was made capable of communion with his Maker, and designed for it; and being designed for it, and made capable of it, he is necessarily unsatisfied and restless without it. For though he has been turned away from God by sin, he retains the same natural relation to God as his end, so that he can enjoy no true repose till he meets with God again. He feels not only sentiments of misery, but of grandeur: and whatever may be employed to quiet and content him, will be found perfectly inadequate; and from every fruitless experiment to supply the cravings of a fallen, yet immortal mind, he will ever be asking, "Who will show us any good?"

There was a time when "the people of God" themselves attempted to live without him in the world. But they were dead while they lived. They were strangers to every thing like satisfaction, till they happily inquired, "Where is God my Maker, who giveth songs in the night?" But since they sought and found him, they have been able to make their boast in the Lord. "The Lord is my portion, saith my soul: therefore will I hope in him."

"Thou shalt guide me with thy counsel, and afterward receive me to glory. Whom have I in heaven but thee? and there is none upon earth that I desire besides thee. My flesh and my heart faileth: but God is the strength of my heart, and my portion for ever." *He*, therefore, is "*their* resting-place," actually, and by conviction, and choice, and enjoyment. And what a resting place is He! There is no repose like that which we possess in Him. It is a peace that passeth all understanding. How then can it be described! Who can express the blessedness of viewing him as our own God, in the covenant of his dear Son, ready to pardon, able to enlighten, to renew, to support, to defend—presiding over all our affairs, and making the most adverse events conduce to our welfare; and promising, on oath, that his grace shall be sufficient for us, and that he will supply all our need from his richness in glory, by Christ Jesus! All we can do is to invite others to come, and learn (it is the only way to know) by experience. "O taste and see that the Lord is good! Blessed is the man that trusteth in him." Incomparable as this resting-place is, it is equally secure and durable. Nothing can destroy: nothing can injure; nothing can invade it. We live in the midst of uncertainty and change; but the Lord changes not. There is, therefore, something sure, something lasting. It is that very one thing, O Christian! upon which thou hast laid all thy hope, and from which thou drawest all thy comfort. The eternal God is thy refuge; and underneath are the everlasting arms.

—And yet they are charged with *forgetting* their resting place. The charge cannot be taken without limitation. As fainting is not death, and as backsliding is not apostacy, so this forgetfulness is not constant and total. But, alas! it cannot be denied that it is occasional and partial. Our ingratitude shows it. This is at once the effect and the proof of our forgetfulness of God, and is therefore expressed by it. "Thou hast forgotten the God that formed thee."

It sometimes appears with regard to the means of grace. In proportion as we feel our need of *Him*, we shall value *them*, because it is in these that God is to be found and enjoyed. Hence it is said "Draw nigh to God, and he will draw nigh to you." But we may read the scriptures less than we did, and be less alone, and less regardful of the Sabbath, and suffer excuse to keep us from the sanctuary that once would have had no influence over us.

It shows itself in our looking to ourselves for what we want, when in the Lord we have righteousness and strength, and from him is our fruit found.

We betray it in our creature dependence. Instead of committing our way unto the Lord, and waiting patiently for him, we weary ourselves for very vanity, in running from creature to creature for help; and learn, by our folly and suffering, that our strength is to sit still. "In returning and rest shall ye be saved; in quietness and in confidence shall be your strength." And do we not forget Him when we faint in the day of adversity? "Oh!" says one, "if such a comfort was removed, mine eye would no more see good." "Oh!" says another, "my loss is irreparable;

my wound is incurable." We do not wish you to be insensible, or to undervalue your deprivations; but is it a lamp, or the sun, of which you have been deprived? David, in the desolations of Ziklag, did not forget his resting place. "Then David encouraged himself in the Lord his God."

Our regard to the world will also show our regard to God. We forget him, just in proportion as the world strikes and allures us; in sight of Him, it can do nothing with us. But where is the spring, when we stoop to the puddle? Are not the consolations of God small with us, when we repair to worldly attractions and delights? But the charge is too obvious to require proof; and every Christian will readily confess,

"Prone to wander, Lord, I feel it;
"Prone to leave the God I love."

But how humiliating is the fact! And how wonderful too! "Can a maid forget her ornaments, or a bride her attire? Yet my people have forgotten me days without number," "who am their beauty, their glory, all their salvation, and all their desire." How little would they themselves have supposed this possible, when they first returned to him, from darkness to light; from bondage to liberty: from a wilderness to the garden of the Lord? "Thus saith the Lord, I remember thee, the kindness of thy youth, the love of thine espousals, when thou wentest after me in the wilderness, in a land that was not sown." And still, after renewed manifestations, and under lively impressions, they are often ready to think they never can be the same dull and ungrateful creatures they have often been.

"When my forgetful soul renews
"The savor of thy grace,
"My heart presumes I cannot lose
"The relish all my days."

"But ere one fleeting hour is past,
"The flattering world employs
"Some sensual bait to seize my taste,
"And to pollute my joys."

"Wretch that I am to wander thus,
"In chase of false delight!
"Let me be fasten'd to thy cross,
"Rather than lose the sight!

"Make haste, my days, to reach the goal,
"And bring my soul to rest
"On the dear centre of my soul—
"My God, my Savior's breast."

NOVEMBER 27.—"Faith and love which is in Christ Jesus."—1 Tim. i, 14

THESE two are often spoken of in the Scriptures. And, if we observe the passages in which they occur, and especially the words of the apostle John, "This is his commandment, that we believe on the name of his Son—and love one another, we shall see, that the first regards Christ, and the second, our brethren.

But let us remark their order. Faith is placed before love—and this is the case without any exception, whenever they are coupled together by the sacred writers. And there is reason for it. The order of the words is the order of the things. Faith precedes all true obedience. It necessarily goes before repentance. I cannot grieve for what I have done amiss, unless I believe I have done wrong: and I cannot sorrow after a godly sort, unless I look on him whom I have pierced, and mourn for *him*. Faith is a radical principle. It is the root of the tree; and all the rest is branch, blossom, and fruit. It is the spring from which every thing else in religion flows, as a stream. Love does not produce faith, but faith love.

Yet there is a connexion between them; and their union is also as invariably expressed as their order. In truth, they are inseparable. Is it conceivable, that when such a scheme as Christianity gets into the soul, it can lie there dead, or even asleep? Is it not compared to a well of water, springing up into everlasting life? to a fire, that converts every thing combustible into its own nature? to leaven hid in meal, that leavens the whole lump? Observe all the believers, who, in the Scripture, encompass us as a great cloud of witnesses. Was their faith a notion? a profession, a form of godliness without the power? Could *such* faith have saved them? True faith overcomes the world. It purifies the heart. And it works by love—not exclusively indeed. It works by hatred, when it regards sin; and by fear when it regards danger—So Noah, by faith, being warned of God, was moved with fear. But love is the disposition the Gospel peculiarly requires. It is the end of the commandment, out of a pure heart, and a good conscience, and faith unfeigned. It also is pre-eminently suited to produce it. What is God? God is love. From what principle did he act in our salvation? God so loved the world that he gave his only begotten Son, that whosoever believeth on him should not perish, but have everlasting life. And if God so loved us, we ought also to love one another. What do we see in the life and death of the Savior, but Divine compassion embodied? a love that passeth knowledge? And what is the inference? "Be ye therefore followers of God, as dear children; and walk in love, as Christ also hath loved us, and hath given himself for us, an offering and a sacrifice to God, for a sweet-smelling savor."

Let us not pass over this. Some people's faith seems to work by selfishness, censoriousness, wrath, malice, and all uncharitableness. But we have no reason to conclude that we have "the faith of God's elect," unless, "as the elect of God, holy and beloved, we put on bowels of mercies, kindness, humbleness of mind, long-suffering, forbearing one another, and forgiving one another, if any man have a quarrel against any: even as Christ forgave you, so also do ye."

It is lamentable to think, how many of our fellow creatures are destitute of these graces. Art thou, O my soul! a stranger to the influence of this faith and love? Let me remember that they are infinitely important and indispensable. "He that believeth on the Son hath everlasting life: and he that believeth not the Son shall not see life; but the wrath of God abideth on him." "We know that we have passed from death unto life, because we love the brethren. He that loveth not his brother abideth in death."

But shall I be satisfied with the reality of this faith and love, regardless of the degree? How desirable—how necessary—how attainable, is more of their vital prevalency! O let me resemble the Thessalonians; of whom the apostle could say, "We are bound to thank God always for you, brethren, as it is meet, because that your faith groweth exceedingly, and charity of every one of you all toward each other aboundeth."

November 28.—" Be thou in the fear of the Lord all the day long."—Proverbs, xxiii, 17.

The mistake of many persons is, that they view religion as something separate from common life, and which can hardly be made to agree with it. But we are to render every thing, not only consistent with godliness, but even a part of it. If Gaius was to bring friends on their way, it was to be done so as to render it not only an act of civility, but of piety. It was to be done "after a godly sort." "On Thee," says David, "do I wait all the day." And Solomon enjoins us to be "in the fear of the Lord all the day long." The day, here, is to be taken, not abstractedly, as a mere period of duration, but in reference to its concerns. There are several things, into contact with which we may expect to come every day. Let us see how the fear of the Lord will influence us, with regard to each of them.

First. It will influence us as to the devotions of the day. If there be an opportunity of repairing to the house of God, and hearing his word, it will dispose us to avail ourselves of it, and so to regulate our affairs as to be able to attend. It will produce morning and evening worship at the family altar. It will also lead us to enter our closets. The principle, also, will not only excite us *to* the performance of devotion, but aid us *in* it—throwing off mere formality, or causing us to mourn over our want of spirituality and life.

Secondly. It will influence us as to the business of the day. It will require us to have some profession or calling in which we are to be employed; and in this it will induce us to be diligent. An idle man cannot be under the power of religion, and lies open to temptation. It will also make us conscientious; governing ourselves by the fair rules of trade; not having divers weights and measures, or different kinds of goods and prices for friends and strangers, the knowing or the ignorant. It will allow us to aim at lawful advantage, but it will regulate and moderate our desire of gain. It will make us content with subsistence and competency, without wealth and independence: "He that maketh haste to be rich shall not be innocent." It will make us feel our reliance upon God for his blessing, without which we may rise early, and sit up late, and eat the bread of sorrows. Upon the same principle it will make us grateful for success, and keep us from burning incense to our own net, and sacrificing to our own drag.

Thirdly. It will influence us as to the relaxations of the day. These we need. Who could bear unceasing, unbending drudgery? The machine would soon be worn out by perpetual friction. All indulgencies are not innocent. We shall, therefore, avoid those that would stain the mind, and wound the conscience, and unfit us for prayer. We shall shun expensive entertainments; the most agreeable and useful recreations are the cheapest; and who can ever be at a loss for these, if they will follow nature instead of fashion? And we shall indulge in none to excess, as to time—of time we must always be frugal. Like the swallow, we must skim the water as we fly; or, like Gideon's followers, we must, in our pursuit, lap with the hand rather than kneel down. The fear of the Lord will make us always watchful with regard to *indulgence*, and *especially* in things lawful; for here we are most liable to be ensnared. God giveth us richly all things to enjoy; but we are not to feast ourselves without fear.

Fourthly. It will influence us as to the company of the day. Are we called to intermix with the wicked? We shall walk in wisdom toward them that are without. We shall endeavor to render our religion, not only impressive, but attractive. We shall keep our mouth as with a bridle: or, if we speak, it will be a word in season. Do we meet with pious connexions? We shall feel toward them as brethren. We shall speak of the things touching the King. We shall not offend against the generation of the upright. Among our immediate relations, and in our family circle, we shall let the Christian appear, and maintain our consistency; but if we rebuke, it will be in the spirit of love. We shall not threaten, but rather entreat. Our religion will be seen much oftener than it is heard; and we shall expect to succeed, not so much by direct effort, as by keeping our charge constantly under the exhibition of whatsoever things are lovely and of good report.

Finally. It will influence us as to the trials of the day. It will not fill us with forebodings, and prevent our enjoying the present comforts of Providence; but it will keep us from forgetting that this is a vale of tears, or thinking it strange if we are called to endure. It will teach us to look beyond instruments—to see and own the hand of God in our afflictions—to inquire wherefore he contendeth with us—to implore grace, not only to support, but to sanctify; and to enable us to honor God, and edify others, by our sufferings; and, avoiding all improper means to escape from trouble, not only hope, but quietly wait, for the salvation of God.

A concern to exemplify all this, is the best evidence of our religion. It is the way of safety, and honor, and advantage. The eye of God is upon us all the day long. He is doing us good all the day long. We may die all the day long—let us, therefore, be in the fear of the Lord all day long.

NOVEMBER 29.—"This is his commandment, That we should believe on the name of his Son Jesus Christ, and love one another, as he gave us commandment."—1 John, iii, 23.

THE *injunction* of the latter of these has given rise to no difficulty. But much dispute has been occasioned by the *commanding* of the former. It is undeniable, however, that the one is enjoined as well as the other, in the same passage, and by the very same authority. He that commands us to love one another, commands us equally to believe on the name of his Son Jesus Christ.

And if so, then faith is a duty. Indeed, if it be not a duty, we are not bound to obey God. If it be not a duty, unbelief is not a sin. Yet the Holy Ghost convinces us of sin—and of sin because we believe not on Christ. Accordingly, in conviction, with the discovery of *this* guilt, we are principally affected; and look on him whom we have pierced, and mourn for him. Hence, unbelief is punishable, and destroys the soul. Indeed, nothing else destroys the soul, under the Gospel. For provision is there made for our fallen condition, and pressed upon our acceptance; but we neglect so great salvation, and turn away from Him that speaketh from heaven. It is true divine influence is necessary. But why is it not possessed! *It is sinful to be without it*, if there be any truth in the Bible. But why should we seek after, or be thankful for assistance, to enable us to do what *we were under no obligation to do?*

This justifies ministers, in calling upon sinners to believe. There are some who condemn and ridicule them for this. But Ezekiel, in the name of God, prophesied to the dry bones, and said unto *them*, "Live." Paul made no scruple to admonish Simon Magus, though in the gall of bitterness and the bond of iniquity, to repent and pray. And to the jailer he said, Believe on the Lord Jesus Christ, and thou *shalt* be saved—for he *then* was not.

As the love of God renders our duty our privilege, so the authority of God renders our privilege our duty. And is not this an advantage? For thus we are left to the calls of self-love, and our own interest; but are bound to pursue our wellfare by the command of God, and a peril arising from a neglect of it.

This also meets the state of the conscience, and affords encouragement to awakened sinners. These, under a sense of their unworthiness and guilt, will be sure to ask, "But *may* I go to him, and trust in him? What *warrant* have I?" Now here is the warrant—the command of God. I may doubt my title to a promise; but I cannot question my obligation to obey a divine command. This fully authorizes me—Yea, it not only secures me from presumption if I comply, but renders me chargeable with disobedience if I refuse. I am not afraid to love another—I never inquire, *May* I do it—I know that I *ought* to do it; because he has commanded it. Why then should I fear to apply to the Savior? And why ask, *May* I believe on him to life everlasting? since this also is his commandment, That we should believe on the name of his Son Jesus Christ?

Lord, I believe—help thou mine unbelief.

NOVEMBER 30.—"Dost thou believe on the Son of God?"—John, ix, 35.

WHOEVER thou art that readest this page, allow the writer to address this question to THEE.

Art thou *young*—Dost *thou* believe on the Son of God? O that you did! How the Scripture extols and recommends early godliness! They that seek me early, says the Savior, shall find me—find me—for there is an emphasis in the promise; find me, as others never will, never can, find me—find me, in a thousand peculiar preservations, honors, advantages, and delights. And what a favorable season do you now enjoy? the body in health and strength—the mind in vigor—the memory retentive—the affections warm—the heart tender—the cares and troubles of life scarcely begun—the days distant in which you will say, "I have no pleasure in them!" Oh! redeem the time. Remember thy Creator in the days of thy youth. Enter immediately a course that is profitable unto all things; having promise of the life that now is, and of that which is to come.

Art thou *old*—Dost *thou* believe on the Son of God? Thy age demands, respect; and I readily pay it—but thy state! Ah! thy state demands all my fidelity. And art thou at the end of sixty, seventy, eighty years, ignorant of the Redeemer, whom to know is life eternal? Have all these departed seasons been passed only in vanity and vice? Is thy day rapidly closing; and thy work, thy journey, not even begun? Does thine eye in looking back, meet with nothing but guilt; and, in looking forward, nothing but gloom? How I pity thy condition! It is time—it is high time—to awake out of sleep. And, blessed be God, it is not too late.

"And, while the lamp holds out to burn, | "The vilest sinner may return."

I announce a Savior who is able to save unto the uttermost; and who converted and pardoned the thief at the eleventh hour—Oh! seek him while he may be found: and call upon him while he is near. But if thou art old in grace, as well as in age, thy hoary head, being found in the way of righteousness, is a crown of glory. And thy salvation nearer than when thou believedst. The night, with thee, is far spent, and the day is at hand. Yet a little while, and what a blessed deliverance—

"All thy sorrows left below, | "And earth exchanged for heaven!"

Till then, let faith and patience have their perfect work. Speak well of his name. Recommend his service to others, from your own knowledge of its excellency. Take a fresh and firmer hold of him, from the proofs you have had of his faithfulness and care: and leaning upon his arm as you descend, say—

"By long experience I have known | "At thy command I venture down
"Thy sovereign power to save, | "Securely to the grave."

Art thou *indulged* by Providence? Dost *thou* believe on the Son of God? Perhaps sickness led you down to the very gates of death; and you looked into eternity, and without hope in that world—you trembled, and cried, Take me not off in the midst of my days—Oh! spare me, that I may recover strength, before I go hence, and be no more. And he heard your cry, and said, Return again, ye children of men. And have you returned again to folly? And have you forgotten that the vows of God are upon you? And what is a recovered body, while the soul is full of moral disease? A reprieve, too, is not a pardon. Dust thou art, and unto dust shalt thou return—is the sentence still suspended; the delayed execution of which will be attended with added terror and remorse. Perhaps thy business flourishes; thy grounds bring forth plentifully; thy cup of prosperity runneth over. We do not wish you to despise the bounties of nature and providence; yea, you ought to be thankful for them. As to their *use*, they are valuable—but what art they as a *portion!* How melancholy is the thought that you must leave them! And you know not how soon you may be torn from all your treasure, And, even in the midst of your fullness, are you not in straits? Do you not sigh over your very enjoyments! Does not success, as well as disappointment, tell you, that this is not your rest? Ah! these failures of hope, these inward uneasinesses, are the inspirations of the Almighty, to give you understanding. They are designed to turn you from creatures, which are all vanity and vexation of spirit, to a Savior who is full of grace and truth. Acquaint now thyself with him, and be at peace; thereby good shall come unto thee.

Art thou subject to *affliction?* Dost *thou* believe on the Son of God? To be poor in the world, and be destitute of true riches; to have no friend below, and no God above; to pass from the sorrows of time into a more miserable eternity, is a state so dreadful, that every feeling of benevolence must be concerned to find a resource for its victims. And such we can open. There is the hope of Israel—the Savior thereof in the time of trouble. His Gospel is sent to bind up the broken-hearted. Perhaps you are at your wit's end. Perhaps ready to curse the day of your birth. Perhaps tempted to destroy yourself. Beware of the devil's relief: that cure will be far worse than the disease. And you need it not. There is One near you whom you know not—O that you did! He is now stretching forth his soft hand; he is now saying, "Come unto me, all ye that labor and are heavy laden, and I will give you rest." This man shall be the peace when the Assyrian cometh into the land.

Art thou a *professor of religion?* Dost thou believe on the Son of God? "Why should you address the inquiry to me? Had not the church been satisfied with my character, and deemed me a believer, they would not have admitted me to their communion." But they might have been mistaken. They could only judge from outward appearance: and it became them to be candid. There is no certainty from this quarter. "But if I had not hoped that I was a real believer in Jesus, I should not have proposed myself as a member of a Christian church, and have come to the Lord's table, where I should have eaten and drunken unworthily. Why, then, do you suspect me?" My friend, I do not suspect you; but I love you—and love, though not suspicious, is cautious. As mistakes are possible, and common, it cannot be improper for you to examine yourself, and prove whether you are in the faith. If the house be built upon the sand, it is well to know it before the storm comes. But if it be built on the rock, the discovery will yield fresh satisfaction, and you will be encouraged to say "I know whom I have believed, and am persuaded that he is able to keep that which I have committed to him against that day."

Or art thou a *real Christian?* Dost *thou* believe on the Son of God? "I know that thou believest." Yet, as pride blends with the humility of the most humble, and impatience with the resignation of the most patient, even so, as an old writer says, what unbelieving believers are the best believers! When our Savior had expressed himself more fully and clearly, his disciples exclaimed, "Now are we sure that thou knowest all things, and needest not that any man should ask thee: by this we believe that thou camest forth from God. Jesus answered them, Do ye now believe?" You think so: but imagination is not reality. I know you better than you know yourselves. And you yourselves, in a little time, will see that you have much less faith than you now profess. "Behold, the hour cometh, yea, is now come, that ye shall be scattered every man to his own, and shall leave me alone; and yet I am not alone, because the Father is with me." And, all may cry out, with tears, Lord, I believe; help thou mine unbelief.

DECEMBER 1.—"Doth Job fear God for nought."—Job, i, 9.

THESE are the words of Satan. Some deny the agency, and even the existence of such a being. But the denial renders the language of the Scripture inexplicable, or absurd; and furnishes a proof of the fact itself, for the god of this world blindeth the minds of them that believe not.

These are the words of Satan. And let us not refuse to consider them, because *he* is the speaker. Truth is the same, whoever utters it.

"Seize upon truth, where'er 'tis found—
"Among your friends, among your foes;
"On Christian, or on heathen ground,
"The flower's divine, where'er it grows,
"Refuse the prickles, and assume the rose."

Alluding to the Scribes, our Savior said to his hearers, "Whatsoever they command you to observe, that observe ye: but do not after their works; for they say, and do not."

These are the words of Satan. But though we should not refuse the truth because it comes from *him;* yet it surely becomes us to examine whether what he says *is* truth; and also for what *purpose* he says it. For even truth may be misapplied and abused. It is thus Antinomians are so injurious; by the most precious doctrines of the Gospel, they turn the grace of our God into lasciviousness, and make Christ the minister of sin. In our Lord's temptation, Satan had a Bible with him, and turned to the passages; or he showed a good memory of the Scripture, for he quoted it very readily; but it was for the vilest design.

Now it is easy to learn his meaning here. God had been extolling his servant Job. "The Lord God said unto Satan, Hast thou considered my servant Job, that there is none like him in the earth, a perfect and an upright man; one that feareth God and escheweth evil! Then Satan answered the Lord, and said, "He is, I acknowledge, a worshipper of thee! And no wonder. He has found it the way to grandeur and wealth. It has procured for him seven thousand sheep, and three thousand camels, and five hundred she asses, and a very great household: so that he is the greatest man in the East. He has found godliness gain, and now makes gain godliness. Doth Job serve God for nought?"

Here we see how well Satan is called the accuser of the brethren. He accuses them to God; and, as many of the articles are true, they would have reason to fear; but they have one in court to nonsuit them—thay have an Advocate with the Father. "Who is he that condemneth? It is Christ that died, yea, rather, that is risen again, who is even at the right hand of God, who also maketh intercession for us?" He accuses them before men. We see, from the early defences of Christianity, how much they were defamed. At their private suppers they devoured their own infants. At their nocturnal meetings they committed every crime that could disgrace human nature. If there was a fire, or a famine, they caused the one, and occasioned the other. In the Acts of the Apostles we read, that Christians were a sect every where spoken against. It is so still; and some of the brightest characters that have adorned the church, and served their generation in modern times, have been blackened by every vileness of imputation.

See the malignant cunning of this adversary, who goeth about seeking whom he may devour or distress. He can bring nothing against Job's conduct, this was undeniably fair and righteous; he, therefore, insinuates a charge against his motive. Are there none that follow his example? "He is so and so; he does so and so, and this would be very well; but it is to please his connexions, to aid his business, and to gain a name. Ah! were it real; but it is all outside—all show—all pretence." Now nothing can be more *devilish* than this. There is a great difference between judging ourselves, and judging others. In the one case we cannot be too severe; in the other we cannot be too candid. Yet the reverse of this commonly prevails. We should not judge ourselves only, or principally, by our actions; but by our motives, which enter so essentially into their morality. But we should judge others wholly by their conduct, and not by their motives, for these are cognizable only to God. It is his prerogative to search the heart. He will not condemn us for our ignorance of it. Charity thinketh no evil. It will always be far more honorable to be mistaken in any of our fellow creatures, than to be suspicious of them.

Satan was right in the principle of his insinuation, viz. That there was little to admire in Job's excellency, had he been a mere mercenary wretch, who, in all he did, had no regard for God, but to his own advantage only. Such actors there have always been. Thus Laban pressed Jacob to continue with him, not from affection or respect, but because, says he, I have learned by experience that the Lord hath blessed me for thy sake. In the same way the Shechemites reasoned: "Shall not their cattle, and their substance, and every beast of theirs, be ours? only let us consent unto them, and they will dwell with us." Jehu said, "See my zeal for the Lord;" but it was to aggrandize himself and his family; and he was even punished for actions which fulfilled the will of God. Our Savior did not commend those who followed him, because they did eat of the loaves and fishes, and early applied a test which would evince a regard for *himself* in those that adhered to him. He that forsaketh not all that he hath, cannot be my disciple. And we always, in the conduct of our fellow creatures, value a trifle that is done from pure regard, while we despise the splendid service that aims at the performer's own advantage. Yet, though there was force in Satan's reasoning; first, nothing could be more vile and false than his application of it to Job. And, therefore, God permitted him to be tried, that his rectitude might be found unto praise, and glory, and honor. Satan said, "Put forth thine hand now, and touch all that he hath, and he will curse thee to thy face." Then says God, Behold, all he *hath* is in thy power; only upon himself put not forth thine hand.

But he bears well the destruction of the whole. Then said Satan, "Skin for skin, yea, all that a man hath, will he give for his life. But put forth thine hand now, and touch his bone and his flesh, and he will curse thee to thy face. And the Lord said unto Satan, Behold, he is in thine hand, but save his life." And he is now covered with sore boils from the crown of his head to the sole of his foot. But in all this he sinneth not, nor charges God foolishly; and instead of cursing him to his face, he exclaims, "Blessed be the name of the Lord!"

And, secondly, we must distinguish between unprincipled selfishness, and excitements to gratitude and encouragement. The supreme reason, as well as the grand rule of obedience, is the will of God. And the language of the Christian is, Lord, what wilt thou have me to do? And the providence of God will often afford him opportunities to evince that the divine glory is dearer to him than his secular advantage. But it cannot be wrong to think of the promises, and be animated in our difficulties by the view of what the Scripture has proposed to us for the very purpose. Thus Moses is not censured for having respect unto the recompense of the reward. And Jesus, for the joy that was set before him, endured the cross, and despised the shame.

And, thirdly, though we ought not to serve God for gain as the motive, we cannot serve God for nought as to the result. He is a good master; and while his work is honorable and glorious, he deals well with his servants; and in keeping his commandments there is great reward. "Godliness is profitable unto all things, having promise of the life that now is, and of that which is to come."

DECEMBER 2.—**"And she said, Truth, Lord; yet the dogs eat of the crumbs which fall from their masters' table."—Matthew, xv, 27.**

To Him, said the dying Jacob, shall the gathering of the people be. To him, said the evangelical Isaiah, shall men come. He is the centre of all attraction, because he is the only source of relief. To whom, in all our ignorance, should we go, but to Him who has the words of eternal life? To whom, in all our guilt and weakness; but to Him in whom we have righteousness and strength? To whom, in all our dangers and misery; but to Him who is the hope of Israel, the Savior thereof in the time of trouble? And, blessed be his name, he is not only mighty to save, but has been pleased to assure us, "Him that cometh unto me, I will in no wise cast out."

—But he may try the confidence. He has bound himself not to disappoint. We have here an application made to him by a woman of Canaan, who cried to him, saying, "Have mercy on me, O Lord, thou son of David; my daughter is grievously vexed with a devil." But observe the discouragements she meets with. First, his silence; "He answered her not a word." Secondly, the address of his disciples. It is not certain that they pleaded for her relief at all; but if they did, it was in a spirit that we cannot admire· betraying impatience, and a wish to get rid of her importunity. "His disciples came and besought him, saying, Lord, send her away, for she crieth after us." Then here is, thirdly, a kind of exclusion, which seems to place her beyond the reach of his commission, if not his pity. "He said, I am not sent but unto the lost sheep of the house of Israel." All this not driving her away, he, fourthly, speaks as if he would add insult to rejection, "Is a dog to be treated like one of the family? It is not meet to take the children's bread, and cast it to dogs?" "And she said, Truth, Lord: yet the dogs eat of the crumbs which fall from their masters' table." Let us consider this as the language of a sinner, applying for mercy, in the prayer of faith.

First. He allows the truth of God's word, however it may reflect upon him—"Truth, Lord." He had in effect, called the woman a dog; and nothing could have been more reproachful. We see this in the question of Hazael; and the offer of Abishai, with regard to Shimei—Among the Jews, too, a dog was an animal unclean, and forbidden in sacrifice; and God's utmost abhorrence of a victim was expressed by cutting off a dog's neck—Yet she says, "Truth, Lord," I acquiesce in the censure. A sinner is called every thing that is vile in the Scripture—a fool, a madman, a rebel, a traitor, unworthy of the least of all God's mercies, and deserving that his wrath should come upon him—And, Lord, says he, it is all true. And thou art justified when thou speakest, and clear when thou judgest.

"Should sudden vengeance seize my breath,
"I must pronounce thee just in death;
"And should my soul be sent to hell,
"Thy righteous law approves it well."

Here, others stand out; but the convinced sinner is brought to add his amen, not only to the truth of God's word in general, but the truth of it with regard to his own personal guilt, depravity, and condemnation. And till we are brought to this, the Gospel can have nothing to do with us. It is a remedy: but a remedy is for the sick, and not for the healthful. The way to attain relief and comfort is, not to deny, conceal, or extenuate our sins, but to confess them in all their heinousness; and, in dealing with God, to stand where his word places us.

Secondly. He draws encouragement from seeming repulse—"Yet, Lord." This is an exercise of spiritual understanding: but the absolute importance of the case makes the man alive to every opening of hope; and he is now under the influence of the Spirit, that is teaching him to be wise unto salvation. Thus, darkness is made light, and crooked things straight. Thus, he rises above difficulties, which would otherwise be insuperable. He distinguishes between appearances and reality. "I know that, behind a frowning providence, he hides a smiling face." Though he slay me, yet will I trust in him. If he wounds, it is to heal. I hope I am his, *because* I am thus. As long as he tries me, he is not saying, Let him alone. He would not thus prune the tree, if he had sentenced it to be cut down. I see what once I did not, and the discovery is painful; but if he was minded to kill me, he would not have showed me such things as these. That be far from him, to trifle with my misery. In vain the enemy says, But thy sins are so numerous and aggravated. They are; but this is the very reason why I should apply for mercy—Pardon mine iniquity, for it is great—

"*Yet*, save a trembling sinner, Lord,
"Whose hope, still hovering round thy word,
"Would light on some sweet promise there,
"Some sure defence against despair."

Thirdly. He prizes the least communication from the Savior, "Truth, Lord: yet the dogs eat of the crumbs which fall from their masters' table;" and this is all I crave. The very same sentiment is put into the mouth of the prodigal—There is bread enough in my father's house, and I perish with hunger; he never thought of the fatted calf, or the best robe, or of the ring on his hand, or shoes on his feet. Oh! let me return to thy dear abode, and I shall not covet the chief room, or the highest seat—Make me as one of thy hired servants. Moses esteemed the reproach of Christ. David wished to be a door-keeper in the house of his God. The least grace is infinitely precious. It is connected with salvation, and makes us the heirs of promise. Blessed are the poor in spirit, for theirs is the kingdom of heaven.

Fourthly. He perceives the affluence and all-sufficiency of the Lord Jesus. Though what I implore is much for me to receive, it is nothing for thee to give. It is no more than a crumb from a king's table—What is this to the viands on the board, and the resources of his wealth! What I implore, thou wilt not miss; and I shall not rob thy children of their portion and plenty.

—Come, therefore, to him, remembering that he is Lord of all; that he is not only rich, but that his riches are unsearchable; not only that he has fulfilled the law, but magnified it, and made it honorable—that his righteousness is the righteousness of God, by faith—that his blood cleanseth from all sin—that in him all fullness dwells.

—And he will give you, not a dog's place, and a dog's portion; but he will put you among the children: he will seat you at his own table: he will say, Eat, O friends, and drink; yea, drink abundantly, O beloved. Was it not so here? Was he not charmed, instead of being displeased with her earnest and continued application? Does he not commend her for not taking a denial; and for urging him, apparently, against his will? "O woman! great is thy faith"—not, great is thy humility, thy importunity, thy perseverance—these *were* great; but *faith* was the root of them all. This, therefore, was what he admired in her. And this is the one thing needful for us. This alone will keep us steady to our purpose, and carry us through all our difficulties. But this will insure our final success, and crown us with praise, and glory, and honor, at the appearing of Jesus Christ. And he said unto her, "Be it unto thee, even as thou wilt." So will he say to you. And you will be foolish indeed, if you do not avail yourselves of the offer, and ask, and receive that your joy may be full.

DECEMBER 3.—"Behold, I am vile."—Job, xl, 4.

VILE, says Johnson's Dictionary, signifies mean, worthless, base, despicable, impure. There is nothing in the world to which this applies so well as sin. And it is to sin the exclaimer here refers.

He does not call himself "vile," because he was reduced and poor. By this, no man of reflection would ever feel himself degraded. A horse is not valued for his trappings, but for his strength or speed. Character is a personal thing, and independent of outward circumstances. If poverty, as some fools seem to judge, made a man vile, how vile were the apostles, who could say, "We hunger, and thirst, and are naked, and are buffeted, and have no certain dwelling-place!" And how vile was He who had not where to lay his head! Nor does he call himself "vile," because he was diseased, and full of sore boils from the crown of his head to the sole of his foot. The Scripture, indeed, calls the body—"this vile body;" and it *is* truly humbling, not only in the putrefaction of the grave, but frequently, also, even in life. How low are some of its appetites! how mortifying some of its infirmities! while some of its diseases are so trying as to require all the force of friendship to discharge the common duties of humanity. But there are no "wounds, bruises, putrefying sores," to be compared with the effects of sin—nothing is so "vile" as this—This makes us abominable to God himself; and is the only thing that does so. And how loathsome must that be, that causes the Creator to abhor the work of his own hands, and the Father of mercies to punish it with everlasting destruction from his presence, and to refuse to pardon it without the sacrifice of his own Son!

But who makes this confession? Is it a profligate wretch, whose iniquity in its effects has been found to be hateful, even to himself? Is it a penitent, newly awakened, and looking into his own heart, that had been concealed from him before? No: but Job, a saint, and a saint of no ordinary magnitude. You have heard of the patience of Job; and know how he is mentioned by Ezekiel, along with Noah and Daniel, as one of three who were pre-eminently righteous, and how God, the Judge of all, calls him "a perfect and an upright man." Yet this is he who cries, "Behold, I am vile!" And what do we learn from hence, but this: that the most gracious characters are the most remote from vain-glory, and are always more affected with their imperfections, than their excellencies? The nearer we approach completeness in any thing, the more easily we shall discern, and the more sensibly we shall feel our remaining deficiencies. A little learning puffeth up; but modesty and diffidence attend profound science. The advancing in knowledge is like sailing down a river, which widens as we proceed, till we find ourselves launched on the sea, and losing sight of the shore. Whoever vaunts himself as sinless, Paul did not: "I have not attained," says he, "I am not already perfect,' "I am less than the least of all saints," "I am the chief of sinners." Not that there is no difference between a saint and a sinner. Job does not mean that he loved sin, or lived in it. His friends accused him of this, but he denied it; and, turning to God, could say, "Thou knowest that I am not wicked." But he knew that in many things he offended, and in every thing came short of the glory of God. He was aware of the remains of sin opposing, hindering, vexing, polluting, his renewed mind; and though they appeared not to the view of others in gross transgressions, they were constantly felt by himself in an evil heart of unbelief, prone to depart from the living God, and constraining him to sigh, "O wretched man that I am! who shall deliver me from the body of this death!"

—And let us observe also when this acknowledgment was made. It was immediately after God's interposition, and appearance, and address: "Then the Lord answered Job out of the whirlwind, and said, Who is this that darkeneth counsel by words without knowledge? Gird up now thy loins like a man; for I will demand of thee, and answer thou me." Then he displayed before him some of his works and perfections. "Moreover the Lord answered Job and said, shall he that contendeth with the Almighty instruct him? He that reproveth God, let him answer it. *Then* Job answered the Lord, and said, Behold, I am vile"—Teaching us, that the more we have to do with God, the more we shall see and feel our nothingness and unworthines. What can make us so sensible of our ignorance, as *His* wisdom; of our weakness, as *His* power; of our pollution, as *His* purity—the purity of Him in whose sight the very heavens are not clean! Those are struck with little things who have never been abroad to see greater ones. But travelling enlarges the mind, and fills it with new and superior images; so that, on our return, we think nothing of the river, and the hill, and the plain of our native village. The Queen of Sheba prided herself upon her magnificence, till she came to Jerusalem, and had seen Solomon in all *his* glory. He that has been introduced to the Lord of all, and has had communion with him, will never think highly of himself again." "The loftiness of man shall be bowed down, and the haughtiness of men shall be made low; and the Lord alone shall be exalted in that day." Ah! said Job, "I have heard of thee by the hearing of the ear; but now mine eye seeth thee. Wherefore I abhor myself, and repent in dust and ashes."

"The more thy glories strike mine eyes,
"The humbler I shall lie."

—And I need not be afraid of this; my pride is the only prevention of my happiness:

"Thus, while *I* sink, my *joys* shall rise,
"Unmeasurably high."

DECEMBER 4.—"Make me to know my transgression and my sin."—Job, xii, 23.

THE desire of knowledge seems natural to every man. The eye is not satisfied with seeing, nor the ear with hearing. But who wishes to know *himself?* Yet this is the knowledge we want. And there are two things concerning ourselves, which it argues a gracious state of mind to be willing to know—our morality, and our depravity. A natural man turns away from both these. But, says David, "Lord, make me to know mine end, and the measure of my days, what it is; that I may know how frail I am." And, says Job, "Make me to know my transgression and my sin."

To explore the offences of others is a common wish. The information not only gratifies curiosity, but feeds malevolence, and furnishes the salt which seasons the conversation of the multitude. But, says Job, "Make me to know *my* transgression and *my* sin."

And what does he wish to know concerning them? Their existence. Their number. Their guilt. Their pollution. Their aggravations.

And this knowledge he seeks from God. He alone can teach us to profit. Conviction is the work of his own Spirit. But he uses means, and shows us our transgression and our sin—by the law, and by the gospel, and by friends and enemies, and by the dispensations of his providence. But he does it gradually. We could not bear all the disclosure at once. It would drive us into distraction or despair. He, therefore, tells us to turn again into the chamber of imagery, and we shall see greater abominations. And this will serve to explain a case in the Christian's experience. He supposes himself to grow worse, because he grows wiser. He seems more sinful, because he is more enlightened. There is not more evil in him, but he sees more.

The effect of this knowledge, in the first instance, will be wonder. It calls us out of darkness into God's marvellous light. We are astonished that He has borne with us so long. We are astonished that we have acted such a foolish, such an ungrateful part. We are astonished that we did not see these things before; for they now strike us with all the force of evidence. And we are astonished that we see them now; since the thousands around us are blind still, and we were once blind also. But the result of the discovery will be as important and useful as it is surprising.

Self-knowledge will produce self-annihilation. Self-vindication will be at an end, and we shall condemn ourselves. Self-complacency will be at an end, and we shall loathe ourselves. Self-dependence will be at an end, and we shall have no confidence in the flesh. "The lofty looks of man shall be humbled, and the haughtiness of men shall be bowed down, and the Lord alone shall be exalted in that day."

—Hence will arise the endearment of the Savior. How precious is the refuge, now the danger is seen! How inviting the healing fountain appears, now we feel our disease! For want of this sensibility, many read and hear of the Lord Jesus with indifference. How can it be otherwise? They that are whole need not the Physician, but they that are sick. The full soul loathes the honeycomb; but to the hungry, every bitter thing is sweet.

—Hence, also, submission, under afflictive dispensations. I will bear the indignation of the Lord, said the church, because I have sinned against him. Why, says Jeremiah, should a living man complain? Aaron's making a calf just before, kept him dumb in the loss of his sons. And David felt, from his adultery and murder, how well it became him to say, in Absalom's rebellion, Here I am; let the Lord do what seemeth him good. If a Christian has nothing criminal in particular to fix upon, he will see enough, in his general temper and walk, to keep him from thinking that God deals hardly with him. The wonder with him will be, not that his trials are so many, but so few—not that so many of his comforts are taken; but that any are left.

—Another advantage will be habitual gratitude. The proud are never thankful. Heap whatever favors upon them, and what reward have ye? They think they deserve it. You are only doing your duty—you are doing justly, rather than loving mercy. But when we are humble, in the same proportion we shall be grateful. When we feel that we are not worthy of the least of all God's mercies, how thankful shall we be for the bread we eat, and the water that we drink! What, then, for the word of his truth! and the Son of his love!

Finally. As we are sensible of our depravity, we shall be tender toward others. Faithful dealing with ourselves will always be accompanied with candid dealing with our fellow creatures. When we are much at home we cannot live much abroad. When we are employed in pulling the beams out of our own eyes, we shall not have much time for finding beams in those of others. If there be a difference between us and them, we shall ascribe it, when we know ourselves, to the mercy and grace of God; He has made us to differ, and we have nothing but what we have received. If we meet with things which are really wrong, and which we cannot deny, we shall not rejoice, but weep. And if a brother be overtaken in a fault, we shall restore such a one in the spirit of meekness, considering ourselves, lest we also be tempted.

Maundrell, in his Fable of the Bee, and Rochefoucault, in his maxims, and many Infidel writers, have shown great acquaintance with the depravity of human nature. But they learned it from the devil—and the scholars felt like the teachers. They delighted in the subject. They love to expose it. It was their interest to degrade and vilify human nature, to draw from it arguments for hatred, injury, selfishness, and distrust. But God teaches us the depravity of human nature, principally through our own depravity. And, with his teaching, he communicates his own Spirit. We therefore pity our common nature. We mourn over its dishonor. We pray for our fellow sinners. We long to save them.

DECEMBER 5.—"This man shall be the peace, when the Assyrian shall come into our land."—Micah, v, 5.

THAT the Messiah is the person here intended will not be denied by those who read the verses immediately preceding, and which speak so expressly of his incarnation and glory. The word *man*, indeed, as the italics apprize us, is not in the original. The sentence therefore reads, "And this shall be the peace"—*i. e.*, this person, of whom the prophet had been just speaking; he who was born as the ruler in Bethlehem, and whose goings forth were from everlasting—"He shall stand and feed in the strength of the Lord, in the majesty of the name of the Lord his God; and they shall abide: for now shall he be great unto the ends of the earth." The translators therefore, should rather have put in the word ruler, or shepherd. But, whatever be the supplement, it all comes to the same, provided *He himself* be understood; who is all our salvation and all our desire—For "this shall be the peace, when the Assyrian shall come into our land." But who is this Assyrian? The word cannot be taken literally; for the Assyrians never entered Judea after the birth of Christ. It is therefore used metaphorically, for some enemy; nothing being more common than for the sacred writers to express, by the name of Egypt, Assyria, or Babylon, any significant adversary; as those powers had distinguished themselves by their hatred, oppression, and enslaving of the Jews. The intimation therefore, is better than if it had been more definite; as we may now include every thing that annoys and alarms; every thing that would injure or destroy—Be the case what it may, he is our principal, our only relief. He does not exempt us from trouble and conflict; but he affords us assistance, comfort, and deliverance. Storms may arise: but he is our strong hold; enemies may assail us; but he will give us victory at last, and even now keep our minds in perfect peace, being stayed on him.

Let us think of several of these Assyrians; and see how when they invade us, and would swallow us up, he is our peace. Does the broken law of God threaten us? I say, the broken law ot God—for a man has nothing to fear from it, when it is perfectly kept; For the man that doeth these things, shall live in them—but the soul that sinneth, it shall die. The curse enters through every breach of transgression. And who is not, therefore, exposed? Who can be so ignorant as to suppose, that he has continued in all things written in the book of the law to do them? Now here is a condition to be in! The commandment coming—sin reviving—hope dying—and nothing expected, but a certain fearful looking for of judgment! But he is our peace who died for our offences and rose again for our justification—

"Go, ye that rest upon the law,
"And toil and seek salvation there,
"Forth to the flames that Moses saw,
"And fear, and tremble, and despair.

"But I'll retire beneath the Cross—
"Savior, at thy dear feet I lie;
"And the keen sword that justice draws,
"Flaming and red, shall pass me by!"

Or, does our adversary the devil terrify? Oh! you say when I think of his wiles, and strength, and his success for near six thousand years: and when I consider myself—here is enough to fill me, not only with dread, but despair—what am I, to the powers of darkness? No more than a "worm to a mountain?" Well be it so: the promise is, "Fear not, thou worm Jacob; for thou shalt thrash the mountains, and beat them small as the dust." In the Lord you have not only righteousness, but strength. Think of him—and take courage. In all these things you are more than conquerors, through him that loved you.

Or do we complain of the sin that dwelleth in us? A christian must feel this, and ought to feel it, and be deeply humbled before God on account of it. Paul felt it; and felt it more than all his sufferings. "O wretched man that I am! who shall deliver me from the body of this death?" But where does he find relief? "I thank God, through Jesus Christ our Lord"—"He will save me from my sins; and not only from their dominion—but their very being. He has begun a good work in me, and he will finish it. My sanctification *will* be as complete, as my justification now is. He is not only able to keep me from falling, but to present me faultless before the presence of his glory with exceeding joy."

Or do we consider the troubles of life? In accordance with this very case, he said to his disciples, In the world ye shall have tribulation; but in me ye shall have peace. And they found it so; and could acknowledge, "As the sufferings of Christ abound in us, so our consolation also aboundeth by Christ." Modern Christians may not be called to suffer persecutions as they did; but they may be the subjects of personal and relative trials, which require the same support and solace; and they equally belong to him; and are never dearer to his heart than in the hour of affliction: and he will not leave them comfortless. Is it nothing to know, that he has removed every thing penal from thy sufferings? that he will never leave thee nor forsake thee? that his grace shall be sufficient for thee? and that all thy sorrows shall yield the peaceable fruits of righteousness?

—But death! Ah! death is called the King of Terrors. Who can wonder that we should feel at the approach of it? And where would be the triumph of faith, if we did not? But it is possible to rise above this enemy. We know it from Scripture. We know it from observation. But whence comes the victory? Persons may die insensibly, or they may banish the subject from their minds; but if a man thinks of it, and thinks of it properly, there is only one relief when this Assyrian approaches us. It is to see him that has "abolished death." It is to hear him saying, "He that believeth in me, though he were dead, yet shall he live; and he that liveth and believeth in me, shall never die." And this is not all. The enemy is not only disarmed by him, but turned into a friend. The curse is converted into a blessing. To die is gain; and gain, too generally, in the experience, as well as always in the result. Well, therefore, could David say, "Yea, though I walk through the valley of the shadow of death, I will fear no evil; for thou art with me: thy rod and thy staff they comfort me."

—Here behold the consolation of Israel. Whatever would dismay us, let us look toward him, and say, "This same shall comfort us." Thanks be unto God for his unspeakable gift.

DECEMBER 6.—"Hast thou not made a hedge about him?"—Job, i, 10.

THIS was the question of Satan. The design of it was crafty and cruel. It was to insinuate that Job's religion was all mercenary. Therefore, no sooner had God extolled him, (who can stand before envy?) than "Satan answered the Lord, and said, Doth Job fear God for nought? Hast thou not made a hedge about him?" But though the motive he ascribes to Job is false, it is otherwise with the condition he represents him to be in. It was true, that God had made a hedge about him; and the same hedge surrounds all believers. Three things may be inferred from it.

First. God's people must be dear and valuable, otherwise he would not make a hedge about them. Men do not incur expense, and take pains to fence in a wilderness, a common, or a dunghill, but only what they set a price upon. "Since," says God, "thou hast been precious in my sight, thou hast been honorable, and I have loved thee." This love "passeth knowledge." His vineyard, his garden, his jewels, his children, his bride, are not so dear and precious to their owner, as all the subjects of divine grace are to God. "The Lord taketh pleasure in them that fear him; in them that hope in his mercy."

Secondly. They must be liable to danger and injury; why else should he make a hedge about them? They are exposed to the same perils with others, but they have many which are peculiar to themselves, because of their new state, and character, and privileges. David admits this. "Thou preparest a table before me, in the presence of my enemies." They were all around him, looking on, ready to seize his comfort, and destroy his person. What is the language of every awakened soul? "Lord, how are they increased that trouble me! Many there be that rise up against me." And as they are numerous, so they are malicious, wise, and powerful, and would soon overcome him; but his help cometh from the name of the Lord, who made heaven and earth.

Thirdly. They must be safe, whatever evils encompass them. For they do not lie open and unguarded—God has made a hedge about them. We have often heard the remark, and it is as true as it is common, "They are well kept whom God keeps." What he does for the safety of his people must be effectual. Therefore, the church says, "Save me, and I shall *be* saved; for thou art my praise." His power is almighty; and he saveth by his right hand them that put their trust in him, from them that rise up against them. He keeps them as the apple of his eye. He that keepeth Israel never slumbers nor sleeps. Lest any hurt them, says he, I will keep them night and day. But how far does this hedge extend? It reaches to his estate, his business, his dwelling place, his family, his reputation, his body, his soul. "Hast not thou made a hedge about *him?* and about his *house?* and about *all* that he hath on *every* side?"

But here it may be asked, How does this subject harmonize with observation and experience? Do not his people sometimes suffer losses and injuries, as well as others? We must distinguish between their spiritual and their temporal condition. With regard to the former their security is absolute. They are kept by the power of God, through faith, unto salvation. But as to the latter, their preservation is conditional. It is never absolutely promised; and the reason is, that it is not essential to their welfare. Yea, sometimes the removal of a temporal good is a greater blessing than the continuance of it, and is even indispensable to some higher advantage. But, with regard to every injury or loss in their temporal interests, there are two things which should always be remembered, and they ought to be sufficient to set their hearts at rest. The one is, that the loss or injury is entirely under the divine permission. Nothing can touch a hair of their head without leave from their heavenly Father. Satan could do nothing against Peter till he had "desired to have him, that he might sift him as wheat." And so here. Satan walked around this hedge, and peeped through, and stood tip-toe to look over, with envy and malice, but could not touch his body, no, nor even one of his servants or sheep, till God, for the trial of Job, allowed him. The other is, that the permission is always, and invariably regulated by the wisdom and goodness of his God, who loves them infinitely better than they love themselves. He that spared not his own Son, will withhold no good thing from them. He does not afflict willingly; but every trial he employs has a purpose to serve, that will evince, in due time, even the kindness of the dispensation, and enable the sufferers to acknowledge, with praise, It is good for me that I have been afflicted.

Let his people, therefore, hearken unto Him, and dwell safely; and be quiet from the fear of evil.

DECEMBER 7.—"And as he was yet a coming, the devil threw him down, and tare him."—Luke, ix, 42.

—FEARFUL of losing his prey, hating to have him cured, and wishing to prevent the display of the Savior's goodness and power. He could not, indeed, hinder the deliverance, but he did what he could.

There is no coming to our Savior now, as persons came in the days of his flesh; for he is no more in the world, as to his bodily presence—But we may come to him spiritually, by faith and prayer. And, in the suffering of this patient, we have an emblem of what we may meet with, as we are approaching. We can never seek him in vain: but our case may seem worse before relief arrives. We may be thrown down and torn in the way. God saw the affliction of Israel, and resolved to save them; but before they left Egypt, their bondage was more sorely felt; and as soon as they had escaped, Pharaoh pursued them, and hemmed them in. As long as people remain regardless of Christ, the enemy keeps them in peace; but when they begin to inquire in earnest after him, then commences the conflict; and this is the language of many an applicant, as "he is a coming"—"O my God! my soul is cast down within me."

Some of his difficulties and discouragements may arise from the opposition of friends and relations. Marvel not, said the Savior, if the world hate you. We have no reason to believe, our religion is the religion of the Bible, if it be palatable to the taste of carnal minds. How often, as soon as a man becomes decided, is he had in derision of all around him, and like one mocked of his neighbor! And is it not trying to proceed in a course that will break up connexions otherwise agreeable? and draw upon him the sneer, or the laugh? the ridicule, or the menace? Yet he must go forth to him without the camp, bearing his reproach. And he ought to rejoice that he is counted worthy to suffer shame for his name. But every thing cannot be expected at first. The trial is greater when a man's foes are those of his own house, when the persecution comes from those he loves, and ought even to obey, only in the Lord. But the trial is greatest, at least to a grateful and ingenuous mind, when the persecution results, not from violence or threatenings, but from kindness, and entreaties and tears. Yet through all this he must press. He that loveth father or mother more than me, is not worthy of me; and he that forsaketh not all that he hath, cannot be my disciple.

Sometimes the coming soul has difficulties arising from ignorance of the method of salvation. These, indeed, will not remain long, when the heart is brought into a proper state, and the man cries, What must I do to be saved? But some are alarmed before they are enlightened, as a person may be awakened in the dark, and not know which way to flee. Or as a patient may be sensible of the danger of his disease, before he knows the physician or the remedy. Some have not had parents who taught them the truth, as it is in Jesus; and they have no access to evangelical preaching, and they are not blessed with such Christian companions as can guide their feet into the path of peace. What wonder, therefore, if such, for a while, should betake themselves (for something, in such cases, will be done, they cannot sit still) to improper expedients, and self-righteous means of relief? For all legalists are not of the same kind. Some are such from disposition, and these are the bitterest adversaries of the Gospel; and the presentation of the truth only draws forth their enmity. But others are such from want of better information only; and when they find the light, they rejoice in it—"Oh! this is what my soul was following hard after—O that I had known it earlier; and, instead of working, had believed on him that justifieth the ungodly; and, instead of attempting to build up a wretched shelter of my own, I had only fled for refuge to the hope set before me!"

Allied to this is another discouragement the coming sinner feels, springing from doubts and fears, when he does perceive the way, and is informed that there is salvation in no other. Pressed down with such a sense of his unworthiness, and with such views of the number and heinousness of his sins, as he never had before, he is ready to conclude, that such immense blessings cannot be for *him;* and that *his* claiming them would be no better than presumption. Let not such a desponding soul refuse to be comforted. Let him ask, What recommendation had Manasseh? Where am *I* excluded from hope! Does he not say, Look unto me, and be ye saved, all the ends of the earth? If I have nothing with which to purchase, am I not invited to "buy without money, and without price?"

" Retreat beneath his wings,
" And in his grace confide;
" This more exalts the King of kings.
" Than all your works beside."

An apprehension, too, of the arduous duties of the Christian life, is frequently very dismaying. The Scripture tells him, that this life is a building and a warfare; and enjoins him, before he begins, to count the cost of the one, and the resources of the other. He does this, and feels himself perfectly inadequate to both. And so he may feel, and ought to feel: for when he is poor, then is he rich; and when he is weak, then is he strong. But fear not, says the Savior; for, I am with thee. My grace is sufficient for thee. As thy day, so shall thy strength be. "Even the youths shall faint and be weary, and the young men shall utterly fall; but they that wait upon the Lord shall renew their strength;

they shall mount up with wings, as eagles; they shall run, and not be weary; and they shall walk, and not faint."

Finally. There are things among the professors of religion, which often perplex and scandalize young converts. Such are the diversities of opinion among them. And their alienation from each other, because of their little distinctions. And the falls of some; and the backslidings of others. Older and wiser Christians know how to account for all this, without shaking their faith and hope—though it often is grievous even to them: but the weak find them stumbling-blocks, over which they often fall. For which reason, the apostle says, to the believing Hebrews, "Lift up the hands which hang down, and the feeble knees; and make straight paths for your feet, lest that which is lame be turned out of the way: but let it rather be healed."

Two things must now be fixed in the mind. The one is--that whatever would impede our coming to Christ, is from Satan; and should be resisted accordingly. The other is—that whatever difficulties we may encounter—come to him we must. It is not a matter of indifference—It is the one thing needful—We perish without it—"Ye will not come unto me that ye might have life."

DECEMBER 8.—"If I must needs glory, I will glory of the things which concern mine infirmities."—2 Cor. xi, 30.

WE may consider these infirmities under two classes:

First; as outward and natural. Thus they include bodily weaknesses and indispositions. Some, by reason of a healthful and firm constitution, know little of these infirmities, and can scarcely sympathize with those who are the subjects of them. But Paul was no stranger to them. I was with you, says he to the Corinthians, in weakness, in fear, and in much trembling. They also include all other external afflictions—whatever lowers a man's condition, and weakens him in the opinion of the world, who always judge after outward appearances. If it were necessary to prove this, we might refer to the apostle's sufferings, as recorded in the preceding verses, and to which he obviously alludes: and also to what he immediately subjoins, as an illustration—in his escape from Damascus, by the wall in a basket; and the thorn in the flesh, the messenger of Satan to buffet him—ending with his noble avowel, "Therefore I take pleasure in infirmities, in reproaches, in necessities, in persecutions, in distresses, for Christ's sake; for when I am weak, then am I strong."

There is something wonderful in this. For all these things are viewed as disadvantages, and give rise to emotions of grief and shame, rather than of joy and glory. People glory in their beauty, not in their deformity; in their strength, not in their weakness; in their dignity, not in their meanness; in their praise, not in their disgrace; in their successes, not in their disappointments. But Paul says, "If I must needs glory *I* will glory of the things which concern mine infirmities." Let us make a distinction here. Absolutely considered, these things are evils in themselves: and it does not become a Christian to pray for them, or go out of his way to meet with them. But when he is called to suffer them according to the will of God, he should remember that there are purposes to be answered by them, which render them *relatively* valuable and excellent. If medicine be regarded only as to its taste, we say it is offensive, and we should decline it: but when the necessity and usefulness of it are perceived, and we think of the health to be restored, and the life to be prolonged by it, we not only consent to take it, but thankfully pay for the otherwise disagreeable remedy. "Now no chastening for the present seemeth to be joyous, but grievous: nevertheless, afterward it yieldeth the peaceable fruit of righteousness unto them which are exercised thereby." So it is here: Paul glories in things which *concern* his infirmities. What are these? We may consider them as preservatives or preventions—Thus when Israel was going astray after her lovers, says God, "I will hedge up her way with thorns, and make a wall that she shall not be able to find her paths." And as restorers. Thus David says, "Before I was afflicted, I went astray; but now I have kept thy word." I was sick, he bled me, and I recovered. And as probations, to evince and display the reality and degree of our religion: the tenderness of God's care, the supports of his grace, and the truth of his word. Of this quality were Job's sufferings. And as preparatives—for usefulness here, and heaven hereafter. How these views of faith alter our estimate of the dispensation, and our feelings under it!

But, secondly; we may consider these infirmities as inward and spiritual. Thus they comprise all those weaknesses and deficiencies of grace under which the best now labor; and which lead them to pray, "Strengthen, O God, that which thou hast wrought for us." Something is wanting in their faith, hope, courage, patience, and spiritual understanding. Even Paul could say, I have not attained: I am not already perfect. But are not these infirmities matter of humiliation, rather than of glorying? Yes; the believer blushes and groans over them. Nor will an apprehension of his security reconcile him to his remaining imperfections. Yea, a persuasion of God's constant love toward him will induce him the more to bewail them. Yet there are things which *concern* these infirmities, for which he feels thankful, and in which he rejoices. Four of these may be mentioned.

First. The means of grace are things which concern our infirmities. They are rendered necessary by them, and are designed to relieve them. In heaven they are laid aside; there they are needless. But the Christian now cries, Send us help from the sanctuary, and strengthen us out of Zion. And by waiting upon the Lord, he renews his strength.

Secondly. The promises are things which concern our infirmities. "To him that hath shall be given." "As thy days, so shall thy strength be." "The righteous shall hold on his way, and he that hath clean hands shall wax stronger and stronger." When we read all this, let the weak say, I am strong. But for these assurances we must despond: but now we read and go on; read, and fight on; read, and suffer on. We rejoice at his word, as one that findeth great spoil.

Thirdly. The influences of the Spirit are things which concern our infirmities. How is a Christian to live, or walk? He lives in the Spirit, and walks in the Spirit. How does he pray? In the Holy Ghost. "The Spirit also helpeth our infirmities: for we know not what we should pray for as we ought; but the Spirit itself maketh intercession for us with groanings which cannot be uttered. And He that searcheth the hearts, knoweth what is the mind of the Spirit, because he maketh intercession for the saints according to the will of God." Observe the ground of the apostle's hope, with regard to himself, in the issue of all his sufferings: "I know that this shall turn to my salvation through your prayer, and the supply of the Spirit of Jesus Christ." And with him here is rich abundance: and in him all fullness dwells; and to him we have always a free and invited access.

Fourthly. The last thing that concerns our infirmities, is the removal of them by death. A certain removal. A removal nigh at hand. An entire removal. Every one of them will be done away with and for ever!

DECEMBER 9.—"I am a burden to myself."—Job, vii, 20.

AND perhaps this is not all—perhaps you are a burden to others also.

—But we will leave this, and inquire whether you are a burden to yourself. We may put the complaint into the mouth of four classes.

It is sometimes the language of the afflicted. Thus it was the exclamation of Job. We talk of trouble. He could say, "Behold, and see if there was sorrow like unto my sorrow." Read the affecting relation; dwell on all the dismal items; and wonder not that *he* should say, "I am a burden to myself." If we cannot approve of the strength of his complaint, we hardly know how to condemn it. God himself overlooks it, and only holds him forth as an example of patience. All sufferers cannot, indeed, say, truly, as he did, "My stroke is heavier than my groanings." Yet the heart's bitterness is known only to itself. We cannot determine the pressure of another's mind under suffering, for the feeling of affliction may be actually much greater, than we should have supposed from the degree of it. But afflictions may be great in themselves, from their number, and frequency, and suddenness, and subject. Is this thy case? Yield not to impatience and despondency. Such afflictions have often introduced a train of mercies, and the Valley of Achor has been a door of hope. How many in heaven, how many on earth, are now thanking God for their trials! He knows how to deliver. Say—Lord, "I am oppressed; undertake for me." Cast thy burden upon the Lord, and he shall sustain thee."

It is sometimes the language of the disengaged and idle. None so little enjoy life, and are such burdens to themselves, as those who have nothing to do—for

"A want of occupation is not rest— | "A mind quite vacant, is a mind distress'd."

Such a man is out of God's order, and opposing his obvious design in the faculties he has given, and the condition in which he has placed him. Nothing, therefore, is promised in the Scripture to the indolent. Take the indolent, with regard to exertion—What indecision! What delay! What reluctance! What apprehension! "The slothful man saith, There is a lion without; I shall be slain in the streets." "The way of a slothful man is as a hedge of thorns; but the way of the righteous is made plain." Take him with regard to health—What sluggishness of circulation! What depression of spirits! What dullness of appetite! What enervation of frame! Take him with regard to temper and enjoyment—Who is pettish and fretful? Who feels wanton and childish cravings? Who is too soft to bear any of the hardships of life? Who broods over every little vexation and inconvenience! Who not only increases real, but conjures up imaginary evils? and gets no sympathy from any one in either? Who feels time wearisome and irksome? Who is devoured by ennui and spleen! Who oppresses others with their company? and their questions, and censorious talk? The active only have the true relish of life. He who knows not what it is to labor, knows not what it is to enjoy. Recreation is only valuable as it unbends us—the idle know nothing of it. It is exertion that renders rest delightful, and sleep sweet and undisturbed. That the happiness of life depends on the regular prosecution of some laudable purpose or lawful calling, which engages, helps, and enlivens, all our powers; let those bear witness who, after spending years in active usefulness, retire, to *enjoy themselves.* Prayers should be offered up for their servants and wives; and for themselves too—they are a burden to themselves.

It is the language of the wicked. Not always, indeed: but much oftener than they are willing to own. It may not come from them in the circle of their companions; but it is sighed out in private, when the charm of amusement has ceased, and conscience tries to be heard. They may pretend (for hypocrisy is not confined to religion) to be peaceful; but they know that one thought of God is sufficient to destroy all the calm. They may profess to admire the world; but they know it affords them no satisfaction. They know they return jaded from all their excursions of avarice, ambition, and sensuality, still asking, Who will show us any good? They know that, in this uncertain state, they are always trembling for the idols of their hearts; that they look for no support in trouble; and dread the approach of death—to the fear of which they are all their life-time subject to bondage. Sin and sorrow are inseparable. God himself has told us that the way of transgressors is hard, and that there is no peace to the wicked. Many sins bring their own punishment along with them. Envy is the rottenness of the bones. "Pride is restless as the wind." What a torment is the spirit of revenge! What must be the apprehension of the thief! and the terror of the murderer! What the remorse of a villain who has seduced a fellow creature from the path of virtue, and made her ignominious and wretched for life! What the feelings of a drunkard, who has ruined his business, and covered his wife and children with rags! How often does the sinner become the contempt of the neighborhood? How often does he contract infirmities and diseases, which lie down with him in the dust! Yes, *he* may well say, I am a burden to myself—and to get rid of the intolerable load, he not rarely lays violent hands upon himself; saying with Cain, my punishment is greater than I can bear.

It may be the language of the godly. We mean, not only or principally as they are afflicted; then they would coincide with the first class of complainants. Many, indeed, are the afflictions of the righteous, and they are not required to be insensible under them. But there are things which they feel more painfully than outward trouble. The temptations of Satan. A world lying in wickedness. The imperfections of their graces. The remains of corruption within them. Wanderings in duty. An evil heart of unbelief. Distrust of their best Friend. The grievings of the Holy Spirit. Another cannot enter into all this. It requires the feelings of a renewed mind; but this induces the believer to say, "I loathe it—I would not live always." O wretched man that I am! said Paul; who shall deliver me from the body of this death?

Is there any relief? The very experience is a token for good. Your case is not peculiar. All your brethren, while in this tabernacle, groan too, being burdened. You will not be a burden to yourself always, or long. You now say, Behold, I am vile: wherefore I abhor myself in dust and ashes. But you will soon be reconciled to yourselves, without pride. Your knowledge will be without obscurity; your services, without imperfections; your pleasure, without pain. And he who is now keeping you from falling, will present you faultless before the presence of his glory, with exceeding joy.

DECEMBER 10.—" I was in the Spirit on the Lord's day."—Rev. i, 10.

THIS proves how early, among Christians, one day in the week was distinguished from the rest. And it is obvious, that the day thus distinguished was the *first* day of the week, for no other is ever styled "the Lord's day," in the New Testament, or by any of the ancient writers. It is called "the Lord's day," not only by way of distinction, but excellency, being appropriated to his service, and consecrated to his honor, as the day of his resurrection from the dead, and entering into his rest from the works of redemption.

To be in the Spirit, often signifies, to be inspired, or to receive communications immediately from God, and it is certain that John was thus honored. But the phrase may be used in reference to a spirituality of mind; and doubtless John experienced this also, and it prepared him for the sublime discoveries he was favored with. Though miracles have ceased, the Spirit is still given in his ordinary influences; and if any man have not the Spirit of Christ, he is none of his. We are required to pray in the Holy Ghost; to worship God in the Spirit; to live and walk in the Spirit. Hence the common notion of our being in the Spirit on the Lord's day is perfectly scriptural. But we must distinguish between our being in the Spirit, and the Spirit being in us. The latter denotes the reality of his influence, the former, the abundance. Thus we say, a man is in love, or in liquor, or in a passion, to intimate that he is entirely seized and governed by it. We are not only to possess the Spirit, but to be possessed by it. "Be ye filled with the Spirit." It is not enough for us to be in a spiritual state—but frame.

We must not, however, confine the import of this expression as some do, who never think of their being in the Spirit on the Lord's day, but when they are relieved, comforted, delighted. We love feeling in religion; but religious feelings are many and various. It is desirable to pass the Sabbath in liveliness, liberty, and joy; and we read of the Spirit of life, and of a free Spirit, and of the comfort of the Holy Ghost. But a mournful Sabbath may be a very profitable one; and we are never more in the Spirit than when we are deeply sensible of our unworthiness, and exclaim, at the foot of the Cross, Behold, I am vile, and hunger and thirst after righteousness. For, is he not the Spirit of truth? the convincer of sin? the Spirit of grace and supplication? And does he not lead us to look upon him whom we have pierced, and to mourn for him?

Who does not know, by experience, that the day and the Spirit are not always thus united? Who has not had Sabbaths devoid of all proper religious affections? This should be a matter of deep humiliation. How piercing should be the thought of a lost Sabbath! Lost, never to return! Lost, yet to be accounted for! But what is a dull and formal attendance on the services of the season, without those influences which the day requires, and is in itself adapted to produce.

As the richest Sabbath, with regard to means and ordinances, may be passed without the Spirit, so we may be in the Spirit on the Lord's day, when the day is attended with few, or none of these advantages. And was it not thus with the beloved disciple? Oh! there are Sabbaths when every thing is attractive; when we go to the house of God in company; when our eyes see our teachers; when our ears hear the joyful sound of salvation by grace! But John's Sabbath was a day of suffering, of privation, of exile, of solitude, in a desert isle—

"Where the sound of the church-going bell,
"Those rocks and those valleys ne'er heard;
"Never sighed at the sound of a knell,
"Or smiled when a Sabbath appeared."

But heaven was opened unto him; and perhaps he never had such a Sabbath on earth before. A Christian may never be less alone, than when alone. His consolations may equal, yea, exceed his sufferings. While his body is fettered, his soul may range in all the glorious liberty of the sons of God.

Yes, you may be in the Spirit on the Lord's day, when denied the privileges of the sanctuary. If you keep away, from indifference, or indolence, or to save expense, when you have the ability to procure accommodation, or from any of those excuses which would detain you from nothing else, you have no reason to expect the Divine sanction. But sometimes travelling, even on the Lord's day, by land or by water, may be unavoidable; or accident, or disease, or infirmity of age, may confine you: in which case the Lord will not despise his prisoners; and they shall know the blessedness of those whose strength is in him, and in whose hearts are the ways of them. It is better to want opportunity and power, than the will, when we serve Him who looketh at the heart. Nothing can be a substitute for him; but he is a substitute for every thing, and he is always accessible; and "if ye, being evil, know how to give good gifts unto your children, how much more shall your heavenly Father give the Holy Spirit to them that ask him!"

December 11.—"And the Lord turned the captivity of Job, when he prayed for his friends."—Job, xiii, 10.

Job was once the greatest man in the East. But he was stripped of every thing, but life; and became as a sufferer, proverbial for ever. How long his calamities continued, we cannot determine. But, at length, the shadow of death was turned into the morning. His troubles were all removed; his losses all repaired; and his latter end blessed more than his beginning. Hence, says the Apostle James, "Ye have heard of the patience of Job, and have seen the end of the Lord; that the Lord is very pitiful, and of tender mercy."

—His state of affliction is called "his captivity." Did, then, the Chaldeans and Sabeans, when they robbed him, make him also a prisoner? The term is metaphorical. Yet there is a striking reality, as the foundation of it. By the permission of Providence, Satan, for a while, had him in his possession, to go as far as he pleased in destroying his substance, and afflicting his body. In consequence of this, a troop of woes seized him; and his feet, as he says, were made fast in the stocks. David also, expresses himself much in the same way—"Bring my soul out of prison." He despises not his prisoners. A state of affliction is not only unpleasant, but confining. Losses in property abridge a man of his former excursions of pleasure, and curtail his entertainments. Sickness arrests a man, and leads him away from company and business, and confines him to a bed of languishing. Yea, it detains a good man from the Sanctuary; and when he thinks of his former freedom and privileges, he pours out his soul in him: for he had gone to the house of God with the voice of joy and praise, with a multitude that kept holy-day.

—His deliverance was of the Lord—"The Lord turned away his captivity." "He that is our God, is the God of salvation; and unto God the Lord belong the issues from death." Some ascribe their deliverances to chance; some to the favor of their fellow creatures; some to their own wisdom and care—all of which is no better than idolatry. Faith will lead us to see and acknowledge the agency of God's hand, whatever means may have been employed. And, till God command deliverance, vain is the help of man. "Behold, he breaketh down, and it cannot be built again; he shutteth up a man, and there can be no opening." But *he* knows how to deliver: and when his time is come, he not only can, but he will, make a way for our escape. "Therefore," says the Church, "I will look unto the Lord; I will wait for the God of my salvation: my God will hear me."

—But it is peculiarly worthy of our remark, that the deliverance was accomplished "when he prayed for his friends." These friends had acted a very unkind part. They had not only mistaken his case, but charged him with hypocrisy, and loaded him with reproach. This was no easy thing to bear. He labors to convince them, but in vain. Yet he felt no resentment, but even prayed for them! This is the best thing we can do, in such cases. It will keep us more than any thing else from the effects of unhallowed passion, and enable us to comply with the command, "Love your enemies." We *cannot* love them *as* we love others; but if we can sincerely *pray* for them, it is a proof we love them, in the sense of the injunction.

But we here see, not only the forgiving temper of Job, but the efficacy of prayer. And it is said, the Lord turned again his captivity *when* he prayed for his friends; it would seem, that the deliverance commenced while he was engaged in the exercise. This is no unusual thing: for, says God, "*While* they call, I will answer." But, if it did not take place *in* the exercise, it followed *immediately after:* and thus it affords a proof, that he is a God hearing prayer, and encourages us to come to the Throne of his Grace.

—And not only for ourselves, but for others also:

—And not only on their behalf, but on our own. Not only because it may avail much for them, but also for ourselves. Thus Job's praying not only obtained pardon for his friends, but deliverance for himself! And though he had often prayed under his afflictions, the prayer honored with his deliverance was not a personal, but relative prayer. Let us forget this, and let us extend it to all other cases of beneficence. If we do no good to those who are the objects, we must do good to those who are the agents. It cannot be in vain, with regard to ourselves. Our prayer, if not successful, will return into our own bosom, and leave a blessing behind it. "Into whatsoever house ye enter, first say, Peace be unto this house. And if the son of peace be there, your peace shall rest upon it; if not, it shall turn to you again."

DECEMBER 12.—"And there was Mary Magdalene, and the other Mary sitting over against the sepulchre."—Matthew, xxvii, 61.

" WHILE upon the Cross He hung,
" The Marys near him staid;
" And when from the tree releas'd,
" Beheld where he was laid:
" Fearless to the place they ran;
" All their hope was buried there;
" And, with grief and wonder, sat
" Before the sepulchre.

" Love it was detain'd them here;
" And sacred was the spot·
" Soon the scene reviv'd their faith
" And mem'ry ne'er forgot.

" From the crowd *I* glad withdraw,
" And, with them, to muse I'm come,
" And prefer to Eden's bliss,
" One tear at such a tomb.

" Here, within this grave, now sleeps
" The best, the only Friend;
" Here, the lips of truth are seal'd,
" And mercy's journeys end.
" Here, the light, the life of men,
" Is early quench'd, and dead;
" How deserveless now appear
" All other tears I've shed.

"Ah! how low his sacred head
"Reposes here for me!
"And how deep, though once so rich,
"Is now his poverty!
"Nought of earth, in life or death,
"His own he never knew;
"Borrow'd was his place of birth;
"His grave was borrow'd too!

"But what terrors seize my frame!
"A trembling shakes the ground;
"And the door, though thrice secured,
"Is now wide open found;
'On the stone the angel sits,
"And frowns the guard to flight;
Yet his looks, and words, to me,
"Speak safety and delight.

"'He thou seekest is not here;
"'Come, view his lowly bed;
"'And, with haste, go tell his friends
"'He's risen from the dead.'
"As I go, himself I meet—
"'All hail,' he greeting cries!
"'I have crush'd sin, death, and hell,
"'And open'd Paradise!

"'I'm alive for evermore!
"'And all that mourn with thee,
"'Like myself, their Head, shall live,
"'For evermore with me.'
"'Tis enough—in every state
"*This* truth myhope revives—
"And, should every comfort die,
"I know my Savior *lives*."

DECEMBER 13.—"And this I pray, That your love may abound yet more and more in knowledge, and in all judgment."—Philippians, i, 9.

ACCORDING to this prayer there is nothing in which we should abound more than love. It is the fulfilling of the law; the end of the gospel commandment; the bond of perfectness. Without it, whatever be our attainments, professions, or sacrifices, we are NOTHING. Yet we are to abound in it *wisely*. This is not found in all religious characters. In one we perceive zeal; in another discretion. One is clear, but cold; another is warm, but inconsiderate. If we could meet with an individual who, in his experience and practice, blended these qualities; who had the heart as well as the head, and the head as well as the heart, of the Christian, *he* would be the prayer of the apostle fulfilled: "I pray, That your love may abound yet more and more in knowledge, and in all judgment."

Our love does not thus abound when we do not distinguish between what is supreme and what is subordinate. There are things in religion which are essential, and things which are only circumstantial. Am I to lay as much stress upon the latter as upon the former? Is the form of the railing of a bridge to be compared with the foundation of the buttresses, or the key-stones of the arch? Is the finger, though useful, of the same importance to the continuance of life, as the heart and the lungs? What is an article about church government, or the mode of administering an ordinance, compared with the doctrine of justification by faith, or redemption by the blood of Christ! I venerate a man who is all diligence to convert sinners from the error of their way, and save souls from death; but I cannot feel the same toward the zealot of bigotry, whose aim is to make proselytes to his own peculiarities, and who regards his community, not as a *part*, but as a *party*.

Persons may not be judicious in their devotional exercises. By the frequency of public attendances they may exclude or abridge the duties of the family, or the closet. They may so lengthen out the worship at the domestic altar, as to produce in children and servants, weariness and aversion. Persons may hazard their health by going forth under bodily indisposition; forgetting that God requires mercy, and not sacrifice; and that when *He* deprives us of the ability, he accepts the ready mind.

Nor does our love abound in knowledge, and in all judgment, when it carries us out of our own places and stations to be useful. Grace always gives us the desire to do good, but Providence must furnish the opportunities. We are not to be unruly, or break the ranks, as the word is; but to march orderly, as good soldiers of Jesus Christ. The Lord puts us where we ought to be, and enjoins us to abide in our calling. There are, indeed, occasional deviations from this rule; but they are exceptions, and must be justified by their own circumstances. When Saul's courtiers reflected upon the Shepherd of Bethlehem as a restless, ambitious young man, who wished to struggle out of obscurity into public life, he was conscious that he followed only the providence of God, and could make this appeal, "Lord, my heart is not haughty, nor mine eyes lofty; neither do I exercise myself in great matters, or in things too high for me." But there is danger, not only of impatience, but pride, in all changes attended with the hope of elevation; and surely it becomes a man to consult some one besides *himself* concerning them. A man, by acting unlawfully, may do good; but the result does not justify the means. Whatever excitements persons may have to act irregularly, they are, upon the whole, far most useful by consistency. Their example, in the latter, *must* do good; but, in the former, it *may* lead astray. I have known men who have been stunned for life by striking their head against a pulpit. I have known preachers who have neglected their families, and left their children to rove wild in the street or the field, while they were teaching in the villages. I have known females who have disregarded their husbands and household affairs, to run unseasonably after favorite ministers. "The wisdom of the prudent," says Solomon, "is to understand *his* way," *i. e.* what becomes *him* to do; whether as a master, or a servant; as a father, or a child; as rich, or as poor—in every relation and condition of life, asking, Lord, what wilt thou have *me* to do?

Many err much in the discharge of the duties they owe to others. Reproof may be more than thrown away, owing to the manner in which it is applied. It is done in anger; but it should flow from the spirit of meekness. It is done in public; but we should tell him his fault alone. We should distinguish, also, between one disposition and another; and become all things to all men, if by any means we may gain some. He that winneth souls is wise—We must therefore walk in wisdom toward them that are without. Wisdom must regulate our discourse. We must know when to speak, what to speak, how to speak—"A word fitly spoken, is like apples of gold in pictures of silver." We shall not talk discouragingly before those that are weak in the faith; nor perplex them with doubtful disputations. We may give strong meat to strong men; but babes require milk.

We may also err in cases of charity. Since we cannot relieve all the necessitous, we must endeavor to ascertain the most proper objects. Alms may become immoral by encouraging vice or idleness. Religious societies are to be encourged and supported; but God abhors robbery, for a burnt-offering. And many an annual subscription, *printed*, robs not only the tradesman, but the poor. Nothing is to incapacitate us to succor the domestic and personal distress which *Providence itself* brings immediately before; and by which some sublimely pass, to attend public meetings—"Whoso hath this world's good, and seeth his brother have need, and shutteth up his bowels of compassion from him, how dwelleth the love of God in him?"

These are not all the instances in which our love is to abound in knowledge and in all judgment. But these are sufficient to show us, that wisdom is profitable to direct. Wherefore, let us not be unwise, but understanding what the will of the Lord is. Let us cultivate our minds. Let us faithfully review our own conduct, and see where we have been mistaken. Let us keep observation alive and awake. Let us walk with wise men. Let us be familiar with the Holy Scriptures, which can furnish us thoroughly unto all good works. Let us often read and study the Proverbs of Solomon. Let us constantly keep in view the life of Jesus, who dealt prudently, and so was exalted, and extolled, and was very nigh. Above all, let us seek the Spirit of Truth—"If any of you lack wisdom, let him ask of God, who giveth to all men liberally, and upbraideth not, and it shall be given him."

DECEMBER 14.—"I will say unto God, do not condemn me."—Job, x, 2.

He could have resolved on nothing better in his affliction than betaking himself to God. It was turning to him that smote him, and resembling the child who, when corrected by the mother, always clings to her knee. We are too fond of talking our complaints to men—

"Were half the breath thus vainly spent,
"To heaven in supplication sent;
"Our cheerful cry would oftener be—
"Hear what the Lord hath done for me."

"If I weep," says Job, "mine eye poureth out tears unto God:" and if I speak, "I will say unto God"—

But what does he say? "Do not condemn me." Now there was no real ground for this fear. Job could say, I know that my Redeemer liveth; and there is no condemnation to them that are in Christ Jesus. Their sins once pardoned, if sought for, shall never be found; and their afflictions, however distressing, have nothing penal in them, they are only like the fire to the gold, and pruning to the vine, and medicine to the patient, and correction to the child. They are chastened of the Lord, that they may not be condemned with the world.

But the language implies, that he knew God could charge him with guilt enough to condemn him, if he should deal with him after his desert. And every child of God feels this. In reviewing even the most innocent periods of his life, and the devoutest services in which he was ever engaged, he exclaims, "Enter not into judgment with thy servant, O Lord; for in thy sight shall no flesh living be justified."

—It shows us also, that a child of God is prone to fear the displeasure of God in his afflictions. The people of the world, as we see in the case of the Barbarians, with regard to Paul's viper;

and the caution of our Lord, with regard to men on whom the tower fell; deem their fellow creatures sinners, because they suffer such things. And though we are much more disposed to judge others by this erroneous rule than ourselves; there is something in calamity, says Madame de Stael, that tends to make all minds superstitious. We would rather say, that tends to revive the remembrance of a moral providence, and the belief of a connexion between sin and punishment. And this is more the case when afflictions are sudden, and unlooked for, and great, and repeated, or have any thing that looks peculiar in them. And even good minds have not been able always to resist such impressions and conclusions. Gideon said, "If the Lord be with us, why then is all this evil befallen us?" And the pious widow of Zarephath, upon the loss of her child, said unto Elijah, "What have I to do with thee, O thou man of God? art thou come unto me to call my sin to remembrance, and to slay my son?" The Poet tells us, and very truly, "Behind a frowning providence, he hides a smiling face"—But he does *hide* it. The frown is visible enough—sense can see this; but the smile can only be apprehended by faith—and whose faith is always in exercise?

We may also remark, that gracious souls deprecate nothing so much as censure from God—Therefore they say unto God, "Do not condemn me. To any thing else I bow. But I cannot bear exclusion from thee. Whom have I in heaven but thee? and there is none on earth I desire besides thee. Thy loving kindness is better than life. In thy presence all my happiness is placed. Use the rod of a father, but let me not feel the sentence of the judge. Correct me; but do not abandon me. Cast me not away from thy presence, and take not thy Holy Spirit from me."

Yes, nothing can relieve the gloom of a follower of God, but the light of his countenance. Nothing can make melody in his troubled conscience, but the sound, Go in peace; thy sins be forgiven thee. O seek such an assurance of divine favor before the evil days come, wherein you will say, we have no pleasure in them: If trouble—and man is born to it as the sparks fly upward: if trouble—and you are not for a moment secure—should fall upon you before you have a good hope, through grace, that God is pacified toward you, your condition will be the most pitiable. You must either stupify the mind with the devil's opiates, or faint in the day of adversity.

And let those that have it, preserve and cherish this sense of divine favor and acceptance. Beware of grieving the Holy Spirit of God. Beware, not only of sin, but of the world. Beware of sloth and sleep. Christian slept, and lost his roll out of his bosom. And while Saul slept, he was deprived of his spear and his cruse. When trouble comes, you should not have to seek what, above all things, you want immediately to use. Without his smiles, even in prosperity, your comforts will not cheer you—but in adversity, without his approbation, how heavily will every stroke fall! and how deeply will every wound be felt!

Let me know always that he is near that justifieth me; that all is well with my soul, and for eternity; that he will support me under my burden; that though he afflicts me, he loves me—and afflicts me *because* he loves me. And I will sing

"Trials must and will befall,
"But with humble faith to see
"Love incribed upon them all,
"This is happiness to me."

DECEMBER 15.—"The Lamb which is in the midst of the throne shall feed them."—Revelations, vii, 17.

THE Lamb. This is an application given the Lord Jesus, for two reasons. The one alluding to his personal qualities; such as purity, innocency, gentleness, meekness, patience: for he was led as a lamb to the slaughter. The other, in reference to the design of his death. Abel offered to God a firstling of the flock. Familiar with the use of such a victim, Isaac asked, "Where is the lamb for a burnt-offering?" Under the law, a lamb was offered every morning and every evening; and on the Sabbath-day, two were offered in the morning, and two in the evening. There was also the Paschal lamb, whose blood was sprinkled, and whose flesh was eaten, at the deliverance of the Jews from the Destroying Angels. And "Christ our passover," says Paul, "is sacrificed for us." And John cried "Behold the Lamb of God, that taketh away the sin of the world!" And it is worthy of our observation, that the name is applied to him, not only in his abasement, but in his exaltation; and that no less than twenty eight times he is called the Lamb, in this Book of the Revelation!

—His glory is much spoken of in the Scripture, but never in stronger language than here; "The Lamb which is in the midst of the Throne"—a station of dignity, dominion, government, full supremacy. Surely, if the sacred writers intended to intimate, that he was a mere creature only, they have expressed themselves in a manner very unguarded and ensnaring. Well; there he is —not only near the throne, but in it—and in the midst of it, in spite of all opposition. Let his enemies tremble, and bewail. They may make war with the Lamb, but the Lamb shall overcome them; for he is a King of kings, and Lord of lords. But let his followers boldly profess him. Why should they be ashamed of a leader that is in the midst of the throne? And why do they not rejoice in his salvation? Surely they must, if they love him, for love always exults in the prosperity of its object. Surely every feeling of their heart prompts the desire—

"Let him be crown'd with majesty,
"That bowed his head to death;
"And be his honors sounded high,
"By all things that have breath."

Well; there he is, in the possession of all power in heaven and in earth, able to save them, to preserve them, to make all things work together for their good.

—And, as is his greatness, so is his condescension and kindness. The Lamb that is in the midst of the throne "shall feed them." The imagery is pastoral. His people are held forth as sheep; and he performs the office of a shepherd. His concern with them begins here. He seeks after them when lost, and brings them to his fold, and furnishes them with supplies. They can rely on the extensiveness of his care, and the continuance of it;

and may individually say, "The Lord is my Shepherd; I shall not want"—

> "While he affords his aid,
> "I cannot yield to fear:
> "Though I should walk through death's dark shade,
> "My Shepherd's with me there."

Nor is this all. When they shall come out of great tribulation; and have washed their robes, and made them white in the blood of the Lamb—when they shall be before the throne, and serve him day and night in his temple, then, even then, he shall feed them, and not as now, by ministers and ordinances, but immediately—not, as now, in the wilderness; but in the heavenly Canaan—not as now, surrounded with enemies; but where all shall be quietness and assurance for ever. The Lamb shall feed them. He shall be the dispenser, and source of their happiness. It will flow from his presence and communications. Therefore, Paul desired to depart, to be with Christ, which was far better. "*He* that sitteth on the throne shall *dwell among them.* They shall hunger no more, neither thirst any more; neither shall the sun light on them, nor any heat: FOR the Lamb which is in the midst of the throne shall feed them, and shall lead them unto living fountains of waters: and God shall wipe away all tears from their eyes."

Poor Burns! This is the representation of heaven, which he says, he could never read from a child, without tears. Oh! let me not admire the description only, but seek after the enjoyment of the blessedness. The language is pathetic, and the scenery is inviting; but is the subject itself more interesting than either? I must be made meet for the inheritance of the saints in light. I cannot hope to attain hereafter what I do not desire and delight in now. A natural man may long for a heaven of release from toil and pain. Do I, O my soul, prize a heaven of which Christ is—all in all!

DECEMBER 16.—"And Jonathan, Saul's son, arose, and went to David into the wood, and strengthened his hand in God."—1 Samuel, xxiii, 16.

WE here see, in the experience of David, that the most eminent of God's people may need encouragement. He was now dejected and dismayed. And we learn from his complaints, in the book of Psalms, that he was frequently the subject of depressions. And to which of the saints recorded in Scripture can we turn, whose hands never hung down, whose knees never trembled? *These*, we are prone to consider as peculiar in their religious attainments: but *they* also were only enlightened and sanctified in part. They also had in them nature, as well as grace. They too, were men of like passions with us, and compassed with infirmities. All those perfect beings now before the throne, were previously in a vale of tears; the spirit indeed willing, but the flesh weak; sometimes rejoicing in God their Savior, but sometimes saying, "I am cast out of his sight."

> "Once they were mourning here below,
> "And wet their couch with tears;
> "They wrestled hard, as we do now,
> "With sins, and doubts, and fears."

In the conduct of Jonathan, we see the duty of real friendship.

A friend is born for adversity: and to him that is afflicted, pity should be shown from his friend." This, however, is not always the case. Many pretenders fail when the day of trial comes; and he who relied upon their attendance, and sympathy, and succor, in trouble, finds his confidence, as Solomon expresses it, "like a broken tooth, or a foot out of joint." Yet let us not say in our haste, all men are liars. See Jonathan, a young prince—surrounded with every indulgence—undertaking, without application, to repair to David—to see and serve his friend at the hazard of his life.

—In the relief derived from this visit, we learn the advantage of pious intercourse. "Come," said Jonathan, "Come, David, remember God's promise. Is it not faithful and true? Think of the anointing oil Samuel poured upon thy head—Can this be in vain? Who enabled thee to conquer Goliath? Who delivered thee from the paw of the lion and the bear? He can turn the shadow of death into the morning. He saveth, by his right hand, them that put their trust in him, from them that rise up against them. He keeps them as the apple of the eye—Encourage thyself in the Lord thy God." The address availed—"He strengthened his hand in God." We have a similar instance in the experience of Paul. He had appealed unto Cæsar, and was now approaching the scene of his trial; and his heart was cast down within him—but the brethren from Rome came down as far as Appii Forum to meet him; "whom, when Paul saw, he thanked God, and took courage." "Two are better than one; because they have a good reward for their labor. For if they fall, the one will lift up his fellow; but wo to him that is alone when he falleth; for he hath not another to lift him up." Who, when dull, has not found a Christian visiter a quickening spirit? "As iron sharpeneth iron, so doth the countenance of a man his friend." Who, in sadness and gloom, has not found refreshment and delight from godly communion? Ointment and perfume rejoice the heart; so doth a man his friend by hearty counsel. Who, like Hagar, has not sometimes been ready to expire with thirst, till some ministering spirit has opened the eyes, and shown him a well?

—And who does not perceive, in the strange circumstances of this consolation, that God can never be at a loss to comfort his followers? He knows, not only how to deliver the godly out of temptation, but to cheer them in it—He is called the God of all comfort. David was now in a state of concealment. Of the few who were with him, no one perhaps knew the state of his mind; for good men, from their regard for the honor of religion, are not always at liberty to lay open many of their distressful feelings. But his God knew what he now suffered, and what his frame of mind required—And what was the instrument He employed? Jonathan, "Saul's son," as it is added; and wisely added. The son of David's bitterest foe. The son, too, that was interested in David's destruction. He was the heir-apparent; and *he* comforts the man who was going to fill a throne, which, by the law of succession, belonged to himself! How wonderful was this! How obviously the work of God! All hearts are in his hand, and he can turn them as he pleases. It is he that gives us favor in the eyes of others; and he can raise us helpers and friends as unlikely to aid us as the ravens were to feed Elijah. Many a situation, also, the most improbable, has been made, by his communications, none other but the house of God and the gate of heaven; and, filled with surprise, we have exclaimed, with Jacob, "Surely God is in this place, and I knew it not!" When are we inaccessible to him? "From the end of the earth," says David, "will I cry unto thee when my heart is overwhelmed." And no wonder, he remembered that Jonathan, Saul's son, arose, and came to him *into the wood*, and strengthened his hand in God. Did he never come to you in a similar condition? "They shall dwell safely in the wilderness, and sleep in the woods." "I will allure her, and bring her into the wilderness, and speak comfortably unto her. And I will give her vineyards from thence; and the Valley of Achor for a door of hope."

DECEMBER 17.—"And a certain Scribe came, and said unto him, Master, I will follow thee whithersoever thou goest. And Jesus saith unto him, The foxes have holes, and the birds of the air have nests; but the Son of man has not wherewith to lay his head."—Matthew, viii, 19, 20.

THE god of this world deludes his followers. He conceals from them every difficulty and danger to which they are exposed in his service, and raises in them expectations which he knows will never be fulfilled—Like Jael, he welcomes in, and spreads the couch, and brings forth butter in a lordly dish—he keeps out of sight the hammer and the nails. Take a man, whose object is to gain a name, to become a leader, and to draw away disciples after him; he courts popularity; he flatters; he employs any means; and he accommodates himself to every disposition, as far as he can, without risking discovery. But it was far otherwise with the Founder of Christianity. His Character was as original as it was excellent. His kingdom was not of this world. His professed object was to instruct, and save, and bless; and no selfish aim was hidden under it. He showed, in his own person, how little his followers were to mind earthly things; and, in dealing with those who came to him, we see that it was not his concern to draw unprincipled crowds into his train. He would form a peculiar people, who should be actuated by the noblest convictions and purposes. He therefore, in order to discriminate, applied a test; he warned them to sit down first and count the cost; and assured them at once, that if any man would be his disciple, he must deny himself, and take up his cross, and forsake all that he had.

—Our Lord now "saw great multitudes about him," so that "he gave commandment to depart unto the other side." But as, in the midst of all these, he was stepping toward the ship, "a certain Scribe came, and said unto him, Master, I will follow thee whithersoever thou goest." A noble resolution, if it had been made from a good motive. But he apprehended our Savior to be a temporal Messiah, who, as he appeared able, from his miracle, to carry every thing before him, would soon have promotions at his disposal; and he hoped to gain some of the loaves and fishes. Our

Lord well knew his thoughts, and said unto him, "The foxes have holes, and the birds of the air have nests; but the Son of man hath not where to lay his head"—What say you now? It is easy to determine what would have been his reply, if he had been sincere and earnest in his application. "O Lord, I come, not to prescribe, but to resign myself entirely to thee. Every thing appears to me less than nothing and vanity, compared with the salvation of my soul; and if, by any means, I can attain it, I shall be satisfied. Whatever—dear and useful as I have deemed it, I cannot retain in following thee, I cheerfully give up. All I fear is, separation from thyself—Entreat me not to leave thee, nor to return from following after thee—Lord I will follow thee to prison and to death." But alas! his mean and mercenary temper was now detected, and we hear no more of him—he left him, having loved this present world.

But the narrative is recorded for our admonition; and the fact which, by way of trial, our Savior addressed to this pretender, is worthy of our attention. It is very affecting and instructive—It is the indigence of Jesus, appearing in the homelessness of his condition. This, as a part, is put for the whole of his abasement; and it is held forth, enhanced, by contrast. The inferior creatures have dwellings, convenient for them, in which they secure themselves, and enjoy repose, and breed up their young. Some of these, man takes, as inmates, under his own roof; such are the faithful dog, and the feathered songster in the cage. He furnishes, also, shelter, as well as provender, for his cattle. But animals that live at large, have also accommodations suited to their kinds. "Foxes have holes." "The young lions gather themselves together, and lie them down in their dens." "The high hills are a refuge for the goats, and the rocks for the conies." "The spider taketh hold with her hand, and is in kings' palaces." "The birds of the air have nests." "The eagle mounts up," and, in rocks inaccessible, "maketh her nest on high." "As for the stork, the fir-trees are her house." Some build on the ground; some in dense thickets; some in boughs depending over the flood; some in isles, secured by water. Some repair to the habitations of men; there the sparrow finds a house, and the swallow a nest for herself, where she may lay her young. And who, in all this, can help admiring the wisdom and kindness of Providence? His tender mercies are over all his works. As he made all, so he careth for them. He giveth their meat in due season. He furnishes them with their powers of defence, or flight; and actuates the skill they display in all their surprising economies. And will he disregard his rational offspring? He teacheth *them* more than the beasts of the earth, and maketh them wiser than the fowls of the air. There is a spirit in man, and the inspiration of the Almighty giveth him understanding. How superior is reason to instinct! How boundless in improvement is human ingenuity! What abodes has it provided for us! And with what conveniences, comforts, pleasures, has it replenished them! From hence, springs the idea of *home.* We cleave to a place where we received our birth, passed the days of infancy, indulged in the sports of youth, where sleep has refreshed our wearied bodies; and where we have smiled at the descending storm, and the piercing cold.

> " —— Home is
> " The lov'd retreat of peace and plenty; where
> " Supporting and supported, polished friends,
> " And dear relations meet, and mingle into bliss."

Well may the same poet represent the man returning at eve, buried in the drifted snow, " Strong with thoughts of home."

A homeless condition, therefore, is the most pitiable. And was this the condition of the Lord Jesus? Not absolutely. During his private life he lived with Joseph and Mary at Nazareth. And after he entered on his public ministry he had friends, who, like Martha, gladly afforded him the accommodations of their own dwellings. But these advantages were occasional, and were of the nature of hospitality. He never possessed a habitation or an apartment he could call his own. He was born in another man's house, and this was a stable, and he was laid in a manger. How often, when my children were about me, have I said, while viewing my sleeping babe:

> " How much better thou art attended
> " Than the Son of God could be,
> " When from heaven he descended,
> " And became a child like thee!
>
> " Soft and easy is thy cradle—
> " Coarse and hard the Savior lay,
> " When his birth-place was a stable
> " And his softest bed was hay!"

How soon was he driven an infant exile into Egypt! Widows ministered to him of their substance. Wearied with his journey, he sat on the well, and said to the woman, Give me to drink. A fish furnished him with money to pay the temple tribute. One night he slept in a fishing boat. Another he continued all night in prayer in a mountain. We read only once of his riding—though he went about doing good; and this was upon a borrowed ass, and a colt, the foal of an ass. He partook of the last passover in a borrowed chamber; and he was wrapped in linen, not his own, when taken down from the Cross, and was buried in another man's garden, and another man's tomb! What does all this teach us?

DECEMBER 18.—" And Jesus saith unto him, The foxes have holes, and the birds of the air have nests; but the Son of man hath not where to lay his head."—Matthew, viii, 20.

THE fact is affecting: but is it not instructive too?

—We may take from it a standard by which to judge of the age and country in which he appeared. Nothing reflects more upon a people than suffering characters, distinguished by the greatest goodness and usefulness, to want. It will always be a reproach to the Corinthian converts, that they allowed such a man as Paul, while preaching and working miracles among them, to work night and day at tent making; but we love and commend the Philippians, who, once and again, when he was in Thessalonica sent to his necessity. Surely we should have said, men will reverence God's Son. At his coming nobles and princes will offer their mansions and palaces. What preparations are made to receive a superior! Yet the honor of the visit is deemed a recompense for the trouble and expense. But *he* was in the world, and the world was made by him, and the world knew him not. He came to his own, and his own received him not. What is man? Let Judea furnish an answer. See the Lord of all, the friend of misery, possessed of every moral perfection, the image of the invisible God, yet not having "where to lay his head!!" But is human nature the same now? Some censure others, and think well of themselves, merely because they have not been tried by the same circumstances, which would equally have displayed their own depravity. "Oh! had we been then living there he should not have been destitute of any accommodation we could have yielded him." Yet you follow the multitude, and the reproach of a name will keep you from owning his truth, and you are backward in giving in the support of his cause. But, by the disposition which you exercise toward his gospel, and house, and ministers, and members, he judges of his attachment or indifference to himself; He that receiveth you, receiveth me—Inasmuch as ye did it not to one of the least of these my brethren, ye did it not to me—Depart.

—Pause, and admire the grace of our Lord Jesus Christ, how that though he was rich, yet for our sakes he became poor, that we through his poverty might be rich. Do not imagine that he did not *feel* his condition. He was really a partaker of flesh and blood, and knew the sensations of hunger, and weariness, and cold, as well as any other man. But the conveniences and comforts which he required, he often found not. Think of his preaching and traveling all the live-long day, and at night not having where to lay his head! The sensibility of his condition was enhanced by his former state of dignity and enjoyment. We are, therefore, more affected when we see a prince reduced, than when we behold an individual suffering who was always indigent. Jesus was higher than the kings of the earth, and had given them all their thrones. Heaven had been his dwelling place, and all the angels his attendants, and adorers too. What condescension was here! Let us remember that he made himself of no reputation, and took upon him the form of a servant. There was no compulsion—it was all voluntary. And not for himself, but for us. And did we deserve such an interposition, such an expensiveness of sacrifice for our comfort? We were viler than the earth—we were enemies by wicked works. Yet he never repented of his engagement; but said, as he was entering all this abasement, Lo! I come! I delight to do thy will! And as his agony approached, he said, "I have a baptism to be baptized with, and how am I straitened till it be accomplished!" It was, therefore, as the apostle calls it, grace—grace the most free and unparalleled. And shall not this love, which passeth knowledge, fix our minds, and fill our hearts? Where is our gratitude, unless we are willing to deny ourselves for him, and to walk worthy of such a divine Benefactor unto all well-pleasing? The lower he descended to save me, the higher shall he rise in my esteem for ever. He is always, and altogether lovely, but never so adorable as when his face is marred more than any man's; and he has not where to lay his head

—Let us also learn not to judge of worth by external advantages. True greatness is personal, and does not depend on power, titles, or wealth. Is a man the more valued of God, because he has a larger field, or a longer purse than his neighbor? Does it give him more virtue, or understanding? A fool, a child of the devil, may be set on the high places of the earth; while the apostles were hungry and naked, and the Son of God had not where to lay his head. While we view him who is higher than the heavens in such an estate, let us learn the vanity of worldly distinctions. Let us see how foolish it is to pride ourselves in a fine house, and splendid furniture, or any of the meanness of the pride of life. Let us despise ourselves, if we have esteemed a man the more for the gold ring and gay clothing, or regarded the poor the less, because he is poor; and remember, that if we had lived in Judea we should have courted Pontius Pilate, and shunned Jesus Christ, who had not where to lay his head.

—Let the Lord's poor take this truth, and apply it, to produce resignation under the privations of life. You talk of penury, but he *was* poor. You have many a comfort you can call your own, but he had not a place where to lay his head. But allowing that your trials were much greater than they are; remember, this is not your rest, and you are rich in faith, and have the honor of conformity to the Lord Jesus. You only know the fellowship of his sufferings. Is it not enough that the servant be as his Master, and the disciple as his Lord? Can the common soldier complain, when he sees the commander-in-chief sharing the same hardships with himself?

—Let it lead us to rejoice in the Savior's present condition. He that descended, is the same also that ascended. He who was crowned with thorns, is crowned with glory and honor. He who had not where to lay his head, has all power in heaven and in earth. How delightful is this assurance to those who love him! for love glories in the exaltation of its object. It is also interesting to their hopes. They are one with him. And because he lives, they shall live also.

DECEMBER 19.—"I will make mention of Rahab and Babylon to them that know me: behold Philistia, and Tyre, and Ethiopia: this man was born there. And of Zion it shall be said, This and that man was born in her." Psalm lxxxvii, 4, 5.

THE Jews, partly from their ignorance, and partly from their aversion to Christianity, strangely pervert this passage, contending that it is designed to intimate, that while other places would produce only now and then a man of note, Jerusalem should abound with all kinds of illustrious characters. But the meaning is this. Zion, in whose name the writer speaks, is foretelling the vocation of the Gentiles, and viewing with ecstacy the accessions that should be made to her of such as should be saved.

Observe to whom she addresses the intelligence: "I will make mention to *them that know me*." That is, to her friends and acquaintances. To such it is natural for us to divulge any thing that is interesting and delightful; as *they* are likely to receive it without envy, and to partake of the pleasure. In the parable the shepherd, having succeeded in his search, not only rejoices himself, but when he cometh home, calls together his neighbors and friends, saying unto them, Rejoice with me, for I have found my sheep which was lost. The Church well knew the mind of the godly, that they would not understand such news, but that it would be to them like cold water to a thirsty soul, or as life from the dead. Thus, in the Acts, when the brethren were informed of the extension of the gospel to the Gentiles, "they glorified God, saying, Then hath God also to the Gentiles granted repentance unto life."

Observe the places from which these additions should come. "I will make mention to them that know me, of *Rahab* and *Babylon;* behold *Philistia*, and *Tyre*, with *Ethiopia*." These are parts put for the whole of the Gentile world; and they are very strikingly put. For all these had been strangers or enemies. Some of them had been her bitterest persecutors, and vilest oppressors. They were all this time lying in wickedness, enveloped in ignorance, and enslaved to idolatry. But they should cast away their idols; and beholding the glory of the Church, abandon their enmity, and take hold of the skirt of him that is a Jew, saying, We will go with you, for we have heard that God is with you. "One shall say, I am the Lord's; and another shall call himself by the name of Jacob; and another shall subscribe with his hand unto the Lord, and surname himself by the name of Israel."

—Mark the change they should experience. "This man was *born there*. And of Zion it shall be said, This and that man was *born there*." They were born, naturally, in Egypt, Philistia, Tyre, and Babylon: but they were to be born, morally, in Zion, by the Word and Spirit of God. They should become new creatures. They should undergo such a conversion in their minds, and hearts, and lives, as should constitute a new birth. For every subject of Divine grace is "born again." And this is properly the date of our existence. We have not lived a moment longer than we have lived "the life of God." "Ye *must* be born again."

By this, therefore, we are to judge whether we are children of Zion, and may rejoice in her King. If we have experienced this change, we are written among the living in Jerusalem. We are enrolled: and though once aliens from the commonwealth of Israel, we shall be regarded as citizens, and have all the honor and advantage of natives: "The Lord shall count, when he writeth up the people, that this man was *born* there."

It was formerly deemed a most enviable privilege to be free of some royal and distinguished city. But what was a citizen of Babylon, or of Rome, compared with a denizen of Mount Zion, the city of the living God, the heavenly Jerusalem? Yea, were you an apostle officially considered only; could you prophesy, and work miracles, and raise the dead; and the Savior met you, elated with your endowments, he would say, "In these things rejoice not, but rather rejoice that your names are written in heaven."

December 20.—" What think ye, that he will not come to the feast ?"—John, xi, 56.

This was the language of many of the Jews who had ascended from the country to Jerusalem, to purify themselves against the passover. It is not easy, or perhaps possible, to determine the principle from which the words were uttered. Perhaps malice uttered them: and they came from persons who wished to discover and apprehend him; for "both the Chief Priests and the Pharisees had given a commandment, that if any man knew where he were, he should show it, that they might take him." Perhaps curiosity uttered them; and they came from persons who were anxious to see whether he had courage enough to appear in public after the threatening of the rulers. Besides this, he was a very extraordinary character, the fame of whose miracles and preaching had spread far and wide; and they naturally desired to see a personage of whom they had heard so much. Perhaps affection uttered them. For, though he was generally despised and rejected of men, there were some who knew his value, and believed him to be the only begotten of the Father, full of grace and truth. They therefore longed for the pleasure, and honor, and advantage of an interview with him at the approaching solemnity. And this is the principle from which, if partakers of divine grace, we are seeking for Jesus. "For Christ our passover," says the apostle, "is sacrificed for us. Let us therefore keep the feast." And it is in reference to the communion of his body and blood, to which we are going to repair, that we issue the inquiry, "What think ye, that he will not come to the feast ?"

This is above every thing desirable. Ordinances are not beneficial, necessarily and of themselves. They derive all their excellency and influence from Him: a truth we learn, not only from Scripture, but experience. What a difference, as to light, and life, and joy, do we feel in the same ordinance—when he is absent or present! This is nothing to the formalist. *He* is satisfied with the outward signs and the service itself. But as to the Christian, intercourse with Christ is the one thing needful. He feels it pleasing to hold communion with the saints: but what he principally wants is fellowship with the Savior. He alone can fill them all: and without him, they would have nothing for each other, or for themselves.

But the inquiry implies doubt. Doubt has two aspects and bearings—the unlikely and the probable—the one exciting fear, and the other encouraging hope. Let us look at each.

—What is there, then, to awaken our supicion and fear that he will *not* be at the feast? And is there not much every way? Without going back to our unconverted days, how have we lived since we have made a profession of his name? Have we walked as those who are not of the world? Have we borne his corrections without murmuring? Have we have been grateful under his mercies? Has he lived in our warmest thoughts? Has he been the chief theme of our conversation? Have we not frequently been ashamed of his cause? Have we recommended him earnestly to others? After all this, how can we expect that he will honor us with his company? Should *we* thus honor any fellow creature, who has treated us as we have treated him? But the cause of alarm is increased, when we consider, not only our conduct at large, but our behavior toward him, with regard to this very feast itself? Have we not suffered trifling excuses to keep us away, when he has been there waiting for us, but waiting in vain? Have we not approached it with the indifference of custom and formality, though angels were there intensely desiring to look into these things? Have we not passed through the divine memorials, mystically eating the flesh, and drinking the blood of the Son of God, with the exercise of no more faith in his death, or love to our brethren, than in an ordinary meal? We need not go on. O blessed Jesus! when we consider all this, and this *only*, we may well question whether thou wilt—ever meet with us again.

But let us look at the other side. Let us see, not only what there is to excite fear, but to encourage hope. Now to induce us to conclude that he will be at the feast. We have his character, his disposition—"His heart is made of tenderness; his bowels melt with love"—"A bruised reed shall he not break, and smoking flax shall he not quench, till he send forth judgment unto victory." We have his past dealings with us. He has tried us, but not forsaken us. We have been often cast down, but never cast off. We have his promise. "Where two or three are gathered together in my name, there am I in the midst of them." In a word, we are sure of the blessing, if we seek it. "Whatsoever ye shall ask in my name, that I will do, that the Father may be glorified in the Son." But is it possible to ascertain when he is with us at the feast? It is. As he is not there corporeally, we cannot apprehend him with our bodily senses. But, as he is there spiritually, we may apprehend him spiritually. They who are new creatures, have new senses, which are exercised to discern both good and evil. They have ears to hear his voice; and eyes to see his glory. They have a holy taste, and holy feelings. Thus his people can be sensible of his arrival. Indeed, he *says*, "I am come." He is not inactive when there. "While the King sitteth at his table, my spikenard sendeth forth the smell thereof."

"And faith, and love, and joy, appear; | "And every grace is active here."

There are impressions and effects which cannot be mistaken, owing to their holy, humbling, heavenly influence. The assurance he has of communion with the Lord in his ordinances, is not evidence for others; but to the believer himself it affords satisfaction; and he is neither to be ridiculed or reasoned out of the conviction. He has the witness in himself.

DECEMBER 21.—"Show me wherefore thou contendest with me."—Job, x, 2.

—A GOOD man perceives, and acknowledges the hand of God in his afflictions. Job sees God contending with him. Though his sufferings were principally from creatures, he said, "The

Lord hath taken away." "Thou hast taken me by my neck, and shaken me to pieces." Whatever may form the twigs of the rod, God is the chastiser, He has a right to correct, and can never err in using it. To realize this is the way, not only to prevent despondency, but to repress all murmuring passions. This satisfied Eli: "It is the Lord, let *him* do what seemeth him good." "Oh!" says the gardener, as he passes down the walks, and priding himself on the beds and borders which he has so carefully cultivated, "who removed that plant? who gathered this flower?" His fellow-servant says, "The master," and he is dumb, and opens not his mouth, because *he* did it.

—Again—God has an end to answer by his contention with us. It is not the display of his sovereignty. There is a distinction between bestowing favors, and inflicting penalties. If a judge condemned a man to show that he *was* a judge, or a king imprisoned a man to show that he *was* a king, every one would cry out against them; but they would be more than justified in employing such measures for the display of justice, and for the advantage of ensample. Paul conveys a degree of censure where we should have looked only for tenderness. The fathers of our flesh chastened us for a few days after their own pleasure. But God, says he, always does it for our profit, that we may be partakers of his holiness. Why is the ship in danger? Because Jonah has fled from the presence of the Lord; and the wind is sent after him. Why does Israel flee before the men of Ai? There is an Achan in the camp. Thus God explains the thing himself: "Behold, the Lord's hand is not shortened, that it cannot save; neither his ear heavy, that it cannot hear; but your iniquities have separated between you and your God, and your sins have hid his face from you, that he will not hear." He therefore does not afflict willingly, nor grieve the children of men. There is some sin indulged, some duty neglected, some idol adored. But his aim may be, not only to rebuke for actual evil, but to hedge up our way with thorns, to keep us from forbidden ground, toward which we were advancing, or to prune us, as vines, that we may bring forth more fruit.

—God alone can discover his own intention in his rebukes. But in doing this, we are not to suppose that he will employ miracles: or speak in an audible voice from heaven, or by a sudden impulse. He acts in a way suited to the nature and improvement of a rational and moral being. He may, therefore, in showing us, use even an enemy. When Shimei cursed him, David considered him as much sent of God to reprove him, as Nathan had been. The will of God may be made known by the admonitions of a pious friend, who sees what we overlook, from habit, or self-love. We should therefore be thankful when the righteous smite us, and not deem them enemies because they tell us the truth. Sometimes the nature and circumstances of the affliction itself proclaim the secret; and we can read the cause in the effect, the sin in the punishment. The faithful word, read or preached, comes home to our case; and conscience cries, Thou art the man. Sometimes the difficulty of discovery is great. But if we address ourselves to the Father of lights, sincerely and importunately, to show us wherefore he contendeth with us, we shall not seek him in vain; but the promise given to Jeremiah shall be fulfilled in us: "Call unto me, and I will answer thee, and show thee great and mighty things, which thou knowest not."

—And very desirable it is that we should know why He contendeth with us. Indeed a good man cannot be satisfied without it. For while the wicked are only anxious to escape from trouble, he wishes to profit by it. He desires this knowledge, therefore, not to gratify curiosity, but to enable him to justify God in his dispensation, and to know how to pray, and to exercise the graces of the condition he is in, and to apply the present duty; and that he may confess whatever is wrong, and watch against it in future, saying, "Surely it is meet to be said unto God, I have borne chastisement, I will not offend any more. That which I see not teach thou me: if I have done iniquity, I will do no more." For there is a tenderness in the conscience of a renewed man that readily responds to God. No sooner did our Lord turn and look upon Peter, than he went out and wept bitterly.

As for an unconverted man to ask God, in his affliction to show wherefore he contends with *him*, it is absurd, and would defeat the end of his suffering, which is not to make him leave a particular sin, but all sin, and to draw him into a new course, and a new state.

But, perhaps, though living in sin, you say, God is not contending with you. So much the worse. He is saying, "They are joined to idols, let them alone." Though he spares you now, he will deal with you hereafter. And the longer the arrear, the severer the reckoning. "And if the righteous scarcely be saved, where shall the ungodly and the sinner appear!"

DECEMBER 22.—**"And call the Sabbath a delight, the holy of the Lord, honorable."—Isaiah, lviii, 13.**

THIS is to characterize the heirs of an exceeding great and precious promise here subjoined. They are to be known, not by their observance of the Lord's day only, but by their endeared and exalted regard for it. They call the Sabbath a delight, and the holy of the Lord, honorable. And what reason they have for all this will appear from its leading aspects and bearings.

Let us connect it with the brute creation. Any thing that tends to make them happier, will be pleasing to a benevolent mind; especially since we know that the whole creation groaneth and travaileth in pain, and was made subject to vanity, not willingly, but by reason of him who hath subjected the same in hope. Though man is lord of this lower world, and all creatures are put under his dominion, he is not to oppress and enslave them. If his power over them be abused, and his tender mercies toward them be cruel, God will resent it; these helpless beings are his creatures, and his care. I love to hear him telling the fretful prophet, as a reason why he spared Nineveh, that there were in it, not only "more than threescore and six thousand persons that could not discern between their right hand and their left," but "also much cattle." I love to hear him forbidding the Jewish husbandmen to muzzle the ox while treading out the corn. I love to read the tenderness of the fourth commandment, " That thine ox and thine ass may rest as well as thou." If the brutes had reason, they would bless God for the Sabbath.

We may view the Sabbath in reference to the business of life. In the sweat of thy brow thou shalt eat bread, till thou return to the dust? was the sentence passed upon man for sin; but, in judgment, God remembers mercy. Who could bear the incessant application and toil? Some change is obviously wanting, to unbend the mind and the body. And man goes forth to his work and to his labor until the evening, when he returns home, and retires to rest, and *his* sleep is sweet, whether he eats little or much. But this is not all. The Sabbath furnishes a fixed pause, a needful relaxation. Those who are in easy circumstances, and, like the lilies of the field, toil not, neither do they spin, feel little interest in the Sabbath, on this account. But let them think of thousands of their fellow creatures. Let them think of those who, by mental pursuits and professional engagements, get their bread by the sweat of the brain. Let them think of those that sit at the loom, stand at the forge, work in the field, drudge under ground. What a relief, what a privilege, is one day in seven, felt by them! How dull would be the monotony of their time, without the break and variety of the Sabbath! What a drag would their life be, if they were to carry their loads unloosened even to the grave! But the day of repose returns—the worn laborer lays down his burden, stretches his limbs, refreshes himself by cleanliness and change of raiment; and after six days, during which time he is almost reduced to the brute, on the seventh he feels himself to be a man. And O ye rigid, if not sanctimonious souls, envy not the sons and daughters of drudgery and confinement a little of the fresh air of heaven, which you, perhaps, can always breathe! nor be too severe with those who only once a week can look forth, and glance on the beauties of nature; the works, too, of Him who ordained the Sabbath!

This day also contributes to the harmony of families. The members may be much divided and dispersed through the week, and have few or slender opportunities of social intercourse. But the Sabbath brings them more fully together, and produces and cherishes those feelings which endear and unite them relatively, and dispose them, by love, to serve one another. Persons and families are, especially among the common people, always unkind, and rude, and savage, both in their temper and manners, where the Sabbath is neglected. But they are respectful, and humane, and tender, where it is observed; because they see each other to advantage, and mingle under moral and religious impressions, which, though not always powerful enough to sanctify, contribute to soften and civilize.

The Sabbath is also a period of devotion and reflection. If we are godly, we shall not go through the week without God. Some pious thoughts and feelings will blend with our busy concerns. But week days are, in a sense, worldly ones, and even our allowed contact with earthly things tends to impair our heavenly impressions, and to make us forgetful of our highest good. We want a day of retreat from this world, that we may think of another, and have opportunities to compare the claims of the objects that court our hearts. We want a day of silence from the passions, to consider more deeply the principles and motives of religion; and to have excited, and carried upward, those affections which cleave unto the dust. To a man concerned to advance in the divine life, how welcome is the return of a day, all for his soul and eternity! in which, by waiting on the Lord, his strength is renewed, his heart is enlarged, and he obtains fresh preparations to meet the temptations, the duties, and the troubles of life.

Again: without the aid of such a day, how would even the face of religion be maintained in the community at large? We may learn from an enemy. When the French wished to destroy every thing like Christianity, they were wise enough to know how much the Sabbath stood in their way; and therefore abolished it, and established their decades. Let any one imagine the Lord's day given up for ten years in our own country. The effect would be a thousand times more injurious to the interests of piety and morality, than all the writings and attempts of infidelity. Let this fence of every thing sacred and useful be broken down, and what an inundation of ignorance and vice of every kind would overspread the land? It is in the services of this day, the rich and the great are reminded of their accountableness; their dependence on God, and their being only on a level with those below them, in their origin and end. This they are too prone to forget: but once in the week, the master is a servant; the king, a subject; the judge, a criminal, crying for mercy. And as to the poor and working classes, how little time have they for religious exercises but the Sabbath! It is then, principally, the Bible is taken down from the shelf; and the child, placed between the knees is heard to read it. Then the children of our Sunday schools cry Hosannas in our temples. Then the family goes to the house of God in company. Then the poor have the Gospel preached unto them, and the common people (unless the preacher mispersonates him) again hear the Savior gladly. How, without these auxiliaries, would a sense of the divine presence, and the moral providence of God, and of a future state, be kept alive on the minds of the multitude? Is not all the knowledge of religion thousands possess, derived from what they read and hear on the Sunday?

And how impressive and interesting is the Sabbath, as the chief period of divine operations! How distinguished will it be in the annals of eternity! How many thousands, how many millions, on this day have been awakened, enlightened, and converted, made new creatures! What triumphs has the cross gained over the powers of darkness! What noble schemes and enterprises, for the glory of God, and the welfare of mankind, have taken their rise, from some impression in the closet, or excitement in the church, on this accepted time, this day of salvation!

Nor is it less delightful and honorable, as an emblem of heaven, and a preparation for it. Philip Henry would often say, at the close of his sabbath devotions, Well, if this be not heaven, it must be the way to it. Yes; it is then Christians often feel themselves, like Jacob in his vision, at the gate. They have earnests and foretastes of the glory to be revealed. Perhaps they are never so willing as then, to go. Many of them have wished to be released on this day; and some have been gratified. But if they do not leave on the earthly sabbath, they enter on the heavenly one. For there remaineth a rest, a sabbatising, as the word is, to the people of God. And what an exchange, for the better! Here we worship with a few; and these like ourselves are imperfect. Here we groan, being burdened; and if we are not weary of our divine work, we are soon wearied in it. And when satisfied with favor and filled with the blessing of the Lord, we can say,

"My willing soul would stay,
" In such a frame as this;"

the world calls us down, and leads us out into its cares, and griefs, and dangers, again. Oh! why do we not sing—

" Thy early Sabbaths, Lord we love;
" But there's a nobler rest above:
" To that our lab'ring souls aspire
" With ardent pangs and strong desire.

"No more fatigue, no more distress,
" Nor sin, nor hell, shall reach the place;
" No groans to mingle with the songs
" That warble from immortal tongues.

" O long expected day begin;
" Dawn on these realms of wo and sin:
" Fain would we leave this weary load,
" And sleep in death, to rest with God!"

DECEMBER 23.—" As well the singers as the players on instruments shall be there; all my springs are in thee."—Psalms lxxxvii, 7.

THIS is spoken of Zion; and shows us the *joy*, and the *attachment*, of her inhabitants.

The joy is expressed in language according with the forms of service in the Jewish worship. They had, in addition to the praises of individuals and families, orders of men, established expressly for the performance of psalmody in the Temple: some vocal, and some instrumental—" As well the singers as the players on instruments shall be there." The meaning is—that Zion, which the world considers the metropolis of sadness and gloom, should be the residence of cheerfulness and mirth; or, in other words, that the church of God should abound with spiritual joy and gladness. This joy may be considered two ways. First, as promised: and so it is to be viewed as a privilege; and we are to look after it in the history and experience of his people. And if we turn, and this is the fairest way, to those whom God has himself described in his word, we shall find them distinguished by nothing more than this experience. They walked in the comfort of the Holy Ghost. Though they had losses and afflictions, yet, believing, they rejoiced with joy unspeakable and full of glory. Secondly, as commanded. Thus they are enjoined to shout aloud for joy, to rejoice in the Lord always, to be filled with the Spirit, speaking to themselves in psalms, and hymns, and spiritual songs, singing and making melody in their hearts to the Lord. And thus it becomes a duty: and, as such we are bound to seek and to preserve it—to study the grounds of it—to guard against every thing that would invade and injure it—to endeavor, by all means, to increase our joy in the Lord—and never *refuse* to be comforted.

All must be singers and players on instruments here. All cannot perform equally well; but all must do something—and pray and strive to show that the religion of Christ is able to make its possessors happy; that it can set their roving hearts at rest; that it can enable them to dispense with the dissipations of the world; that it can sustain them under the trials of life, and raise them above the fears of death—and thus adorn the doctrine of God their Savior in all things.

But here is attachment, as well as joy—"All my springs are in thee." No affection was ever more sincere than that which the pious Jews bore to their native land. Jerusalem was the source of their hope and glory; the circle and the centre of all the endearments of life. They breathed out their very soul when they said, "Peace be within thy walls, and prosperity within thy palaces." They deemed nothing too dear to be parted with, for its ornament or defence. In its welfare, they forgot their personal and relative sorrows; and when it was taken and destroyed, they abandoned themselves to grief, hung up their harps upon the willows, and felt life a burden. Even in its reduced state, they "took pleasure in her stones, and favored the dust thereof"—Each of them sighing, "If I forget thee, O Jerusalem, let my right hand forget her cunning; let my tongue cleave to the roof of my mouth, if I prefer not Jerusalem above my chief joy." And is there less intenseness of regard in Christians, toward Jerusalem, which is above, and free, and the mother of us all? No—all their springs are there—All that refreshes me—can each of them say; all that reviews, all that enlivens, all that inspires, "all my springs are in thee."

Where are all the springs of a worldly man? In the world. To all his interests there he is alive; his heart is glad when his corn and wine increase; and his joy fails with them. His losses are the taking away of his goods—and what has he more? But what is the experience of the Christian? In the word of God, and the ordinances of his house, and communion with his people, and the consolations of his Spirit—here it is, says he, I find my Heaven! If this cannot touch and animate him, nothing for the time can. On the other hand, this can make him joyful, even in tribulation. This seems to indemnify him under every earthly disappointment. What is it, says he, that my schemes fail, if His flourish? Yea, in spiritual darkness; and when he is ready to conclude that he has no part or lot in the matter, and that his heart cannot be right in the sight of God, his countenance is illumined, and the tear of joy starts into his eye, when he hears that the word of the Lord hath free course and is glorified; that sinners are fleeing to the Savior, as doves to their windows; that the order to Zion is issued, Enlarge the place of thy tent, lengthen her cords, strengthen her stakes. In this, says he, I rejoice; yea, and will rejoice. And so, when there are apostacies and backslidings, and professors cause the way of truth to be evil spoken of, he is "sorrowful for the solemn assembly, and the reproach of it is his burden." And his fear, as well as his hope, and his grief as well as his pleasure, show where the attraction of his heart lies. And if any thing is to be done for Zion, he feels a courage that is not natural to him. His tongue is as the pen of a ready writer. His hand gets unawares into his pocket; and to his power, yea, and beyond his power, he is willing to communicate; and his zeal, as well as all his other feelings, justify his saying, "All my springs are in thee."

December 24.—"Through the tender mercy of our God; whereby the dayspring from on high hath visited us, to give light to them that sit in dark ness and in the shadow of death, to guide our feet in the way of peace."—Luke, i, 78, 79.

"Well," said David, "what is man, that thou art mindful of him; and the son of man, that thou visitest him?" He does this in a thousand ways; and each of us may acknowledge, with Job, "Thou hast granted me life and favor, and thy visitation hath preserved my spirit." But what a visit is here! Twice does Zacharias, under different allusions, expressly mention it in his thanksgiving song. "Blessed be the Lord God of Israel, for he hath visited and redeemed his people, and hath raised up a horn of salvation for us in the house of his servant David." "Through the tender mercy of our God, whereby the dayspring from on high hath visited us, to give light to them that sit in darkness and in the shadow of death, to guide our feet into the way of peace."

Observe the image under which he views the coming of the Savior—"The dayspring from on high." The springing of the day is produced, and only can be produced, by the rising of the sun. There is only one sun in nature, and there is only one Sun in grace; and to them that fear my name, said God, by the prophet Malachi, shall the Sun of Righteousness arise with healing in his wings.

—See the state in which he finds us—"Sitting in darkness and the shadow of death." Darkness is ignorance, Some ignorance is of little importance; but here we are destroyed for lack of knowledge. The darkness is connected with the shadow of death, a state of terror and danger, and nearness to perdition; for the shadow cannot be far from the reality. It is not only vain, but injurious, to deny the truth of this representation, when there is so much to prove it; and, without the admission, Christianity must be needless and absurd.

But see the benefit he is designed to communicate, "To give light" to them that are in darkness, and the shadow of death. Accordingly, his coming has shed a lustre upon every subject interesting to our duty and welfare. So that every individual under the gospel knows far more than all the heathen philosophers put together, and also far more than the most illuminated among the Jews. Hence our Savior "turned unto his disciples, and said privately, Blessed are the eyes which see the things that ye see; for I tell you, that many prophets and kings have desired to see those things which ye see, and have not seen them; and to hear those things which ye hear, and have not heard them." It is, therefore, called, not only "the true light," but "a great light." It has two properties. It is *practical.* It is "to guide our feet." We were "sitting" before; inactive, like persons in the dark, and afraid to move; but when the light comes we are set in motion, and in motion with our feet. The doctrine of Christ is not a mere speculation; he that receives it feels an influence like that of the orb of day, which is vital, as well as enlightening. He walks in the Spirit. In the fear of the Lord. In the truth. It is also *blessed*. It is to guide our feet "into the path of peace." There is something very pleasing in the word peace, as it intends reconciliation, and especially reconciliation with God. And God was in Christ reconciling the world unto himself, not imputing their trespasses unto them. And being justified by faith, we have peace with God through our Lord Jesus Christ. This peace is essential to every other blessing, and every other blessing is sure to follow it. The word, therefore, is often used for every kind of good and of happiness. It is finely expressed by the apostle, "We who have believed do enter into rest;" and yet more fully David, "Blessed is the people that know the joyful sound; they shall walk, O Lord, in the light of thy countenance. In thy name shall they rejoice all the day: and in thy righteousness shall they be exalted. For thou art the glory of their strength: and in thy favor our horn shall be exalted."

But what is the source of all this blessedness? "The tender mercy of our God." As we are guilty and condemned creatures, every gift we enjoy must be from mercy. This is true of our daily and outward comforts; and, therefore, Jacob calls them all "mercies," and acknowledges that he is not worthy of the "least" of them. How true it is, then, that, not by works of righteousness which we have done, but by his mercy he saved us! Neither are we to imagine, that God was made merciful by the incarnation and sufferings of Christ. It is from injudicious representations of this kind, that the enemies of the atonement are furnished with their strongest objection. But, in the Scripture, we are told, that God so loved the world, that he gave his only begotten Son, that whosoever believeth on him should not perish, but have everlasting life. What he requires he provides. He would not pardon Job's friends, but through his intercessions; but he prescribed his prayer for the very purpose, and accepted it, and thus we are "justified freely by his grace, *through* the redemption that is in Christ Jesus."

Let us bless God for this tender mercy. "God is the Lord, which hath showed us light: bind the sacrifice with cords, even unto the horns of the altar." Let us improve the advantages it has afforded us, and walk as children of the light. Let us pray that his way be made known on earth, and his saving health among all nations.

December 25.—"**And it came to pass in those days, that there went out a decree from Cæsar Augustus, that all the world should be taxed. (And this taxing was first made when Cyrenius was governor of Syria.) And all went to be taxed, every one into his own city. And Joseph also went up from Galilee, out of the city of Nazareth, into Judea, unto the city of David, which is called Bethlehem; (because he was of the house and lineage of David;) to be taxed with Mary his espoused wife, being great with child. And so it was, that while they were there, the days were accomplished that she should be delivered.**"—Luke, ii, 1—16.

The birth of Christ is so wonderful and important, that every circumstance attending it is worthy of our attention, and capable of improvement. We are here informed of the *time* and the *place.*

As to the *time*, it was under the reign of Angustus. Luke could not have distinguished it by a more illustrious mark than the name of a man, the greatest prince then in the world, as he governed the Roman empire, which had extended itself over the largest and fairest portions of the inhabited earth. What is related indefinitely is liable to dispute and mistake, whereas particularity tends to gain credence, and renders falsehood easier of detection. Hence the evangelist mentions a remarkable fact attending the period: " And it came to pass in those days, that there went out a decree from Cæsar Augustus, that all the world should be taxed," and adds, " And this taxing was first made when Cyrenius was governor of Syria." Here, however, a difficulty occurs, which infidelity, always alive to the worst of causes, and feeling the paucity and poverty of its resources, has readily laid hold of.

It must be granted that Cyrenius, as Josephus, and all the Greek and Latin historians agree, was not governor of Syria, till eleven years after. But, first, it is supposable, that though he was not the actual governor, he presided on this occasion by a special commission from Augustus. This agrees with the history of the emperor, which shows us that, in several instances, he sent his particular friends to superintend the enrolment, without leaving it to the care of the ordinary governors of the province. Did not David do the same when he wished to number the people? There were rulers over all the tribes of Israel; yet he sent Joab, who went through all the land, and brought him the result at the end of nine months and twenty days. Secondly; Dr. Campbell renders it, " And this enrollment *first took effect* when Cyrenius was governor of Syria." Though our version reads taxing, it is, in the margin, enrolling. There was some difference between these. For though the registering was generally with a view to the taxing, yet the latter did not always immediately follow the former; it only laid the foundation for it, by showing the number and wealth of his subjects, whenever he chose to demand soldiers or money. Now, though the decree for enrollment was issued eleven years before, it was not *acted upon* till Cyrenius *was* governor of Syria; and the Roman power, on the expulsion of Archelaus from Judea, first levied the tax on the Jewish people. We have a similar instance in our own history. William the Conqueror wished to make a survey of the kingdom; this was done in what is called the Doomsday Book, and which is still extant; it was *six years in making in England only, and no payment of taxes was made upon it till twelve years after.* Either of these solutions is perfectly satisfactory, and there is no inconsistency between them; the one does not invalidate the other. And when to this we add, that the fact itself was notorious, and that Luke could not be deceived, and must have known that he could not be misunderstood at the time, we see another instance of the weakness of infidel objections. But Luke mentions this affair, not only to authenticate the truth of his narrative, but the

Messiahship of Christ. His coming had not only been foretold, but the time of it. We allude to the prophetical declaration of the dying Jacob, when, speaking of Judah, he said, "The sceptre shall not depart from Judah, nor a lawgiver from between his feet, until Shiloh come; and unto him shall the gathering of the people be." That is—when he should come, the supreme power should be dislodged from their possession. And here we see the accomplishment: for the supreme power had now fallen into the hands of Herod the Idumean, who was exercising his vile tyranny under the favor of the Roman Sovereign, master of Syria and Palestine.

The *place* was Bethlehem. It is called the city of David because there David was born. But the word city, which the Jews used so differently from us, should not mislead us: it was only a small village, in which nothing had occurred to aggrandize it. Here he was brought forth, and not in Jerusalem, or Rome, or any other illustrious place. Was this to intimate, that his kingdom was not of this world? What cannot ennoble greatness, greatness can ennoble. How has the birth-place of the Mantuan Bard been noticed! How many cities contended for the honor of Homer's birth! The birth of Jesus instantly drew to this village a new star, and sages from the East, and the angel of the Lord, and a multitude of the heavenly host, and has made it to be remembered in all generations. Therefore, said the prophet Micah, "Thou, Bethlehem, Ephratah, though thou be little among the thousands of Judah, yet out of thee shall He come forth unto me that is to be ruler in Israel; whose goings forth have been from old, from everlasting." That he was to be born here, was known and expected, not only by the chief priests and scribes, as we see in their answer to Herod, but also by even the common people, who argued against him, when they supposed that he was *not* born there. "Hath not the Scripture said, That Christ cometh of the seed of David, and out of the town of Bethlehem, where David was?" But let us not forget the occasion of the event. For it was, humanly speaking, the most unlikely thing in the world, that Jesus should be born here. For Bethlehem was not the place of Joseph's residence; but Nazareth, in Galilee. But, the decree requiring that every one should repair to his own patrimonial city to be enrolled, Joseph, being of the house and lineage of David, goes up from Galilee, out of the city of Nazareth, into Judea, unto the city of David, which is called Bethlehem, and Mary with him, being great with child: and so it was, that while they were there, waiting for his registry, the days were accomplished that she should be delivered! Mary thought of nothing, but accompanying Joseph. Joseph thought of nothing, but obeying the order of the Governor. The Governor thought of nothing, but the mandate of the Emperor. The Emperor only obeyed his vanity and pride; and yet all these ignorantly, but unitedly, conduced to fulfill the determinate counsel and foreknowledge of God. How freely men can act! and yet how necessarily! How real, and yet inexplicable, is the concord between human liberty, and the certainty of events! What is contingent, where divine veracity is concerned? How impossible is it that the Scriptures can be broken! How wonderful is the providence of God! By what methods does it conduct its plans to their completion! How easily, and yet how uncontrollably, does it bend to its pleasure all the dispositions and movements of creatures, who, like men in a boat, look one way, and row another!

DECEMBER 26.—"**And there were in the same country shepherds abiding in the field, keeping watch over their flock by night: and lo, the angel of the Lord came upon them, and the glory of the Lord shone round about them; and they were sore afraid.**"—Luke, ii, 8, 9.

Two classes of men were led to Bethlehem, to witness the new born Messiah. The wise men from the East, and the shepherds. The former were versed in the works of nature; they were espepecially astronomers and star gazers: and God conducts them by a star. The latter were Jews; they had the Scriptures in their hands; and these were directed by an angel. God has various methods of manifesting himself to his creatures: but none of them are arbitrary. They all evince his "wisdom and prudence," and are adapted to the state and circumstances of the beings with whom he has to do.

Angels are all ministering spirits. And if they attend the heirs of salvation, how much more the Author of it! if they wait on the servants, how much more on the Son, who is Lord of all! When he bringethh his first begotten into the world, he saith, Yea, and let all the angels of God worship him. He was seen of angels.

—We might have expected that this glorious messenger would have been sent to persons of rank and authority—to the rulers; to the doctors of the law; to the ministers of the sanctuary; to Herod; to the High Priest. But God's thoughts are not our thoughts. He seeth not as man seeth. Man judgeth after the outward appearance; but the Lord looketh to the heart. He is no respecter of persons. The distinctions of life, which, owing to folly, are the sources of so much pride to some, and envy to others, are nothing to Him. He is equally "nigh unto *all* them that call upon him," whatever be their outward condition; as the sun shines in the valley as well as on the hill. It was to these shepherds the angel of the Lord appeared. And may not this be considered an intimation of the persons for whom the dispensation was principally designed, and by whom it would be chiefly received? Hence we read, "The poor have the Gospel preached unto them"—"The common people heard him gladly"—"Have any of the rulers believed on him?" "Thou hast hid these things from the wise and prudent, and hast revealed them unto babes." Not that the rich and great are excluded. And there always have been a few who have humbled themselves, to be exalted: but "not many wise men after the flesh, not many mighty, not many noble, are called: but God hath chosen the foolish things of the world to confound the wise; and God hath chosen the weak things of the world to confound the things which are mighty; and base things of the world, and things which are despised hath God chosen; yea, and things which are not, to bring to nought things that are: that no flesh should glory in his presence."

—We have much reason to conclude, that these shepherds were among the number of those who were looking for redemption in Jerusalem. While many of their countrymen, in ceiled houses, were seeking their consolation in the world, they, like Simeon, were waiting for the consolation of Israel. Perhaps at this very moment they were silently musing, or perhaps conversing with each other (for they were obviously together) "when the kingdom of God should come;" and sighing out the words of David, "O that the salvation of Israel were come out of Zion! When God bringeth back the captivity of his people, Jacob shall rejoice, and Israel shall be glad"—when, "lo! the angel of the Lord came upon them! and the glory of the Lord shone round about them!"

And this angel, by his example, teaches us, however much we may be placed above them, not to overlook the poor, nor refuse to visit them, especially God's poor; for they are rich in faith, and heirs of the kingdom which he has promised to them that love him. It is a character of the citizen of Zion, that in his eyes a vile person is contemned, however high; but he honors them that fear the Lord, though they may not have the gold ring, and the gay clothing.

The sacred historian has not failed to tell us how these men were engaged, at the time of their being thus distinguished. They were in the field, keeping watch over their flocks by night. Thus they were abiding in their calling, and faithfully and actively discharging the duties of it. Never mind how humble your occupation may be,

"Honor and shame from no condition rise;
"Act well your part—there all the honor lies."

Be attentive and diligent, and you are useful and respectable. *They* ought to blush, who do nothing, or have nothing to do. Their mode of living is as inconsistent with the life of a Christian required in the Gospel, as a life of vice. The tree that bringeth forth no *good* fruit, is hewn down and cast into the fire. The servant that hid his Lord's talent in a napkin, did not abuse it; but because he was an unprofitable servant, he was a wicked one, and therefore punished. The case of these shepherds is not a solitary one. Go through the Scriptures, and make out a list of all those whom God favored and dignified with his visits; and show me one among them all that was a drone in the community, or not properly and usefully employed. *Other* beings are more likely to appear to the useless and idle. "Our idle days," says Bishop Hall, "are the devil's busy ones."

"For Satan finds some mischief still,
"For idle hands to do."

It was well said by an old Puritan, "I find diligence the best preservative from temptation: for when Satan comes to me with his proposals, I say to him, I cannot attend to thee now—I am so busy."

"The labors of the righteous tend to life." "The soul of the sluggard desireth, and hath nothing; but the soul of the diligent shall be made fat."

DECEMBER 27.—"Let us now go even unto Bethlehem, and see this thing which is come to pass."—Luke, ii, 15.

THIS was the language of the Shepherds. And it was not a vain curiosity that led them. While keeping their flocks by night, the angel of the Lord appeared to them, and said, "Fear not: for behold, I bring you good tidings of great joy, which shall be to all people. For unto you is born this day, in the city of David, a Savior, which is Christ the Lord. And this shall be a sign unto you. Ye shall find the babe wrapped in swaddling clothes, lying in a manger." This they considered as it really was, in order to repair, to ascertain and report the fact. And they would have set off instantly. But there suddenly descended a multitude of the heavenly host, praising God and saying, Glory to God in the highest; on earth peace, good will toward men. We know not how long this melody continued; but who can wonder at their staying till it was over! But no sooner were the angels gone away into heaven, than "the shepherds said one to another, Let us now go even unto Bethlehem, and see this thing which is come to pass." Let us accompany them, and contemplate a scene which will induce us to exclaim, with Moses, on a very marvellous, but very inferior occasion—"For ask now of the days that are past, which were before thee, since the day that God created man upon the earth, and ask from the one side of heaven unto the other, whether there hath been any such thing as this great thing is, or hath been heard like it?"

In this thing which is come to pass, we behold a very striking display of divine truth. The coming of the Messiah was called, "*The* truth of God." Many things evinced the divine veracity: but this was the main pledge. It was the chief promise ever given to man. It was also the earliest assurance; it was given as early as the Fall. And what a length of time the assurance seemed to hang in suspense; a year—a hundred years—a thousand years—another thousand, and another, rolled away before the seed of the woman appeared! Hath he forgotten to be gracious? Doth his promise fail for evermore? But at the end of four thousand years it was proclaimed. His councils of old are faithfulness and truth. How many also were, what we may call the minute parts of the promise. It was foretold that he should descend from a particular nation—the nation of the Jews: a particular tribe—the tribe of Judah: a particular family—the family of David: a particular mother—a virgin. On how many things does the veracity of God now depend, the failure of any one of which would prove him a liar. The place of his residence was foretold—it was Bethlehem. The prophecy had been recorded for ages, and was acknowledged at the time of his birth. But how many things were necessary to this; and how accidental seemed the fulfillment! For Joseph and Mary were residing at Nazareth. And had not Judea been under the Roman dominions; and had not Cæsar Augustus proudly wished to know the number and wealth of his subjects; and had Mary been delivered a few days sooner or later: he would have been born elsewhere, and the word of God would have been of none effect. All these occurrences appear casual, and they were so to the parties themselves; but not to God, who knows all his works from the beginning. All these events seemed loosely connected, but they were links, making an adamantine chain. The truth of God was the pivot on which all turned; the centre in which all united; the end to which all referred. Let us see here, not only how willing, but how able he is to accomplish his word; and be strong in faith, giving glory to God. Let no apparent delay, no opposing difficulties, no interfering interests, affect our minds. His purpose is secretly, yet uncontrollably, moving on; and the most unlikely instruments are contributing to its execution. How much depends on our confidence in the truth of God!

We see in the thing which has come to pass, a wonderful combination. A combination of natures—I admit his humanity; and why should I question his divinity? I find many things ascribed to him, which cannot belong to him as God; and I find others ascribed to him, which cannot pertain to him as man: and here is the solution of the difficulty—"God was manifest in the flesh." A combination of grandeur and abasement. Whose birth could have been more obscure and degrading? What welcome was given him? What preparation was made for him? "The world was made by him, and the world knew him not. He came unto his own, and his own received him not." A poor young female was his mother; a stable his chamber, and a manger his cradle—because there was no room at the inn. But whose birth was ever so glorious? Ye gods of the earth, bring forth your first born—but no new star sparkles over where the young child is, no wise men come miraculously from the east to worship him, no angel comes down, no heavenly choir sing his birth, no command is given, Yea, and let all the angels of God worship him, no spirit of prophecy breathes inspiration; no Simeon waits for him as the consolation of Israel, no Anna speaks of him to all those who look for redemption.

We also see a prodigy of benevolence. Every thing says behold a love which passeth knowledge. His former condition—he *was* rich and *became* poor. His independence and choice: he was not *constrained* to enter such a state—Lo! I *come*, says he: he *gave* his life a ransom for us. The principle that moved him—it was not our desert, but his own *mercy*. He came into the world to save *sinners*: he died for the ungodly: in his love and pity he redeemed us. His not waiting for our application, arising from a sense of our need of him—His engaging, in foresight of all the degree and extent of his sufferings—His going through the whole without repenting of the expensive undertaking—His accomplishing it with delight.

"Oh! for this love let rocks and hills
"Their lasting silence break;
"And all harmonious human tongues
"The Savior's praises speak!"

Here, also, we see an example for our imitation. Did he thus despise worldly distinctions? and shall we admire them? Shall we seek great things for ourselves?- Such a Christian by the side of the manger! Having food and raiment, let us be therewith content. Shall we find it difficult to condescend to men of low estate, and to exercise self-denial in doing good? "Let this mind be in you which was also in Christ Jesus: who being in the form of God, thought it not robbery to be equal with God: but made himself of no reputation, and took upon him the form of a servant, and was made in the likeness of men." Did he not only stoop so low, but suffer so much for us; and shall we not be willing to endure any privations, and incur any sacrifices for our brethren? "Be ye therefore followers of God, as dear children; and walk in love, as Christ also hath loved us, and hath given himself for us, as an offering and sacrifice to God for a sweet-smelling savor."

Great as this thing is which has come to pass, there are many who will refuse to take a step to see it. Even at the very festival, which is the commemoration of it, they will be found any where rather than at Bethlehem; and be attracted to every thing, rather than to that sight, which the Shepherds left their flocks, and made haste to see; which the Eastern sages came such a vast distance to behold; and which drew all heaven down to earth. Some, while they observe the day by a freedom from labor, not only neglect, but insult the subject of it; and by intemperance and riot, revive the works of the devil, which the Son of God was maifested to destroy.

But let us call off our attention from the little, debasing, vexing, defiling things of the world, and repair to the Infant of Bethlehem, the desire of all nations. Let us give him the glory which is due unto his holy name, and say, "Unto us a child is born, unto us a son is given; and the government shall be upon his shoulder; and his name shall be called Wonderful, Counsellor, The mighty God, the Everlasting Father, the Prince of Peace." Let us behold in him provision made for our recovery, the most suitable to our wants, and adequate to our relief, and placed entirely within our reach. Let us embrace him, and exclaim, "Lo, this is our God; we have waited for him, and he will save us: this is the Lord; we have waited for him; we will be glad, and rejoice in his salvation."

And let our zeal and gratitude be equal to our joy. And let us follow the shepherds, not only in our going, but in our return: "And when they had seen it, they made known abroad the saying which was told them concerning the child;" "And they returned glorifying and praising God for all things that they had heard and seen."

DECEMBER 28.—"And they were both righteous before God, walking in all the commandments and ordinances of the Lord, blameless."—Luke, i, 6.

THIS worthy couple are known as the father and mother of a very illustrious personage, of whom the Judge of all said, "Among them that are born of women, there hath not risen a greater than John the Baptist." But while Zacharias and Elizabeth derive distinction from their son, they are worthy of attention, personally considered. Though not distinguished by worldly grandeur, they were great in the sight of the Lord; and though their names are not recorded in the annals of national history, their characters will be had in everlasting remembrance in the Scriptures of truth. Five things are here said of their piety.

—It was sincere; they were righteous *before God.* Many are righteous before men, who only look on the outward appearance; but the Lord, who searcheth the heart, and sees actions in their motives, disowns them. A large assembly may be convened together, and be engaged in the same exercises; but they only worship Him, who worship him in Spirit and in truth. What are we in His estimation? He that judgeth us is the Lord.

—It was practical; they *walked in the commandments and ordinances of the Lord.* Divine truth is important; yet, if we know these things, happy are we only if we do them. Practice is nothing without principle; and what proof have we of the reality and excellency of principle without practice? "I will put my Spirit within you, and cause you to walk in my statutes, and ye shall keep my judgments, and do them." We do not undervalue experience; but the Scripture requires something more than good feelings: "Let your light so shine before men, that they may see your good works, and glorify your Father which is in heaven." A good conscience will always be accompanied with a good conversation. He is a vain man who says he has faith, and hath not works. Can such faith save him?

—It was impartial; they walked in *all* the commandments and ordinances of the Lord. None are universally wicked. Vices are often inconsistent with each other; prodigality opposes avarice, and covetousness complains of extravagance. All do something, for conscience must be appeased; but they are determined in their *selections* by the easiness of the thing, or its relation to some one of their interests. They have no regard to the will of God; for if their observance sprang from a regard to his pleasure, this would lead them to avoid every thing which he has forbidden, and to inquire after every thing he has enjoined. "Then shall I not be ashamed, when I have respect unto all thy commandments." "Blessed is every one that feareth the Lord, that walketh in his ways."

—It was irreproachable; they walked in all the commandments and ordinances of the Lord, *blameless.* It is not said, they were sinless. The subjects of divine grace will always have enough to bewail before God, instead of saying, I have attained, I am already perfect. But it is a mercy (and this is possible) to be preserved from those falls which injure our reputation and influence; and also from those imprudencies which draw upon a man the reproach of folly and weakness, when he is not taxable with sin, and from those veerings of opinion which are yet consistent with some degree of fixed principle in higher things. It is well when our good cannot be evil spoken of; and we are without offence till the day of Christ.

—It was mutual; they were both righteous before God, walking in all the commandments and ordinances of the Lord, blameless. This is not the case in every family. In some houses there is no fear of God in either master or mistress, father or mother, husband or wife. In others, there is one of these relations godly, and only one. They are joined together by marriage, but not in the Lord. This difference may be accounted for in three ways. One of the parties may have been called after their affinity, neither of them knowing God at the time of contracting it. Or one of the parties may have deceived the other; and some are guarded and crafty; and those who are upright themselves, are generally free from suspicion. Or the religious individual was, perhaps, (how strange!) careless upon this subject, and did not feel religion, in his choice, the one thing needful; or was bribed, against his conviction, by other things. The two former cases deserve pity; but this, censure—and his error will correct him. For nothing can be more desirable and important than the godliness of *both* parties. How near is the relation! How constant and influential the intercourse! How lamentable, in a course where we need every assistance, to meet with impediments! How can two walk together, except they be agreed? And are there servants? are there children? Each will have their adherents. And it is not difficult to conclude, from the depravity of human nature, which will be more readily followed—the one who would lead into the world, or the one who would lead out of it.

But the case would be more awful still, if one of the parties was an official character. Surely, a Zacharias should have an Elisabeth. What disgrace and injury may result from the union of a preacher with an irreligious or indiscreet companion! The apostle therefore describes the character of a minister's wife, as well as his own: and naturally concludes, that he who proclaims his want of piety and judgment in a case so plain and momentous, *tells* how unqualified he is for other matters—"For if a man know not how to rule his own house, how shall he take care of the church of God?"

DECEMBER 29.—"Though he slay me, yet will I trust in him."—Job, xiii, 15.

THIS is a noble resolution. It supposes suffering. Slaying here, stands for every loss and infliction he could suffer or forbode. Slaying, literally means death; and Job does not exclude this from his supposition. He more than once seems to apprehend it as the consequence of his present malady—I know thou wilt bring me to death—My breath is corrupt; my days are extinct. The graves are ready for me. Indeed there is not much for him to slay. He has slain my cattle, my servants, my children; he has slain the tenderness of my wife, and the confidence of my friends; he has slain my health; and if there be any thing more, let him slay it. I can trust him down to the grave, and through it—for I know that my Redeemer liveth, and that in my flesh I shall see God, though my reins be consumed within me.

—It professes confidence—"Though he slay me, yet will I *trust in him*." It is obvious, from hence, that he did not think God was really his enemy. If he had, how could he have trusted in him? He knew nothing of the language of a mystic—"Though I perish, I shall serve thee still—If thou send me to hell, I shall love thee there." These are the sayings of religious madness; and one hour of the suffering they make so light of, would bring them to the use of their senses. By the very law of my nature, it is impossible for me to regard a Being that I believe determined to make me miserable for ever; and God himself has commanded me to seek after my salvation and happiness—I could not therefore acquiesce in my misery, without violating his will. Such a state of sublime self-annihilation, therefore, is not possible, if it were proper; and it is not proper, if it were possible. But if it is both proper and possible to believe, that natural evil may be converted into moral good; that bodily pain may conduce to spiritual profit; that though no chastening for the present is joyous, but grievous, it may afterward yield the peaceable fruit of righteousness to them that are exercised therewith; that behind a frowning providence he may hide a smiling face; that though he amputates a limb, it is to save life; and that in ways beyond all my conceptions, he can, he will, make all things work together for good to them that love him. And this is what Job means by his confidence.

—But it also intimates difficulty—*Though* he slay me, *yet* will I trust in him. For there is much in searching and awful dispensations to try and check confidence, and to awaken suspicion and fear. When things are agreeable and prosperous, we feel but comparatively little difficulty. But when the scene is changed, and the sky overspread, and the clouds return after the rain; when we are stripped, bereaved, abandoned, then we are cast out of his sight, our way is perished from the Lord; and we think our eye will no more see good! When troubles befall others, we go to them, and strengthen their hands in God. We readily deal out the promises to them, and feel inclined to reprove, if they refuse to be comforted.

We tell them, God is only waiting to be gracious; and will appear to their joy. But when we come into the same condition ourselves, we are unable to follow the advice we have given, and to receive the encouragements we have administered. Thus we incur the censure, "Behold, thou hast instructed many, and thou hast strengthened the weak hands; thy words have upholden him that was fallen, and thou hast strengthened the feeble knees; but now it is come upon thee, and thou faintest; it toucheth thee, and thou art troubled." Let us not be too severe with people in affliction. To trust God, when we know not what he is doing; when he seems to oppose us, and his word too; when he presents a sword even to our bosom, and we feel its point—it is then, verily, no easy thing to hope in the Lord, and wait patiently for him. But Job did this. Yea, says he, in the midst of every killing providence, though he slay me, yet will I trust in him. Let us therefore seek after this confidence in God. For, first, there is nothing so honorable to God. Secondly, there is nothing so beneficial to ourselves. Thirdly, there is nothing so reasonable in itself—for, whatever view we take of God, whether we consider his perfections, or his relations, or his promise, or his past dealings with others and ourselves, the more we shall be induced to say, "What time I am afraid, I will trust in Thee." So true is it—They that *know* his Name, will put their trust in him.

DECEMBER 30.—" Are not my days few?"—Job, x, 20.

—NOT years, months, weeks, but days—Life is to be reckoned by *days*. Are not my days *few?* They are so in every respect—relatively, comparatively; absolutely. It will not be necessary to prove this; as no one denies it—or can deny it. Yet how much depends upon the proper use of a truth so obvious, and a reflection so simple! Are not my days few?

—But how came they so? All men die, but not willingly. Skin for skin, yea all that a man hath, will he give for his life: but he cannot continue it. He hates, he dreads death—It is the king of terrors. The thought of it imbitters his comforts, and keeps him always subject to bondage. And could this have been the natural state of man as he came from the hands of his Maker? The Deist meets with this fact as well as we: and as he cannot deny it, let him account for it under the empire and agency of a Being who is "omnipotent benevolence." Revelation gives us the only rational and convincing account—" The body is dead because of sin." "By one man sin entered into the world, and death by sin; and so death hath passed upon all men, because all have sinned." It is not "a debt due to nature." It is the consequence of a judicial and penal infliction: "For all our days are passed away in thy wrath." We are not struck with this, because we are accustomed to the result, and it gradually takes place. But could we have seen the Deluge destroying the whole world at once, we should not have questioned the provocation of God by some mighty cause. But where is the difference, as to primitive justice, whether all the criminals are executed together, or led forth one by one? Are not my days few?

—Do not then render them fewer. What! you are ready to exclaim, do you think we are going to turn self-murderers? Yet how many are continually reported as having destroyed themselves! But violence is not the only mode of shortening life. One of our most eminent physicians has affirmed, that "the board destroys more than the sword." Another has said, "Though all men are mortal, not one in a thousand dies a purely natural death." Many enervate themselves by lying late in bed; and living (if it deserves the name of life) in lazy inactiveness, as injurious to health as to virtue. Envy is the rottenness of the bones. Fretfulness and anxiety corrode. Anger and malice consume. It is needless to mention intemperance and sensuality, the effects o which so often lie down with the sinner in an early grave. Godliness has the promise of the life that now is. By freeing us from the malignant passions—which are always injurious to ourselves, as well as to others; and by inducing the affectionate and benevolent ones, which are always beneficial: by the peace it sheds abroad in the bosom, and the hope and confidence it authorizes and inspires, as well as by surrounding us with the care of Providence; it is, as David calls it, "the health of the countenance:" and justifies the admonition of his son—"Fear the Lord, and depart from evil. It shall be health to thy navel, and marrow to thy bones." Are not my days few?

—Why then moderate your attachment to every thing that depends upon their brevity. Who would set their heart on that which is not? Who would load with treasure a vessel rotten or full of holes? All the admired distinctions and possessions of the world are very uncertain in themselves, and often leave us. But if they continue with us, we cannot continue with them. We brought nothing with us into the world, and it is certain that we can carry nothing out—Yet, stripped and naked as we shall go—go we must—and the time of our departure is at hand. Oh? what shall we think, a few "days" hence, of those pursuits which now so much engross us! "To-morrow we die;" and what will it signify, whether we are carried to the grave from a cottage, or a mansion; or leave behind us much or little? Endeavor to think always as you will feel soon. "Brethren, the time is short: it remaineth, that both they that have wives be as though they had none; and they that weep, as though they wept not; and they that rejoice, as though they rejoiced not; and they that buy, as though they possessed not; and they that use this world, as not abusing it: for the fashion of this world passeth away." Are not my days few?

—Then let us well employ and improve them. This is what Moses prayed for: "So teach us to number our days, that we may apply our hearts unto wisdom." And what is wisdom? This must be determined by circumstances. What is wise conduct in one man, may be folly in another, because of their different relations and circumstances. But it is easy to determine what is wisdom in a man who numbers his days, and finds them to be few: and who has, during their continuance, an all-important interest to secure: and has no other opportunity. If he is guilty, it must be wise in him to seek forgiveness. If he is lost, it must be wise in him to seek salvation: and if he be unable to save himself, it must be wise in him to apply to another who is appointed for the very purpose. And in our case, such a one there is. His name is Jesus. He is mighty to save. He is willing to save. Instead of complaining of your application, he only complains of your neglect—Ye will not come to me, that ye might have life. Many have tried his power and his love, and recommended him from their own happy experience. He is now on the Throne of Grace; but he will not be always there—He will soon ascend the tribunal of justice. Oh! seek him while he may be found, and call upon him while he is near. Behold, *now* is the accepted time; behold *now* is the day of salvation.

This part of our subject branches itself into another line of duty. As you are to *gain* good, so you are to *do* good. And this, too, is equally enforced by the fewness of your days. Life is yours; and it affords you one privilege above the saints in light. It is the opportunity of beneficence—of relieving the poor, of instructing the ignorant, of converting the sinner. But remember two things. *Their* days are few, and therefore they will soon be gone beyond the possibility of receiving relief. And *your* days are few; and you will soon be placed beyond the possibility of affording it. Wing your zeal, therefore, with the thought, "The night cometh, wherein no man can work."

--Oh! there is a way of lengthening life. It is—not by duration, but by diligence—it is by "filling our days." It is by doing much business in a little time. Some live longer in a week than others do in a year.

DECEMBER 31.—"**He thanked God and took courage.**"—*Acts, xxviii, 15.*

GRATITUDE and confidence are individually excellent; but their union is admirable. They adorn, and recommend, and aid, each other. There is no one they so well become as the Christian. And when he is without cause for both? When has he not, if truth examines his condition, a thousand excitements to praise, and encouragements to hope?

It can never be more proper to exercise these, than at the interesting period of the last day of the year; when we are naturally and unavoidably led to think of the past and the future. Let us therefore follow the example of Paul, when he met the brethren at Appii Forum. Let us thank God, and take courage.

What can be more reasonable than to thank God when we review the past? While many have been cut off—and not a few in their sins—we have been carried through another year in safety. We have been exposed to accidents and diseases, as well as they who are now in the dust; and our frame has been as delicate, as frail as theirs. But we are the living, the living to praise Him, as it is this day: and all our bones can say, Who is a God like unto thee? While he has holden our souls in life, he has also continued our mercies—and these mercies have been new every morning. Of the least of all these, we have been unworthy. And had we been dealt with according to our desert, we should have been the most wretched beings on earth. But we have been fed at his table, and clothed from his wardrobe. We have had, not only the necessaries, but the comforts and the indulgences of life. He has given us richly all things to enjoy. He has made the outgoings of our mornings and evenings to rejoice. He has given us the succession of the seasons. He has blessed the springing of the earth. He has charmed us in the field, and in the garden, with melody, and fragrance, and colors, and tastes. What relative attachment! What endearments of friendship! What pleasing interchange of solitude and society! of labor and of rest! We have not only to acknowedge private, but public mercies. How has he preserved and blessed our country, notwithstanding all our national provocations! He has not only blessed us personally, but relatively. He has been the benefactor of our families and our friends. Yea, he has blessed us, not only in the kindness of his providence, but in the means of grace. We have had our Sabbaths. Our eyes have seen our teachers. We have been made joyful in his house of prayer. He has fed us with the finest of the wheat, and with oil out of the rock has he satisfied us. Bless the Lord, O my soul, and forget not all his benefits!

—We have had trials; but even these, instead of checking gratitude, if properly reviewed, will increase it. They have been few, compared with our comforts. They have been light, compared with the sufferings of others. They have been variously alleviated. In measure, when they shot forth, he debated with them: he stayed his rough wind in the day of the east wind. They have all been founded in a regard to our welfare. They have imbittered sin, and endeared the Scriptures, and the Throne of Grace, and the sympathy of Him who is touched with the feelings of our infirmities. They have weaned us from the world. They have told us that this is not our rest. They have also told us that he knows how to support and to deliver. Aaron's rod blossomed—so shall ours; and yield the peaceable fruit of righteousness. There was honey at the end of Jonathan's rod—and there is sweetness at the end of ours. Yea, already we can say, It is good for me that I have been afflicted. Surely a gratitude is required, on this occasion, that will not expire on mere acknowledgments; but induce me to dedicate myself to his service, and walk before me in newness of life.

And what can be more reasonable than to take courage when we look forward? We enter, indeed, on the year commencing, not knowing what a day may bring forth: and darkness is apt to gender dread. Duties *will* arise; and we must meet their claims. Afflictions *may* arise—indeed they are almost unavoidable. Does not every path of life lead through a vale of tears? Is not every thing here uncertain? My health may be assailed. My friends may be removed. This year I may die.

—But I will pore on this no longer. I will not sour my present mercies, by suspicion, or fear, or anxiety. It is my duty, it is my privilege, to be careful for nothing; but to cast all my care on Him who careth for me. I take courage from his former dispensations. Has he ever forsaken or forgotten me? Because he has been my help, therefore, under the shadow of his wings will I rejoice. I take courage from his providence. I am not in "a fatherless world." Nothing is left to chance. My ways are continually before Him; and the very hairs of my head are all numbered. I take courage from his power. Nothing is too hard for him. He can make even mine enemies be at peace with me. He can render every loss a gain. He can make all things work together for my good. I take courage from his promises. They are all faithfulness and truth. And what case do they leave unnoticed, unprovided for, from which despondency can spring? I will therefore trust, and not be afraid—but go forward, cheerfully—with Him who has said—I will never leave thee, nor forsake thee.

"Beneath his smiles my heart has lived,
"And part of heaven possessed:
"I praise his name for grace received,
"And trust him for the rest."

THE END.

Scripture Index

Depravity - 12/4

Affliction - Aug 21, Sept 25, 10/1
Aging - June 11, Aug 2
Assurance - Sept 13
Benevolence - June 9
Christ
Sufferings - Aug 24
Communion c God 1/15, 1/29, 10/9
Curiosity - Aug 3,
Compassion - Sept 25
Devil - June 21
Dying - P.44-45 (VI) - Jan 21, Aug 2, 9/29
Evangelism - 9/27
Fear of God - Aug 30, 11/28
Faith (March 27) - May 17, 11/27
vs. works - 4/18

Fatherhood of God - 48-49 (VI)
Friendship - 73-74 (VI)
God's dwelling - 24 (VI)

Fore Knowing - 10/9

God:
Goodness - March 27
Love - Oct 28
Resting in - Nov 26
Grace - 4/18
day of. - 4/24

Holy Spirt, grieve - May 25
Joy - PS 16 - April 7
Justifaction - May - 22, Jul. 8,
Jesus -
Priesthood - 10/5
Suficiency - 12/6
Knowledge - of God - 9/19
Life - 10/22-23
Love - 111-112, 11/27
Liberty - 10/25

Marytordom - Aug 2
Mercy - July 18, Aug 14
Miracles - Sept. 17

Moderation, - 10/3

Omniscience - Aug 16

Peace, July 14
Perseverance - July 27
Prayer - May. 30, Aug 8, 10/8, 10/29
Pilgrims on earth - 10/6, 10/10

Presence of God c us - May 18
Prosperity - Oct 14
Provision of God - Aug 16

Repentance P. 2 8, (VI)
Rest, Sept 29
Rescurection - P. 48, (VI); April 8; 11/10
Rod - May 14
Sickness - P. 47 (VI)
Sabbath - 12/22
Voltaire - P. 28-29, (VI)

Teachablness. P 120. (VI)
Temptation - June 21, 12/6
Trial of Your Faith - 5/9, 10/29, 11/3
Trust - July - 23

Recommended Other Reading

Available Through Calvary Press...

The Heart of Anger

Lou Priolo

Do you have an angry child? Do you know someone who does? Did you know that parents often unknowingly provoke their children to the point of anger? This is a manual for parents seeking to correct or prevent the development of those angry responses which characterize what the Bible calls "an angry man." Children can easily habituate themselves to think, act, and be motivated with anger— especially if parents do not have the biblical knowledge and wisdom to prevent or intervene to correct such problems of the heart. These pages contain the practical help and real hope for all those facing these vital concerns. Says Jay Adams, "The Church in general will be in Lou's debt for writing it. It is a book whose time has come."

Shepherding A Child's Heart

Tedd Tripp

Pastor John MacArthur writes: "With the plethora of material on parenting and the family, it is distressing to see how few are genuinely biblical. Here is a refreshing exception. Tedd Tripp offers solid, trustworthy, biblical help for parents. If you're looking for the right perspective and practical help on the divine plan for parenting, you won't find a more excellent guide." In an age when the subject of child-rearing is often intertwined with notions of pop-psychology this book will become your definitive guide to a bible based understanding of the parent's role and responsibilities. A landmark book on this subject. If you are a parent or anticipate being one or are involved with children as an educator or caretaker let this be the one book you own if none else.

From Forgiven to Forgiving
Jay Adams

Without a doubt, this is the best book on biblical forgiveness available today. An attractive and affordable soft-cover edition, it is destined to become a classic work on this subject. A must for the library of the pastor, professional counselor and lay person alike. We've grown up learning many popular misconceptions about forgiveness from our parents, society and even our churches. This book has been greatly used by God and will continue to be instrumental in the saving of marriages, friendships, church memberships, and any relationship where issues of forgiveness have not been understood or dealt with properly. An excellent book to use for group study or a church Sunday school study.

The Person and Work of the Holy Spirit
Benjamin B. Warfield

In our present day the person and the work of the Holy Spirit is too often misunderstood. Whole denominations hold to and promote unscriptural doctrines concerning God's Spirit and His operation in the lives of Christians today. So how can one know with certainty the character and the ways and means by which the Holy Spirit works in the Church of God? Would it not be by seeking our answer from God Himself? In this volume, are assembled for the first time anywhere the completeworks of Benjamin B. Warfield regarding the Holy Spirit. The sermons, articles and book reviews contained in this book will instruct you and challenge you to know the Holy Spirit as He has revealed Himself— through the scriptures.

An Obedient & Patient Faith

An Exposition of 1st Peter
by Robert Leighton

This classic commentary has been considered by many to be the most valuable single commentary on scripture ever written. Spurgeon considered it a "heavenly work...a favorite with all spiritual men." The depth of First Peter is glorious and the depth and thoroughness by which Leighton exposits and explains it is fantastic. In an age when the study of Theology was the universal and highest pursuit, Leighton was preeminent.

Within these pages lies a banquet of precious and delightful truths to be savored, every page is full of the flavor and aroma of deep piety and judicious instruction. No student of the scriptures should be without this invaluable commentary.

From Religion to Christ

Peter Jeffery

Under the cover of a dark night, a gray-haired Jewish Rabbi approached a much younger man to inquire about matters which were deeply troubling him. That conversation between Nicodemus and Jesus of Nazareth has intrigued God's people for the past two millennia. In this book, we are taken back to that night's conversation and are shown how the words Jesus spoke to Nicodemus on a Jerusalem hillside some two thousand years past are essential to our salvation today. The author is deeply concerned that millions of people are just like Nicodemus was that night— religious, but not redeemed by God. A careful and prayerful reading of this book can be used of God to open the eyes of many to see clearly that their religion is empty and vain, but salvation can and will be found in Jesus Christ alone.

The Mission of Calvary Press

The ministry of Calvary Press is firmly committed to printing quality Christian literature relevant to the dire needs of the church and the world at the close of the 20th century. We unashamedly stand upon the foundation stones of the Reformation of the 16th century— Scripture alone, Faith alone, Grace alone, Christ alone, and God's Glory alone!

Our prayer for this ministry is found in two portions taken from the Psalms: "And let the beauty of the LORD our God be upon us, And establish the work of our hands for us; Yes, establish the work of our hands." (Psalm 90:17) & "Not unto us, O LORD, not unto us, but to Your name give glory." (Psalm 115:1)

Calvary Press is thankful to anyone who has a burden for sound doctrine and literature such as that published by this ministry. If you would like to help our efforts by making a donation to this ministry we would greatly appreciate it. Calvary Press is a not-for-profit ministry of Grace Reformed Baptist Church of Long Island, N.Y., all donations will be recognized with a tax-deductible receipt. Thank You in advance for any assistance you would seek to give us in our labors.